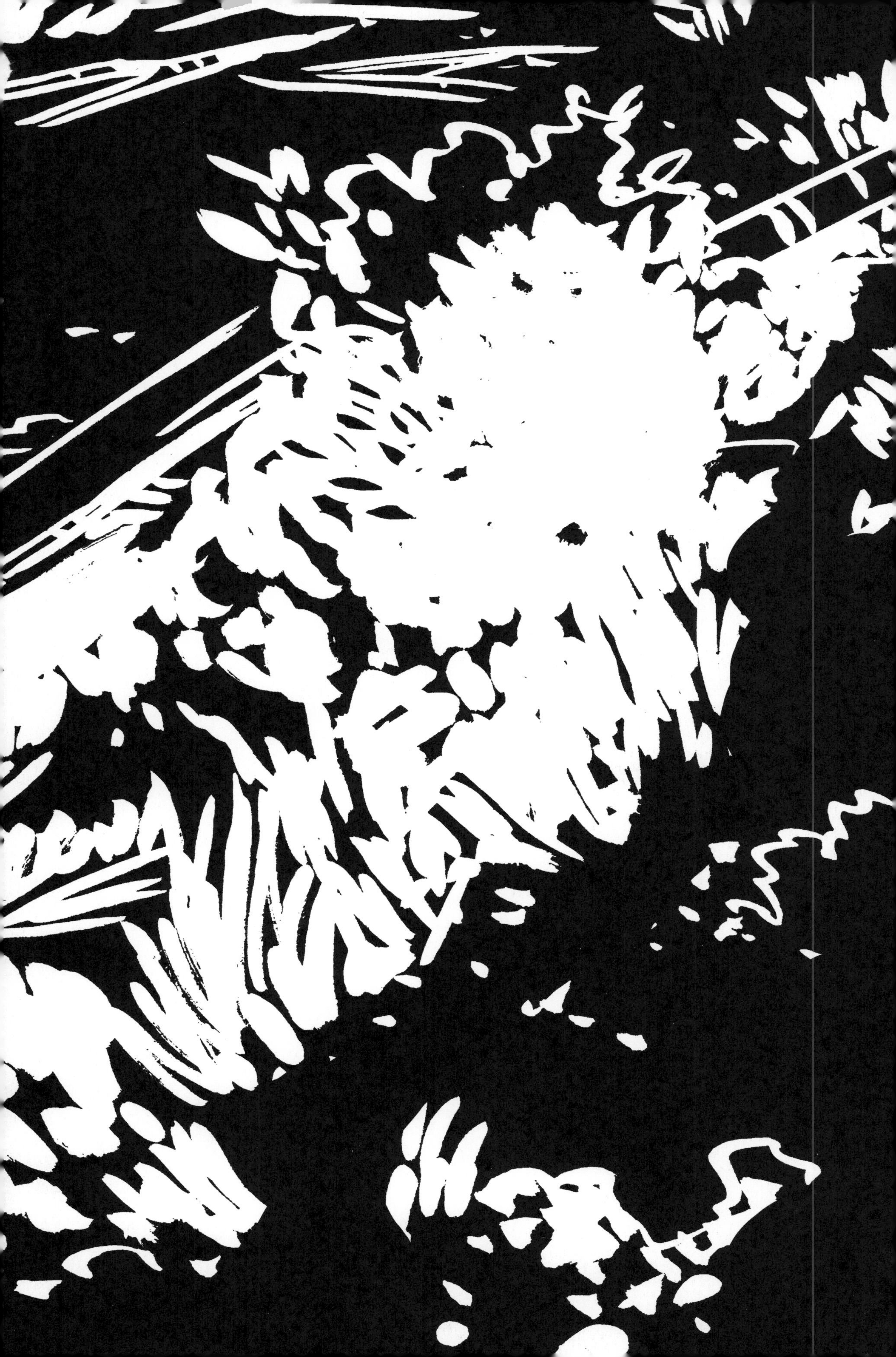

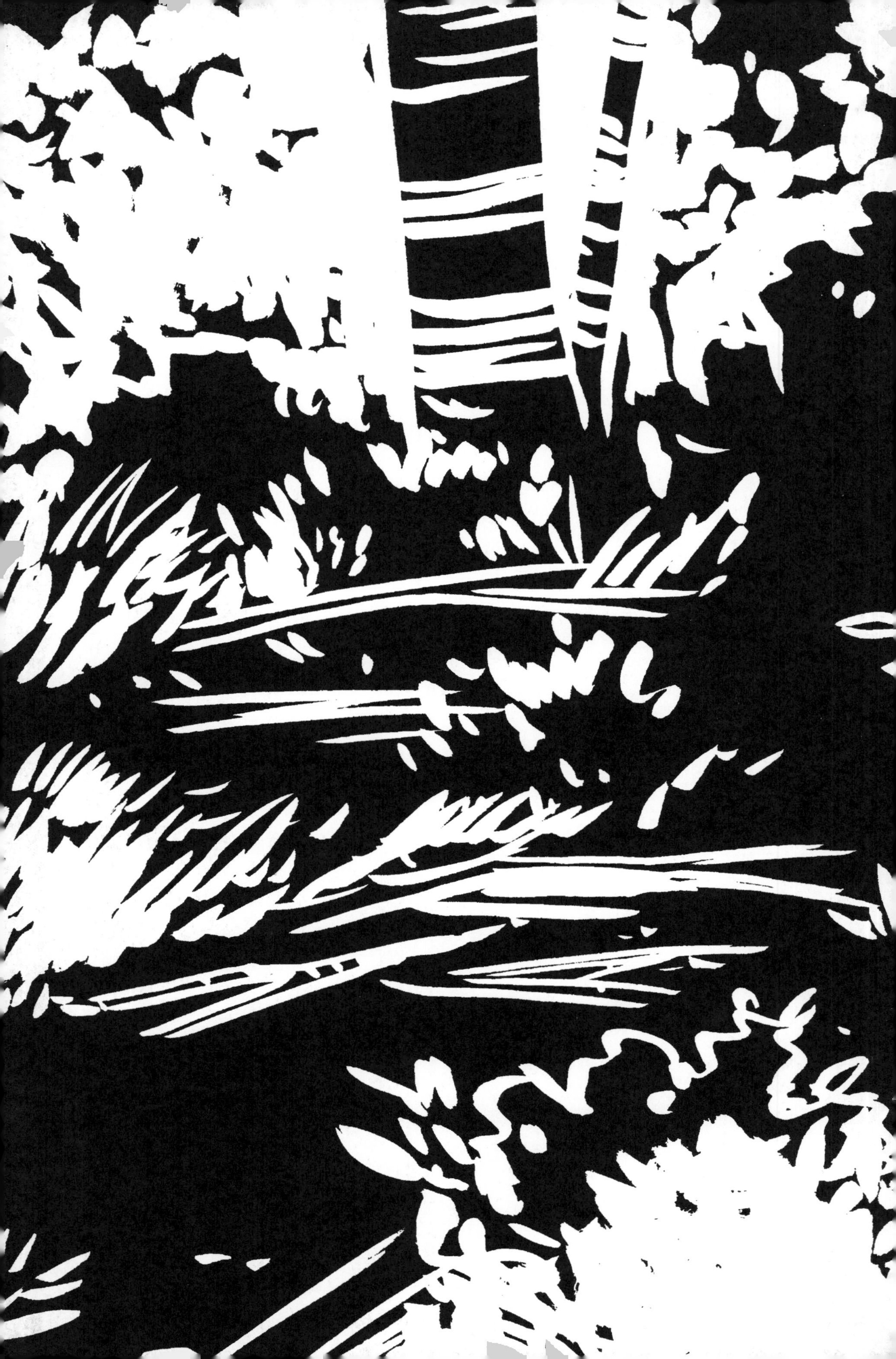

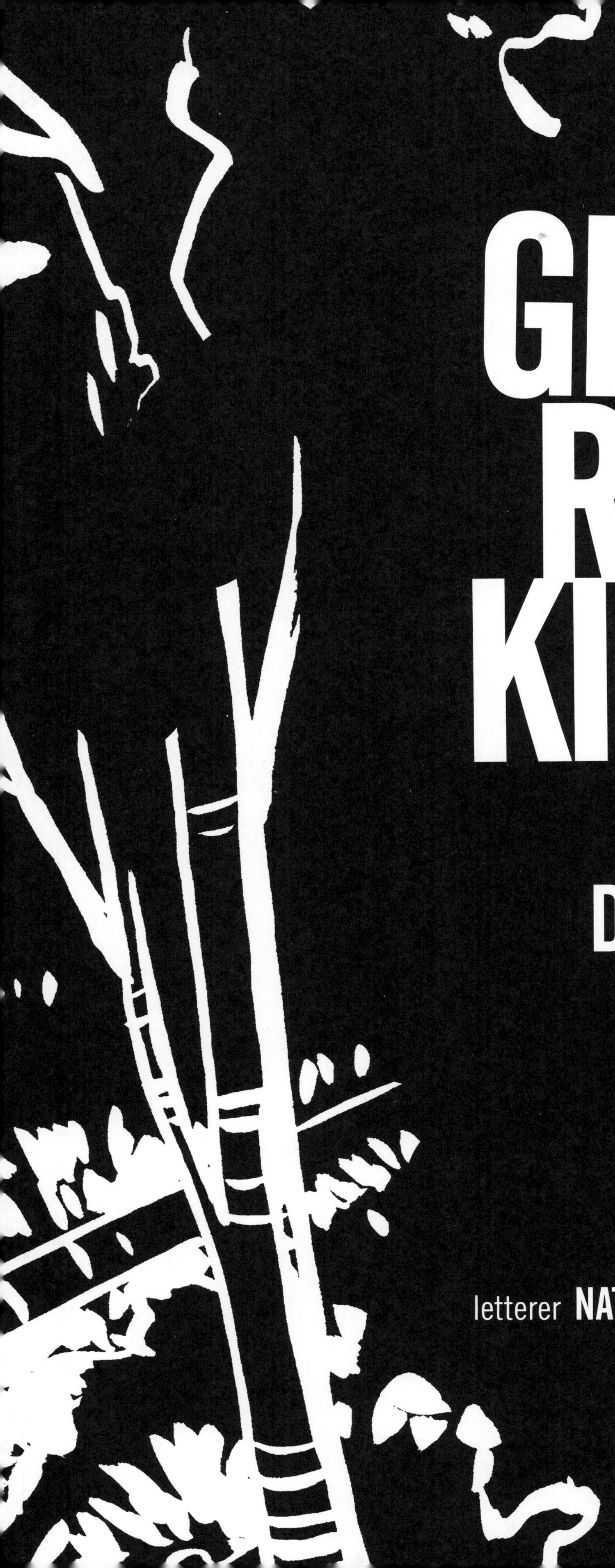

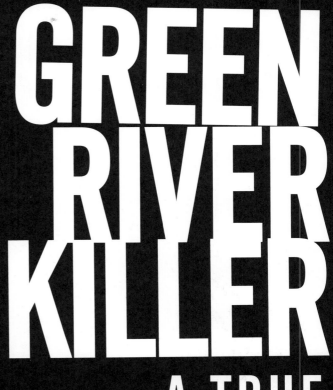

GREEN RIVER KILLER

A TRUE DETECTIVE STORY

writer **JEFF JENSEN**

artist **JONATHAN CASE**

letterer **NATE PIEKOS OF BLAMBOT®**

DARK HORSE BOOKS

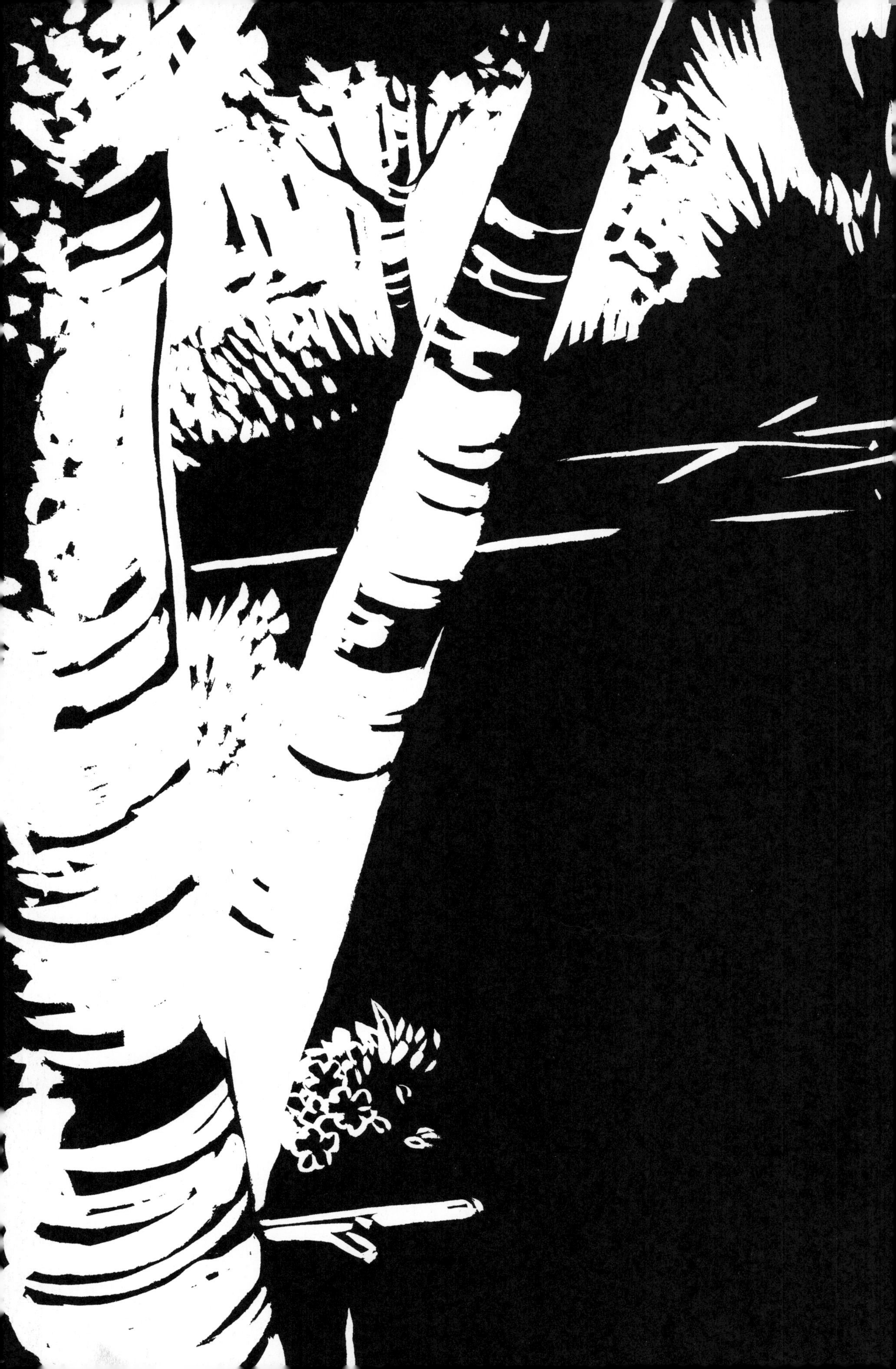

INTRODUCTION

I have a very powerful and potent memory about the earliest moments of the creation of this graphic novel . . . which is very weird because I had absolutely nothing to do with the creation of this graphic novel. Also, I am not friends or really know anybody involved with this book. Oh, also I am not the Green River Killer. Just felt like throwing that out there now in case you thought I might be building to it.

My memory about this GN is so innocuous on the surface, yet so potent and detailed in my mind, that I often wonder why I remember it so clearly. Not to brag, but I have a life. I have four kids and five full-time jobs. I have things to remember. So I often wonder why my brain remembers what I am about to tell you as often as it does and so clearly.

Jeff Jensen. Sometimes when you read an introduction like this the writers are good friends or a favor is owed. Not in this case. I am just a very big fan of this material and I've made it very clear to anyone who would listen. In fact, I don't think I've spoken to Jeff in years. I've only spoken to Jeff a few times in my life. He was a reporter for *Entertainment Weekly* and *Entertainment Weekly* has always been very kind to me for some reason. Well, except once.

Every time I would get on the phone with Jeff, it was always a great deal of fun because immediately we were speaking from the same points of reference. I am sure you have people in your life like that. People you know you could have been friends with if—if only . . . Sometimes for comics people it makes all the difference when the reporter is "one of us." Jeff knew his comics and genre. Jeff was the real deal.

It was just after one of our fun, professional interview conversations that Jeff said to me:

JEFF: Hey, can I ask you for some advice? Off the record.

BRIAN: Sure, what's up?

JEFF: I think I have an idea for a graphic novel.

For comic creators that sentence can be a bit of a record scratch because it's usually followed by the most not-good idea EVER. No offense to anyone who has ever spoken to me. And I'm sorry if this sounds rude, but you haven't heard the parade of pitches I have heard.

But every once in a while, someone really has something. I held my breath. Jeff is a writer. He knows story. Please don't be a pitch about an entertainment reporter who secretly has the power of God.

JEFF: So . . . my dad was the lead detective working the Green River Killer case.

Beat. Pause. Wow. Is it weird that I was immediately jealous? I'll answer, "Yes." And it wasn't that I was jealous that he had a father and I didn't. You *think* that would be the reason. Oh no. I'm a broken writer person. I was jealous that he had a father with enough material in him for a potentially GREAT GRAPHIC NOVEL. Pro tip, if there's a story to share that others could be inspired by . . . writers get weird. It's morbid. It is not cool. It is horrible. But it is also the backbone of every writer's room of every hour-long drama on TV. Ever.

Jeff started to tell me some of the more personal details that you are about to read in this book. Jeff started to whisper to me little moments of such personal truth that I realized he maybe had more than a story, he had something close to actual art.

Jeff had a story in front of him that only he could tell. There are stories out there that many people can tell but then there are stories only one, or two, people can tell and those are obviously more precious. For this story to exist it had to be Jeff. There was no one else. It had to be that person at that place at that time who, also, had developed an ability to tell a story this rich.

From that early conversation I could tell he was building up the guts to tell the true story. Now the true story involves really reflecting on the relationship between himself and his father and his father to the world around him.

It's a story ABOUT truth. So you have to be true. That is some weird advice to give to someone you don't know, but, in retrospect, I think that's why he was asking me, a professional stranger. He wanted someone who didn't know him or his father to tell him to do it.

I highly doubt I am the only person that he talked to about this. I am sure I was one of a chorus of professional creative people who told him the same thing. But I'm the only one writing this intro so I'll make it about me :-).

I compared it, in theory, to *Maus*. Which is REALLY obnoxious. The man hasn't even started the GN yet and I come along and say "Oh, your thing sounds like it could be as good as one of the greatest comics ever!"

I did it. I was excited. I officially apologize. But I was right.

One of the reasons *Maus* elevates so high above so many other powerful stories about the Holocaust is because it really was a story about the relationship between Art Spiegelman and his father. And it wasn't a "sugarcoated" one. It was a struggle. Like they all are. It was truth. A truth people of many lifestyles and experience could relate to.

It was a good conversation. I remember the pang of jealousy. "*Man! He is sitting on gold.*" But, the fact of the matter is, a lot of people tell a lot of people a lot of ideas, good or bad, and they just drift away into the ether. It's hard to sit down and make something. And it's super hard to make something this honest.

But miracle upon miracles . . . he did it. They both did it.

Yes, the truly magnificent artist Jonathan Case, whose line work and authority over character acting and no-nonsense approach to storytelling would make Will Eisner stand up and applaud. Jonathan's work is about to speak for itself in ways I could never express here.

But why? Why do I remember this conversation from years ago with such precision and detail?

I think it's because I was witness to the pure act of Jeff and Jonathan achieving all the goals of any creative person.

They found their truth.

Perfectly.

I don't care who you are or where you're from . . . you don't forget a thing like that.

BENDIS!
Portland, Oregon 2018

For my father, with love, admiration, and deep gratitude.
This is what you get for teaching me how to read with *Batman* comics.

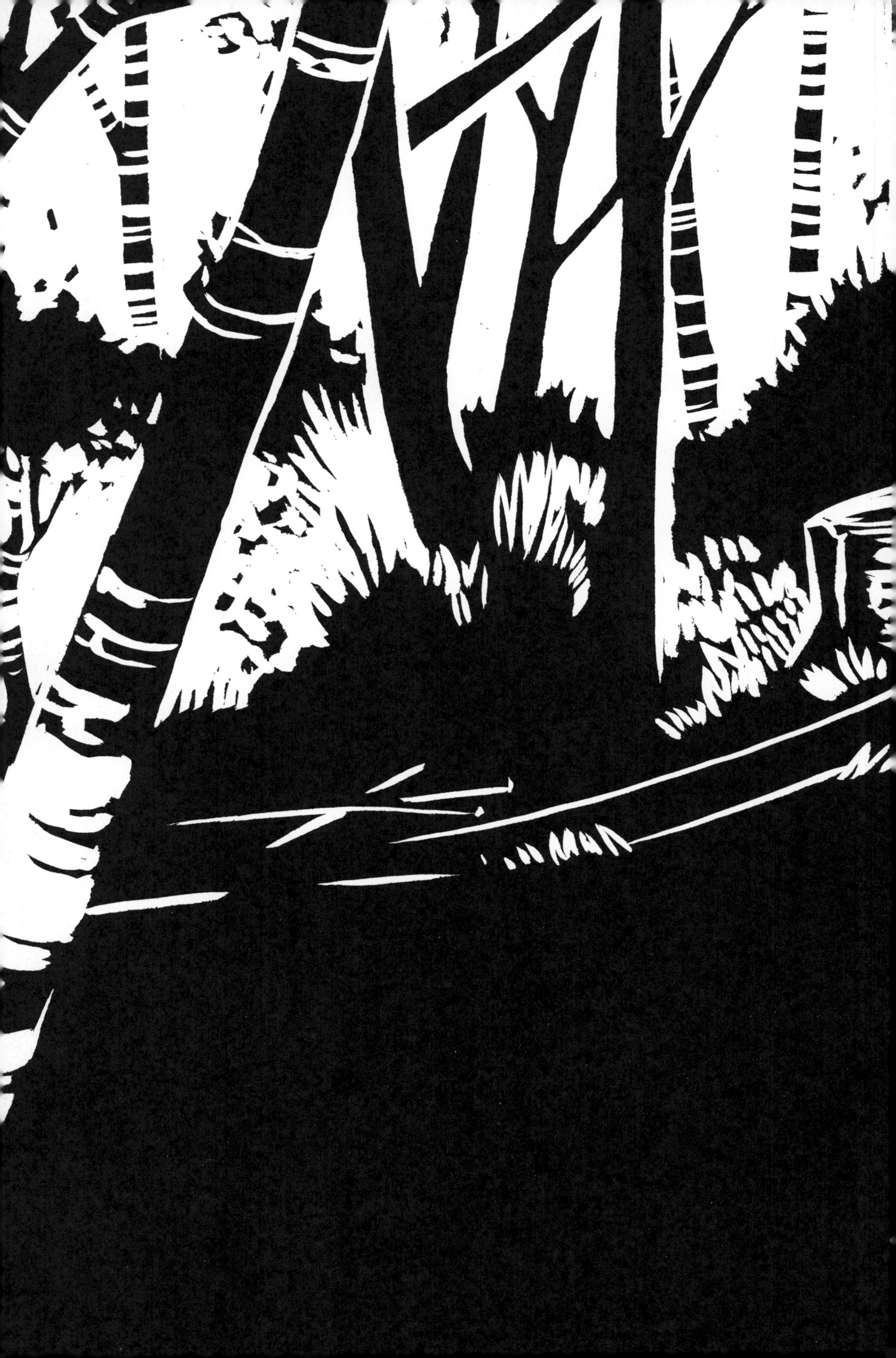

PROLOGUE: 1965

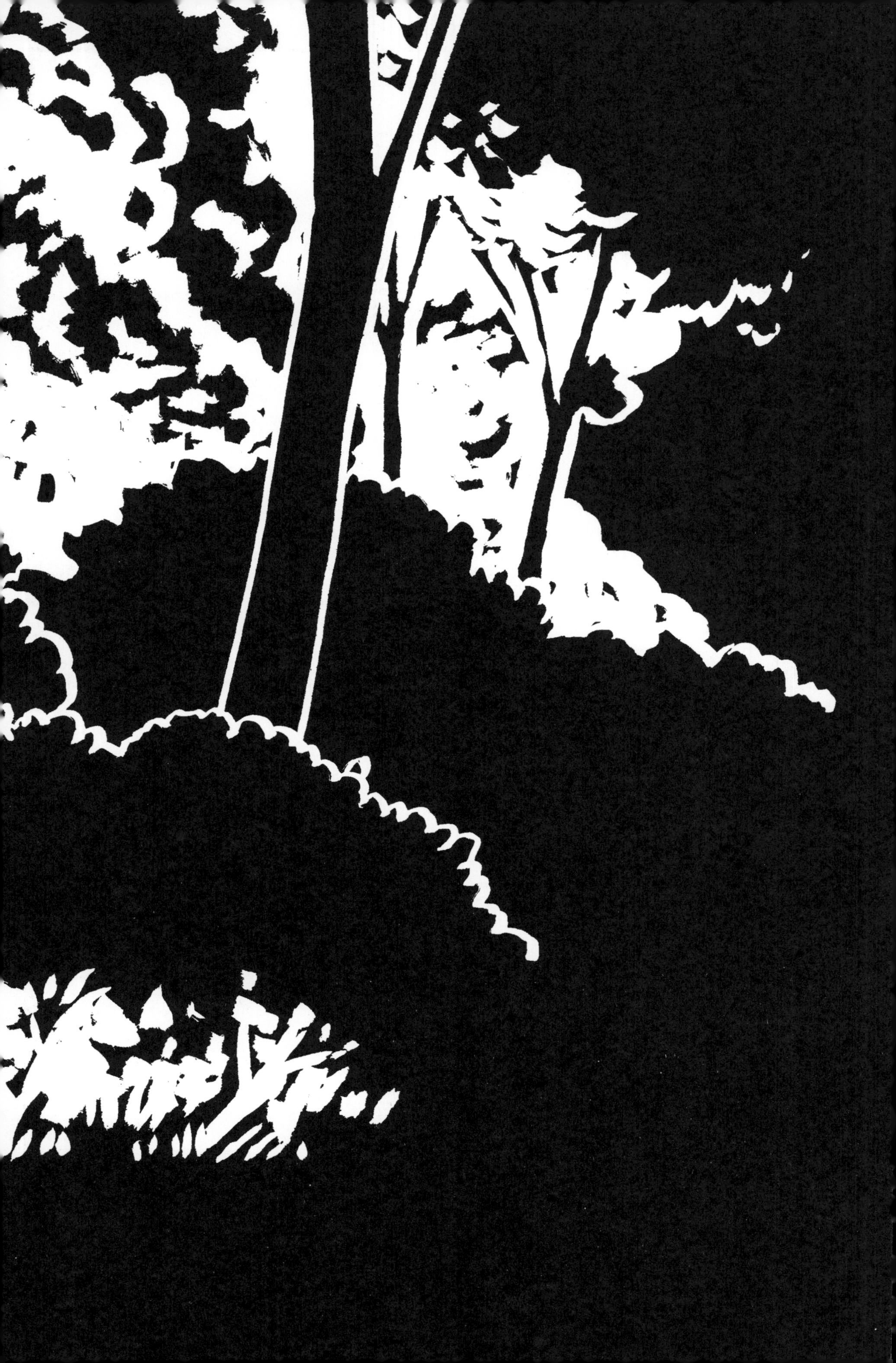

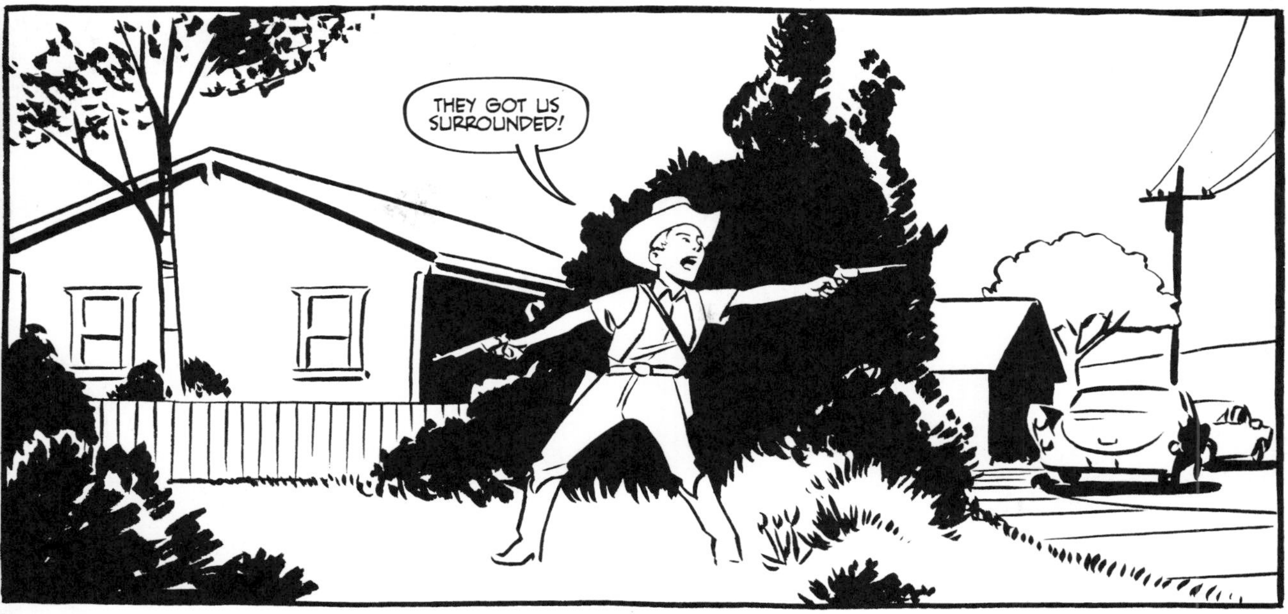
THEY GOT US SURROUNDED!

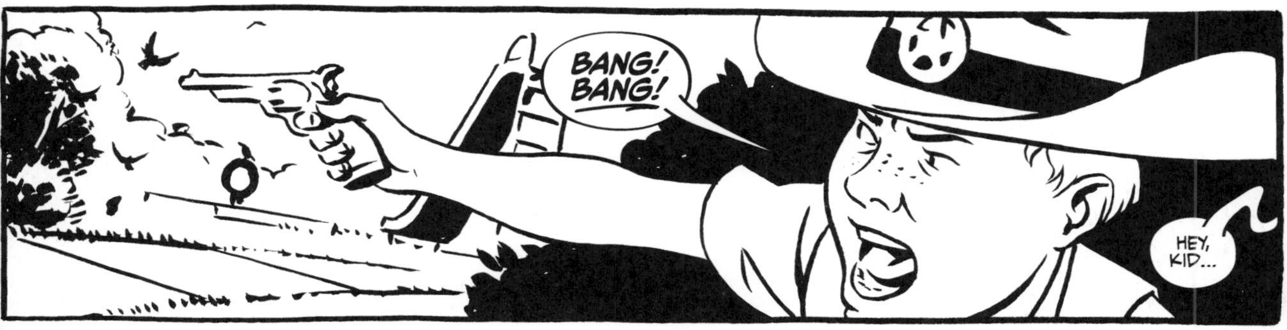
BANG! BANG!
HEY, KID...

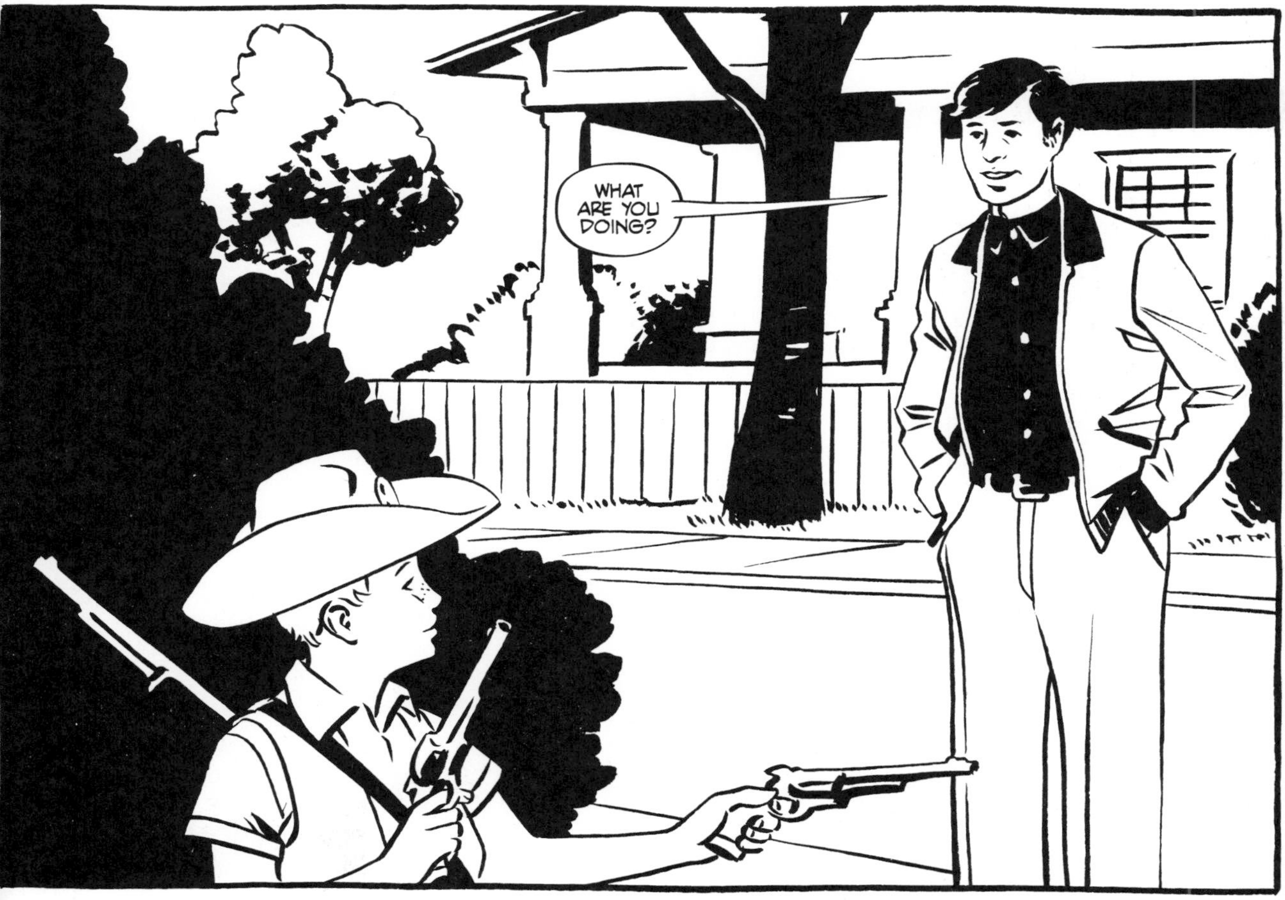
WHAT ARE YOU DOING?

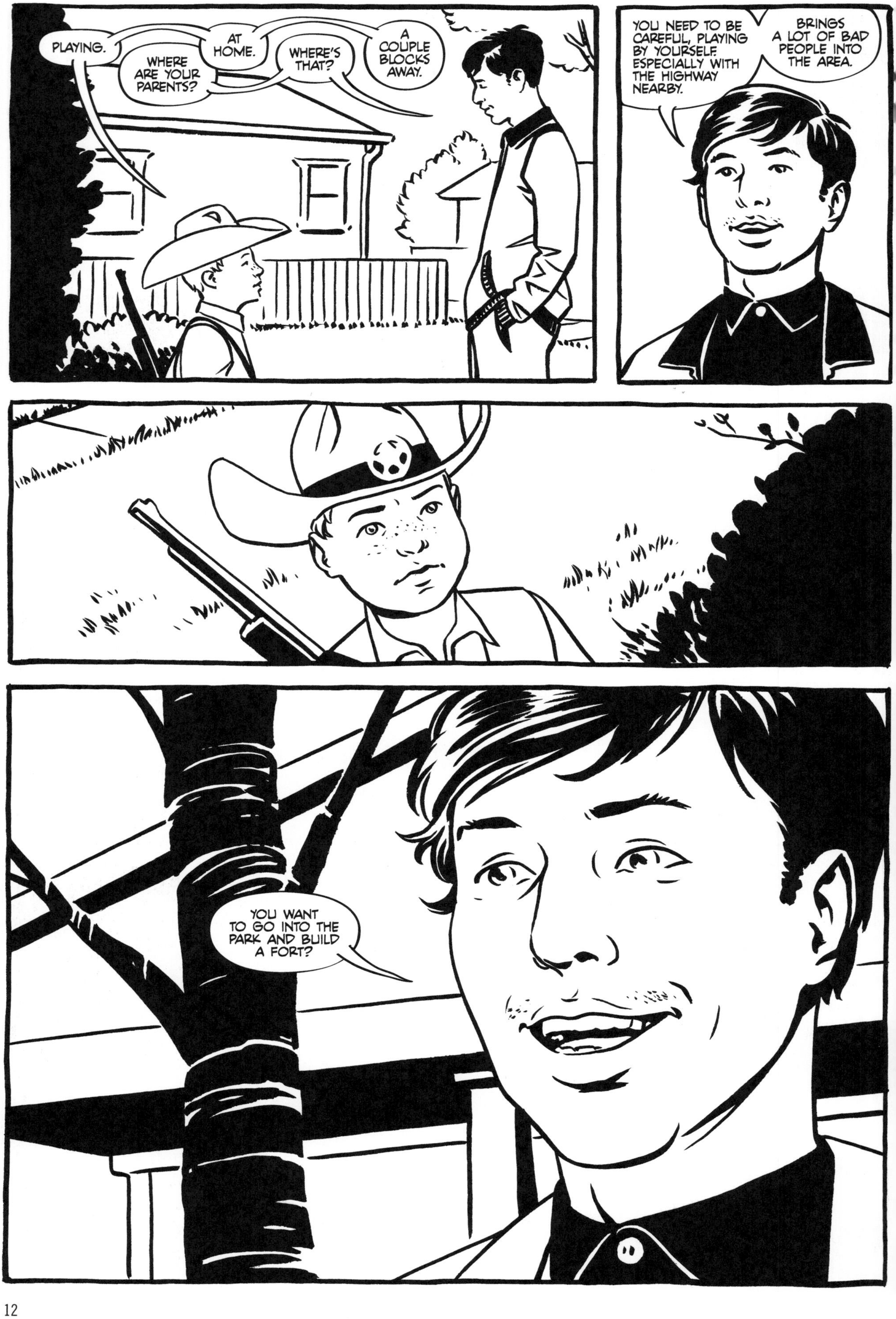
PLAYING.
WHERE ARE YOUR PARENTS?
AT HOME.
WHERE'S THAT?
A COUPLE BLOCKS AWAY.
YOU NEED TO BE CAREFUL, PLAYING BY YOURSELF. ESPECIALLY WITH THE HIGHWAY NEARBY.
BRINGS A LOT OF BAD PEOPLE INTO THE AREA.
YOU WANT TO GO INTO THE PARK AND BUILD A FORT?

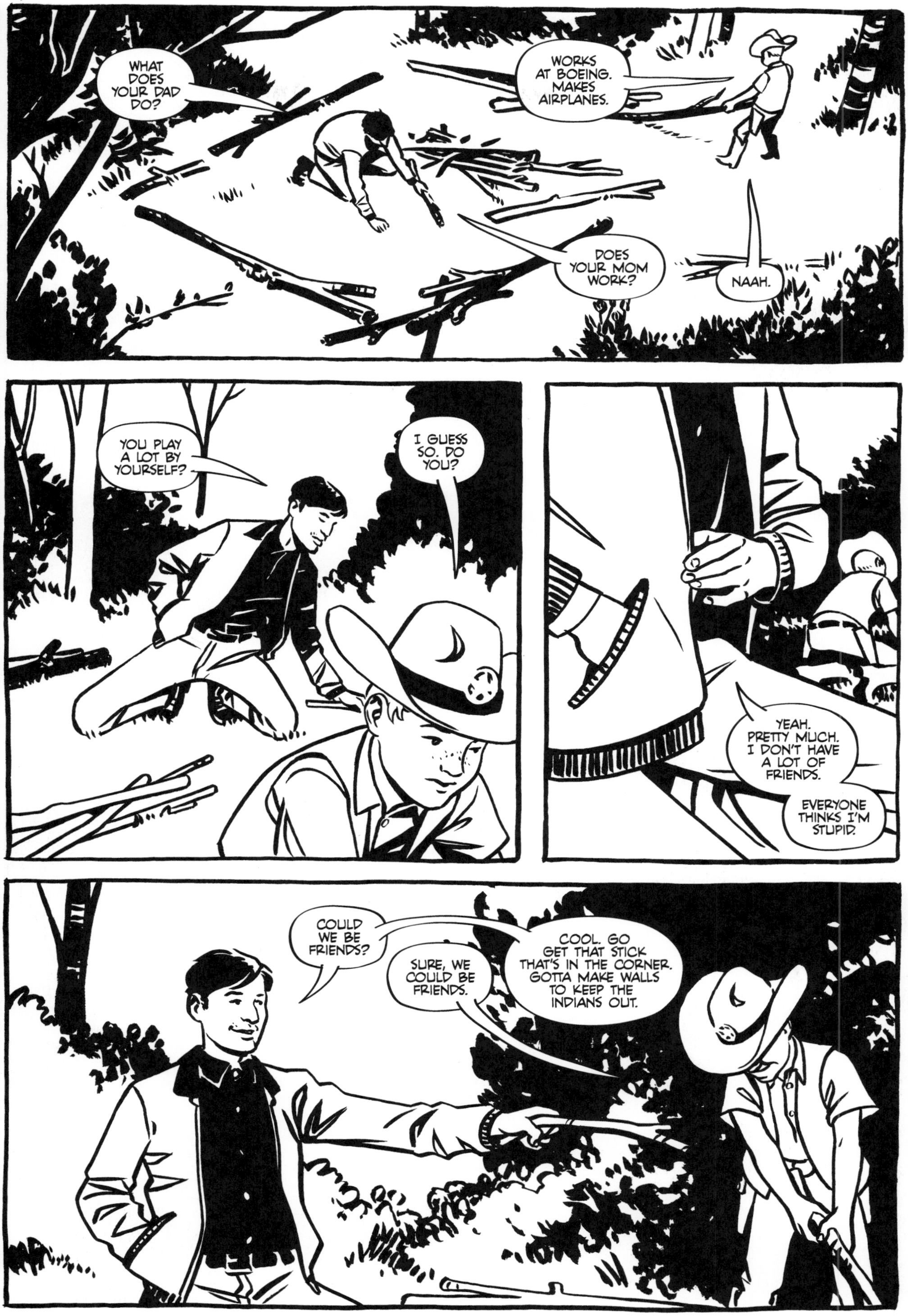
WHAT DOES YOUR DAD DO?
WORKS AT BOEING. MAKES AIRPLANES.
DOES YOUR MOM WORK?
NAAH.
YOU PLAY A LOT BY YOURSELF?
I GUESS SO. DO YOU?
YEAH. PRETTY MUCH. I DON'T HAVE A LOT OF FRIENDS.
EVERYONE THINKS I'M STUPID.
COULD WE BE FRIENDS?
SURE, WE COULD BE FRIENDS.
COOL. GO GET THAT STICK THAT'S IN THE CORNER. GOTTA MAKE WALLS TO KEEP THE INDIANS OUT.

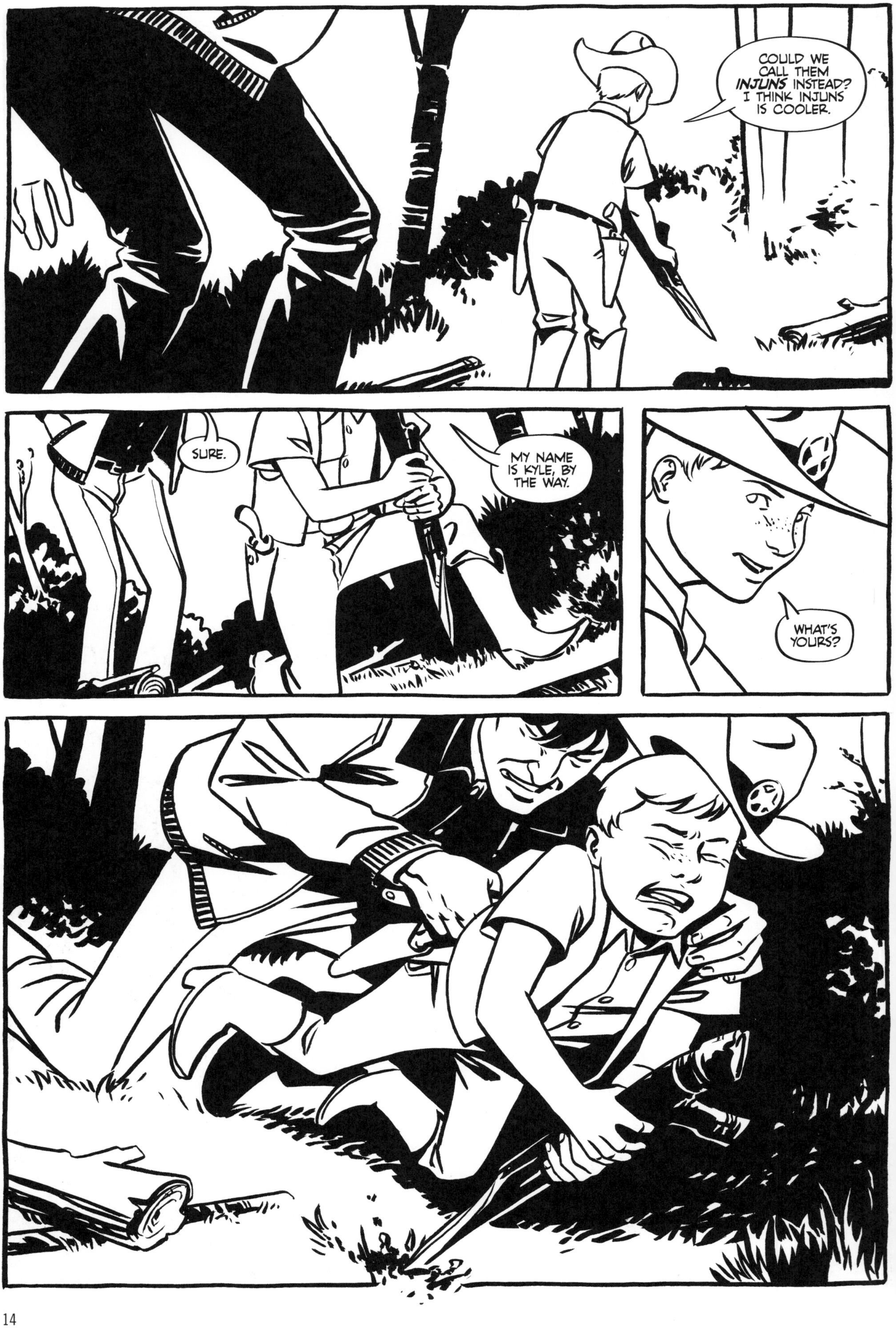
COULD WE CALL THEM *INJUNS* INSTEAD? I THINK INJUNS IS COOLER.
SURE.
MY NAME IS KYLE, BY THE WAY.
WHAT'S YOURS?

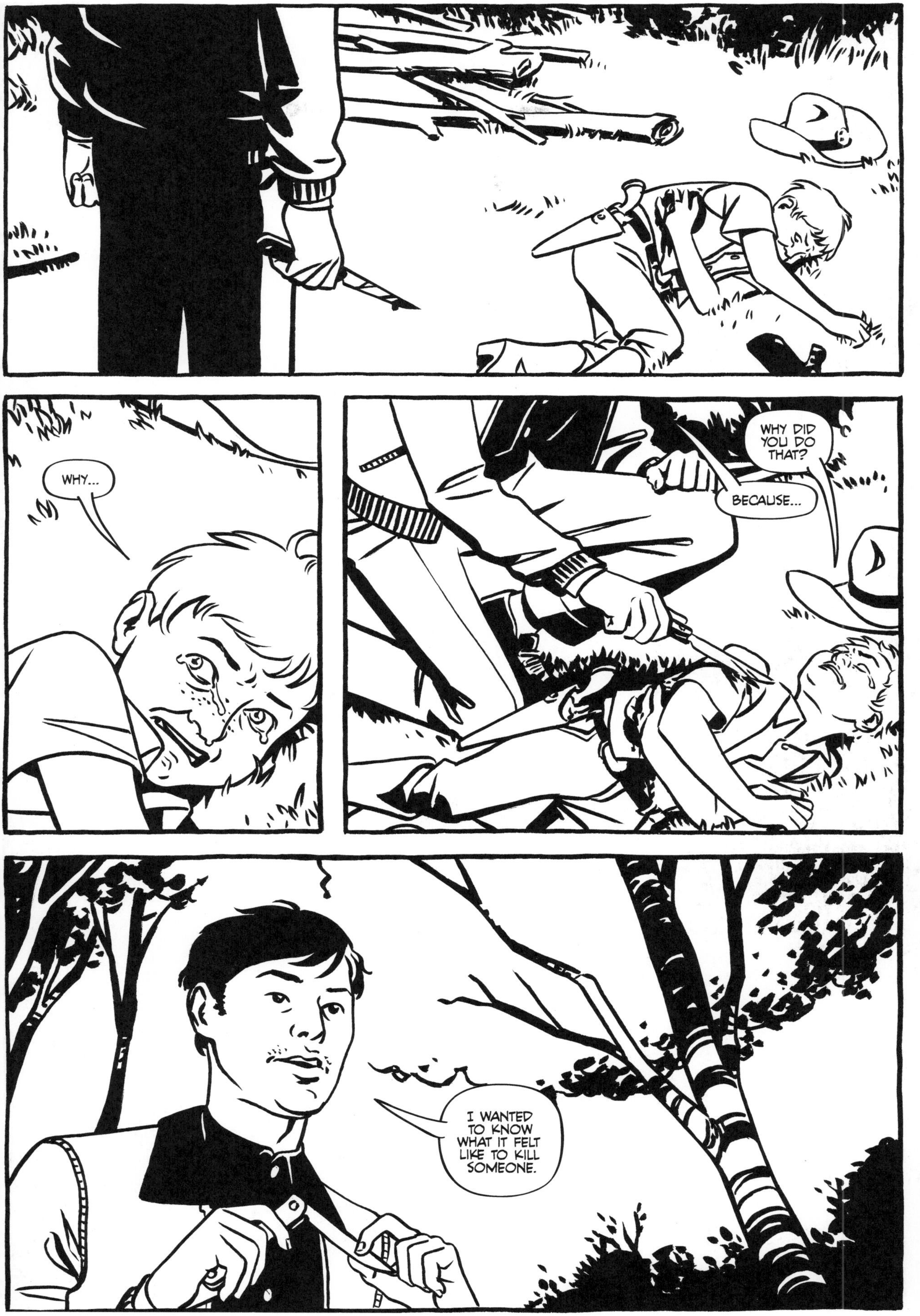
WHY...
WHY DID YOU DO THAT?
BECAUSE...
I WANTED TO KNOW WHAT IT FELT LIKE TO KILL SOMEONE.

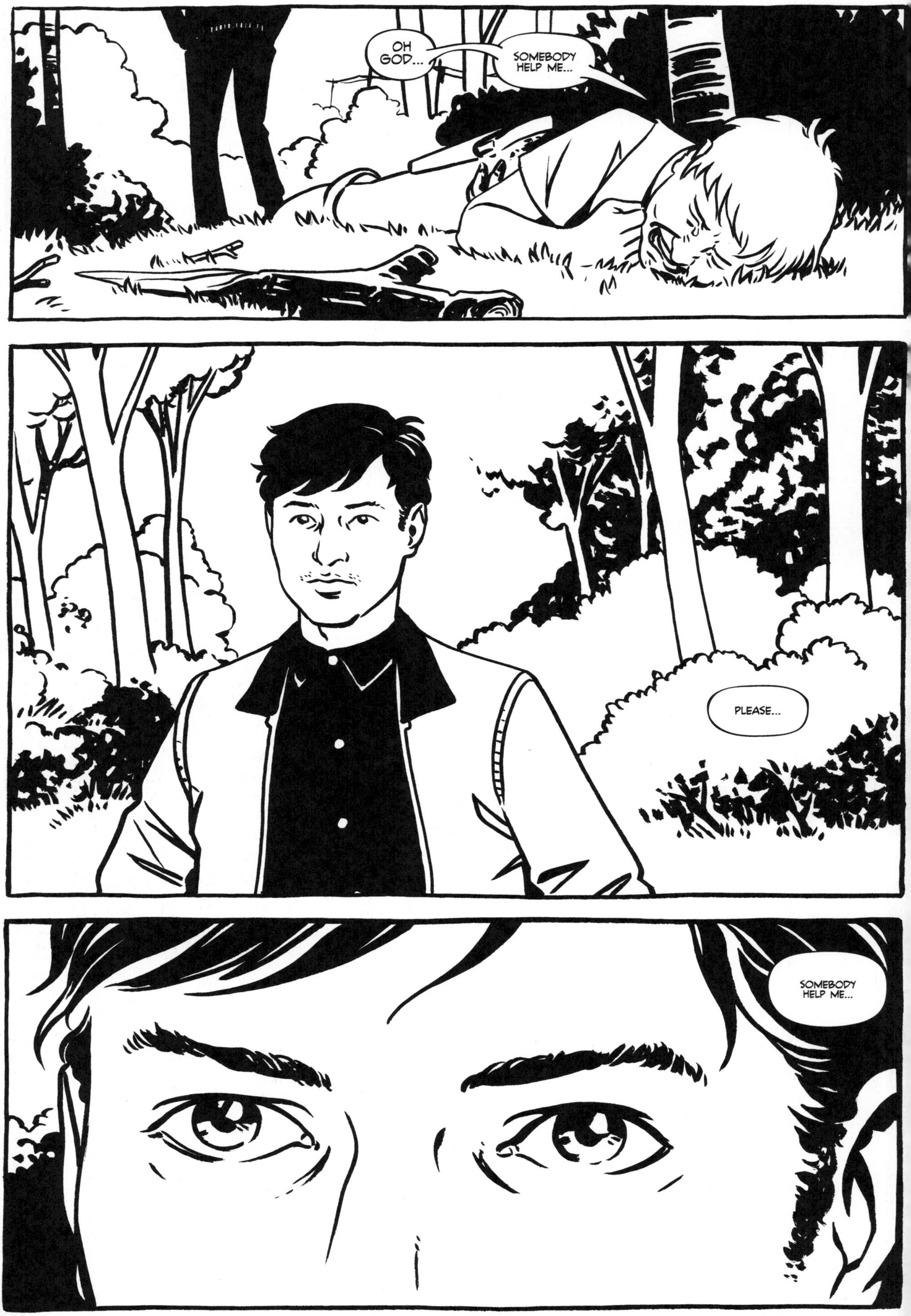
OH GOD...
SOMEBODY HELP ME...
PLEASE...
SOMEBODY HELP ME...

DAY ONE: ORIENTATION

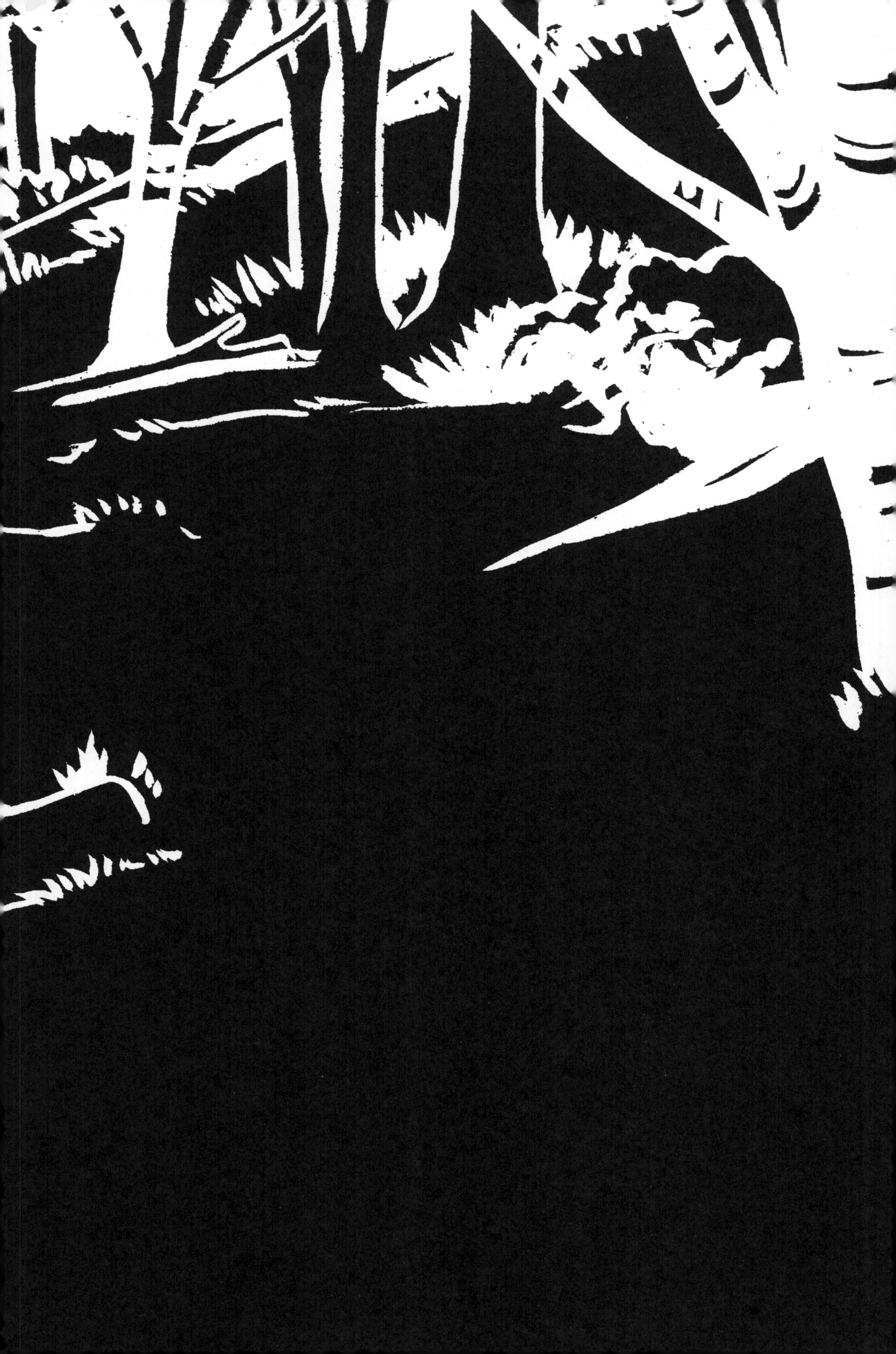

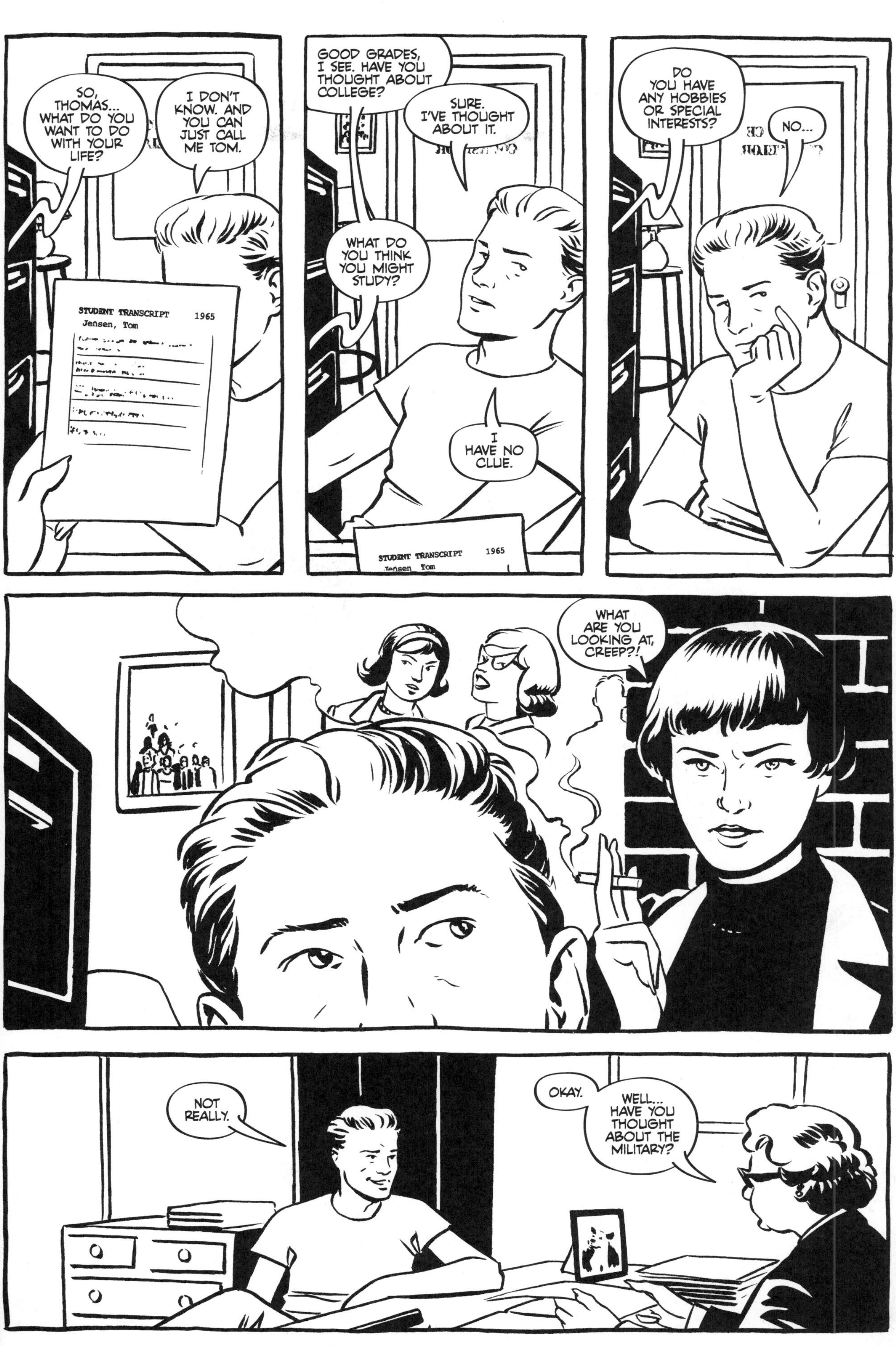
SO, THOMAS... WHAT DO YOU WANT TO DO WITH YOUR LIFE?
I DON'T KNOW. AND YOU CAN JUST CALL ME TOM.
STUDENT TRANSCRIPT 1965
Jensen, Tom
GOOD GRADES, I SEE. HAVE YOU THOUGHT ABOUT COLLEGE?
SURE. I'VE THOUGHT ABOUT IT.
WHAT DO YOU THINK YOU MIGHT STUDY?
I HAVE NO CLUE.
STUDENT TRANSCRIPT 1965
Jensen Tom
DO YOU HAVE ANY HOBBIES OR SPECIAL INTERESTS?
NO...
WHAT ARE YOU LOOKING AT, CREEP?!
NOT REALLY.
OKAY.
WELL... HAVE YOU THOUGHT ABOUT THE MILITARY?

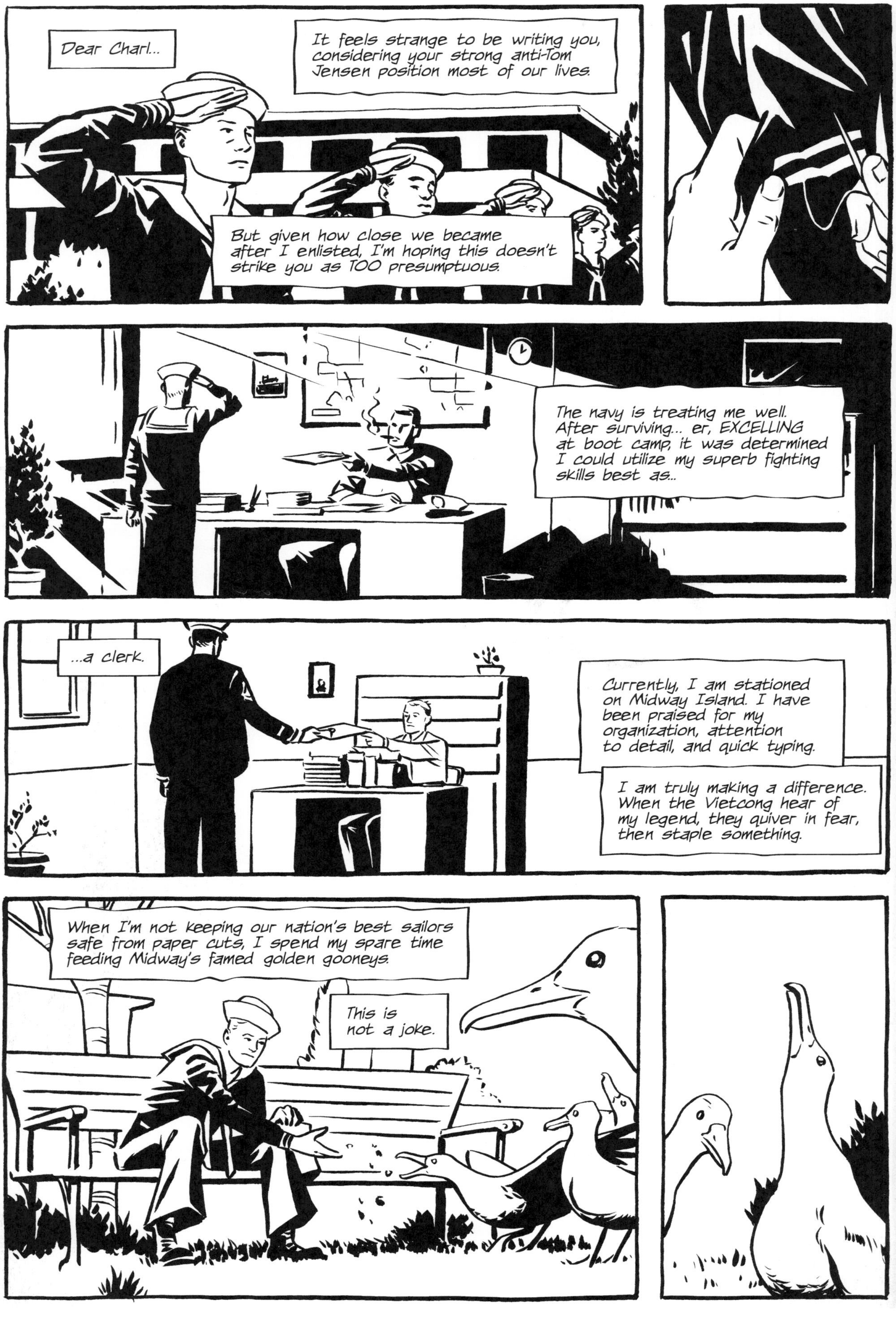
Dear Charl...
It feels strange to be writing you, considering your strong anti-Tom Jensen position most of our lives.
But given how close we became after I enlisted, I'm hoping this doesn't strike you as TOO presumptuous.
The navy is treating me well. After surviving... er, EXCELLING at boot camp, it was determined I could utilize my superb fighting skills best as...
...a clerk.
Currently, I am stationed on Midway Island. I have been praised for my organization, attention to detail, and quick typing.
I am truly making a difference. When the Vietcong hear of my legend, they quiver in fear, then staple something.
When I'm not keeping our nation's best sailors safe from paper cuts, I spend my spare time feeding Midway's famed golden gooneys.
This is not a joke.

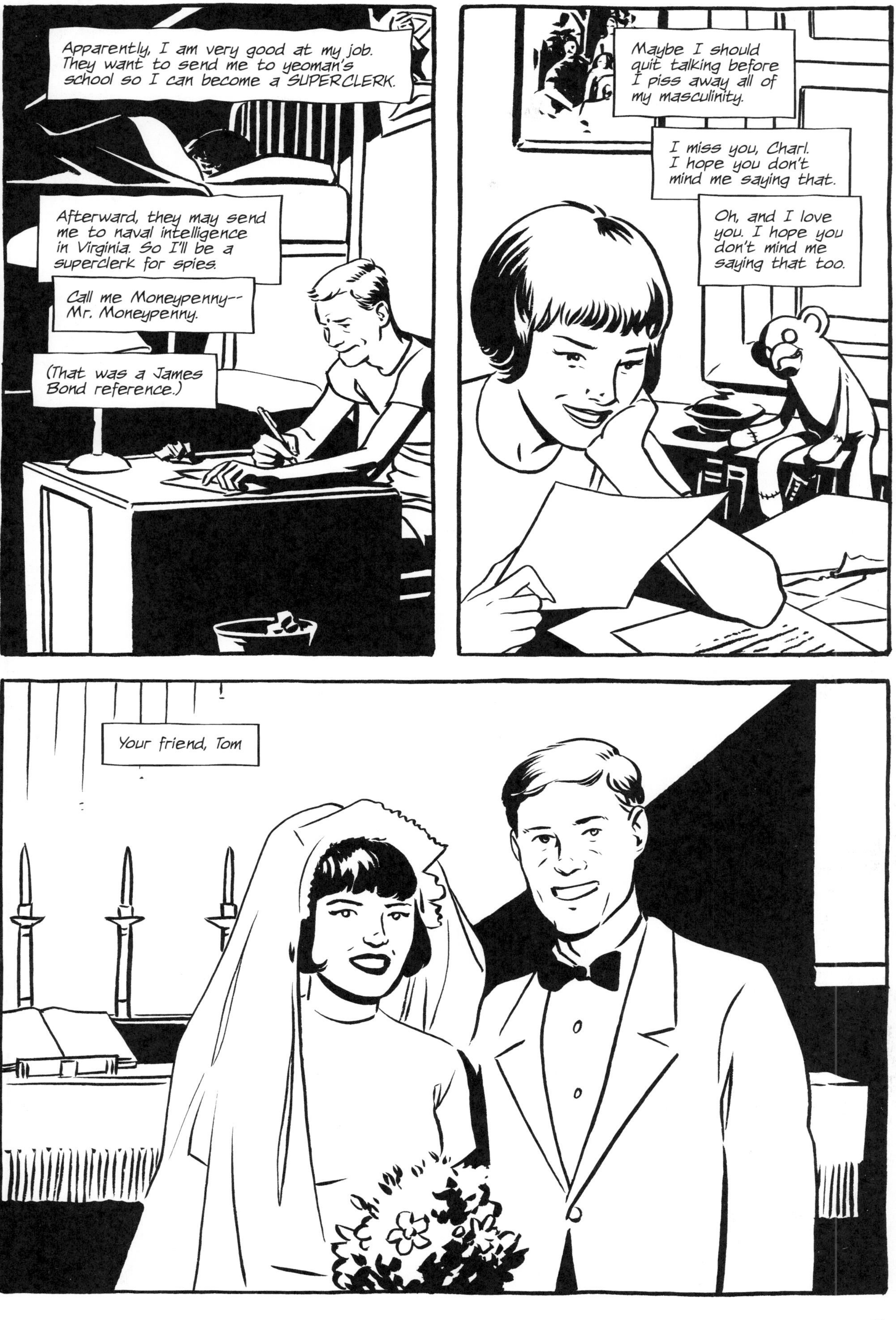
Apparently, I am very good at my job. They want to send me to yeoman's school so I can become a SUPERCLERK.
Afterward, they may send me to naval intelligence in Virginia. So I'll be a superclerk for spies.
Call me Moneypenny-- Mr. Moneypenny.
(That was a James Bond reference.)
Maybe I should quit talking before I piss away all of my masculinity.
I miss you, Charl. I hope you don't mind me saying that.
Oh, and I love you. I hope you don't mind me saying that too.
Your friend, Tom

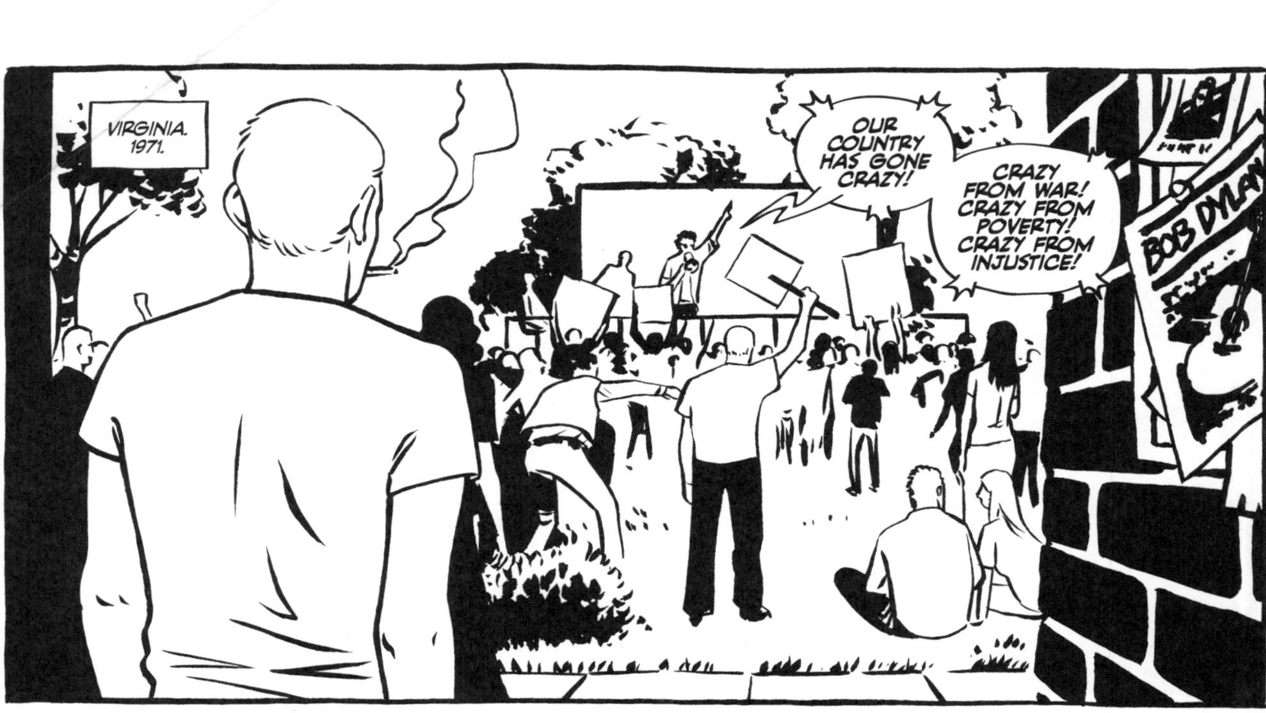
VIRGINIA. 1971.
OUR COUNTRY HAS GONE CRAZY!
CRAZY FROM WAR! CRAZY FROM POVERTY! CRAZY FROM INJUSTICE!
BOB DYLAN

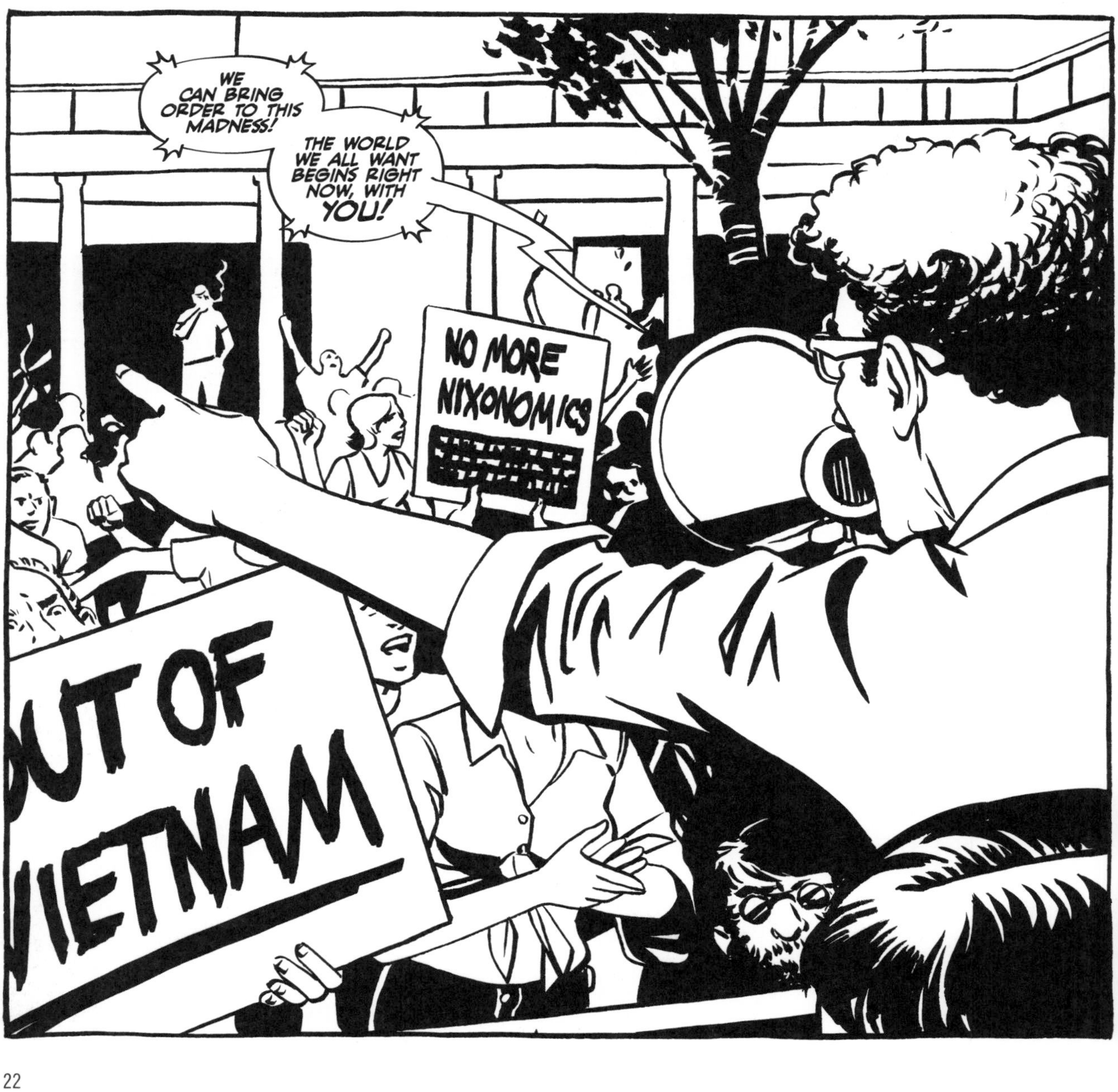
WE CAN BRING ORDER TO THIS MADNESS!
THE WORLD WE ALL WANT BEGINS RIGHT NOW, WITH YOU!
NO MORE NIXONOMICS
OUT OF VIETNAM

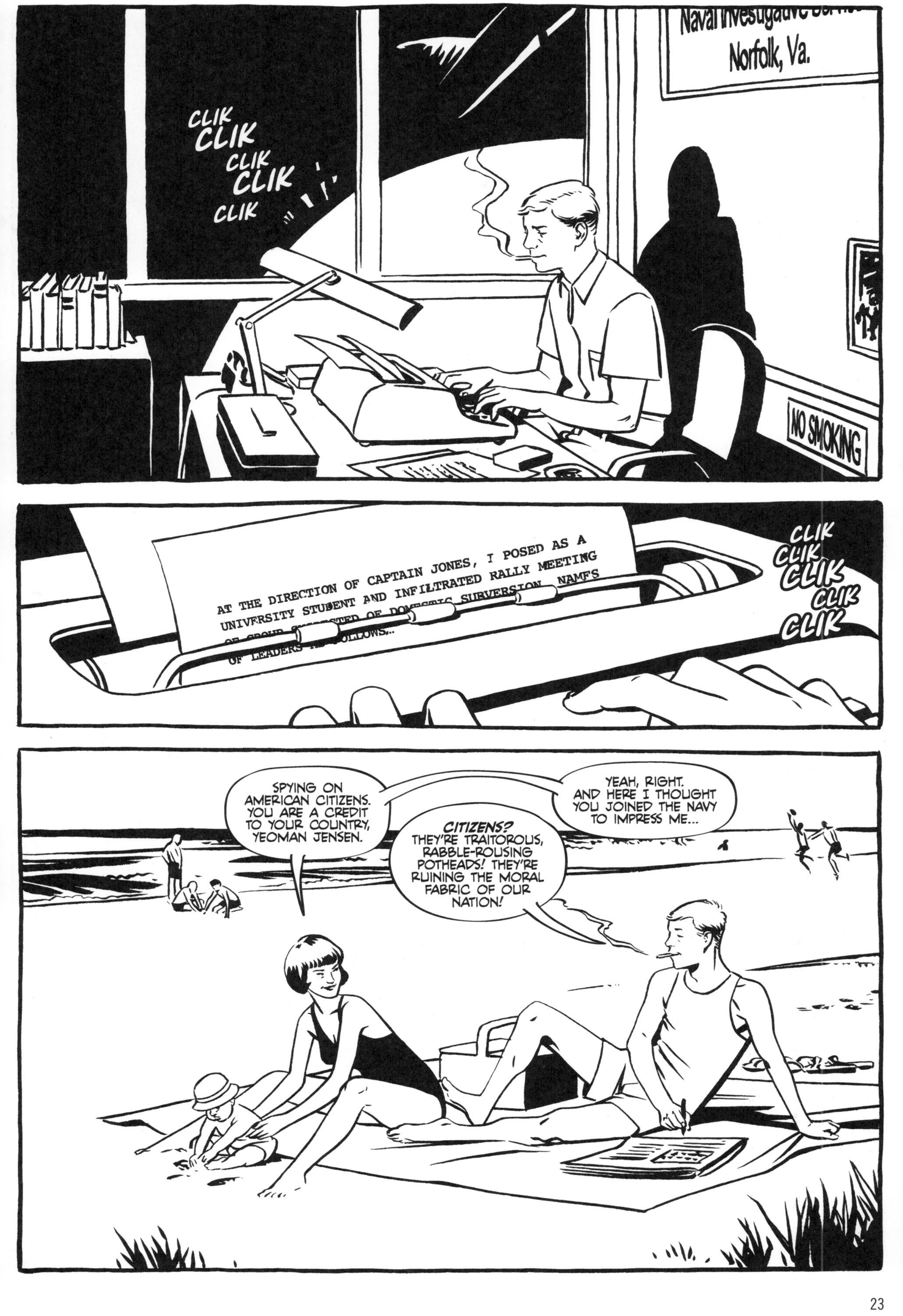
Naval Investigative Service
Norfolk, Va.
CLIK CLIK CLIK CLIK CLIK
NO SMOKING
AT THE DIRECTION OF CAPTAIN JONES, I POSED AS A
UNIVERSITY STUDENT AND INFILTRATED RALLY MEETING
CLIK CLIK CLIK CLIK CLIK
SPYING ON AMERICAN CITIZENS. YOU ARE A CREDIT TO YOUR COUNTRY, YEOMAN JENSEN.
CITIZENS? THEY'RE TRAITOROUS, RABBLE-ROUSING POTHEADS! THEY'RE RUINING THE MORAL FABRIC OF OUR NATION!
YEAH, RIGHT. AND HERE I THOUGHT YOU JOINED THE NAVY TO IMPRESS ME...

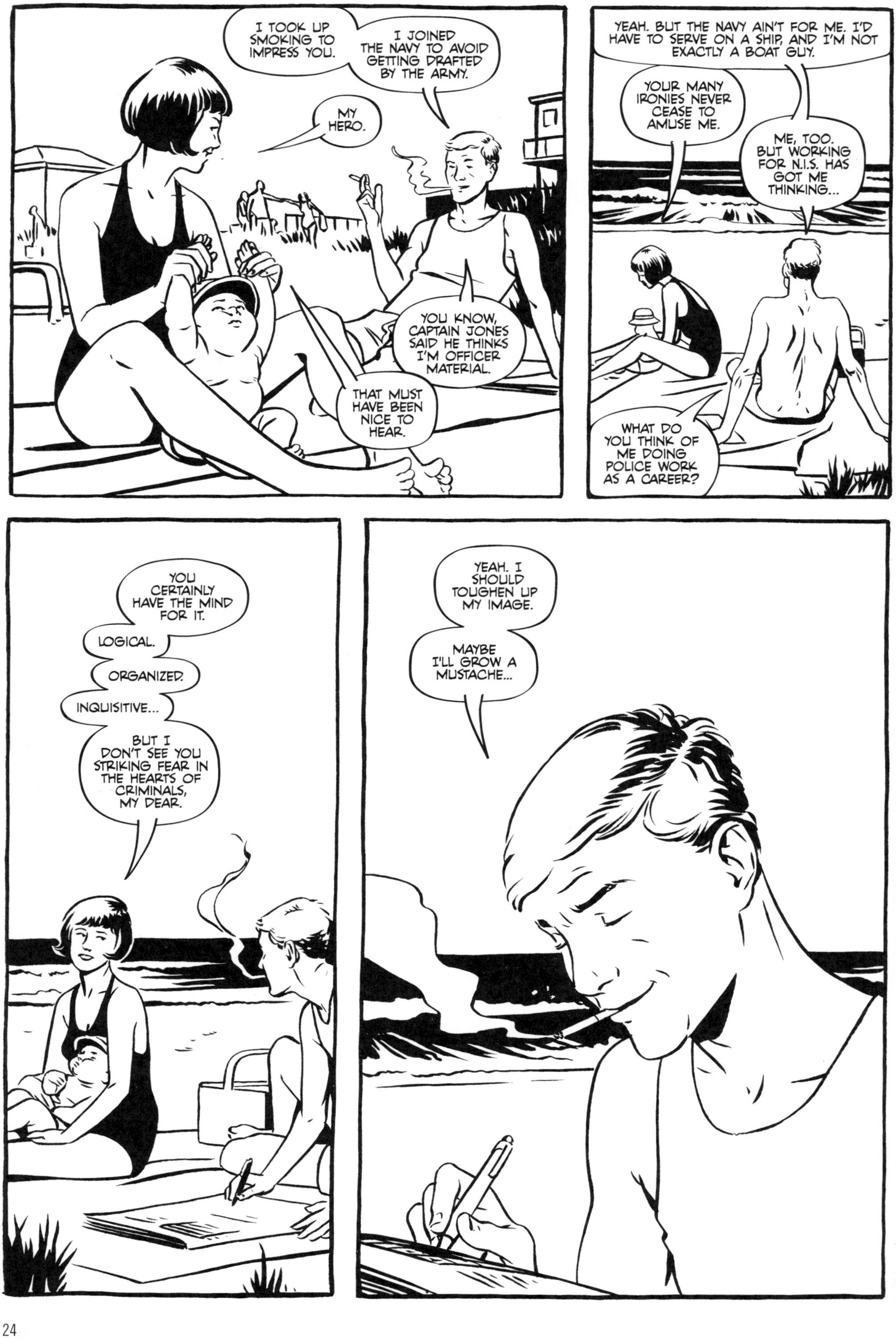
I TOOK UP SMOKING TO IMPRESS YOU.
I JOINED THE NAVY TO AVOID GETTING DRAFTED BY THE ARMY.
MY HERO.
YOU KNOW, CAPTAIN JONES SAID HE THINKS I'M OFFICER MATERIAL.
THAT MUST HAVE BEEN NICE TO HEAR.
YEAH. BUT THE NAVY AIN'T FOR ME. I'D HAVE TO SERVE ON A SHIP, AND I'M NOT EXACTLY A BOAT GUY.
YOUR MANY IRONIES NEVER CEASE TO AMUSE ME.
ME, TOO. BUT WORKING FOR N.I.S. HAS GOT ME THINKING...
WHAT DO YOU THINK OF ME DOING POLICE WORK AS A CAREER?
YOU CERTAINLY HAVE THE MIND FOR IT.
LOGICAL.
ORGANIZED.
INQUISITIVE...
BUT I DON'T SEE YOU STRIKING FEAR IN THE HEARTS OF CRIMINALS, MY DEAR.
YEAH. I SHOULD TOUGHEN UP MY IMAGE.
MAYBE I'LL GROW A MUSTACHE...

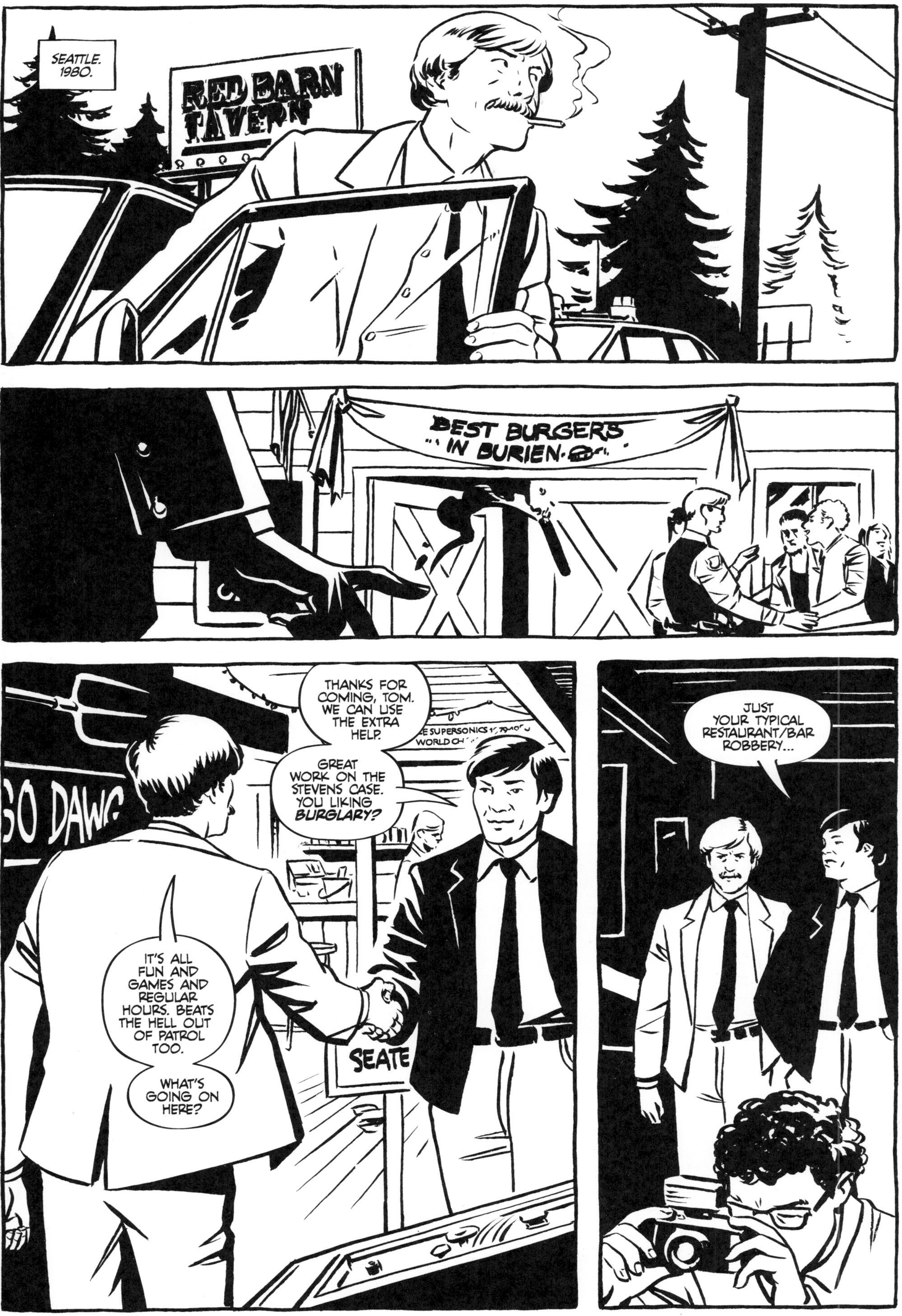
SEATTLE. 1980.
RED BARN TAVERN
BEST BURGERS IN BURIEN
THANKS FOR COMING, TOM. WE CAN USE THE EXTRA HELP.
GREAT WORK ON THE STEVENS CASE. YOU LIKING *BURGLARY?*
IT'S ALL FUN AND GAMES AND REGULAR HOURS. BEATS THE HELL OUT OF PATROL TOO.
WHAT'S GOING ON HERE?
JUST YOUR TYPICAL RESTAURANT/BAR ROBBERY...

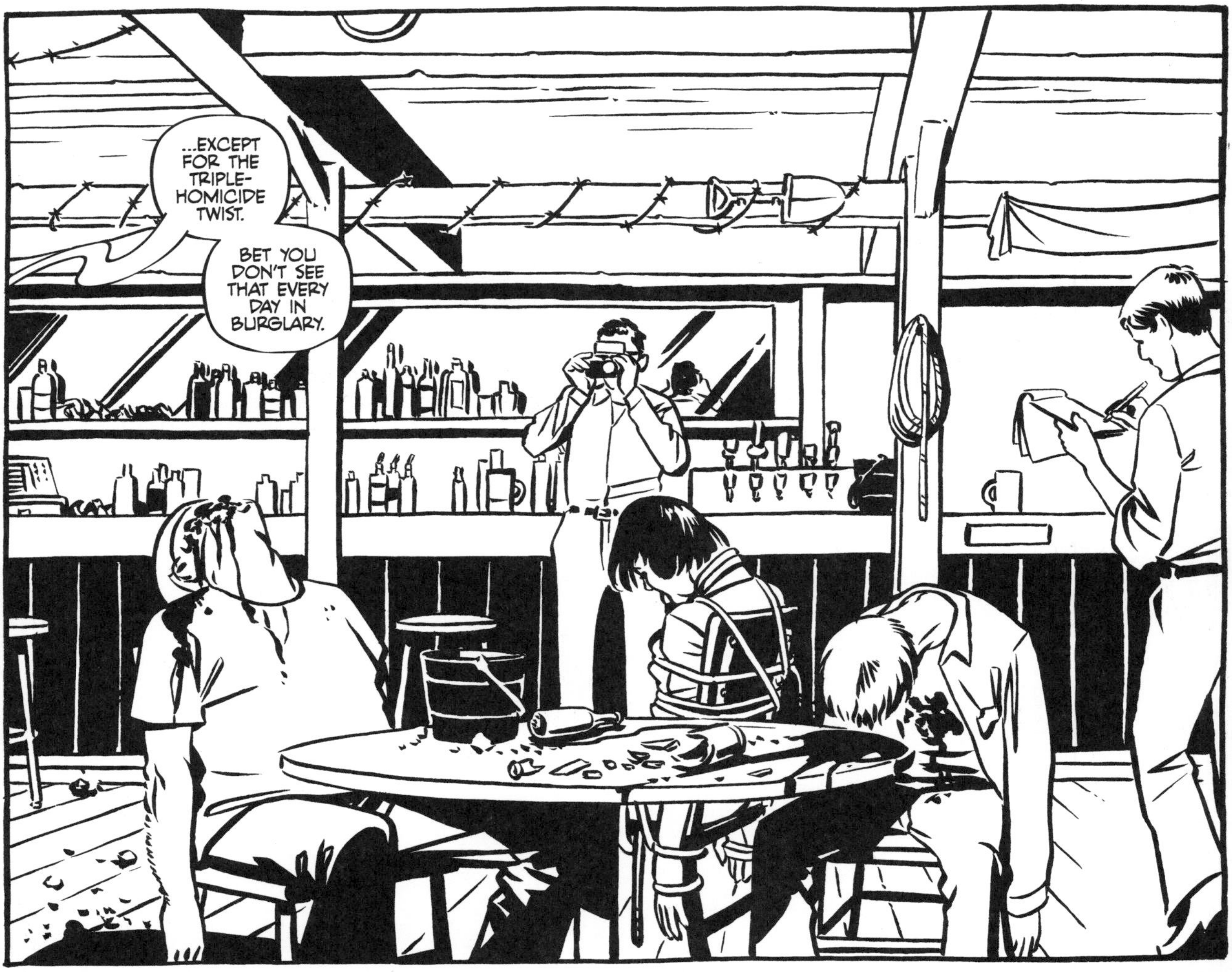
...EXCEPT FOR THE TRIPLE-HOMICIDE TWIST.
BET YOU DON'T SEE THAT EVERY DAY IN BURGLARY.

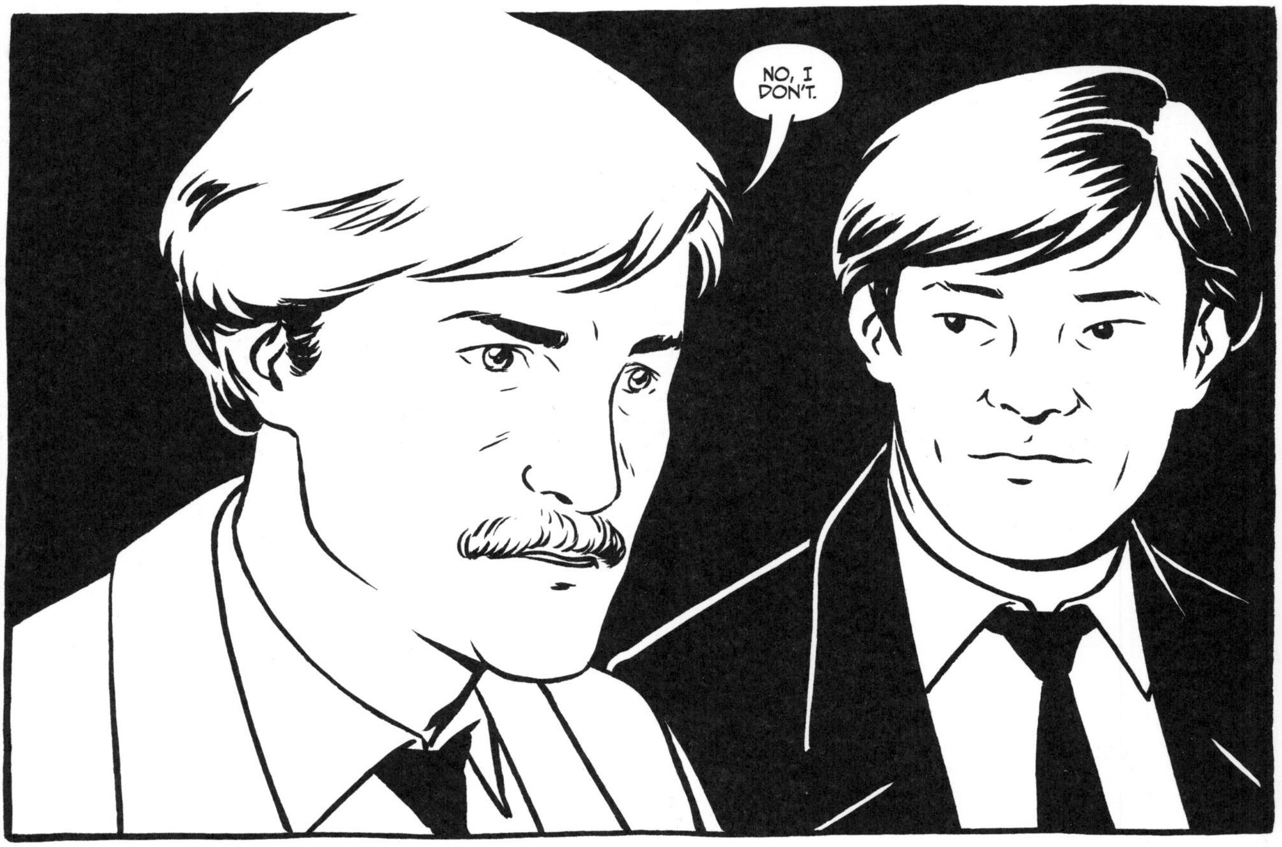
NO, I DON'T.

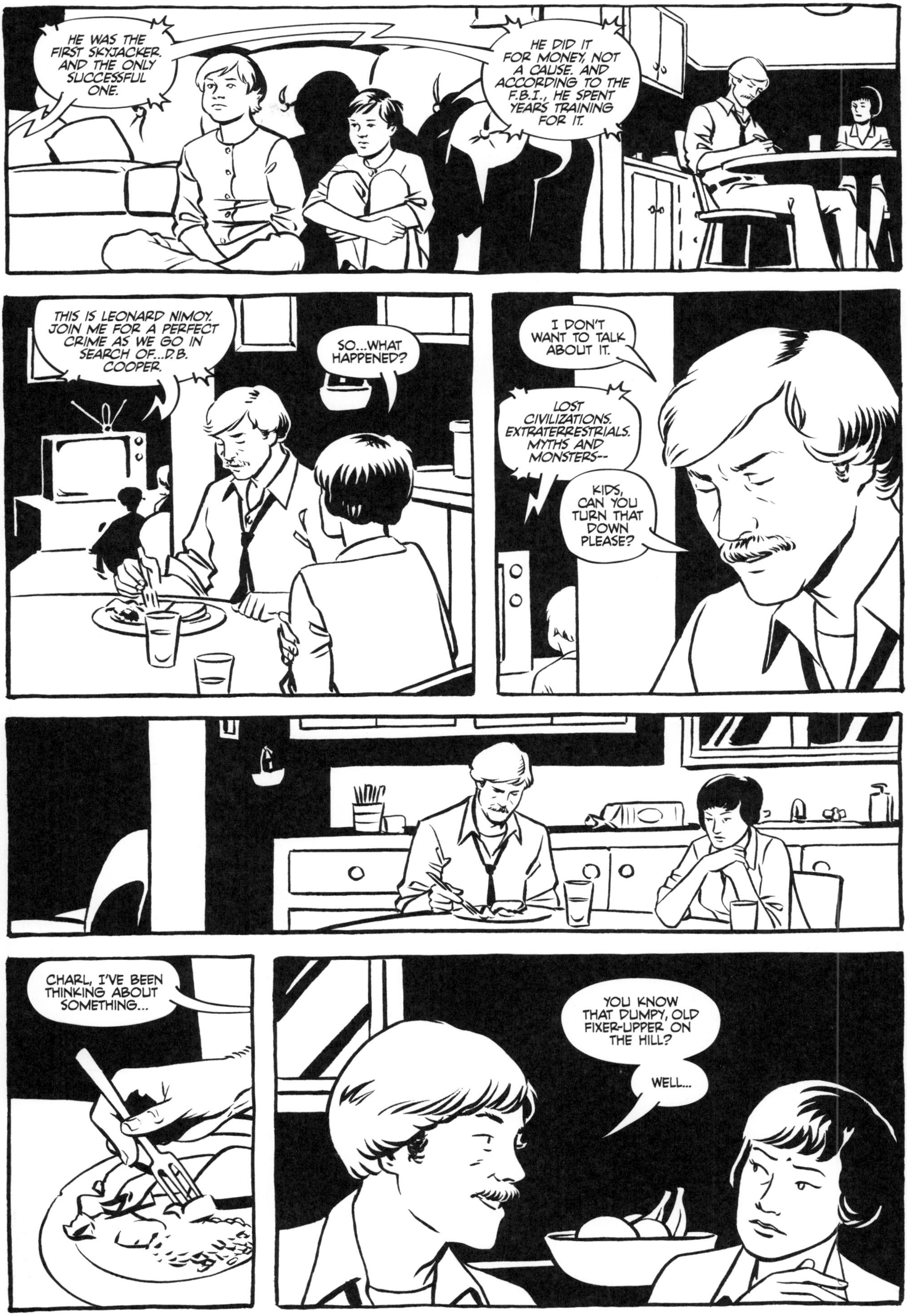
HE WAS THE FIRST SKYJACKER. AND THE ONLY SUCCESSFUL ONE.
HE DID IT FOR MONEY, NOT A CAUSE. AND ACCORDING TO THE F.B.I., HE SPENT YEARS TRAINING FOR IT.
THIS IS LEONARD NIMOY. JOIN ME FOR A PERFECT CRIME AS WE GO IN SEARCH OF...D.B. COOPER.
SO...WHAT HAPPENED?
I DON'T WANT TO TALK ABOUT IT.
LOST CIVILIZATIONS. EXTRATERRESTRIALS. MYTHS AND MONSTERS--
KIDS, CAN YOU TURN THAT DOWN PLEASE?
CHARL, I'VE BEEN THINKING ABOUT SOMETHING...
YOU KNOW THAT DUMPY, OLD FIXER-UPPER ON THE HILL?
WELL...

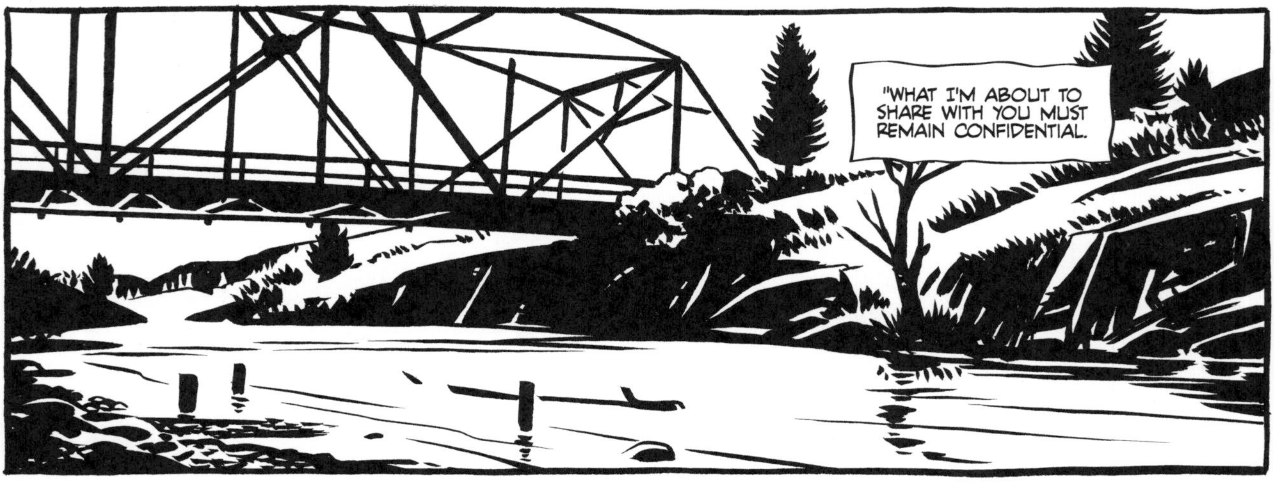
"WHAT I'M ABOUT TO SHARE WITH YOU MUST REMAIN CONFIDENTIAL.

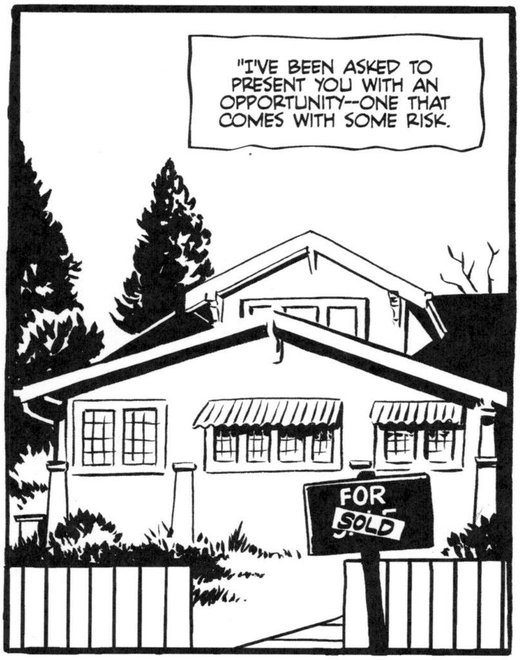
"I'VE BEEN ASKED TO PRESENT YOU WITH AN OPPORTUNITY--ONE THAT COMES WITH SOME RISK.
FOR
SOLD

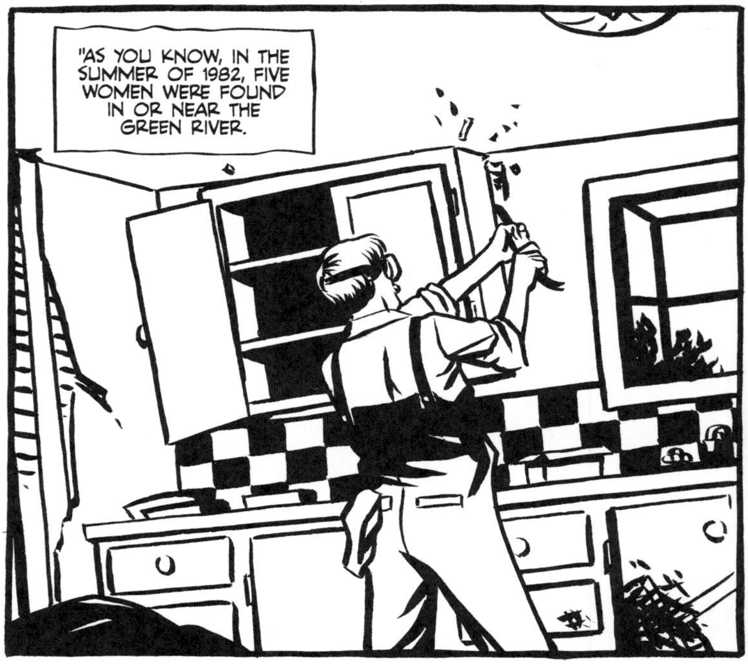
"AS YOU KNOW, IN THE SUMMER OF 1982, FIVE WOMEN WERE FOUND IN OR NEAR THE GREEN RIVER.

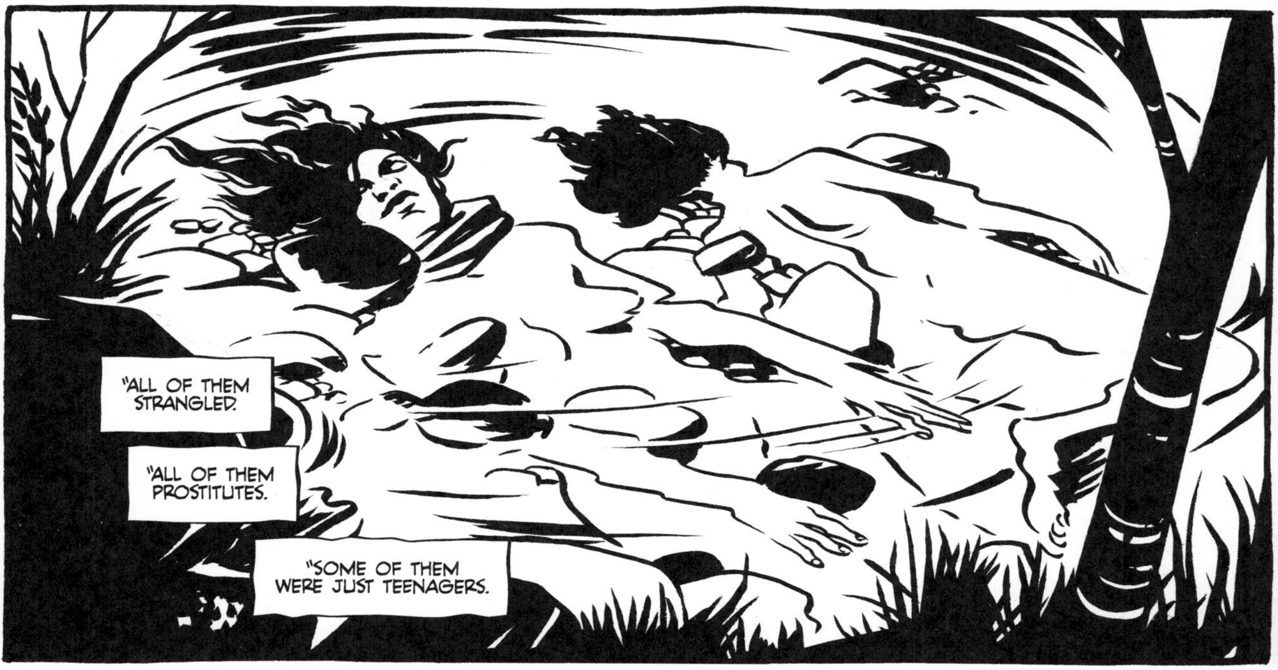
"ALL OF THEM STRANGLED.
"ALL OF THEM PROSTITUTES.
"SOME OF THEM WERE JUST TEENAGERS.

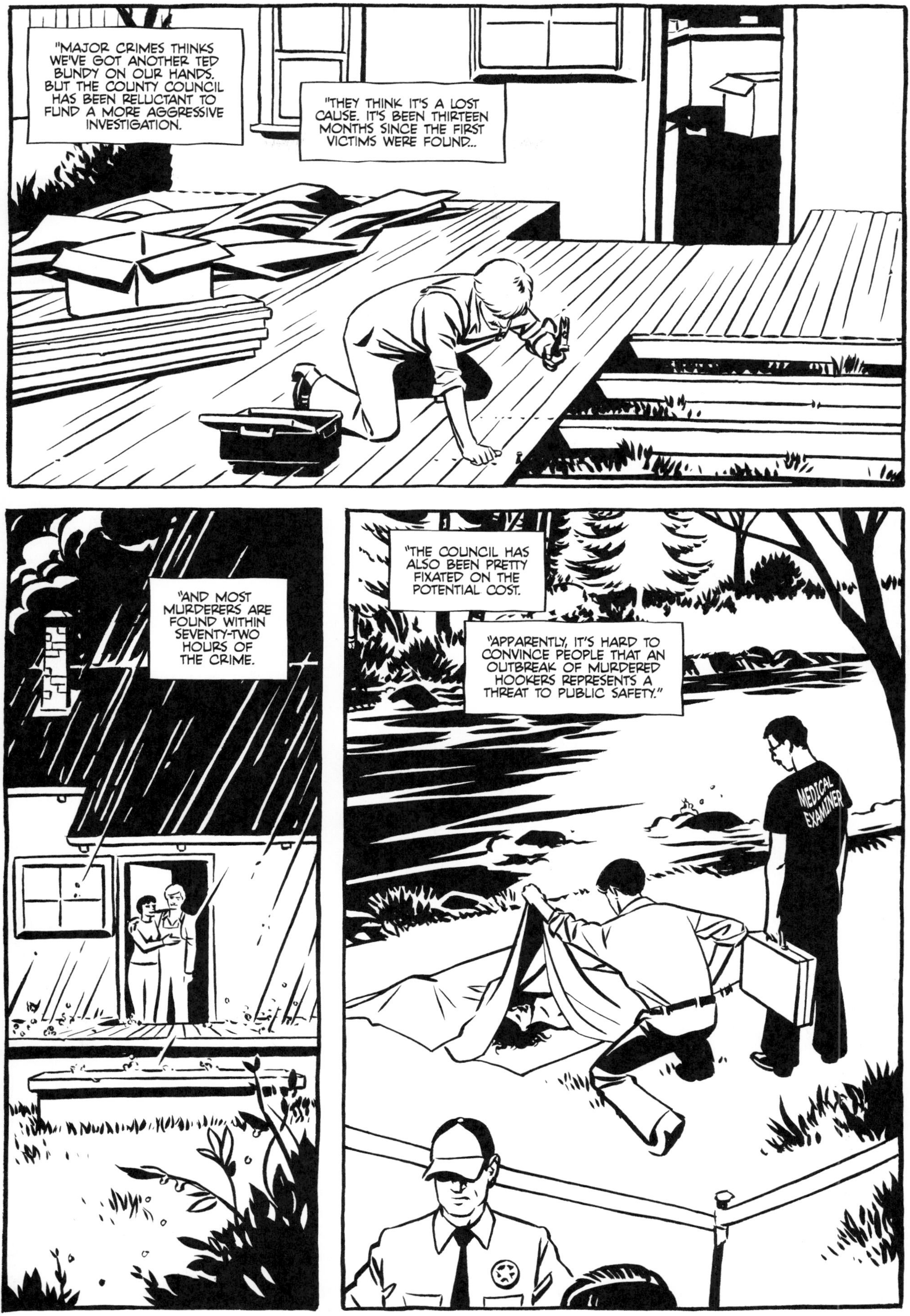
"MAJOR CRIMES THINKS WE'VE GOT ANOTHER TED BUNDY ON OUR HANDS. BUT THE COUNTY COUNCIL HAS BEEN RELUCTANT TO FUND A MORE AGGRESSIVE INVESTIGATION.
"THEY THINK IT'S A LOST CAUSE. IT'S BEEN THIRTEEN MONTHS SINCE THE FIRST VICTIMS WERE FOUND...
"AND MOST MURDERERS ARE FOUND WITHIN SEVENTY-TWO HOURS OF THE CRIME.
"THE COUNCIL HAS ALSO BEEN PRETTY FIXATED ON THE POTENTIAL COST.
"APPARENTLY, IT'S HARD TO CONVINCE PEOPLE THAT AN OUTBREAK OF MURDERED HOOKERS REPRESENTS A THREAT TO PUBLIC SAFETY."
MEDICAL EXAMINER

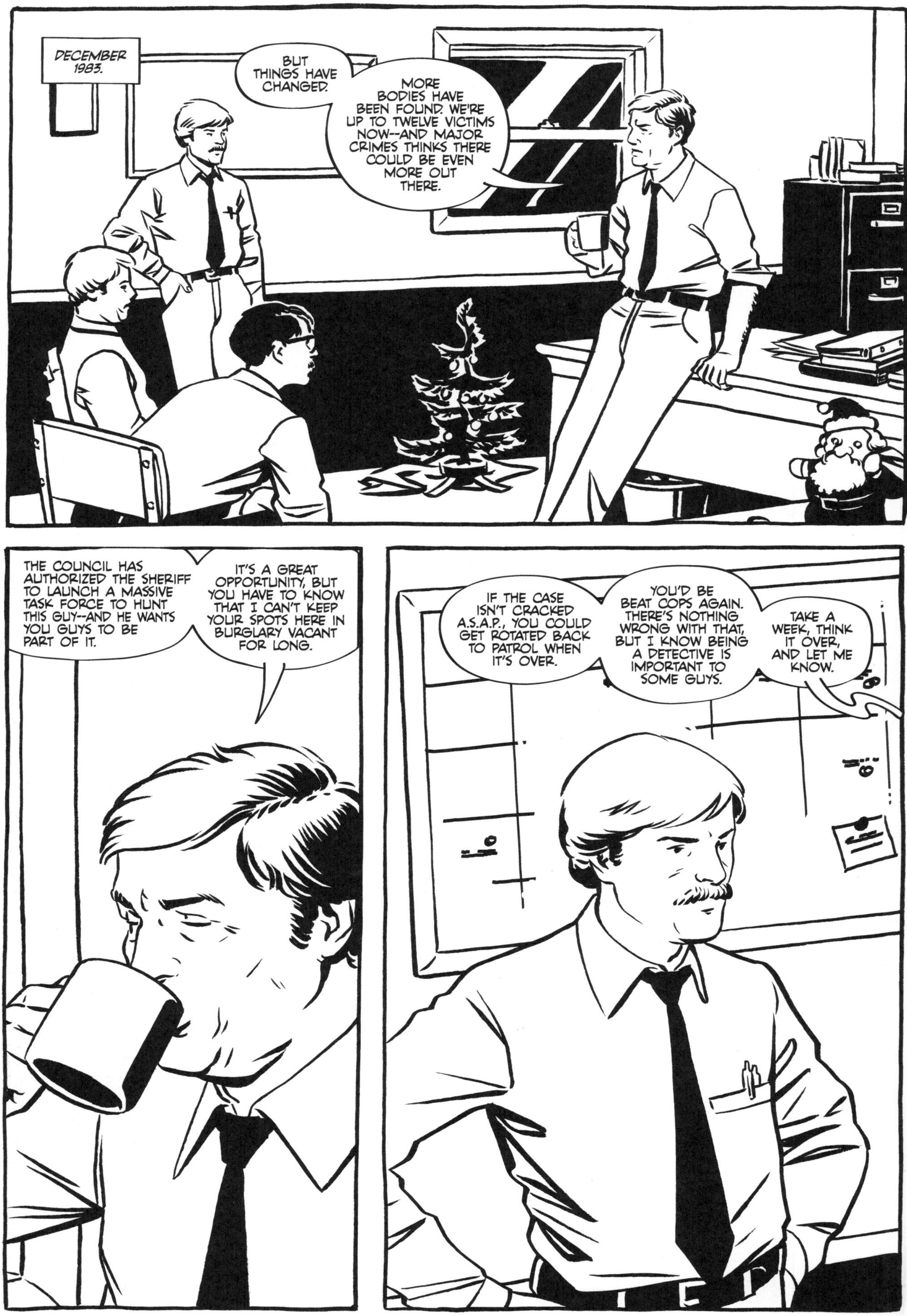
DECEMBER 1983.
BUT THINGS HAVE CHANGED.
MORE BODIES HAVE BEEN FOUND. WE'RE UP TO TWELVE VICTIMS NOW--AND MAJOR CRIMES THINKS THERE COULD BE EVEN MORE OUT THERE.
THE COUNCIL HAS AUTHORIZED THE SHERIFF TO LAUNCH A MASSIVE TASK FORCE TO HUNT THIS GUY--AND HE WANTS YOU GUYS TO BE PART OF IT.
IT'S A GREAT OPPORTUNITY, BUT YOU HAVE TO KNOW THAT I CAN'T KEEP YOUR SPOTS HERE IN BURGLARY VACANT FOR LONG.
IF THE CASE ISN'T CRACKED A.S.A.P., YOU COULD GET ROTATED BACK TO PATROL WHEN IT'S OVER.
YOU'D BE BEAT COPS AGAIN. THERE'S NOTHING WRONG WITH THAT, BUT I KNOW BEING A DETECTIVE IS IMPORTANT TO SOME GUYS.
TAKE A WEEK, THINK IT OVER, AND LET ME KNOW.

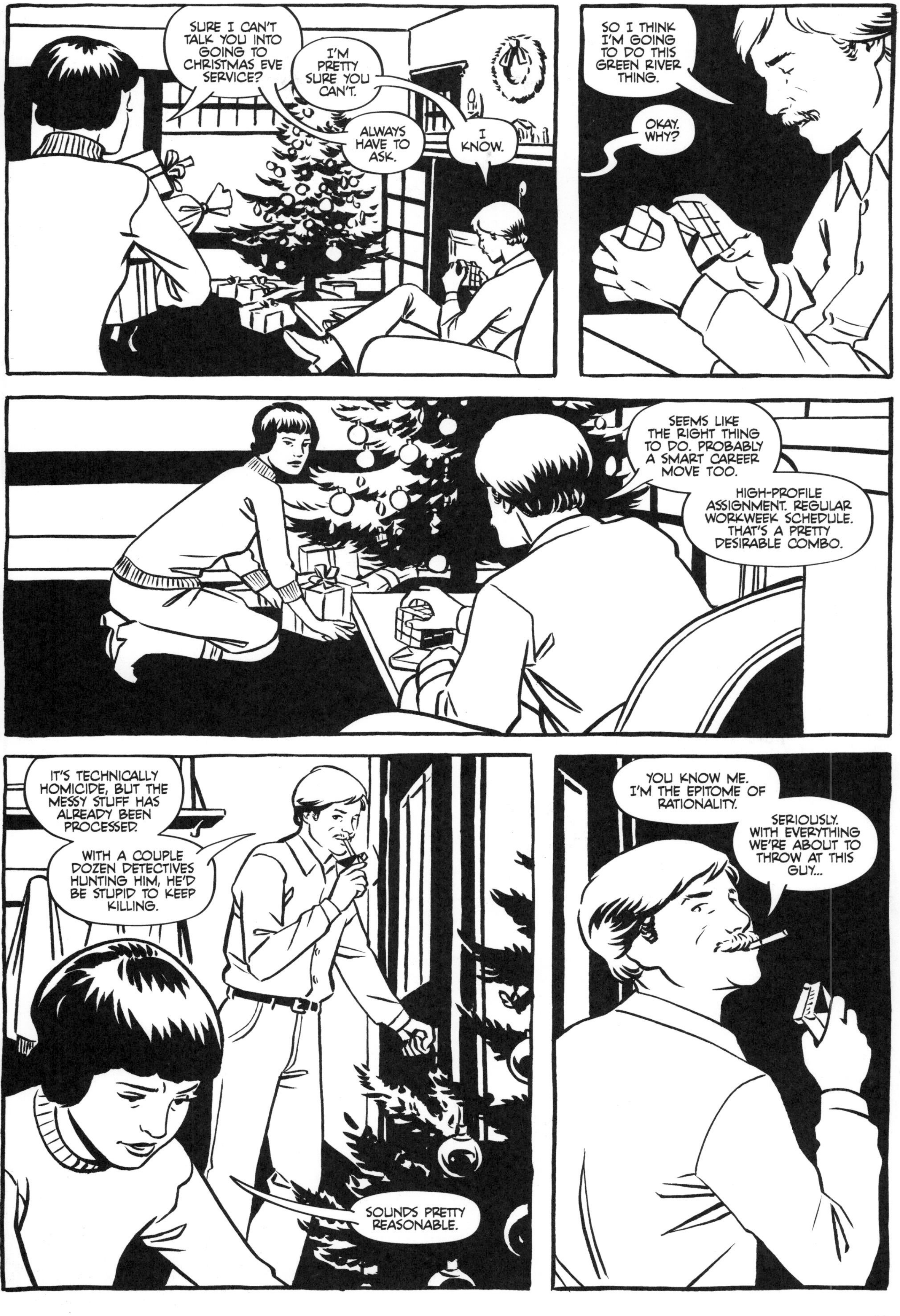
SURE I CAN'T TALK YOU INTO GOING TO CHRISTMAS EVE SERVICE?
I'M PRETTY SURE YOU CAN'T.
ALWAYS HAVE TO ASK.
I KNOW.
SO I THINK I'M GOING TO DO THIS GREEN RIVER THING.
OKAY. WHY?
SEEMS LIKE THE RIGHT THING TO DO. PROBABLY A SMART CAREER MOVE TOO.
HIGH-PROFILE ASSIGNMENT. REGULAR WORKWEEK SCHEDULE. THAT'S A PRETTY DESIRABLE COMBO.
IT'S TECHNICALLY HOMICIDE, BUT THE MESSY STUFF HAS ALREADY BEEN PROCESSED.
WITH A COUPLE DOZEN DETECTIVES HUNTING HIM, HE'D BE STUPID TO KEEP KILLING.
SOUNDS PRETTY REASONABLE.
YOU KNOW ME. I'M THE EPITOME OF RATIONALITY.
SERIOUSLY. WITH EVERYTHING WE'RE ABOUT TO THROW AT THIS GUY...

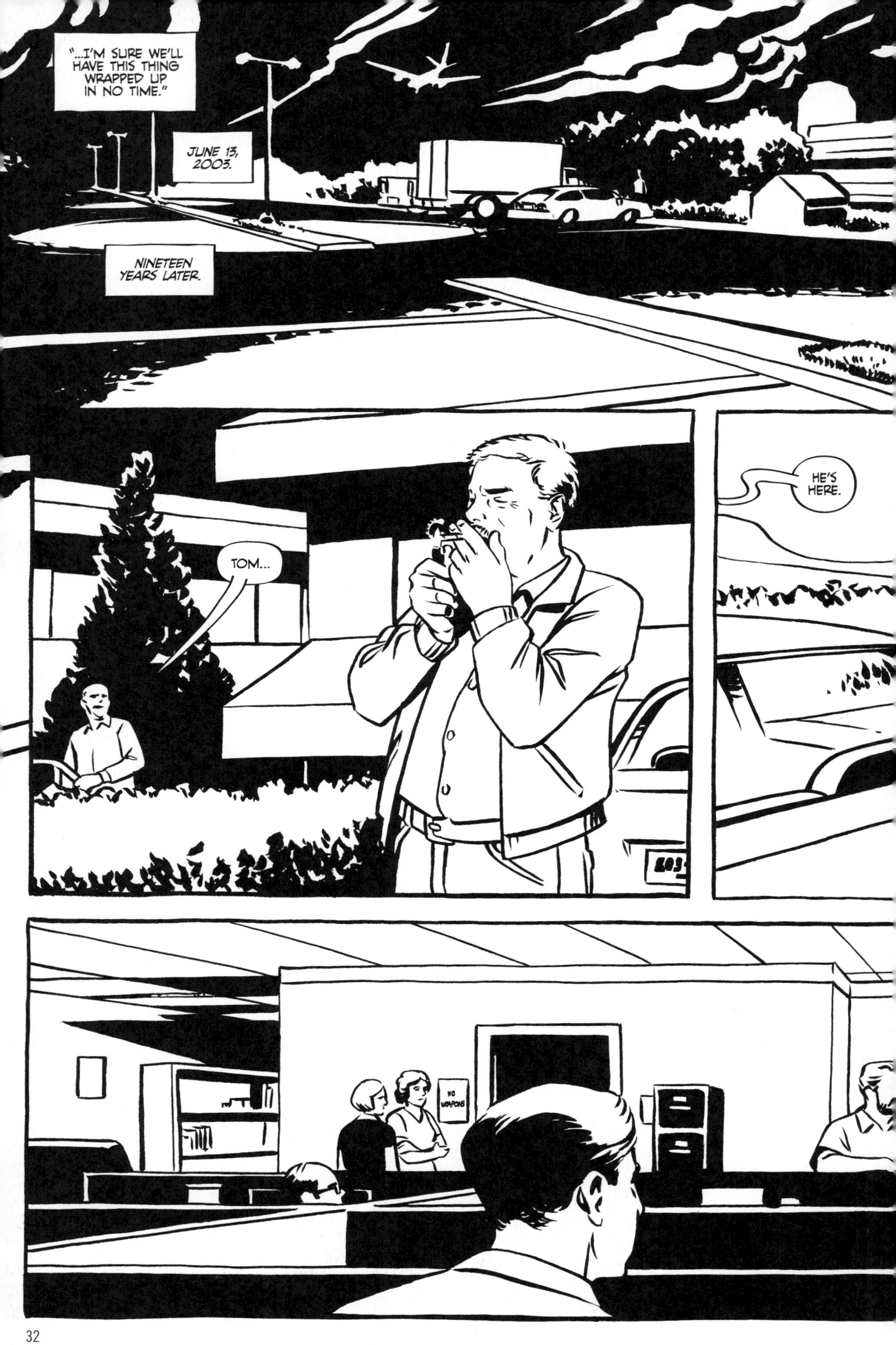
"...I'M SURE WE'LL HAVE THIS THING WRAPPED UP IN NO TIME."
JUNE 13, 2003.
NINETEEN YEARS LATER.
TOM...
HE'S HERE.
NO WEAPONS

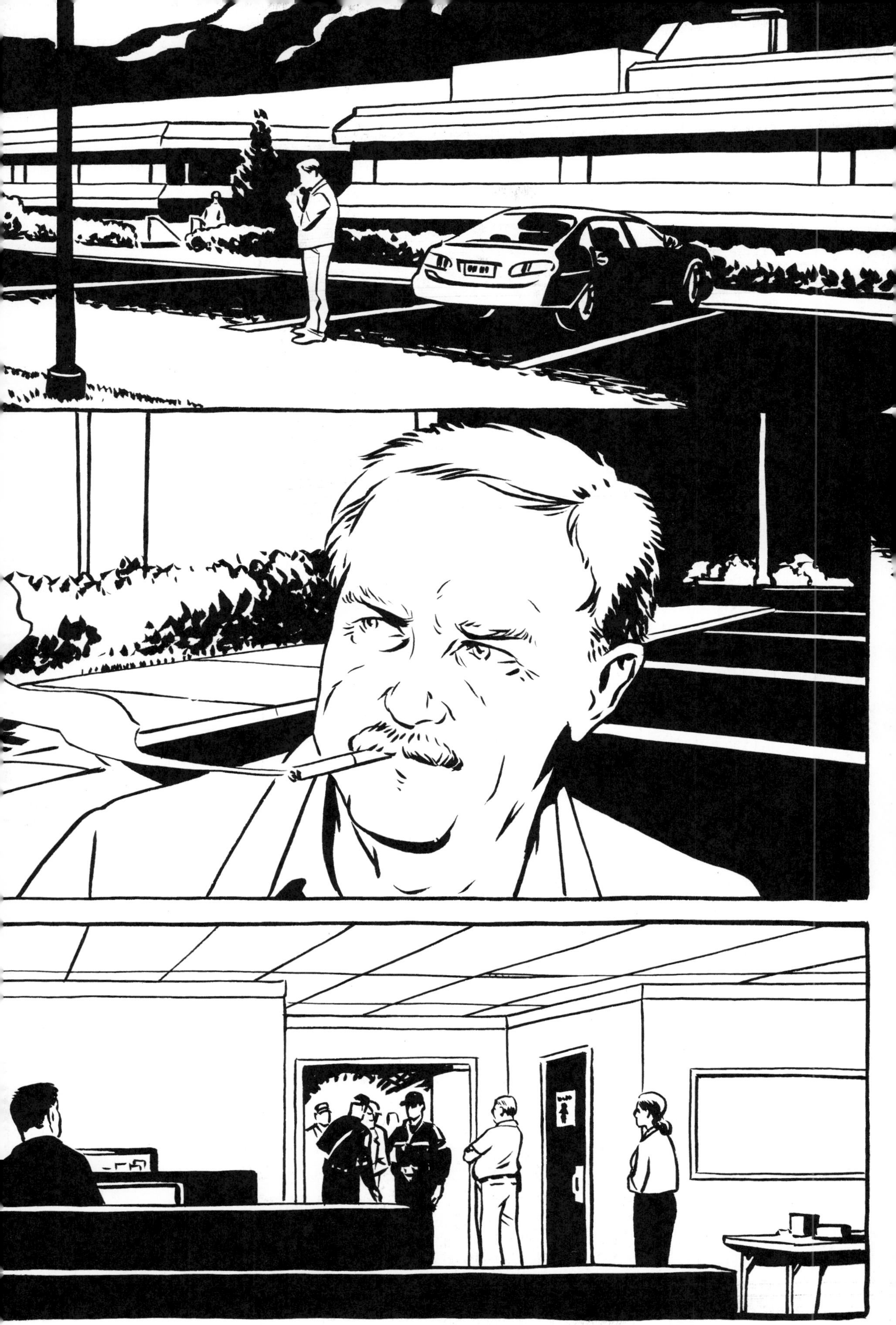

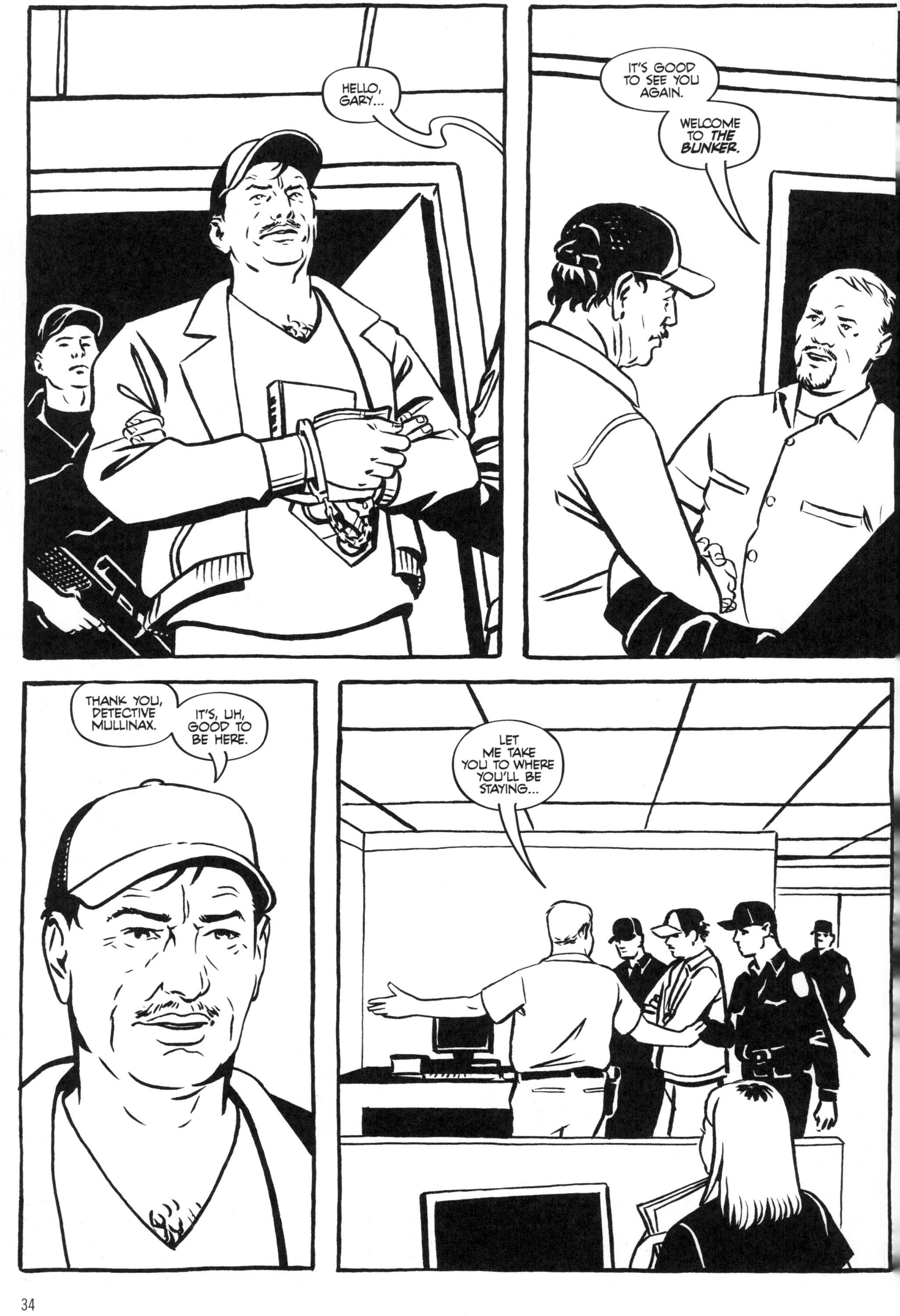
HELLO, GARY...
IT'S GOOD TO SEE YOU AGAIN.
WELCOME TO THE BUNKER.
THANK YOU, DETECTIVE MULLINAX.
IT'S, UH, GOOD TO BE HERE.
LET ME TAKE YOU TO WHERE YOU'LL BE STAYING...

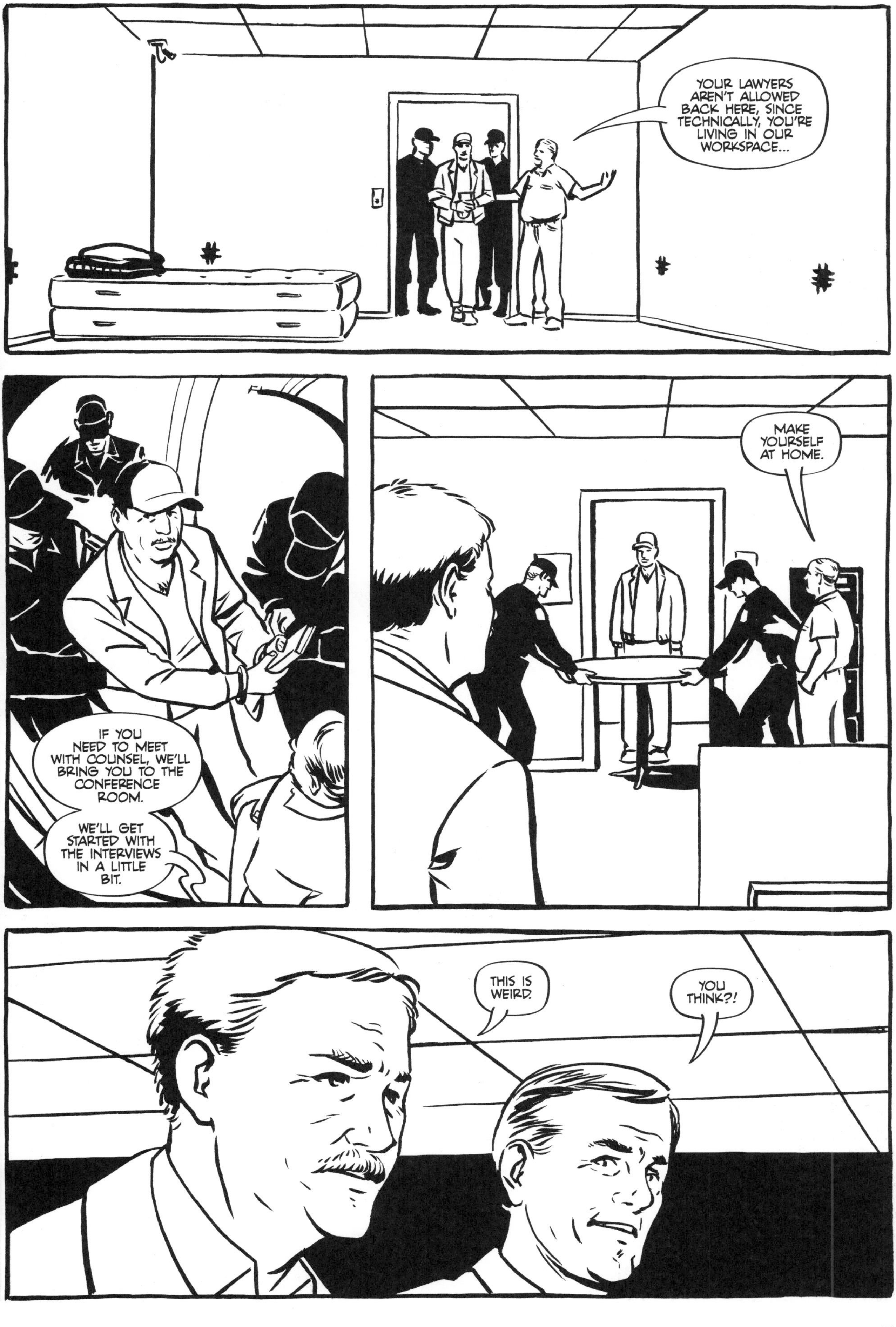
YOUR LAWYERS AREN'T ALLOWED BACK HERE, SINCE TECHNICALLY, YOU'RE LIVING IN OUR WORKSPACE...
IF YOU NEED TO MEET WITH COUNSEL, WE'LL BRING YOU TO THE CONFERENCE ROOM.
WE'LL GET STARTED WITH THE INTERVIEWS IN A LITTLE BIT.
MAKE YOURSELF AT HOME.
THIS IS WEIRD.
YOU THINK?!

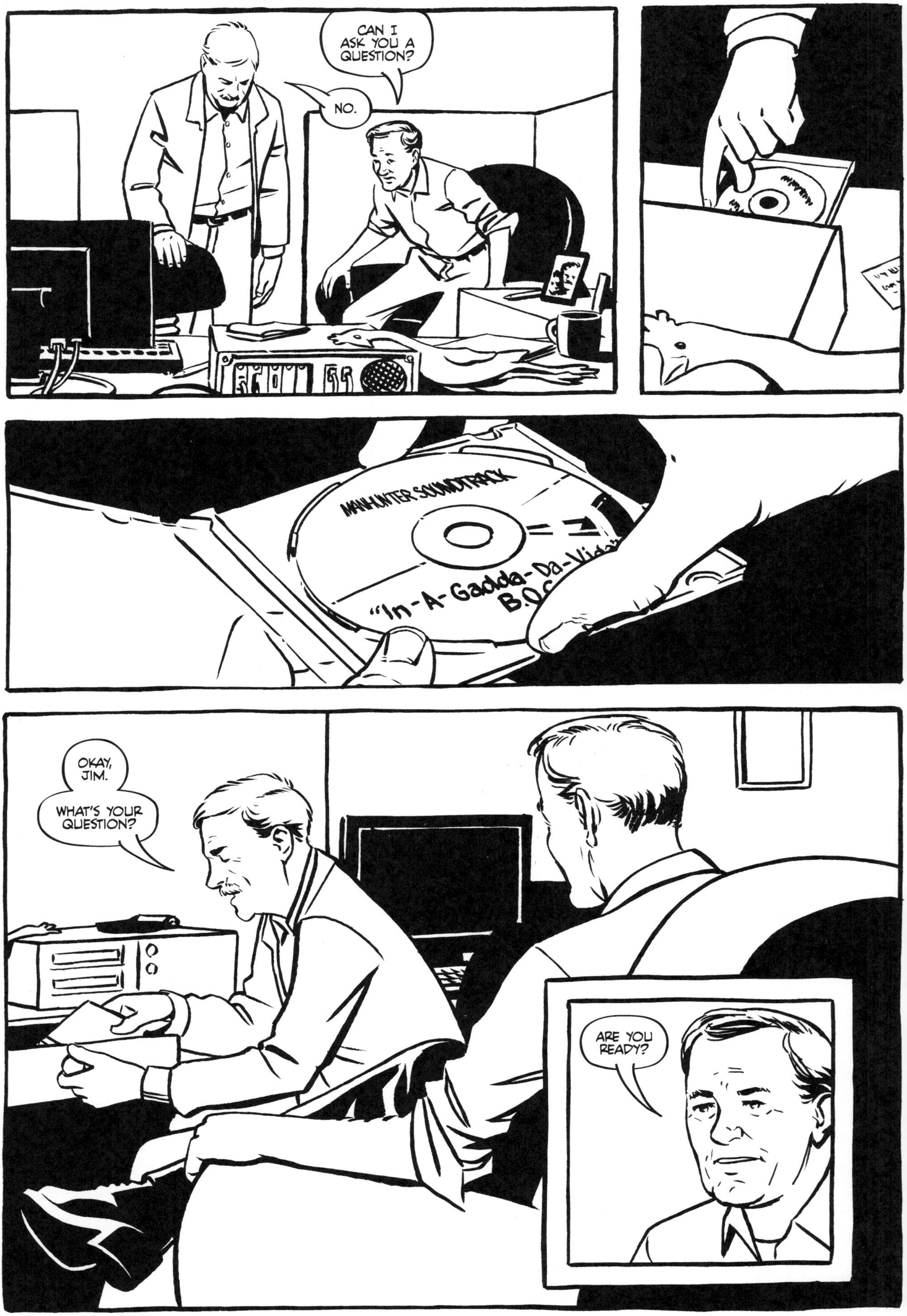
CAN I ASK YOU A QUESTION?
NO.
MANHUNTER SOUNDTRACK
“In-A-Gadda-Da-
OKAY, JIM.
WHAT'S YOUR QUESTION?
ARE YOU READY?

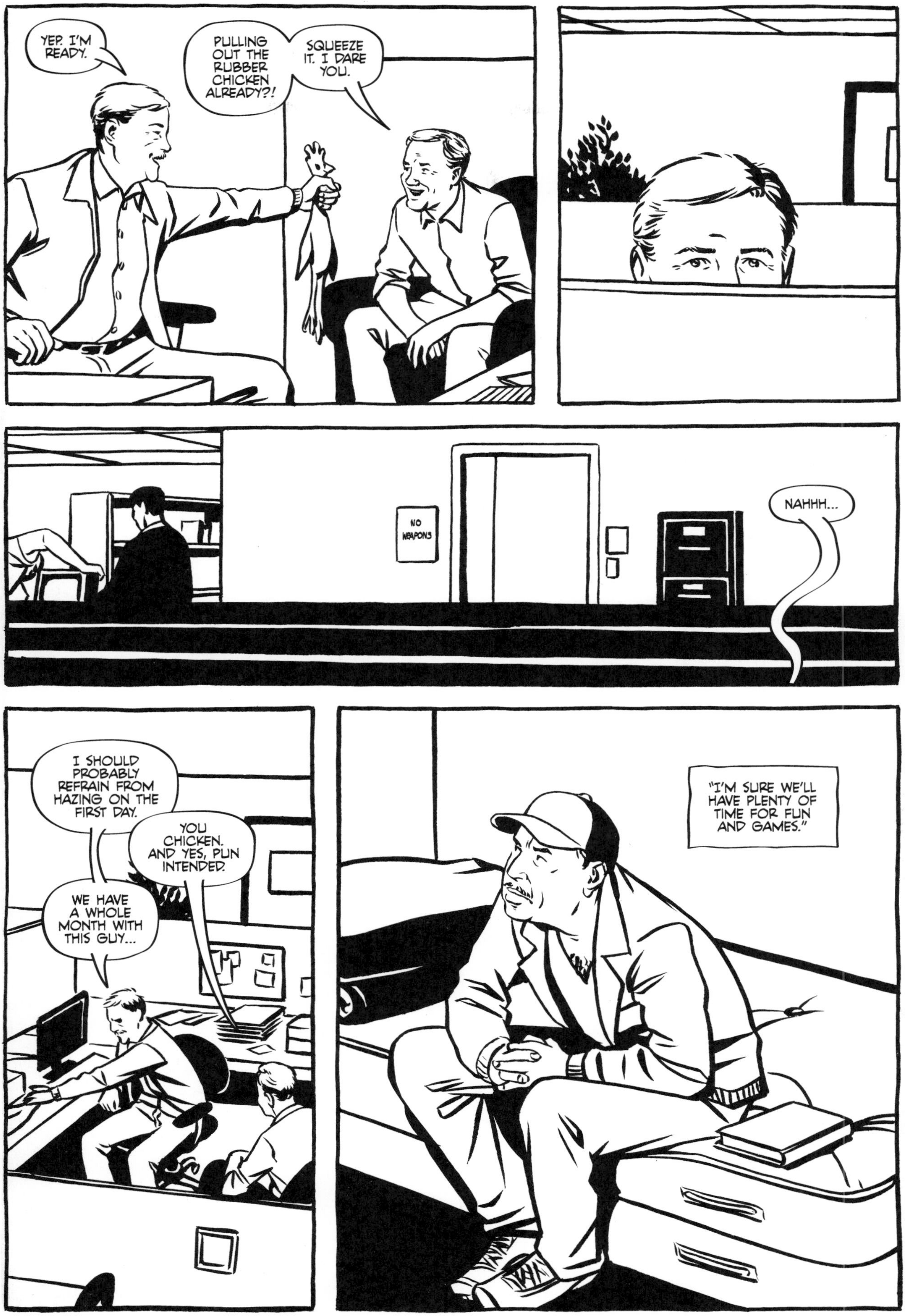
YEP. I'M READY.
PULLING OUT THE RUBBER CHICKEN ALREADY?!
SQUEEZE IT. I DARE YOU.
NO WEAPONS
NAHHH...
I SHOULD PROBABLY REFRAIN FROM HAZING ON THE FIRST DAY.
YOU CHICKEN. AND YES, PUN INTENDED.
WE HAVE A WHOLE MONTH WITH THIS GUY...
"I'M SURE WE'LL HAVE PLENTY OF TIME FOR FUN AND GAMES."

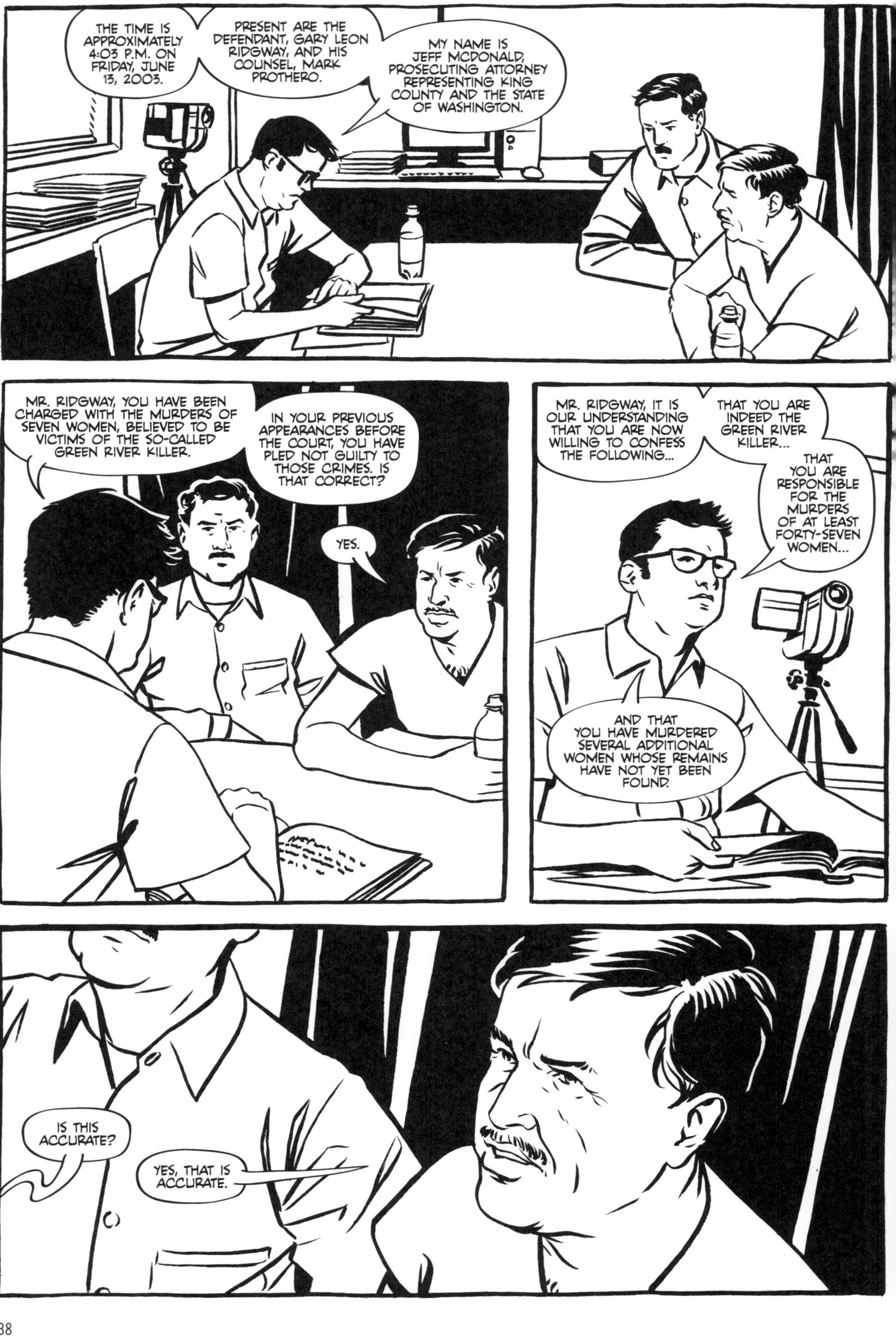
THE TIME IS APPROXIMATELY 4:03 P.M. ON FRIDAY, JUNE 13, 2003.
PRESENT ARE THE DEFENDANT, GARY LEON RIDGWAY, AND HIS COUNSEL, MARK PROTHERO.
MY NAME IS JEFF MCDONALD, PROSECUTING ATTORNEY REPRESENTING KING COUNTY AND THE STATE OF WASHINGTON.
MR. RIDGWAY, YOU HAVE BEEN CHARGED WITH THE MURDERS OF SEVEN WOMEN, BELIEVED TO BE VICTIMS OF THE SO-CALLED GREEN RIVER KILLER.
IN YOUR PREVIOUS APPEARANCES BEFORE THE COURT, YOU HAVE PLED NOT GUILTY TO THOSE CRIMES. IS THAT CORRECT?
YES.
MR. RIDGWAY, IT IS OUR UNDERSTANDING THAT YOU ARE NOW WILLING TO CONFESS THE FOLLOWING...
THAT YOU ARE INDEED THE GREEN RIVER KILLER...
THAT YOU ARE RESPONSIBLE FOR THE MURDERS OF AT LEAST FORTY-SEVEN WOMEN...
AND THAT YOU HAVE MURDERED SEVERAL ADDITIONAL WOMEN WHOSE REMAINS HAVE NOT YET BEEN FOUND.
IS THIS ACCURATE?
YES, THAT IS ACCURATE.

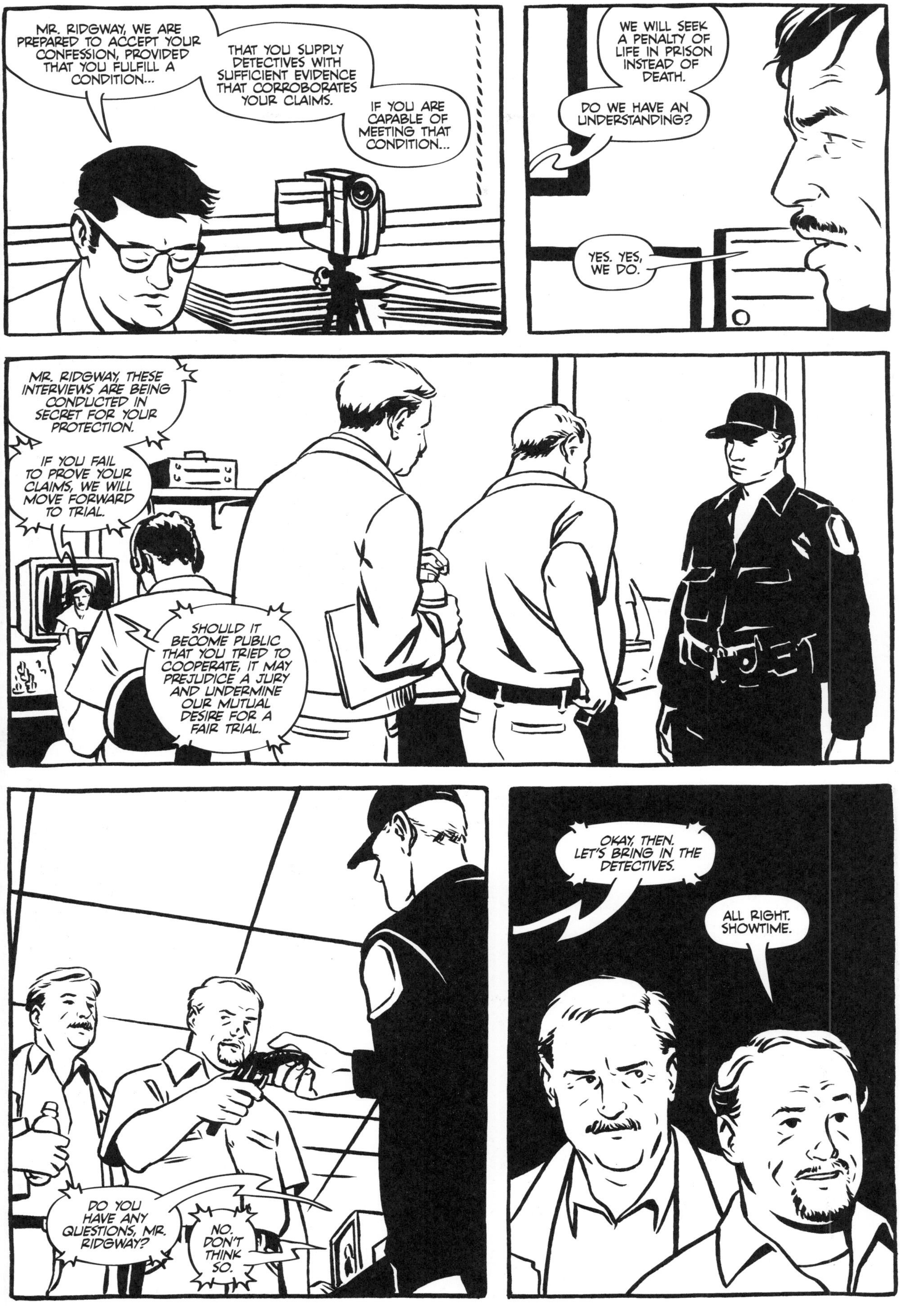
MR. RIDGWAY, WE ARE PREPARED TO ACCEPT YOUR CONFESSION, PROVIDED THAT YOU FULFILL A CONDITION...
THAT YOU SUPPLY DETECTIVES WITH SUFFICIENT EVIDENCE THAT CORROBORATES YOUR CLAIMS.
IF YOU ARE CAPABLE OF MEETING THAT CONDITION...
WE WILL SEEK A PENALTY OF LIFE IN PRISON INSTEAD OF DEATH.
DO WE HAVE AN UNDERSTANDING?
YES. YES, WE DO.
MR. RIDGWAY, THESE INTERVIEWS ARE BEING CONDUCTED IN SECRET FOR YOUR PROTECTION.
IF YOU FAIL TO PROVE YOUR CLAIMS, WE WILL MOVE FORWARD TO TRIAL.
SHOULD IT BECOME PUBLIC THAT YOU TRIED TO COOPERATE, IT MAY PREJUDICE A JURY AND UNDERMINE OUR MUTUAL DESIRE FOR A FAIR TRIAL.
DO YOU HAVE ANY QUESTIONS, MR. RIDGWAY?
NO. DON'T THINK SO.
OKAY, THEN. LET'S BRING IN THE DETECTIVES.
ALL RIGHT. SHOWTIME.

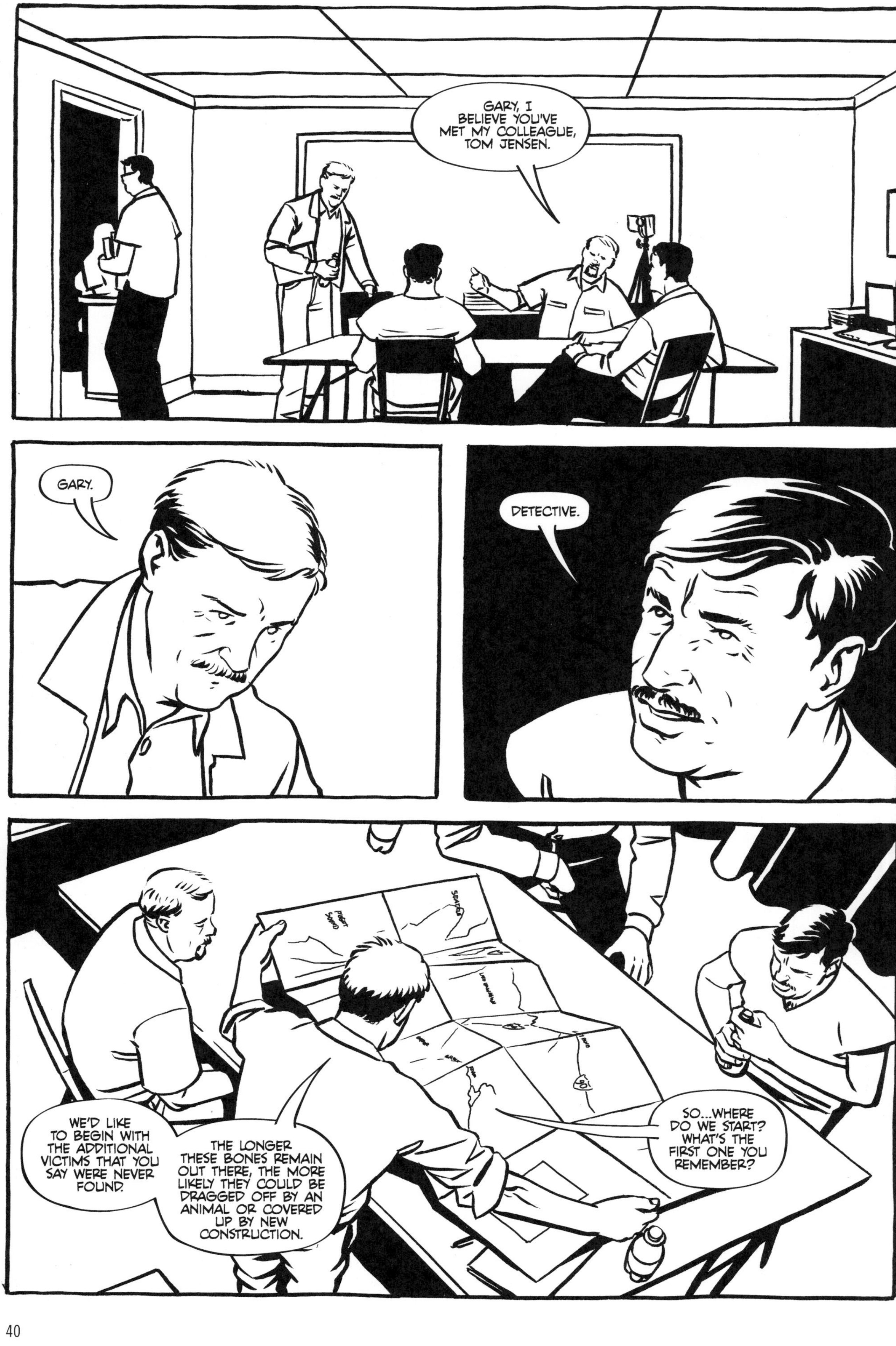
GARY, I BELIEVE YOU'VE MET MY COLLEAGUE, TOM JENSEN.
GARY.
DETECTIVE.
WE'D LIKE TO BEGIN WITH THE ADDITIONAL VICTIMS THAT YOU SAY WERE NEVER FOUND.
THE LONGER THESE BONES REMAIN OUT THERE, THE MORE LIKELY THEY COULD BE DRAGGED OFF BY AN ANIMAL OR COVERED UP BY NEW CONSTRUCTION.
SO...WHERE DO WE START? WHAT'S THE FIRST ONE YOU REMEMBER?

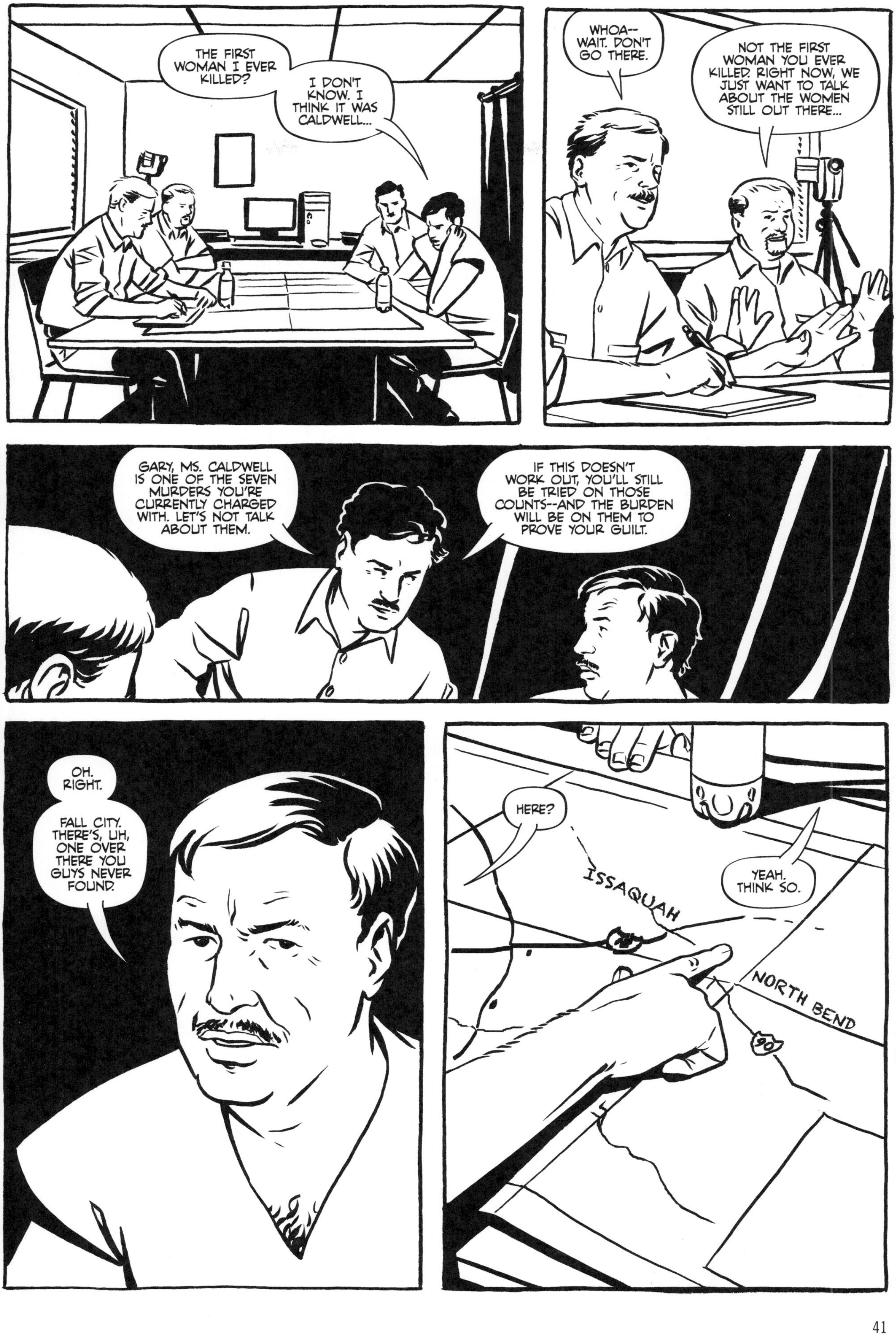
THE FIRST WOMAN I EVER KILLED?
I DON'T KNOW. I THINK IT WAS CALDWELL...
WHOA-- WAIT. DON'T GO THERE.
NOT THE FIRST WOMAN YOU EVER KILLED. RIGHT NOW, WE JUST WANT TO TALK ABOUT THE WOMEN STILL OUT THERE...
GARY, MS. CALDWELL IS ONE OF THE SEVEN MURDERS YOU'RE CURRENTLY CHARGED WITH. LET'S NOT TALK ABOUT THEM.
IF THIS DOESN'T WORK OUT, YOU'LL STILL BE TRIED ON THOSE COUNTS--AND THE BURDEN WILL BE ON THEM TO PROVE YOUR GUILT.
OH. RIGHT.
FALL CITY. THERE'S, UH, ONE OVER THERE YOU GUYS NEVER FOUND.
HERE?
YEAH. THINK SO.
ISSAQUAH
NORTH BEND
90

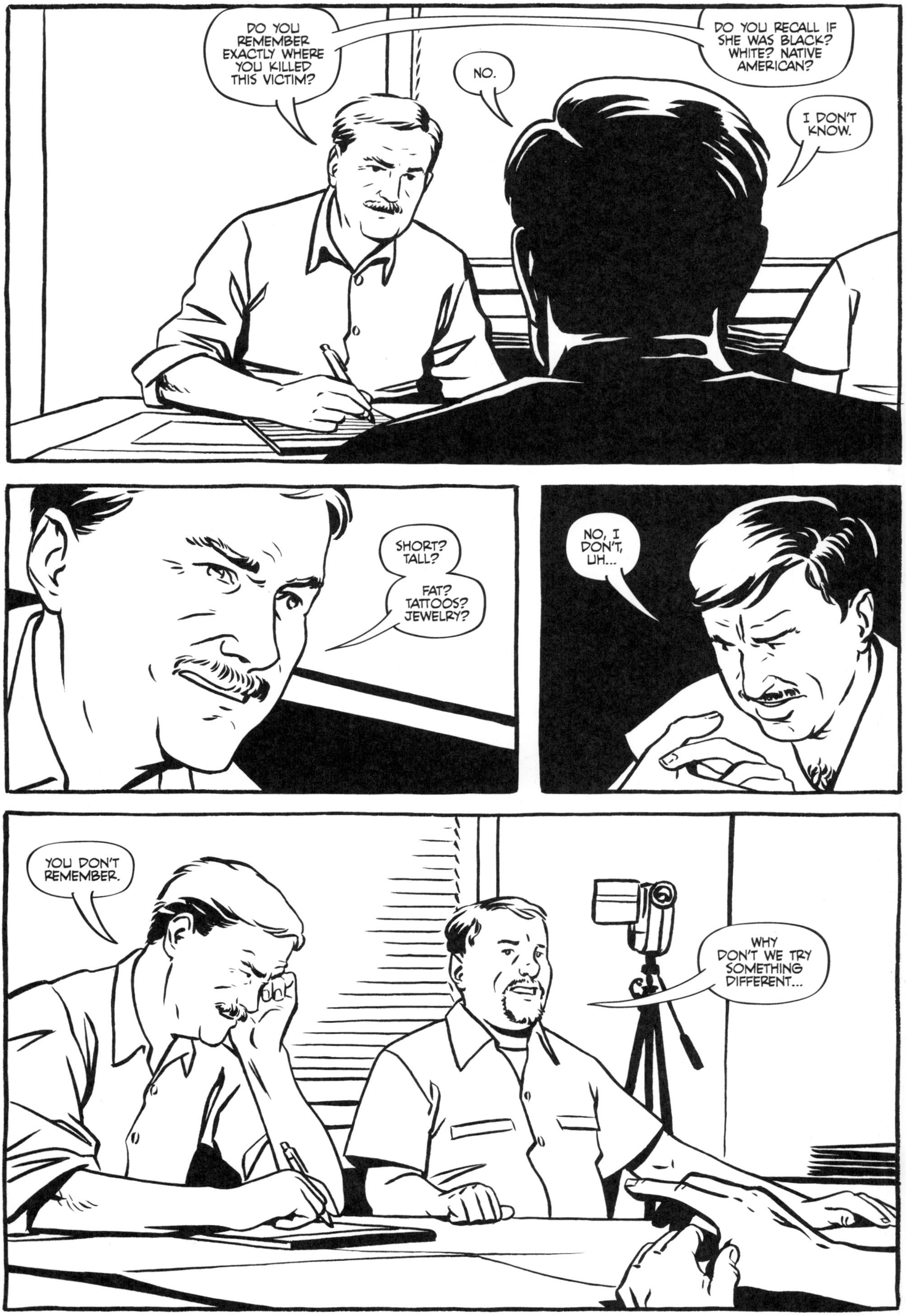
DO YOU REMEMBER EXACTLY WHERE YOU KILLED THIS VICTIM?
NO.
DO YOU RECALL IF SHE WAS BLACK? WHITE? NATIVE AMERICAN?
I DON'T KNOW.
SHORT? TALL?
FAT? TATTOOS? JEWELRY?
NO, I DON'T, UH...
YOU DON'T REMEMBER.
WHY DON'T WE TRY SOMETHING DIFFERENT...

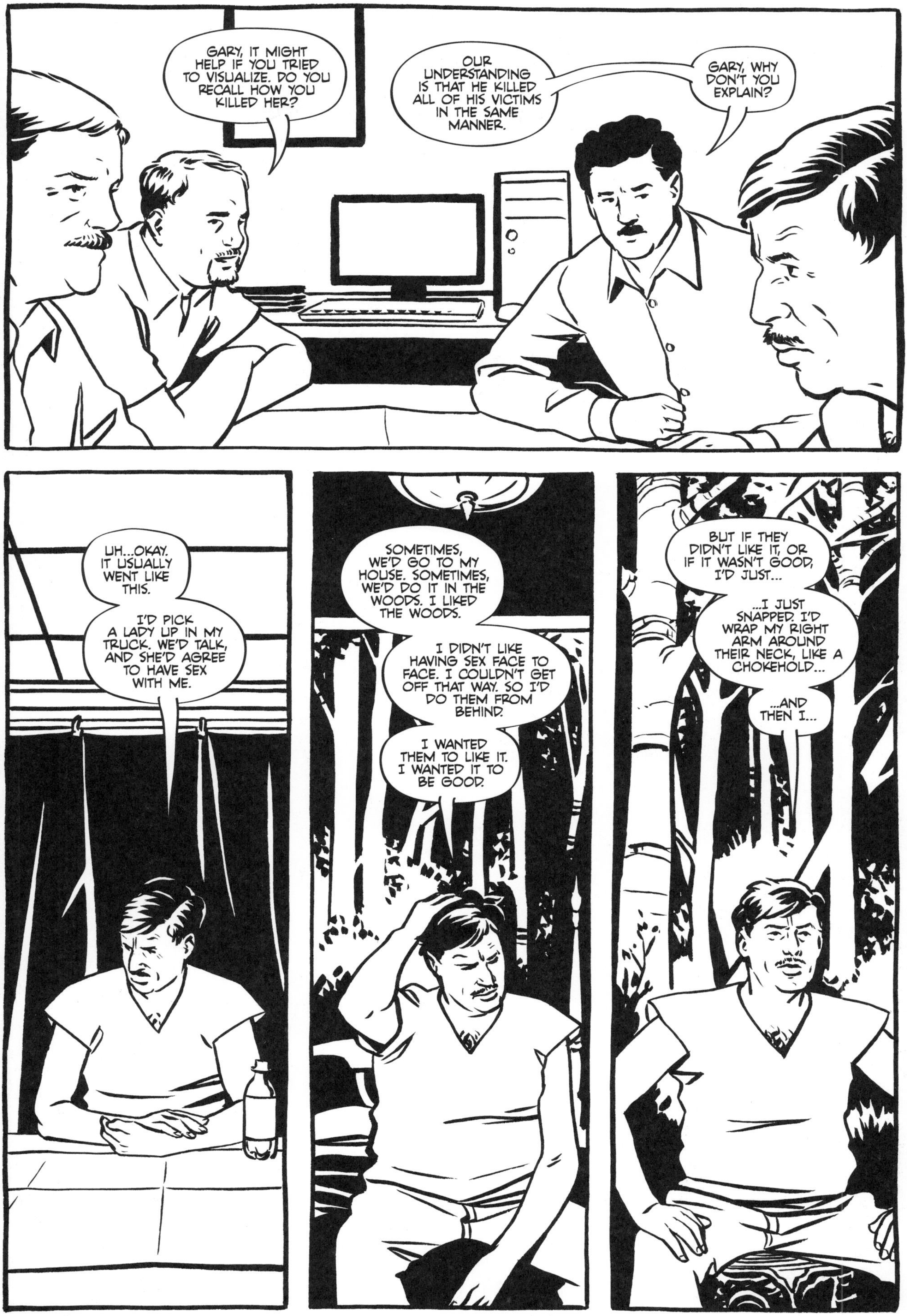
GARY, IT MIGHT HELP IF YOU TRIED TO VISUALIZE. DO YOU RECALL HOW YOU KILLED HER?
OUR UNDERSTANDING IS THAT HE KILLED ALL OF HIS VICTIMS IN THE SAME MANNER.
GARY, WHY DON'T YOU EXPLAIN?
UH...OKAY. IT USUALLY WENT LIKE THIS.
I'D PICK A LADY UP IN MY TRUCK. WE'D TALK, AND SHE'D AGREE TO HAVE SEX WITH ME.
SOMETIMES, WE'D GO TO MY HOUSE. SOMETIMES, WE'D DO IT IN THE WOODS. I LIKED THE WOODS.
I DIDN'T LIKE HAVING SEX FACE TO FACE. I COULDN'T GET OFF THAT WAY. SO I'D DO THEM FROM BEHIND.
I WANTED THEM TO LIKE IT. I WANTED IT TO BE GOOD.
BUT IF THEY DIDN'T LIKE IT, OR IF IT WASN'T GOOD, I'D JUST...
...I JUST SNAPPED. I'D WRAP MY RIGHT ARM AROUND THEIR NECK, LIKE A CHOKEHOLD...
...AND THEN I...

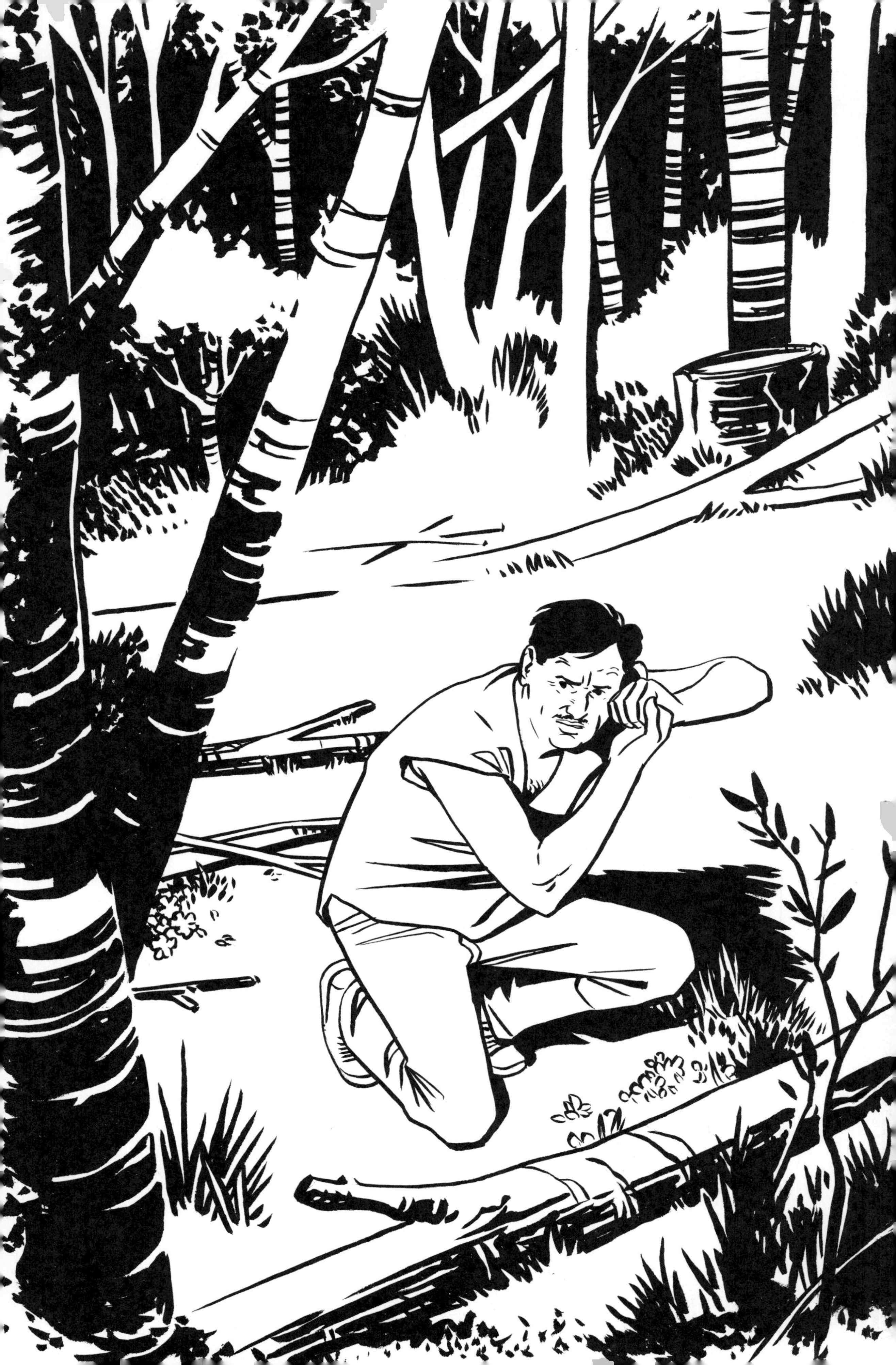

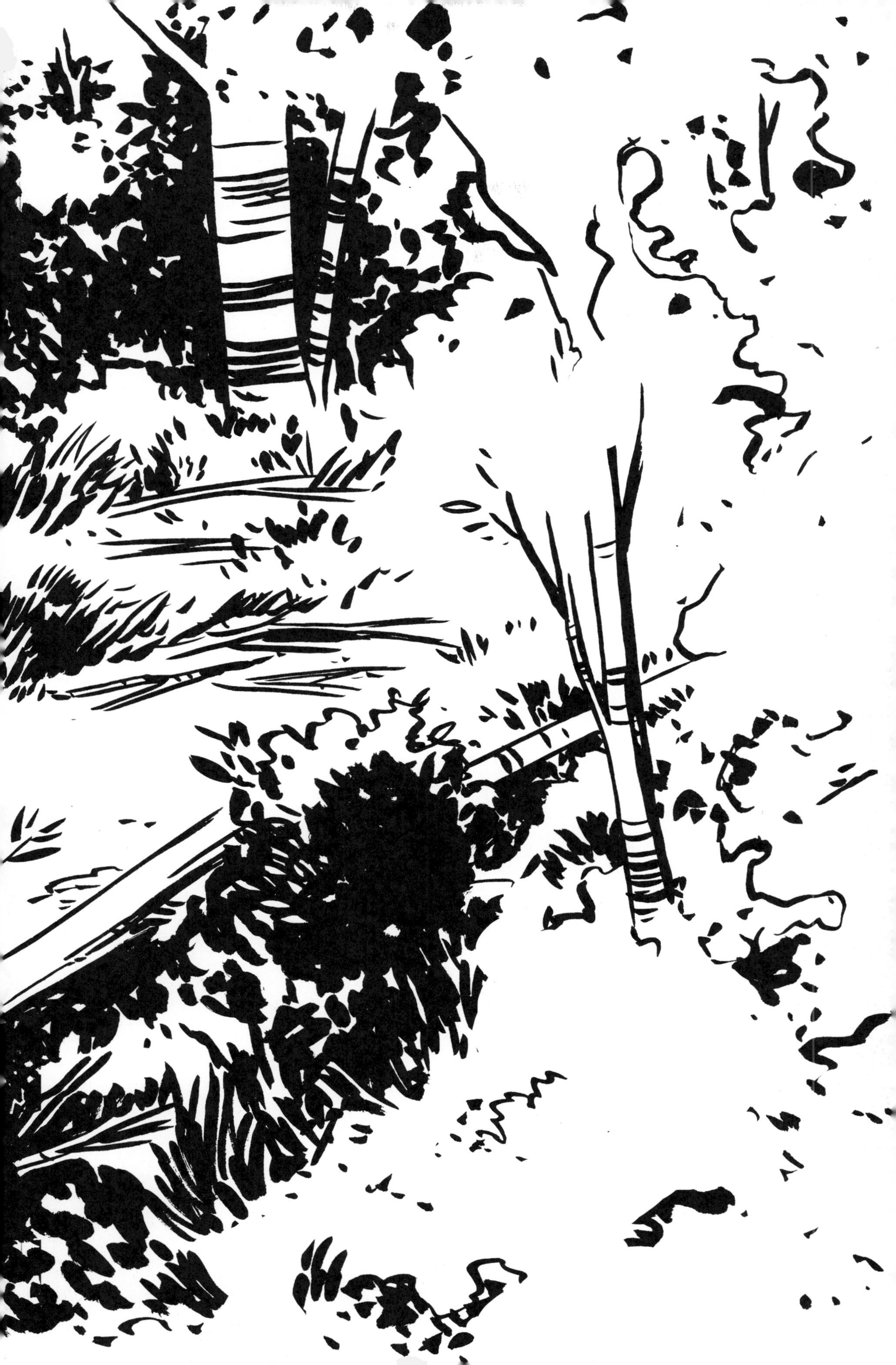

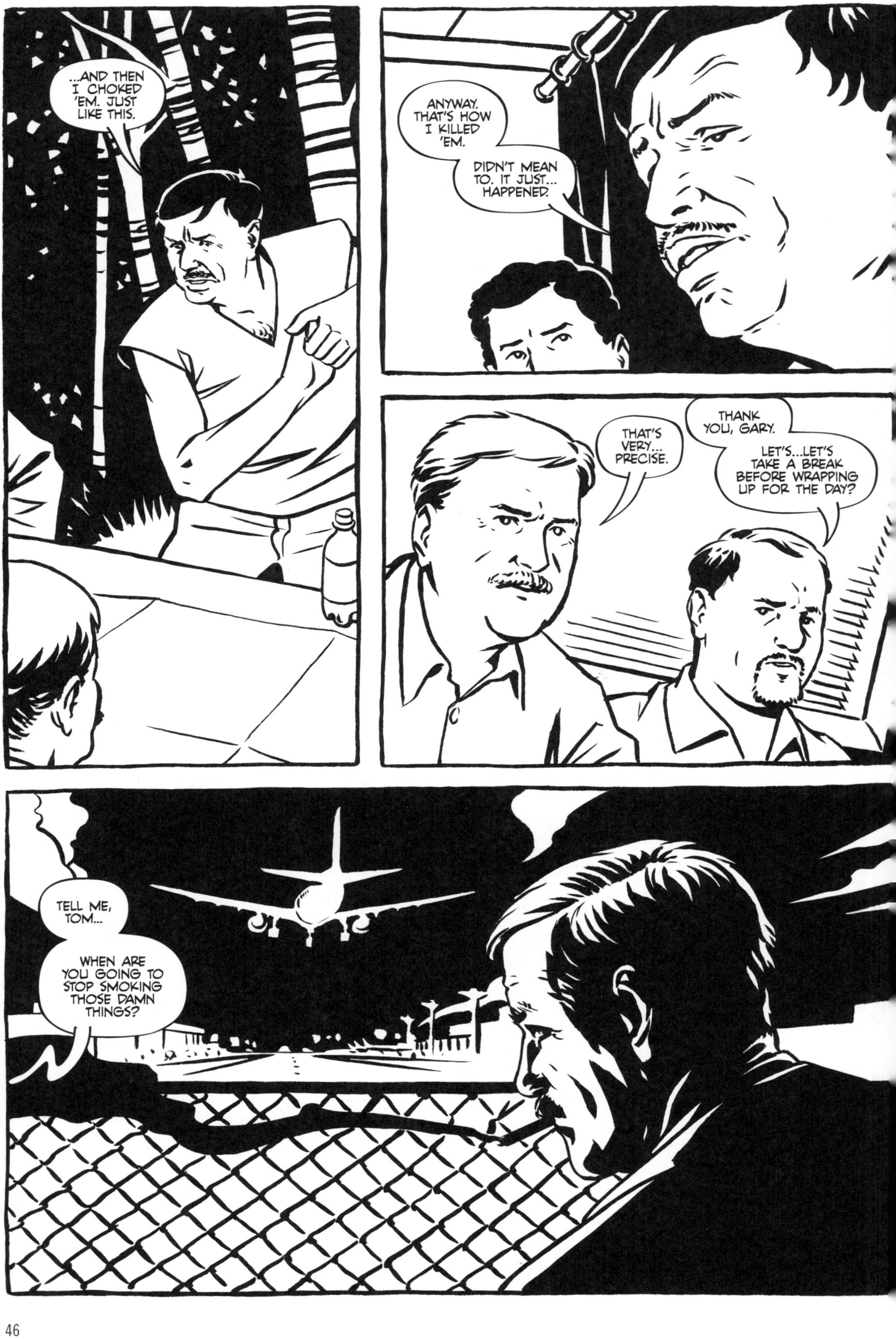

...AND THEN I CHOKED 'EM. JUST LIKE THIS.
ANYWAY. THAT'S HOW I KILLED 'EM.
DIDN'T MEAN TO. IT JUST... HAPPENED.
THAT'S VERY... PRECISE.
THANK YOU, GARY.
LET'S...LET'S TAKE A BREAK BEFORE WRAPPING UP FOR THE DAY?
TELL ME, TOM...
WHEN ARE YOU GOING TO STOP SMOKING THOSE DAMN THINGS?

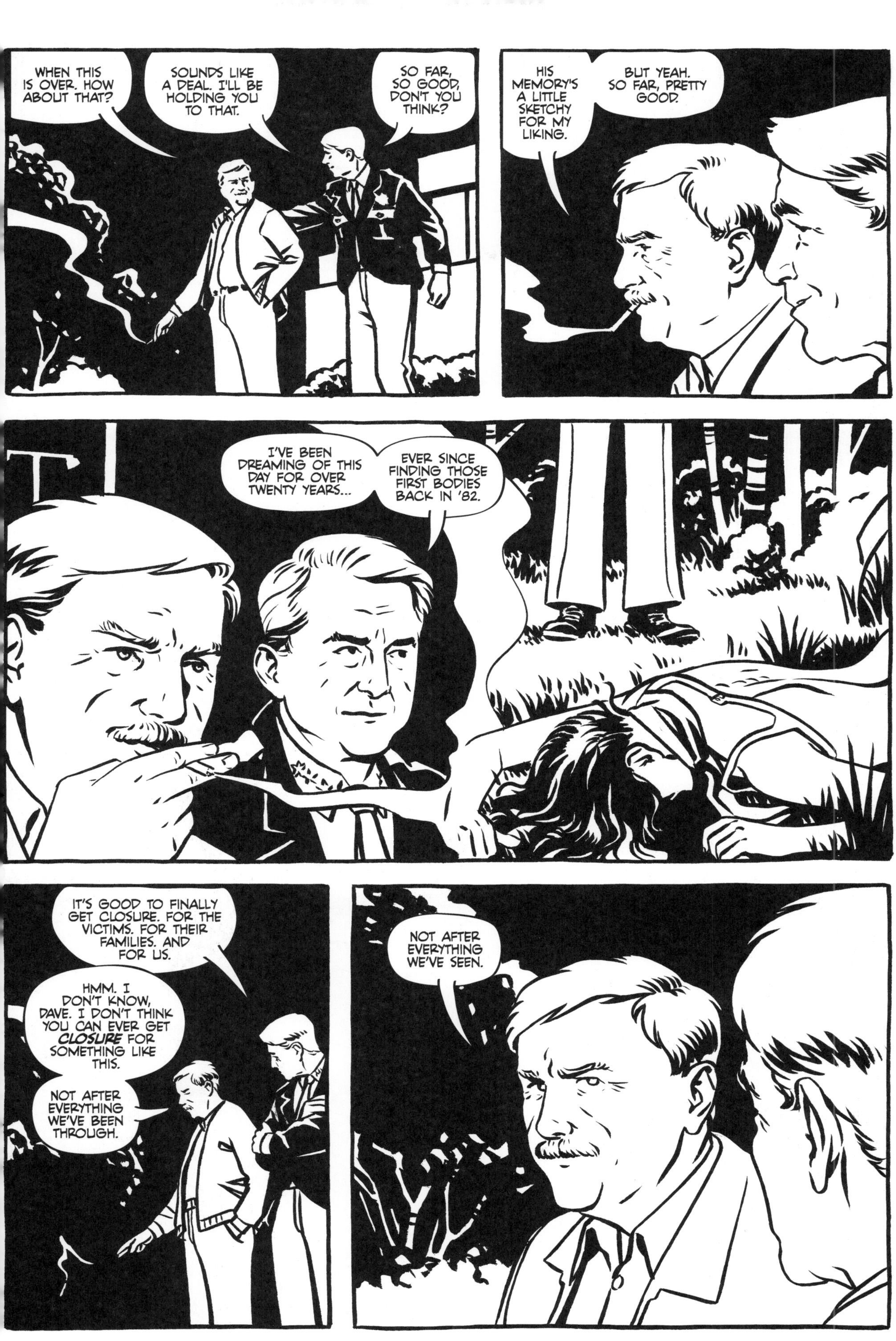
WHEN THIS IS OVER. HOW ABOUT THAT?
SOUNDS LIKE A DEAL. I'LL BE HOLDING YOU TO THAT.
SO FAR, SO GOOD, DON'T YOU THINK?
HIS MEMORY'S A LITTLE SKETCHY FOR MY LIKING.
BUT YEAH. SO FAR, PRETTY GOOD.
I'VE BEEN DREAMING OF THIS DAY FOR OVER TWENTY YEARS...
EVER SINCE FINDING THOSE FIRST BODIES BACK IN '82.
IT'S GOOD TO FINALLY GET CLOSURE. FOR THE VICTIMS. FOR THEIR FAMILIES. AND FOR US.
HMM. I DON'T KNOW, DAVE. I DON'T THINK YOU CAN EVER GET CLOSURE FOR SOMETHING LIKE THIS.
NOT AFTER EVERYTHING WE'VE BEEN THROUGH.
NOT AFTER EVERYTHING WE'VE SEEN.

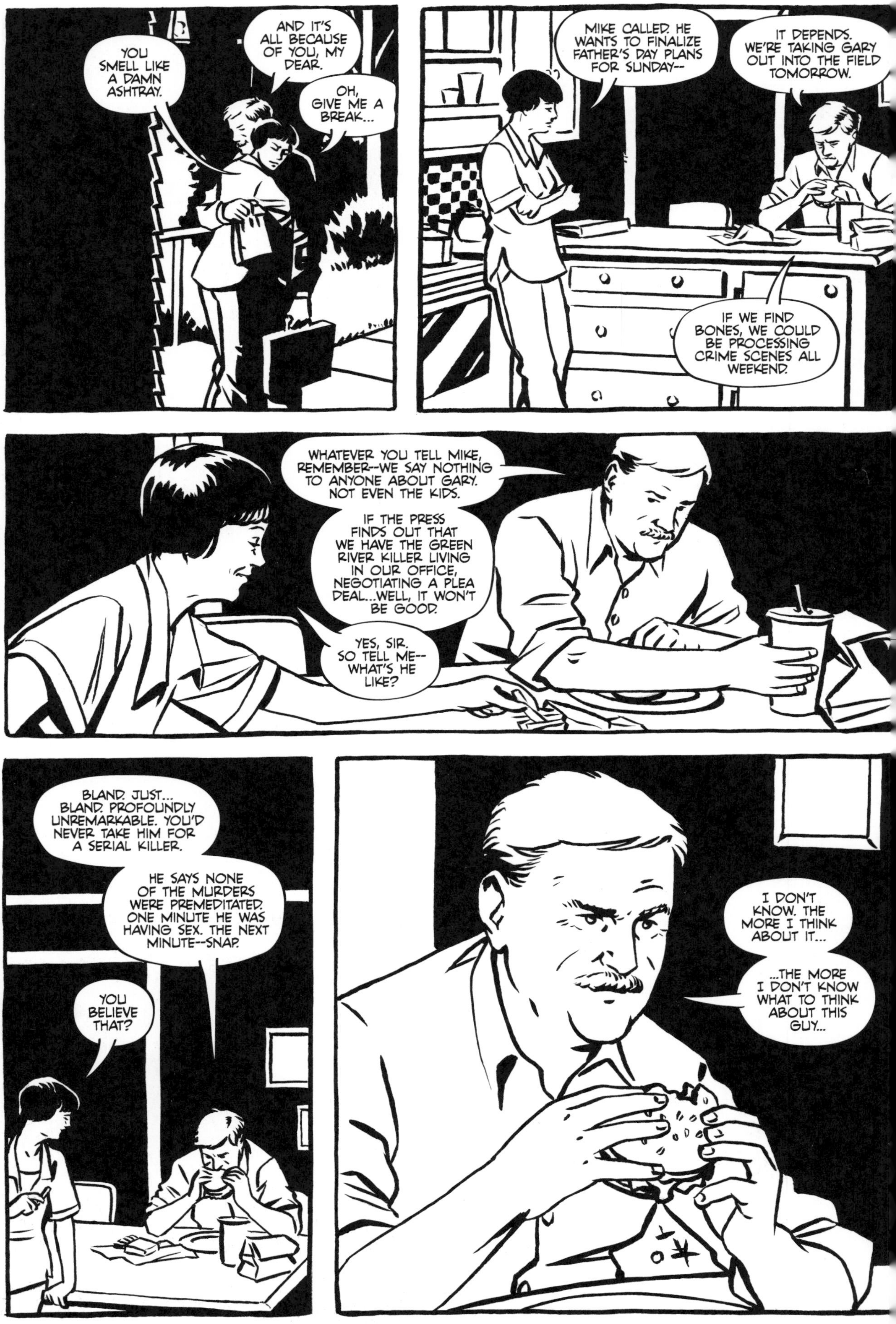

YOU SMELL LIKE A DAMN ASHTRAY.
AND IT'S ALL BECAUSE OF YOU, MY DEAR.
OH, GIVE ME A BREAK...
MIKE CALLED. HE WANTS TO FINALIZE FATHER'S DAY PLANS FOR SUNDAY--
IT DEPENDS. WE'RE TAKING GARY OUT INTO THE FIELD TOMORROW.
IF WE FIND BONES, WE COULD BE PROCESSING CRIME SCENES ALL WEEKEND.
WHATEVER YOU TELL MIKE, REMEMBER--WE SAY NOTHING TO ANYONE ABOUT GARY. NOT EVEN THE KIDS.
IF THE PRESS FINDS OUT THAT WE HAVE THE GREEN RIVER KILLER LIVING IN OUR OFFICE, NEGOTIATING A PLEA DEAL...WELL, IT WON'T BE GOOD.
YES, SIR. SO TELL ME-- WHAT'S HE LIKE?
BLAND. JUST... BLAND. PROFOUNDLY UNREMARKABLE. YOU'D NEVER TAKE HIM FOR A SERIAL KILLER.
HE SAYS NONE OF THE MURDERS WERE PREMEDITATED. ONE MINUTE HE WAS HAVING SEX. THE NEXT MINUTE--SNAP.
YOU BELIEVE THAT?
I DON'T KNOW. THE MORE I THINK ABOUT IT...
...THE MORE I DON'T KNOW WHAT TO THINK ABOUT THIS GUY...

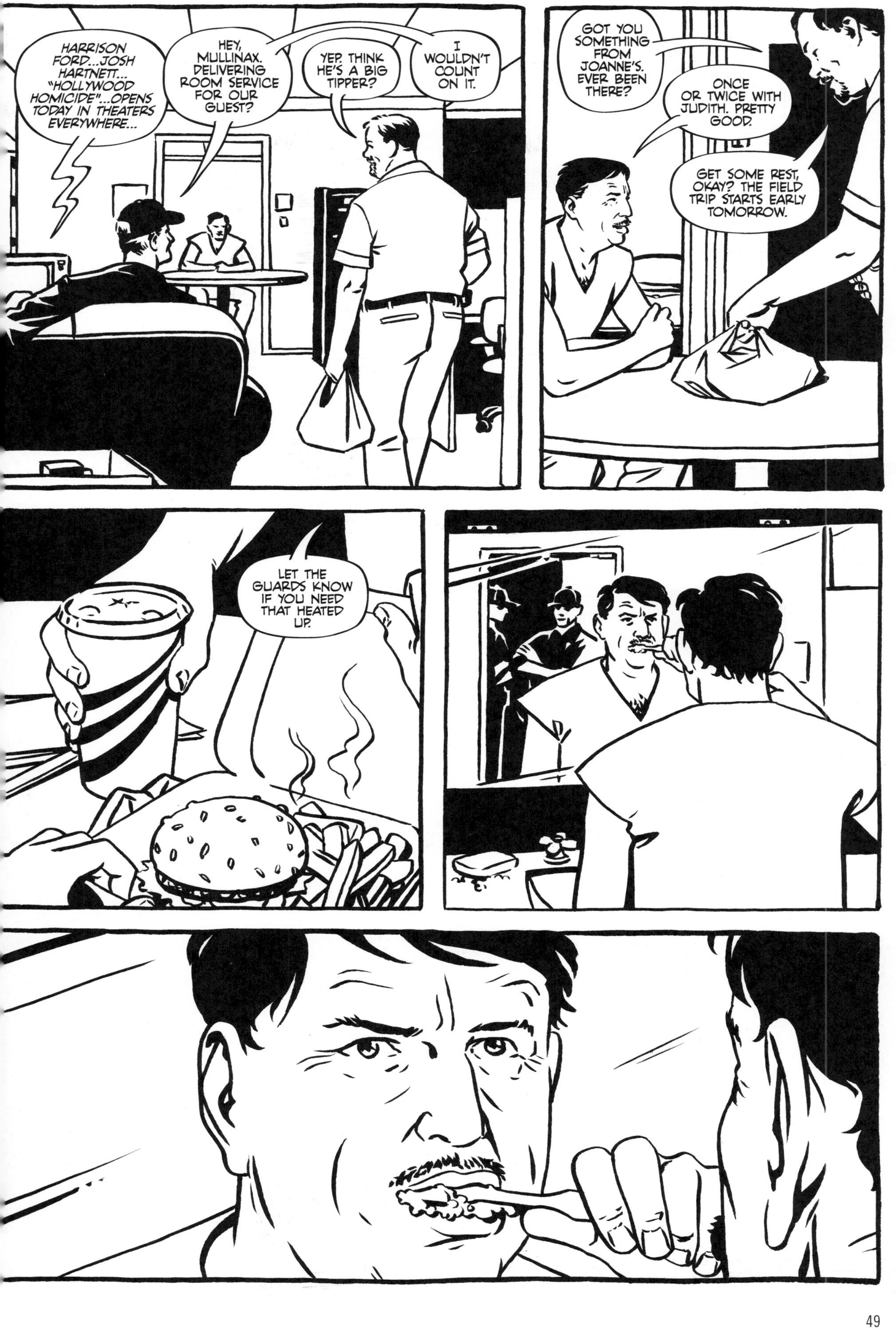
HARRISON FORD...JOSH HARTNETT... "HOLLYWOOD HOMICIDE"...OPENS TODAY IN THEATERS EVERYWHERE...
HEY, MULLINAX. DELIVERING ROOM SERVICE FOR OUR GUEST?
YEP. THINK HE'S A BIG TIPPER?
I WOULDN'T COUNT ON IT.
GOT YOU SOMETHING FROM JOANNE'S. EVER BEEN THERE?
ONCE OR TWICE WITH JUDITH. PRETTY GOOD.
GET SOME REST, OKAY? THE FIELD TRIP STARTS EARLY TOMORROW.
LET THE GUARDS KNOW IF YOU NEED THAT HEATED UP.

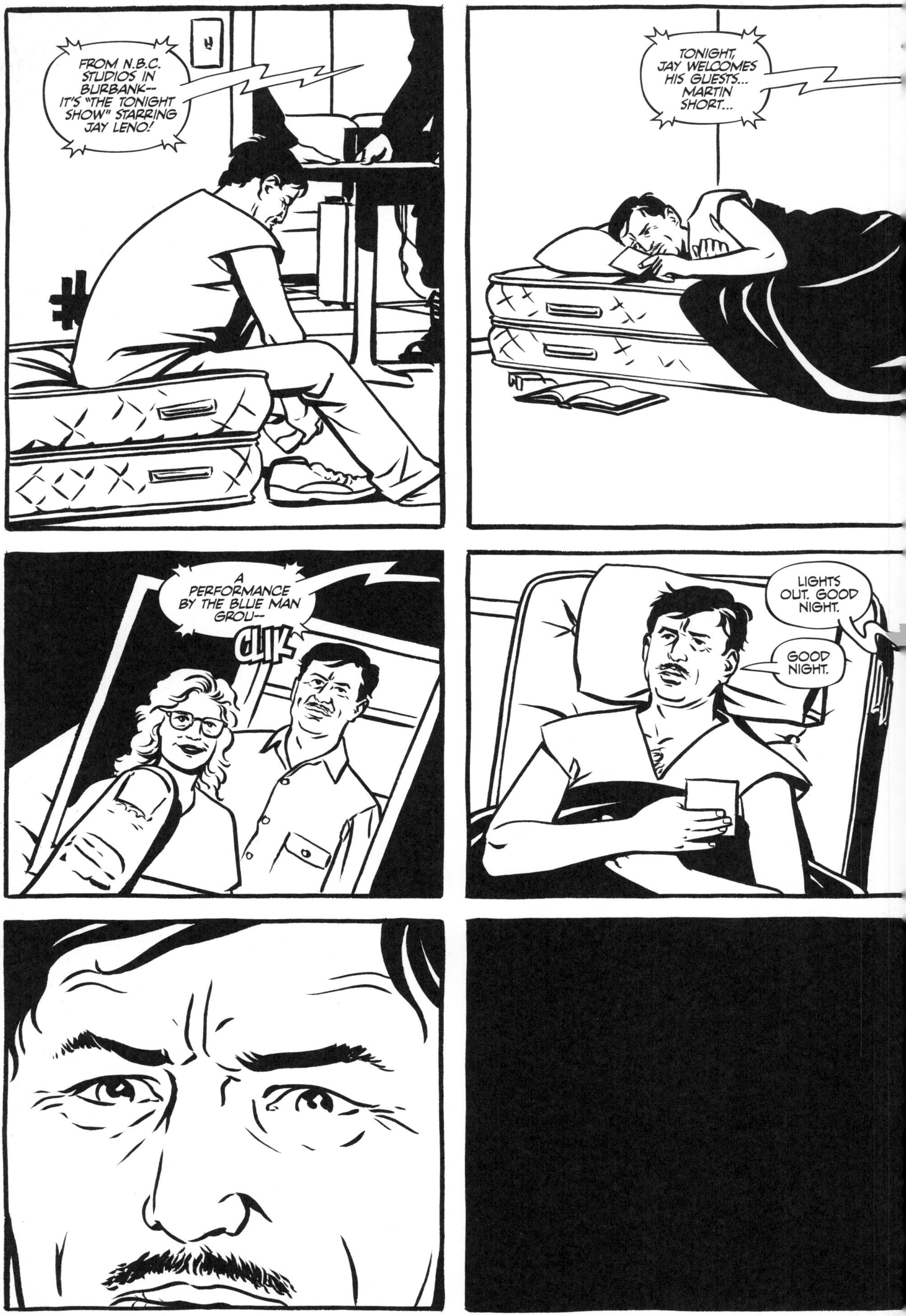
FROM N.B.C. STUDIOS IN BURBANK-- IT'S "THE TONIGHT SHOW" STARRING JAY LENO!
TONIGHT, JAY WELCOMES HIS GUESTS... MARTIN SHORT...
A PERFORMANCE BY THE BLUE MAN GROU--
CLIK
LIGHTS OUT. GOOD NIGHT.
GOOD NIGHT.

DAY TWO: FIELD TRIPS

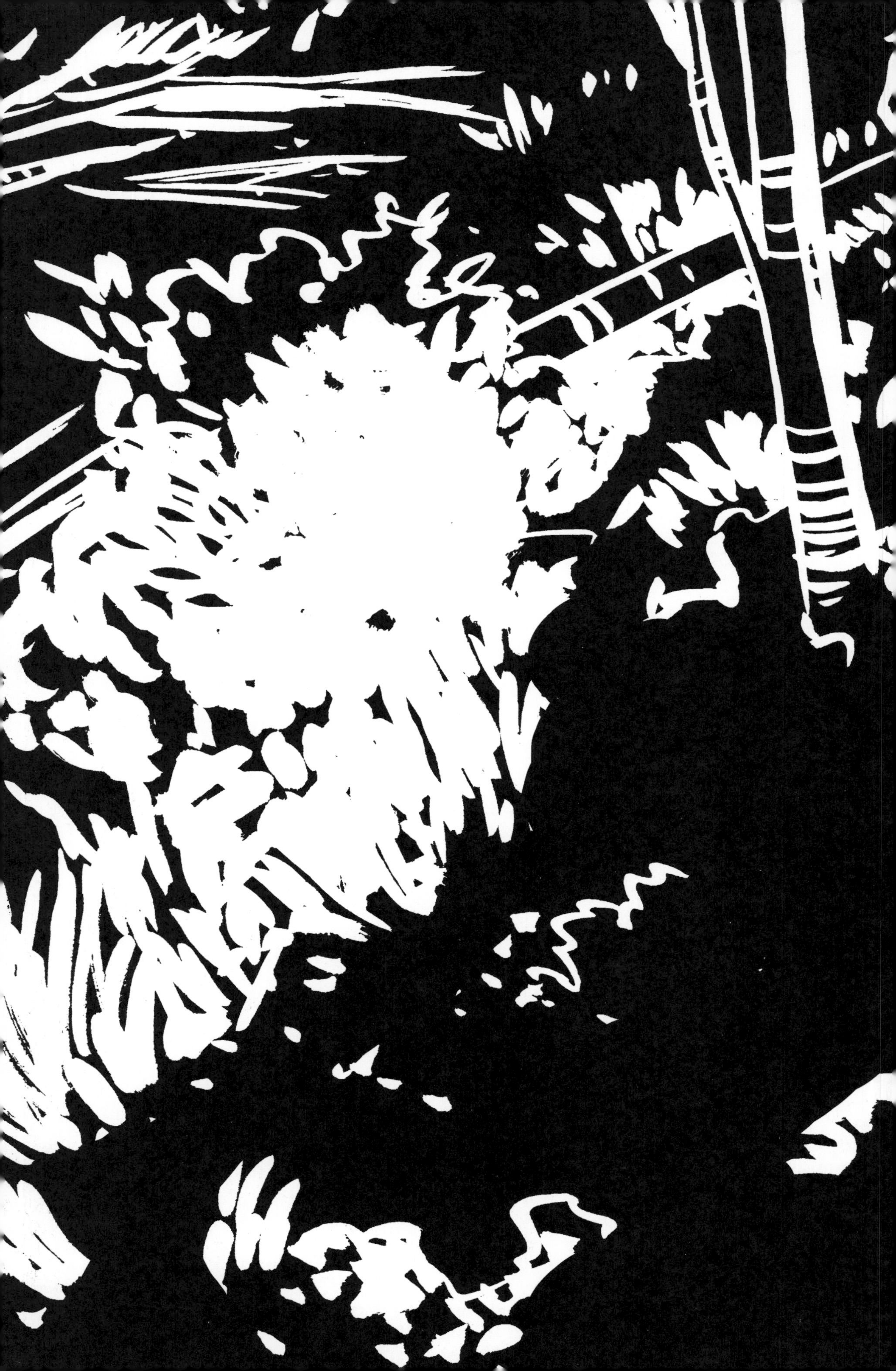

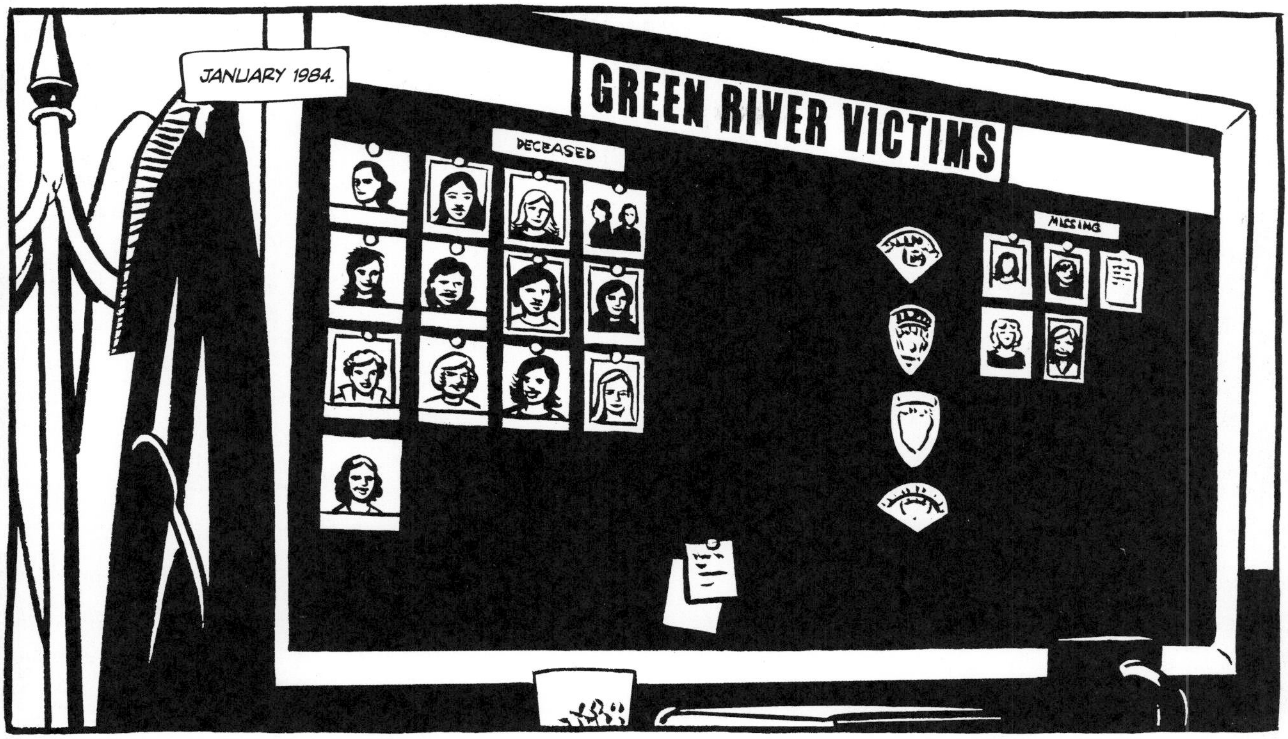
JANUARY 1984.
GREEN RIVER VICTIMS
DECEASED
MISSING

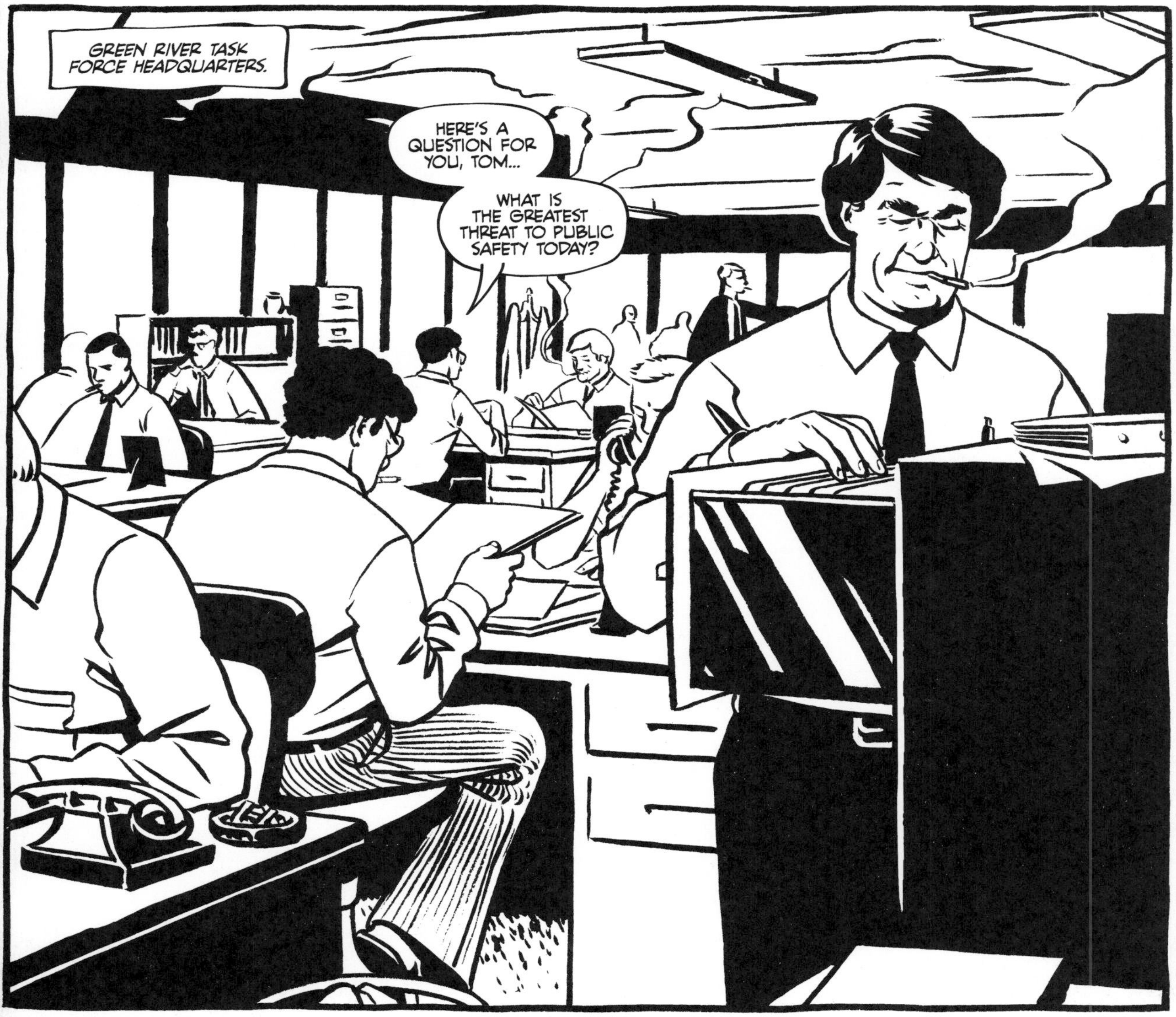
GREEN RIVER TASK FORCE HEADQUARTERS.
HERE'S A QUESTION FOR YOU, TOM...
WHAT IS THE GREATEST THREAT TO PUBLIC SAFETY TODAY?

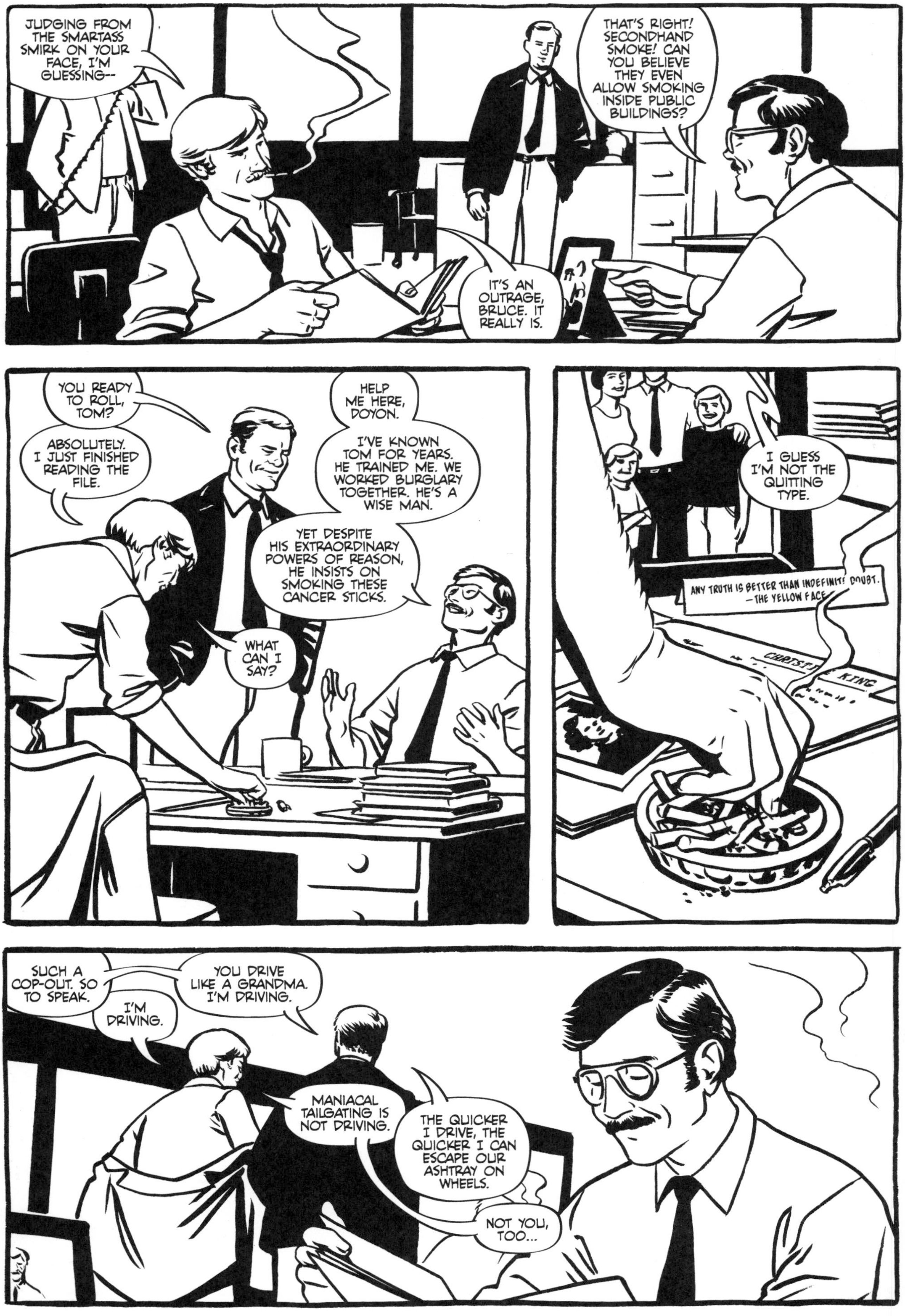
JUDGING FROM THE SMARTASS SMIRK ON YOUR FACE, I'M GUESSING--
THAT'S RIGHT! SECONDHAND SMOKE! CAN YOU BELIEVE THEY EVEN ALLOW SMOKING INSIDE PUBLIC BUILDINGS?
IT'S AN OUTRAGE, BRUCE. IT REALLY IS.
YOU READY TO ROLL, TOM?
ABSOLUTELY. I JUST FINISHED READING THE FILE.
HELP ME HERE, DOYON.
I'VE KNOWN TOM FOR YEARS. HE TRAINED ME. WE WORKED BURGLARY TOGETHER. HE'S A WISE MAN.
YET DESPITE HIS EXTRAORDINARY POWERS OF REASON, HE INSISTS ON SMOKING THESE CANCER STICKS.
WHAT CAN I SAY?
I GUESS I'M NOT THE QUITTING TYPE.
ANY TRUTH IS BETTER THAN INDEFINIT DOUBT.
—THE YELLOW FACE
SUCH A COP-OUT. SO TO SPEAK.
I'M DRIVING.
YOU DRIVE LIKE A GRANDMA. I'M DRIVING.
MANIACAL TAILGATING IS NOT DRIVING.
THE QUICKER I DRIVE, THE QUICKER I CAN ESCAPE OUR ASHTRAY ON WHEELS.
NOT YOU, TOO...

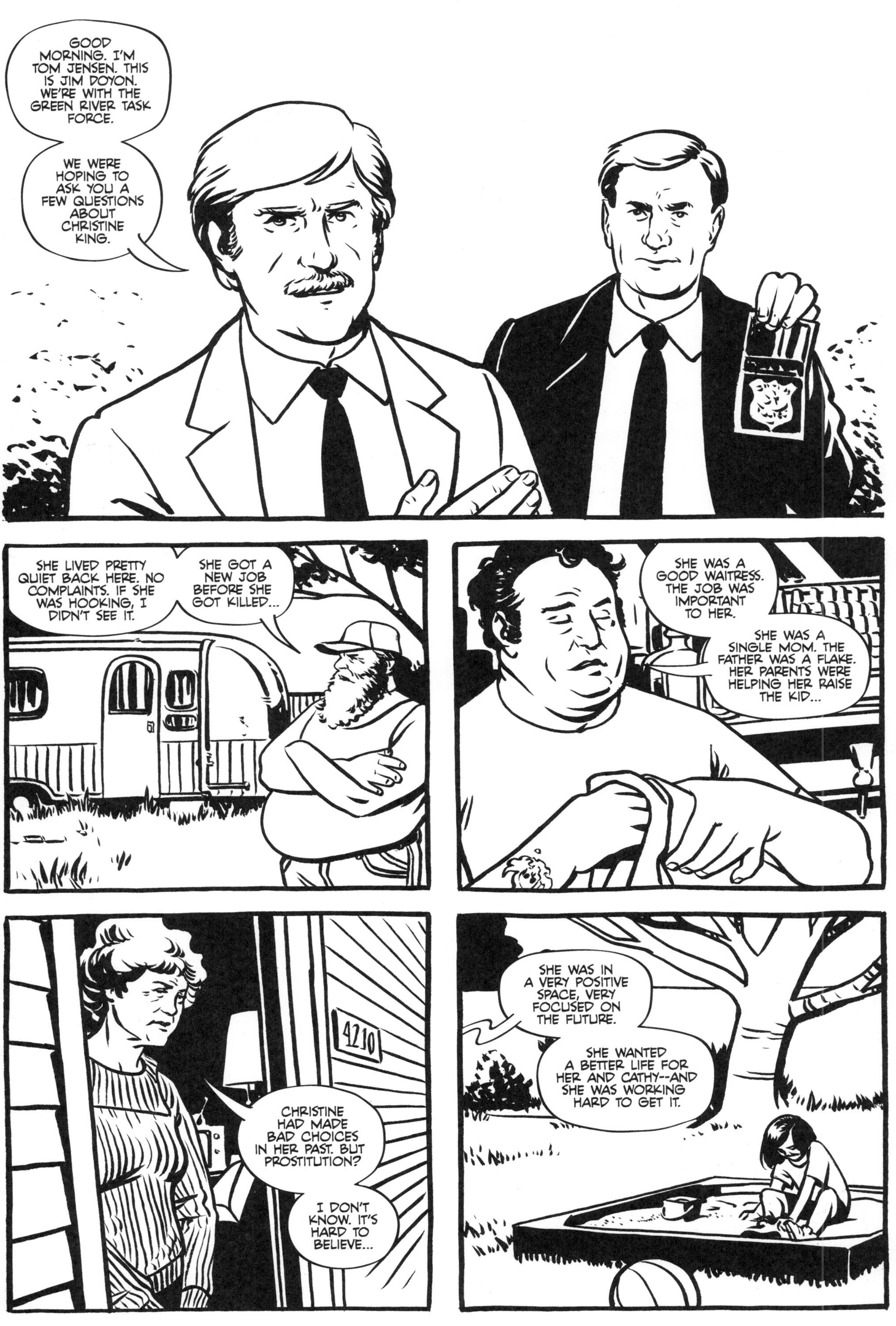
GOOD MORNING. I'M TOM JENSEN. THIS IS JIM DOYON. WE'RE WITH THE GREEN RIVER TASK FORCE.
WE WERE HOPING TO ASK YOU A FEW QUESTIONS ABOUT CHRISTINE KING.
SHE LIVED PRETTY QUIET BACK HERE. NO COMPLAINTS. IF SHE WAS HOOKING, I DIDN'T SEE IT.
SHE GOT A NEW JOB BEFORE SHE GOT KILLED...
SHE WAS A GOOD WAITRESS. THE JOB WAS IMPORTANT TO HER.
SHE WAS A SINGLE MOM. THE FATHER WAS A FLAKE. HER PARENTS WERE HELPING HER RAISE THE KID...
4210
CHRISTINE HAD MADE BAD CHOICES IN HER PAST. BUT PROSTITUTION?
I DON'T KNOW. IT'S HARD TO BELIEVE...
SHE WAS IN A VERY POSITIVE SPACE, VERY FOCUSED ON THE FUTURE.
SHE WANTED A BETTER LIFE FOR HER AND CATHY--AND SHE WAS WORKING HARD TO GET IT.

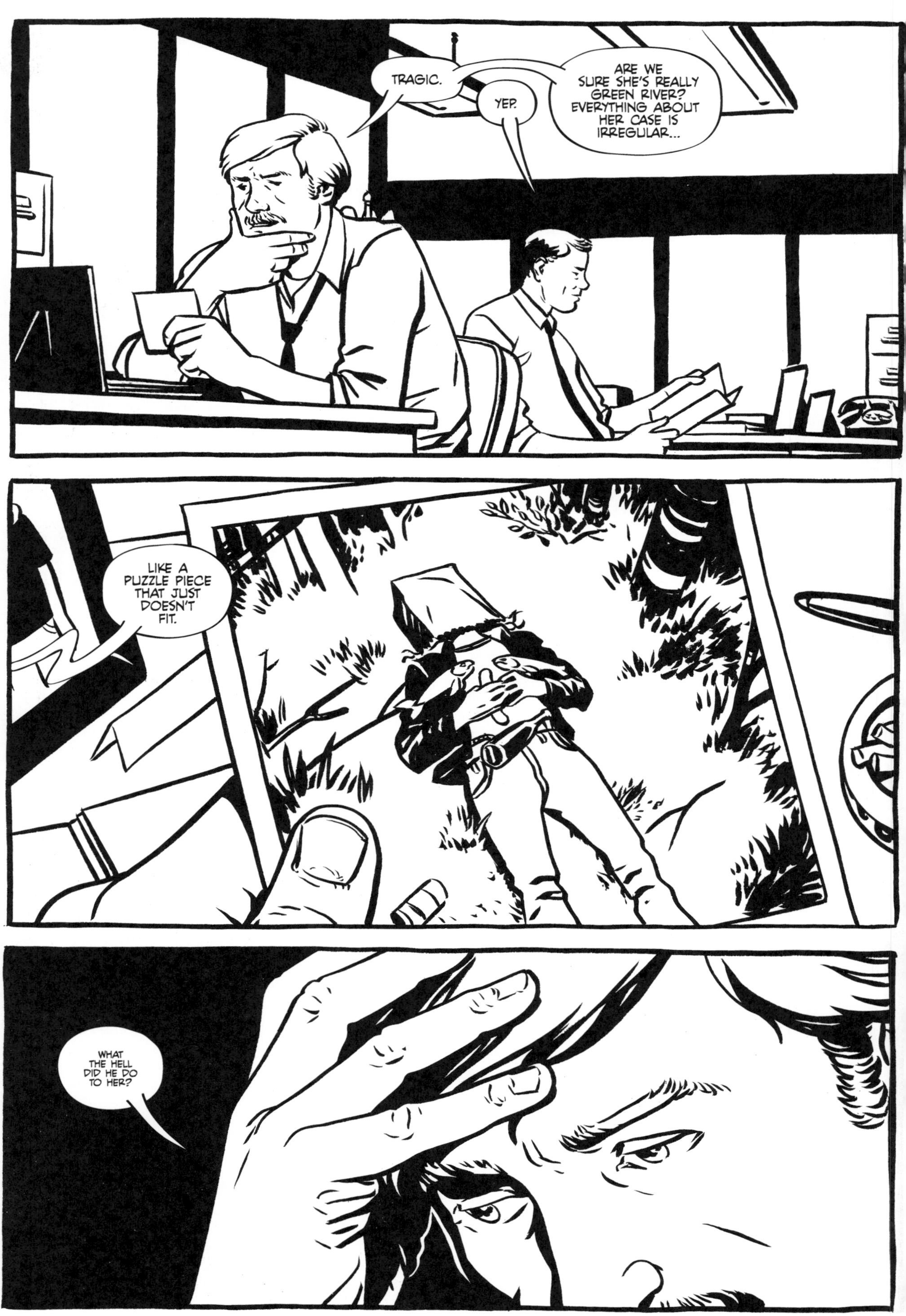
TRAGIC.
YEP.
ARE WE SURE SHE'S REALLY GREEN RIVER? EVERYTHING ABOUT HER CASE IS IRREGULAR...
LIKE A PUZZLE PIECE THAT JUST DOESN'T FIT.
WHAT THE HELL DID HE DO TO HER?

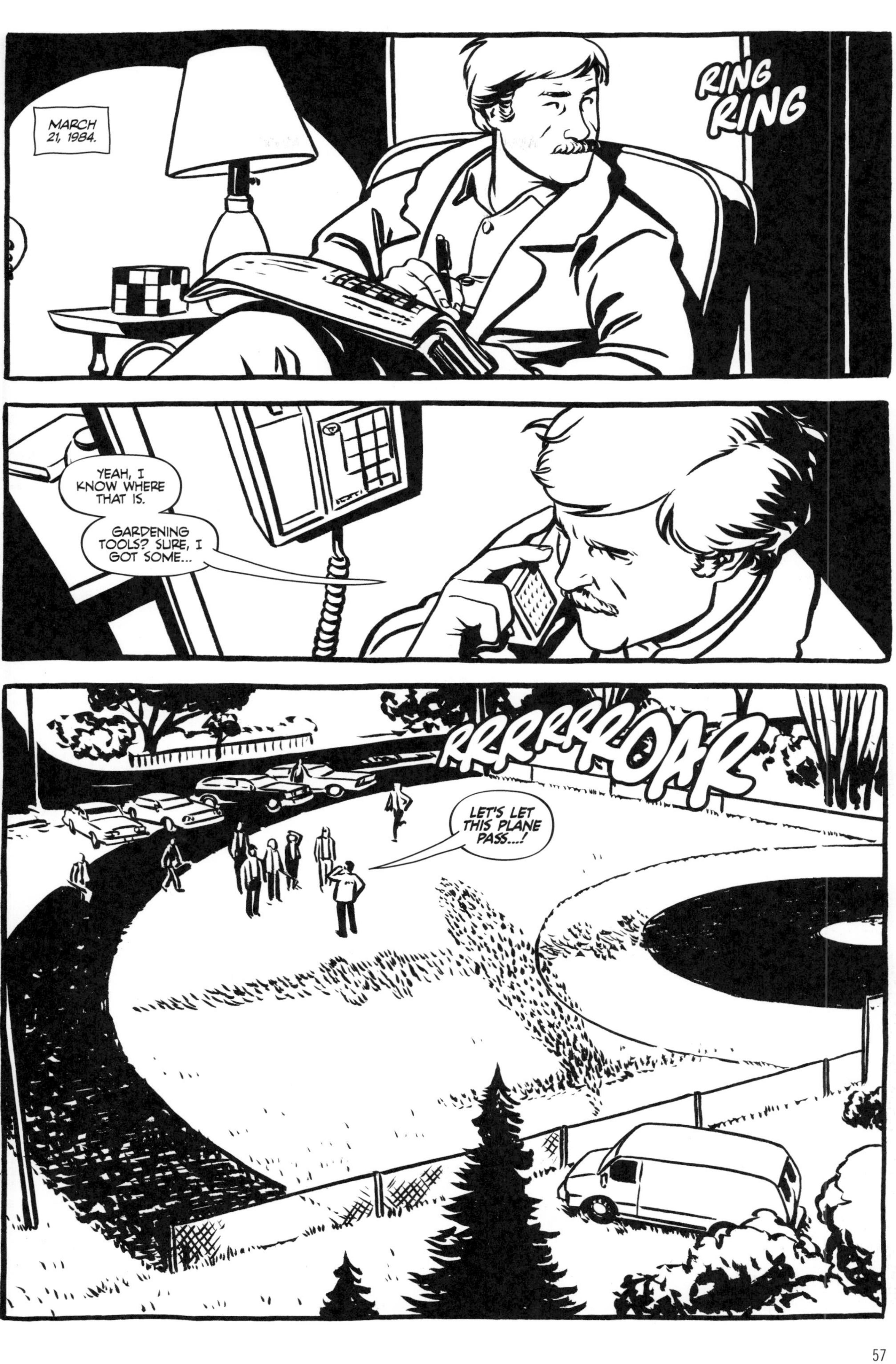
MARCH 21, 1984.
RING RING
YEAH, I KNOW WHERE THAT IS.
GARDENING TOOLS? SURE, I GOT SOME...
RRRRRROAR
LET'S LET THIS PLANE PASS...!

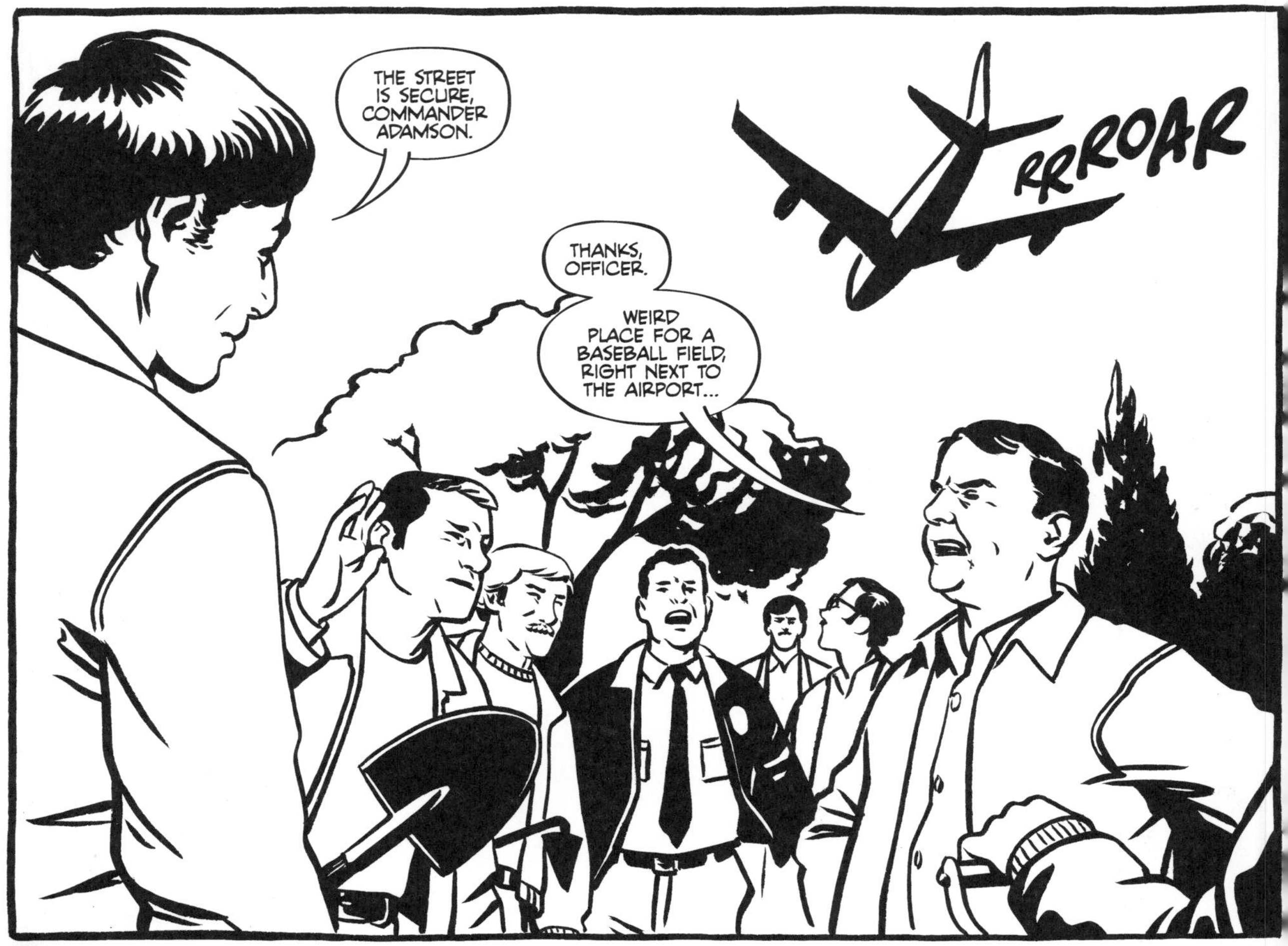
THE STREET IS SECURE, COMMANDER ADAMSON.
RRROAR
THANKS, OFFICER.
WEIRD PLACE FOR A BASEBALL FIELD, RIGHT NEXT TO THE AIRPORT...

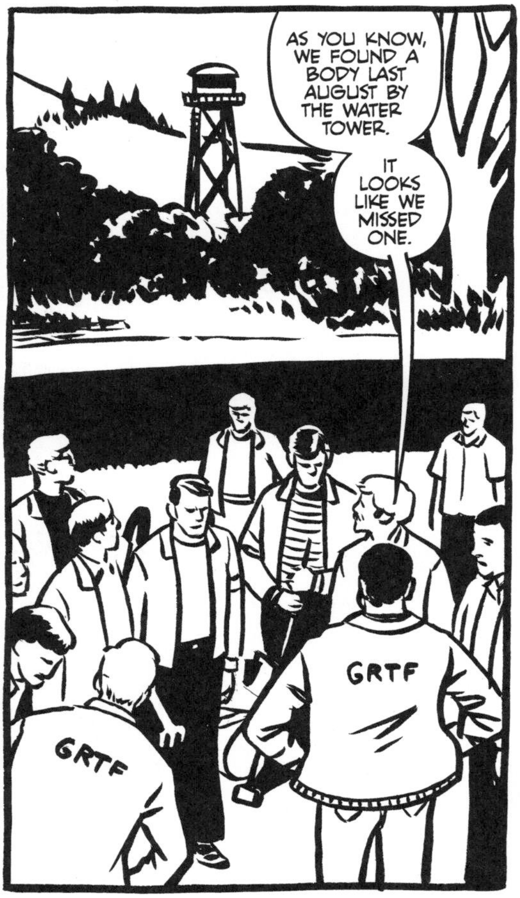
AS YOU KNOW, WE FOUND A BODY LAST AUGUST BY THE WATER TOWER.
IT LOOKS LIKE WE MISSED ONE.
GRTF
GRTF

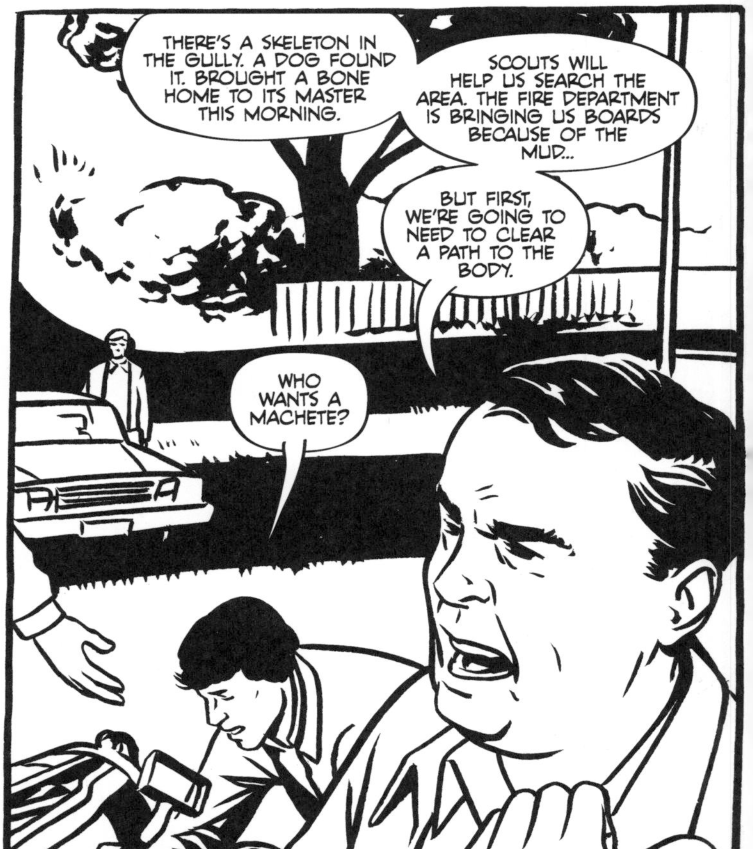
THERE'S A SKELETON IN THE GULLY. A DOG FOUND IT. BROUGHT A BONE HOME TO ITS MASTER THIS MORNING.
SCOUTS WILL HELP US SEARCH THE AREA. THE FIRE DEPARTMENT IS BRINGING US BOARDS BECAUSE OF THE MUD...
BUT FIRST, WE'RE GOING TO NEED TO CLEAR A PATH TO THE BODY.
WHO WANTS A MACHETE?

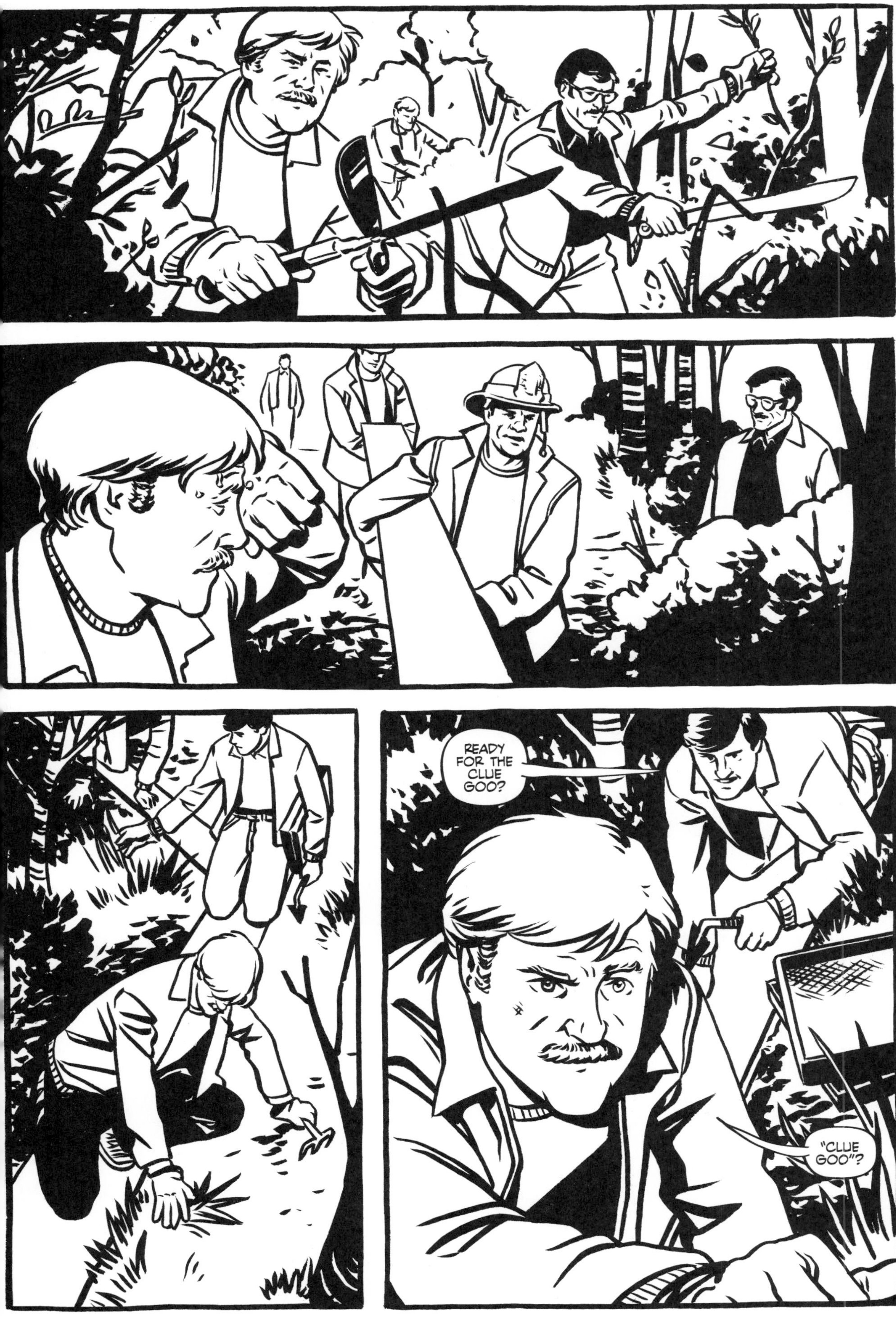
READY FOR THE CLUE GOO?
"CLUE GOO"?

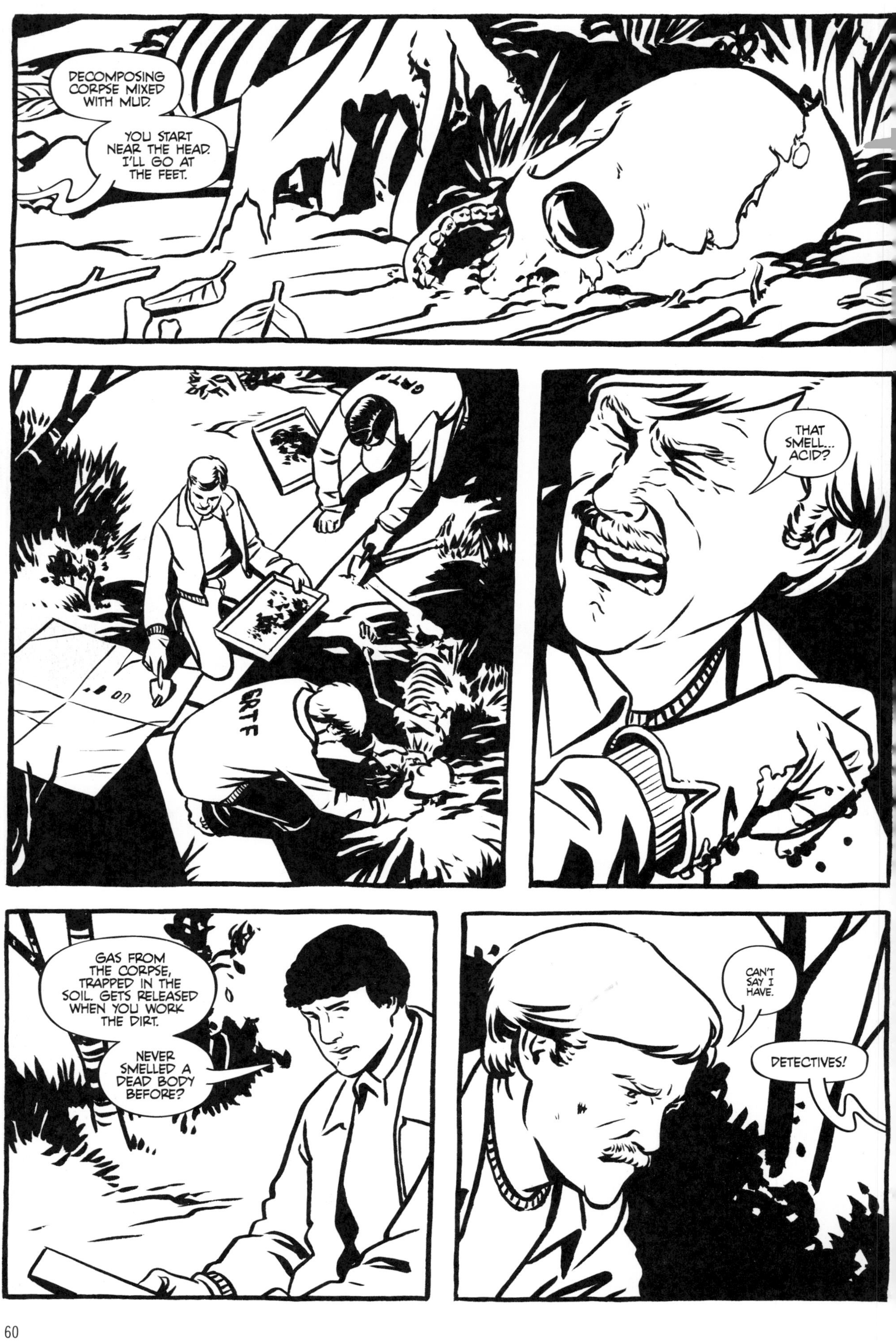
DECOMPOSING CORPSE MIXED WITH MUD.
YOU START NEAR THE HEAD. I'LL GO AT THE FEET.
GRTF
GRTF
THAT SMELL... ACID?
GAS FROM THE CORPSE, TRAPPED IN THE SOIL. GETS RELEASED WHEN YOU WORK THE DIRT.
NEVER SMELLED A DEAD BODY BEFORE?
CAN'T SAY I HAVE.
DETECTIVES!

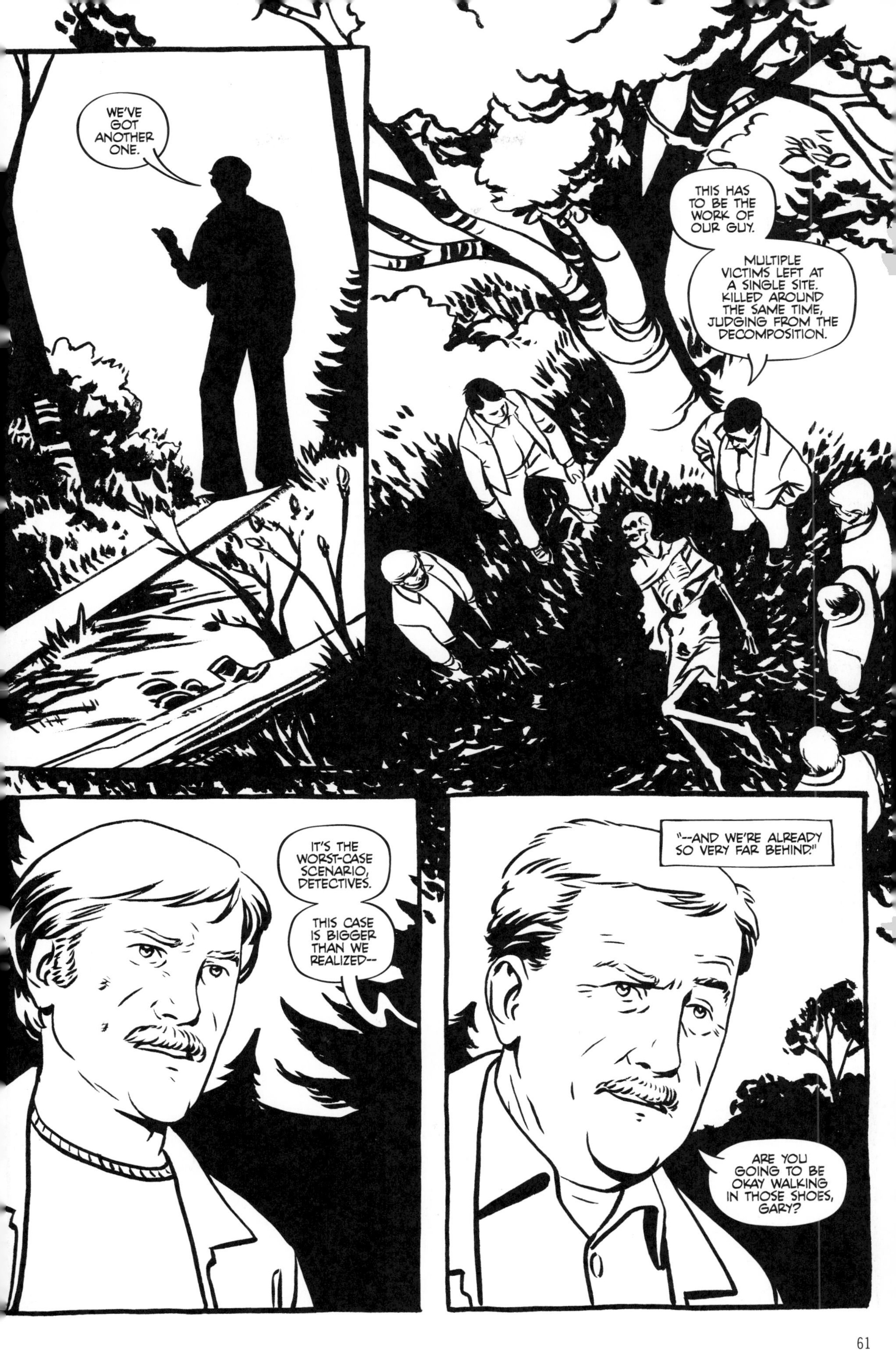

WE'VE GOT ANOTHER ONE.
THIS HAS TO BE THE WORK OF OUR GUY.
MULTIPLE VICTIMS LEFT AT A SINGLE SITE. KILLED AROUND THE SAME TIME, JUDGING FROM THE DECOMPOSITION.
IT'S THE WORST-CASE SCENARIO, DETECTIVES.
THIS CASE IS BIGGER THAN WE REALIZED--
"--AND WE'RE ALREADY SO VERY FAR BEHIND."
ARE YOU GOING TO BE OKAY WALKING IN THOSE SHOES, GARY?

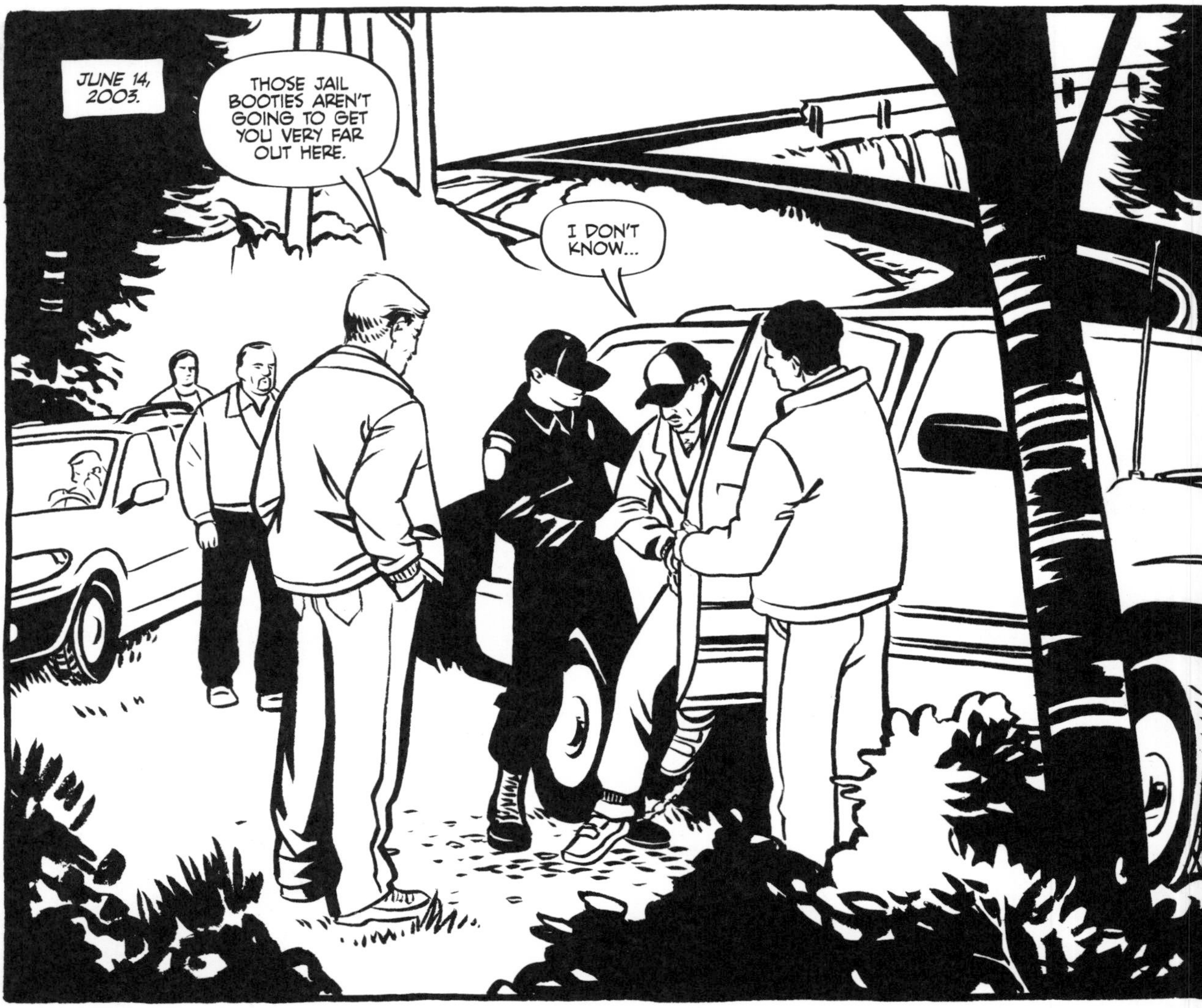
JUNE 14, 2003.
THOSE JAIL BOOTIES AREN'T GOING TO GET YOU VERY FAR OUT HERE.
I DON'T KNOW...

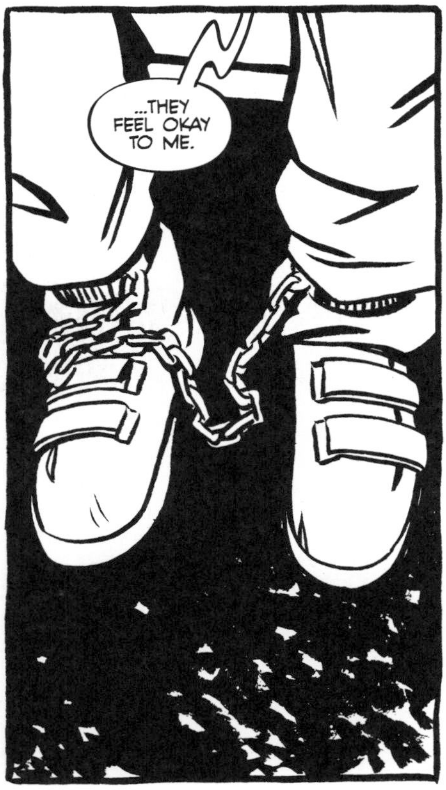
...THEY FEEL OKAY TO ME.

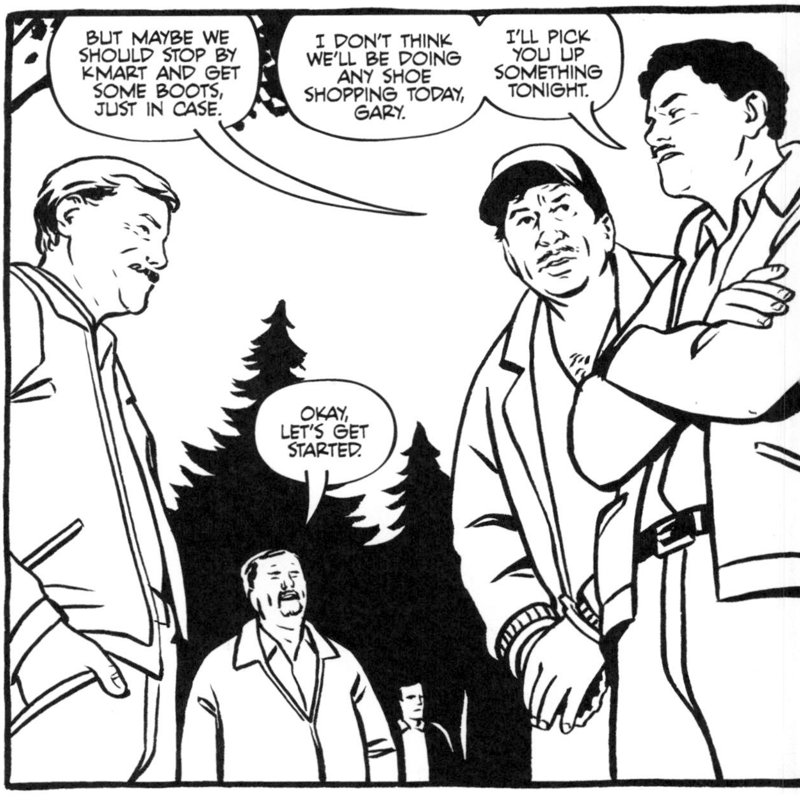
BUT MAYBE WE SHOULD STOP BY KMART AND GET SOME BOOTS, JUST IN CASE.
I DON'T THINK WE'LL BE DOING ANY SHOE SHOPPING TODAY, GARY.
I'LL PICK YOU UP SOMETHING TONIGHT.
OKAY, LET'S GET STARTED.

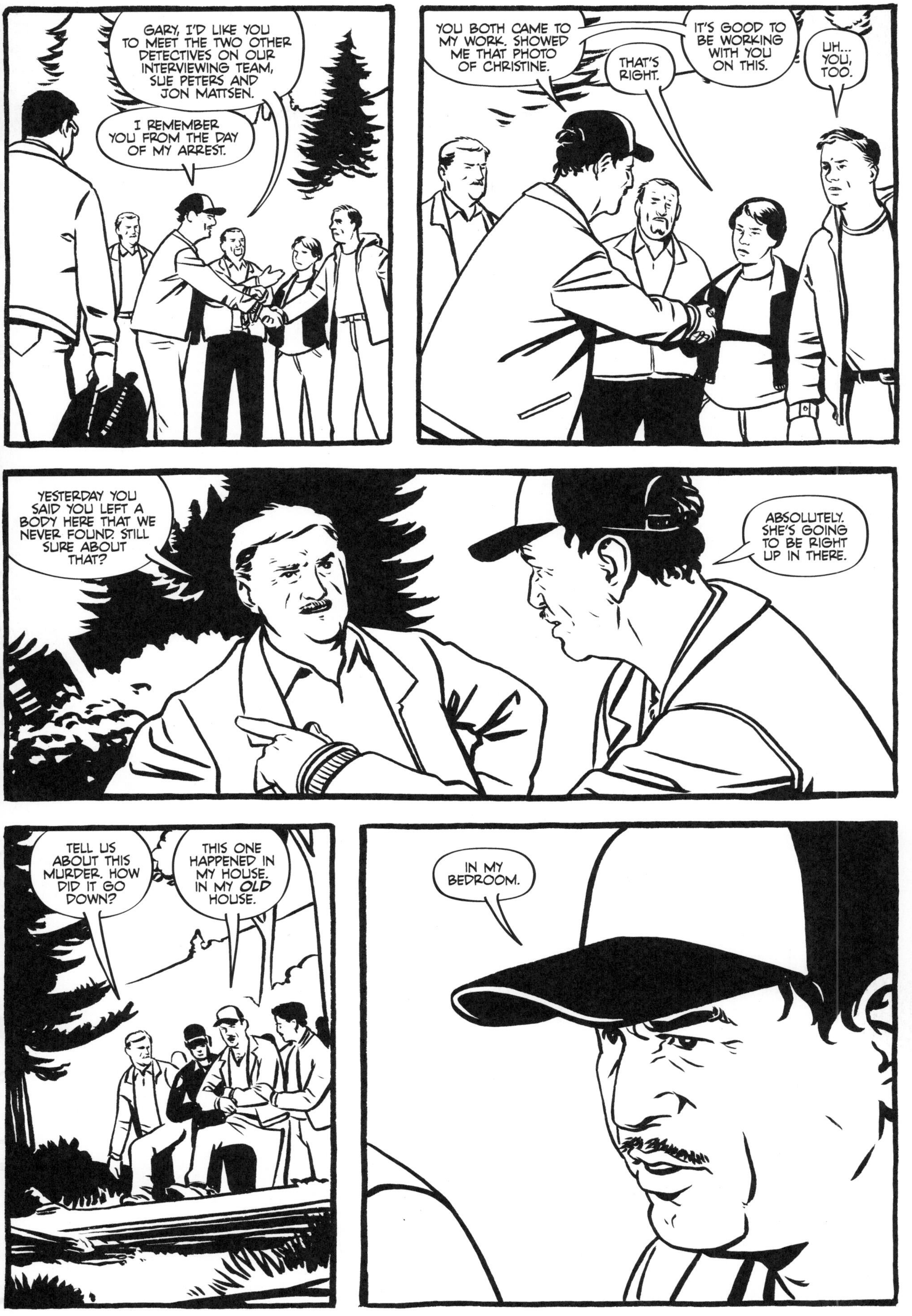
GARY, I'D LIKE YOU TO MEET THE TWO OTHER DETECTIVES ON OUR INTERVIEWING TEAM, SUE PETERS AND JON MATTSEN.
I REMEMBER YOU FROM THE DAY OF MY ARREST.
YOU BOTH CAME TO MY WORK. SHOWED ME THAT PHOTO OF CHRISTINE.
THAT'S RIGHT.
IT'S GOOD TO BE WORKING WITH YOU ON THIS.
UH... YOU, TOO.
YESTERDAY YOU SAID YOU LEFT A BODY HERE THAT WE NEVER FOUND. STILL SURE ABOUT THAT?
ABSOLUTELY. SHE'S GOING TO BE RIGHT UP IN THERE.
TELL US ABOUT THIS MURDER. HOW DID IT GO DOWN?
THIS ONE HAPPENED IN MY HOUSE. IN MY *OLD* HOUSE.
IN MY BEDROOM.

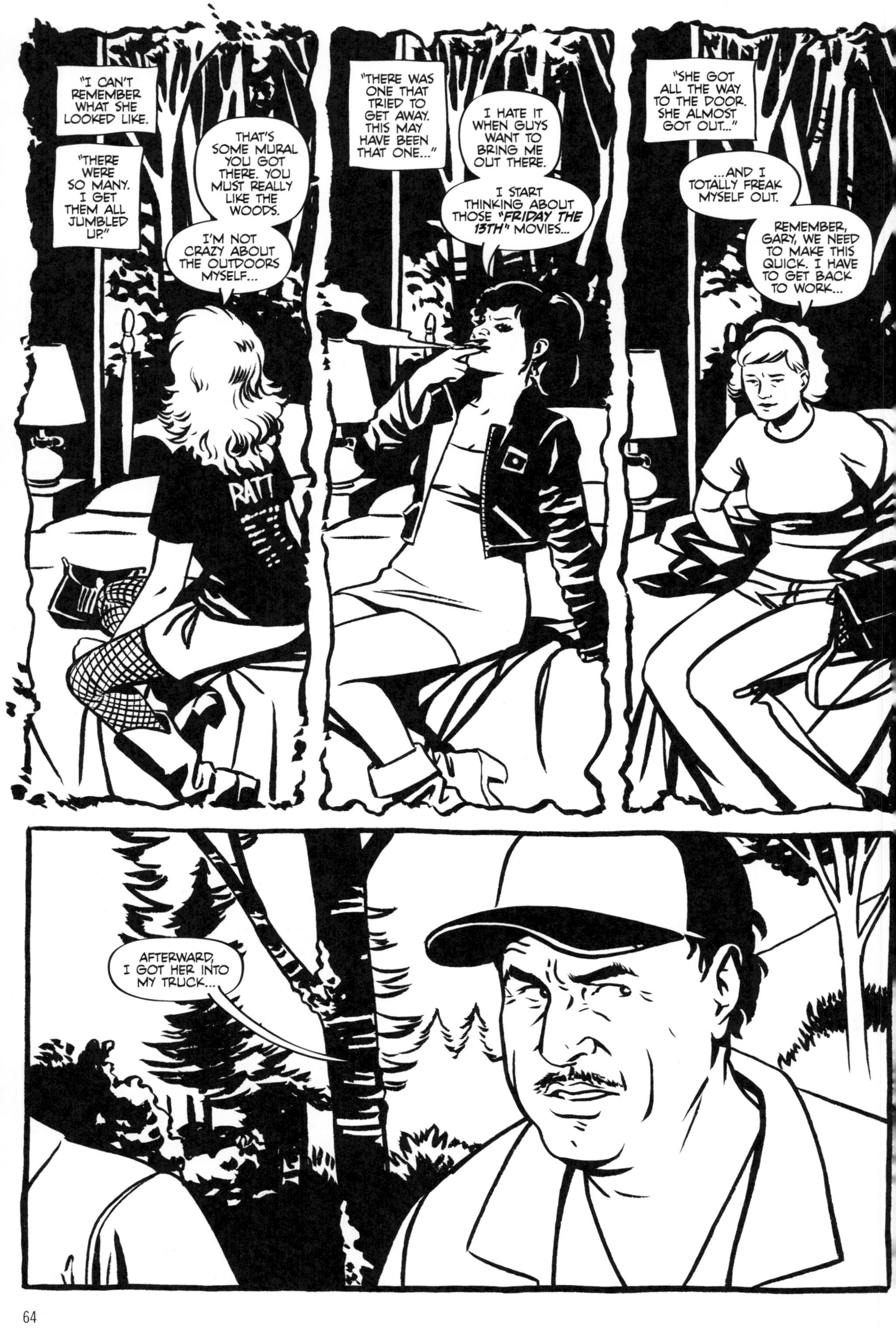
"I CAN'T REMEMBER WHAT SHE LOOKED LIKE.
"THERE WERE SO MANY. I GET THEM ALL JUMBLED UP."
THAT'S SOME MURAL YOU GOT THERE. YOU MUST REALLY LIKE THE WOODS.
I'M NOT CRAZY ABOUT THE OUTDOORS MYSELF...
RATT
"THERE WAS ONE THAT TRIED TO GET AWAY. THIS MAY HAVE BEEN THAT ONE..."
I HATE IT WHEN GUYS WANT TO BRING ME OUT THERE.
I START THINKING ABOUT THOSE "FRIDAY THE 13TH" MOVIES...
"SHE GOT ALL THE WAY TO THE DOOR. SHE ALMOST GOT OUT..."
...AND I TOTALLY FREAK MYSELF OUT.
REMEMBER, GARY, WE NEED TO MAKE THIS QUICK. I HAVE TO GET BACK TO WORK...
AFTERWARD, I GOT HER INTO MY TRUCK...

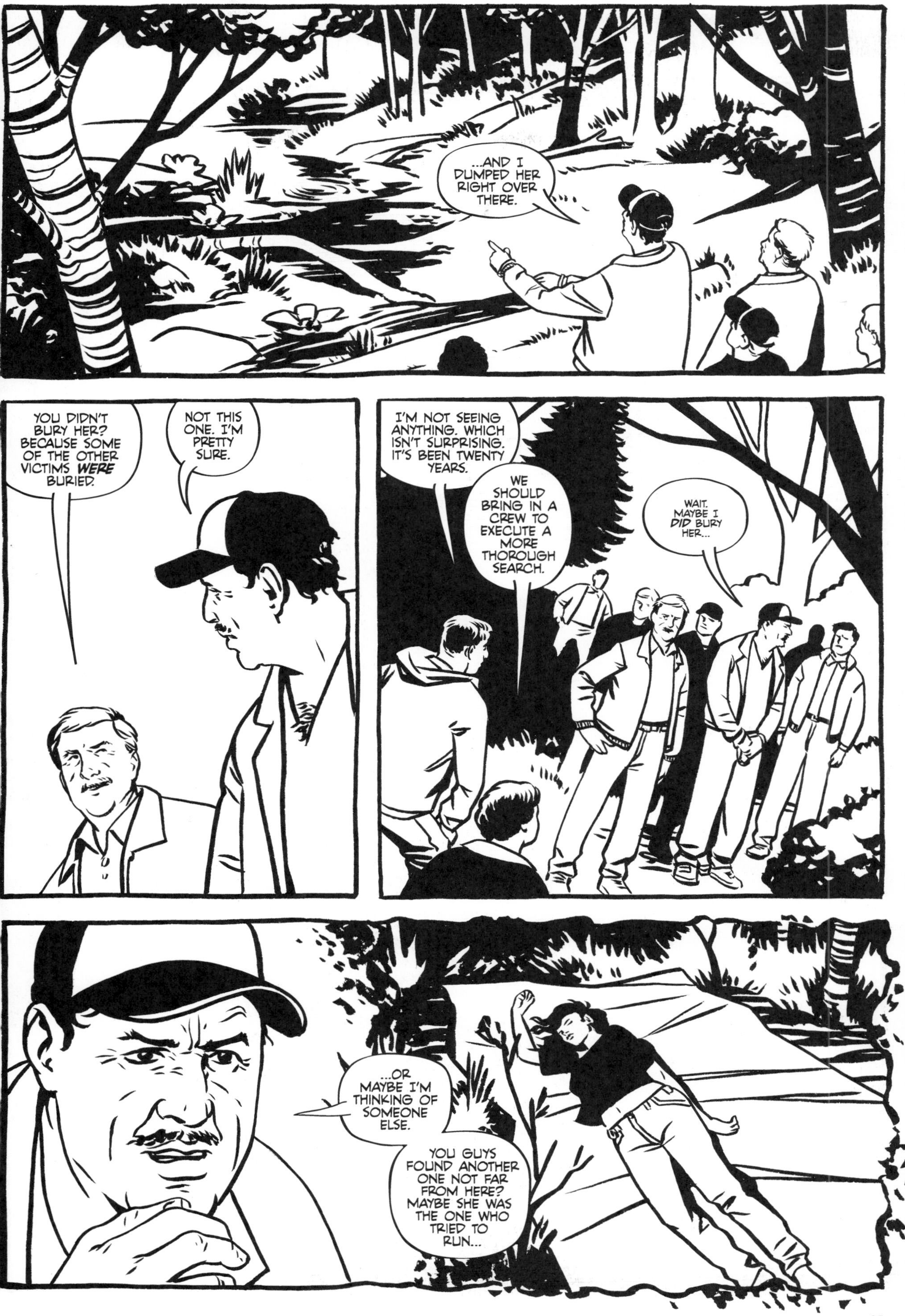
...AND I DUMPED HER RIGHT OVER THERE.
YOU DIDN'T BURY HER? BECAUSE SOME OF THE OTHER VICTIMS *WERE* BURIED.
NOT THIS ONE. I'M PRETTY SURE.
I'M NOT SEEING ANYTHING. WHICH ISN'T SURPRISING. IT'S BEEN TWENTY YEARS.
WE SHOULD BRING IN A CREW TO EXECUTE A MORE THOROUGH SEARCH.
WAIT. MAYBE I *DID* BURY HER...
...OR MAYBE I'M THINKING OF SOMEONE ELSE.
YOU GUYS FOUND ANOTHER ONE NOT FAR FROM HERE? MAYBE SHE WAS THE ONE WHO TRIED TO RUN...

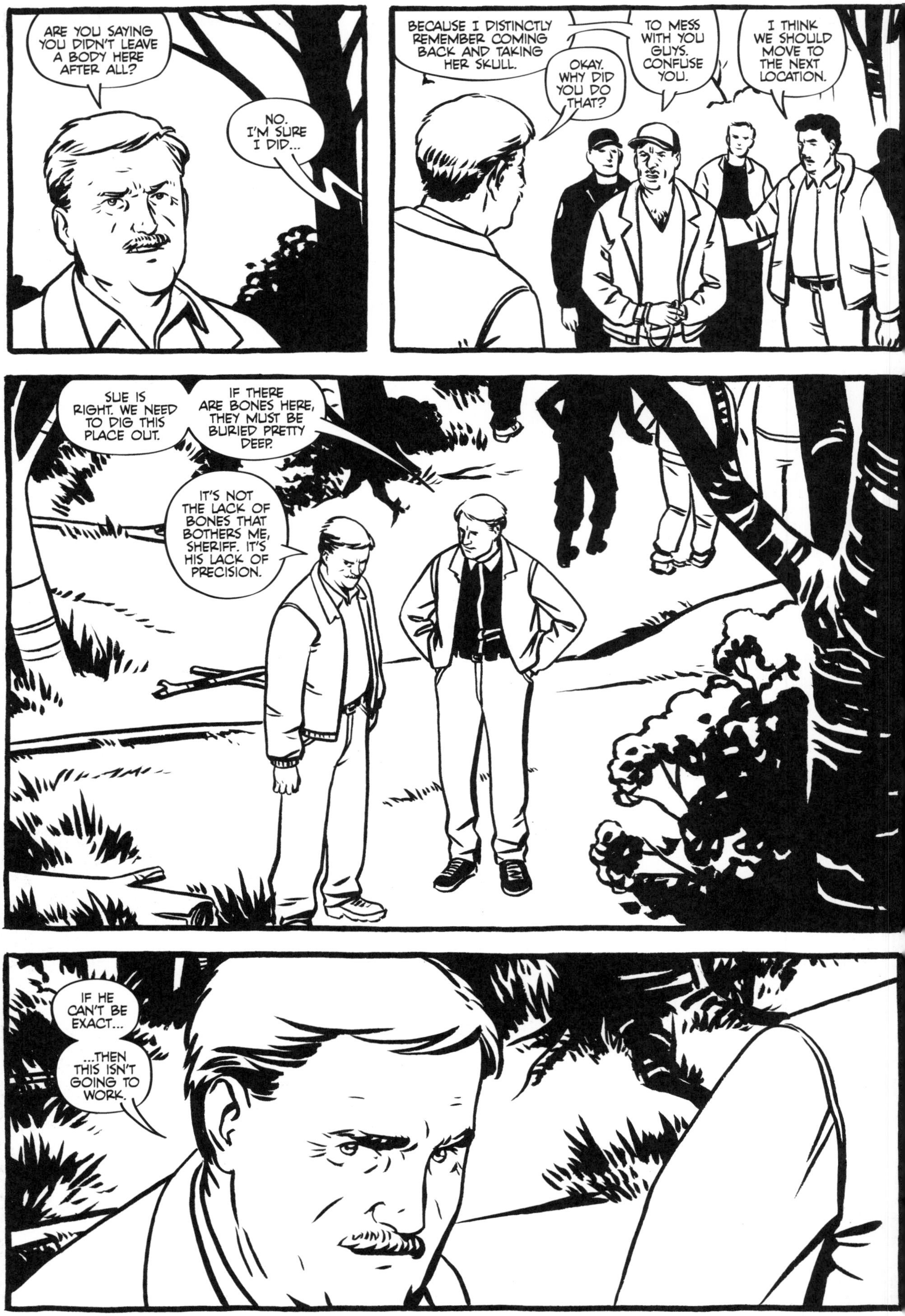
ARE YOU SAYING YOU DIDN'T LEAVE A BODY HERE AFTER ALL?
NO. I'M SURE I DID...
BECAUSE I DISTINCTLY REMEMBER COMING BACK AND TAKING HER SKULL.
OKAY. WHY DID YOU DO THAT?
TO MESS WITH YOU GUYS. CONFUSE YOU.
I THINK WE SHOULD MOVE TO THE NEXT LOCATION.
SUE IS RIGHT. WE NEED TO DIG THIS PLACE OUT.
IF THERE ARE BONES HERE, THEY MUST BE BURIED PRETTY DEEP.
IT'S NOT THE LACK OF BONES THAT BOTHERS ME, SHERIFF. IT'S HIS LACK OF PRECISION.
IF HE CAN'T BE EXACT...
...THEN THIS ISN'T GOING TO WORK.

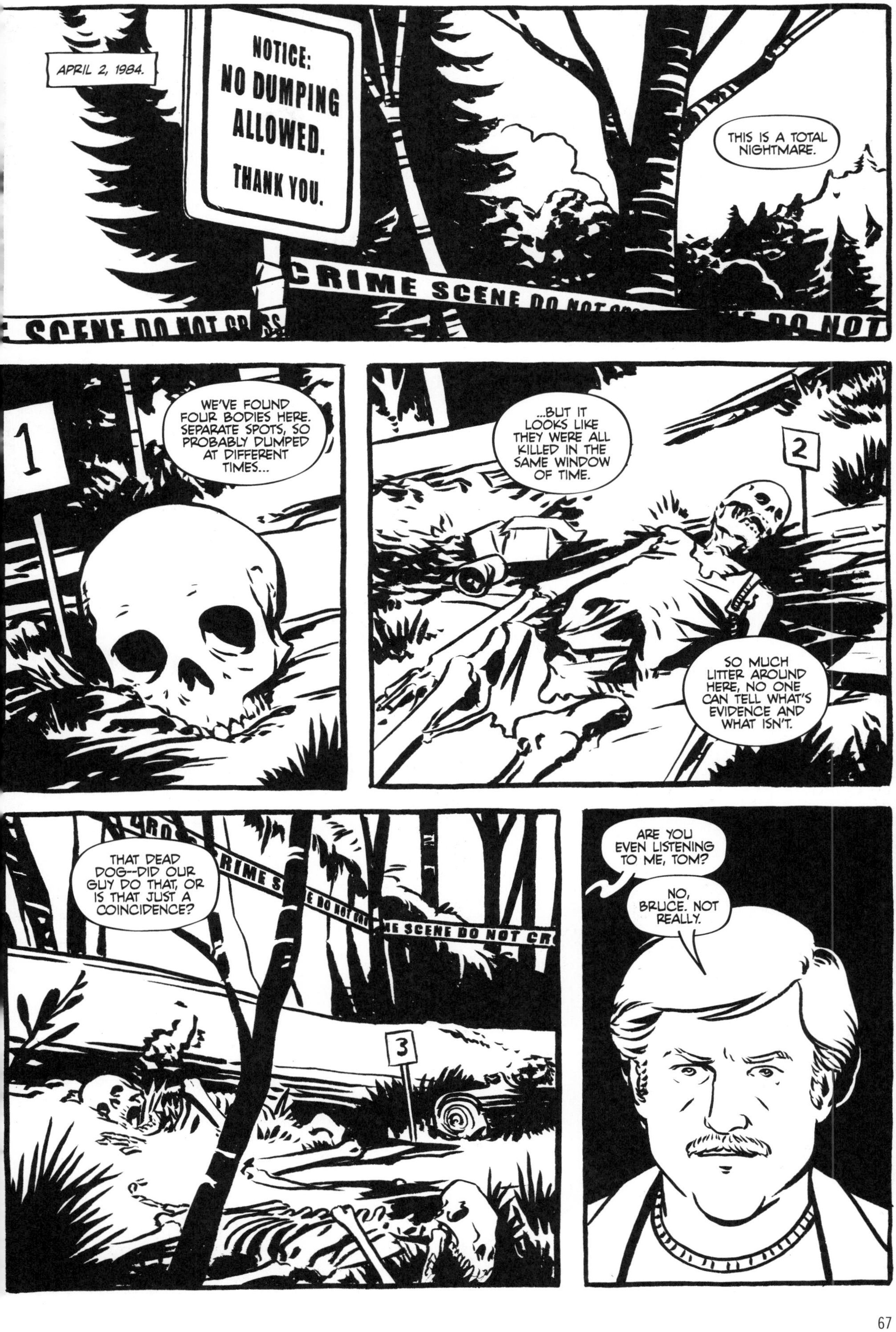
APRIL 2, 1984.
NOTICE: NO DUMPING ALLOWED. THANK YOU.
CRIME SCENE
THIS IS A TOTAL NIGHTMARE.
1
WE'VE FOUND FOUR BODIES HERE. SEPARATE SPOTS, SO PROBABLY DUMPED AT DIFFERENT TIMES...
...BUT IT LOOKS LIKE THEY WERE ALL KILLED IN THE SAME WINDOW OF TIME.
2
SO MUCH LITTER AROUND HERE, NO ONE CAN TELL WHAT'S EVIDENCE AND WHAT ISN'T.
THAT DEAD DOG--DID OUR GUY DO THAT, OR IS THAT JUST A COINCIDENCE?
3
ARE YOU EVEN LISTENING TO ME, TOM?
NO, BRUCE. NOT REALLY.

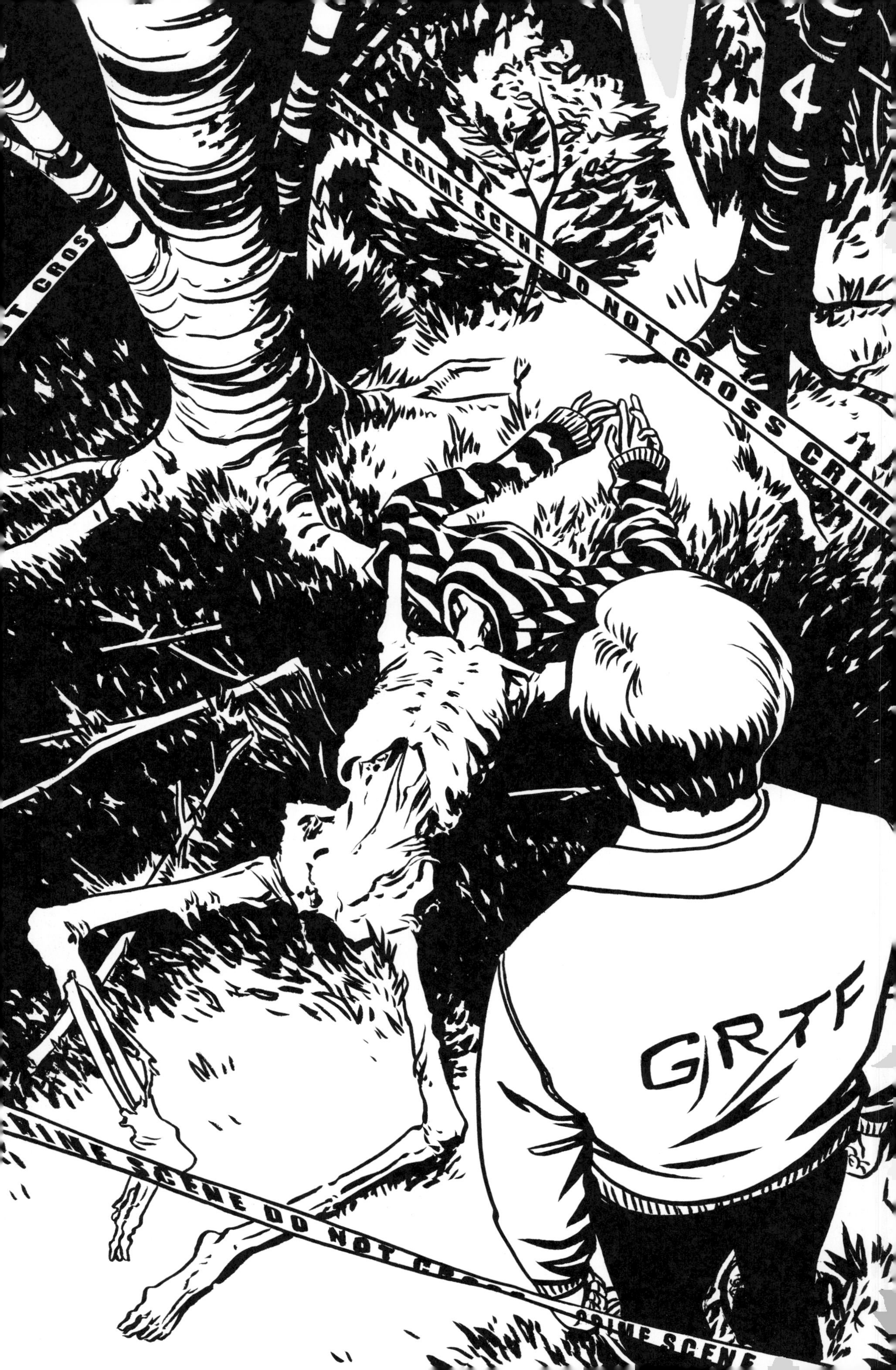
CRIME SCENE DO NOT CROSS CRIM
T CROS
GRTF
CRIME SCENE DO NOT CROSS
CRIME SCENE

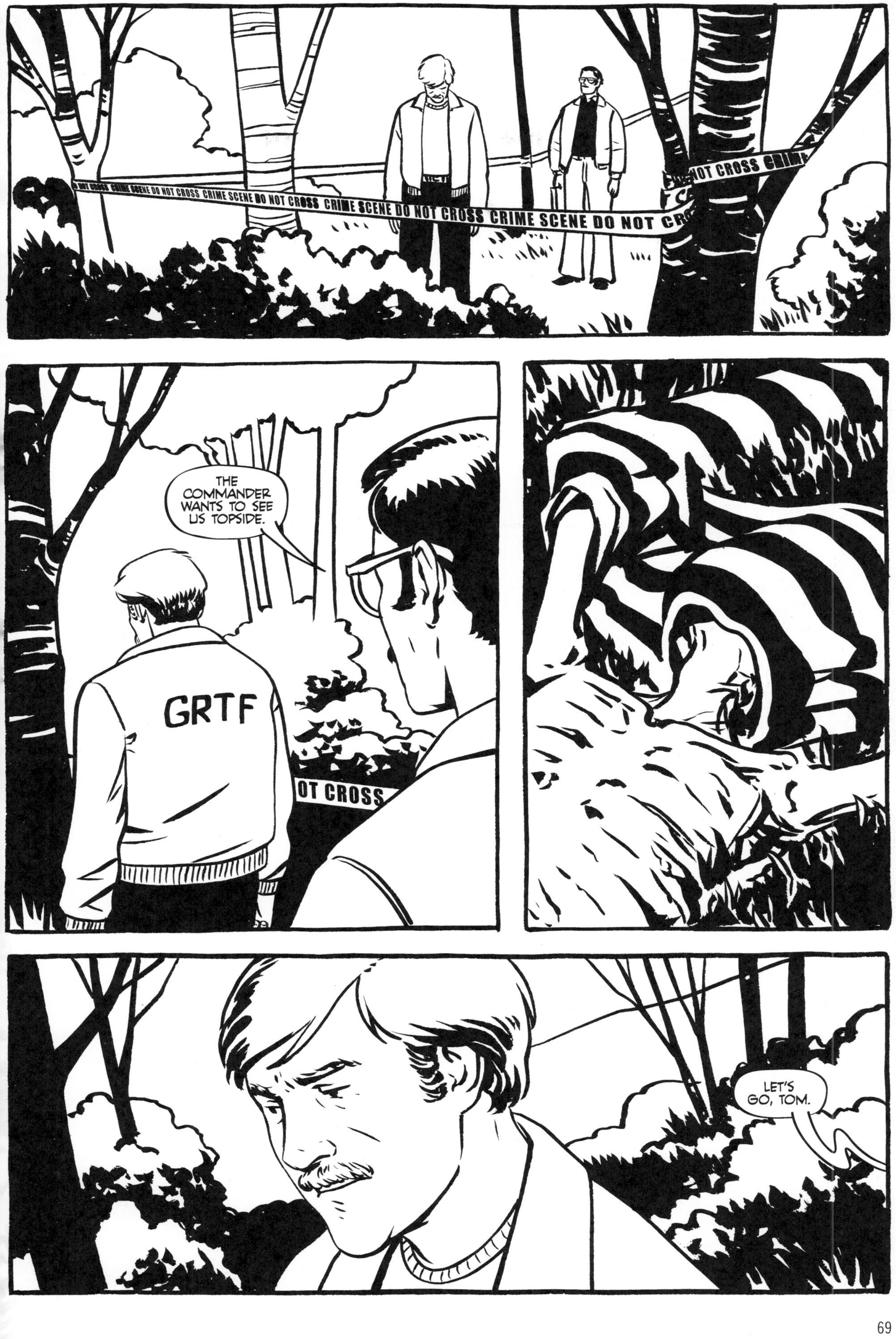

CRIME SCENE DO NOT CROSS CRIME SCENE DO NOT CR
NOT CROSS CRIME
THE COMMANDER WANTS TO SEE US TOPSIDE.
GRTF
OT CROSS
LET'S GO, TOM.

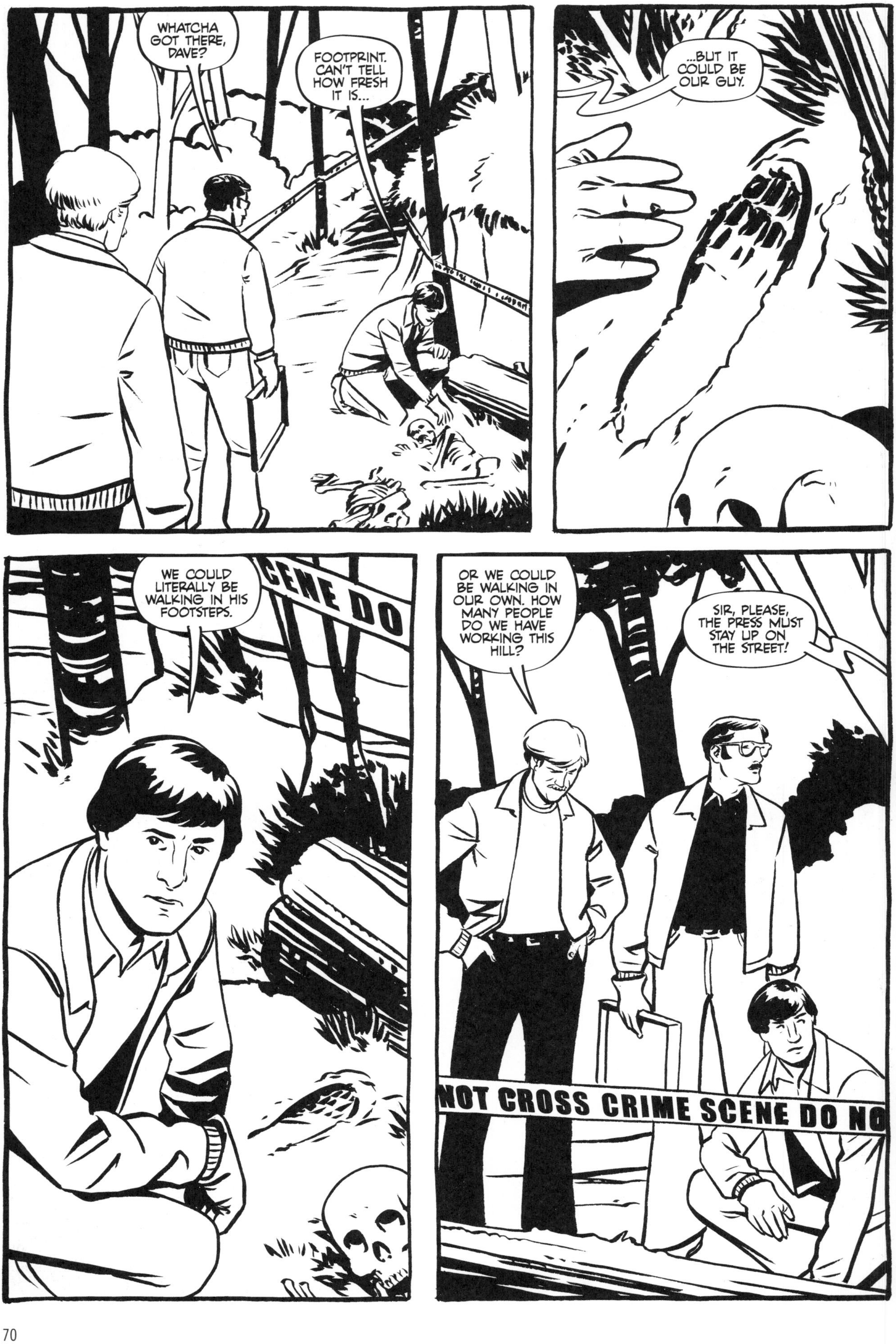
WHATCHA GOT THERE, DAVE?
FOOTPRINT. CAN'T TELL HOW FRESH IT IS...
...BUT IT COULD BE OUR GUY.
WE COULD LITERALLY BE WALKING IN HIS FOOTSTEPS.
GENE DO
OR WE COULD BE WALKING IN OUR OWN. HOW MANY PEOPLE DO WE HAVE WORKING THIS HILL?
SIR, PLEASE, THE PRESS MUST STAY UP ON THE STREET!
NOT CROSS CRIME SCENE DO NO

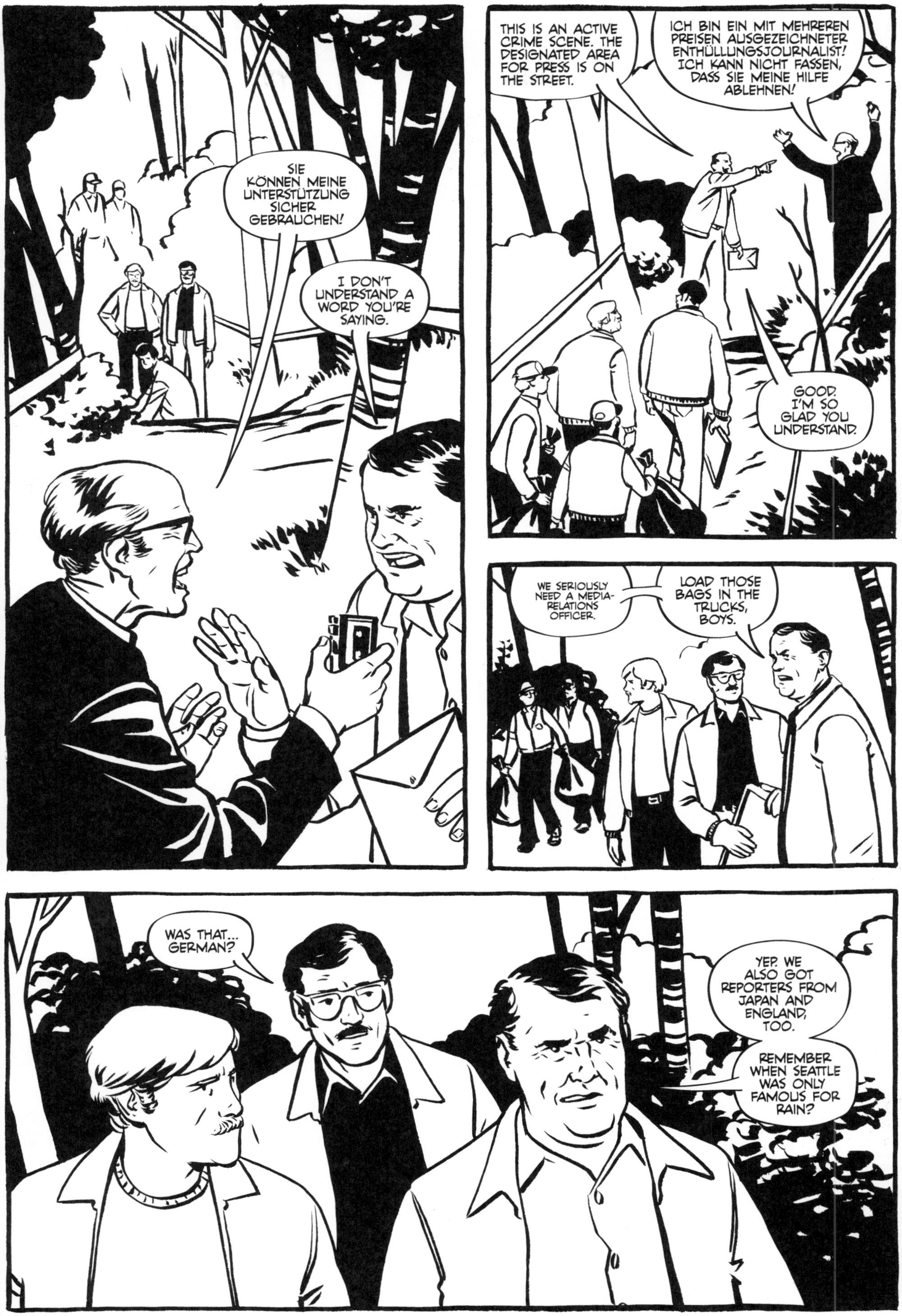
SIE KÖNNEN MEINE UNTERSTÜTZUNG SICHER GEBRAUCHEN!
I DON'T UNDERSTAND A WORD YOU'RE SAYING.
THIS IS AN ACTIVE CRIME SCENE. THE DESIGNATED AREA FOR PRESS IS ON THE STREET.
ICH BIN EIN MIT MEHREREN PREISEN AUSGEZEICHNETER ENTHÜLLUNGSJOURNALIST! ICH KANN NICHT FASSEN, DASS SIE MEINE HILFE ABLEHNEN!
GOOD. I'M SO GLAD YOU UNDERSTAND.
WE SERIOUSLY NEED A MEDIA-RELATIONS OFFICER.
LOAD THOSE BAGS IN THE TRUCKS, BOYS.
WAS THAT... GERMAN?
YEP. WE ALSO GOT REPORTERS FROM JAPAN AND ENGLAND, TOO.
REMEMBER WHEN SEATTLE WAS ONLY FAMOUS FOR RAIN?

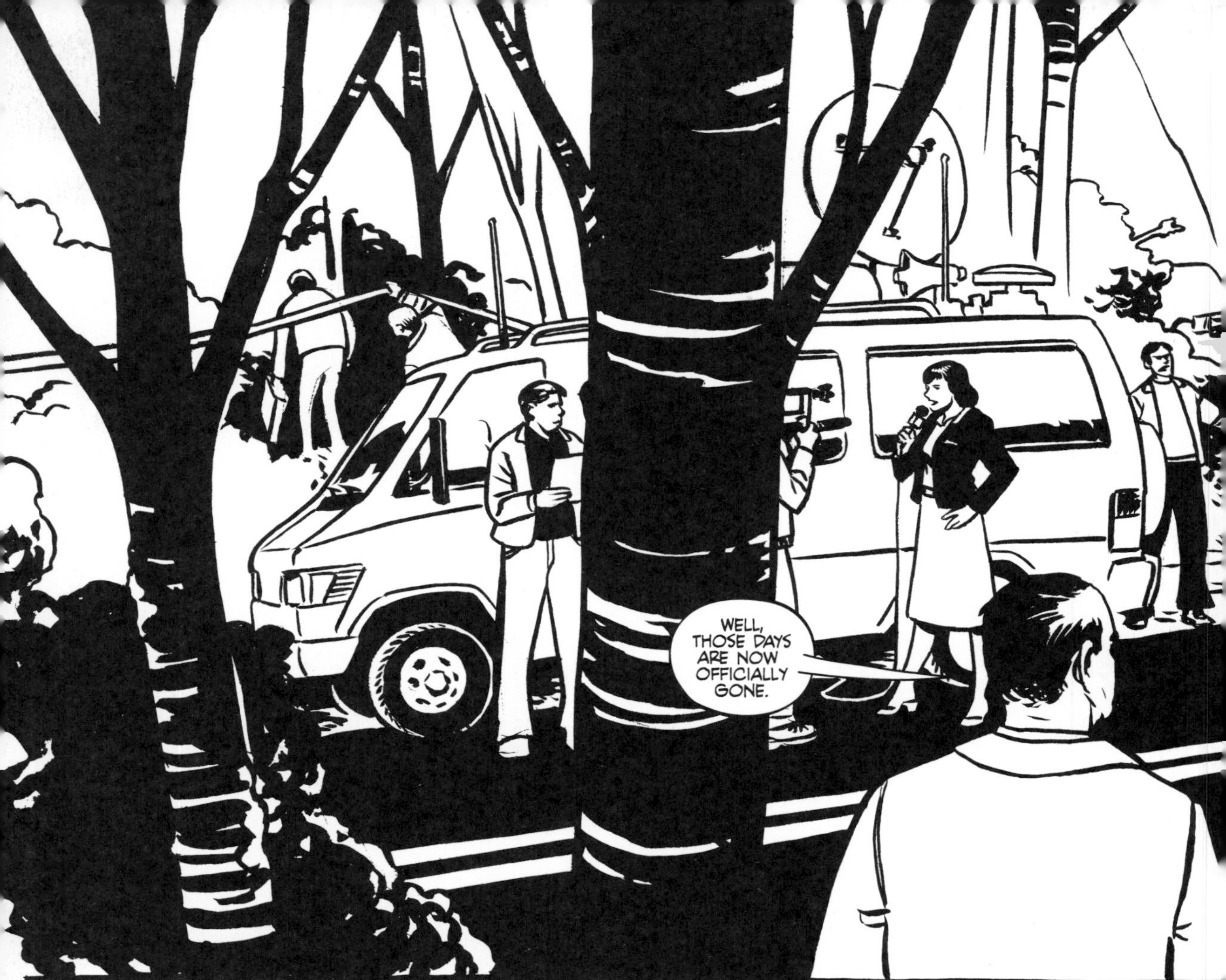
WELL, THOSE DAYS ARE NOW OFFICIALLY GONE.

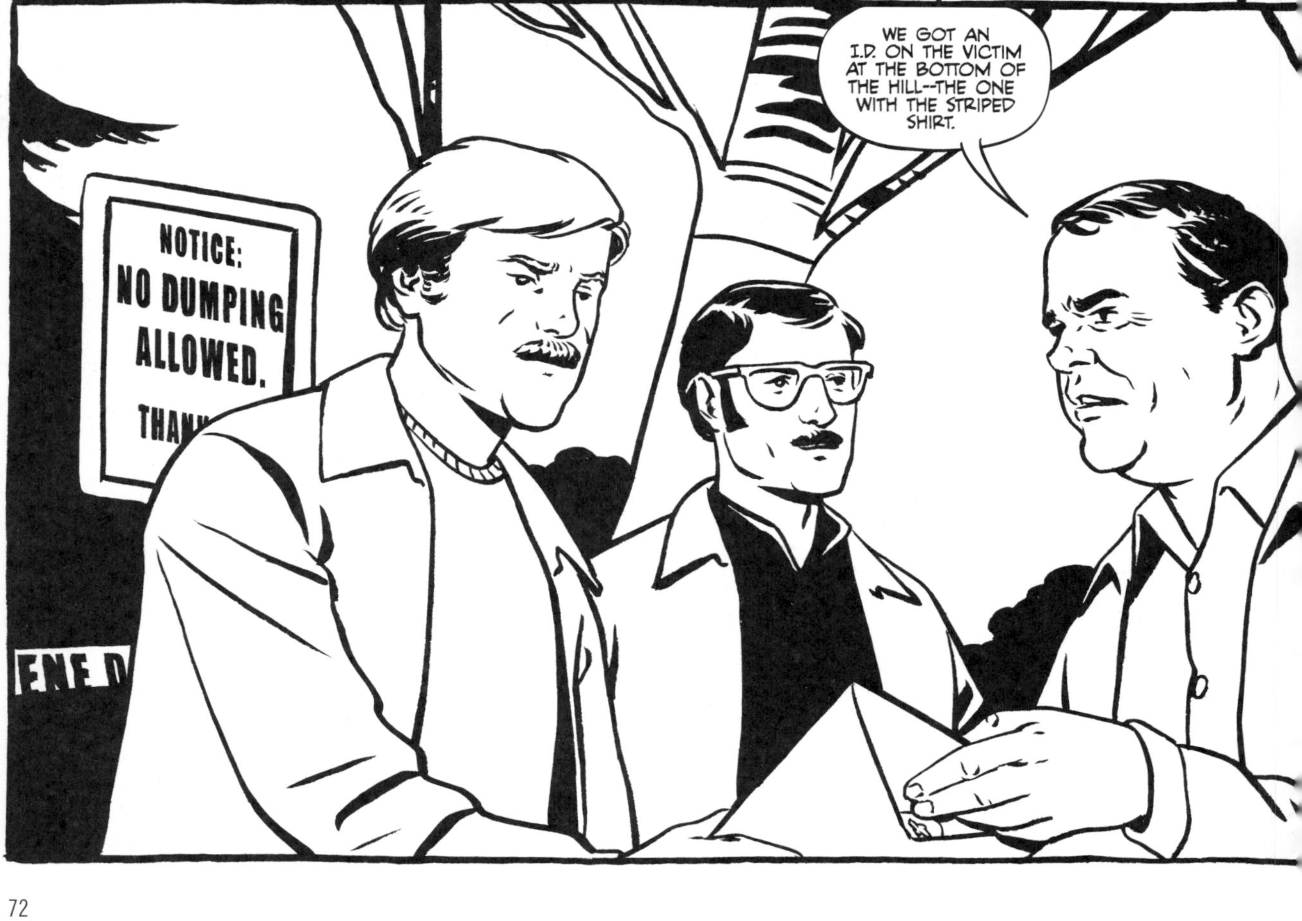
WE GOT AN I.D. ON THE VICTIM AT THE BOTTOM OF THE HILL--THE ONE WITH THE STRIPED SHIRT.
NOTICE:
NO DUMPING ALLOWED.

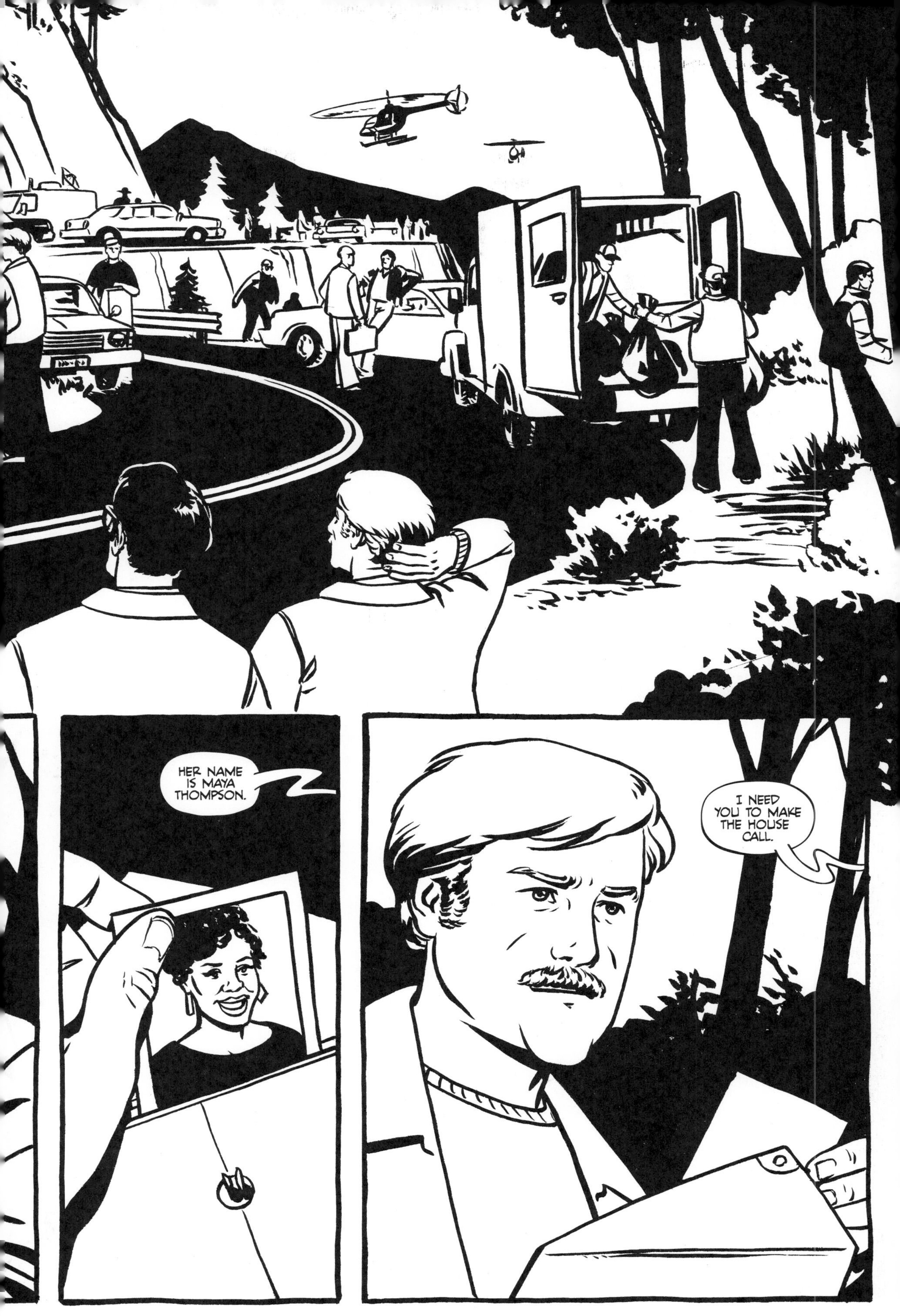
HER NAME IS MAYA THOMPSON.
I NEED YOU TO MAKE THE HOUSE CALL.

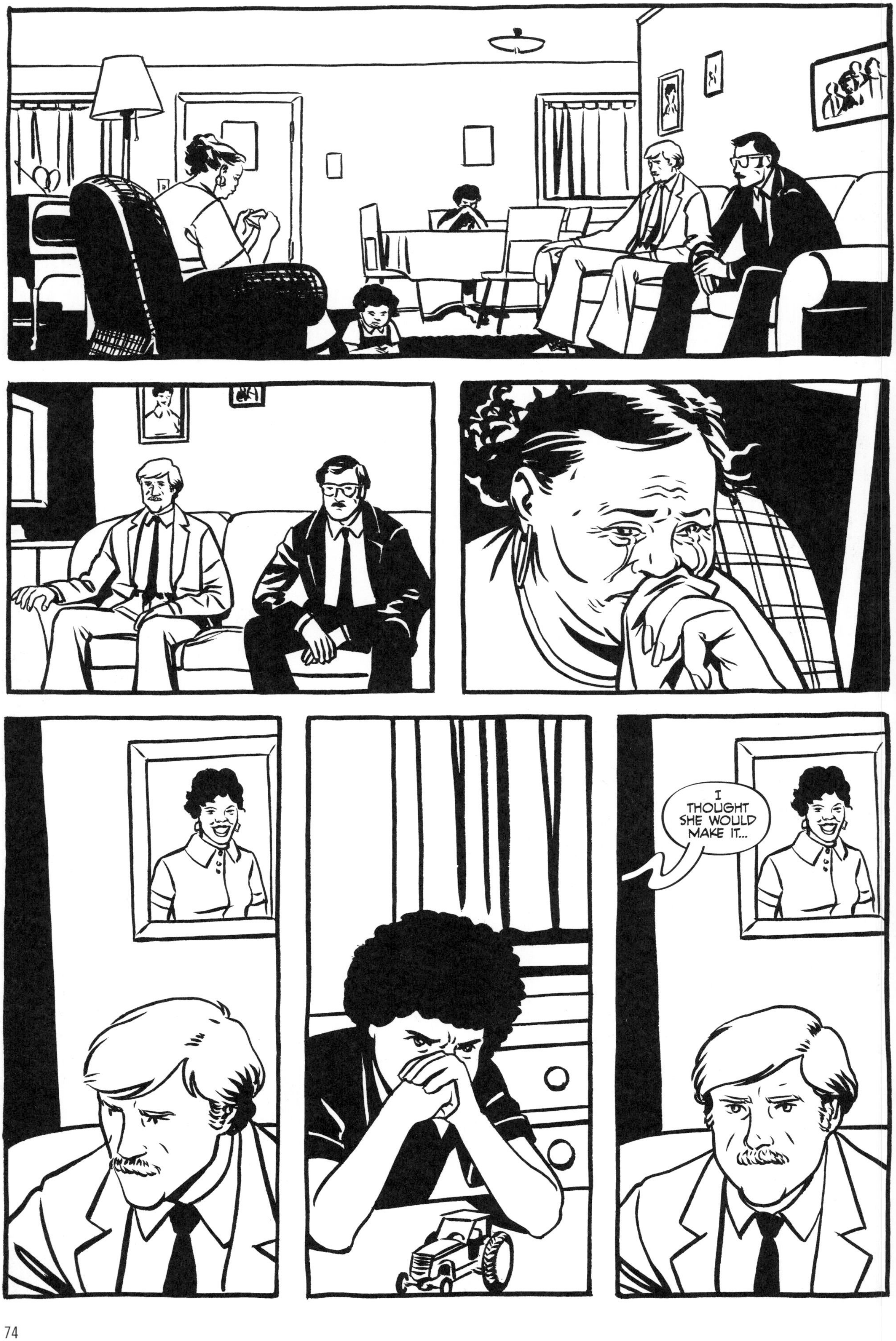
I THOUGHT SHE WOULD MAKE IT...

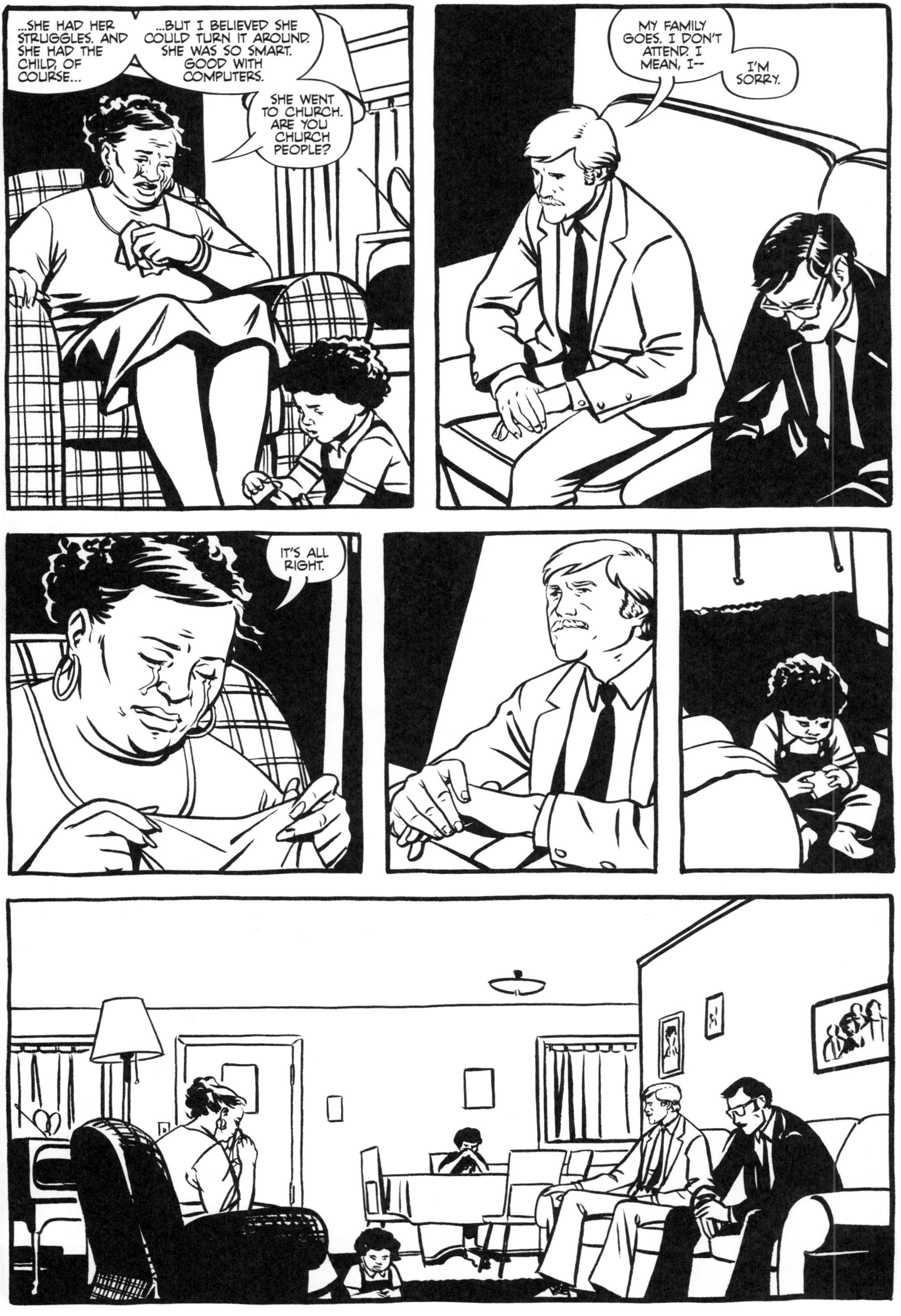
...SHE HAD HER STRUGGLES. AND SHE HAD THE CHILD, OF COURSE...
...BUT I BELIEVED SHE COULD TURN IT AROUND. SHE WAS SO SMART. GOOD WITH COMPUTERS.
SHE WENT TO CHURCH. ARE YOU CHURCH PEOPLE?
MY FAMILY GOES. I DON'T ATTEND. I MEAN, I--
I'M SORRY.
IT'S ALL RIGHT.

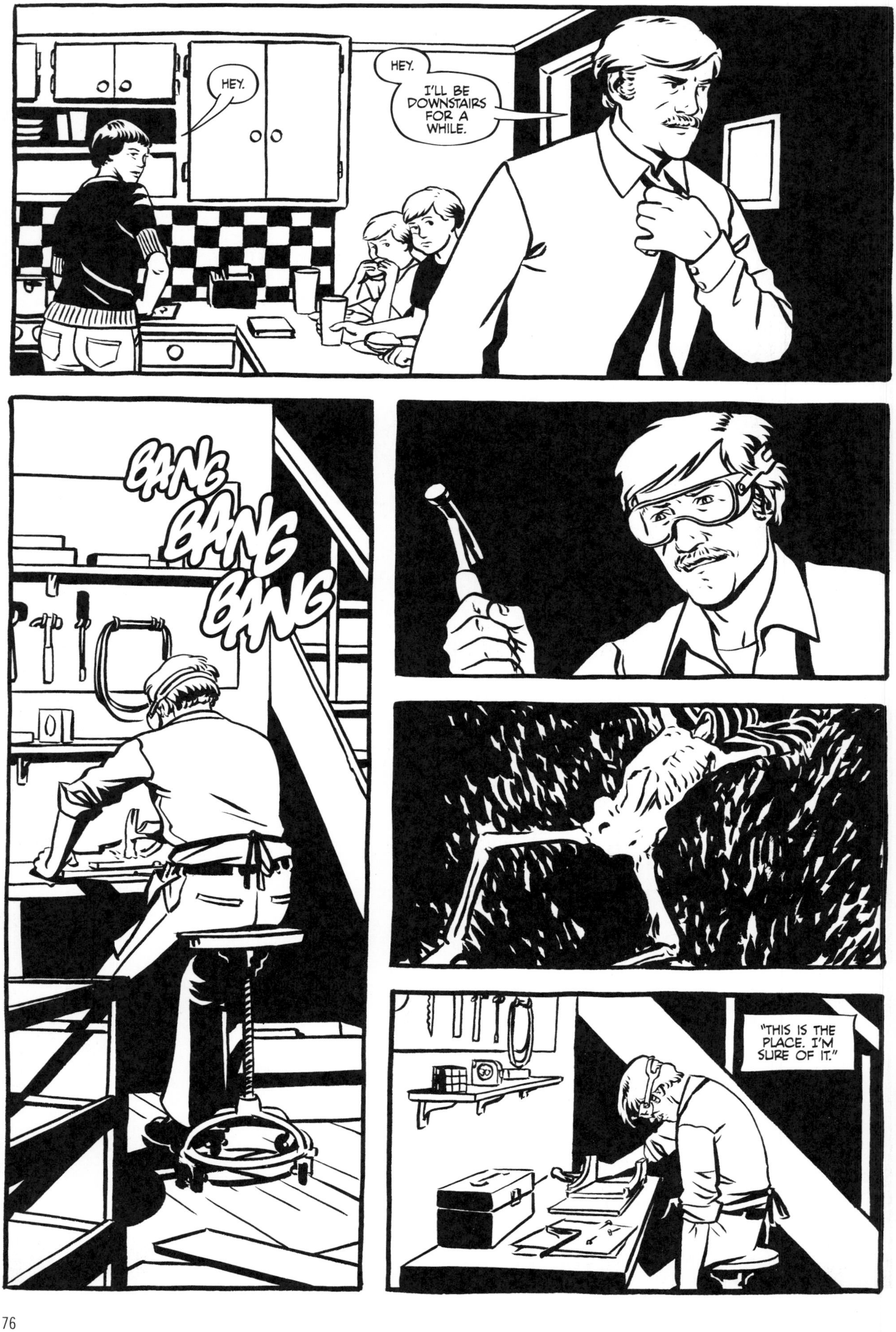
HEY.
HEY.
I'LL BE DOWNSTAIRS FOR A WHILE.
BANG BANG BANG
"THIS IS THE PLACE. I'M SURE OF IT."

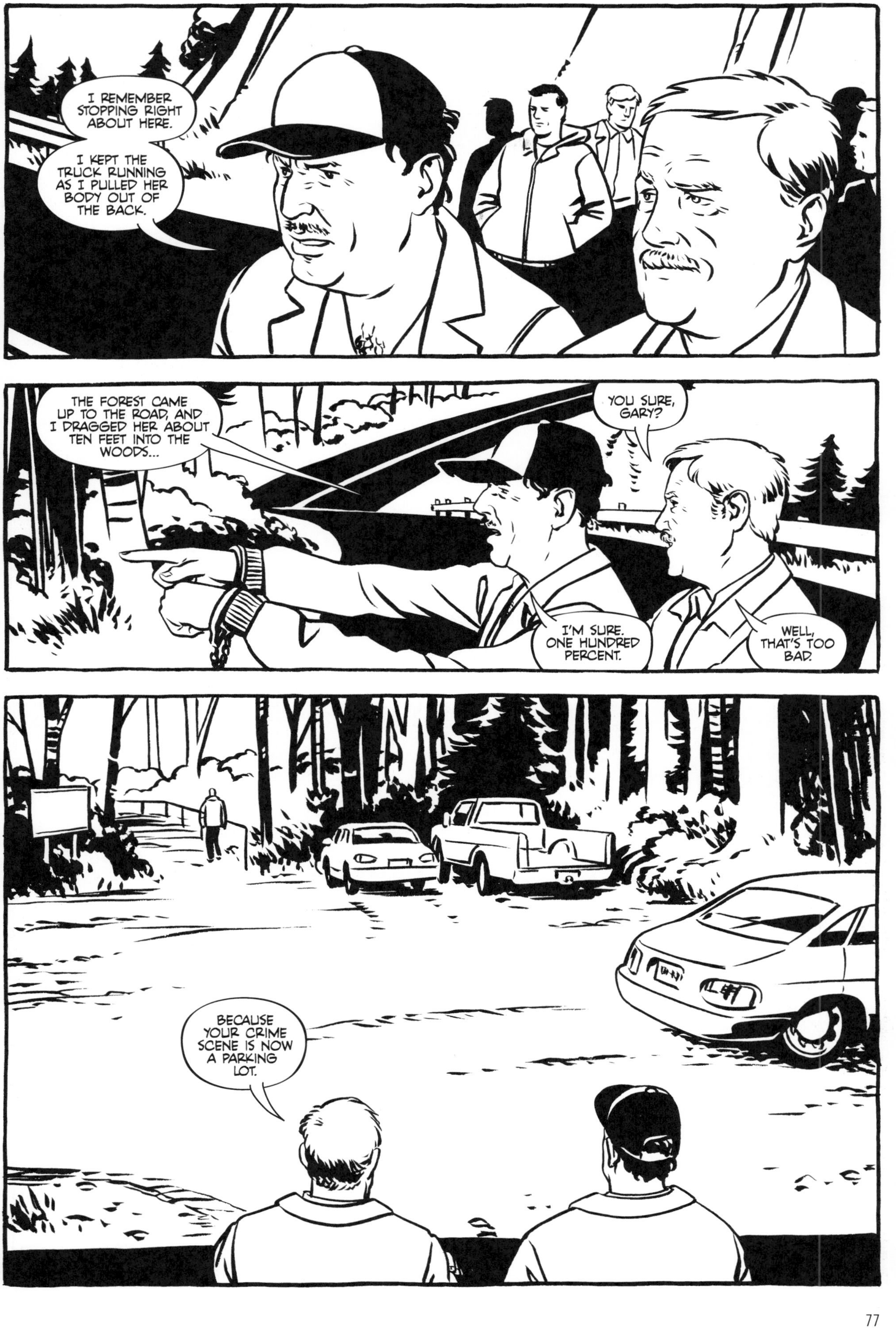
I REMEMBER STOPPING RIGHT ABOUT HERE.
I KEPT THE TRUCK RUNNING AS I PULLED HER BODY OUT OF THE BACK.
THE FOREST CAME UP TO THE ROAD, AND I DRAGGED HER ABOUT TEN FEET INTO THE WOODS...
YOU SURE, GARY?
I'M SURE. ONE HUNDRED PERCENT.
WELL, THAT'S TOO BAD.
BECAUSE YOUR CRIME SCENE IS NOW A PARKING LOT.

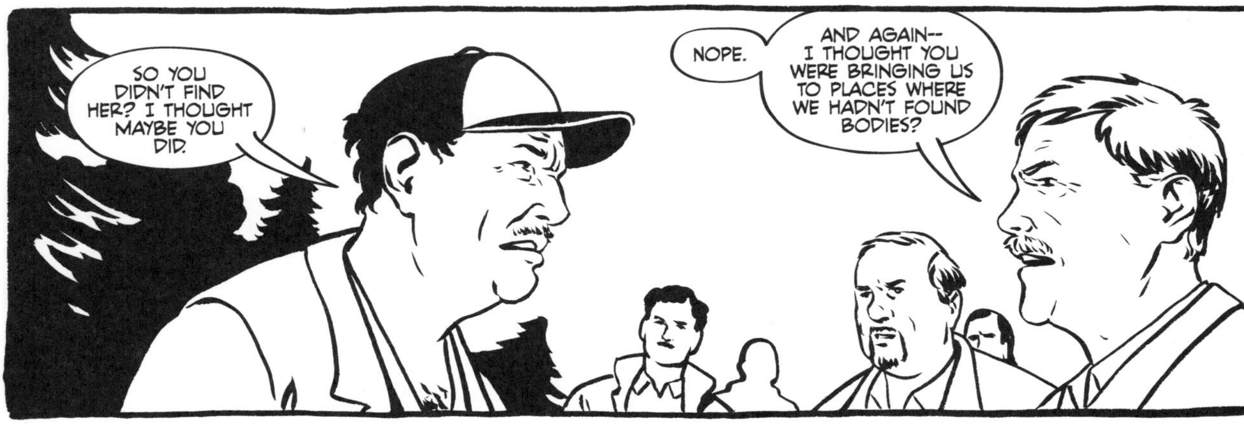
SO YOU DIDN'T FIND HER? I THOUGHT MAYBE YOU DID.
NOPE.
AND AGAIN-- I THOUGHT YOU WERE BRINGING US TO PLACES WHERE WE HADN'T FOUND BODIES?

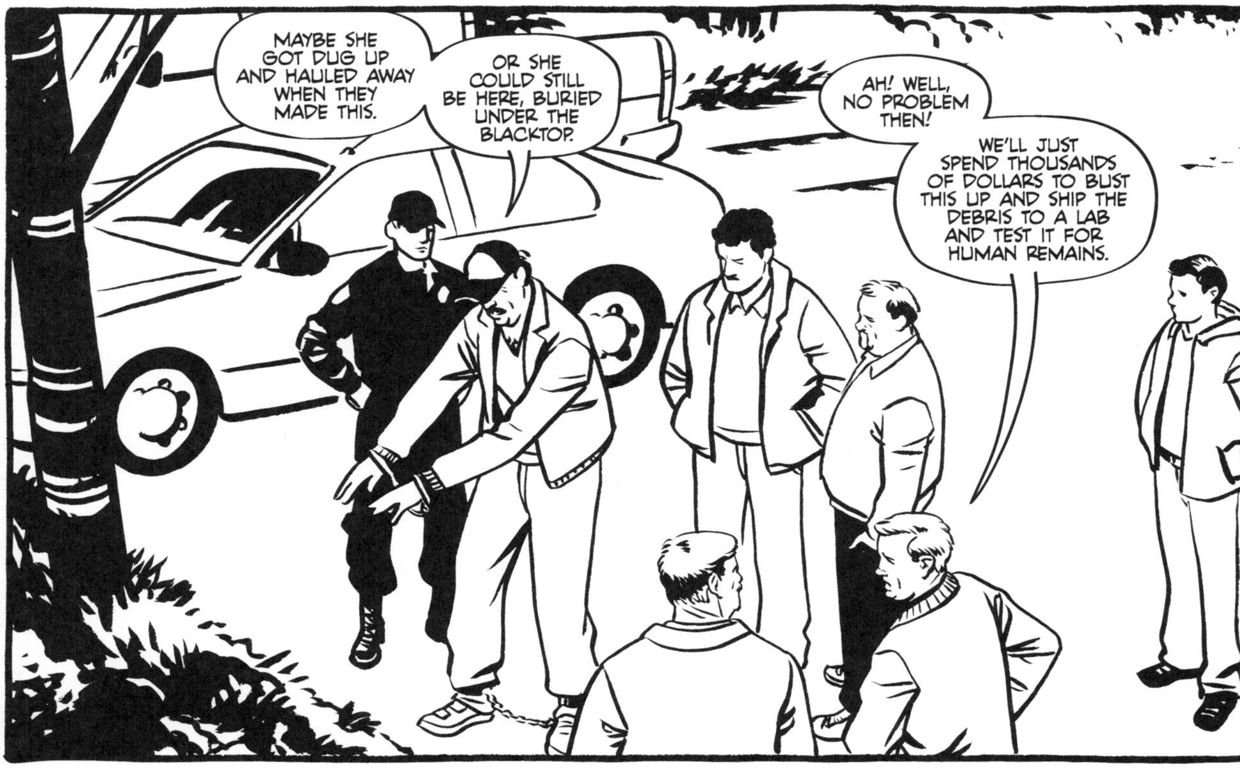
MAYBE SHE GOT DUG UP AND HAULED AWAY WHEN THEY MADE THIS.
OR SHE COULD STILL BE HERE, BURIED UNDER THE BLACKTOP.
AH! WELL, NO PROBLEM THEN!
WE'LL JUST SPEND THOUSANDS OF DOLLARS TO BUST THIS UP AND SHIP THE DEBRIS TO A LAB AND TEST IT FOR HUMAN REMAINS.

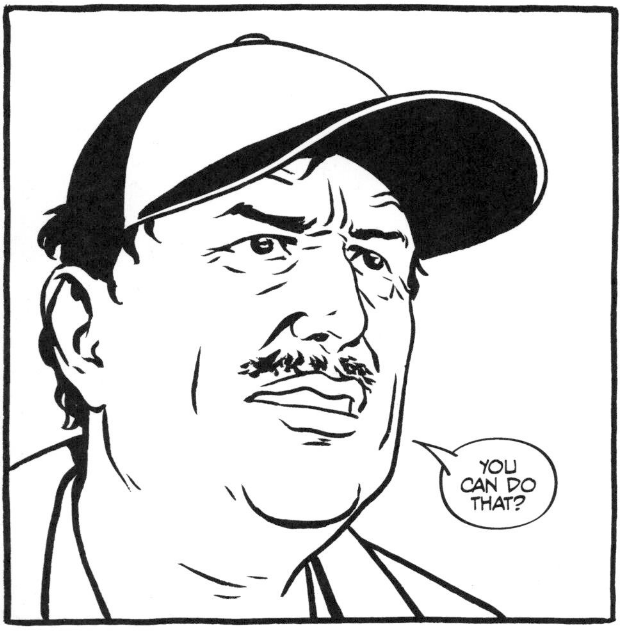
YOU CAN DO THAT?

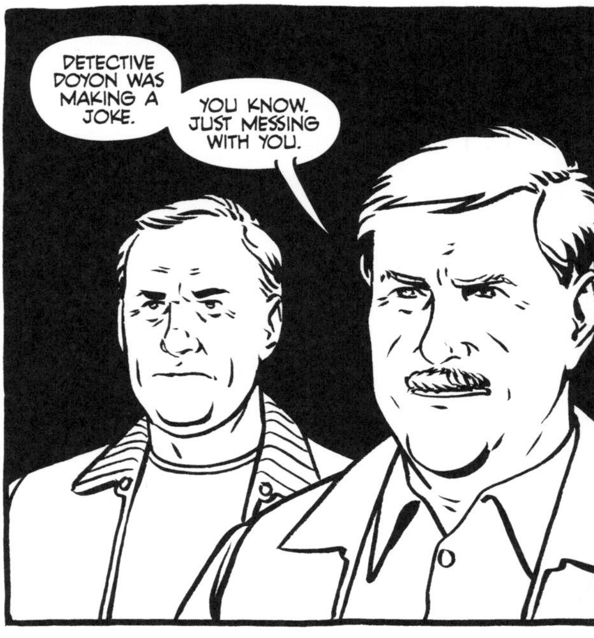
DETECTIVE DOYON WAS MAKING A JOKE.
YOU KNOW. JUST MESSING WITH YOU.

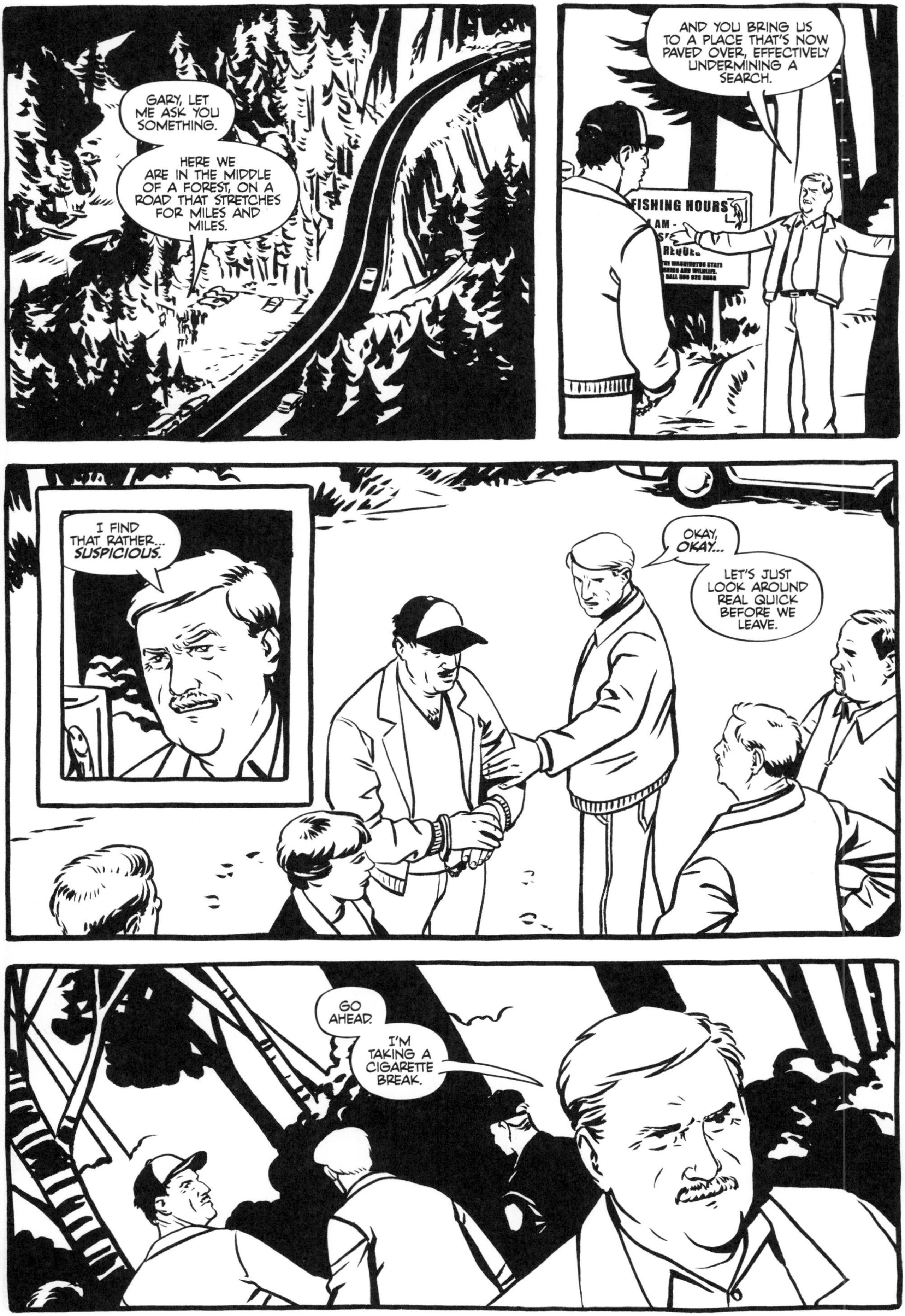
GARY, LET ME ASK YOU SOMETHING.
HERE WE ARE IN THE MIDDLE OF A FOREST, ON A ROAD THAT STRETCHES FOR MILES AND MILES.
AND YOU BRING US TO A PLACE THAT'S NOW PAVED OVER, EFFECTIVELY UNDERMINING A SEARCH.
FISHING HOURS
I FIND THAT RATHER... *SUSPICIOUS.*
OKAY, *OKAY...*
LET'S JUST LOOK AROUND REAL QUICK BEFORE WE LEAVE.
GO AHEAD.
I'M TAKING A CIGARETTE BREAK.

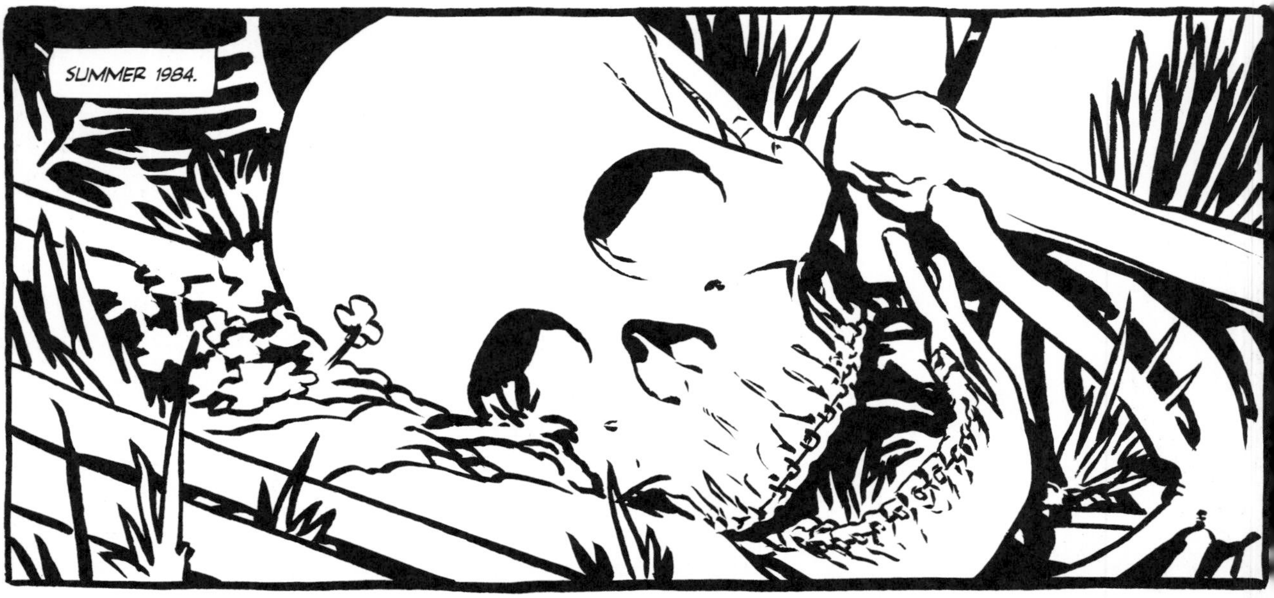
SUMMER 1984.

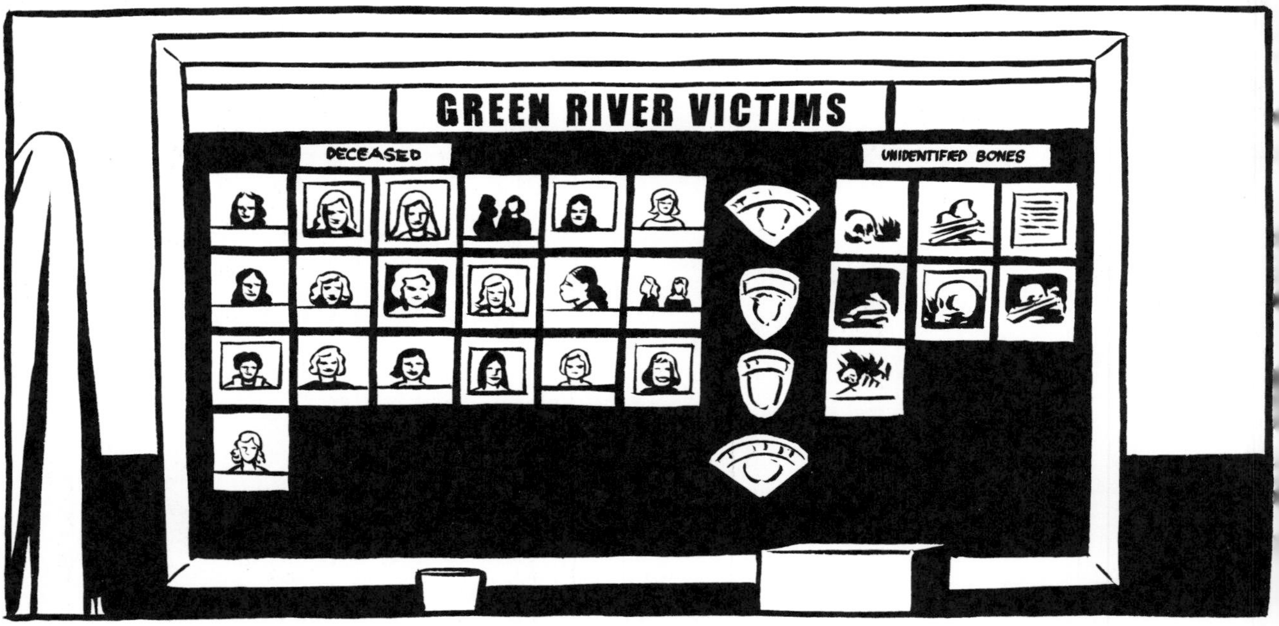
GREEN RIVER VICTIMS
DECEASED
UNIDENTIFIED BONES

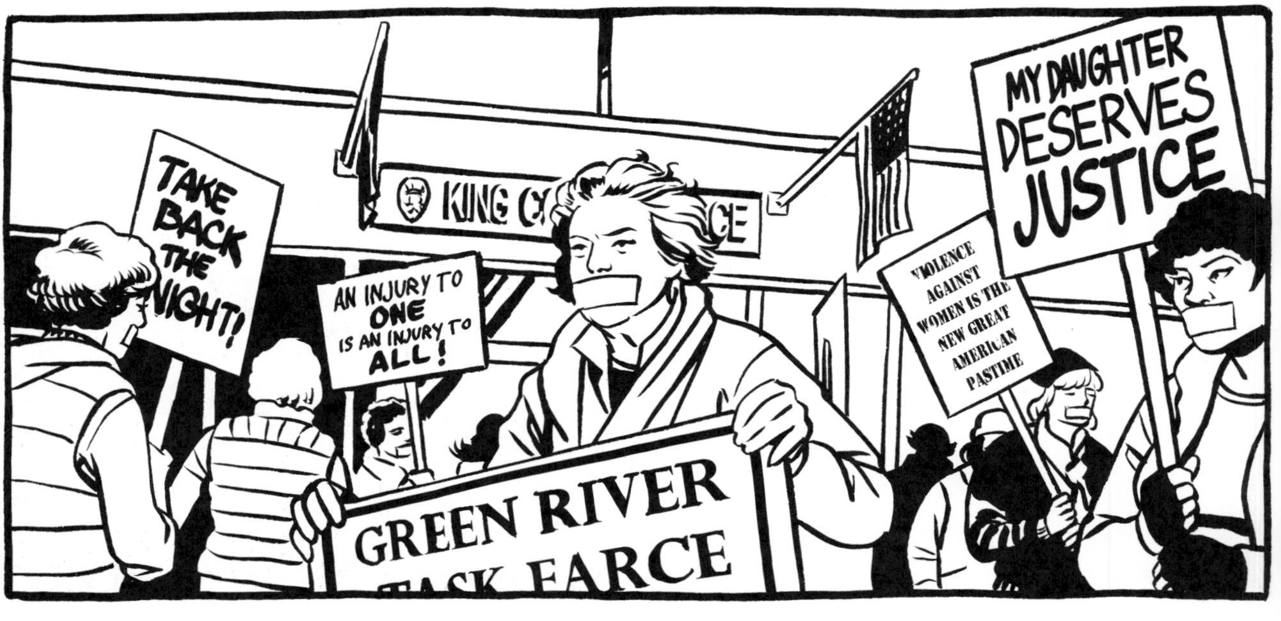
TAKE BACK THE NIGHT!
AN INJURY TO ONE IS AN INJURY TO ALL!
MY DAUGHTER DESERVES JUSTICE
VIOLENCE AGAINST WOMEN IS THE NEW GREAT AMERICAN PASTIME
GREEN RIVER

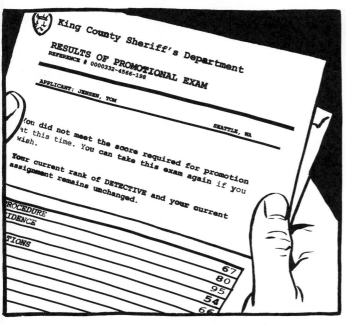

King County Sheriff's Department

RESULTS OF PROMOTIONAL EXAM

REFERENCE # 0000332-4566-198

APPLICANT: JENSEN, TOM

SEATTLE, WA

You did not meet the score required for promotion at this time. You can take this exam again if you wish.

Your current rank of DETECTIVE and your current assignment remains unchanged.

PROCEDURE

IDENCE

TIONS

67
80
95
54
66

MY DAUGHTER DESERVES JUSTICE

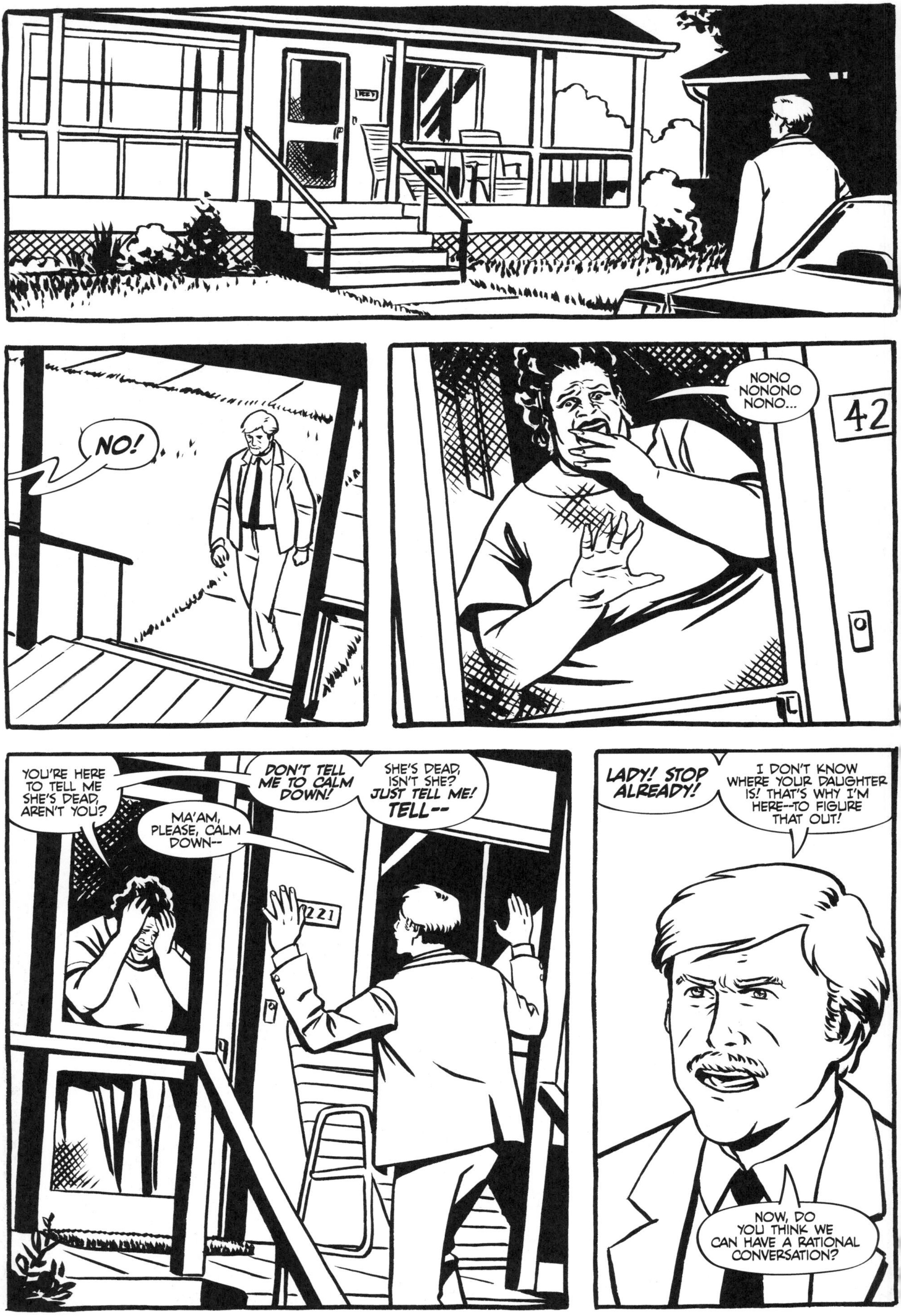
NO!
NONO NONONO NONO...
42
YOU'RE HERE TO TELL ME SHE'S DEAD, AREN'T YOU?
MA'AM, PLEASE, CALM DOWN--
DON'T TELL ME TO CALM DOWN!
SHE'S DEAD, ISN'T SHE? JUST TELL ME! TELL--
LADY! STOP ALREADY!
I DON'T KNOW WHERE YOUR DAUGHTER IS! THAT'S WHY I'M HERE--TO FIGURE THAT OUT!
NOW, DO YOU THINK WE CAN HAVE A RATIONAL CONVERSATION?

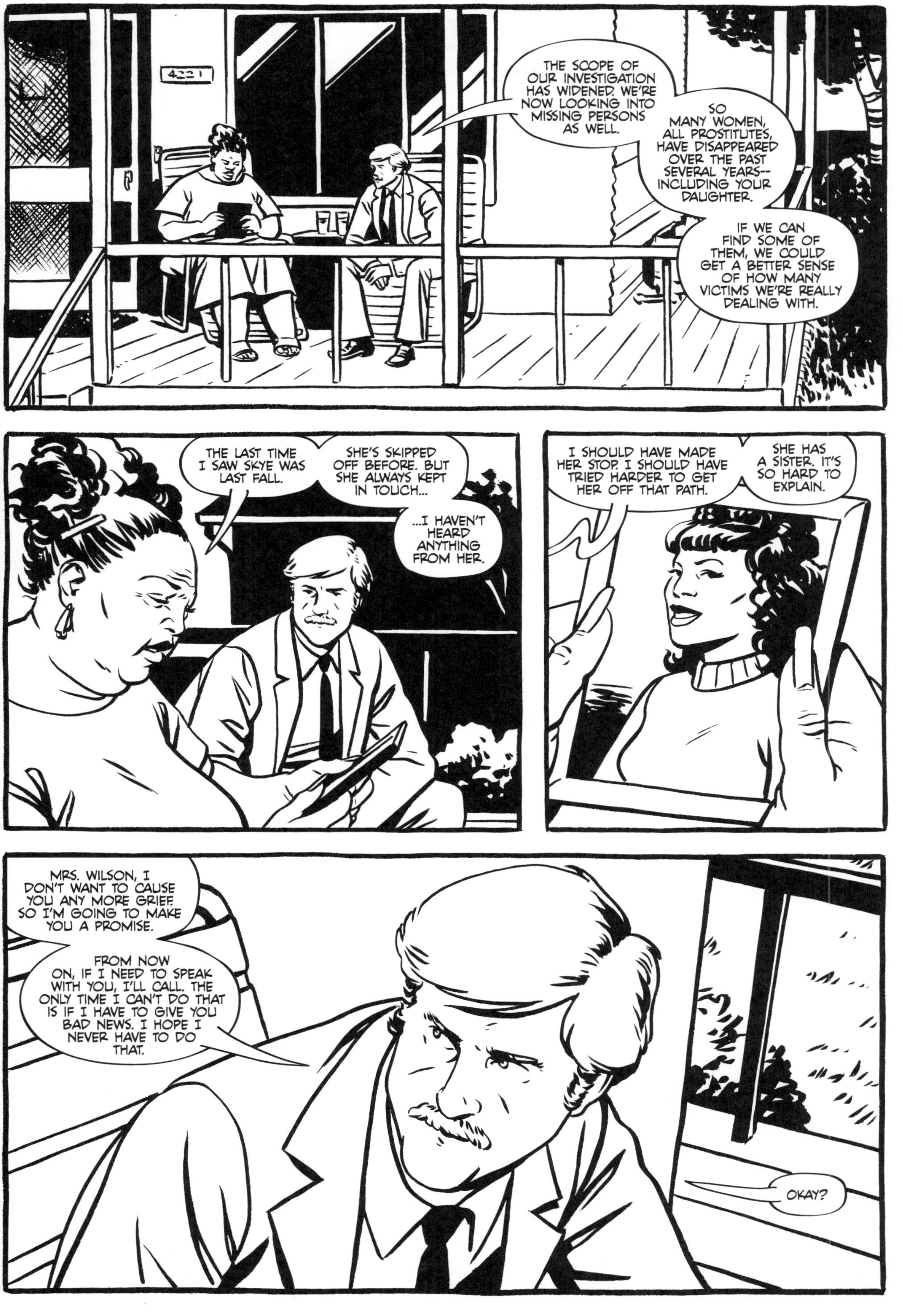

4221
THE SCOPE OF OUR INVESTIGATION HAS WIDENED. WE'RE NOW LOOKING INTO MISSING PERSONS AS WELL.
SO MANY WOMEN, ALL PROSTITUTES, HAVE DISAPPEARED OVER THE PAST SEVERAL YEARS-- INCLUDING YOUR DAUGHTER.
IF WE CAN FIND SOME OF THEM, WE COULD GET A BETTER SENSE OF HOW MANY VICTIMS WE'RE REALLY DEALING WITH.
THE LAST TIME I SAW SKYE WAS LAST FALL.
SHE'S SKIPPED OFF BEFORE. BUT SHE ALWAYS KEPT IN TOUCH...
...I HAVEN'T HEARD ANYTHING FROM HER.
I SHOULD HAVE MADE HER STOP. I SHOULD HAVE TRIED HARDER TO GET HER OFF THAT PATH.
SHE HAS A SISTER. IT'S SO HARD TO EXPLAIN.
MRS. WILSON, I DON'T WANT TO CAUSE YOU ANY MORE GRIEF. SO I'M GOING TO MAKE YOU A PROMISE.
FROM NOW ON, IF I NEED TO SPEAK WITH YOU, I'LL CALL. THE ONLY TIME I CAN'T DO THAT IS IF I HAVE TO GIVE YOU BAD NEWS. I HOPE I NEVER HAVE TO DO THAT.
OKAY?

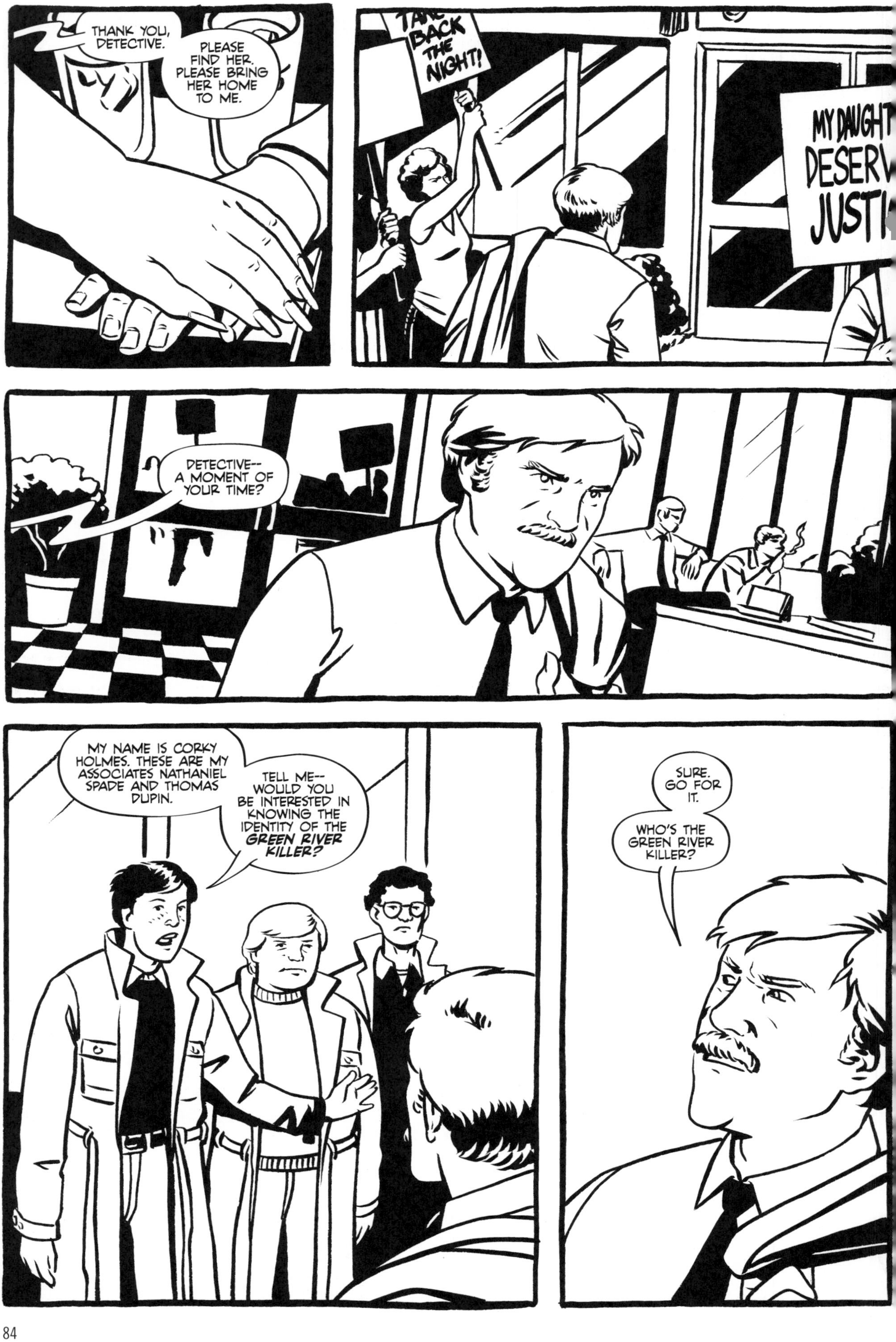
THANK YOU, DETECTIVE.
PLEASE FIND HER. PLEASE BRING HER HOME TO ME.
TAKE BACK THE NIGHT!
MY DAUGHT DESERV JUSTI
DETECTIVE-- A MOMENT OF YOUR TIME?
MY NAME IS CORKY HOLMES. THESE ARE MY ASSOCIATES NATHANIEL SPADE AND THOMAS DUPIN.
TELL ME-- WOULD YOU BE INTERESTED IN KNOWING THE IDENTITY OF THE *GREEN RIVER KILLER?*
SURE. GO FOR IT.
WHO'S THE GREEN RIVER KILLER?

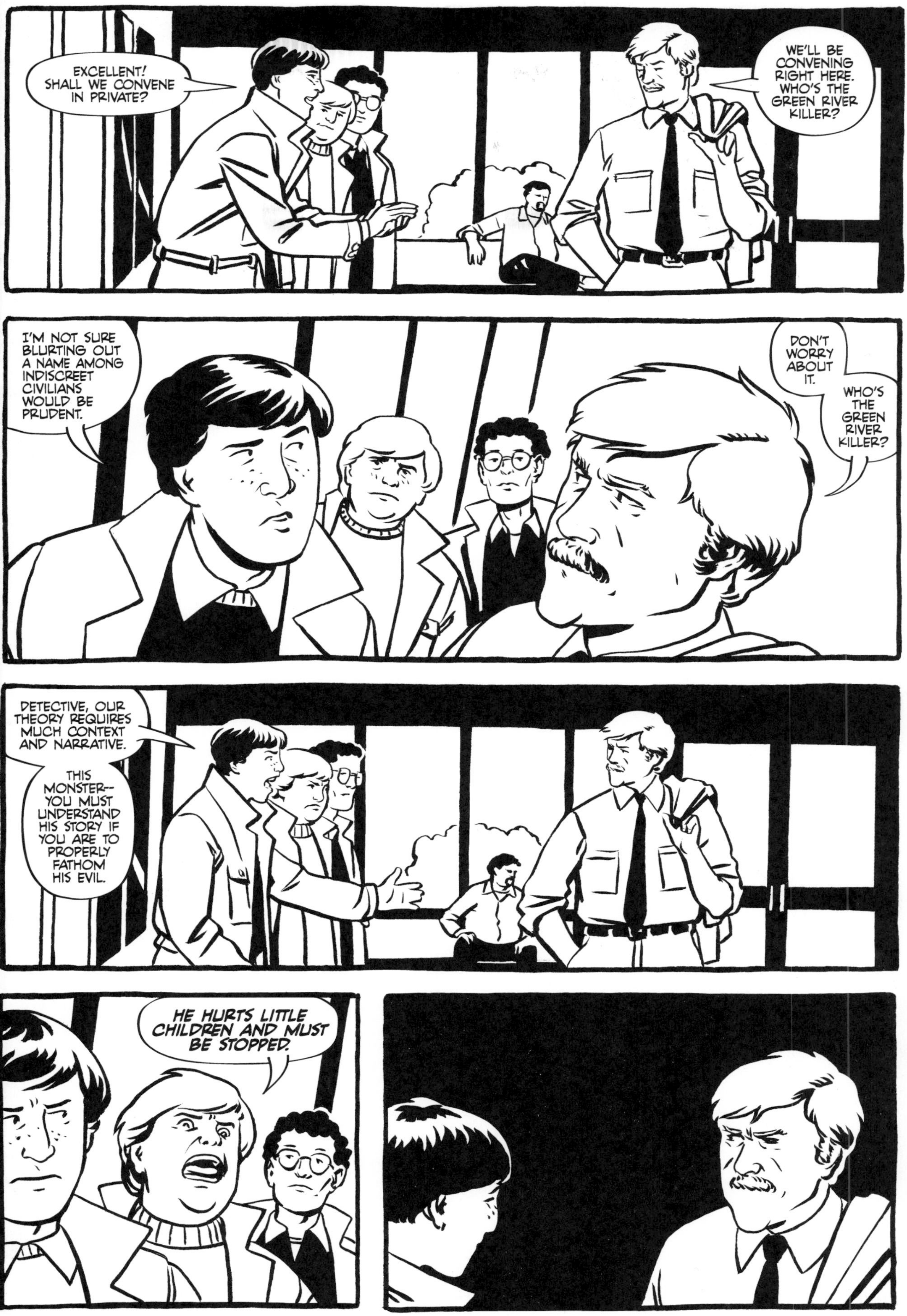

EXCELLENT! SHALL WE CONVENE IN PRIVATE?
WE'LL BE CONVENING RIGHT HERE. WHO'S THE GREEN RIVER KILLER?
I'M NOT SURE BLURTING OUT A NAME AMONG INDISCREET CIVILIANS WOULD BE PRUDENT.
DON'T WORRY ABOUT IT.
WHO'S THE GREEN RIVER KILLER?
DETECTIVE, OUR THEORY REQUIRES MUCH CONTEXT AND NARRATIVE.
THIS MONSTER-- YOU MUST UNDERSTAND HIS STORY IF YOU ARE TO PROPERLY FATHOM HIS EVIL.
HE HURTS LITTLE CHILDREN AND MUST BE STOPPED.

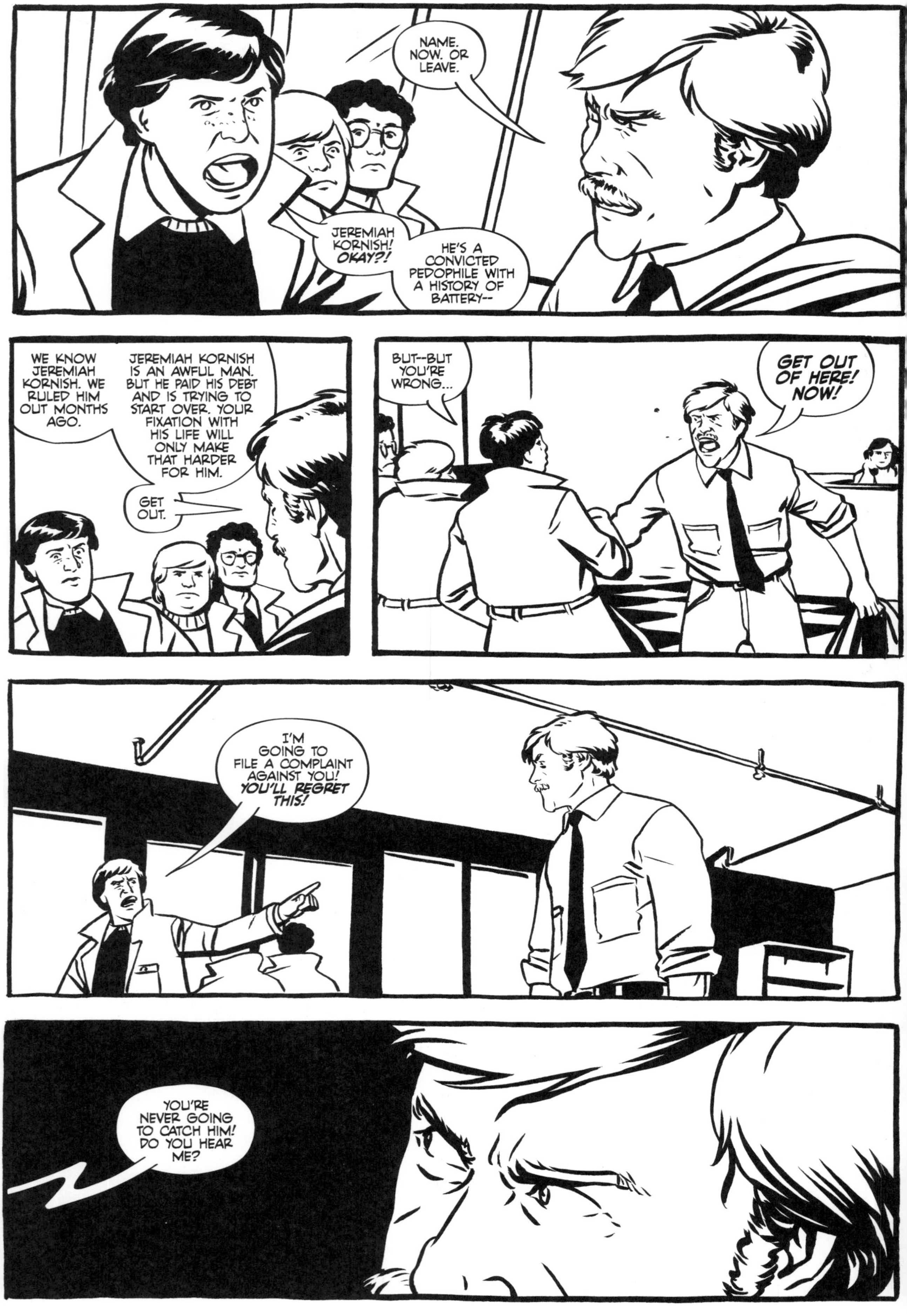
NAME. NOW. OR LEAVE.
JEREMIAH KORNISH! OKAY?!
HE'S A CONVICTED PEDOPHILE WITH A HISTORY OF BATTERY--
WE KNOW JEREMIAH KORNISH. WE RULED HIM OUT MONTHS AGO.
JEREMIAH KORNISH IS AN AWFUL MAN. BUT HE PAID HIS DEBT AND IS TRYING TO START OVER. YOUR FIXATION WITH HIS LIFE WILL ONLY MAKE THAT HARDER FOR HIM.
GET OUT.
BUT--BUT YOU'RE WRONG...
GET OUT OF HERE! NOW!
I'M GOING TO FILE A COMPLAINT AGAINST YOU! YOU'LL REGRET THIS!
YOU'RE NEVER GOING TO CATCH HIM! DO YOU HEAR ME?

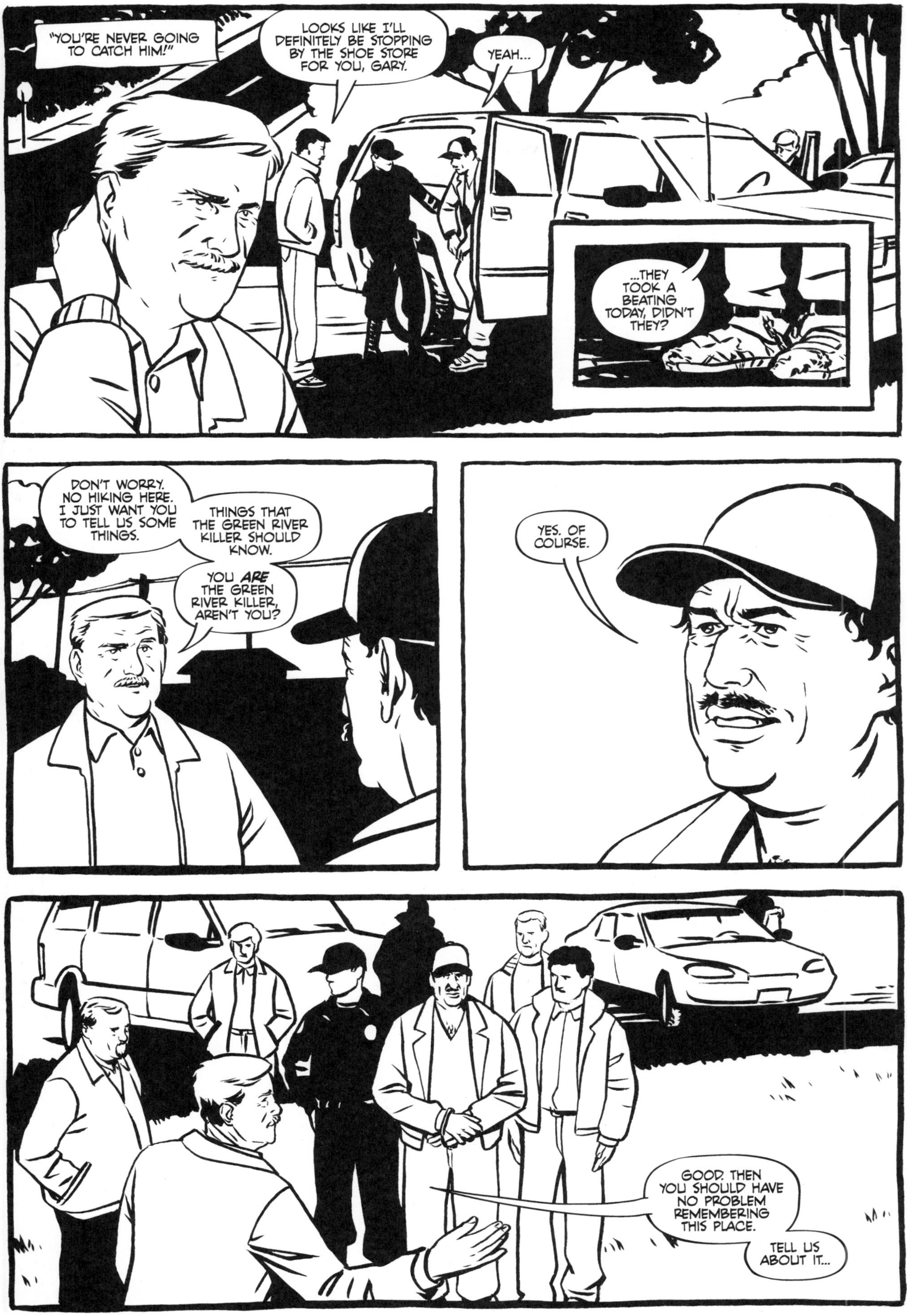
"YOU'RE NEVER GOING TO CATCH HIM!"
LOOKS LIKE I'LL DEFINITELY BE STOPPING BY THE SHOE STORE FOR YOU, GARY.
YEAH...
...THEY TOOK A BEATING TODAY, DIDN'T THEY?
DON'T WORRY. NO HIKING HERE. I JUST WANT YOU TO TELL US SOME THINGS.
THINGS THAT THE GREEN RIVER KILLER SHOULD KNOW.
YOU **ARE** THE GREEN RIVER KILLER, AREN'T YOU?
YES. OF COURSE.
GOOD. THEN YOU SHOULD HAVE NO PROBLEM REMEMBERING THIS PLACE.
TELL US ABOUT IT...

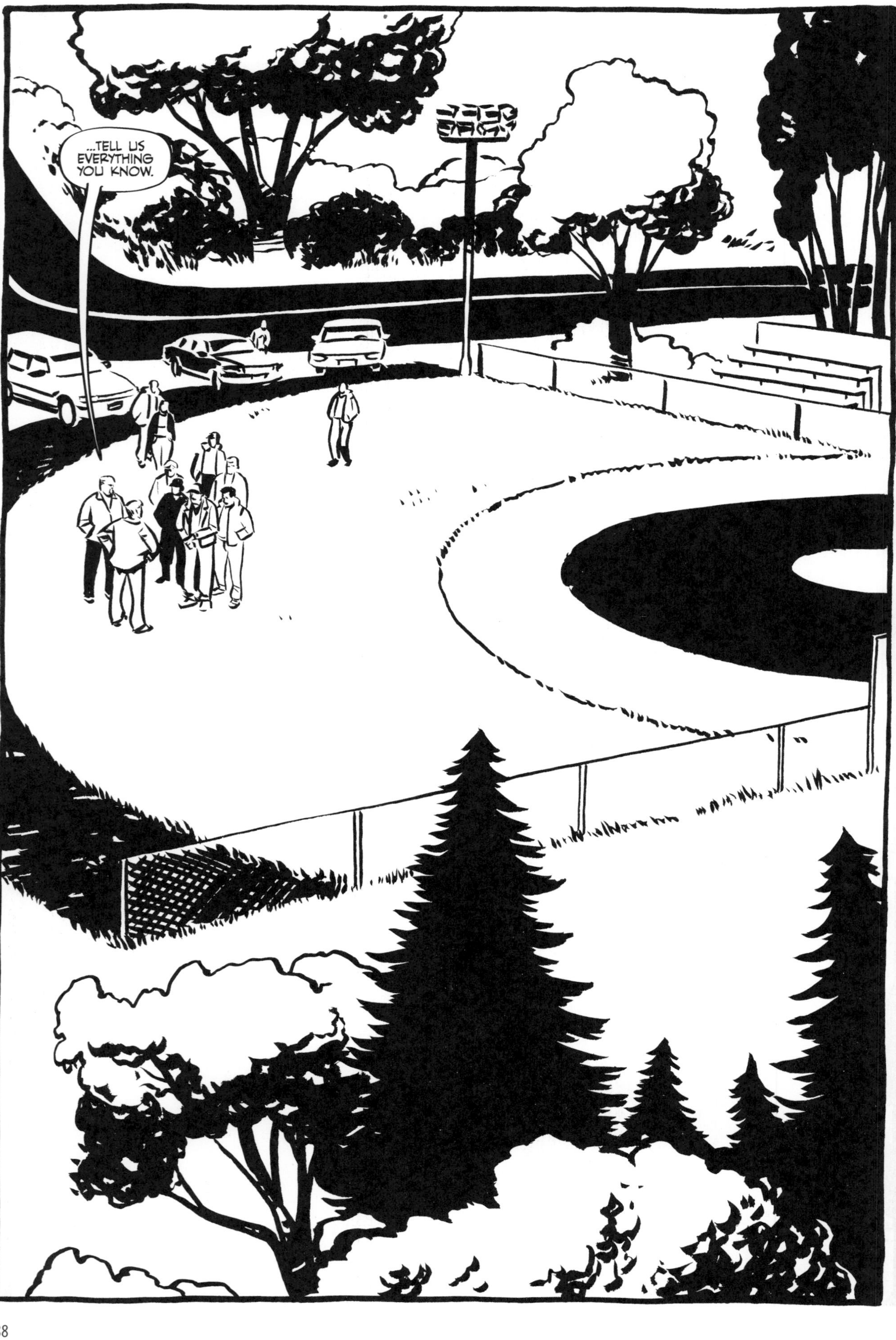
...TELL US EVERYTHING YOU KNOW.

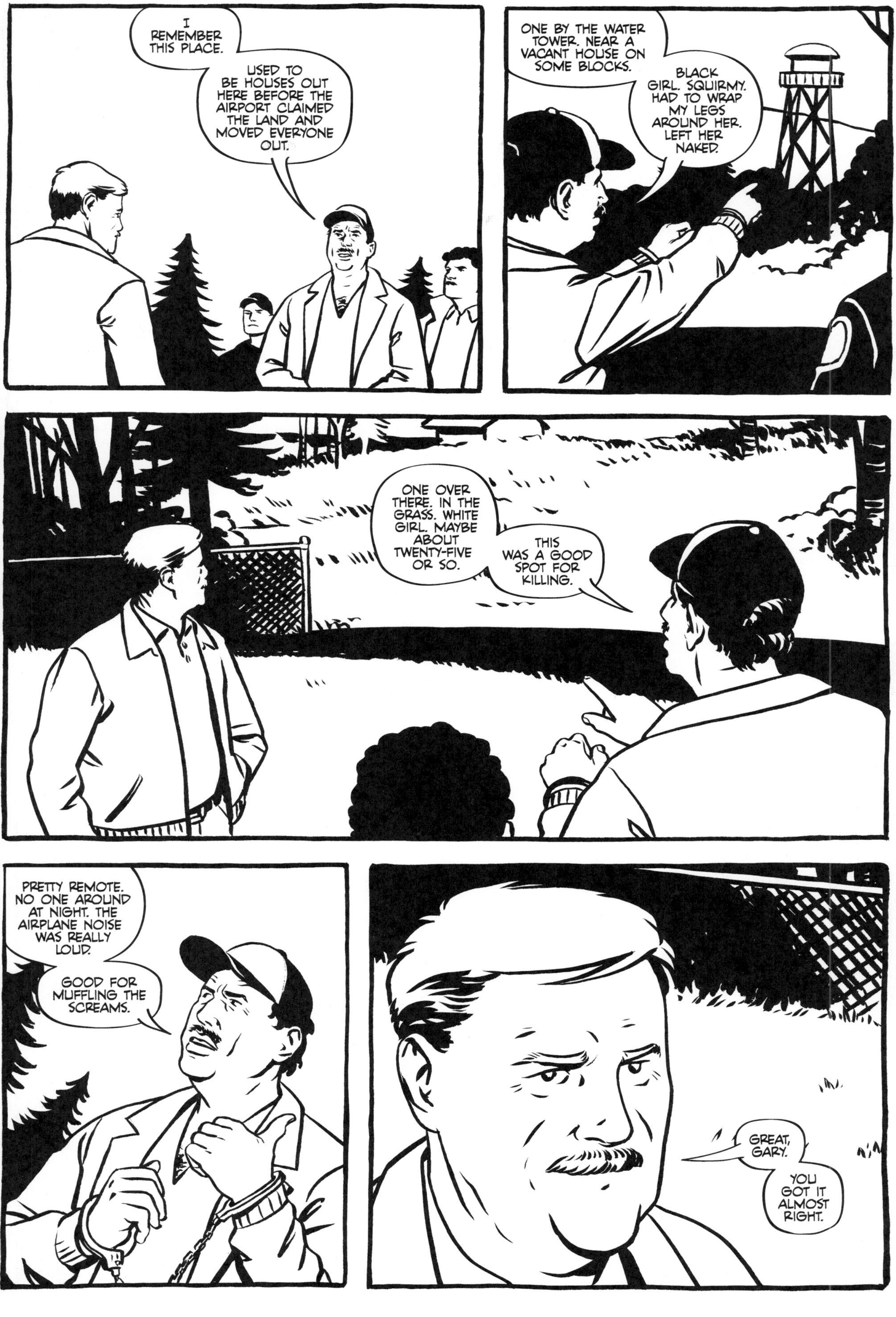
I REMEMBER THIS PLACE.
USED TO BE HOUSES OUT HERE BEFORE THE AIRPORT CLAIMED THE LAND AND MOVED EVERYONE OUT.
ONE BY THE WATER TOWER. NEAR A VACANT HOUSE ON SOME BLOCKS.
BLACK GIRL. SQUIRMY. HAD TO WRAP MY LEGS AROUND HER. LEFT HER NAKED.
ONE OVER THERE. IN THE GRASS. WHITE GIRL. MAYBE ABOUT TWENTY-FIVE OR SO.
THIS WAS A GOOD SPOT FOR KILLING.
PRETTY REMOTE. NO ONE AROUND AT NIGHT. THE AIRPLANE NOISE WAS REALLY LOUD.
GOOD FOR MUFFLING THE SCREAMS.
GREAT, GARY.
YOU GOT IT ALMOST RIGHT.

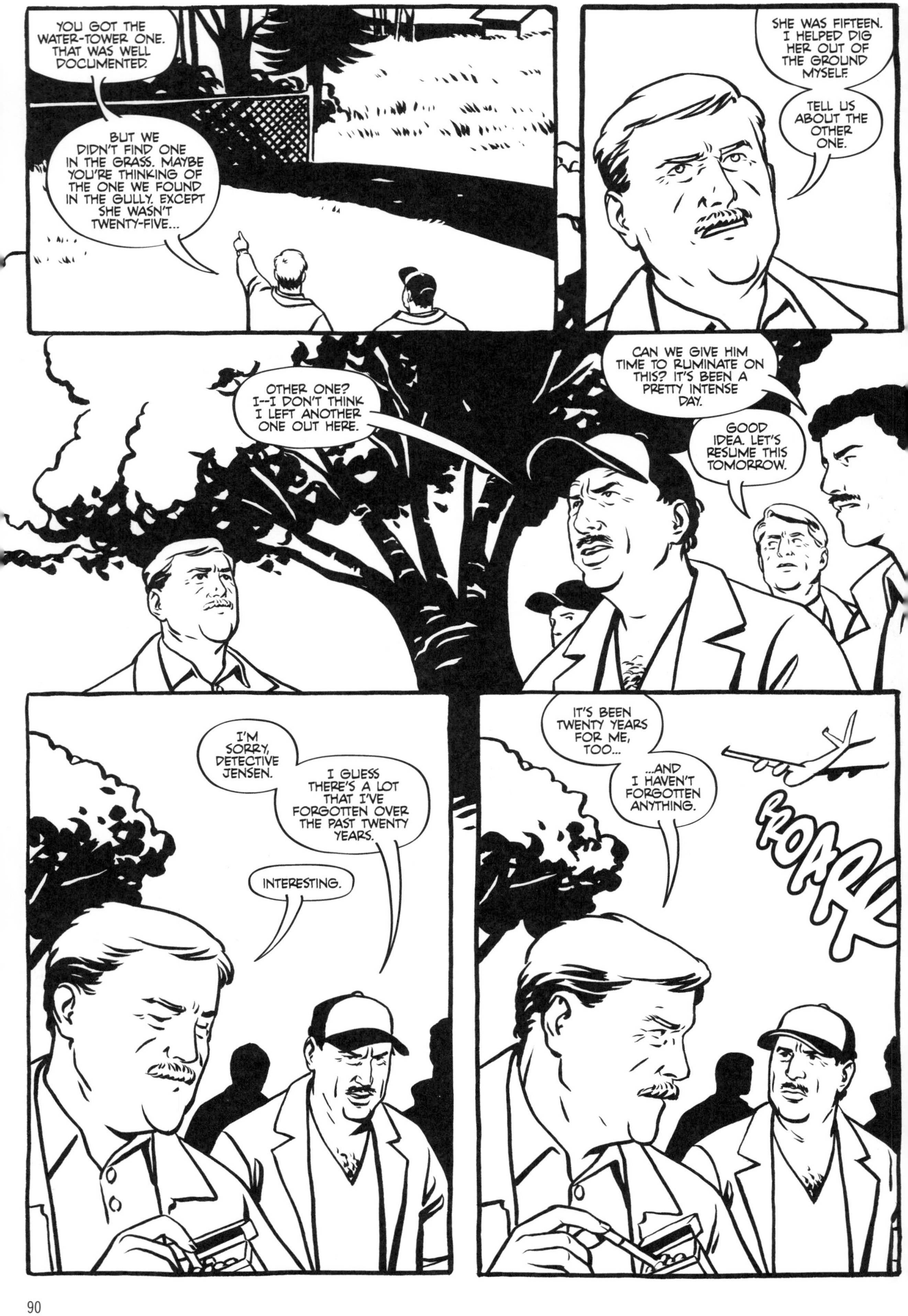
YOU GOT THE WATER-TOWER ONE. THAT WAS WELL DOCUMENTED.
BUT WE DIDN'T FIND ONE IN THE GRASS. MAYBE YOU'RE THINKING OF THE ONE WE FOUND IN THE GULLY. EXCEPT SHE WASN'T TWENTY-FIVE...
SHE WAS FIFTEEN. I HELPED DIG HER OUT OF THE GROUND MYSELF.
TELL US ABOUT THE OTHER ONE.
OTHER ONE? I--I DON'T THINK I LEFT ANOTHER ONE OUT HERE.
CAN WE GIVE HIM TIME TO RUMINATE ON THIS? IT'S BEEN A PRETTY INTENSE DAY.
GOOD IDEA. LET'S RESUME THIS TOMORROW.
I'M SORRY, DETECTIVE JENSEN.
I GUESS THERE'S A LOT THAT I'VE FORGOTTEN OVER THE PAST TWENTY YEARS.
INTERESTING.
IT'S BEEN TWENTY YEARS FOR ME, TOO...
...AND I HAVEN'T FORGOTTEN ANYTHING.
ROARR

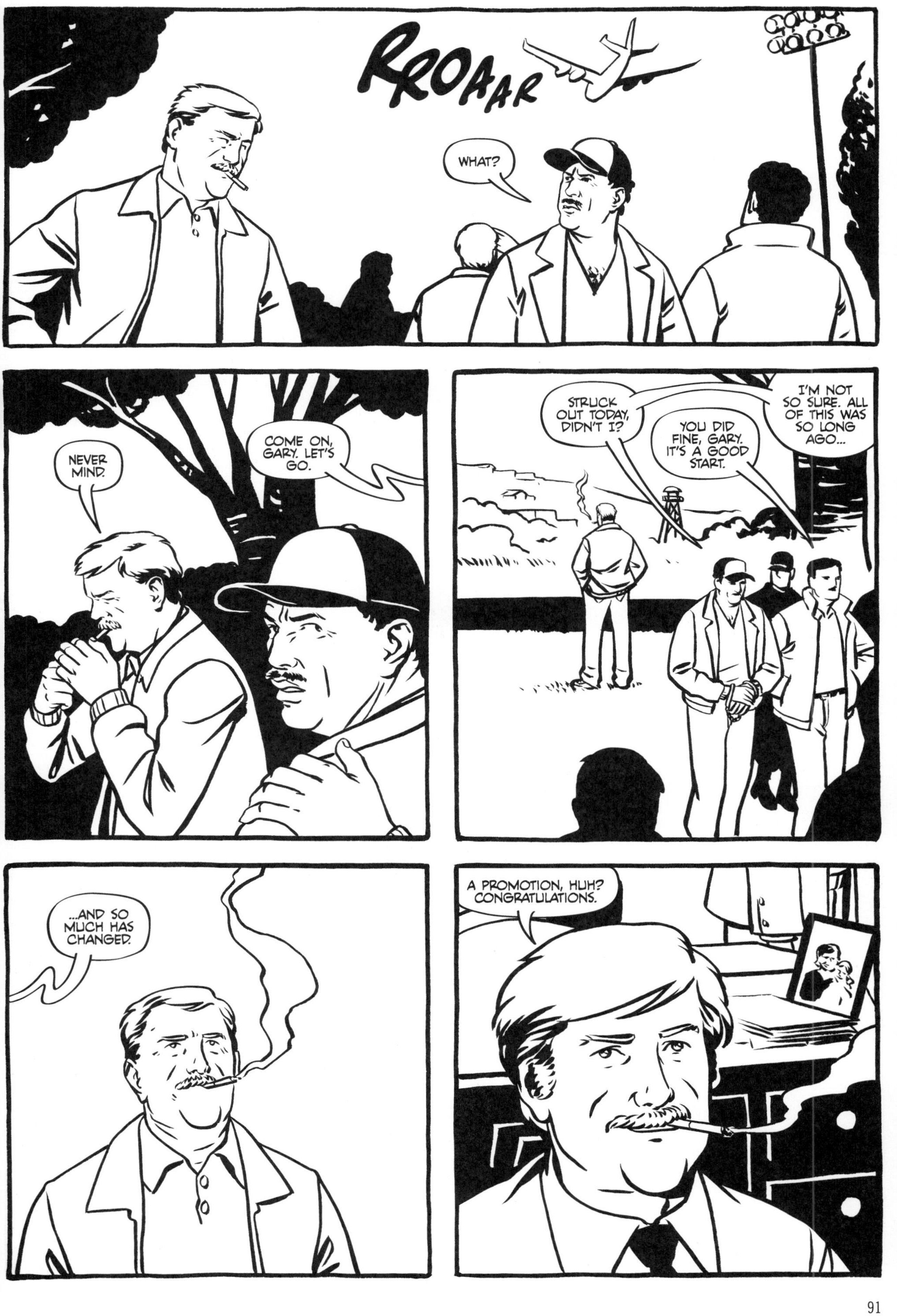
RROAAAR
WHAT?
NEVER MIND.
COME ON, GARY. LET'S GO.
STRUCK OUT TODAY, DIDN'T I?
YOU DID FINE, GARY. IT'S A GOOD START.
I'M NOT SO SURE. ALL OF THIS WAS SO LONG AGO...
...AND SO MUCH HAS CHANGED.
A PROMOTION, HUH? CONGRATULATIONS.

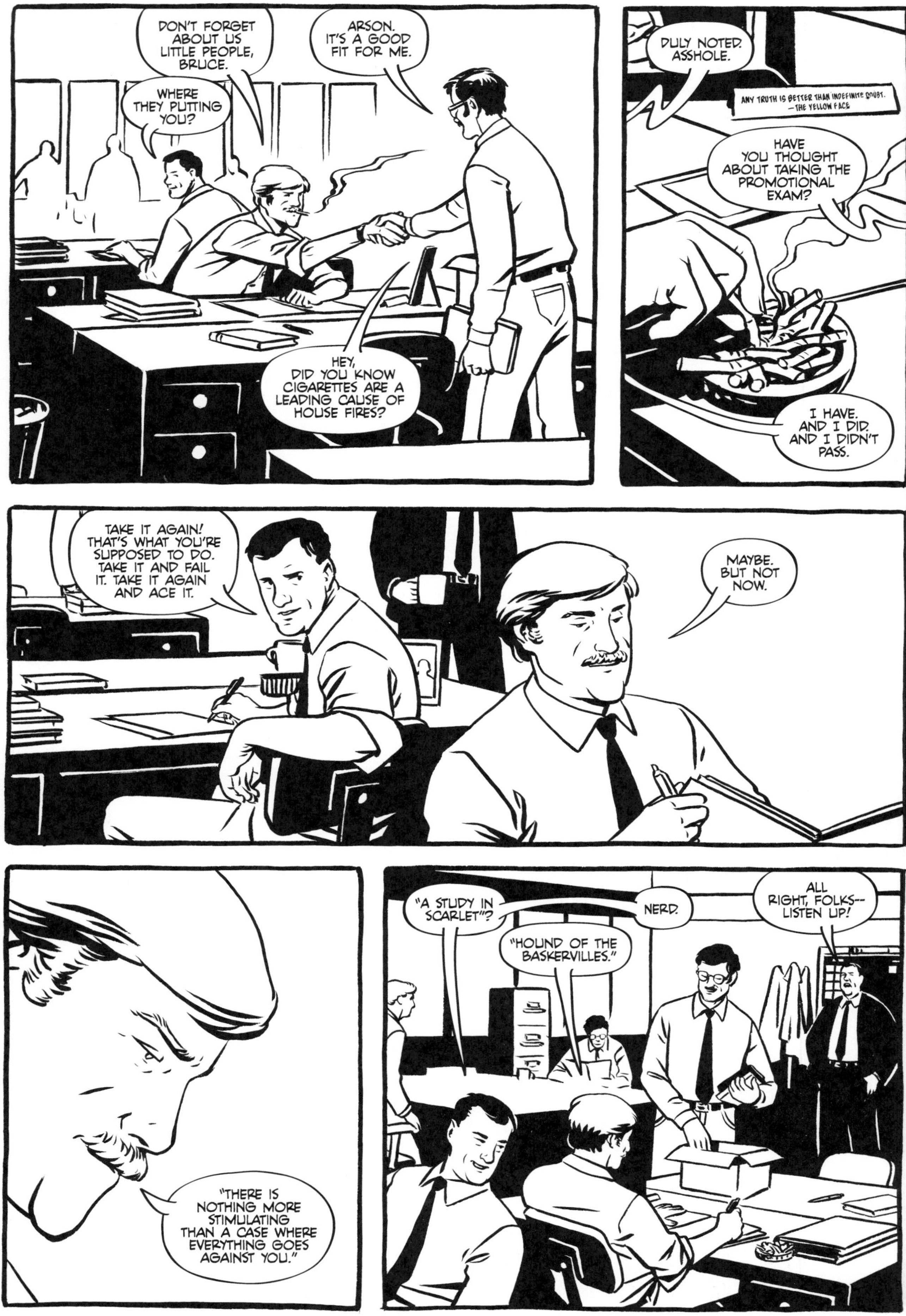
DON'T FORGET ABOUT US LITTLE PEOPLE, BRUCE.
WHERE THEY PUTTING YOU?
ARSON. IT'S A GOOD FIT FOR ME.
HEY, DID YOU KNOW CIGARETTES ARE A LEADING CAUSE OF HOUSE FIRES?
DULY NOTED. ASSHOLE.
ANY TRUTH IS BETTER THAN INDEFINITE DOUBT. —THE YELLOW FACE
HAVE YOU THOUGHT ABOUT TAKING THE PROMOTIONAL EXAM?
I HAVE. AND I DID. AND I DIDN'T PASS.
TAKE IT AGAIN! THAT'S WHAT YOU'RE SUPPOSED TO DO. TAKE IT AND FAIL IT. TAKE IT AGAIN AND ACE IT.
MAYBE. BUT NOT NOW.
"THERE IS NOTHING MORE STIMULATING THAN A CASE WHERE EVERYTHING GOES AGAINST YOU."
"A STUDY IN SCARLET"?
NERD.
"HOUND OF THE BASKERVILLES."
ALL RIGHT, FOLKS-- LISTEN UP!

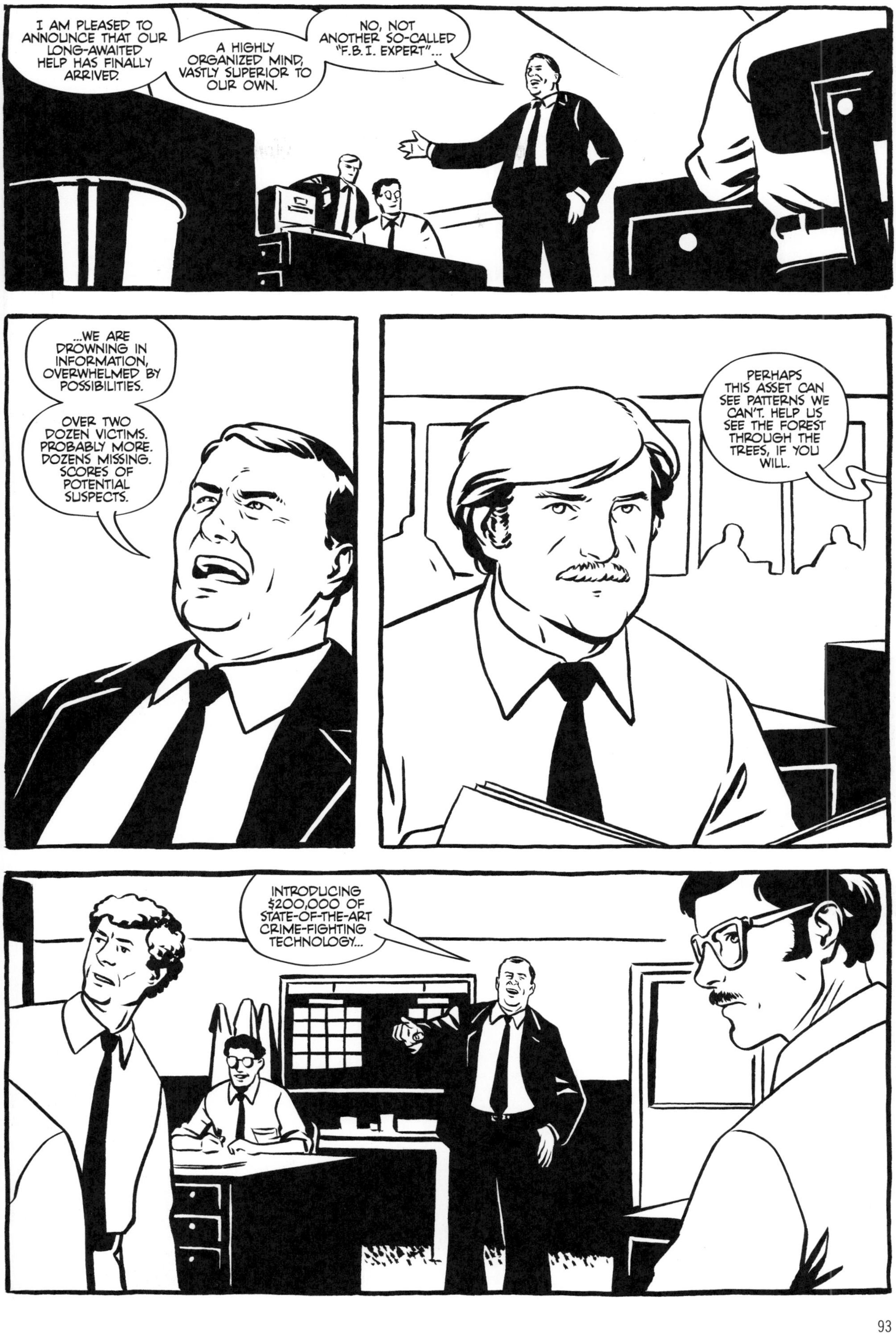
I AM PLEASED TO ANNOUNCE THAT OUR LONG-AWAITED HELP HAS FINALLY ARRIVED.
A HIGHLY ORGANIZED MIND, VASTLY SUPERIOR TO OUR OWN.
NO, NOT ANOTHER SO-CALLED "F.B.I. EXPERT"...
...WE ARE DROWNING IN INFORMATION, OVERWHELMED BY POSSIBILITIES.
OVER TWO DOZEN VICTIMS. PROBABLY MORE. DOZENS MISSING. SCORES OF POTENTIAL SUSPECTS.
PERHAPS THIS ASSET CAN SEE PATTERNS WE CAN'T. HELP US SEE THE FOREST THROUGH THE TREES, IF YOU WILL.
INTRODUCING $200,000 OF STATE-OF-THE-ART CRIME-FIGHTING TECHNOLOGY...

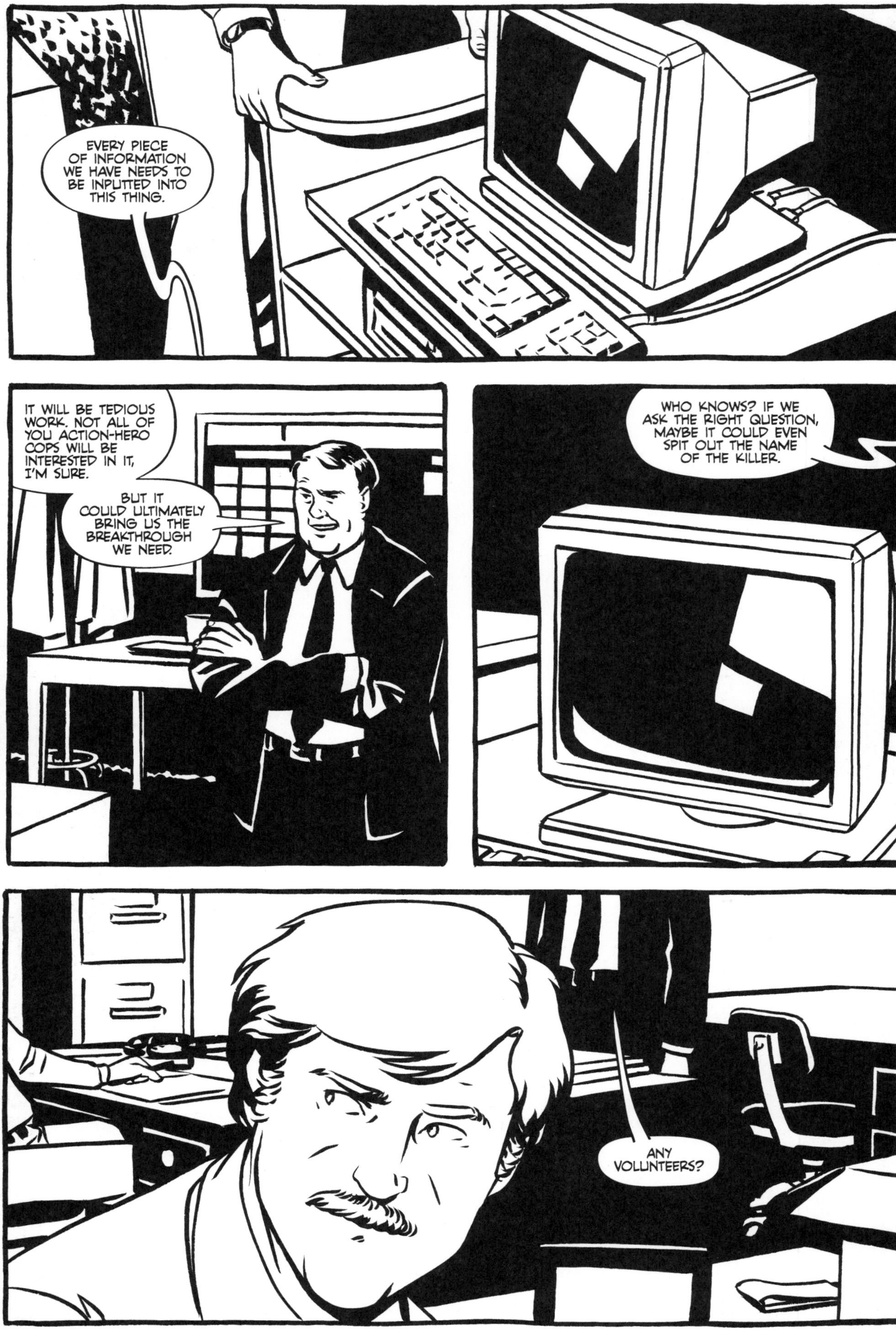
EVERY PIECE OF INFORMATION WE HAVE NEEDS TO BE INPUTTED INTO THIS THING.
IT WILL BE TEDIOUS WORK. NOT ALL OF YOU ACTION-HERO COPS WILL BE INTERESTED IN IT, I'M SURE.
BUT IT COULD ULTIMATELY BRING US THE BREAKTHROUGH WE NEED.
WHO KNOWS? IF WE ASK THE RIGHT QUESTION, MAYBE IT COULD EVEN SPIT OUT THE NAME OF THE KILLER.
ANY VOLUNTEERS?

DAY THREE: FATHER'S DAY

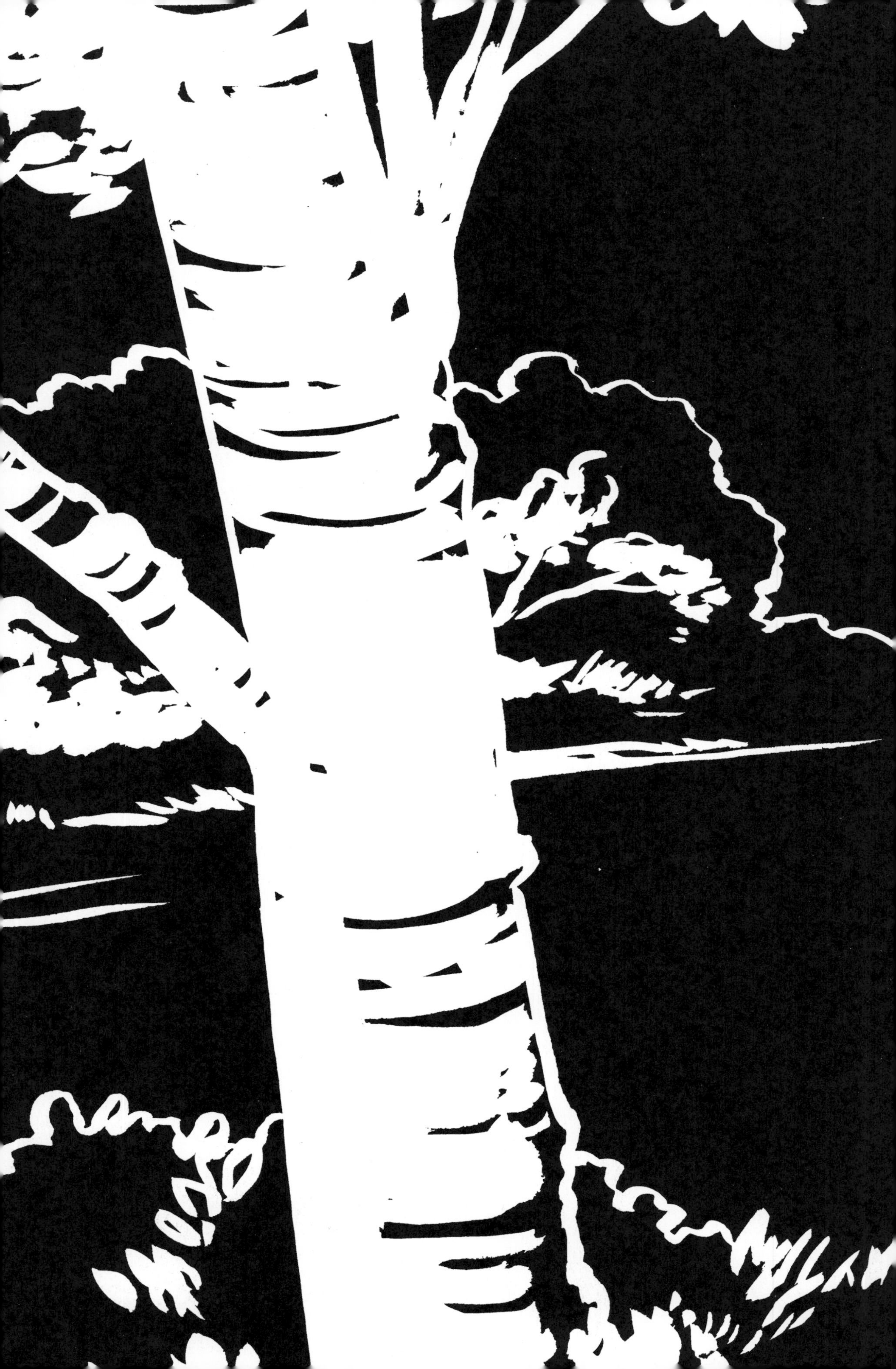

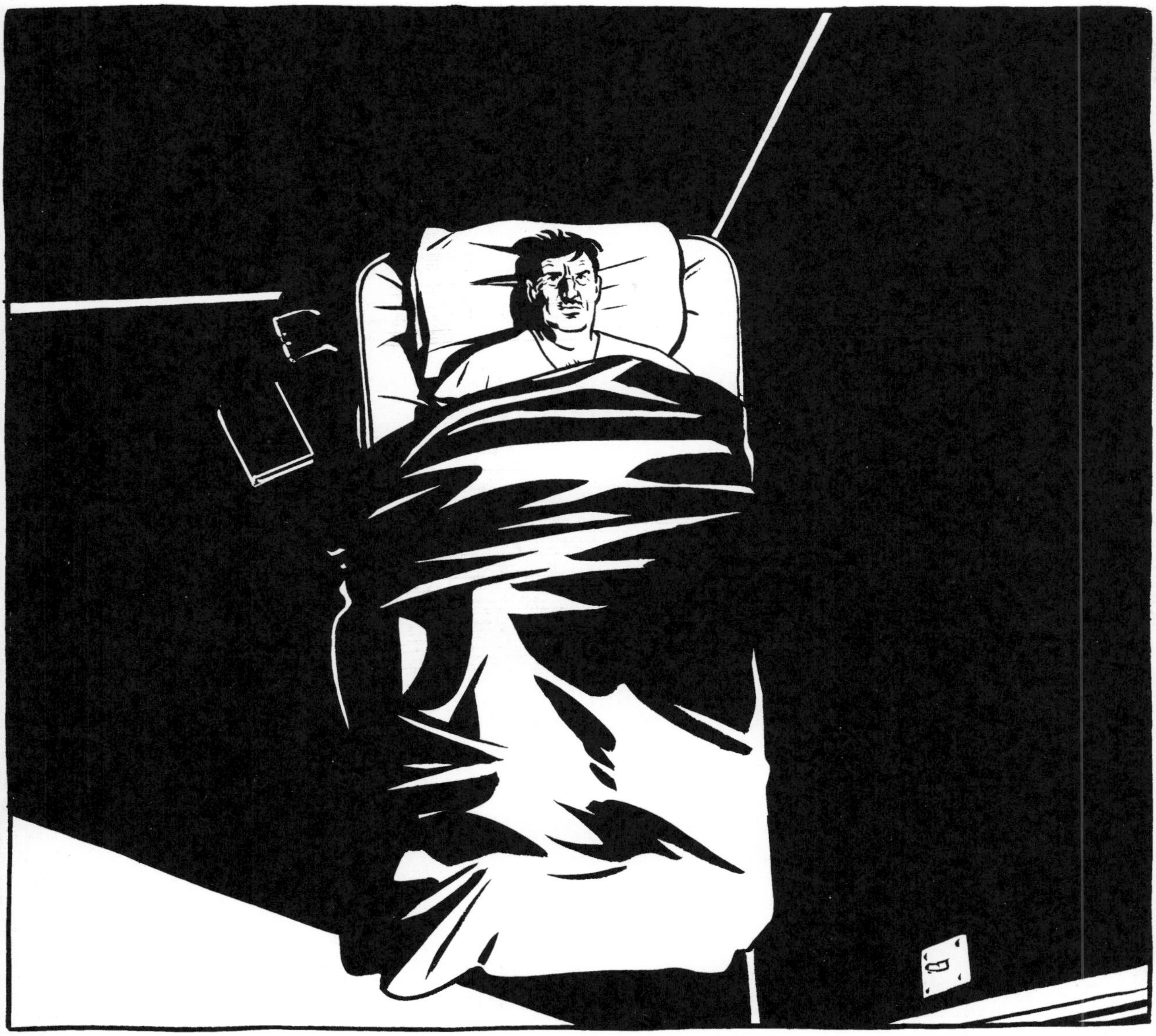

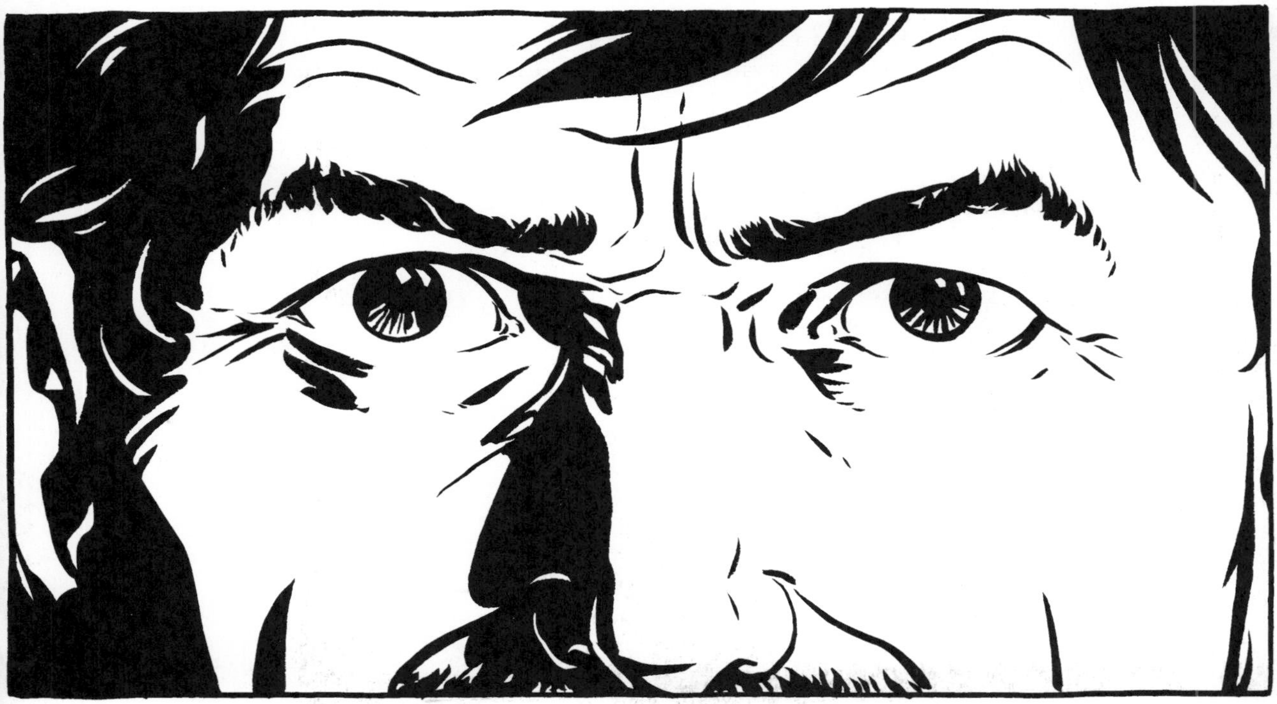

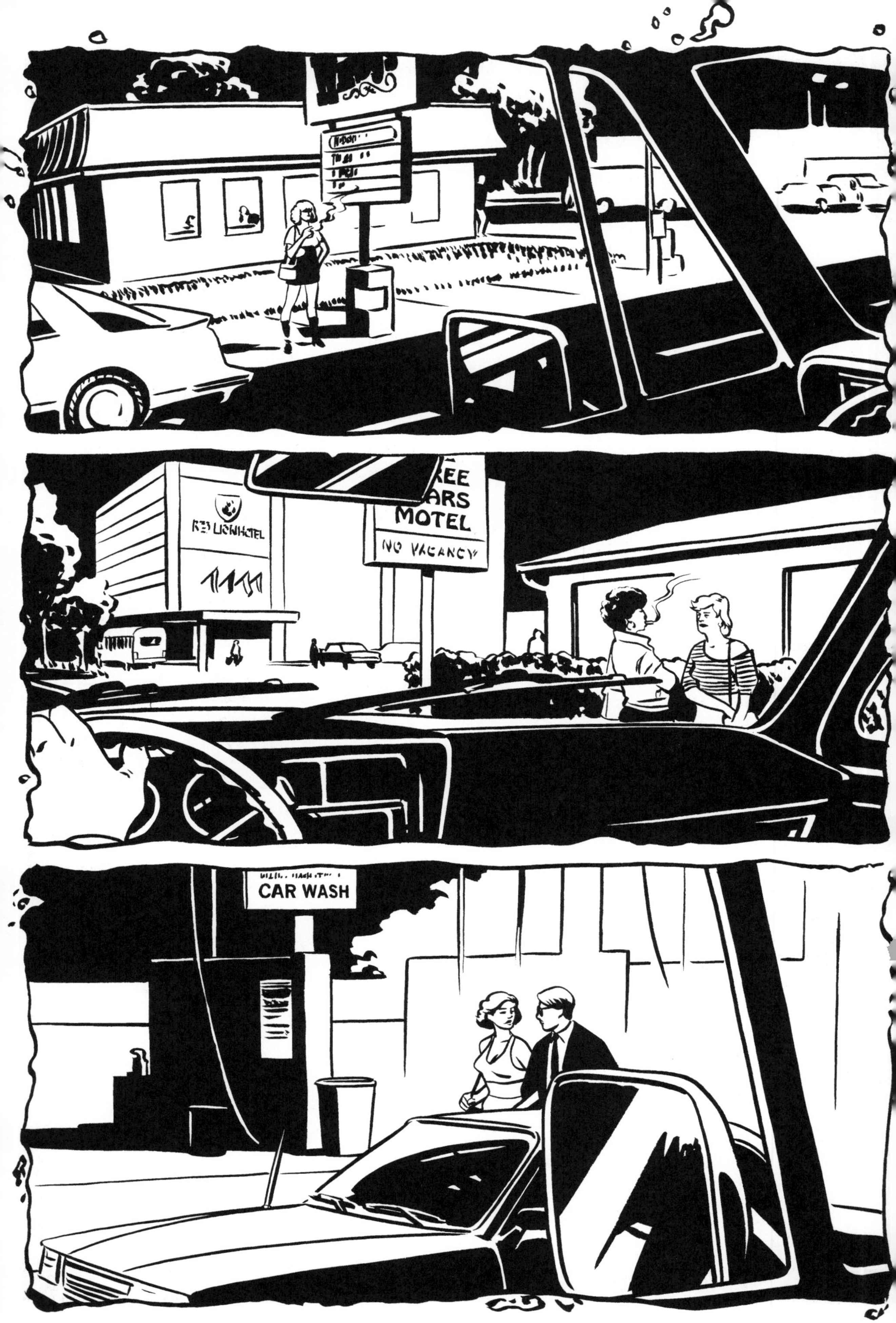
RED LION HOTEL
MOTEL
NO VACANCY
CAR WASH

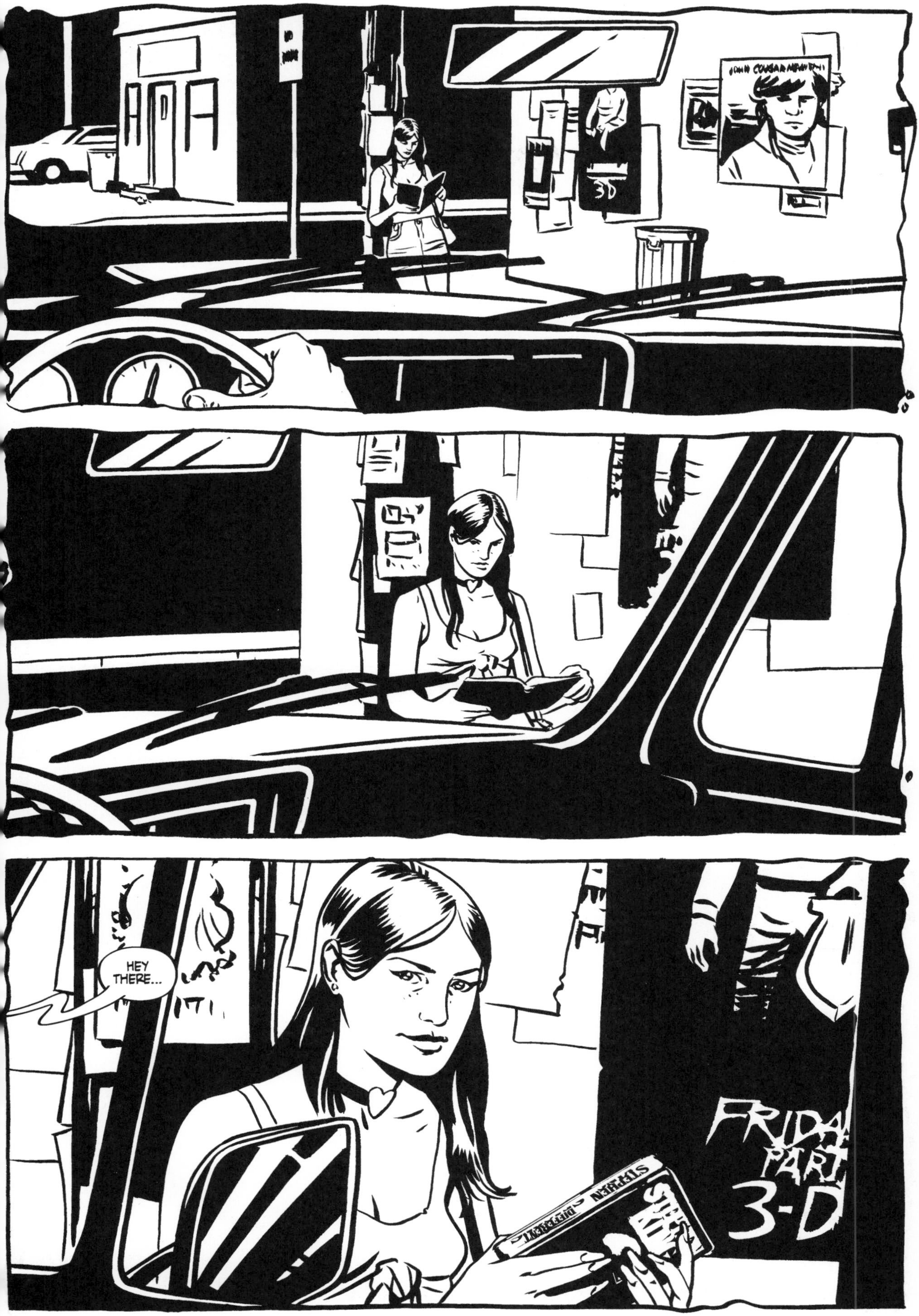
HEY THERE...
3-D

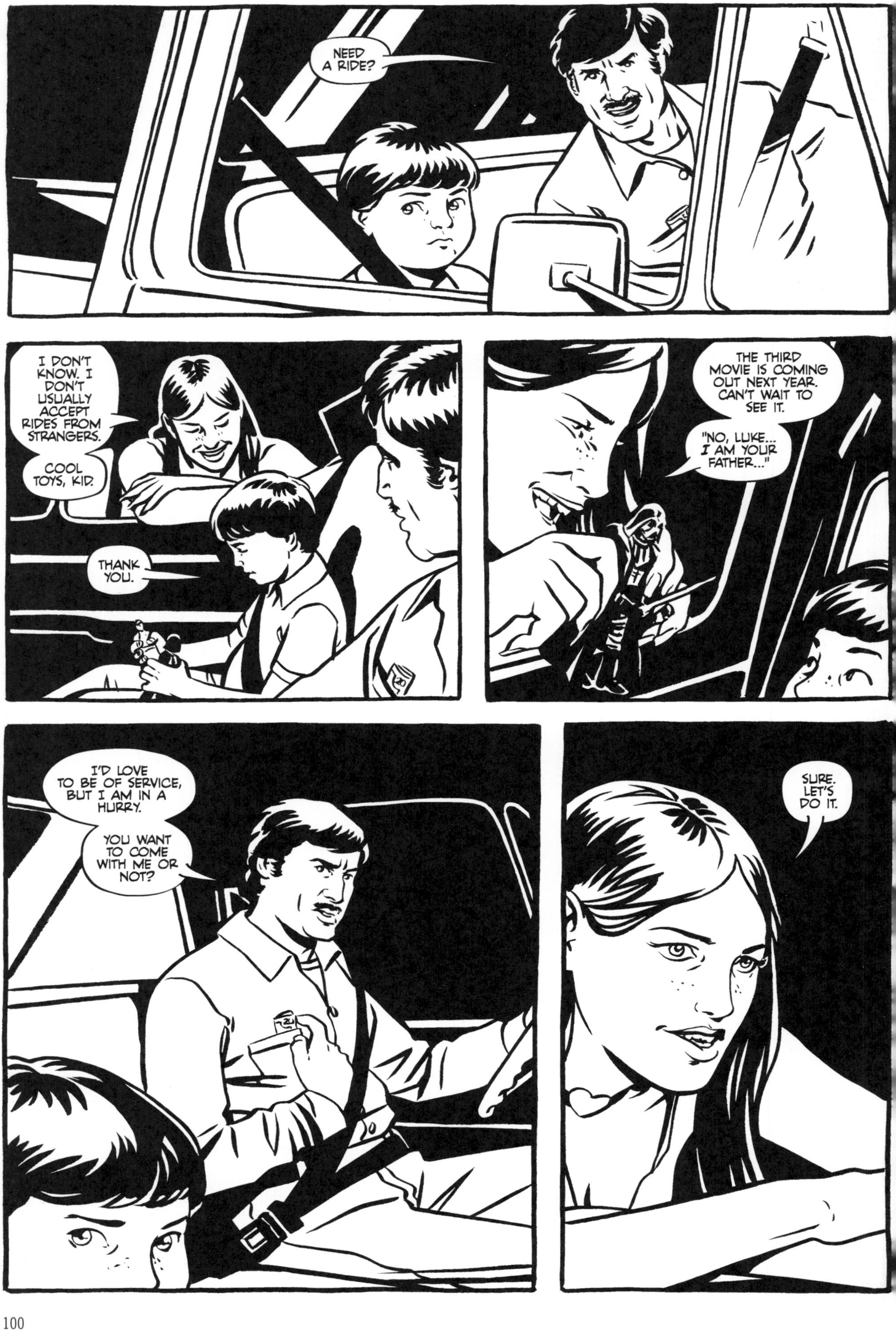
NEED A RIDE?
I DON'T KNOW. I DON'T USUALLY ACCEPT RIDES FROM STRANGERS.
COOL TOYS, KID.
THANK YOU.
THE THIRD MOVIE IS COMING OUT NEXT YEAR. CAN'T WAIT TO SEE IT.
"NO, LUKE... I AM YOUR FATHER..."
I'D LOVE TO BE OF SERVICE, BUT I AM IN A HURRY.
YOU WANT TO COME WITH ME OR NOT?
SURE. LET'S DO IT.

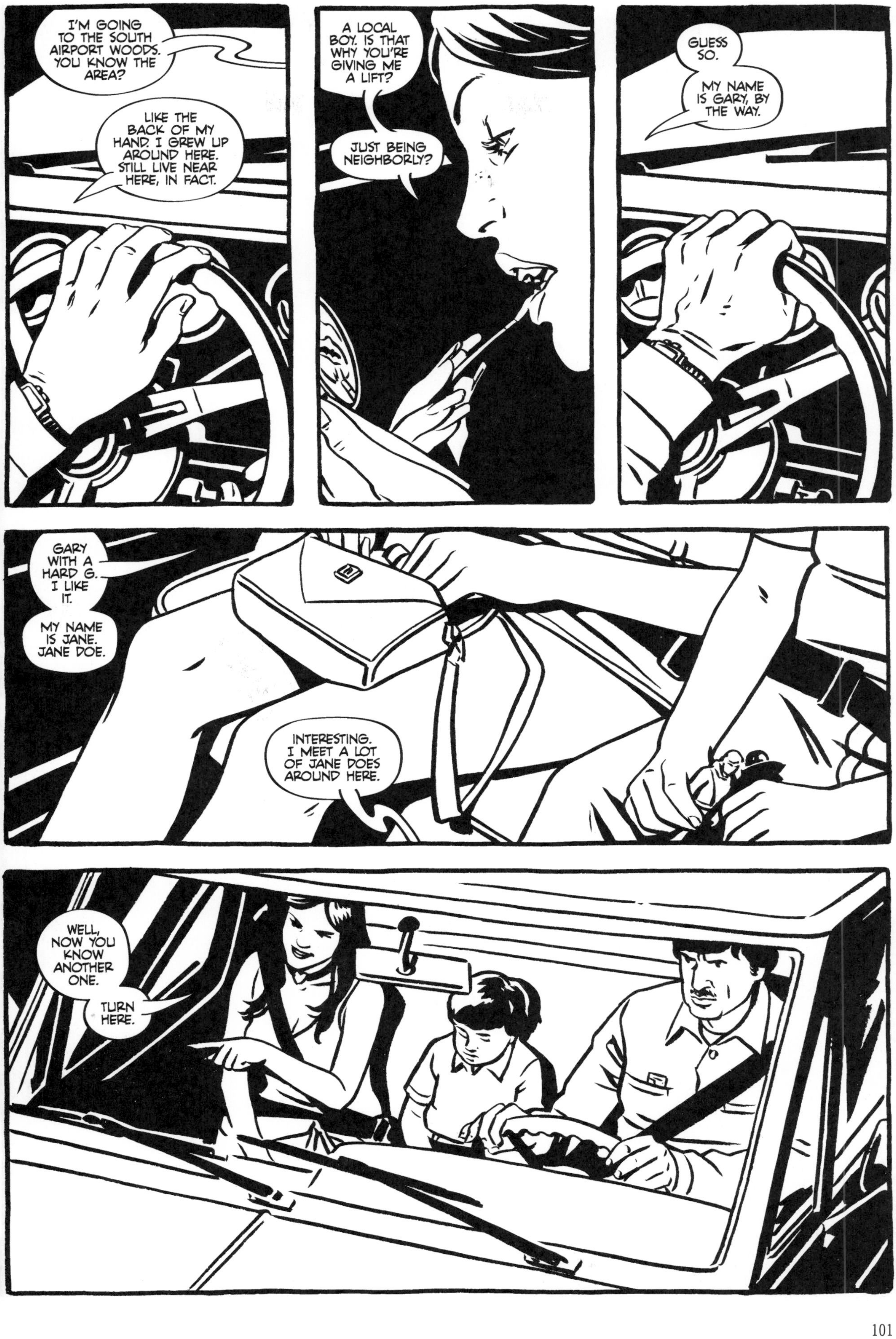

I'M GOING TO THE SOUTH AIRPORT WOODS. YOU KNOW THE AREA?
LIKE THE BACK OF MY HAND. I GREW UP AROUND HERE. STILL LIVE NEAR HERE, IN FACT.
A LOCAL BOY. IS THAT WHY YOU'RE GIVING ME A LIFT?
JUST BEING NEIGHBORLY?
GUESS SO.
MY NAME IS GARY, BY THE WAY.
GARY WITH A HARD G. I LIKE IT.
MY NAME IS JANE. JANE DOE.
INTERESTING. I MEET A LOT OF JANE DOES AROUND HERE.
WELL, NOW YOU KNOW ANOTHER ONE.
TURN HERE.

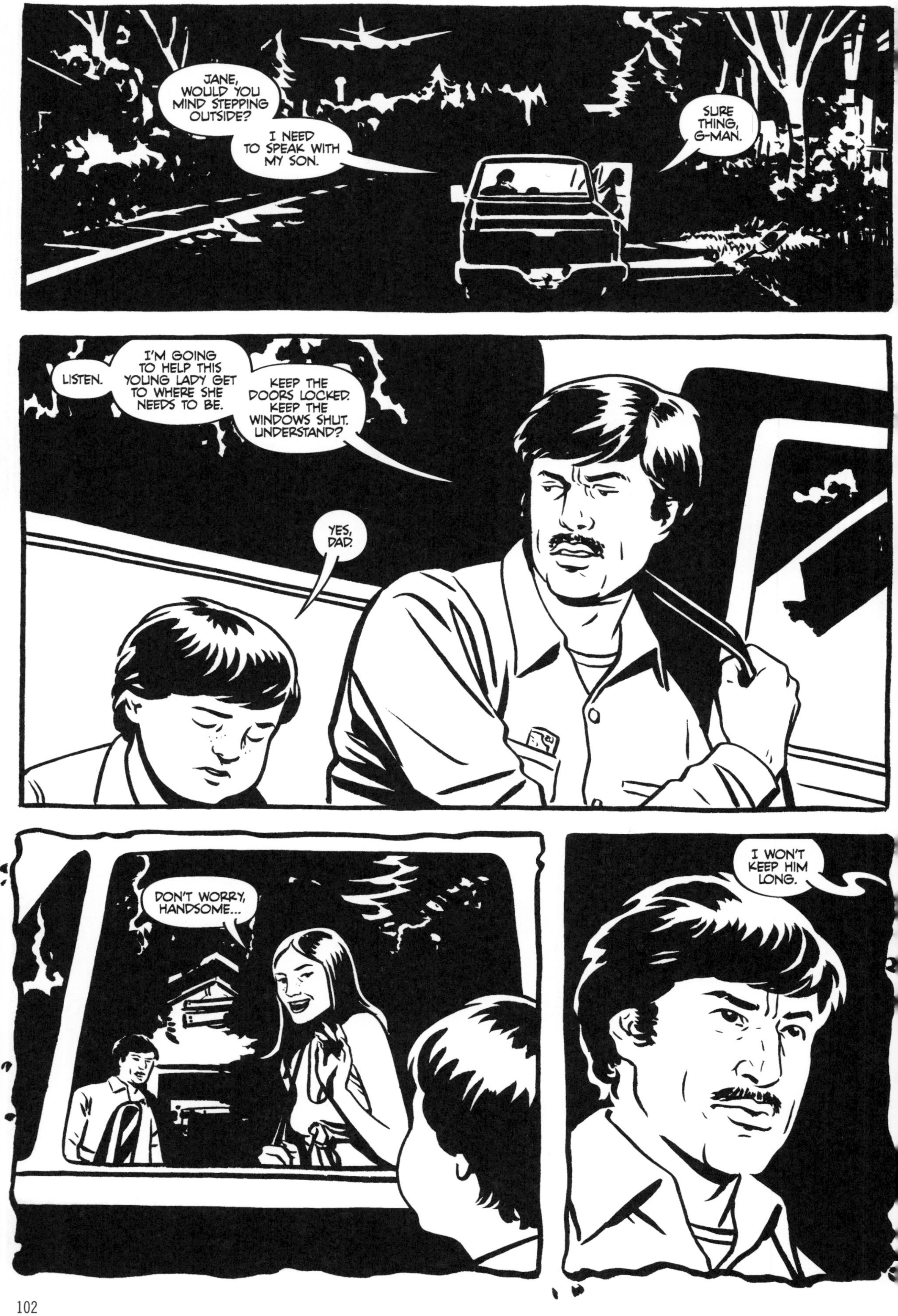
JANE, WOULD YOU MIND STEPPING OUTSIDE?
I NEED TO SPEAK WITH MY SON.
SURE THING, G-MAN.
LISTEN.
I'M GOING TO HELP THIS YOUNG LADY GET TO WHERE SHE NEEDS TO BE.
KEEP THE DOORS LOCKED. KEEP THE WINDOWS SHUT. UNDERSTAND?
YES, DAD.
DON'T WORRY, HANDSOME...
I WON'T KEEP HIM LONG.

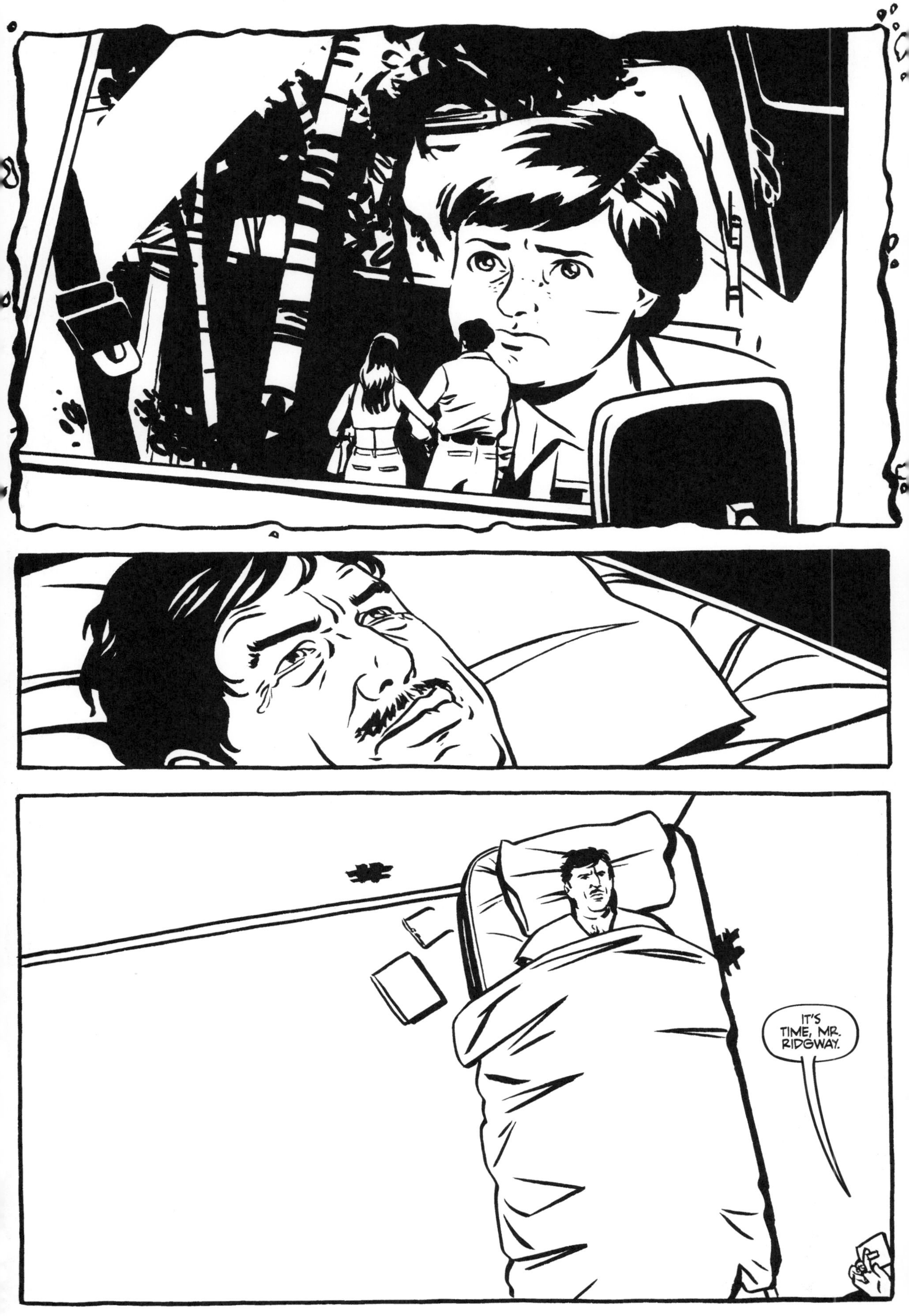
IT'S TIME, MR. RIDGWAY.

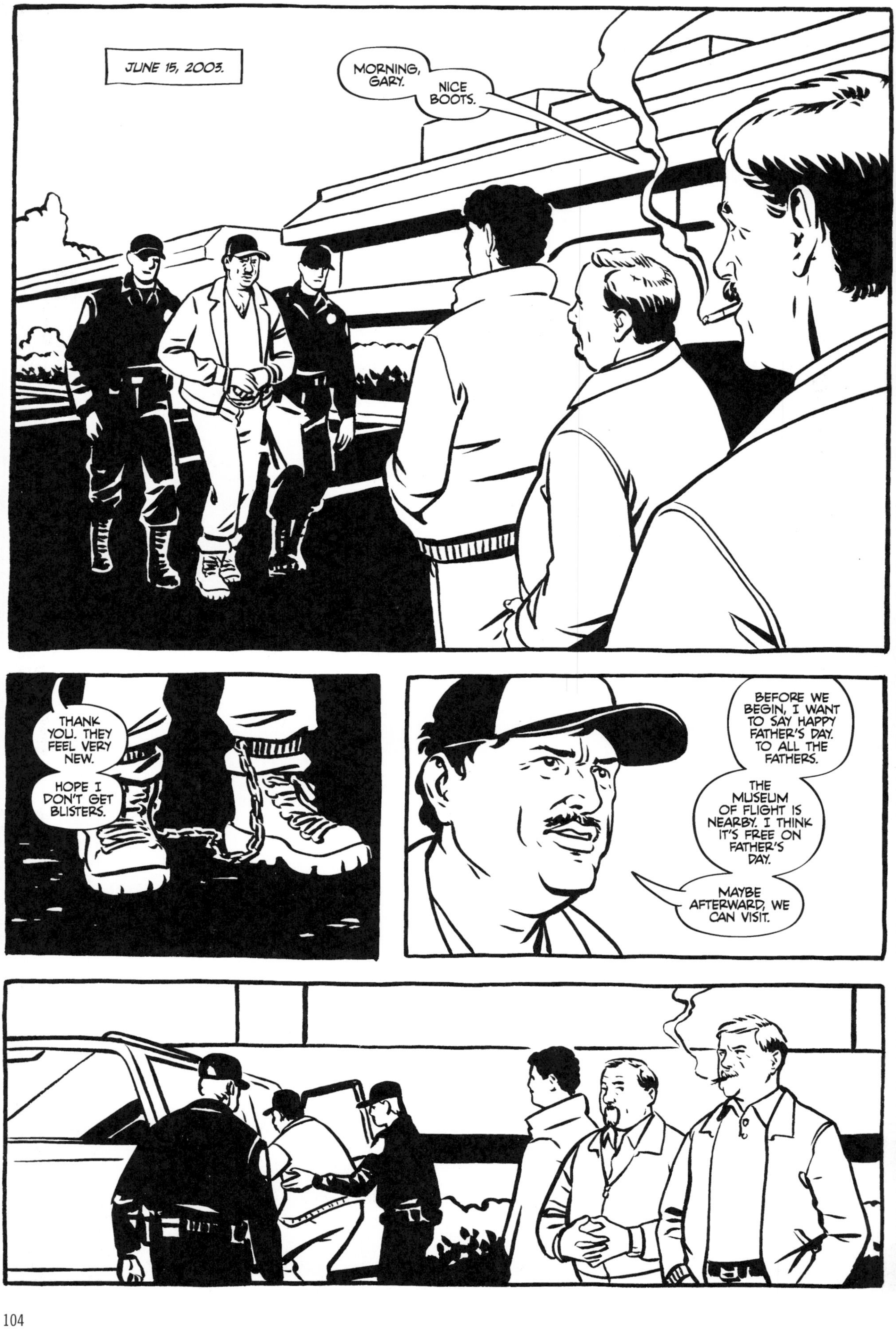
JUNE 15, 2003.
MORNING, GARY.
NICE BOOTS.
THANK YOU. THEY FEEL VERY NEW.
HOPE I DON'T GET BLISTERS.
BEFORE WE BEGIN, I WANT TO SAY HAPPY FATHER'S DAY. TO ALL THE FATHERS.
THE MUSEUM OF FLIGHT IS NEARBY. I THINK IT'S FREE ON FATHER'S DAY.
MAYBE AFTERWARD, WE CAN VISIT.

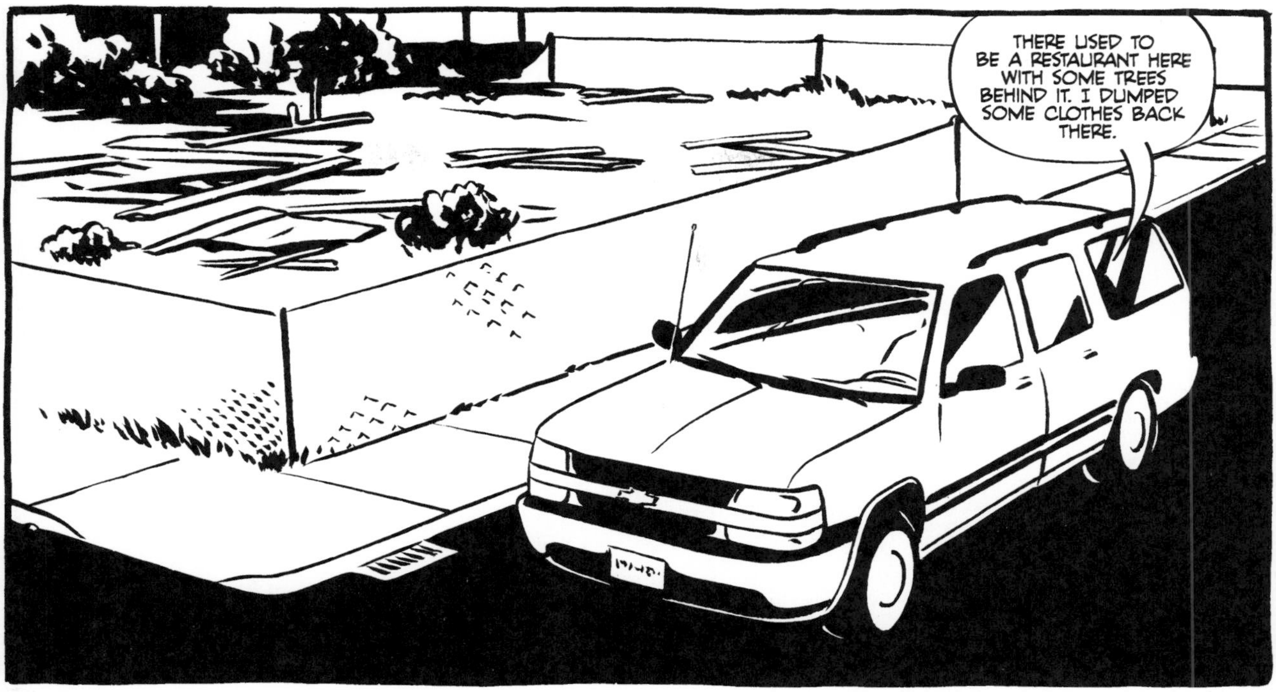
THERE USED TO BE A RESTAURANT HERE WITH SOME TREES BEHIND IT. I DUMPED SOME CLOTHES BACK THERE.

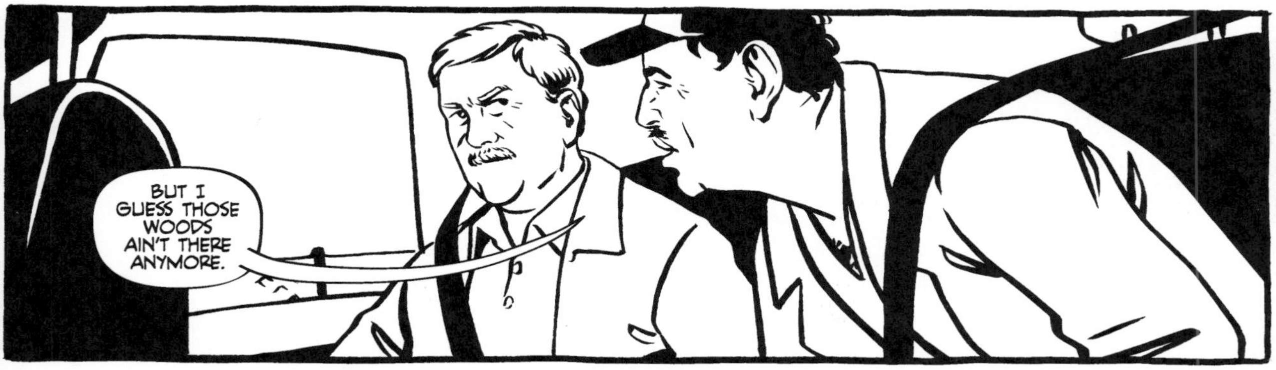
BUT I GUESS THOSE WOODS AIN'T THERE ANYMORE.

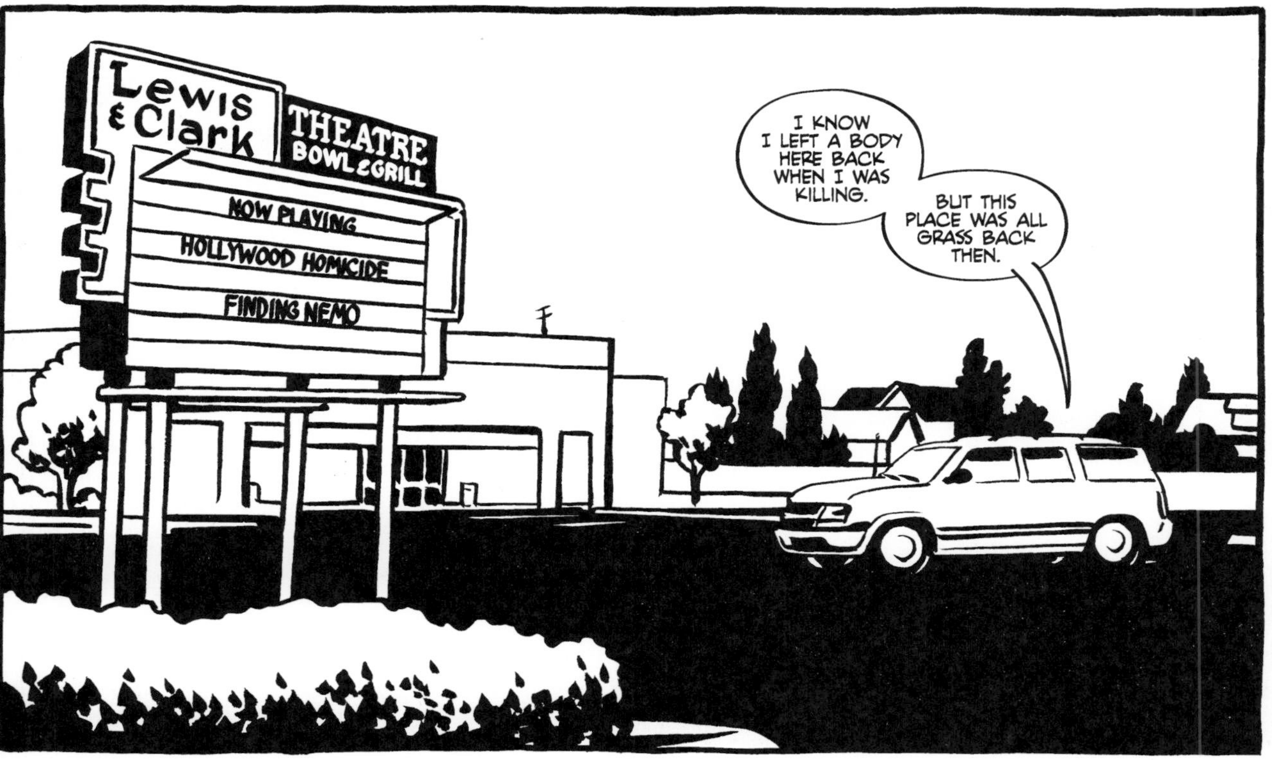
Lewis & Clark
THEATRE
BOWL & GRILL
NOW PLAYING
HOLLYWOOD HOMICIDE
FINDING NEMO
I KNOW I LEFT A BODY HERE BACK WHEN I WAS KILLING.
BUT THIS PLACE WAS ALL GRASS BACK THEN.

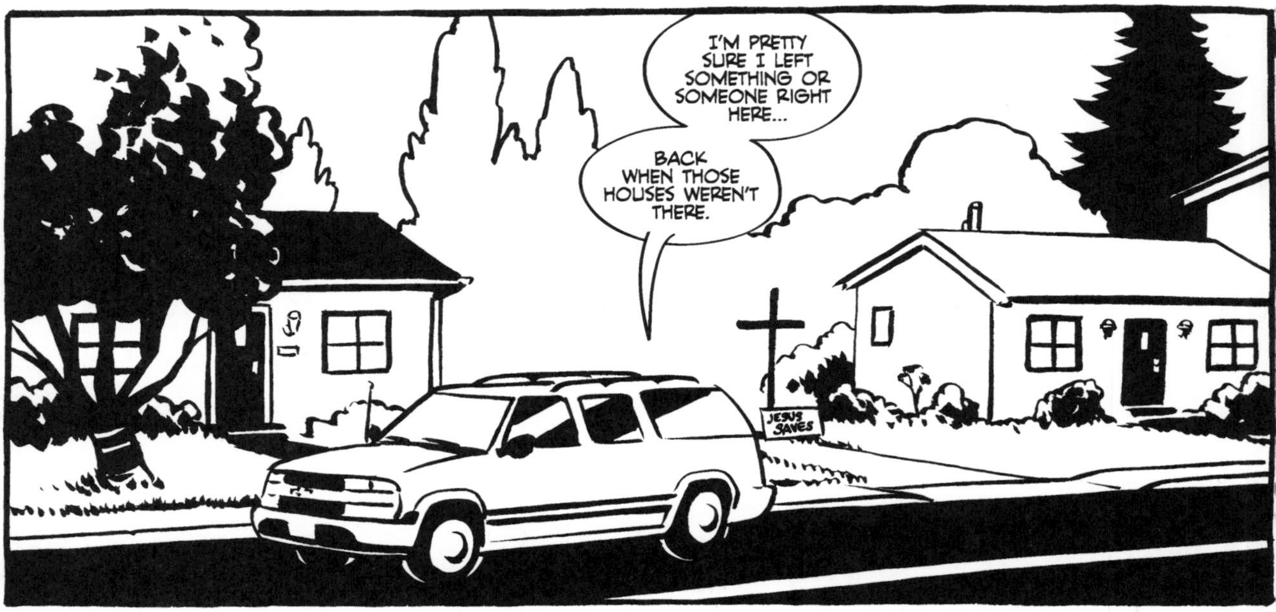
I'M PRETTY SURE I LEFT SOMETHING OR SOMEONE RIGHT HERE...
BACK WHEN THOSE HOUSES WEREN'T THERE.
JESUS SAVES

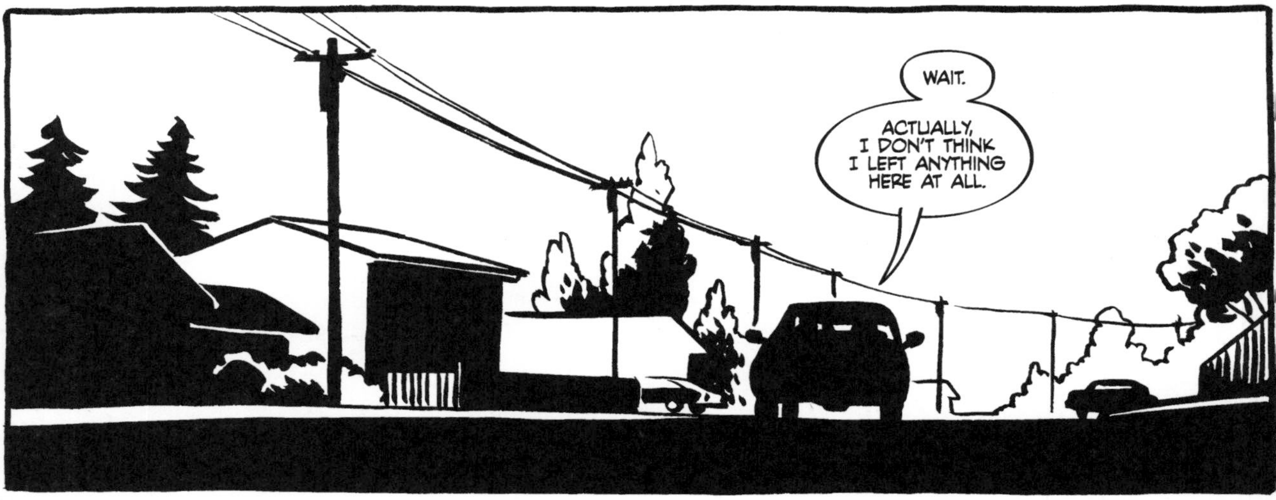
WAIT.
ACTUALLY, I DON'T THINK I LEFT ANYTHING HERE AT ALL.

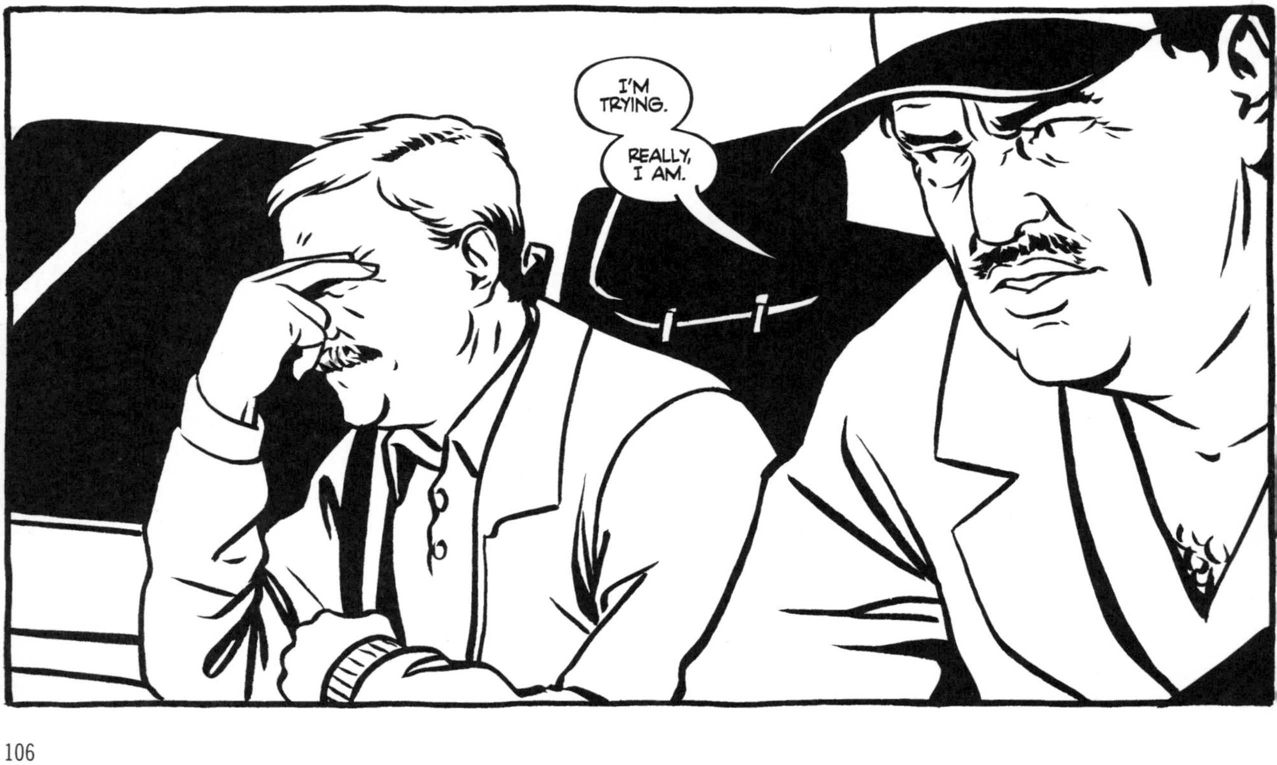
I'M TRYING.
REALLY, I AM.

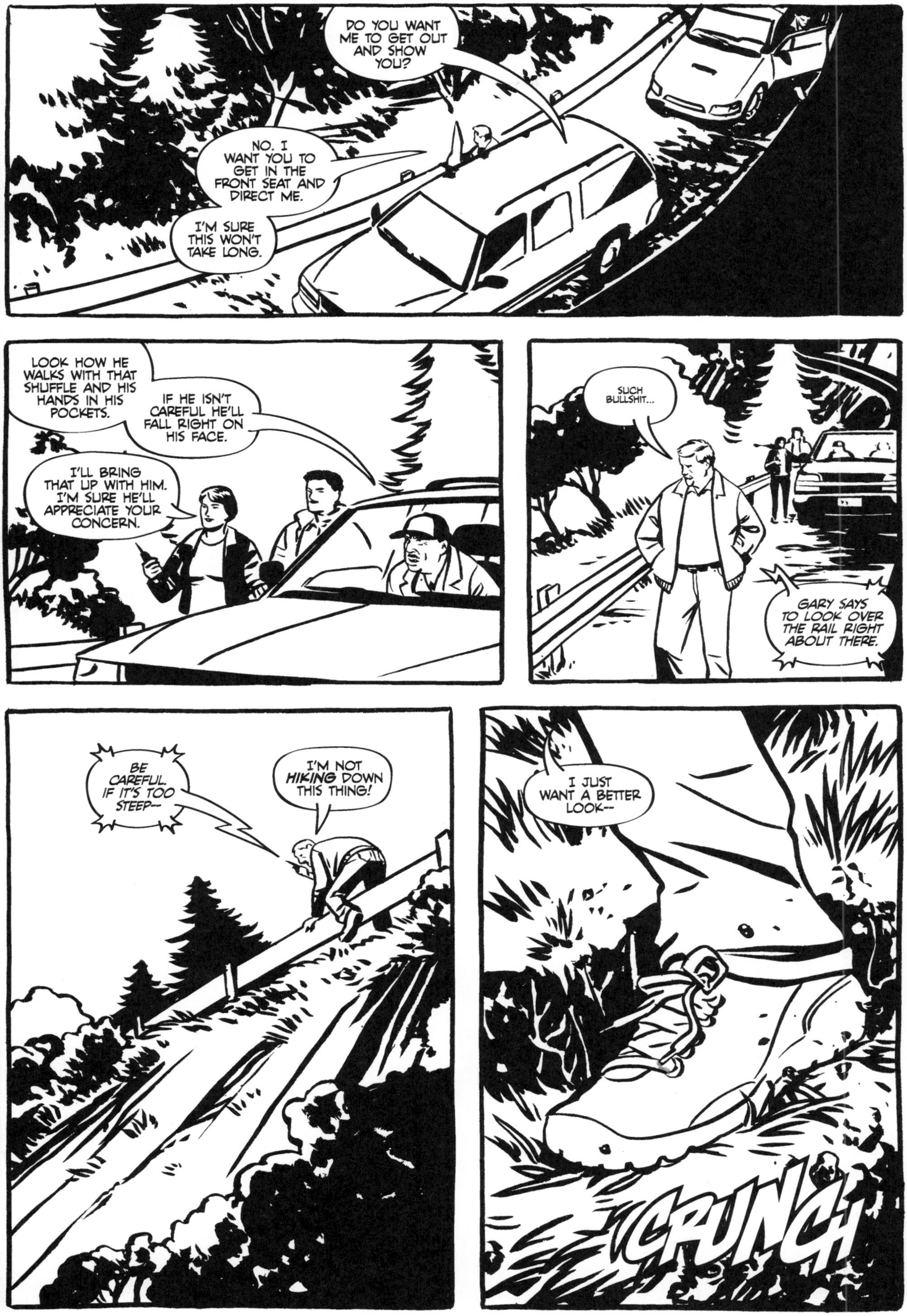

DO YOU WANT ME TO GET OUT AND SHOW YOU?
NO. I WANT YOU TO GET IN THE FRONT SEAT AND DIRECT ME.
I'M SURE THIS WON'T TAKE LONG.
LOOK HOW HE WALKS WITH THAT SHUFFLE AND HIS HANDS IN HIS POCKETS.
IF HE ISN'T CAREFUL HE'LL FALL RIGHT ON HIS FACE.
I'LL BRING THAT UP WITH HIM. I'M SURE HE'LL APPRECIATE YOUR CONCERN.
SUCH BULLSHIT...
GARY SAYS TO LOOK OVER THE RAIL RIGHT ABOUT THERE.
BE CAREFUL. IF IT'S TOO STEEP--
I'M NOT HIKING DOWN THIS THING!
I JUST WANT A BETTER LOOK--
CRUNCH

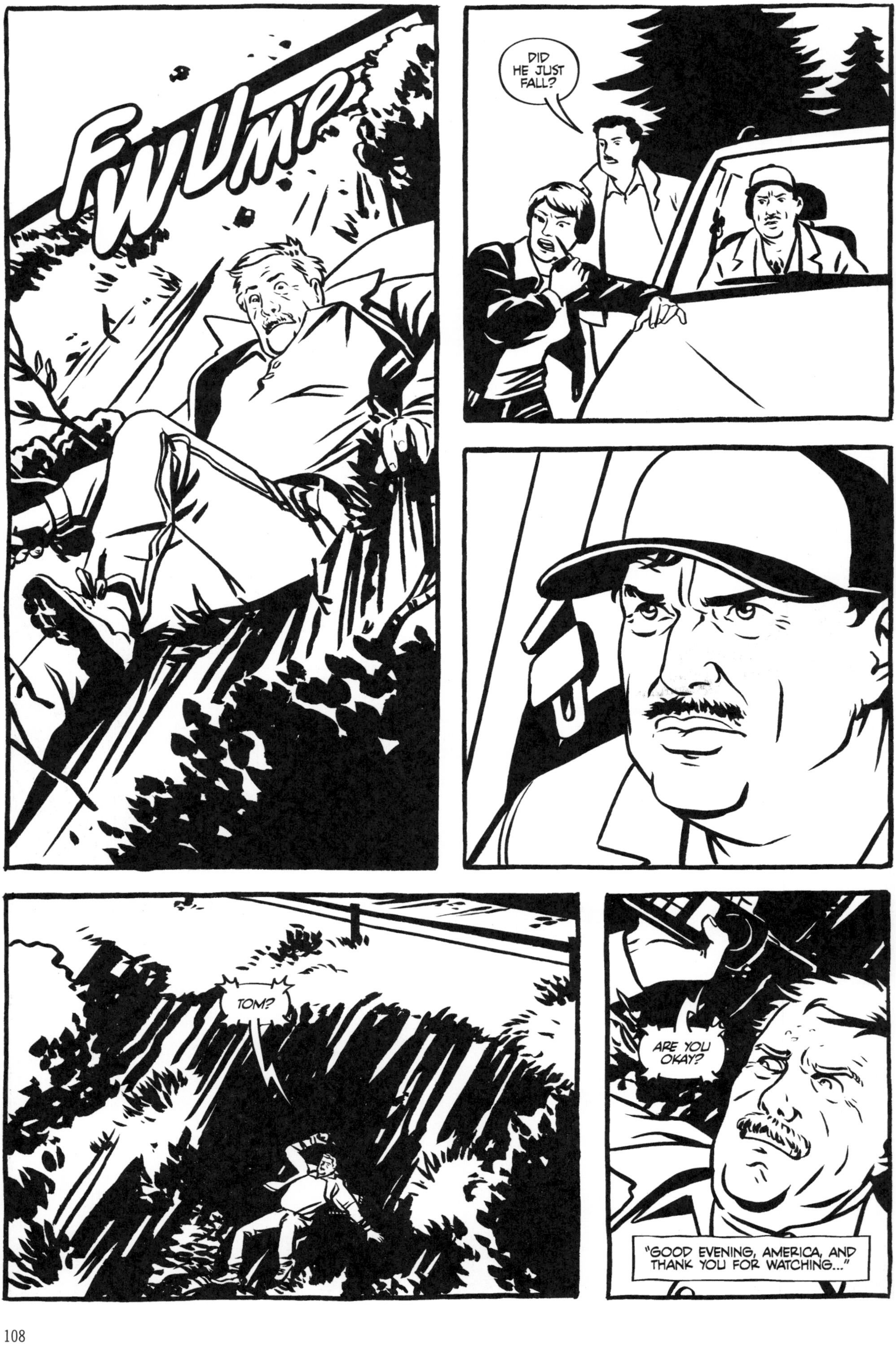
FWUMP
DID HE JUST FALL?
TOM?
ARE YOU OKAY?
"GOOD EVENING, AMERICA, AND THANK YOU FOR WATCHING..."

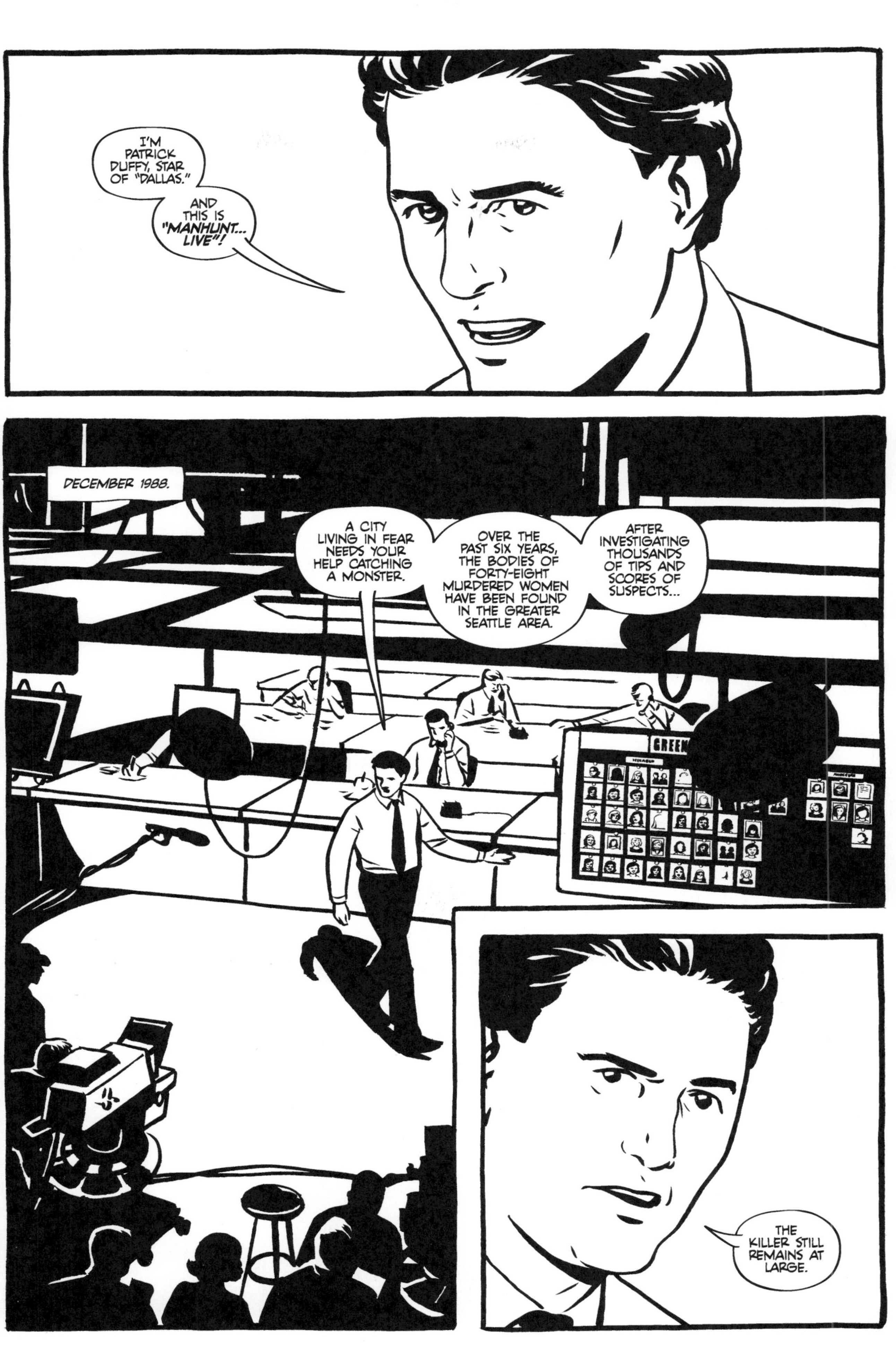
I'M PATRICK DUFFY, STAR OF "DALLAS."
AND THIS IS "MANHUNT... LIVE"!
DECEMBER 1988.
A CITY LIVING IN FEAR NEEDS YOUR HELP CATCHING A MONSTER.
OVER THE PAST SIX YEARS, THE BODIES OF FORTY-EIGHT MURDERED WOMEN HAVE BEEN FOUND IN THE GREATER SEATTLE AREA.
AFTER INVESTIGATING THOUSANDS OF TIPS AND SCORES OF SUSPECTS...
THE KILLER STILL REMAINS AT LARGE.

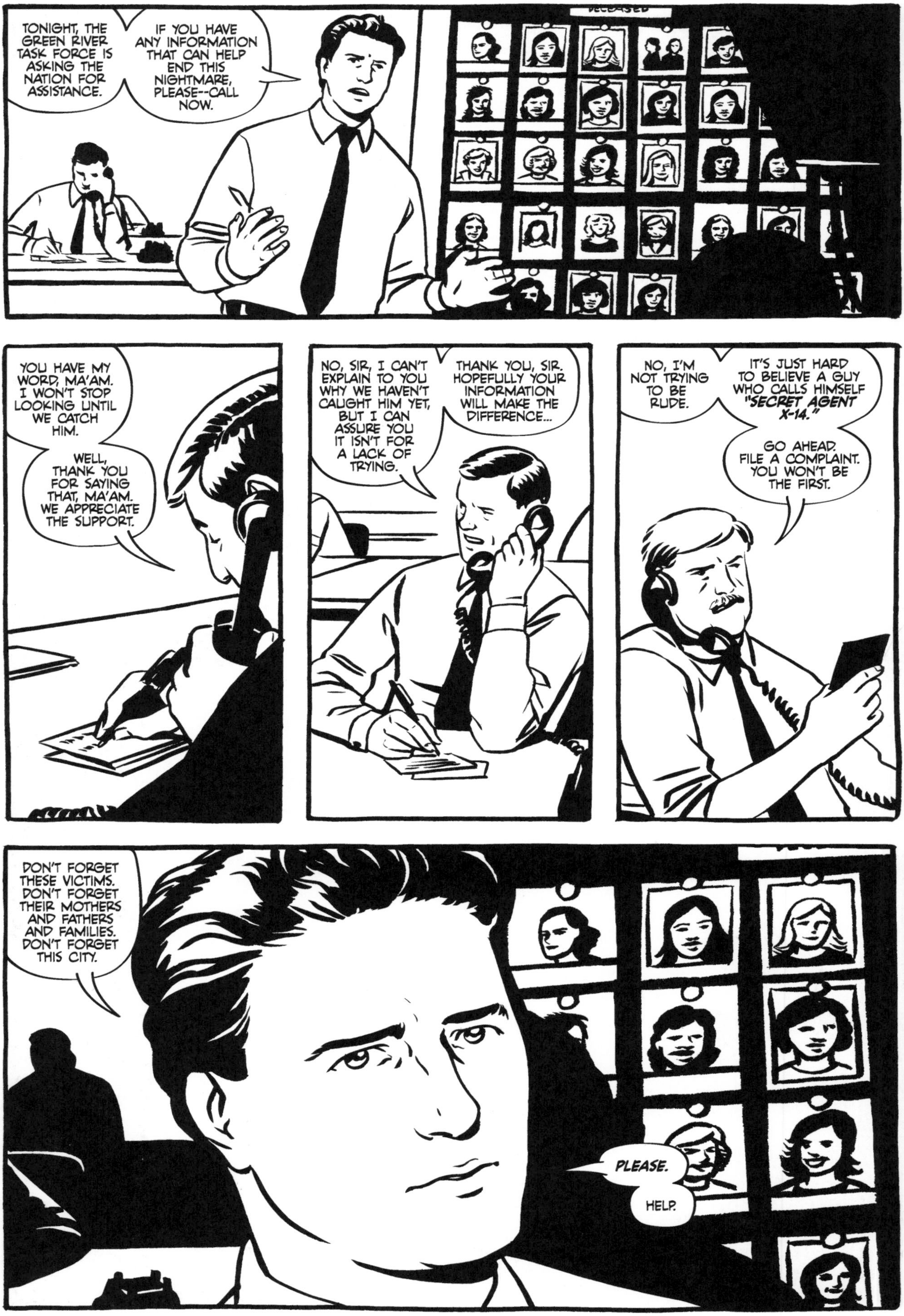
TONIGHT, THE GREEN RIVER TASK FORCE IS ASKING THE NATION FOR ASSISTANCE.
IF YOU HAVE ANY INFORMATION THAT CAN HELP END THIS NIGHTMARE, PLEASE--CALL NOW.
YOU HAVE MY WORD, MA'AM. I WON'T STOP LOOKING UNTIL WE CATCH HIM.
WELL, THANK YOU FOR SAYING THAT, MA'AM. WE APPRECIATE THE SUPPORT.
NO, SIR, I CAN'T EXPLAIN TO YOU WHY WE HAVEN'T CAUGHT HIM YET, BUT I CAN ASSURE YOU IT ISN'T FOR A LACK OF TRYING.
THANK YOU, SIR. HOPEFULLY YOUR INFORMATION WILL MAKE THE DIFFERENCE...
NO, I'M NOT TRYING TO BE RUDE.
IT'S JUST HARD TO BELIEVE A GUY WHO CALLS HIMSELF *"SECRET AGENT X-14."*
GO AHEAD. FILE A COMPLAINT. YOU WON'T BE THE FIRST.
DON'T FORGET THESE VICTIMS. DON'T FORGET THEIR MOTHERS AND FATHERS AND FAMILIES. DON'T FORGET THIS CITY.
PLEASE.
HELP.

SIX YEARS, $15 MILLION, OUR BEST GUYS, AND A STATE-OF-THE-ART COMPUTER...

CONTACT: Juliet Gale
PHONE: 481-516-2342
SUSPECT: Ben Cassidy
COMMENTS: C... claims
harassing re...
predator/sta...

...AND IT COMES DOWN TO A HAIL MARY THROWN BY BOBBY EWING.

QUITE A SHOW, THOUGH.

NAME: JULIET
SUSPECT: BEN CA...

COMMENTS:

NO ONE OUTSIDE OF SEATTLE WOULD HAVE GUESSED HOW LAME WE REALLY ARE.

CONTACT: Gayle Wa...
PHONE: 206-555-8020
SUSPECT: Michael V...
COMMENTS: Claim...
d "obse..." w...
crime st...

OUR BUDGET'S BEEN GUTTED. OUR STAFF KEEPS GETTING CUT. THE MEDIA HAS DECLARED US TOTALLY INCOMPETENT...

IF THERE'S A RING IN HELL RESERVED FOR DETECTIVES, I THINK WE'RE STUCK IN IT.

CONTACT: Marc Petersen
PHONE: 503-555-3627
SUSPECT: Unknown
COMMENTS: Bar owner witnessed assault of prostitute by frequent, "strange" customer.
HIGH PRIORITY

YOU'RE NOT LISTENING TO ME, ARE YOU?

NO, DOYON. I'M BUSY. BEING A DETECTIVE.

HONK

OSCAR, FELIX, IF I MAY INTERRUPT...

111

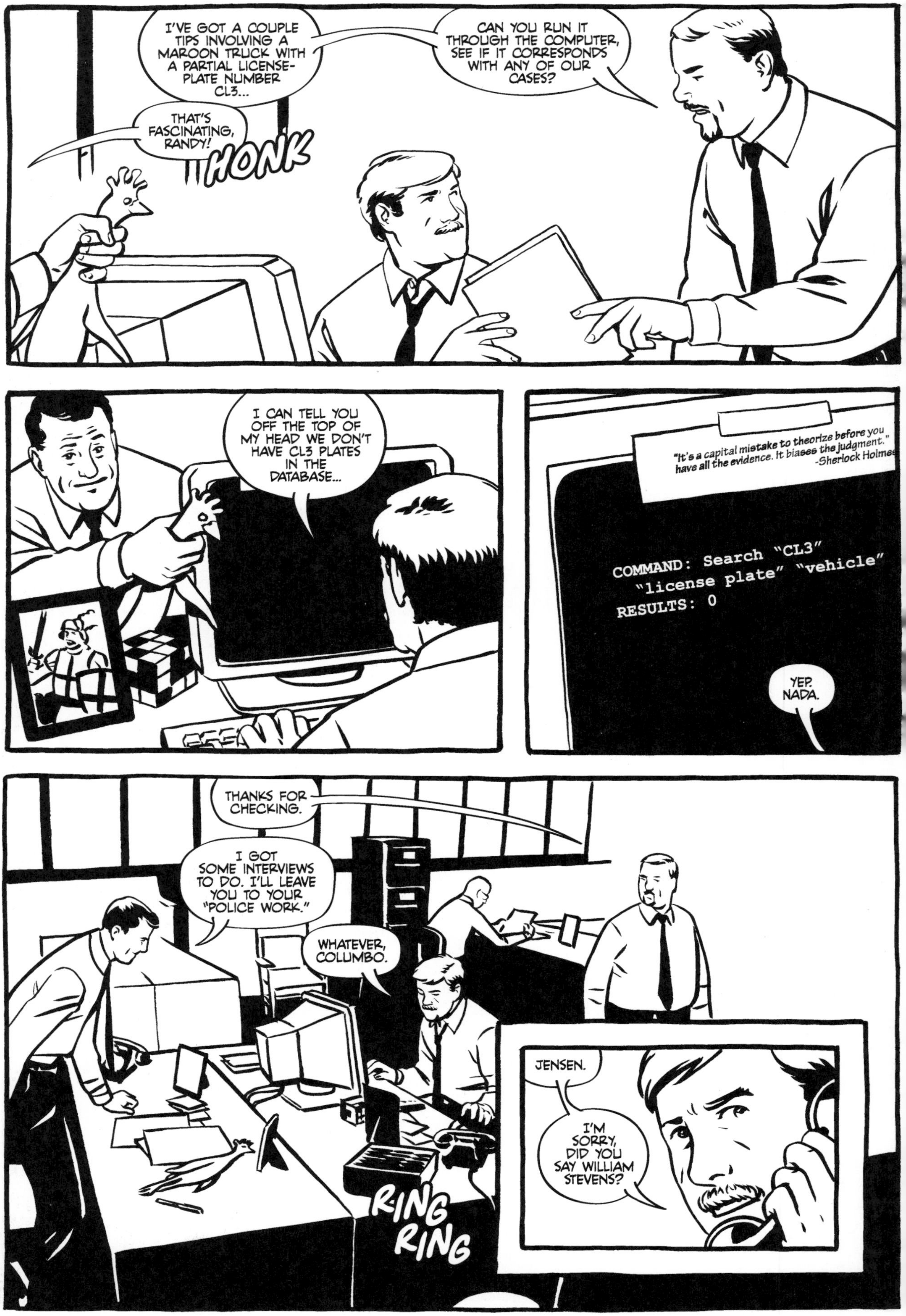
I'VE GOT A COUPLE TIPS INVOLVING A MAROON TRUCK WITH A PARTIAL LICENSE-PLATE NUMBER CL3...
CAN YOU RUN IT THROUGH THE COMPUTER, SEE IF IT CORRESPONDS WITH ANY OF OUR CASES?
THAT'S FASCINATING, RANDY!
HONK
I CAN TELL YOU OFF THE TOP OF MY HEAD WE DON'T HAVE CL3 PLATES IN THE DATABASE...
"It's a capital mistake to theorize before you have all the evidence. It biases the judgment." -Sherlock Holmes
COMMAND: Search "CL3" "license plate" "vehicle"
RESULTS: 0
YEP. NADA.
THANKS FOR CHECKING.
I GOT SOME INTERVIEWS TO DO. I'LL LEAVE YOU TO YOUR "POLICE WORK."
WHATEVER, COLUMBO.
JENSEN.
I'M SORRY, DID YOU SAY WILLIAM STEVENS?
RING RING

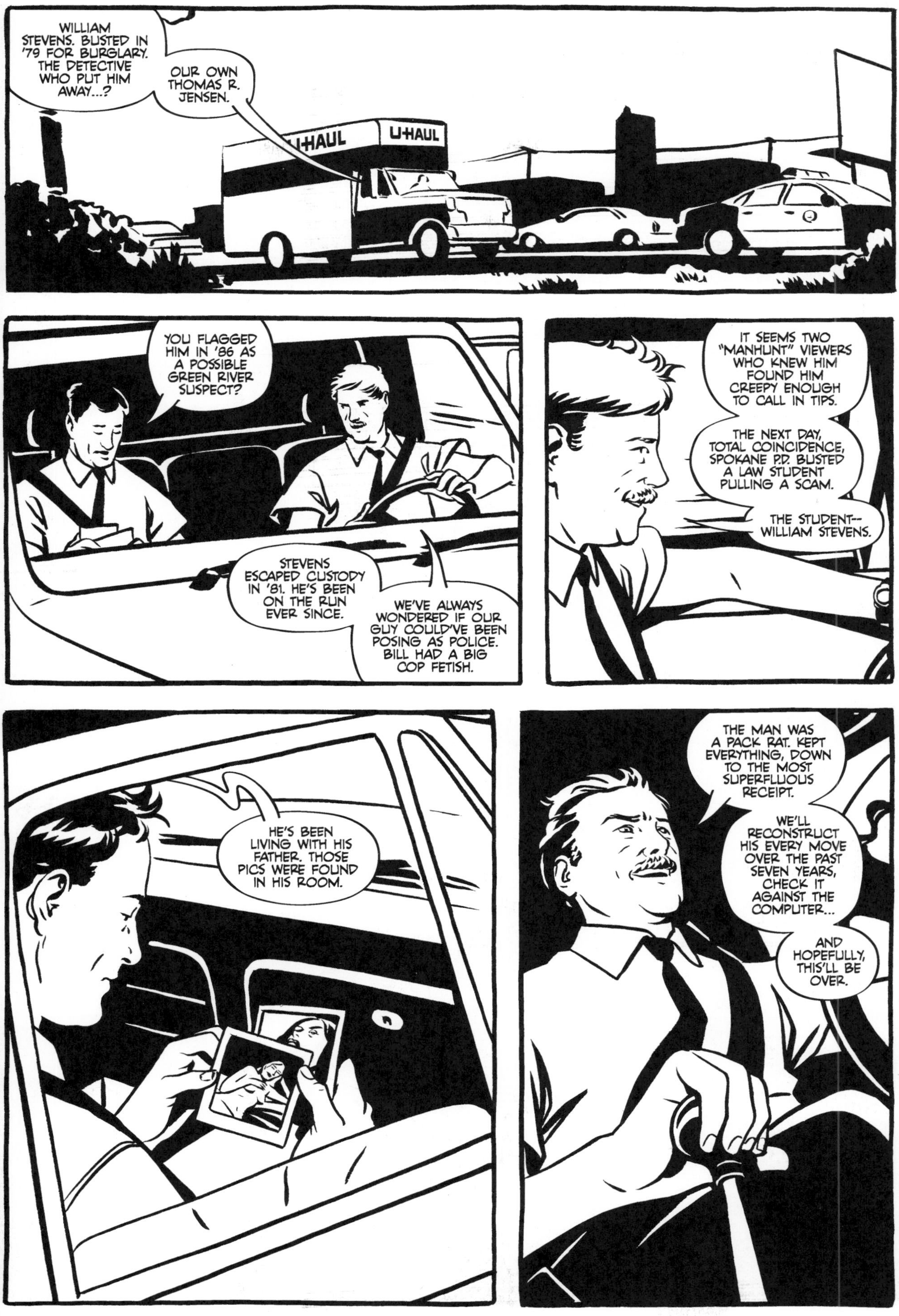

WILLIAM STEVENS. BUSTED IN '79 FOR BURGLARY. THE DETECTIVE WHO PUT HIM AWAY...?
OUR OWN THOMAS R. JENSEN.
U-HAUL
U-HAUL
YOU FLAGGED HIM IN '86 AS A POSSIBLE GREEN RIVER SUSPECT?
STEVENS ESCAPED CUSTODY IN '81. HE'S BEEN ON THE RUN EVER SINCE.
WE'VE ALWAYS WONDERED IF OUR GUY COULD'VE BEEN POSING AS POLICE. BILL HAD A BIG COP FETISH.
IT SEEMS TWO "MANHUNT" VIEWERS WHO KNEW HIM FOUND HIM CREEPY ENOUGH TO CALL IN TIPS.
THE NEXT DAY, TOTAL COINCIDENCE, SPOKANE P.D. BUSTED A LAW STUDENT PULLING A SCAM.
THE STUDENT-- WILLIAM STEVENS.
HE'S BEEN LIVING WITH HIS FATHER. THOSE PICS WERE FOUND IN HIS ROOM.
THE MAN WAS A PACK RAT. KEPT EVERYTHING, DOWN TO THE MOST SUPERFLUOUS RECEIPT.
WE'LL RECONSTRUCT HIS EVERY MOVE OVER THE PAST SEVEN YEARS, CHECK IT AGAINST THE COMPUTER...
AND HOPEFULLY, THIS'LL BE OVER.

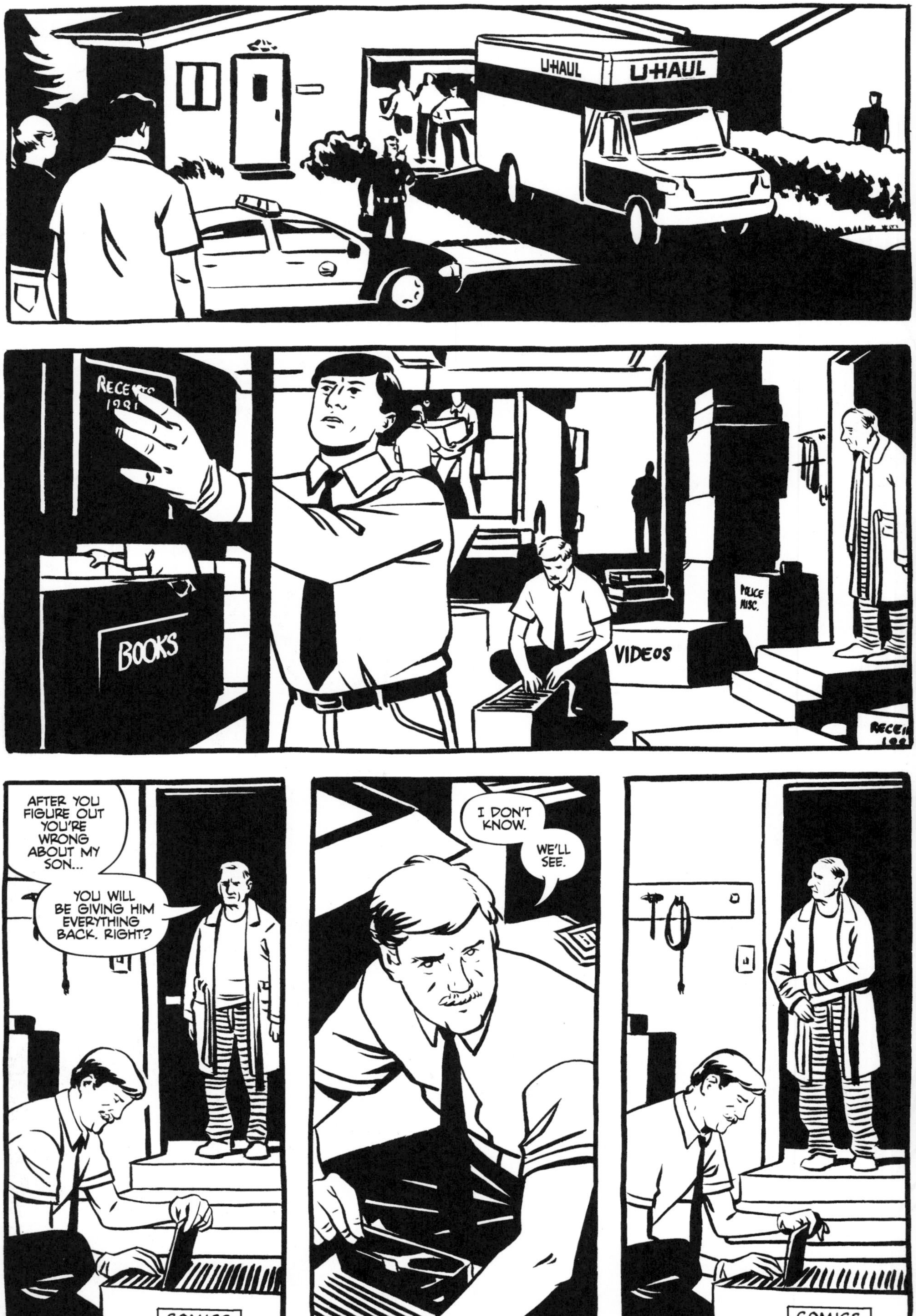
U-HAUL
U-HAUL
BOOKS
VIDEOS
POLICE MISC.
AFTER YOU FIGURE OUT YOU'RE WRONG ABOUT MY SON...
YOU WILL BE GIVING HIM EVERYTHING BACK. RIGHT?
I DON'T KNOW.
WE'LL SEE.
COMICS
COMICS

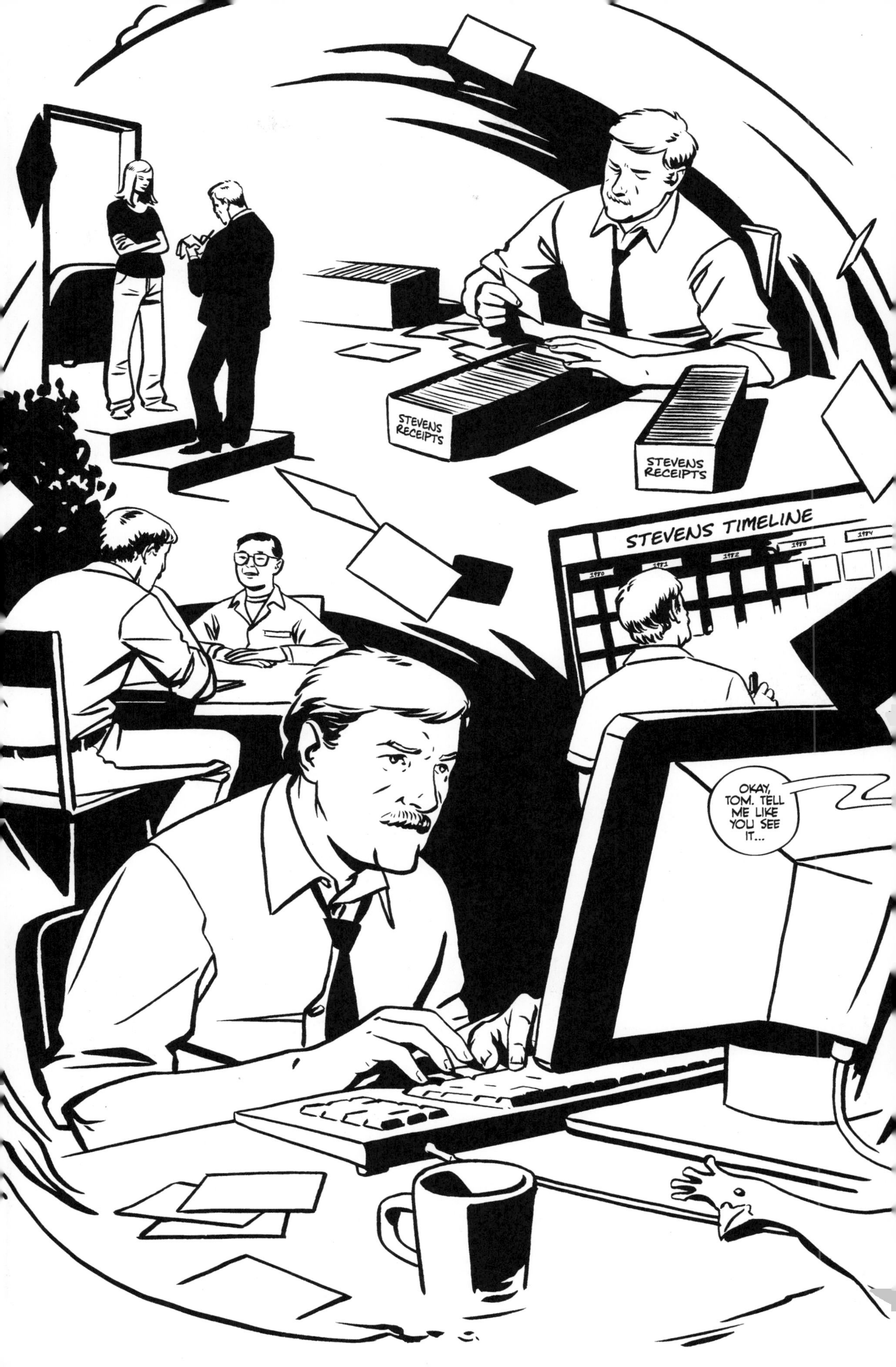
STEVENS RECEIPTS
STEVENS RECEIPTS
STEVENS TIMELINE
1980
1981
1982
1983
1984
OKAY, TOM. TELL ME LIKE YOU SEE IT...

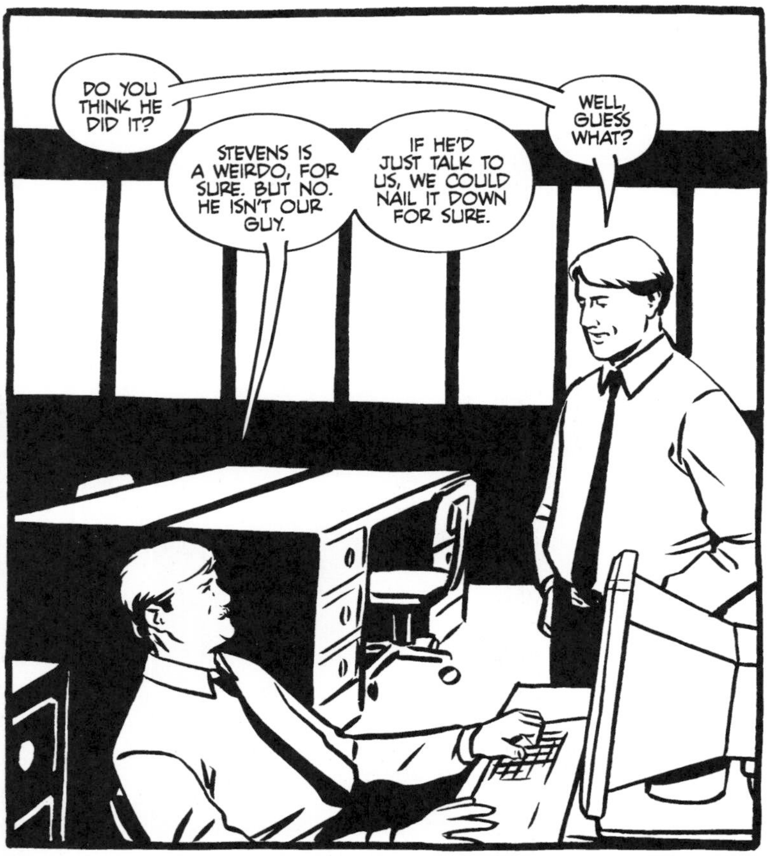
DO YOU THINK HE DID IT?
STEVENS IS A WEIRDO, FOR SURE. BUT NO. HE ISN'T OUR GUY.
IF HE'D JUST TALK TO US, WE COULD NAIL IT DOWN FOR SURE.
WELL, GUESS WHAT?

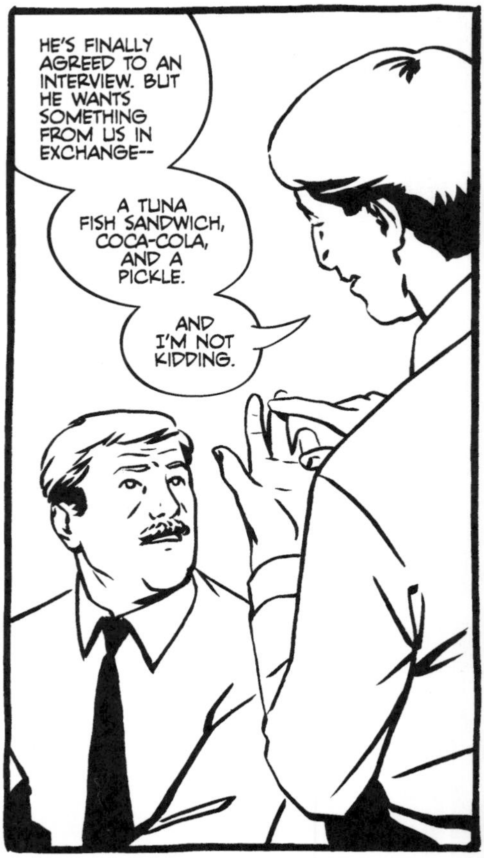
HE'S FINALLY AGREED TO AN INTERVIEW. BUT HE WANTS SOMETHING FROM US IN EXCHANGE--
A TUNA FISH SANDWICH, COCA-COLA, AND A PICKLE.
AND I'M NOT KIDDING.

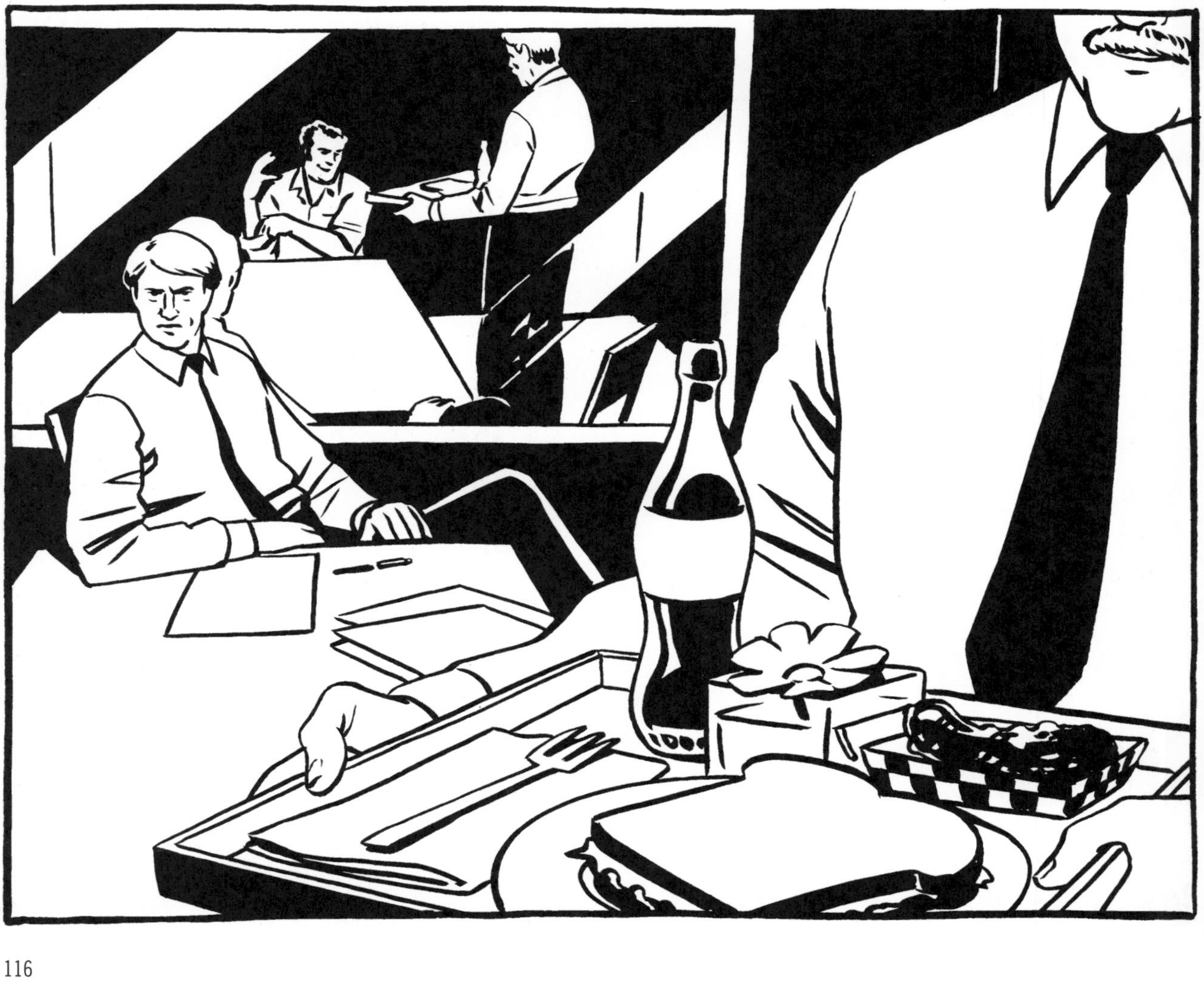

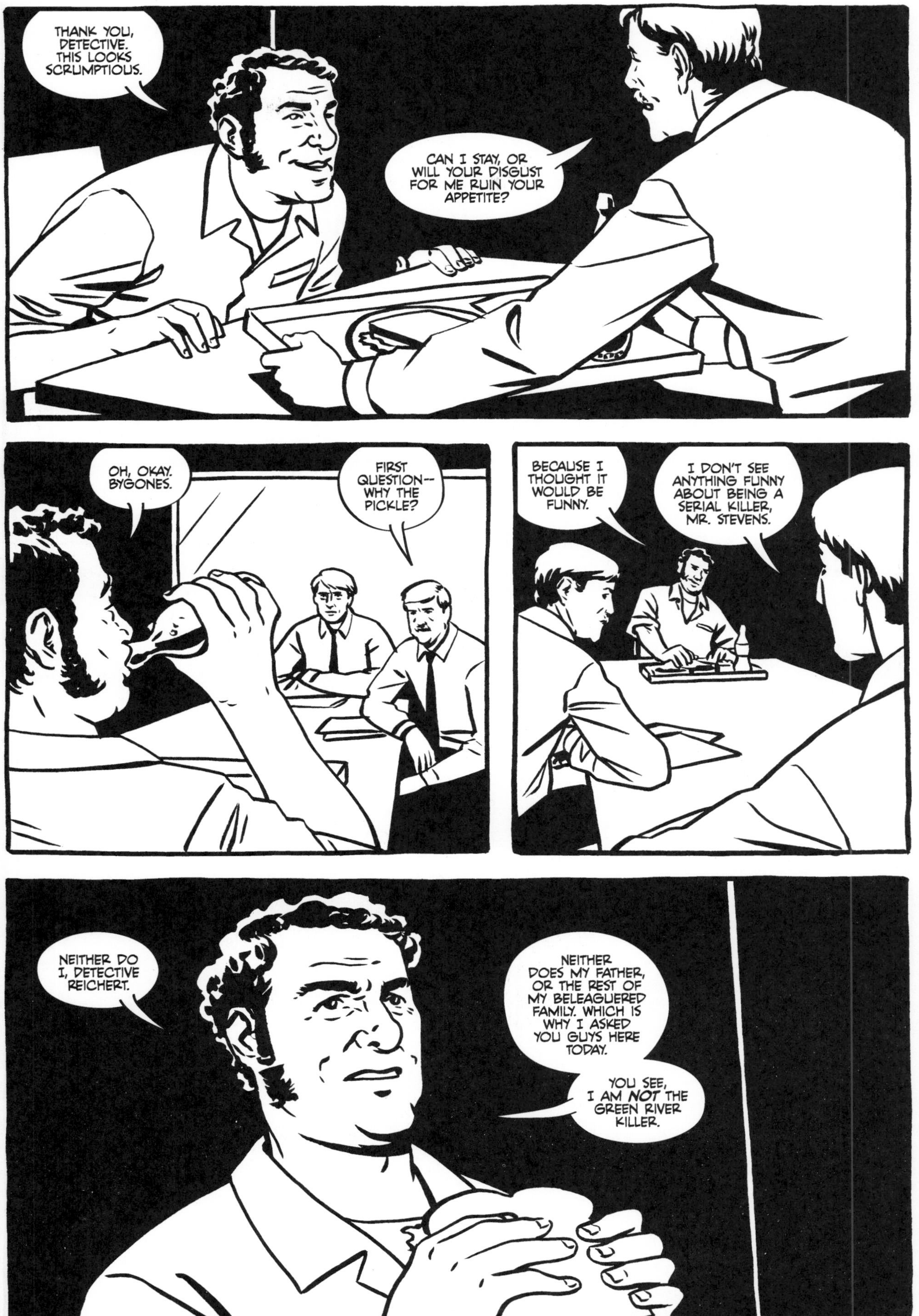
THANK YOU, DETECTIVE. THIS LOOKS SCRUMPTIOUS.
CAN I STAY, OR WILL YOUR DISGUST FOR ME RUIN YOUR APPETITE?
OH, OKAY. BYGONES.
FIRST QUESTION-- WHY THE PICKLE?
BECAUSE I THOUGHT IT WOULD BE FUNNY.
I DON'T SEE ANYTHING FUNNY ABOUT BEING A SERIAL KILLER, MR. STEVENS.
NEITHER DO I, DETECTIVE REICHERT.
NEITHER DOES MY FATHER, OR THE REST OF MY BELEAGUERED FAMILY. WHICH IS WHY I ASKED YOU GUYS HERE TODAY.
YOU SEE, I AM *NOT* THE GREEN RIVER KILLER.

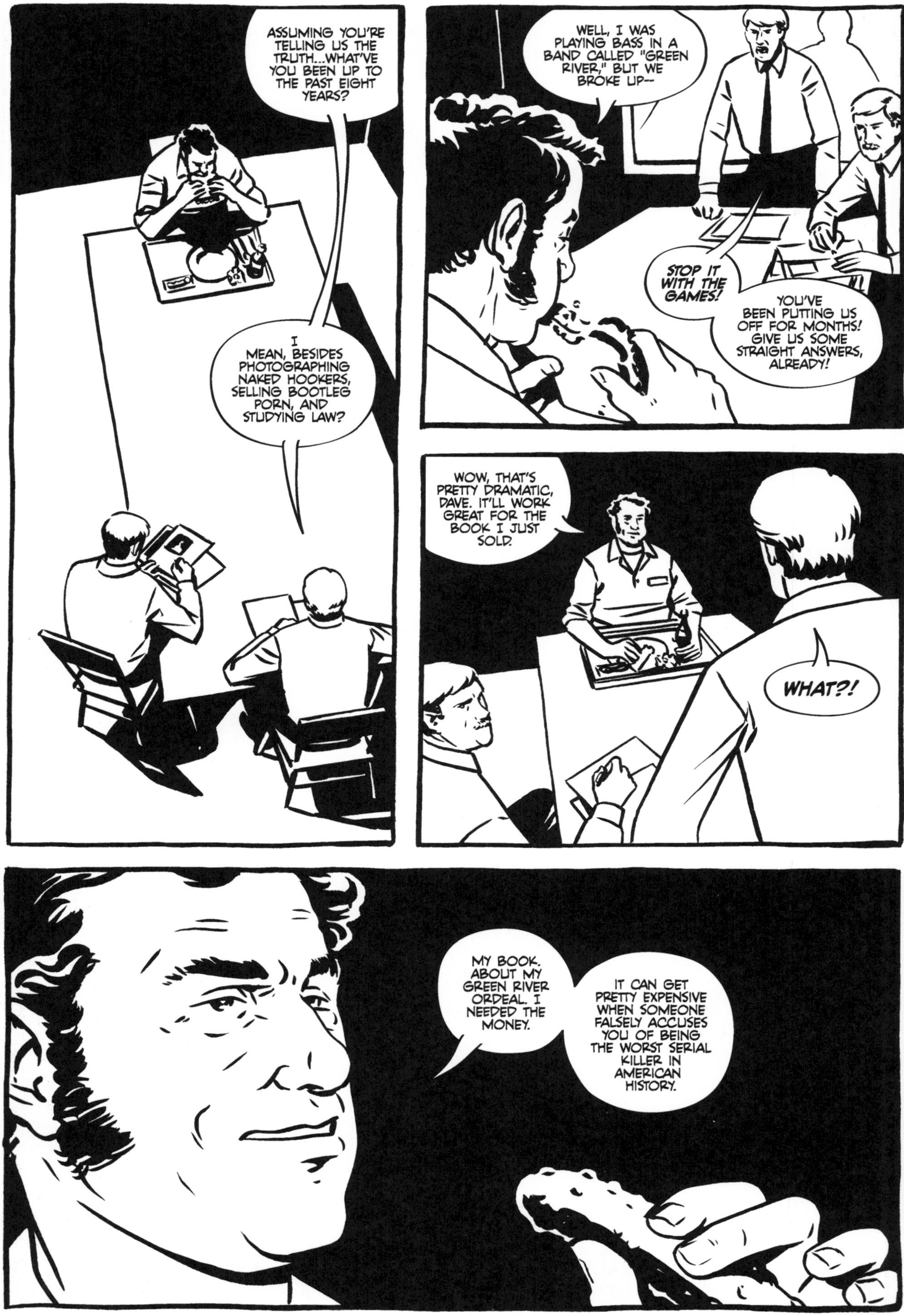
ASSUMING YOU'RE TELLING US THE TRUTH...WHAT'VE YOU BEEN UP TO THE PAST EIGHT YEARS?
I MEAN, BESIDES PHOTOGRAPHING NAKED HOOKERS, SELLING BOOTLEG PORN, AND STUDYING LAW?
WELL, I WAS PLAYING BASS IN A BAND CALLED "GREEN RIVER," BUT WE BROKE UP--
STOP IT WITH THE GAMES!
YOU'VE BEEN PUTTING US OFF FOR MONTHS! GIVE US SOME STRAIGHT ANSWERS, ALREADY!
WOW, THAT'S PRETTY DRAMATIC, DAVE. IT'LL WORK GREAT FOR THE BOOK I JUST SOLD.
WHAT?!
MY BOOK. ABOUT MY GREEN RIVER ORDEAL. I NEEDED THE MONEY.
IT CAN GET PRETTY EXPENSIVE WHEN SOMEONE FALSELY ACCUSES YOU OF BEING THE WORST SERIAL KILLER IN AMERICAN HISTORY.

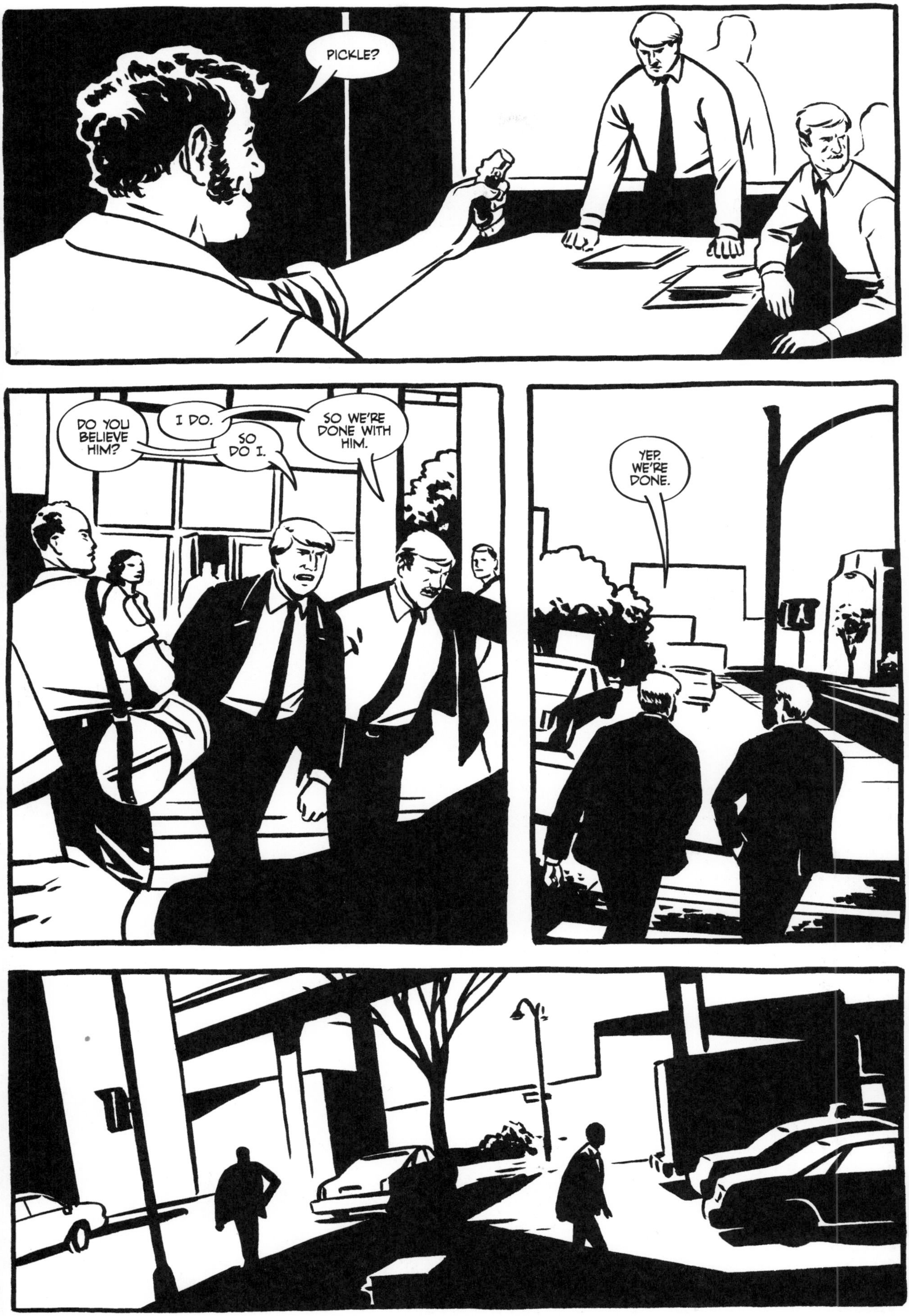
PICKLE?
DO YOU BELIEVE HIM?
I DO.
SO DO I.
SO WE'RE DONE WITH HIM.
YEP. WE'RE DONE.

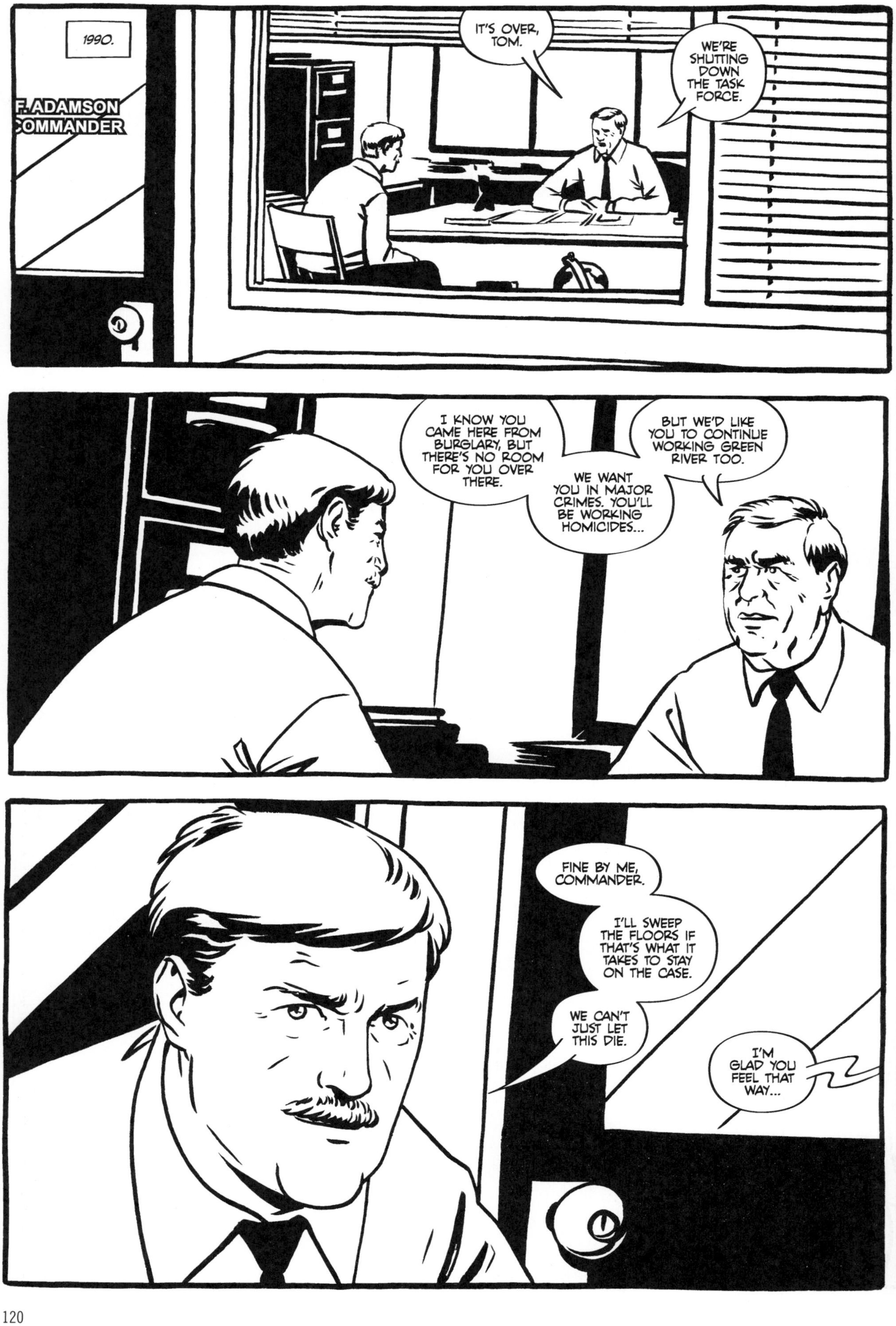
1990.
F. ADAMSON COMMANDER
IT'S OVER, TOM.
WE'RE SHUTTING DOWN THE TASK FORCE.
I KNOW YOU CAME HERE FROM BURGLARY, BUT THERE'S NO ROOM FOR YOU OVER THERE.
WE WANT YOU IN MAJOR CRIMES. YOU'LL BE WORKING HOMICIDES...
BUT WE'D LIKE YOU TO CONTINUE WORKING GREEN RIVER TOO.
FINE BY ME, COMMANDER.
I'LL SWEEP THE FLOORS IF THAT'S WHAT IT TAKES TO STAY ON THE CASE.
WE CAN'T JUST LET THIS DIE.
I'M GLAD YOU FEEL THAT WAY...

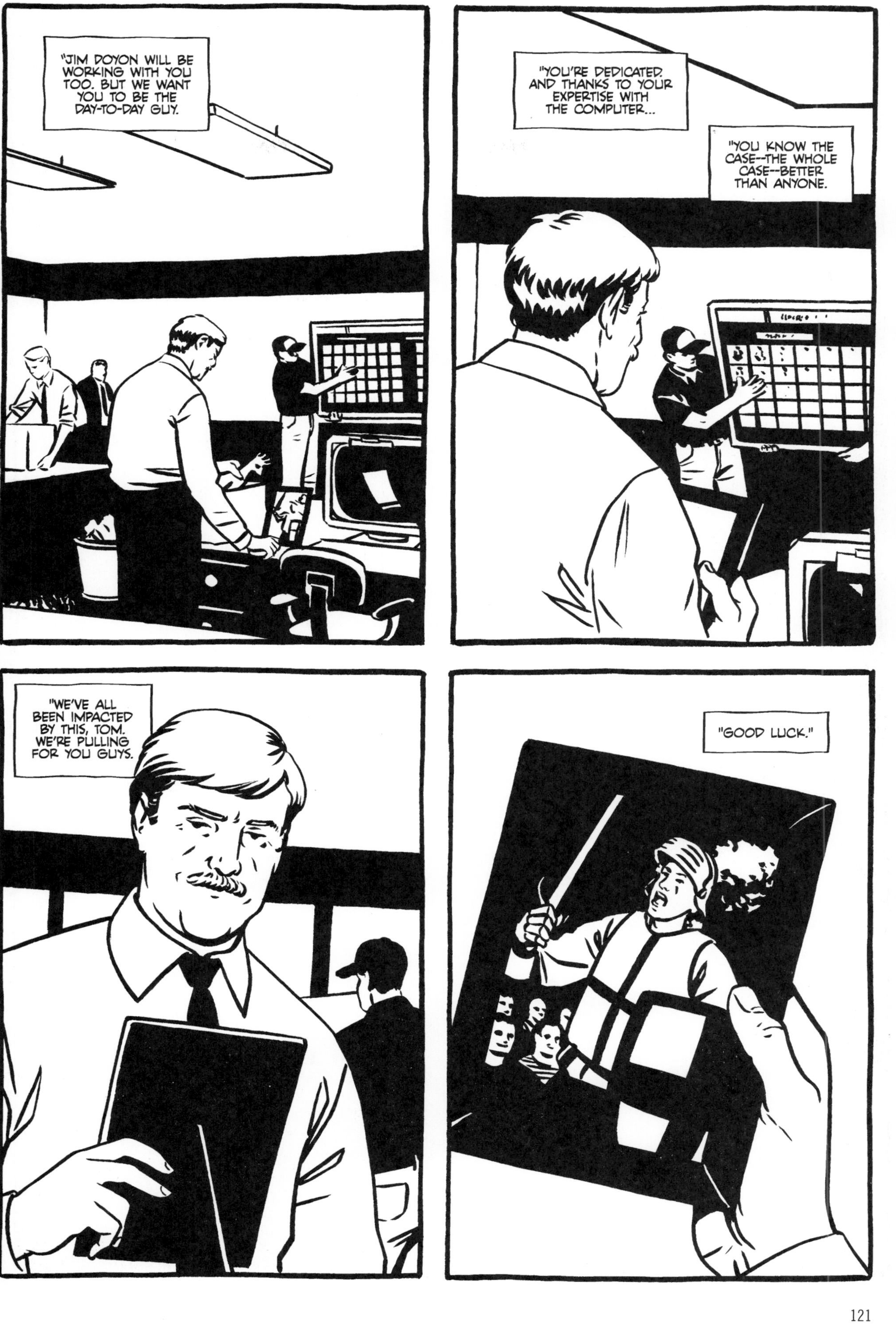
"JIM DOYON WILL BE WORKING WITH YOU TOO. BUT WE WANT YOU TO BE THE DAY-TO-DAY GUY.
"YOU'RE DEDICATED. AND THANKS TO YOUR EXPERTISE WITH THE COMPUTER...
"YOU KNOW THE CASE--THE WHOLE CASE--BETTER THAN ANYONE.
"WE'VE ALL BEEN IMPACTED BY THIS, TOM. WE'RE PULLING FOR YOU GUYS.
"GOOD LUCK."

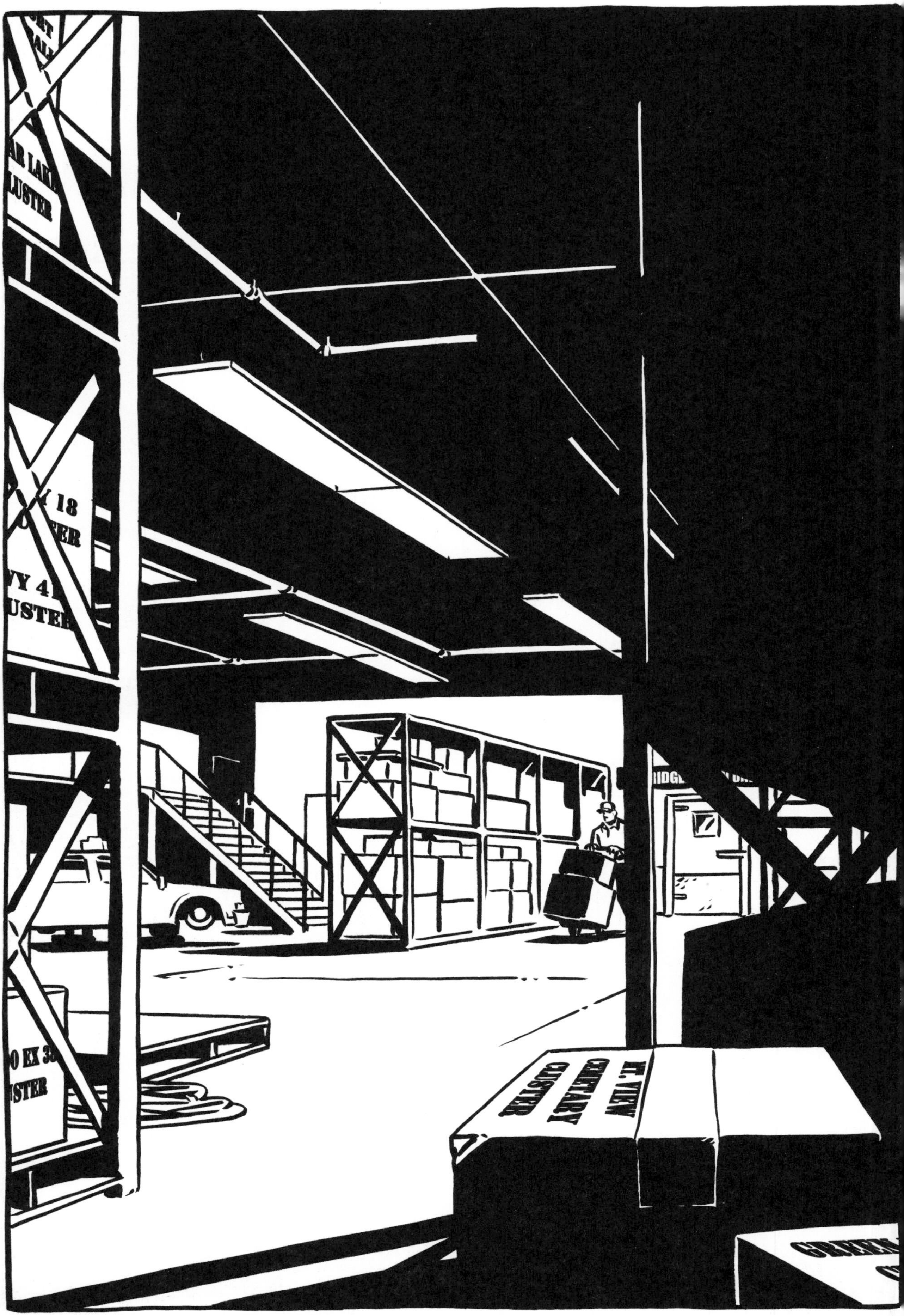
MT. VIEW
CEMETARY
CLUSTER

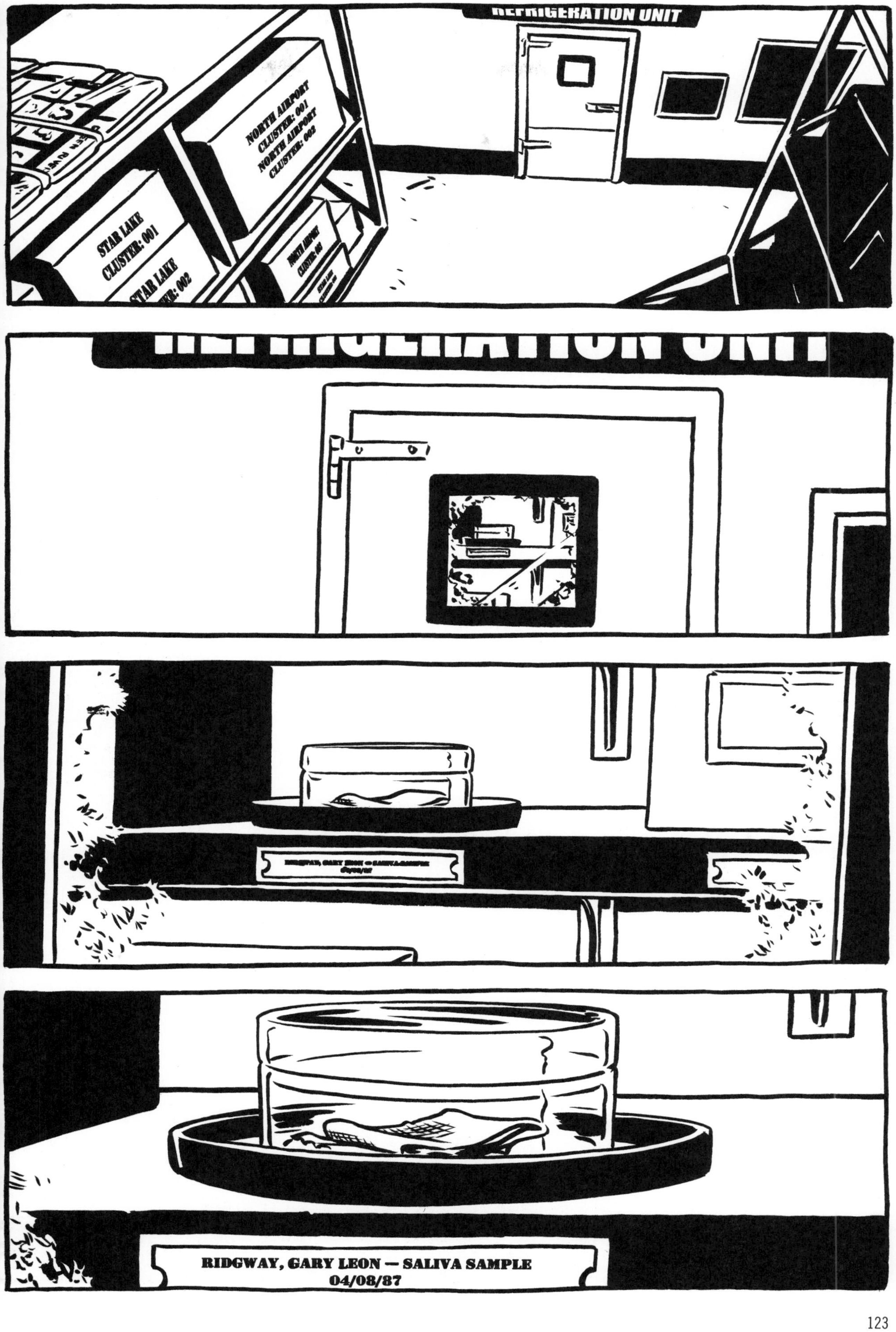
REFRIGERATION UNIT
NORTH AIRPORT
CLUSTER: 001
NORTH AIRPORT
CLUSTER: 002
STAR LAKE
CLUSTER: 001
RIDGWAY, GARY LEON — SALIVA SAMPLE
04/08/87

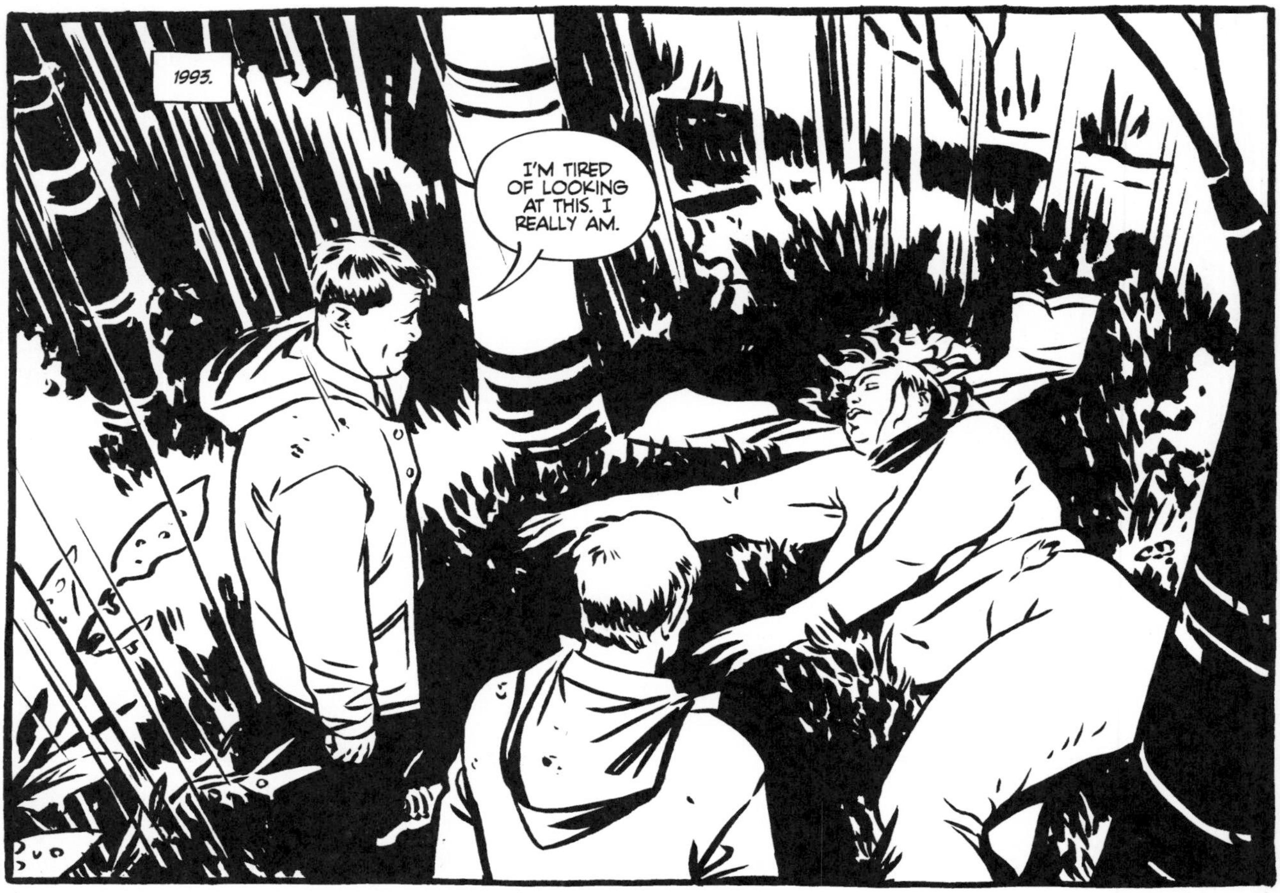
1993.
I'M TIRED OF LOOKING AT THIS. I REALLY AM.

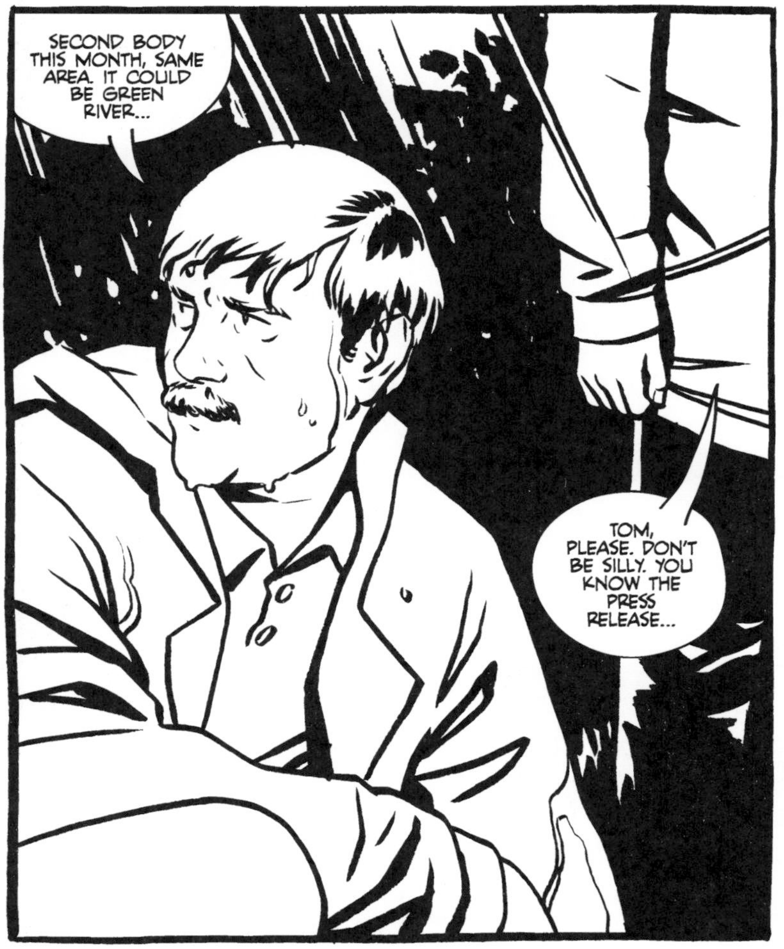
SECOND BODY THIS MONTH, SAME AREA. IT COULD BE GREEN RIVER...
TOM, PLEASE. DON'T BE SILLY. YOU KNOW THE PRESS RELEASE...

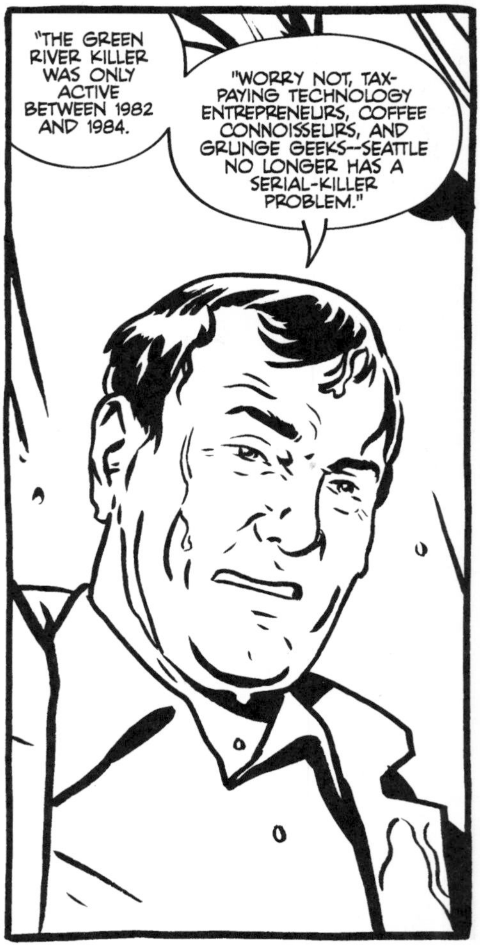
"THE GREEN RIVER KILLER WAS ONLY ACTIVE BETWEEN 1982 AND 1984.
"WORRY NOT, TAX-PAYING TECHNOLOGY ENTREPRENEURS, COFFEE CONNOISSEURS, AND GRUNGE GEEKS--SEATTLE NO LONGER HAS A SERIAL-KILLER PROBLEM."

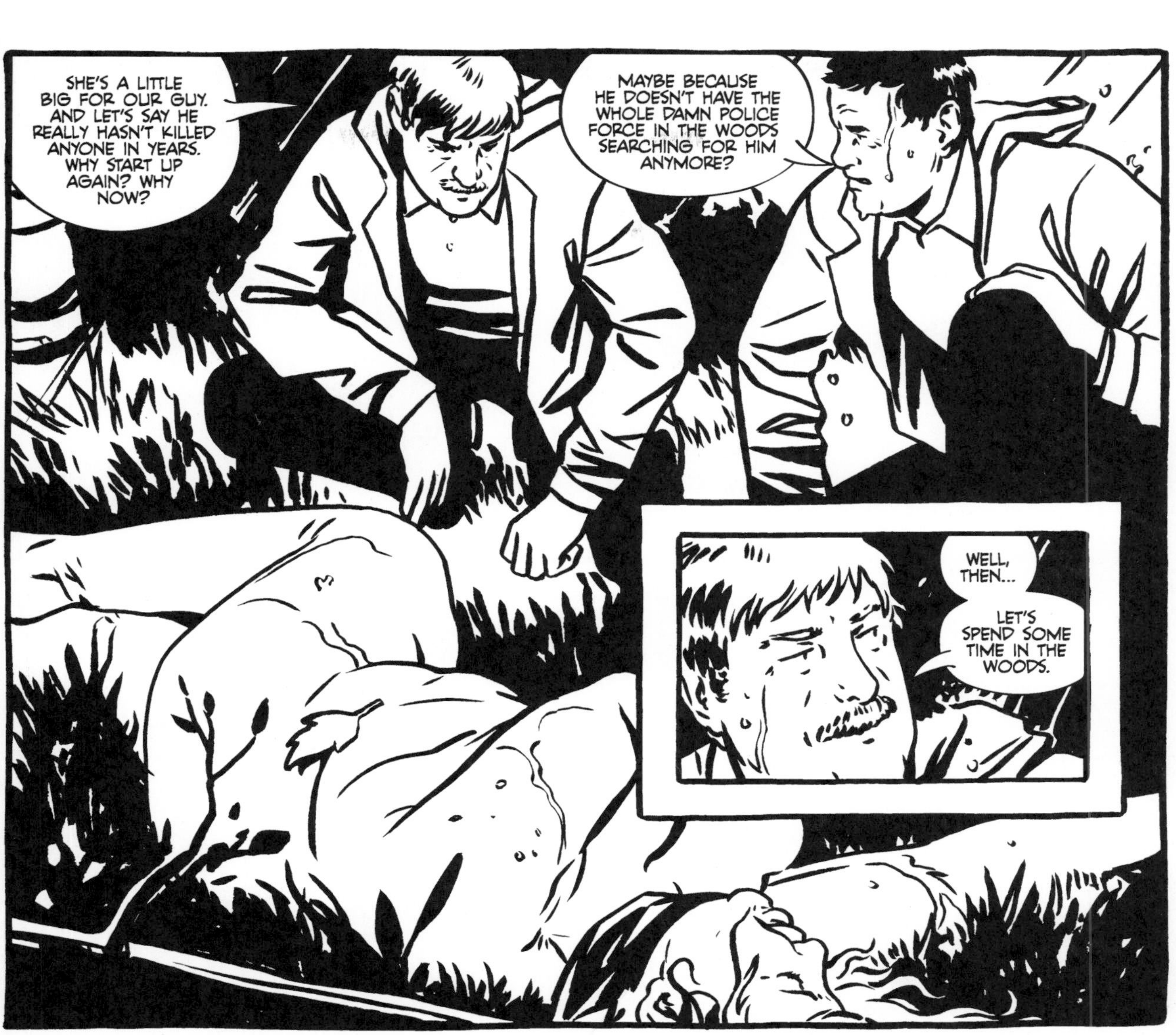
SHE'S A LITTLE BIG FOR OUR GUY. AND LET'S SAY HE REALLY HASN'T KILLED ANYONE IN YEARS. WHY START UP AGAIN? WHY NOW?
MAYBE BECAUSE HE DOESN'T HAVE THE WHOLE DAMN POLICE FORCE IN THE WOODS SEARCHING FOR HIM ANYMORE?
WELL, THEN...
LET'S SPEND SOME TIME IN THE WOODS.

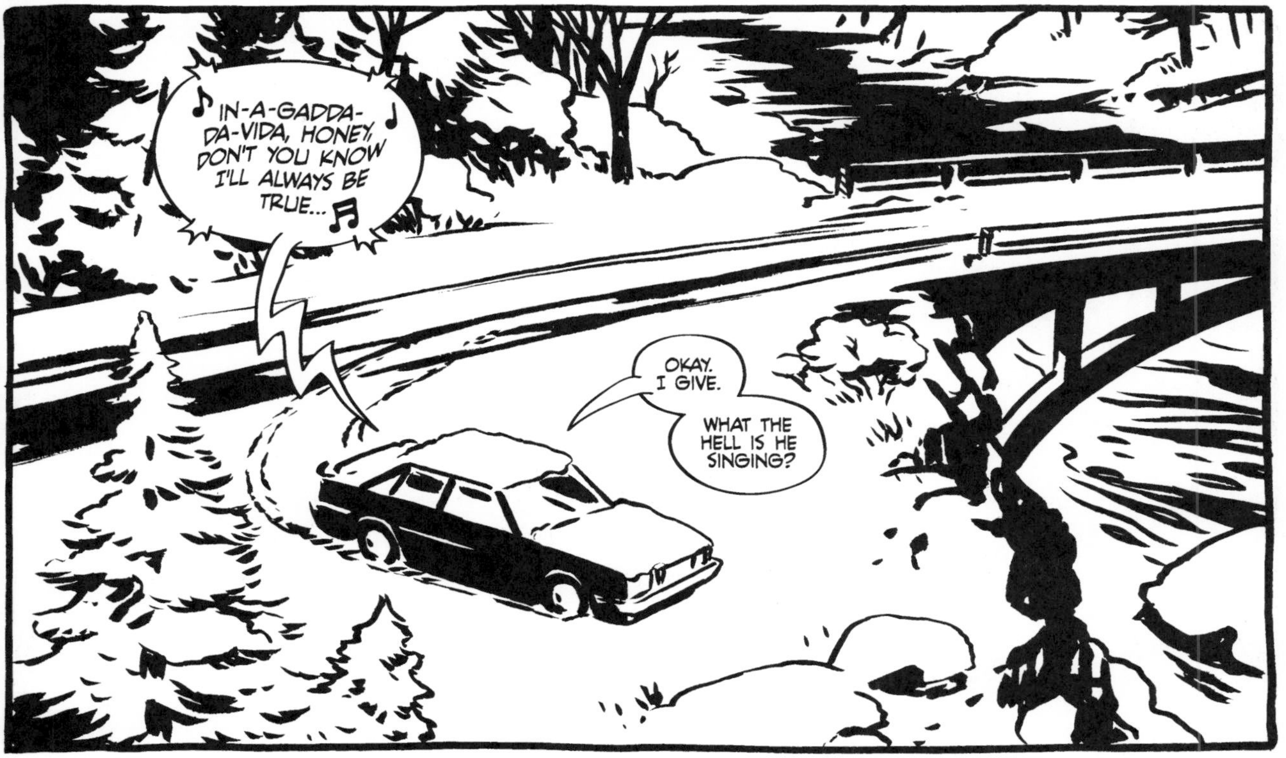
IN-A-GADDA-DA-VIDA, HONEY, DON'T YOU KNOW I'LL ALWAYS BE TRUE...
OKAY. I GIVE.
WHAT THE HELL IS HE SINGING?

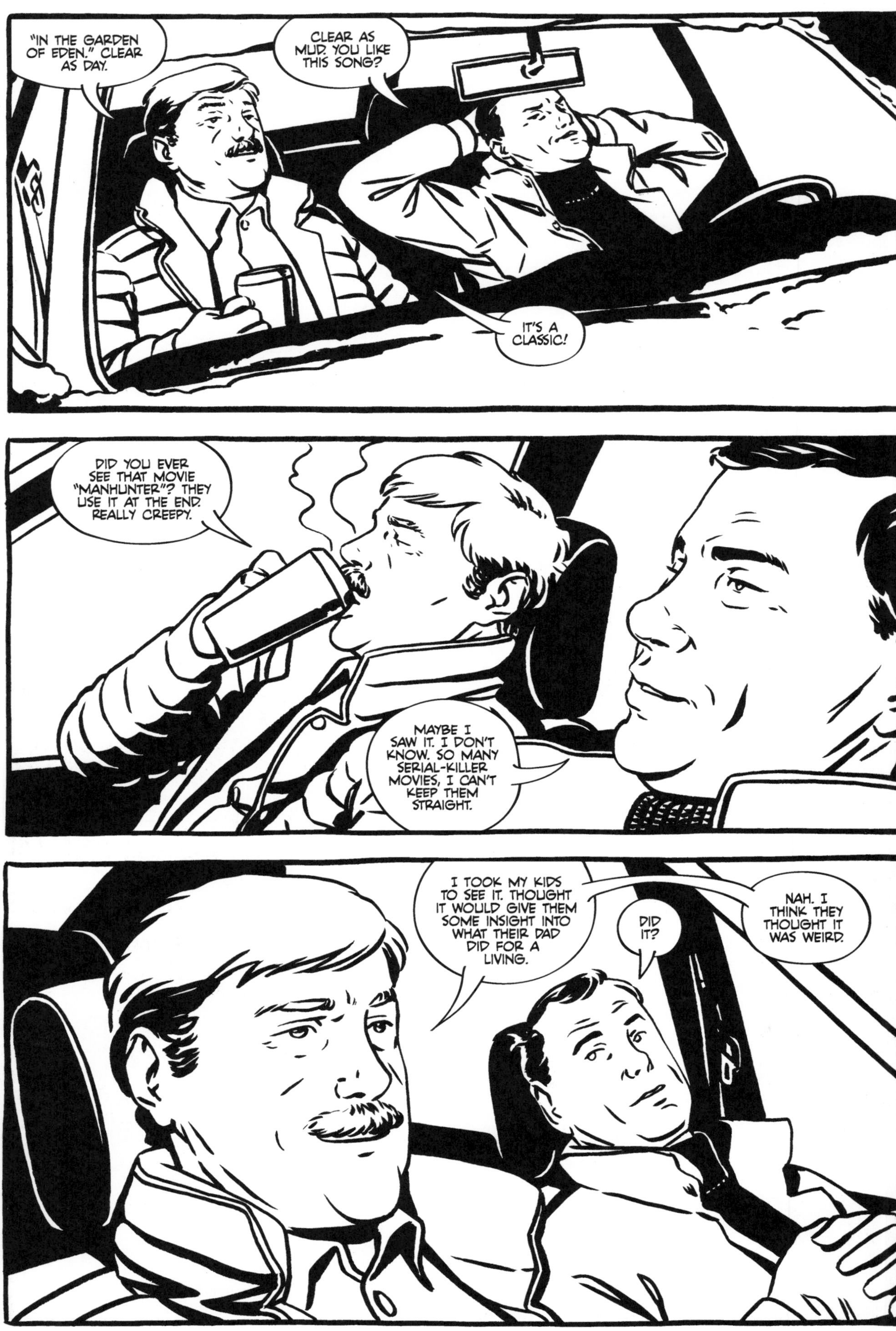
"IN THE GARDEN OF EDEN." CLEAR AS DAY.
CLEAR AS MUD. YOU LIKE THIS SONG?
IT'S A CLASSIC!
DID YOU EVER SEE THAT MOVIE "MANHUNTER"? THEY USE IT AT THE END. REALLY CREEPY.
MAYBE I SAW IT. I DON'T KNOW. SO MANY SERIAL-KILLER MOVIES, I CAN'T KEEP THEM STRAIGHT.
I TOOK MY KIDS TO SEE IT. THOUGHT IT WOULD GIVE THEM SOME INSIGHT INTO WHAT THEIR DAD DID FOR A LIVING.
DID IT?
NAH. I THINK THEY THOUGHT IT WAS WEIRD.

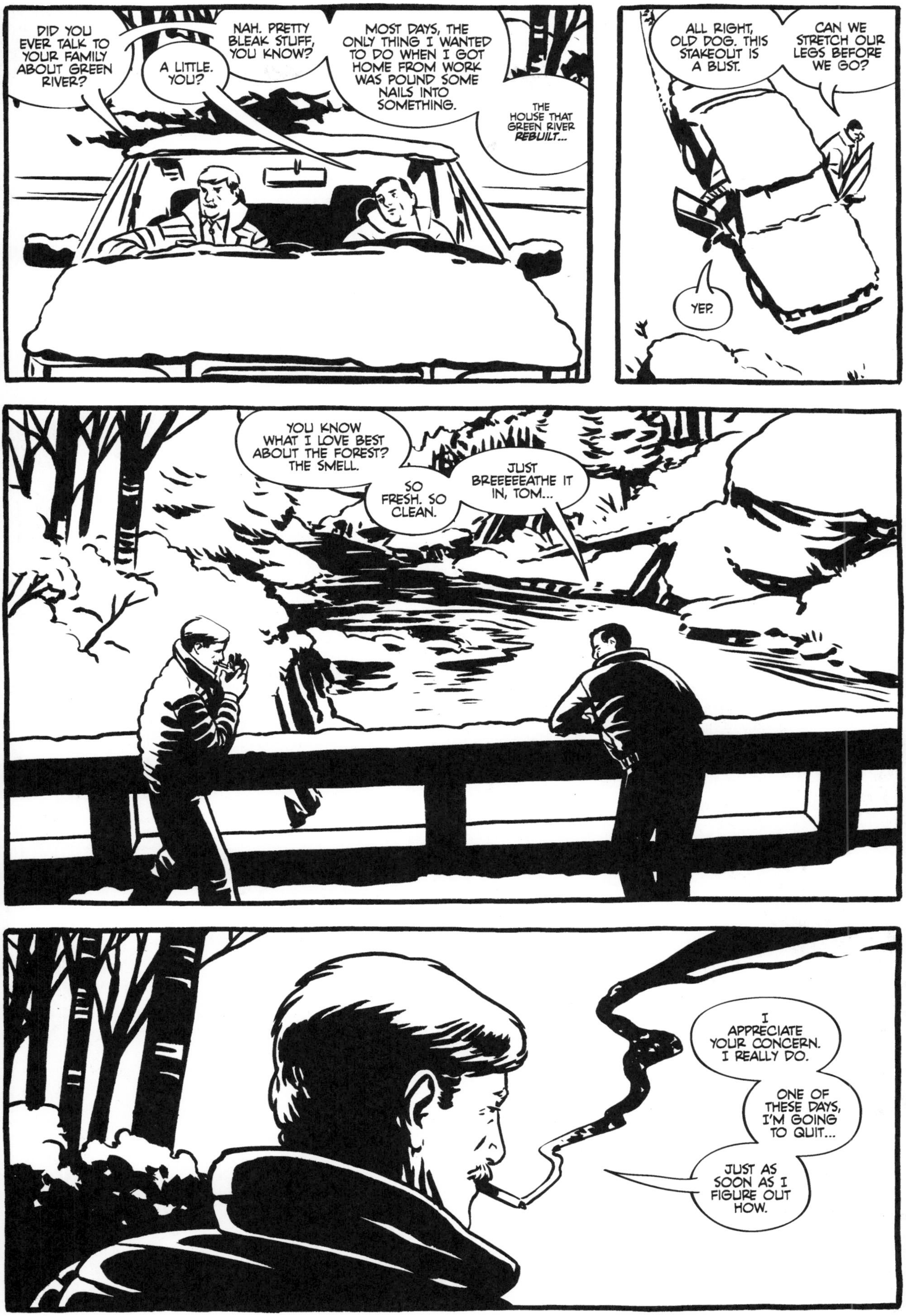
DID YOU EVER TALK TO YOUR FAMILY ABOUT GREEN RIVER?
A LITTLE. YOU?
NAH. PRETTY BLEAK STUFF, YOU KNOW?
MOST DAYS, THE ONLY THING I WANTED TO DO WHEN I GOT HOME FROM WORK WAS POUND SOME NAILS INTO SOMETHING.
THE HOUSE THAT GREEN RIVER *REBUILT...*
ALL RIGHT, OLD DOG. THIS STAKEOUT IS A BUST.
CAN WE STRETCH OUR LEGS BEFORE WE GO?
YEP.
YOU KNOW WHAT I LOVE BEST ABOUT THE FOREST? THE SMELL.
SO FRESH. SO CLEAN.
JUST BREEEEEATHE IT IN, TOM...
I APPRECIATE YOUR CONCERN. I REALLY DO.
ONE OF THESE DAYS, I'M GOING TO QUIT...
JUST AS SOON AS I FIGURE OUT HOW.

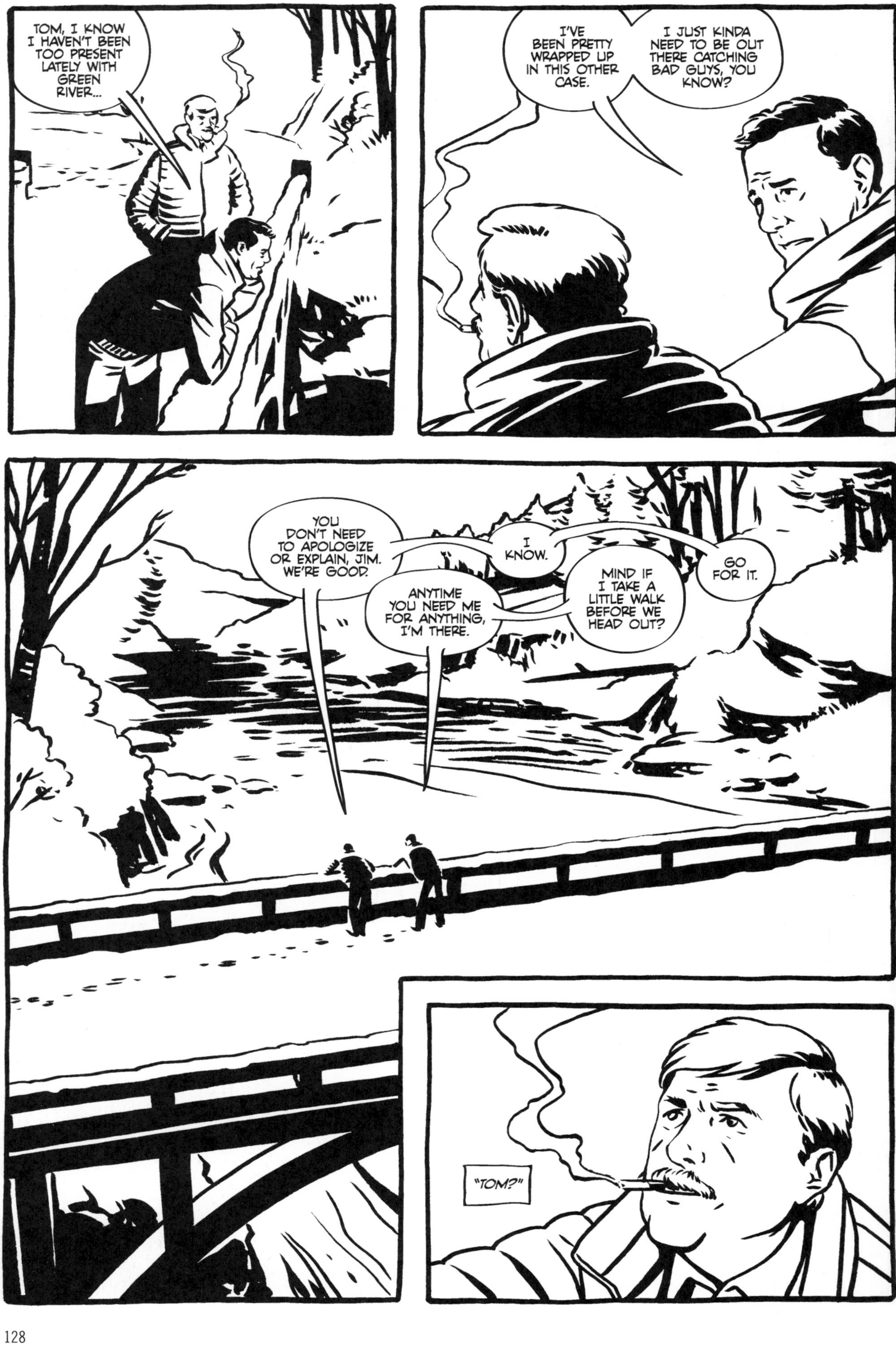
TOM, I KNOW I HAVEN'T BEEN TOO PRESENT LATELY WITH GREEN RIVER...
I'VE BEEN PRETTY WRAPPED UP IN THIS OTHER CASE.
I JUST KINDA NEED TO BE OUT THERE CATCHING BAD GUYS, YOU KNOW?
YOU DON'T NEED TO APOLOGIZE OR EXPLAIN, JIM. WE'RE GOOD.
I KNOW.
ANYTIME YOU NEED ME FOR ANYTHING, I'M THERE.
MIND IF I TAKE A LITTLE WALK BEFORE WE HEAD OUT?
GO FOR IT.
"TOM?"

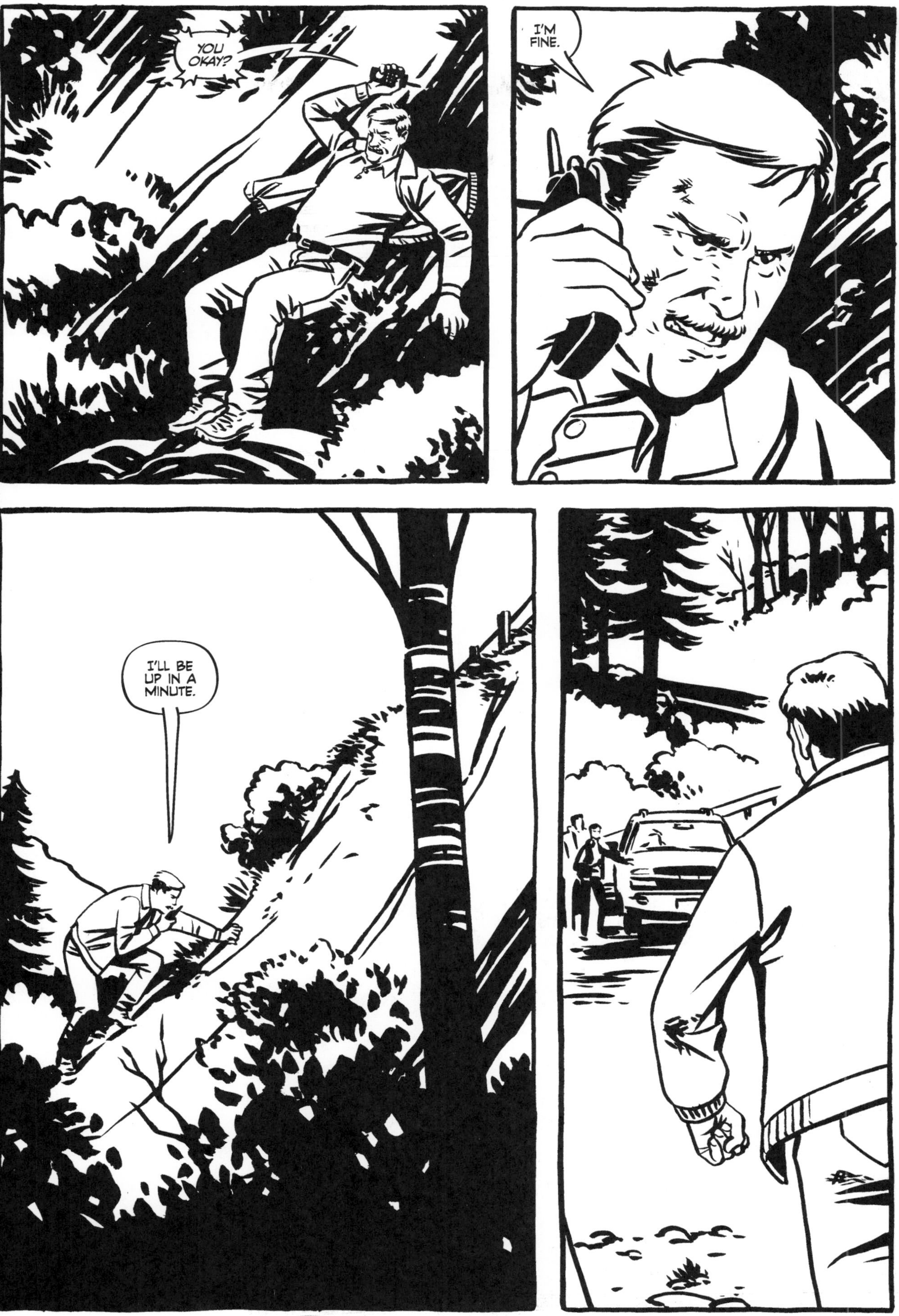
YOU OKAY?
I'M FINE.
I'LL BE UP IN A MINUTE.

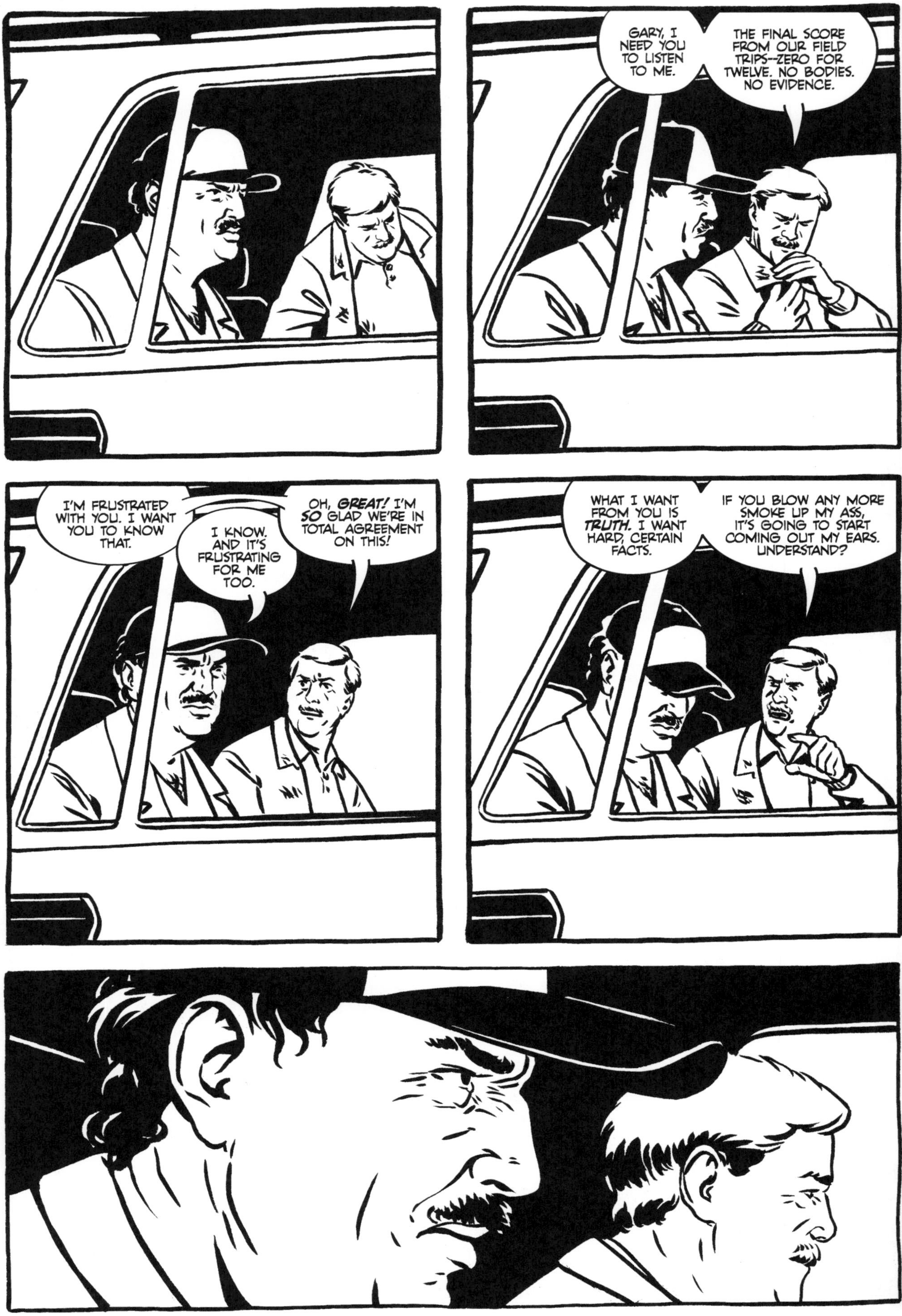
GARY, I NEED YOU TO LISTEN TO ME.
THE FINAL SCORE FROM OUR FIELD TRIPS--ZERO FOR TWELVE. NO BODIES. NO EVIDENCE.
I'M FRUSTRATED WITH YOU. I WANT YOU TO KNOW THAT.
I KNOW. AND IT'S FRUSTRATING FOR ME TOO.
OH, GREAT! I'M SO GLAD WE'RE IN TOTAL AGREEMENT ON THIS!
WHAT I WANT FROM YOU IS TRUTH. I WANT HARD, CERTAIN FACTS.
IF YOU BLOW ANY MORE SMOKE UP MY ASS, IT'S GOING TO START COMING OUT MY EARS. UNDERSTAND?

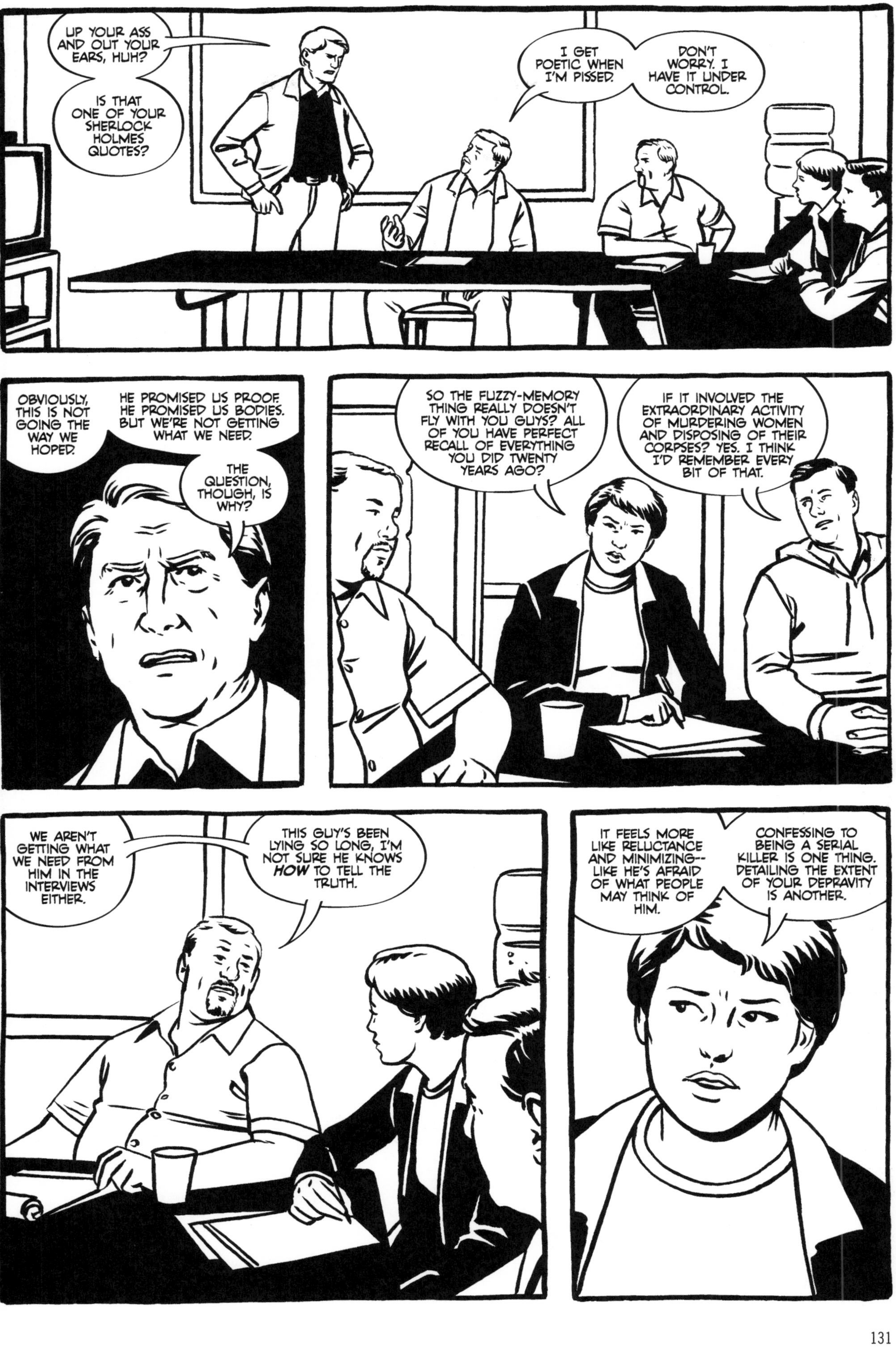
UP YOUR ASS AND OUT YOUR EARS, HUH?
IS THAT ONE OF YOUR SHERLOCK HOLMES QUOTES?
I GET POETIC WHEN I'M PISSED.
DON'T WORRY. I HAVE IT UNDER CONTROL.
OBVIOUSLY, THIS IS NOT GOING THE WAY WE HOPED.
HE PROMISED US PROOF. HE PROMISED US BODIES. BUT WE'RE NOT GETTING WHAT WE NEED.
THE QUESTION, THOUGH, IS WHY?
SO THE FUZZY-MEMORY THING REALLY DOESN'T FLY WITH YOU GUYS? ALL OF YOU HAVE PERFECT RECALL OF EVERYTHING YOU DID TWENTY YEARS AGO?
IF IT INVOLVED THE EXTRAORDINARY ACTIVITY OF MURDERING WOMEN AND DISPOSING OF THEIR CORPSES? YES. I THINK I'D REMEMBER EVERY BIT OF THAT.
WE AREN'T GETTING WHAT WE NEED FROM HIM IN THE INTERVIEWS EITHER.
THIS GUY'S BEEN LYING SO LONG, I'M NOT SURE HE KNOWS *HOW* TO TELL THE TRUTH.
IT FEELS MORE LIKE RELUCTANCE AND MINIMIZING-- LIKE HE'S AFRAID OF WHAT PEOPLE MAY THINK OF HIM.
CONFESSING TO BEING A SERIAL KILLER IS ONE THING. DETAILING THE EXTENT OF YOUR DEPRAVITY IS ANOTHER.

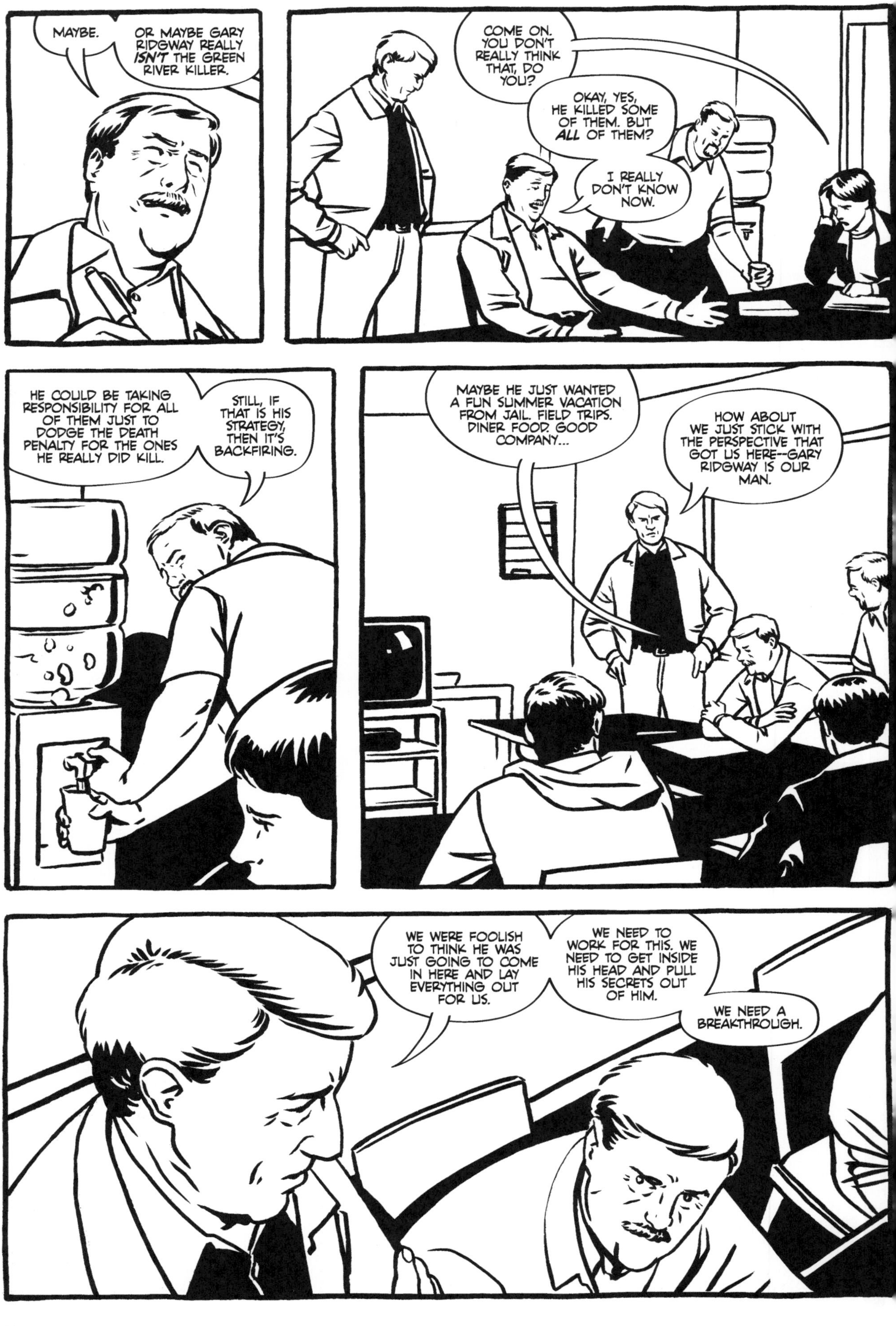
MAYBE.
OR MAYBE GARY RIDGWAY REALLY *ISN'T* THE GREEN RIVER KILLER.
COME ON. YOU DON'T REALLY THINK THAT, DO YOU?
OKAY, YES, HE KILLED SOME OF THEM. BUT *ALL* OF THEM?
I REALLY DON'T KNOW NOW.
HE COULD BE TAKING RESPONSIBILITY FOR ALL OF THEM JUST TO DODGE THE DEATH PENALTY FOR THE ONES HE REALLY DID KILL.
STILL, IF THAT IS HIS STRATEGY, THEN IT'S BACKFIRING.
MAYBE HE JUST WANTED A FUN SUMMER VACATION FROM JAIL. FIELD TRIPS. DINER FOOD. GOOD COMPANY...
HOW ABOUT WE JUST STICK WITH THE PERSPECTIVE THAT GOT US HERE--GARY RIDGWAY IS OUR MAN.
WE WERE FOOLISH TO THINK HE WAS JUST GOING TO COME IN HERE AND LAY EVERYTHING OUT FOR US.
WE NEED TO WORK FOR THIS. WE NEED TO GET INSIDE HIS HEAD AND PULL HIS SECRETS OUT OF HIM.
WE NEED A BREAKTHROUGH.

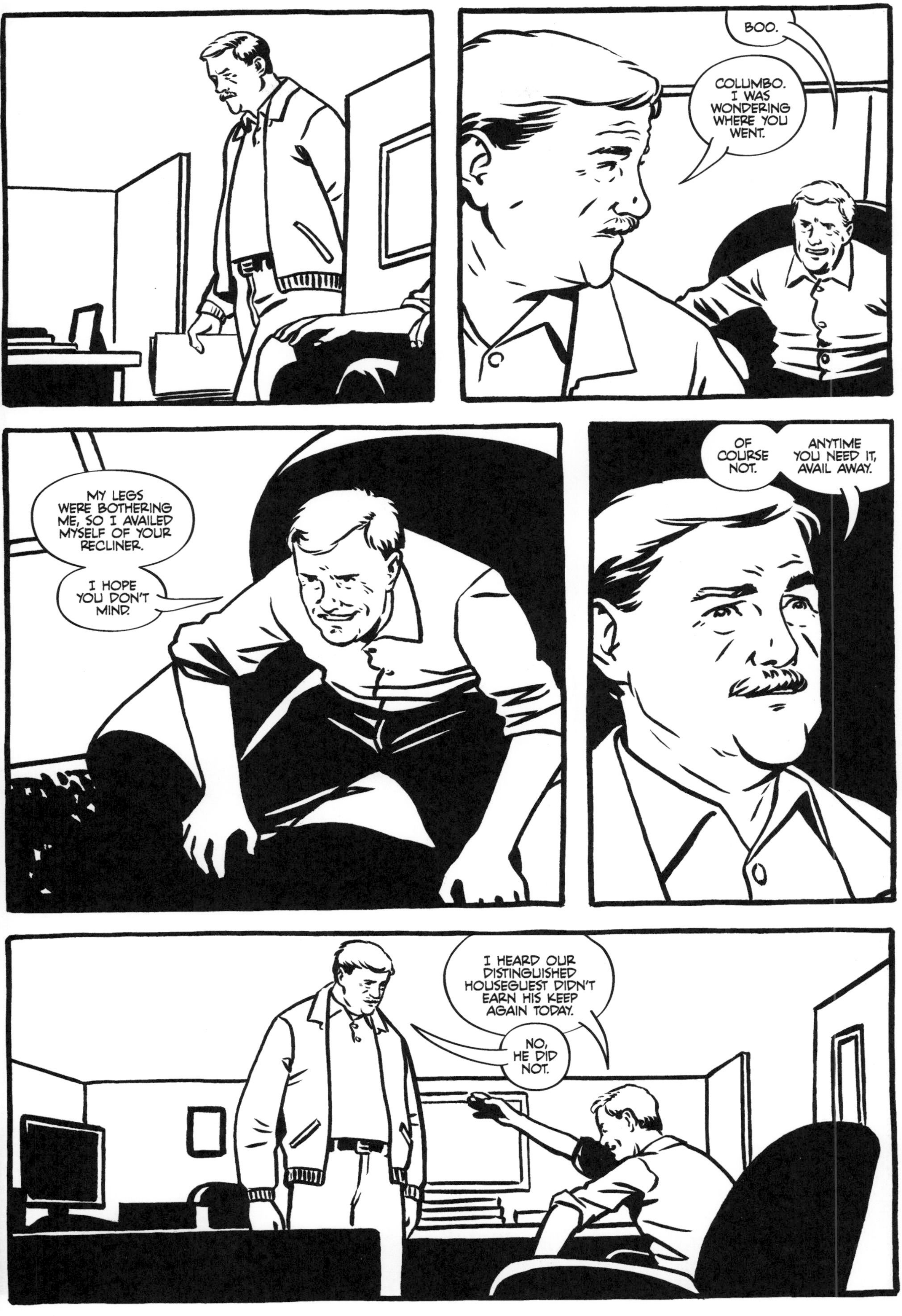
BOO.
COLUMBO. I WAS WONDERING WHERE YOU WENT.
MY LEGS WERE BOTHERING ME, SO I AVAILED MYSELF OF YOUR RECLINER.
I HOPE YOU DON'T MIND.
OF COURSE NOT.
ANYTIME YOU NEED IT, AVAIL AWAY.
I HEARD OUR DISTINGUISHED HOUSEGUEST DIDN'T EARN HIS KEEP AGAIN TODAY.
NO, HE DID NOT.

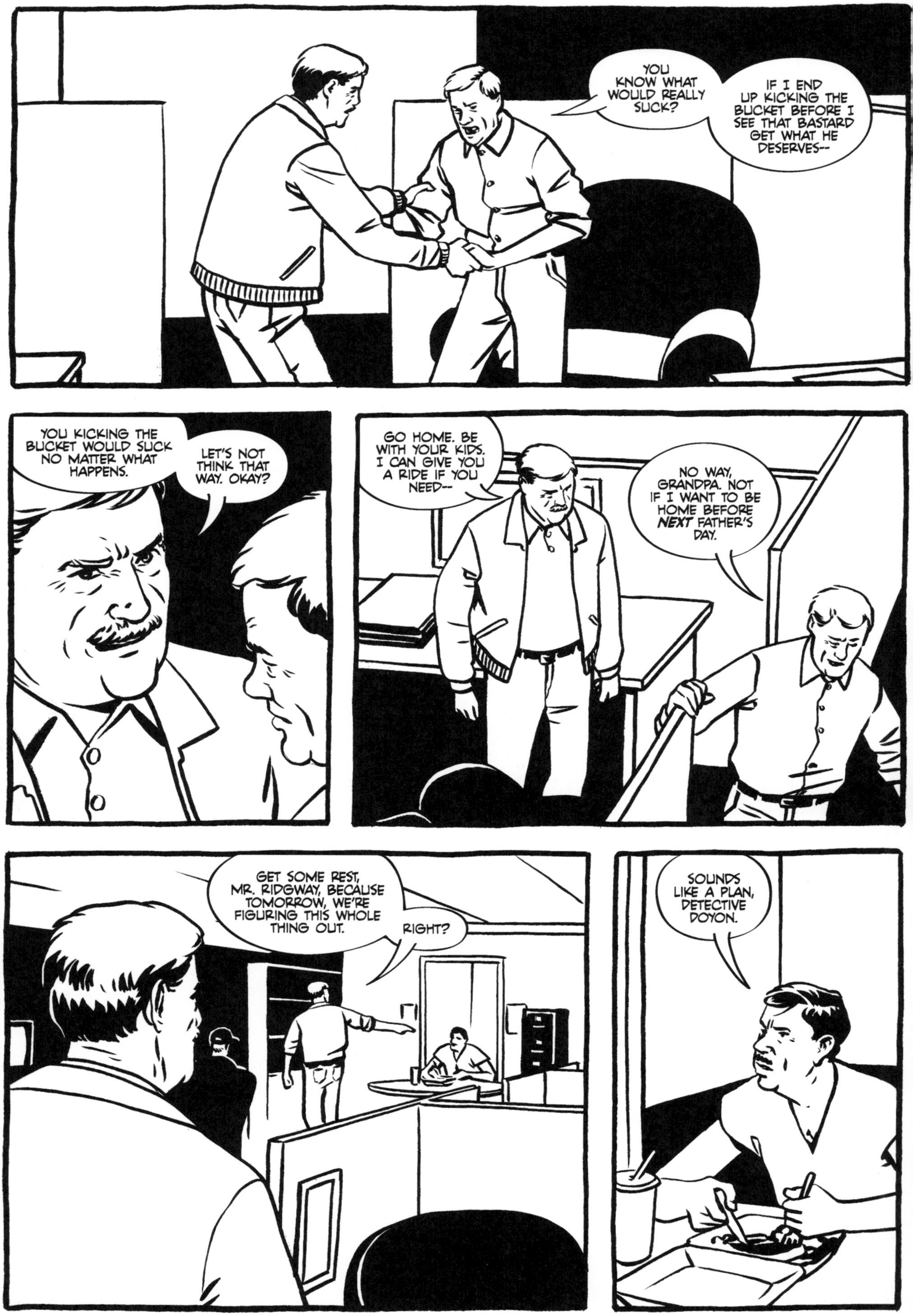
YOU KNOW WHAT WOULD REALLY SUCK?
IF I END UP KICKING THE BUCKET BEFORE I SEE THAT BASTARD GET WHAT HE DESERVES--
YOU KICKING THE BUCKET WOULD SUCK NO MATTER WHAT HAPPENS.
LET'S NOT THINK THAT WAY. OKAY?
GO HOME. BE WITH YOUR KIDS. I CAN GIVE YOU A RIDE IF YOU NEED--
NO WAY, GRANDPA. NOT IF I WANT TO BE HOME BEFORE *NEXT* FATHER'S DAY.
GET SOME REST, MR. RIDGWAY, BECAUSE TOMORROW, WE'RE FIGURING THIS WHOLE THING OUT.
RIGHT?
SOUNDS LIKE A PLAN, DETECTIVE DOYON.

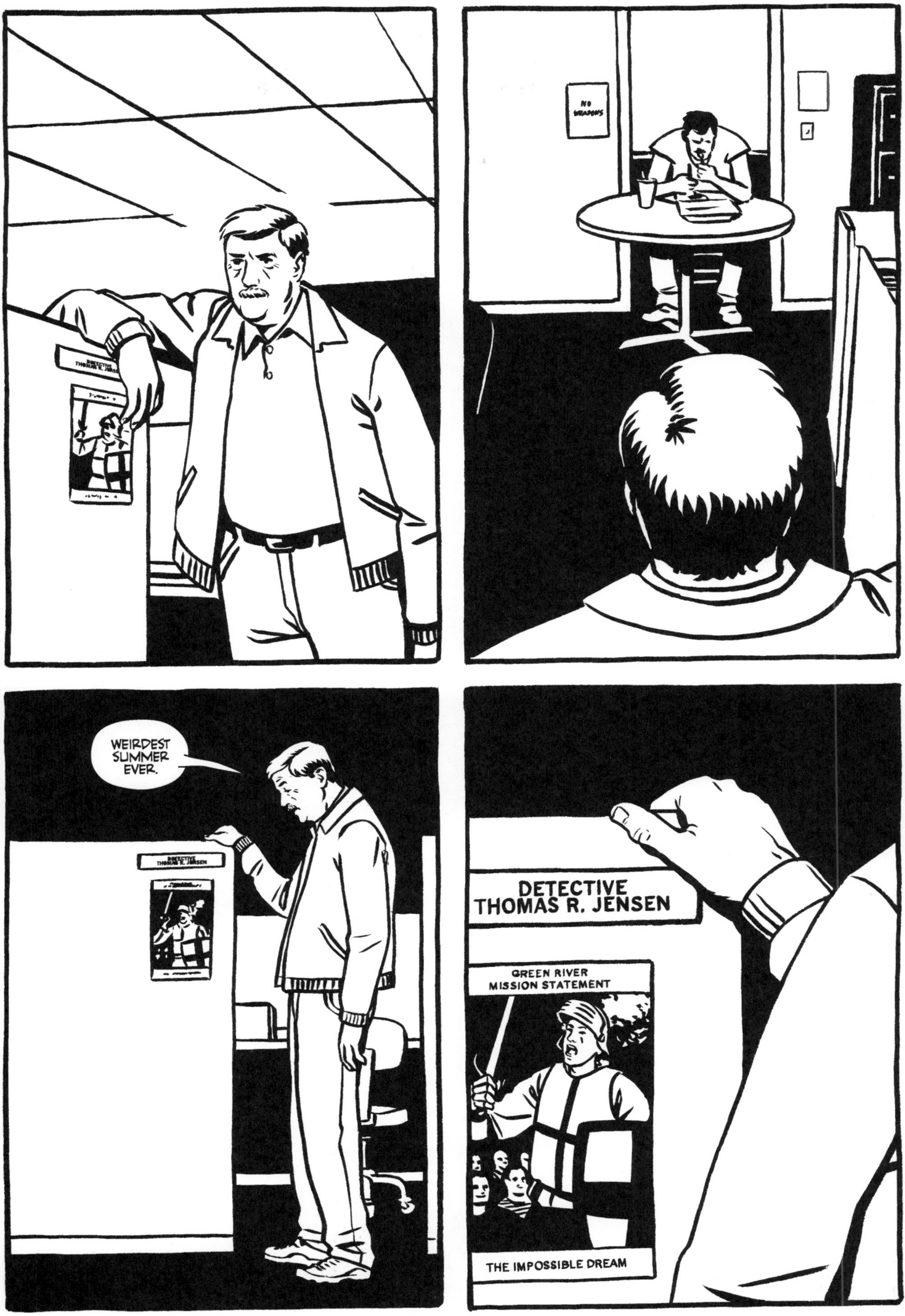
NO WEAPONS
WEIRDEST SUMMER EVER.
DETECTIVE THOMAS R. JENSEN
GREEN RIVER MISSION STATEMENT
THE IMPOSSIBLE DREAM

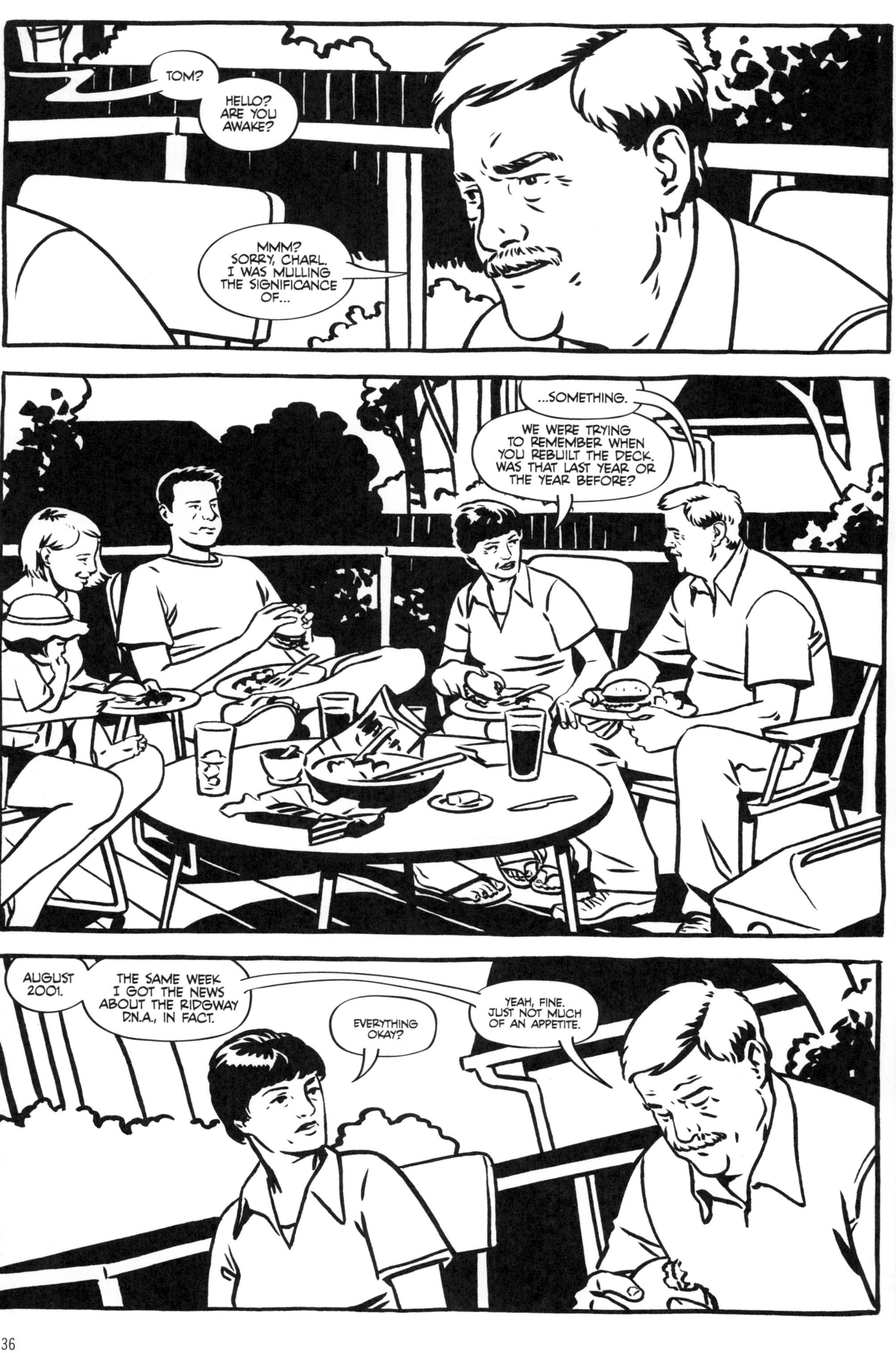
TOM?
HELLO? ARE YOU AWAKE?
MMM? SORRY, CHARL. I WAS MULLING THE SIGNIFICANCE OF...
...SOMETHING.
WE WERE TRYING TO REMEMBER WHEN YOU REBUILT THE DECK. WAS THAT LAST YEAR OR THE YEAR BEFORE?
AUGUST 2001.
THE SAME WEEK I GOT THE NEWS ABOUT THE RIDGWAY D.N.A., IN FACT.
EVERYTHING OKAY?
YEAH, FINE. JUST NOT MUCH OF AN APPETITE.

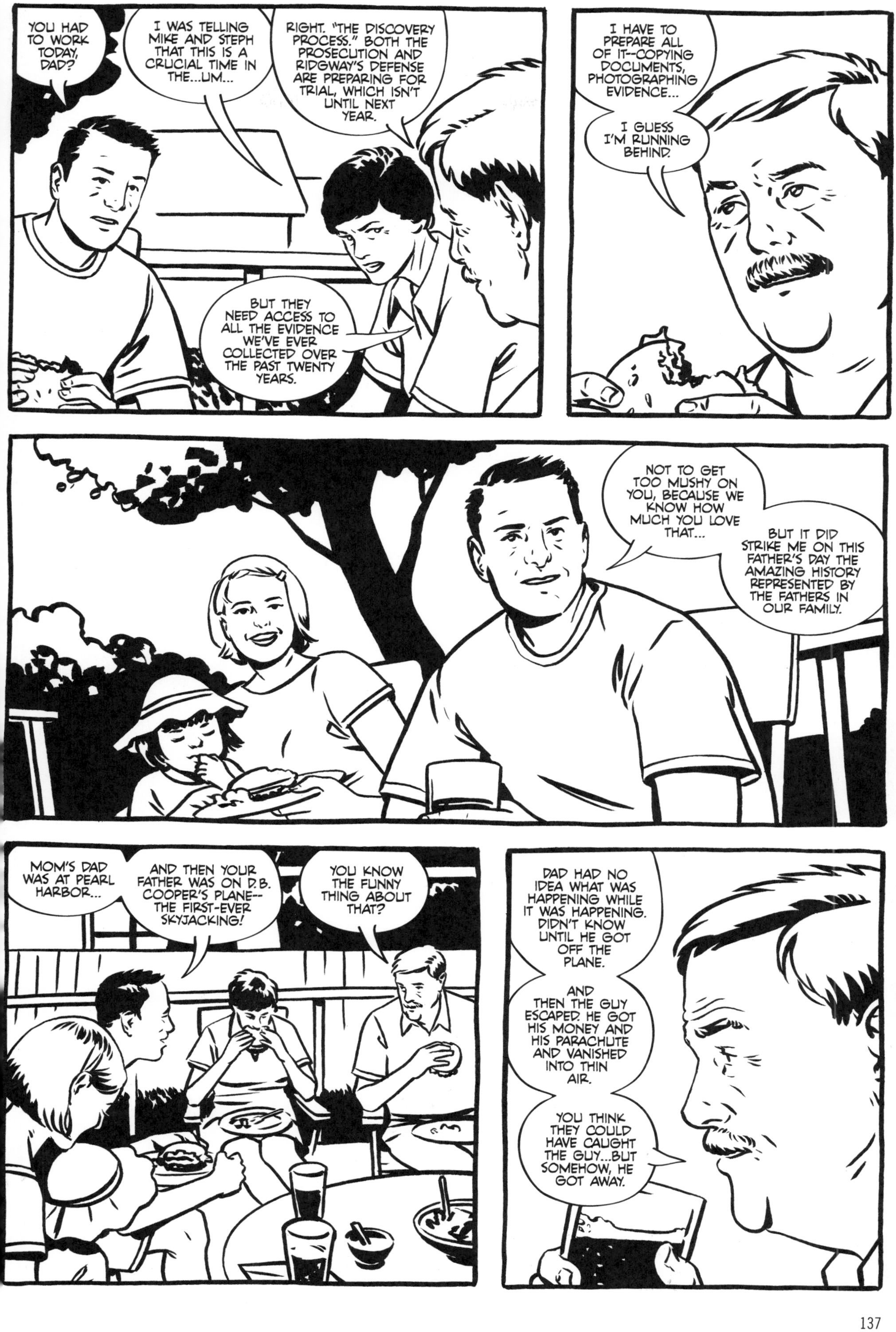

YOU HAD TO WORK TODAY, DAD?
I WAS TELLING MIKE AND STEPH THAT THIS IS A CRUCIAL TIME IN THE...UM...
RIGHT. "THE DISCOVERY PROCESS." BOTH THE PROSECUTION AND RIDGWAY'S DEFENSE ARE PREPARING FOR TRIAL, WHICH ISN'T UNTIL NEXT YEAR.
BUT THEY NEED ACCESS TO ALL THE EVIDENCE WE'VE EVER COLLECTED OVER THE PAST TWENTY YEARS.
I HAVE TO PREPARE ALL OF IT--COPYING DOCUMENTS, PHOTOGRAPHING EVIDENCE...
I GUESS I'M RUNNING BEHIND.
NOT TO GET TOO MUSHY ON YOU, BECAUSE WE KNOW HOW MUCH YOU LOVE THAT...
BUT IT DID STRIKE ME ON THIS FATHER'S DAY THE AMAZING HISTORY REPRESENTED BY THE FATHERS IN OUR FAMILY.
MOM'S DAD WAS AT PEARL HARBOR...
AND THEN YOUR FATHER WAS ON D.B. COOPER'S PLANE-- THE FIRST-EVER SKYJACKING!
YOU KNOW THE FUNNY THING ABOUT THAT?
DAD HAD NO IDEA WHAT WAS HAPPENING WHILE IT WAS HAPPENING. DIDN'T KNOW UNTIL HE GOT OFF THE PLANE.
AND THEN THE GUY ESCAPED. HE GOT HIS MONEY AND HIS PARACHUTE AND VANISHED INTO THIN AIR.
YOU THINK THEY COULD HAVE CAUGHT THE GUY...BUT SOMEHOW, HE GOT AWAY.

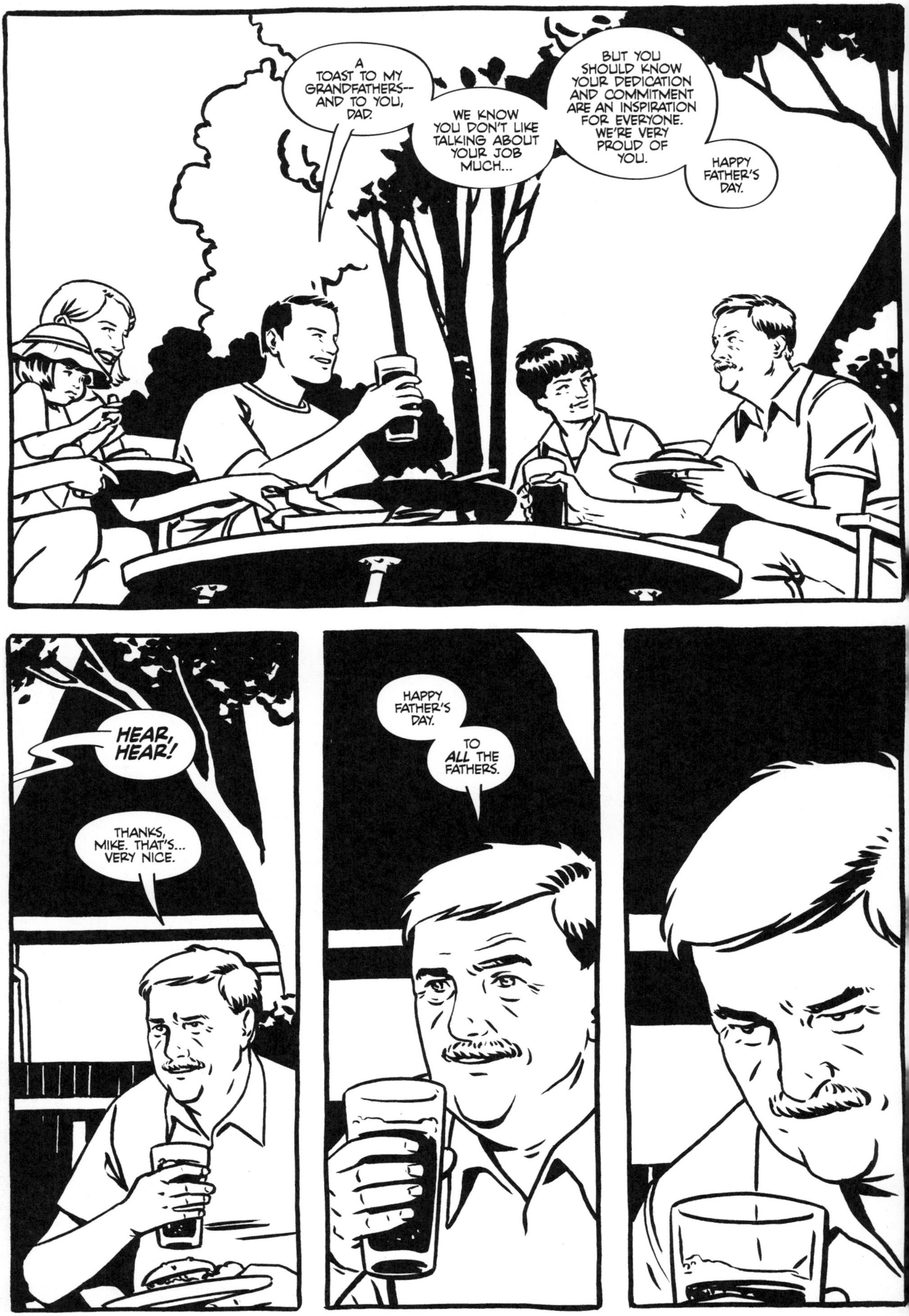
A TOAST TO MY GRANDFATHERS-- AND TO YOU, DAD.
WE KNOW YOU DON'T LIKE TALKING ABOUT YOUR JOB MUCH...
BUT YOU SHOULD KNOW YOUR DEDICATION AND COMMITMENT ARE AN INSPIRATION FOR EVERYONE. WE'RE VERY PROUD OF YOU.
HAPPY FATHER'S DAY.
HEAR, HEAR!
THANKS, MIKE. THAT'S... VERY NICE.
HAPPY FATHER'S DAY.
TO ALL THE FATHERS.

DAY FOUR: BURDEN OF PROOF

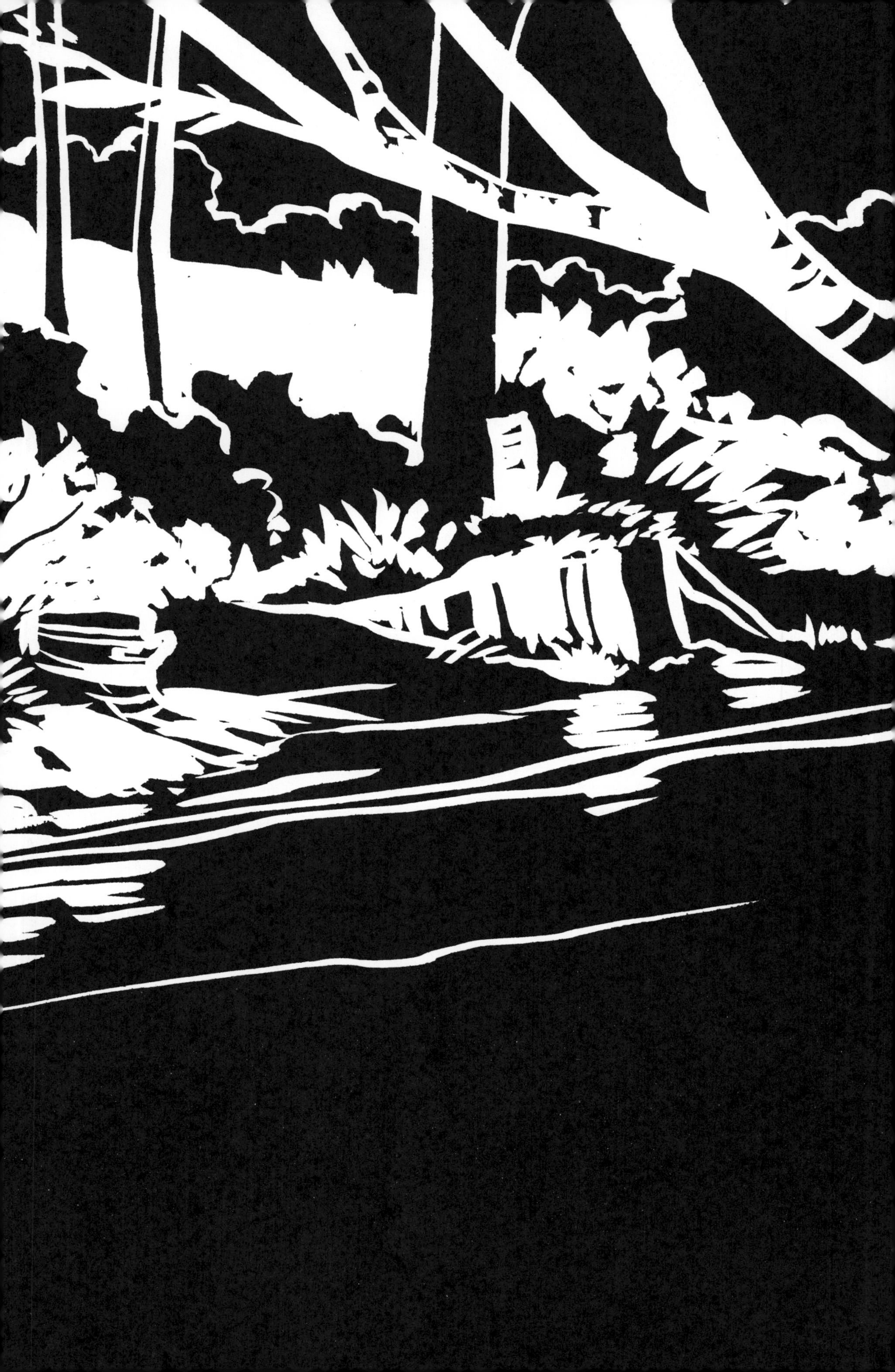

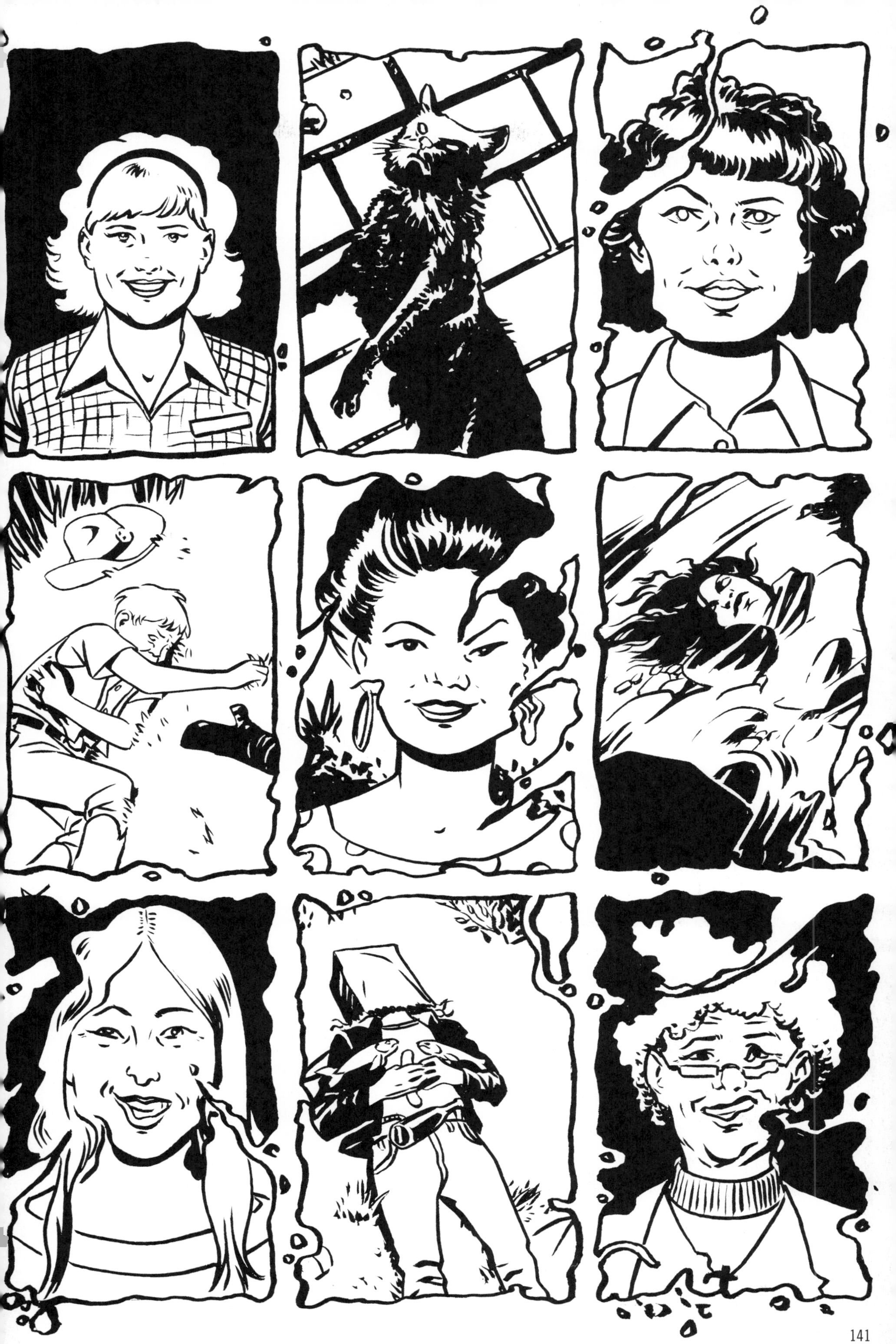

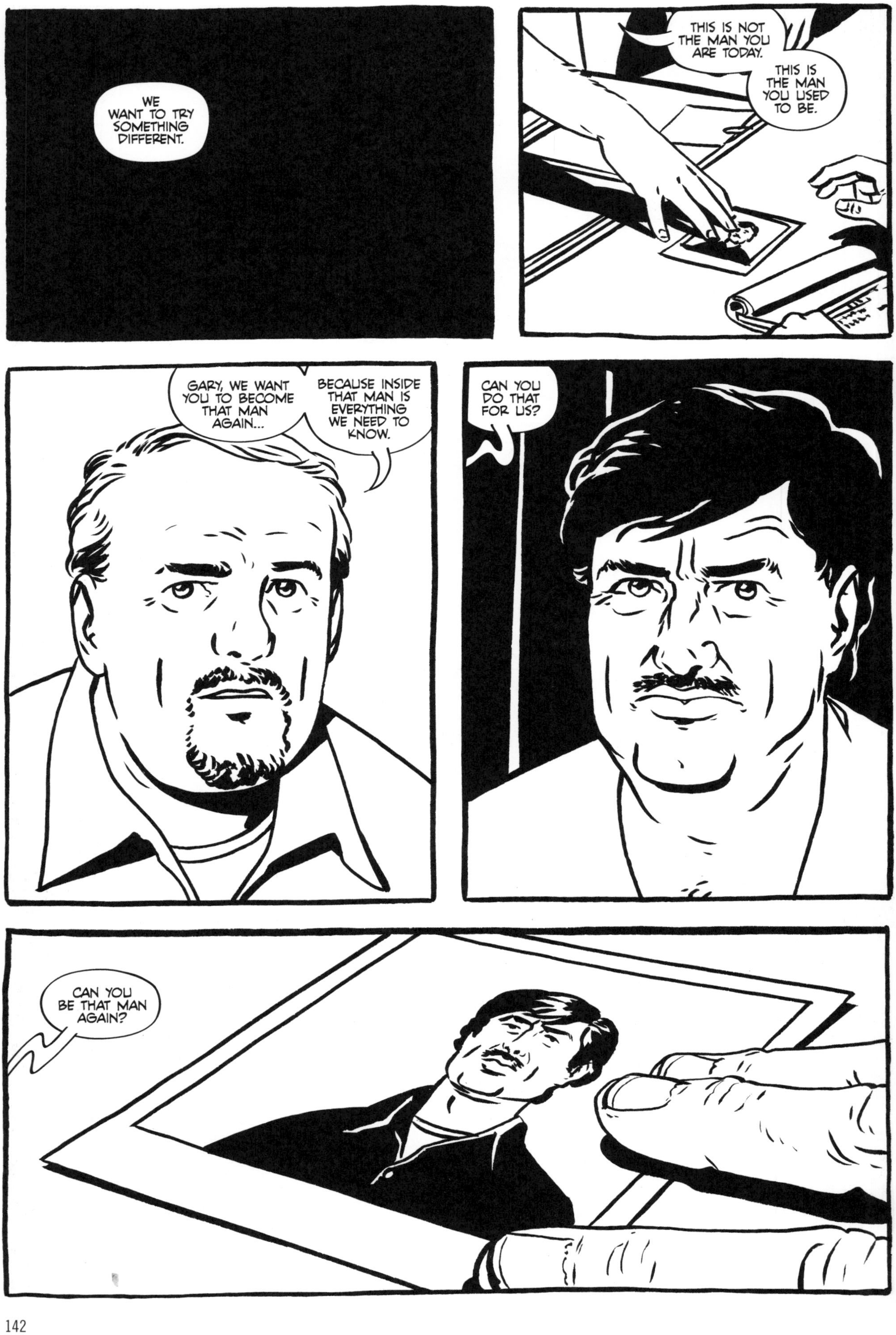
WE WANT TO TRY SOMETHING DIFFERENT.
THIS IS NOT THE MAN YOU ARE TODAY.
THIS IS THE MAN YOU USED TO BE.
GARY, WE WANT YOU TO BECOME THAT MAN AGAIN...
BECAUSE INSIDE THAT MAN IS EVERYTHING WE NEED TO KNOW.
CAN YOU DO THAT FOR US?
CAN YOU BE THAT MAN AGAIN?

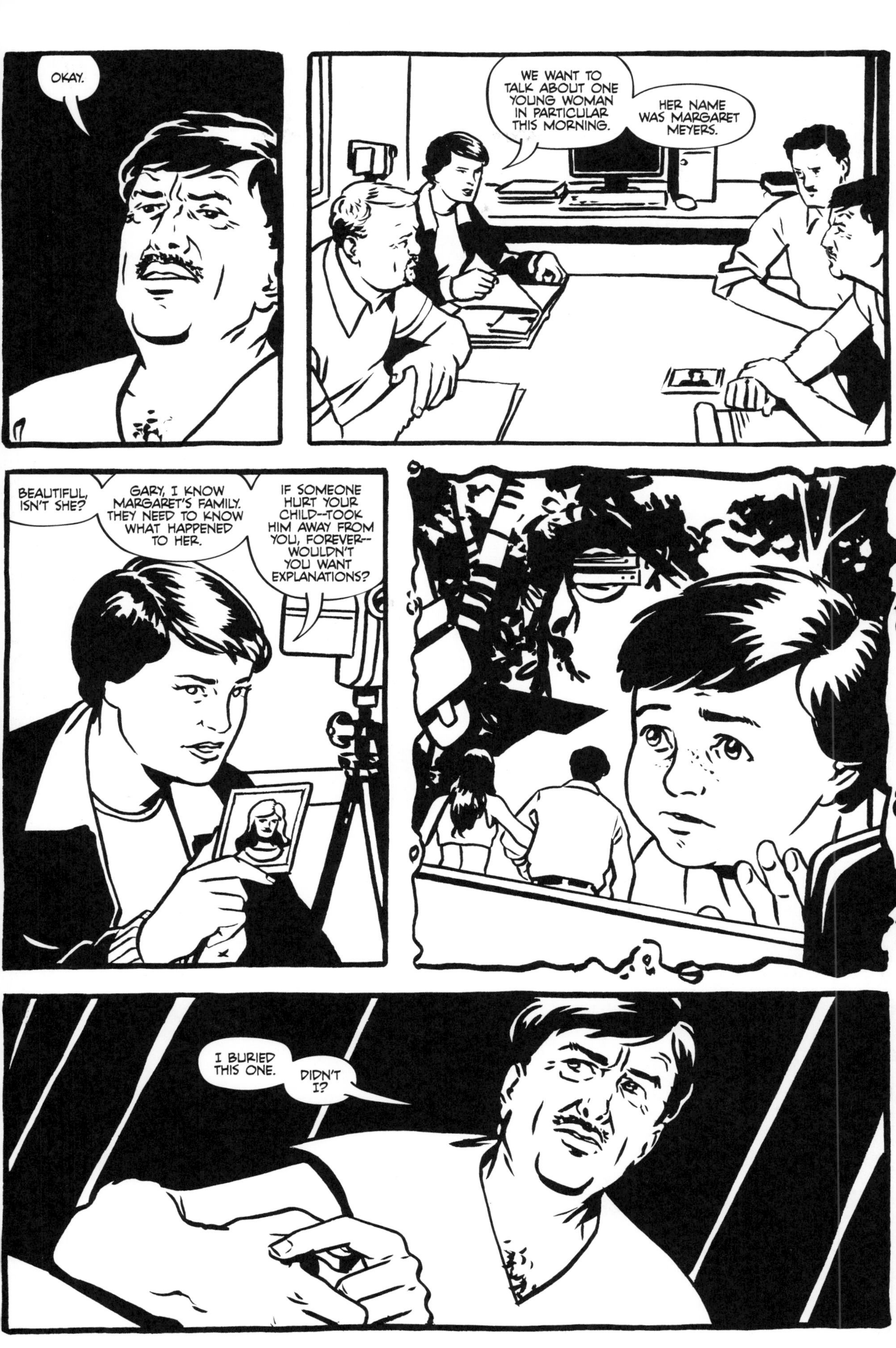
OKAY.
WE WANT TO TALK ABOUT ONE YOUNG WOMAN IN PARTICULAR THIS MORNING.
HER NAME WAS MARGARET MEYERS.
BEAUTIFUL, ISN'T SHE?
GARY, I KNOW MARGARET'S FAMILY. THEY NEED TO KNOW WHAT HAPPENED TO HER.
IF SOMEONE HURT YOUR CHILD--TOOK HIM AWAY FROM YOU, FOREVER-- WOULDN'T YOU WANT EXPLANATIONS?
I BURIED THIS ONE.
DIDN'T I?

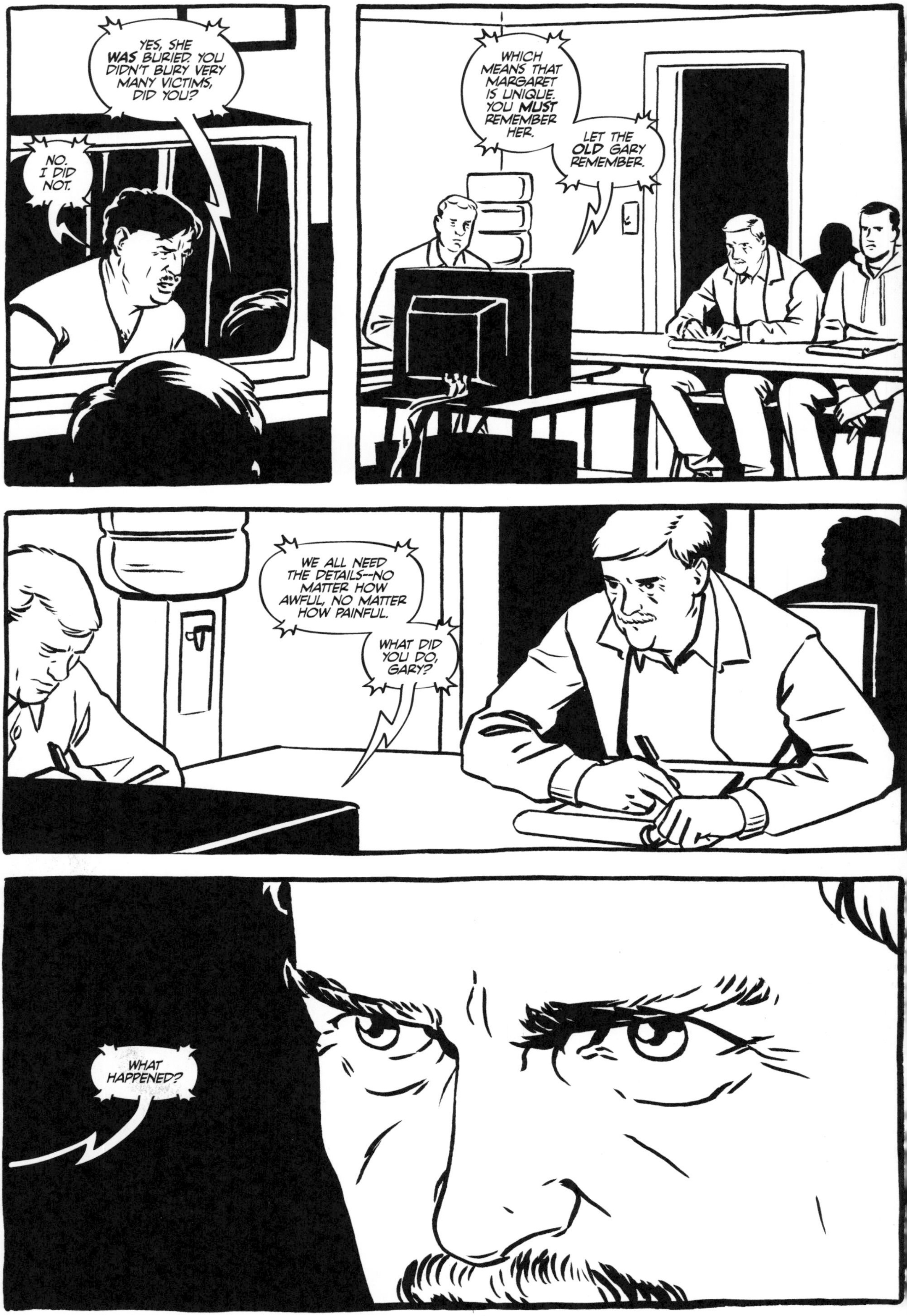
YES, SHE WAS BURIED. YOU DIDN'T BURY VERY MANY VICTIMS, DID YOU?
NO. I DID NOT.
WHICH MEANS THAT MARGARET IS UNIQUE. YOU MUST REMEMBER HER.
LET THE OLD GARY REMEMBER.
WE ALL NEED THE DETAILS--NO MATTER HOW AWFUL, NO MATTER HOW PAINFUL.
WHAT DID YOU DO, GARY?
WHAT HAPPENED?

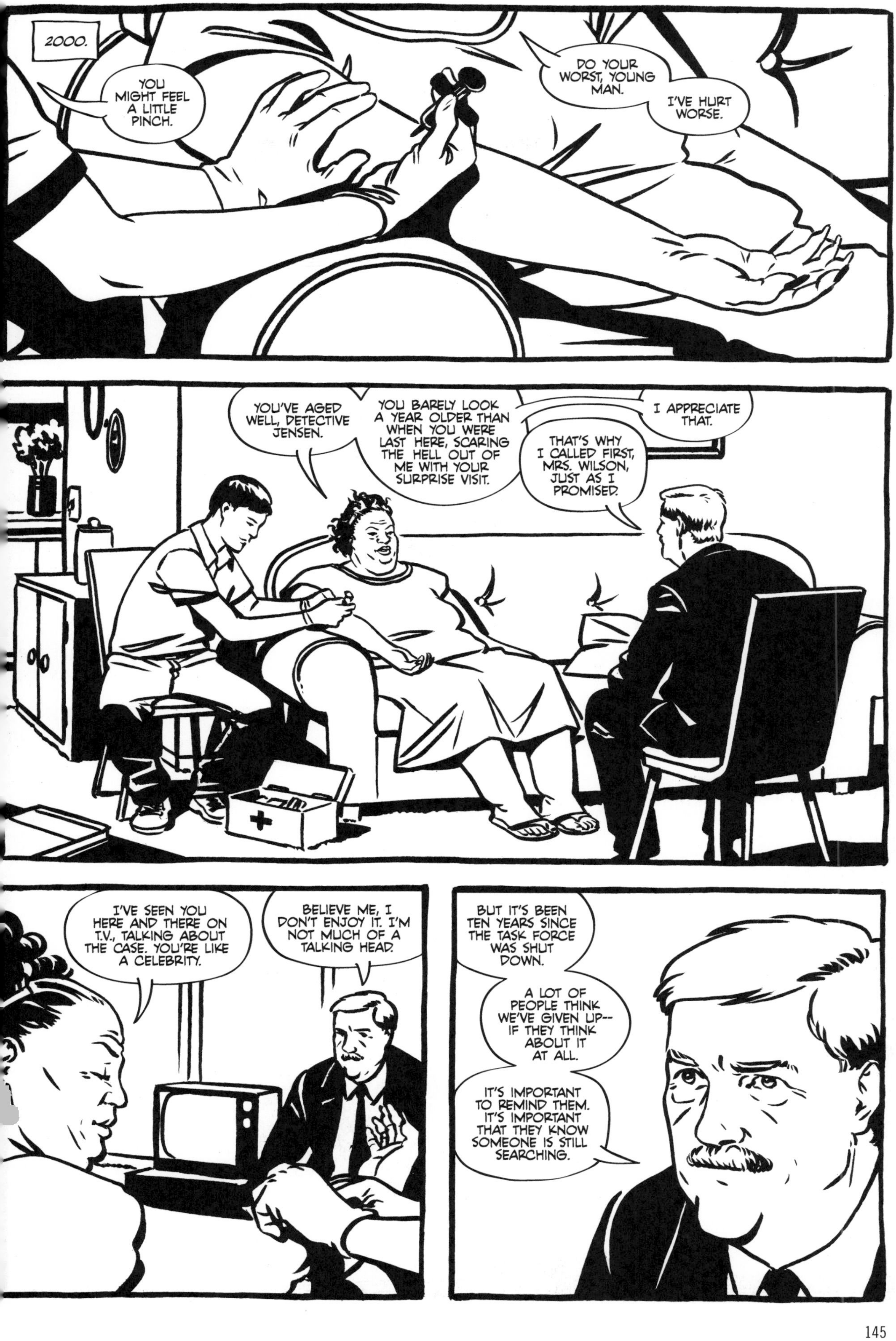
2000.
YOU MIGHT FEEL A LITTLE PINCH.
DO YOUR WORST, YOUNG MAN.
I'VE HURT WORSE.
YOU'VE AGED WELL, DETECTIVE JENSEN.
YOU BARELY LOOK A YEAR OLDER THAN WHEN YOU WERE LAST HERE, SCARING THE HELL OUT OF ME WITH YOUR SURPRISE VISIT.
I APPRECIATE THAT.
THAT'S WHY I CALLED FIRST, MRS. WILSON, JUST AS I PROMISED.
I'VE SEEN YOU HERE AND THERE ON T.V., TALKING ABOUT THE CASE. YOU'RE LIKE A CELEBRITY.
BELIEVE ME, I DON'T ENJOY IT. I'M NOT MUCH OF A TALKING HEAD.
BUT IT'S BEEN TEN YEARS SINCE THE TASK FORCE WAS SHUT DOWN.
A LOT OF PEOPLE THINK WE'VE GIVEN UP-- IF THEY THINK ABOUT IT AT ALL.
IT'S IMPORTANT TO REMIND THEM. IT'S IMPORTANT THAT THEY KNOW SOMEONE IS STILL SEARCHING.

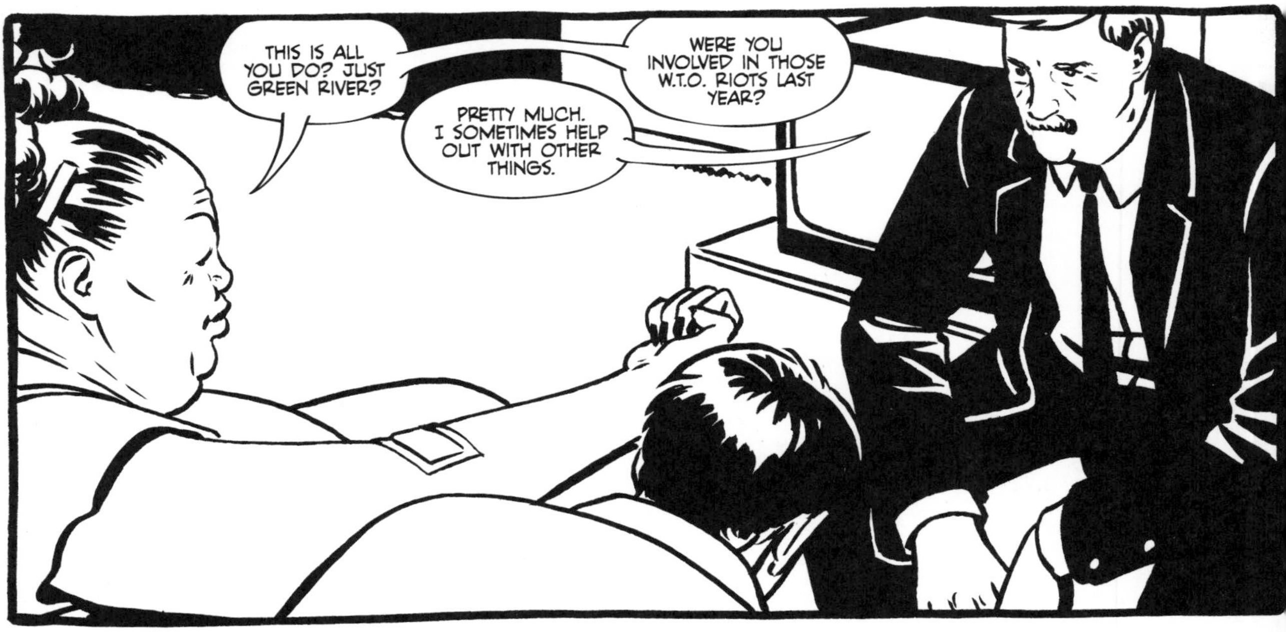
THIS IS ALL YOU DO? JUST GREEN RIVER?
PRETTY MUCH. I SOMETIMES HELP OUT WITH OTHER THINGS.
WERE YOU INVOLVED IN THOSE W.T.O. RIOTS LAST YEAR?

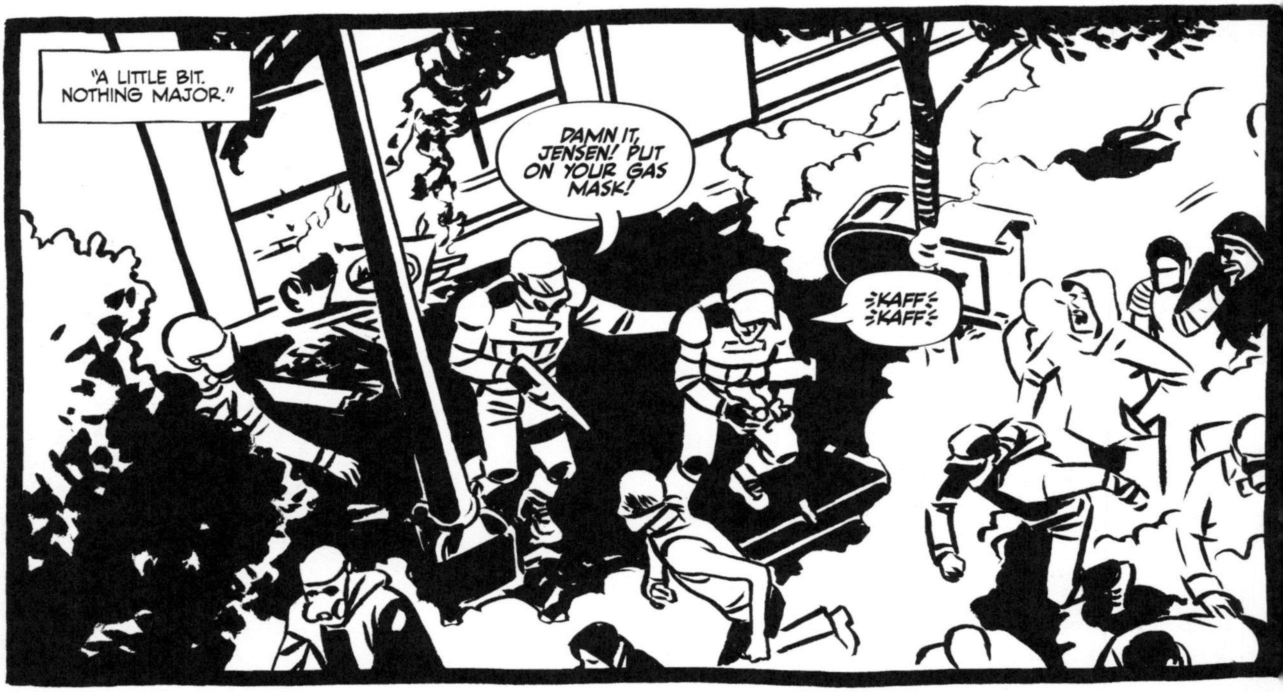
"A LITTLE BIT. NOTHING MAJOR."
DAMN IT, JENSEN! PUT ON YOUR GAS MASK!
KAFF KAFF

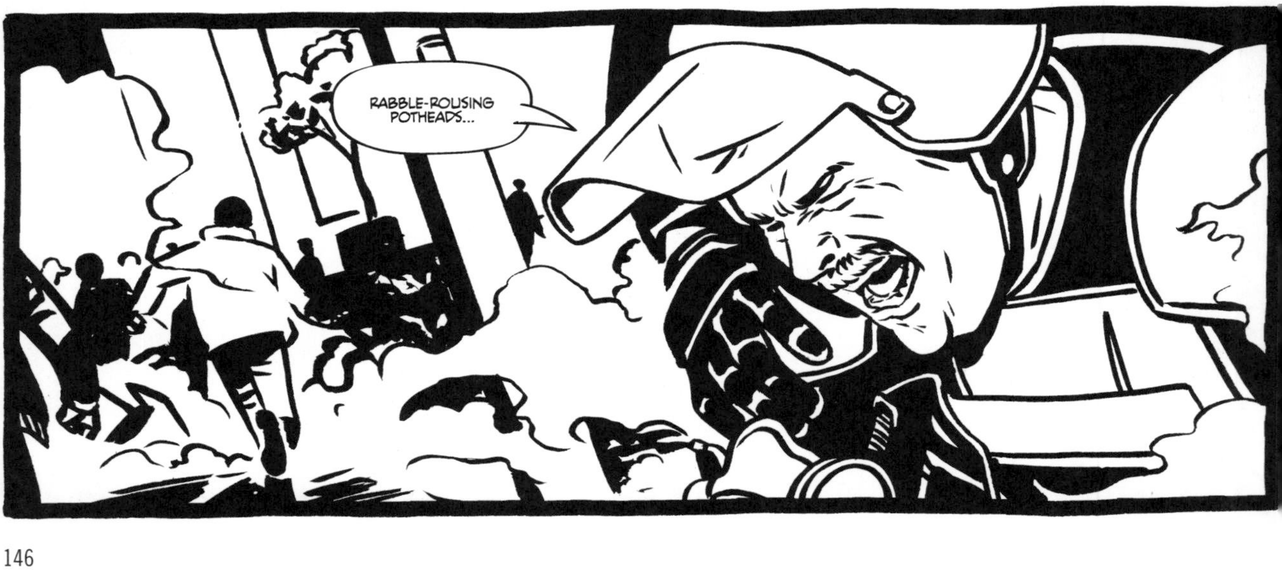
RABBLE-ROUSING POTHEADS...

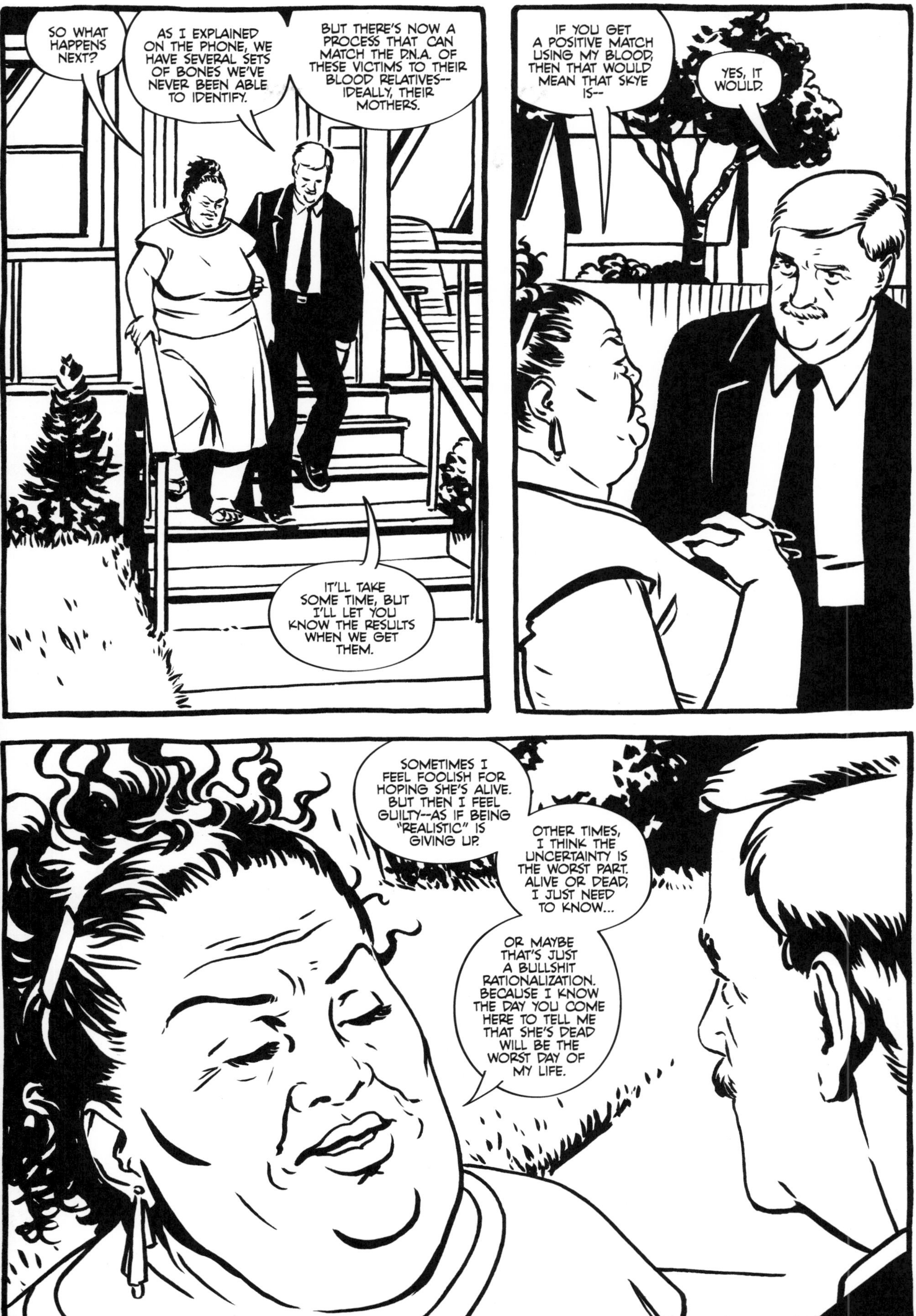
SO WHAT HAPPENS NEXT?
AS I EXPLAINED ON THE PHONE, WE HAVE SEVERAL SETS OF BONES WE'VE NEVER BEEN ABLE TO IDENTIFY.
BUT THERE'S NOW A PROCESS THAT CAN MATCH THE D.N.A. OF THESE VICTIMS TO THEIR BLOOD RELATIVES--IDEALLY, THEIR MOTHERS.
IT'LL TAKE SOME TIME, BUT I'LL LET YOU KNOW THE RESULTS WHEN WE GET THEM.
IF YOU GET A POSITIVE MATCH USING MY BLOOD, THEN THAT WOULD MEAN THAT SKYE IS--
YES, IT WOULD.
SOMETIMES I FEEL FOOLISH FOR HOPING SHE'S ALIVE. BUT THEN I FEEL GUILTY--AS IF BEING "REALISTIC" IS GIVING UP.
OTHER TIMES, I THINK THE UNCERTAINTY IS THE WORST PART. ALIVE OR DEAD, I JUST NEED TO KNOW...
OR MAYBE THAT'S JUST A BULLSHIT RATIONALIZATION. BECAUSE I KNOW THE DAY YOU COME HERE TO TELL ME THAT SHE'S DEAD WILL BE THE WORST DAY OF MY LIFE.

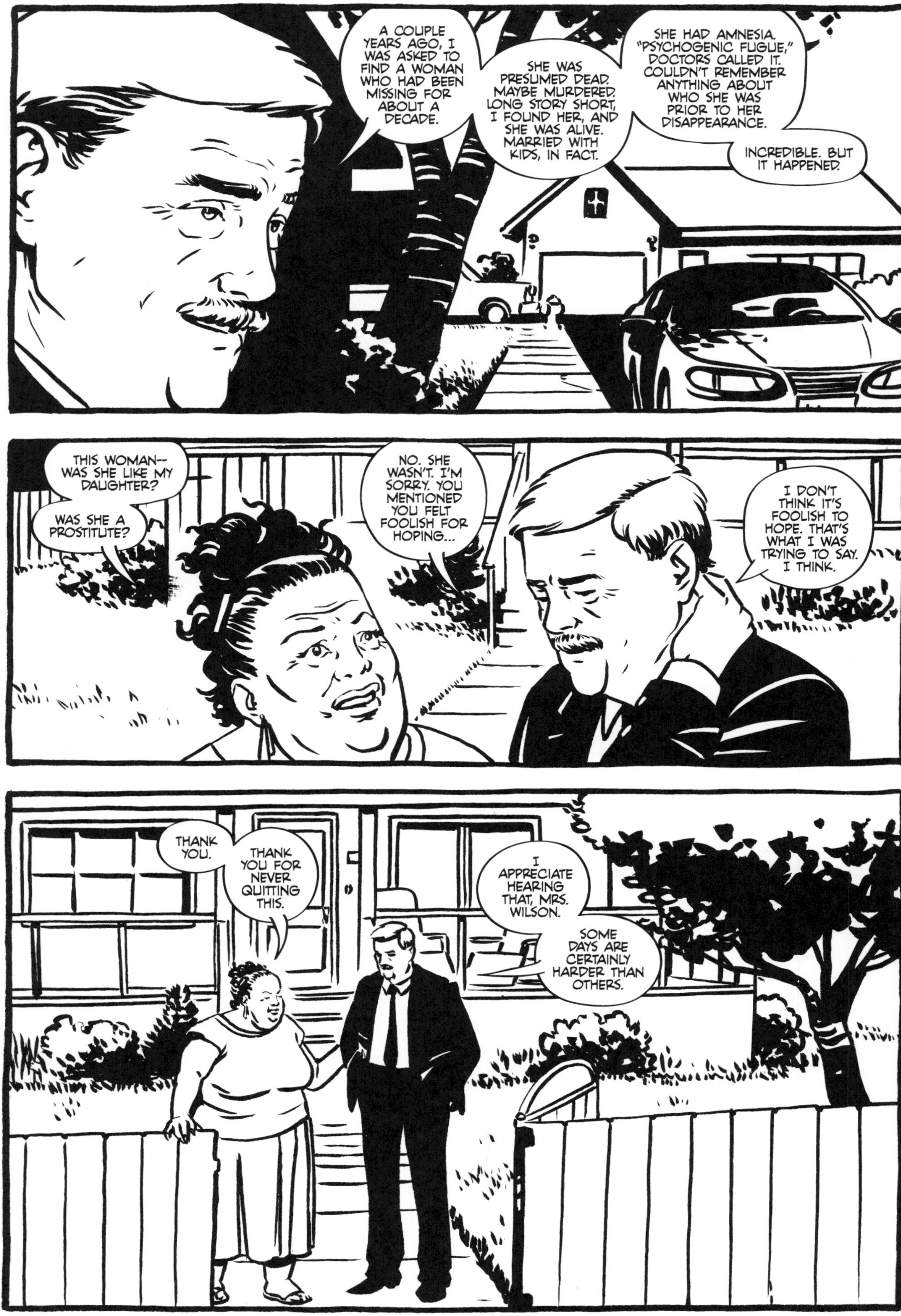

A COUPLE YEARS AGO, I WAS ASKED TO FIND A WOMAN WHO HAD BEEN MISSING FOR ABOUT A DECADE.
SHE WAS PRESUMED DEAD. MAYBE MURDERED. LONG STORY SHORT, I FOUND HER, AND SHE WAS ALIVE. MARRIED WITH KIDS, IN FACT.
SHE HAD AMNESIA. "PSYCHOGENIC FUGUE," DOCTORS CALLED IT. COULDN'T REMEMBER ANYTHING ABOUT WHO SHE WAS PRIOR TO HER DISAPPEARANCE.
INCREDIBLE. BUT IT HAPPENED.
THIS WOMAN-- WAS SHE LIKE MY DAUGHTER?
WAS SHE A PROSTITUTE?
NO. SHE WASN'T. I'M SORRY. YOU MENTIONED YOU FELT FOOLISH FOR HOPING...
I DON'T THINK IT'S FOOLISH TO HOPE. THAT'S WHAT I WAS TRYING TO SAY. I THINK.
THANK YOU.
THANK YOU FOR NEVER QUITTING THIS.
I APPRECIATE HEARING THAT, MRS. WILSON.
SOME DAYS ARE CERTAINLY HARDER THAN OTHERS.

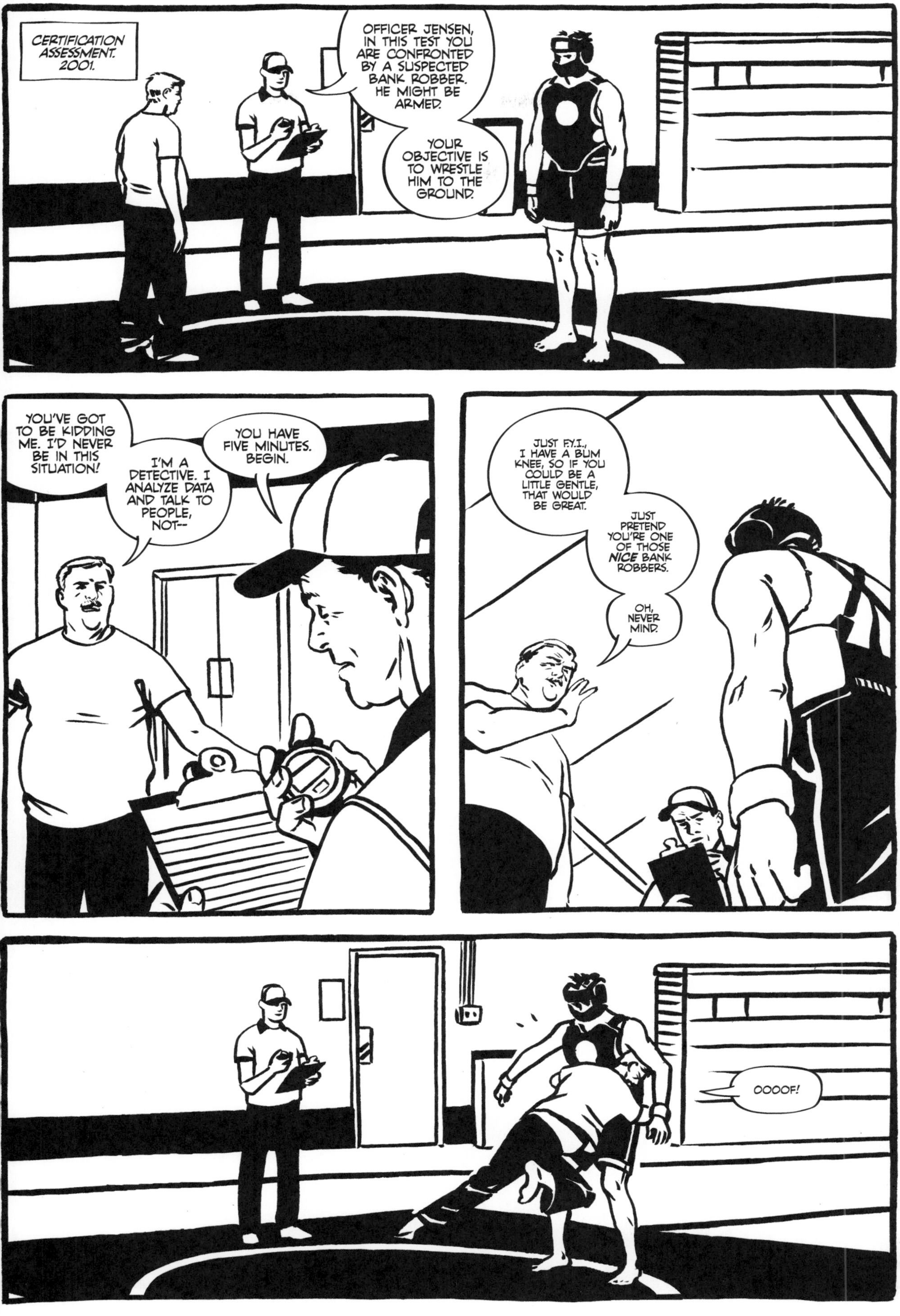
CERTIFICATION ASSESSMENT. 2001.
OFFICER JENSEN, IN THIS TEST YOU ARE CONFRONTED BY A SUSPECTED BANK ROBBER. HE MIGHT BE ARMED.
YOUR OBJECTIVE IS TO WRESTLE HIM TO THE GROUND.
YOU'VE GOT TO BE KIDDING ME. I'D NEVER BE IN THIS SITUATION!
I'M A DETECTIVE. I ANALYZE DATA AND TALK TO PEOPLE, NOT--
YOU HAVE FIVE MINUTES. BEGIN.
JUST F.Y.I., I HAVE A BUM KNEE, SO IF YOU COULD BE A LITTLE GENTLE, THAT WOULD BE GREAT.
JUST PRETEND YOU'RE ONE OF THOSE NICE BANK ROBBERS.
OH, NEVER MIND.
OOOOF!

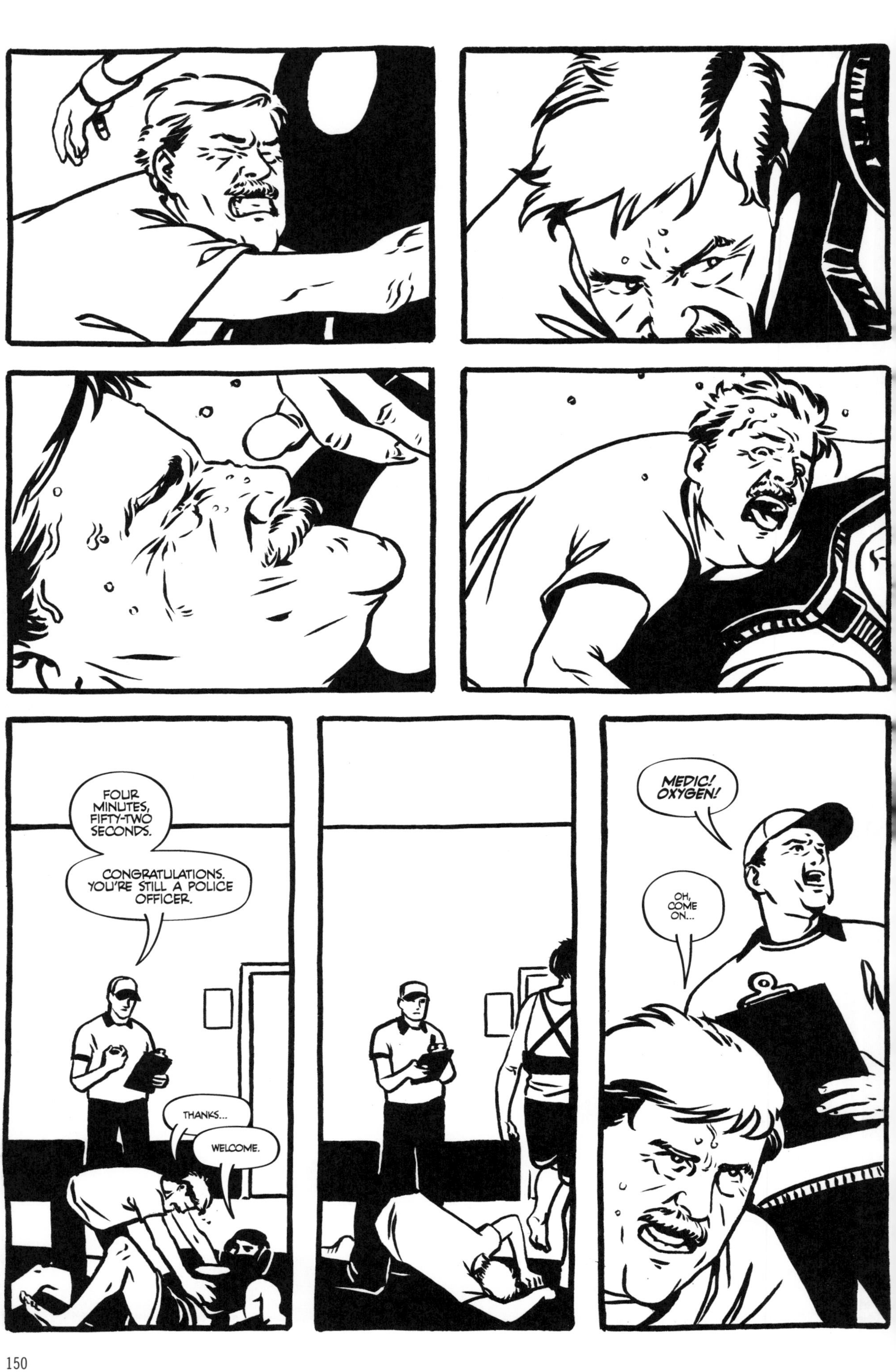
FOUR MINUTES, FIFTY-TWO SECONDS.
CONGRATULATIONS. YOU'RE STILL A POLICE OFFICER.
THANKS...
WELCOME.
MEDIC! OXYGEN!
OH, COME ON...

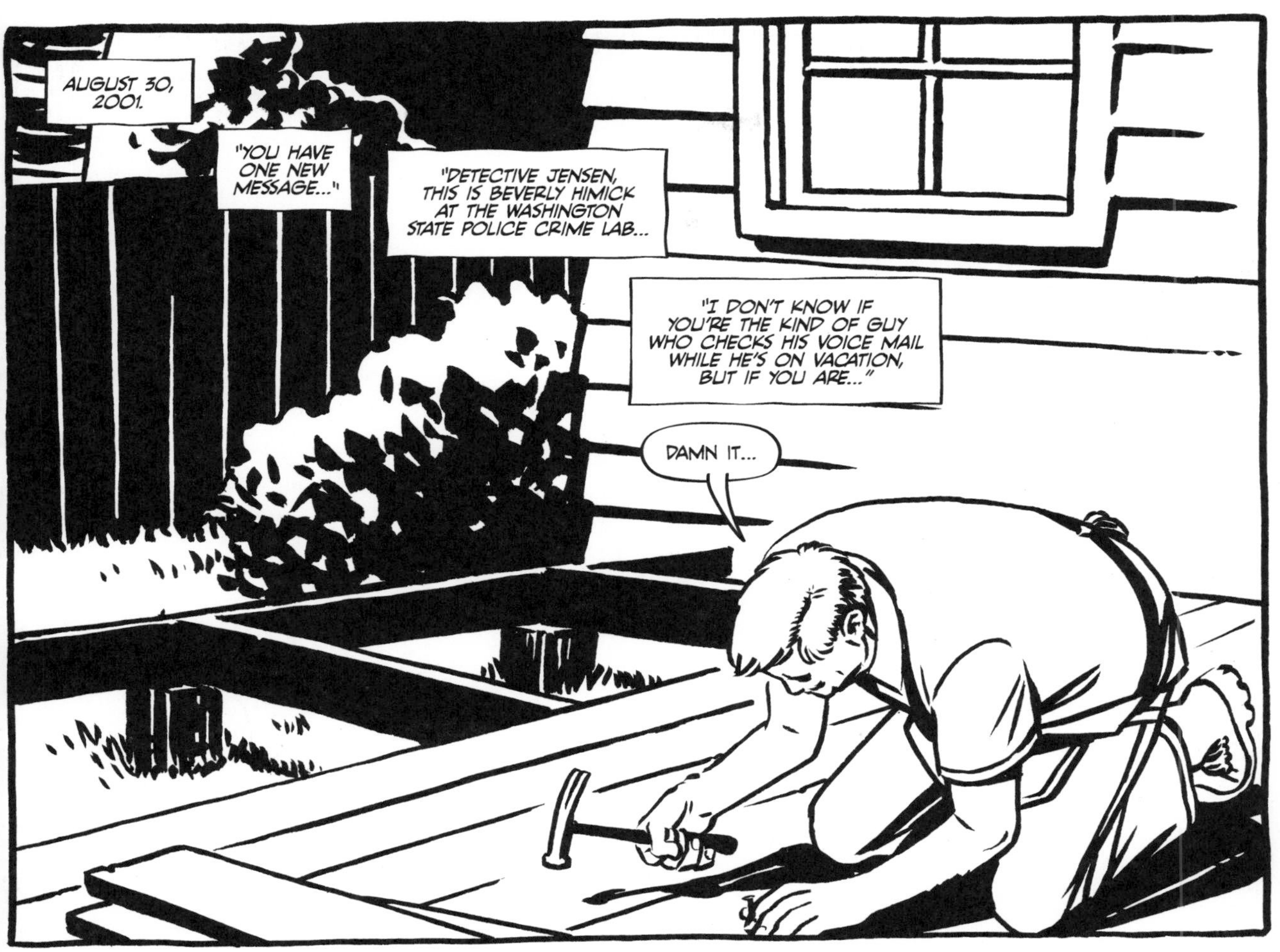
AUGUST 30, 2001.
"YOU HAVE ONE NEW MESSAGE..."
"DETECTIVE JENSEN, THIS IS BEVERLY HIMICK AT THE WASHINGTON STATE POLICE CRIME LAB...
"I DON'T KNOW IF YOU'RE THE KIND OF GUY WHO CHECKS HIS VOICE MAIL WHILE HE'S ON VACATION, BUT IF YOU ARE..."
DAMN IT...

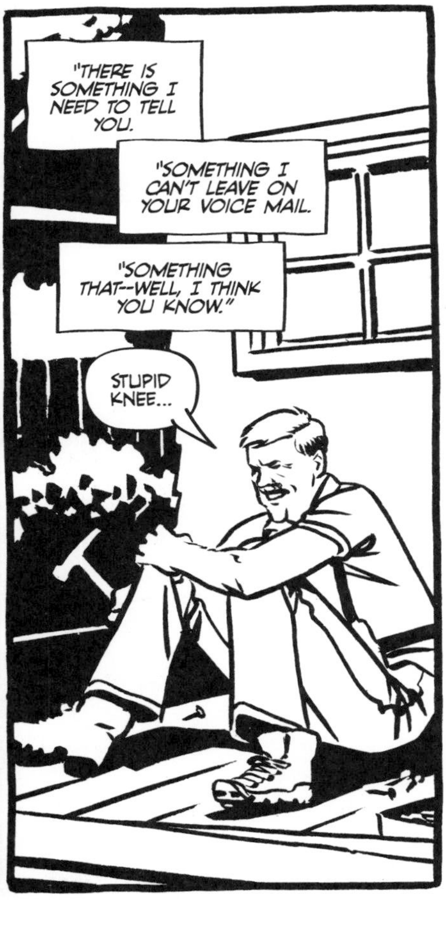
"THERE IS SOMETHING I NEED TO TELL YOU.
"SOMETHING I CAN'T LEAVE ON YOUR VOICE MAIL.
"SOMETHING THAT--WELL, I THINK YOU KNOW."
STUPID KNEE...

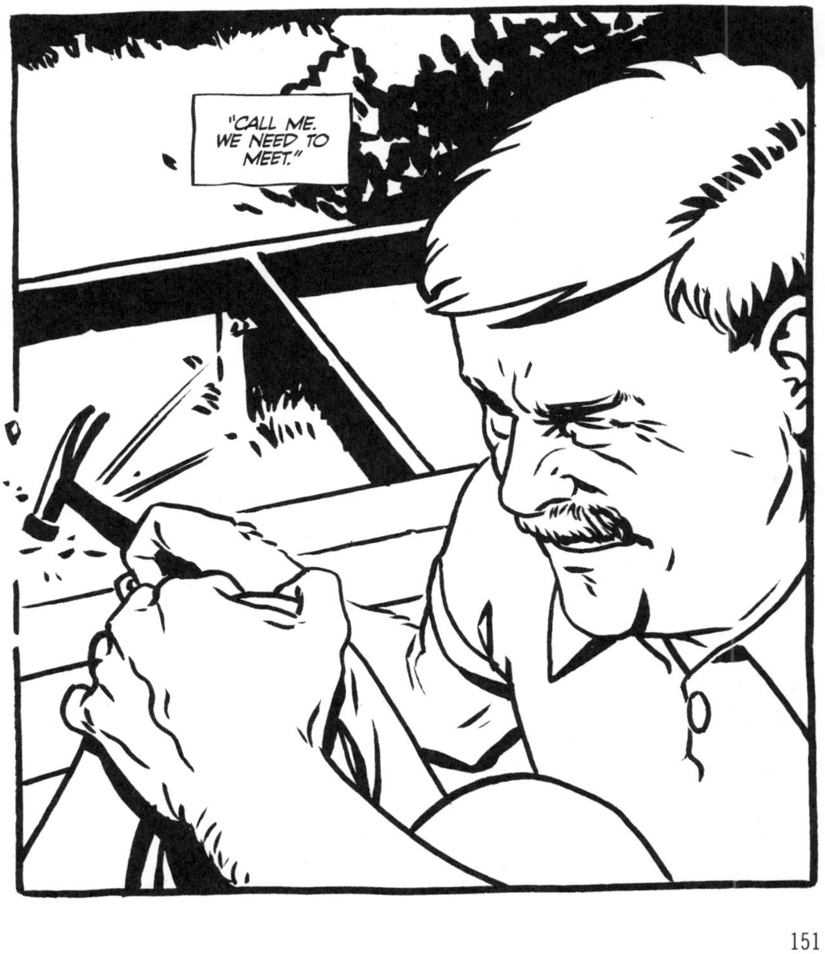
"CALL ME. WE NEED TO MEET."

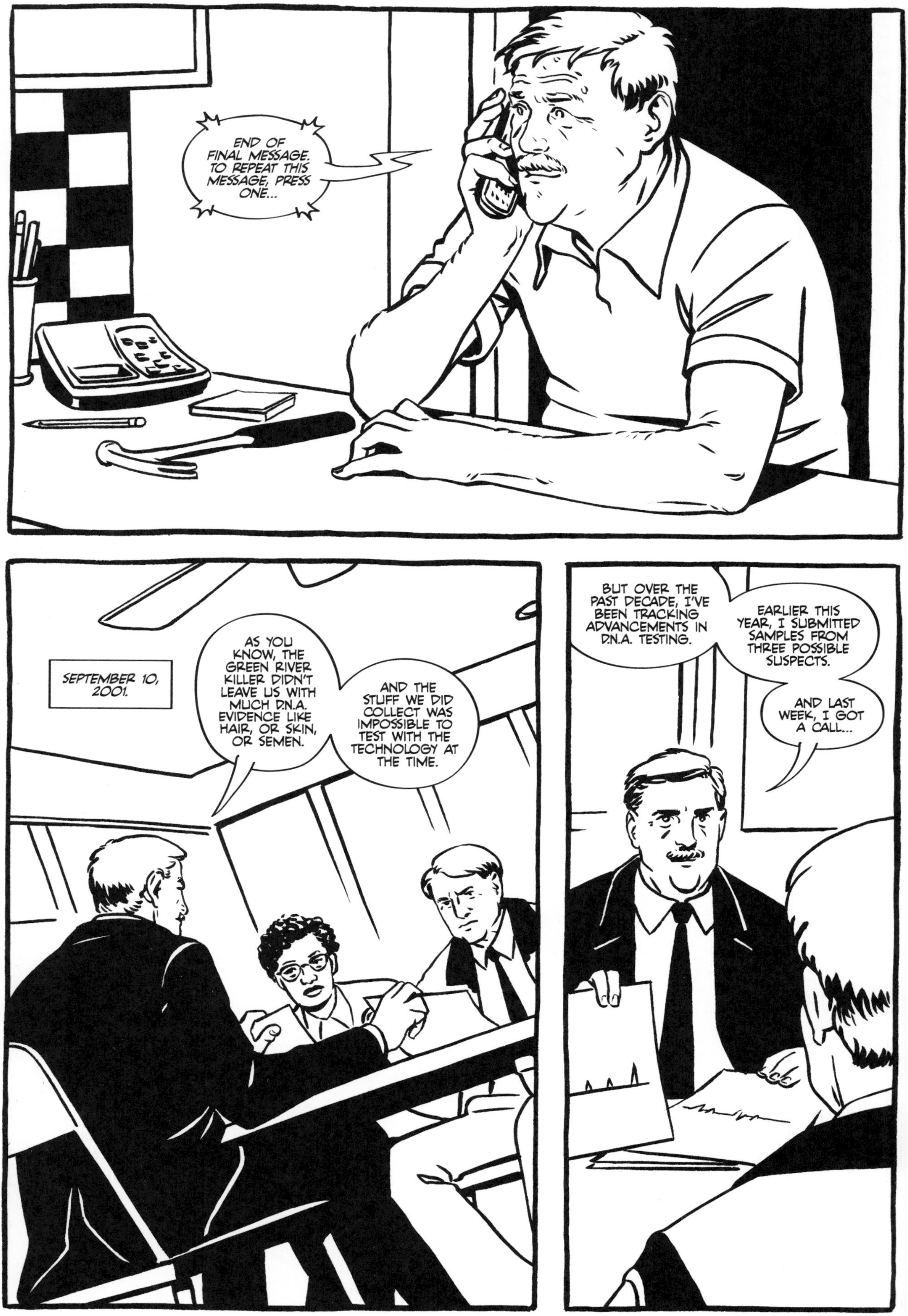
END OF FINAL MESSAGE. TO REPEAT THIS MESSAGE, PRESS ONE...
SEPTEMBER 10, 2001.
AS YOU KNOW, THE GREEN RIVER KILLER DIDN'T LEAVE US WITH MUCH D.N.A. EVIDENCE LIKE HAIR, OR SKIN, OR SEMEN.
AND THE STUFF WE DID COLLECT WAS IMPOSSIBLE TO TEST WITH THE TECHNOLOGY AT THE TIME.
BUT OVER THE PAST DECADE, I'VE BEEN TRACKING ADVANCEMENTS IN D.N.A. TESTING.
EARLIER THIS YEAR, I SUBMITTED SAMPLES FROM THREE POSSIBLE SUSPECTS.
AND LAST WEEK, I GOT A CALL...

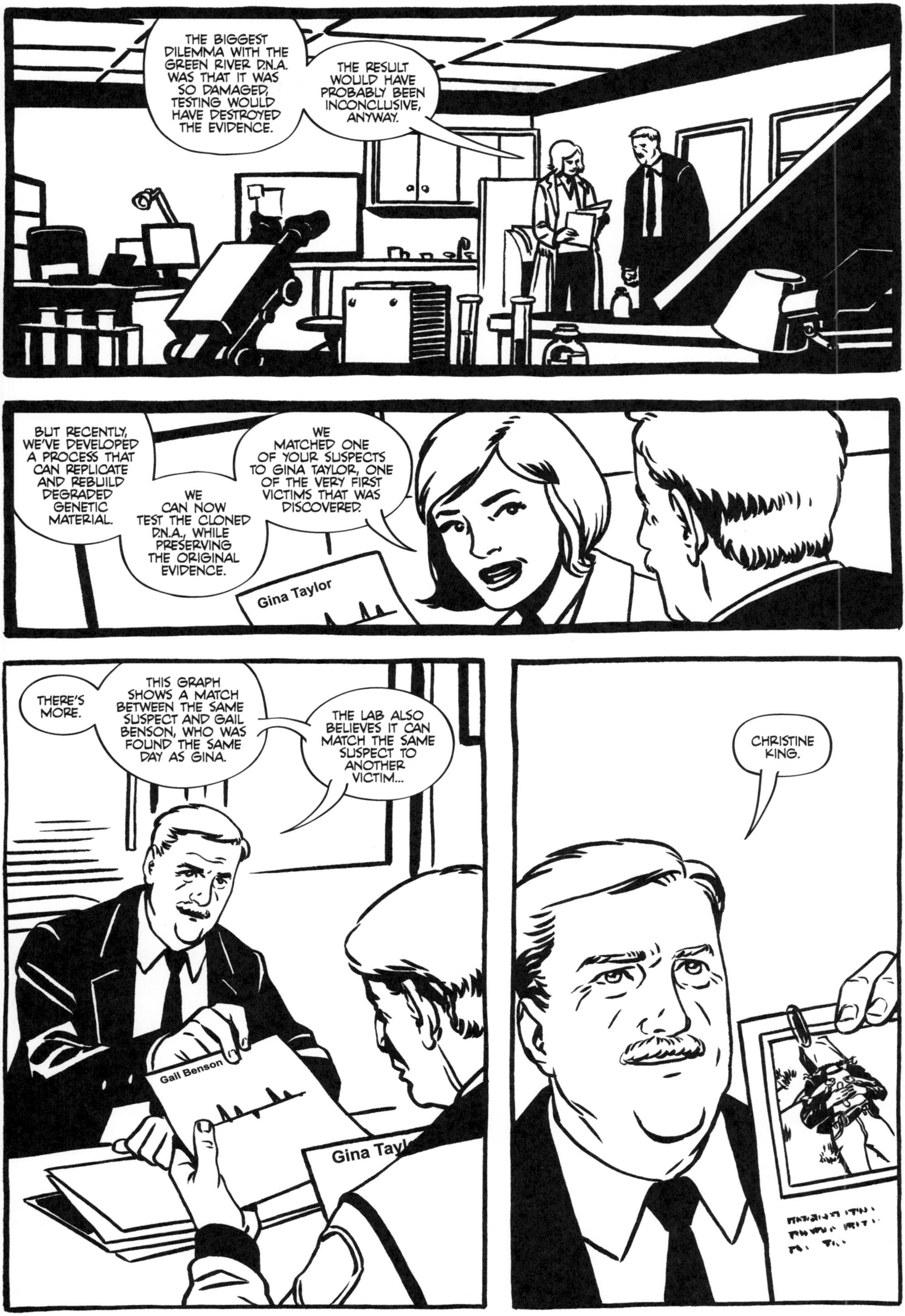

THE BIGGEST DILEMMA WITH THE GREEN RIVER D.N.A. WAS THAT IT WAS SO DAMAGED, TESTING WOULD HAVE DESTROYED THE EVIDENCE.
THE RESULT WOULD HAVE PROBABLY BEEN INCONCLUSIVE, ANYWAY.
BUT RECENTLY, WE'VE DEVELOPED A PROCESS THAT CAN REPLICATE AND REBUILD DEGRADED GENETIC MATERIAL.
WE CAN NOW TEST THE CLONED D.N.A., WHILE PRESERVING THE ORIGINAL EVIDENCE.
WE MATCHED ONE OF YOUR SUSPECTS TO GINA TAYLOR, ONE OF THE VERY FIRST VICTIMS THAT WAS DISCOVERED.
Gina Taylor
THERE'S MORE.
THIS GRAPH SHOWS A MATCH BETWEEN THE SAME SUSPECT AND GAIL BENSON, WHO WAS FOUND THE SAME DAY AS GINA.
THE LAB ALSO BELIEVES IT CAN MATCH THE SAME SUSPECT TO ANOTHER VICTIM...
Gail Benson
Gina Tayl
CHRISTINE KING.

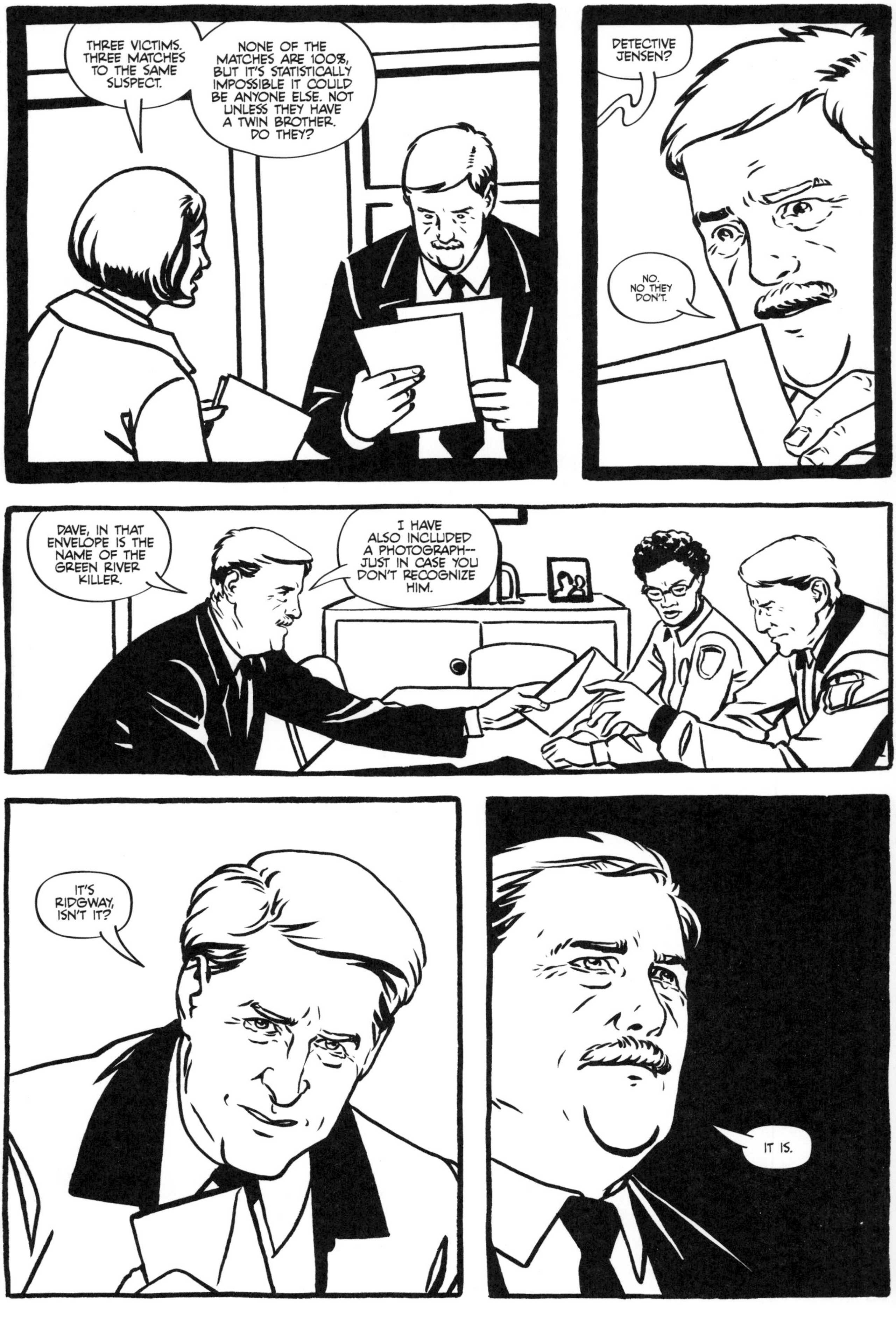
THREE VICTIMS. THREE MATCHES TO THE SAME SUSPECT.
NONE OF THE MATCHES ARE 100%, BUT IT'S STATISTICALLY IMPOSSIBLE IT COULD BE ANYONE ELSE. NOT UNLESS THEY HAVE A TWIN BROTHER. DO THEY?
DETECTIVE JENSEN?
NO. NO THEY DON'T.
DAVE, IN THAT ENVELOPE IS THE NAME OF THE GREEN RIVER KILLER.
I HAVE ALSO INCLUDED A PHOTOGRAPH-- JUST IN CASE YOU DON'T RECOGNIZE HIM.
IT'S RIDGWAY, ISN'T IT?
IT IS.

I DON'T KNOW HOW TO FEEL ABOUT THIS, FAYE.

THIS IS VINDICATION--OF WHAT YOU AND I STARTED NINETEEN YEARS AGO WHEN WE INVESTIGATED THOSE FIRST MURDERS, OF THE WORK DONE BY THE TASK FORCE TO IDENTIFY THIS MONSTER. AT THE SAME TIME...

HE GOT AWAY. WE HAD HIM, AND HE GOT AWAY.

WHO ELSE BUT US KNOWS?

I TOLD THE HEADS OF MAJOR CRIMES LAST WEEK WHEN I GOT THE RESULTS.

WE WANTED TO TELL YOU, BUT YOU WERE ON VACATION.

HELL OF A WAY TO COME BACK.

WE NEED TO ASSEMBLE A TEAM. LET'S KEEP IT SMALL AND BE QUIET ABOUT IT.

WE'LL MEET ON WEDNESDAY TO DRAW UP A BATTLE PLAN.

SUNDAY, SEPTEMBER 8, 2001

MONDAY, SEPTEMBER 9, 2001

TUESDAY, SEPTEMBER 11, 2001

WEDNESDAY, SEPTEMBER 12, 2001

THURSDAY, SEPTEMBER 2001

THE NIGHTMARE IS ALMOST OVER.

THANK YOU, GOD.

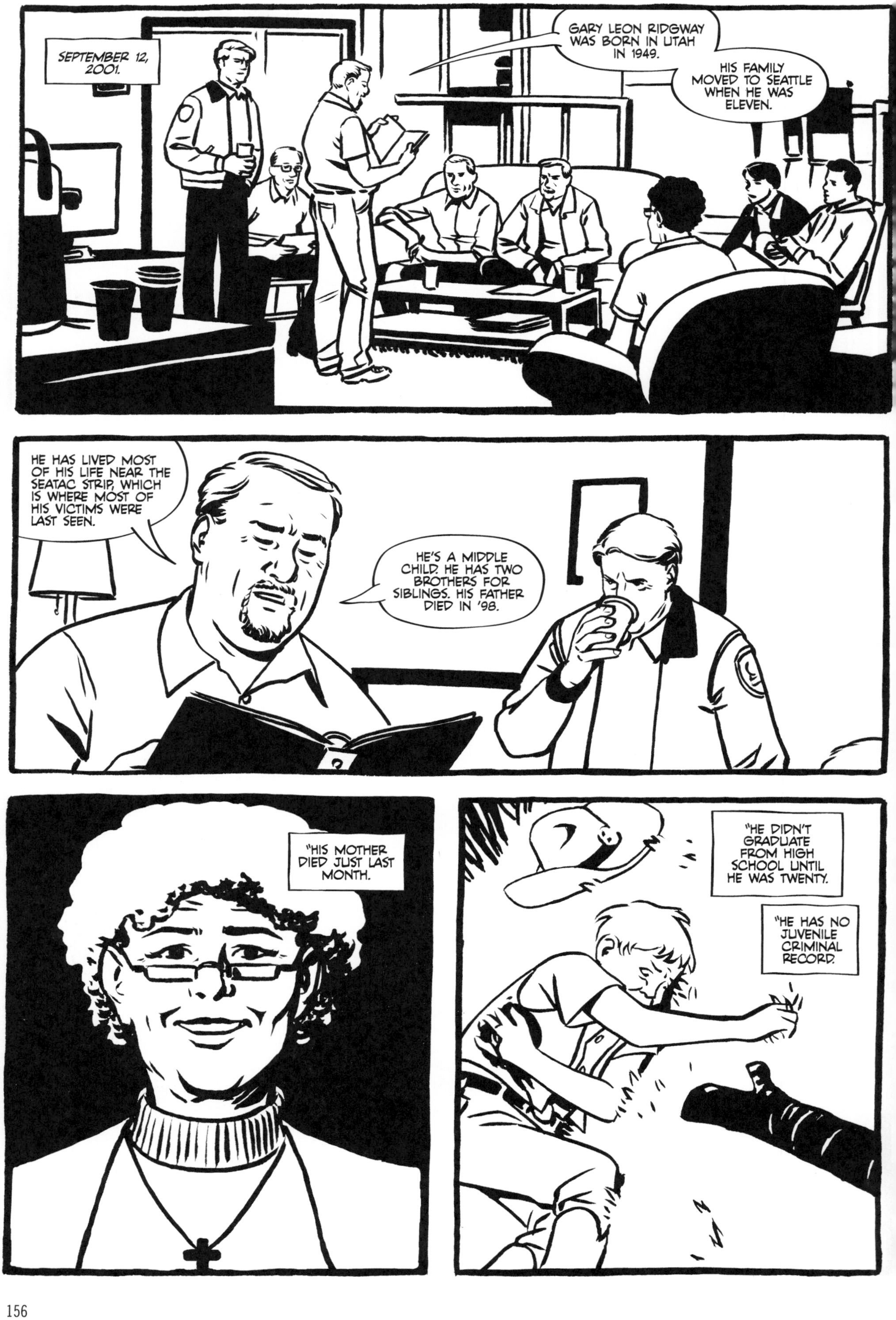
SEPTEMBER 12, 2001.
GARY LEON RIDGWAY WAS BORN IN UTAH IN 1949.
HIS FAMILY MOVED TO SEATTLE WHEN HE WAS ELEVEN.
HE HAS LIVED MOST OF HIS LIFE NEAR THE SEATAC STRIP, WHICH IS WHERE MOST OF HIS VICTIMS WERE LAST SEEN.
HE'S A MIDDLE CHILD. HE HAS TWO BROTHERS FOR SIBLINGS. HIS FATHER DIED IN '98.
"HIS MOTHER DIED JUST LAST MONTH.
"HE DIDN'T GRADUATE FROM HIGH SCHOOL UNTIL HE WAS TWENTY.
"HE HAS NO JUVENILE CRIMINAL RECORD.

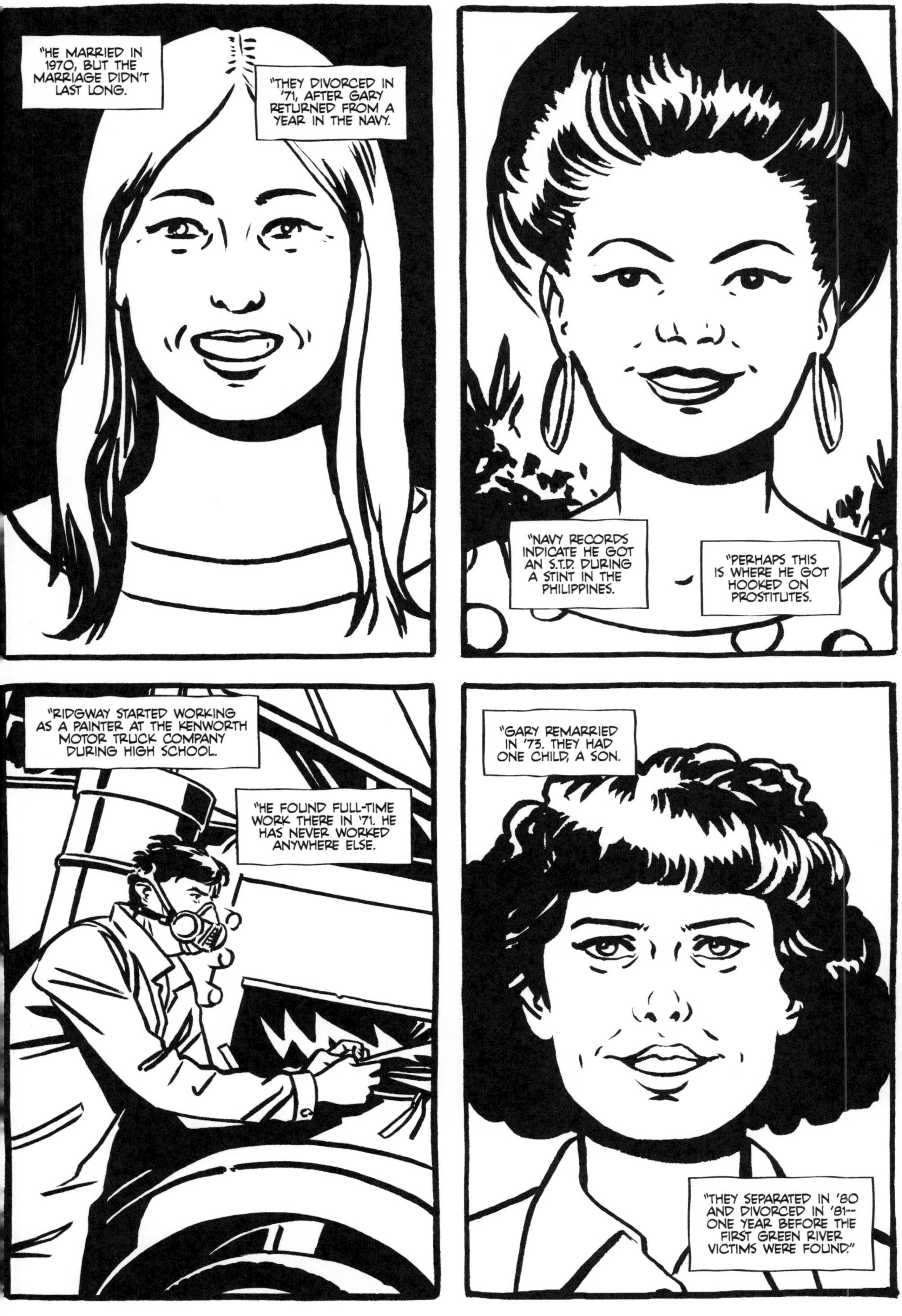
"HE MARRIED IN 1970, BUT THE MARRIAGE DIDN'T LAST LONG.
"THEY DIVORCED IN '71, AFTER GARY RETURNED FROM A YEAR IN THE NAVY.
"NAVY RECORDS INDICATE HE GOT AN S.T.D. DURING A STINT IN THE PHILIPPINES.
"PERHAPS THIS IS WHERE HE GOT HOOKED ON PROSTITUTES.
"RIDGWAY STARTED WORKING AS A PAINTER AT THE KENWORTH MOTOR TRUCK COMPANY DURING HIGH SCHOOL.
"HE FOUND FULL-TIME WORK THERE IN '71. HE HAS NEVER WORKED ANYWHERE ELSE.
"GARY REMARRIED IN '73. THEY HAD ONE CHILD, A SON.
"THEY SEPARATED IN '80 AND DIVORCED IN '81-- ONE YEAR BEFORE THE FIRST GREEN RIVER VICTIMS WERE FOUND."

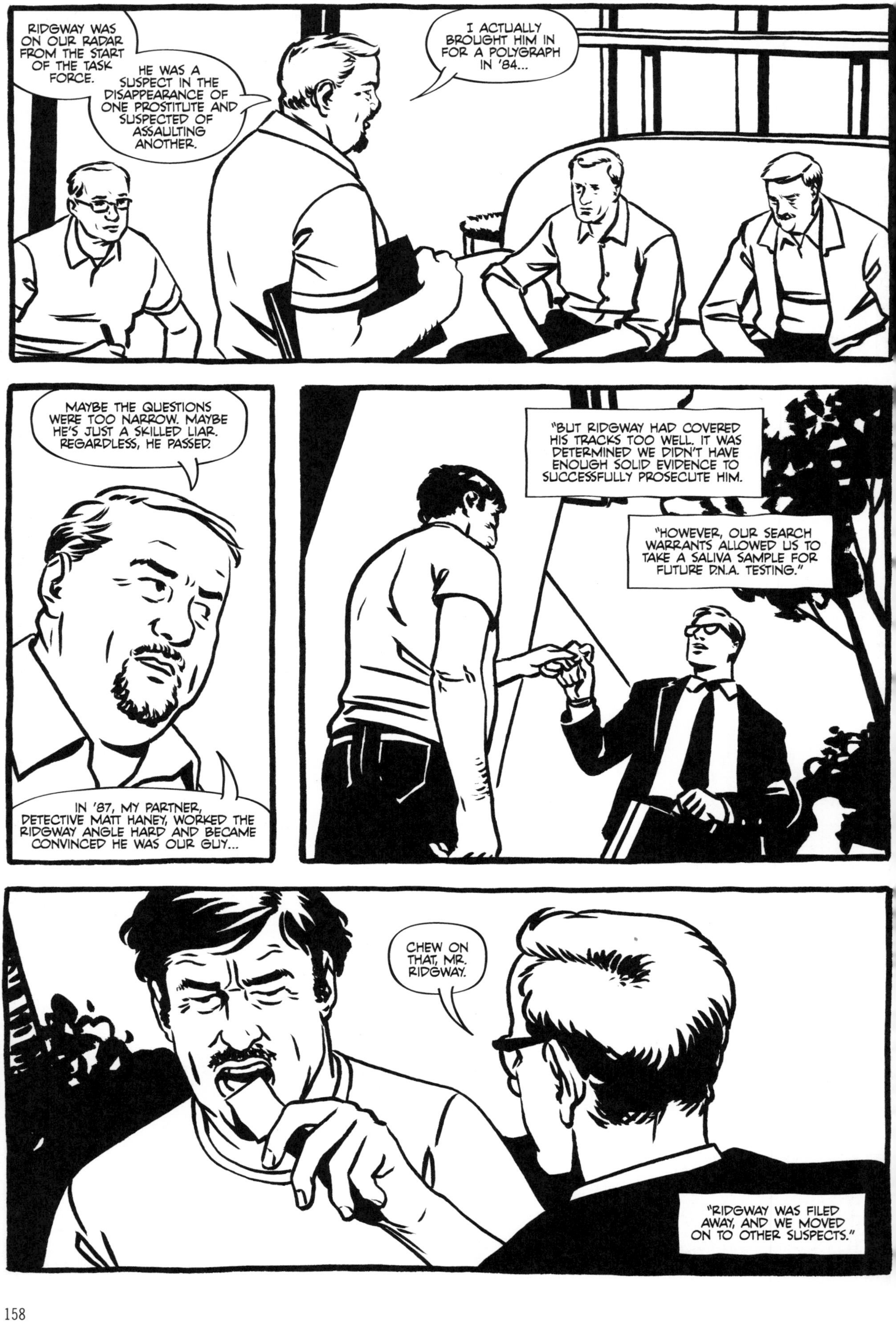
RIDGWAY WAS ON OUR RADAR FROM THE START OF THE TASK FORCE.
HE WAS A SUSPECT IN THE DISAPPEARANCE OF ONE PROSTITUTE AND SUSPECTED OF ASSAULTING ANOTHER.
I ACTUALLY BROUGHT HIM IN FOR A POLYGRAPH IN '84...
MAYBE THE QUESTIONS WERE TOO NARROW. MAYBE HE'S JUST A SKILLED LIAR. REGARDLESS, HE PASSED.
IN '87, MY PARTNER, DETECTIVE MATT HANEY, WORKED THE RIDGWAY ANGLE HARD AND BECAME CONVINCED HE WAS OUR GUY...
"BUT RIDGWAY HAD COVERED HIS TRACKS TOO WELL. IT WAS DETERMINED WE DIDN'T HAVE ENOUGH SOLID EVIDENCE TO SUCCESSFULLY PROSECUTE HIM.
"HOWEVER, OUR SEARCH WARRANTS ALLOWED US TO TAKE A SALIVA SAMPLE FOR FUTURE D.N.A. TESTING."
CHEW ON THAT, MR. RIDGWAY.
"RIDGWAY WAS FILED AWAY, AND WE MOVED ON TO OTHER SUSPECTS."

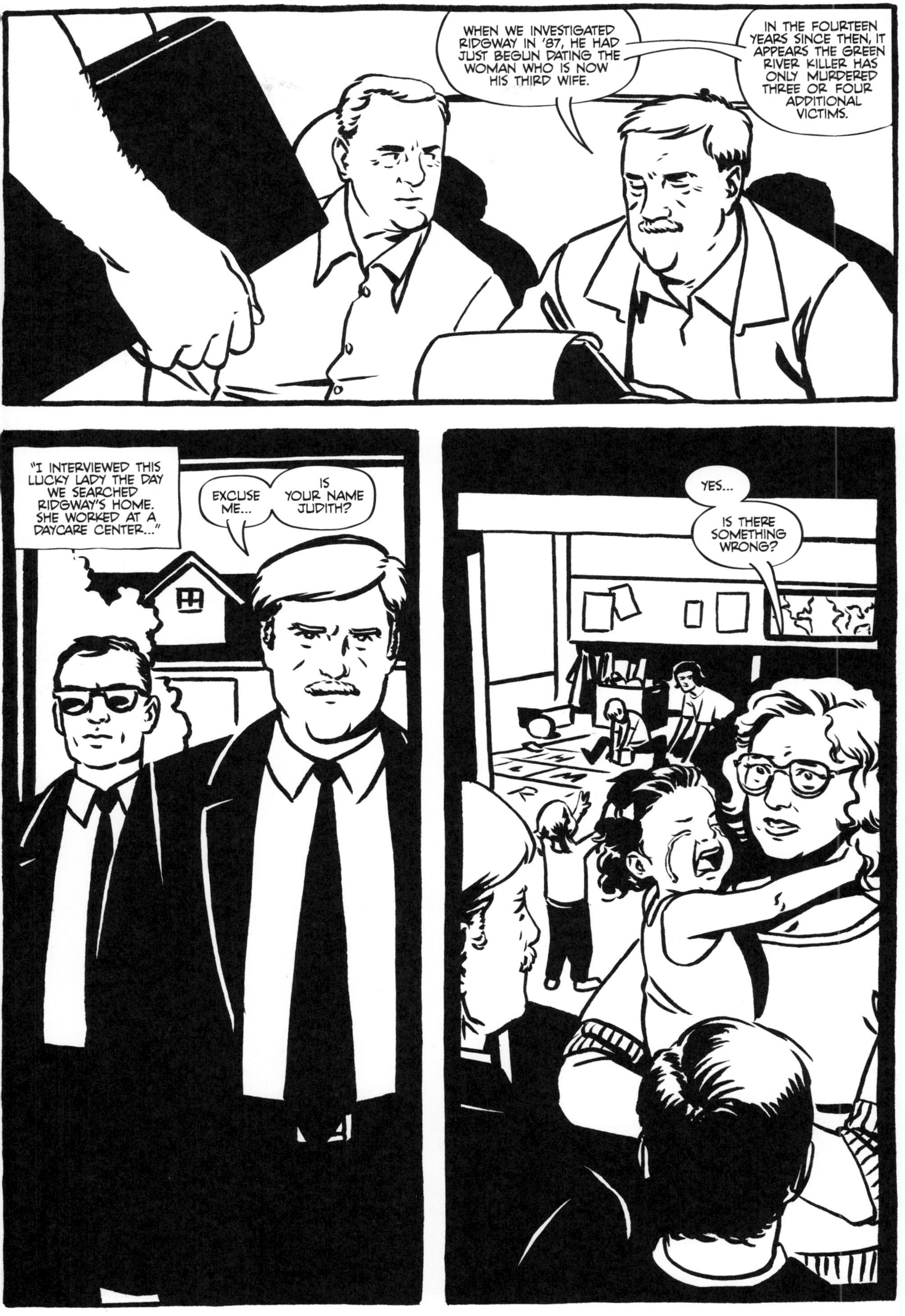
WHEN WE INVESTIGATED RIDGWAY IN '87, HE HAD JUST BEGUN DATING THE WOMAN WHO IS NOW HIS THIRD WIFE.
IN THE FOURTEEN YEARS SINCE THEN, IT APPEARS THE GREEN RIVER KILLER HAS ONLY MURDERED THREE OR FOUR ADDITIONAL VICTIMS.
"I INTERVIEWED THIS LUCKY LADY THE DAY WE SEARCHED RIDGWAY'S HOME. SHE WORKED AT A DAYCARE CENTER..."
EXCUSE ME...
IS YOUR NAME JUDITH?
YES...
IS THERE SOMETHING WRONG?

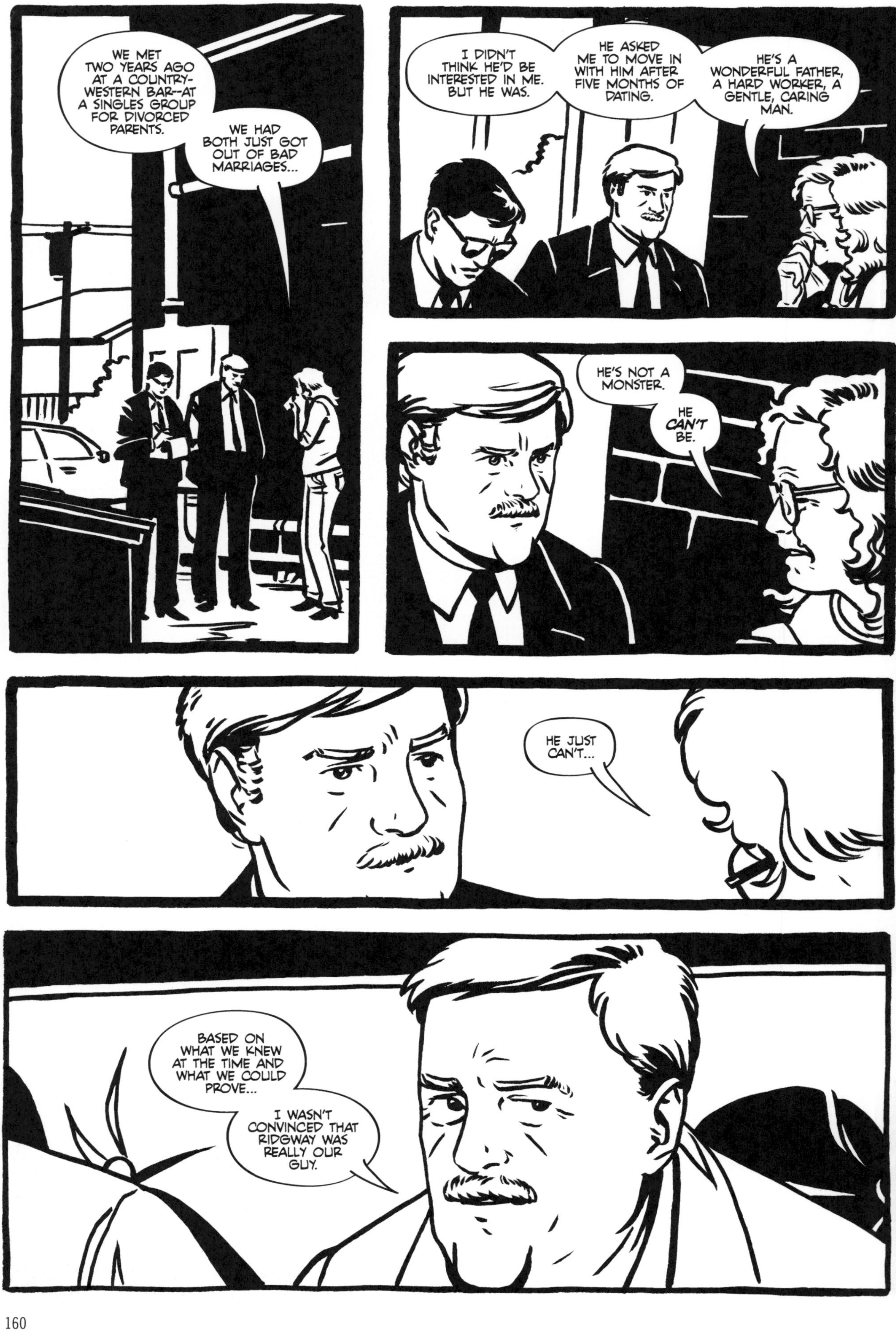
WE MET TWO YEARS AGO AT A COUNTRY-WESTERN BAR--AT A SINGLES GROUP FOR DIVORCED PARENTS.
WE HAD BOTH JUST GOT OUT OF BAD MARRIAGES...
I DIDN'T THINK HE'D BE INTERESTED IN ME. BUT HE WAS.
HE ASKED ME TO MOVE IN WITH HIM AFTER FIVE MONTHS OF DATING.
HE'S A WONDERFUL FATHER, A HARD WORKER, A GENTLE, CARING MAN.
HE'S NOT A MONSTER.
HE *CAN'T* BE.
HE JUST CAN'T...
BASED ON WHAT WE KNEW AT THE TIME AND WHAT WE COULD PROVE...
I WASN'T CONVINCED THAT RIDGWAY WAS REALLY OUR GUY.

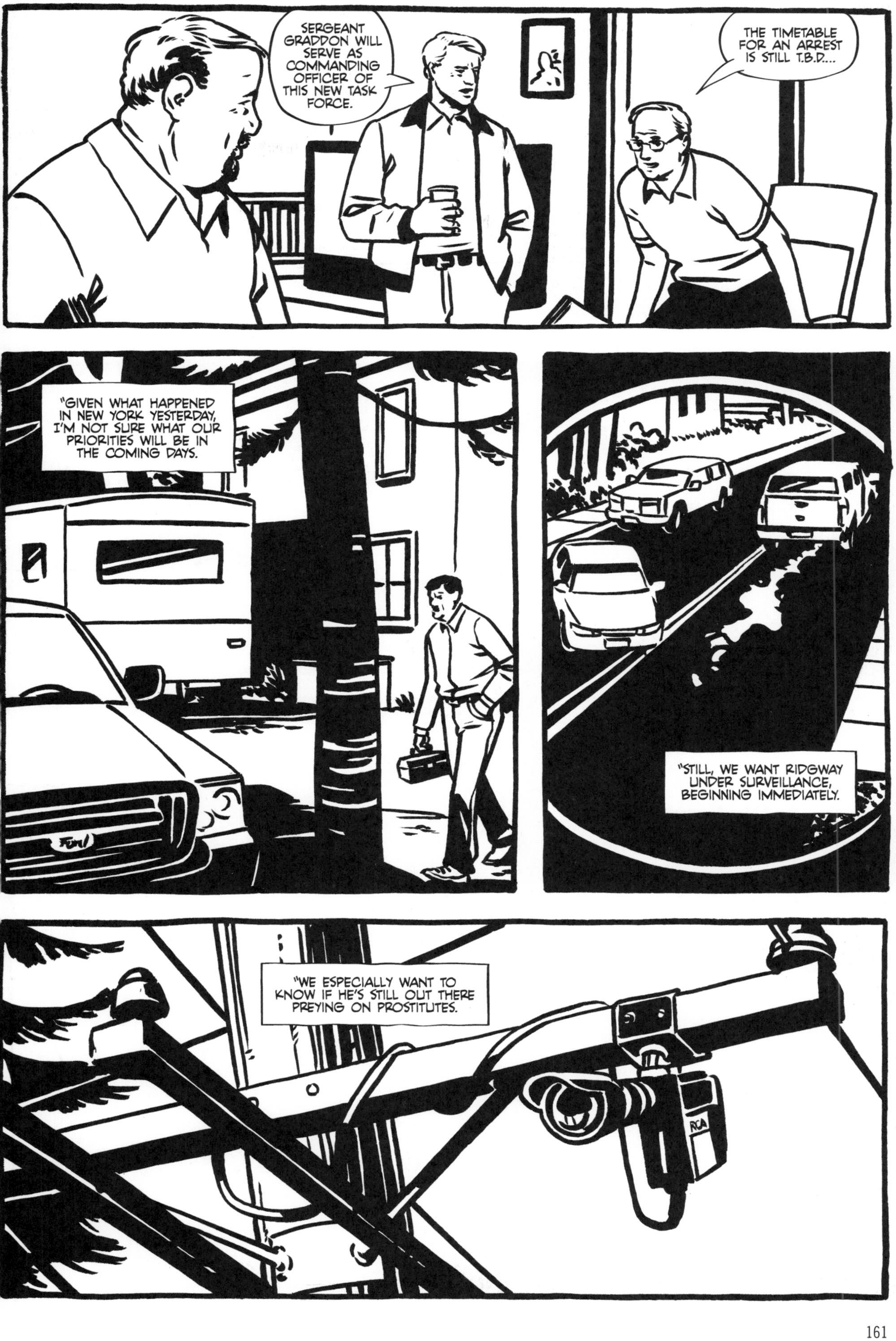
SERGEANT GRADDON WILL SERVE AS COMMANDING OFFICER OF THIS NEW TASK FORCE.
THE TIMETABLE FOR AN ARREST IS STILL T.B.D....
"GIVEN WHAT HAPPENED IN NEW YORK YESTERDAY, I'M NOT SURE WHAT OUR PRIORITIES WILL BE IN THE COMING DAYS.
"STILL, WE WANT RIDGWAY UNDER SURVEILLANCE, BEGINNING IMMEDIATELY.
"WE ESPECIALLY WANT TO KNOW IF HE'S STILL OUT THERE PREYING ON PROSTITUTES.
RCA

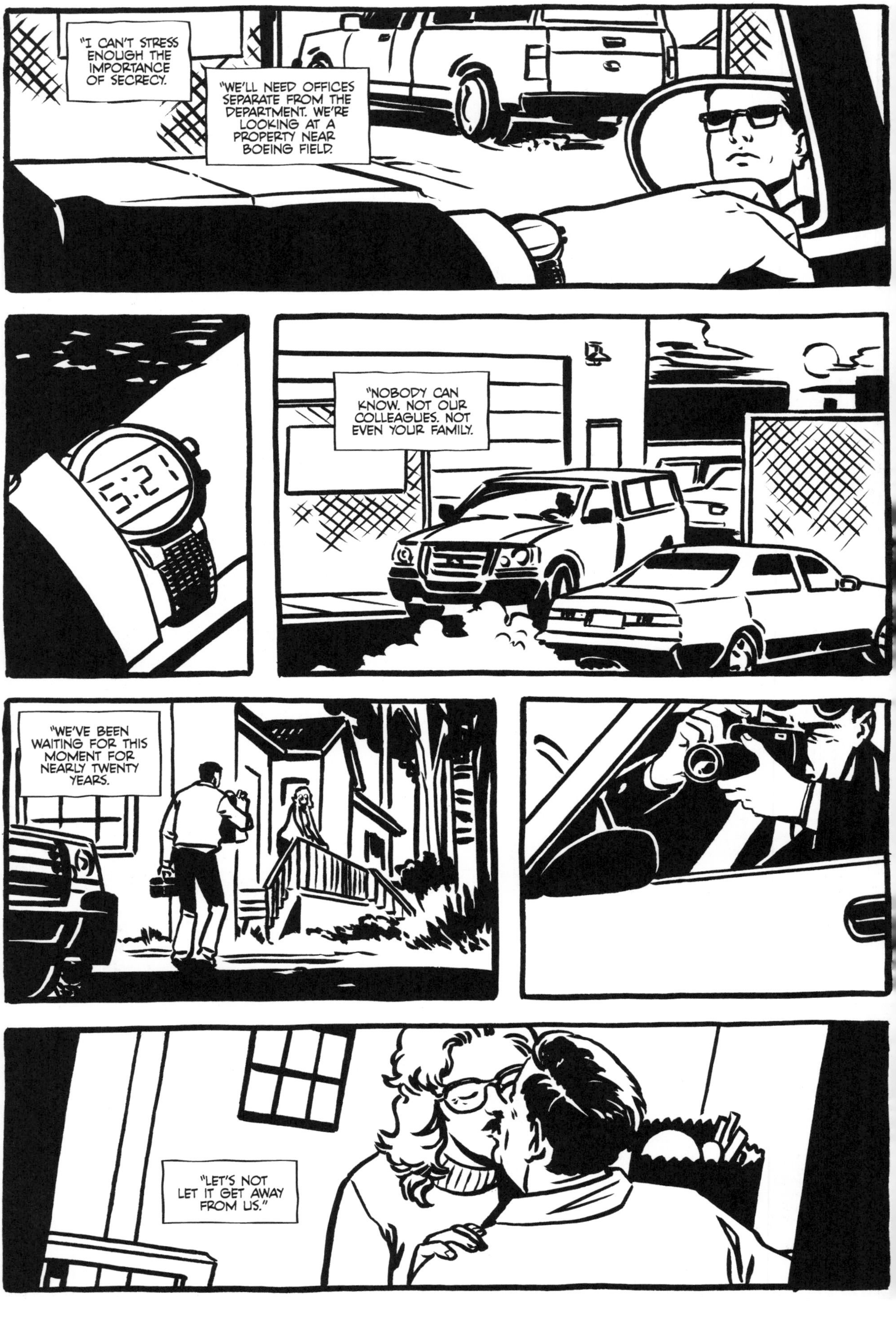
"I CAN'T STRESS ENOUGH THE IMPORTANCE OF SECRECY.
"WE'LL NEED OFFICES SEPARATE FROM THE DEPARTMENT. WE'RE LOOKING AT A PROPERTY NEAR BOEING FIELD.
5:21
"NOBODY CAN KNOW. NOT OUR COLLEAGUES. NOT EVEN YOUR FAMILY.
"WE'VE BEEN WAITING FOR THIS MOMENT FOR NEARLY TWENTY YEARS.
"LET'S NOT LET IT GET AWAY FROM US."

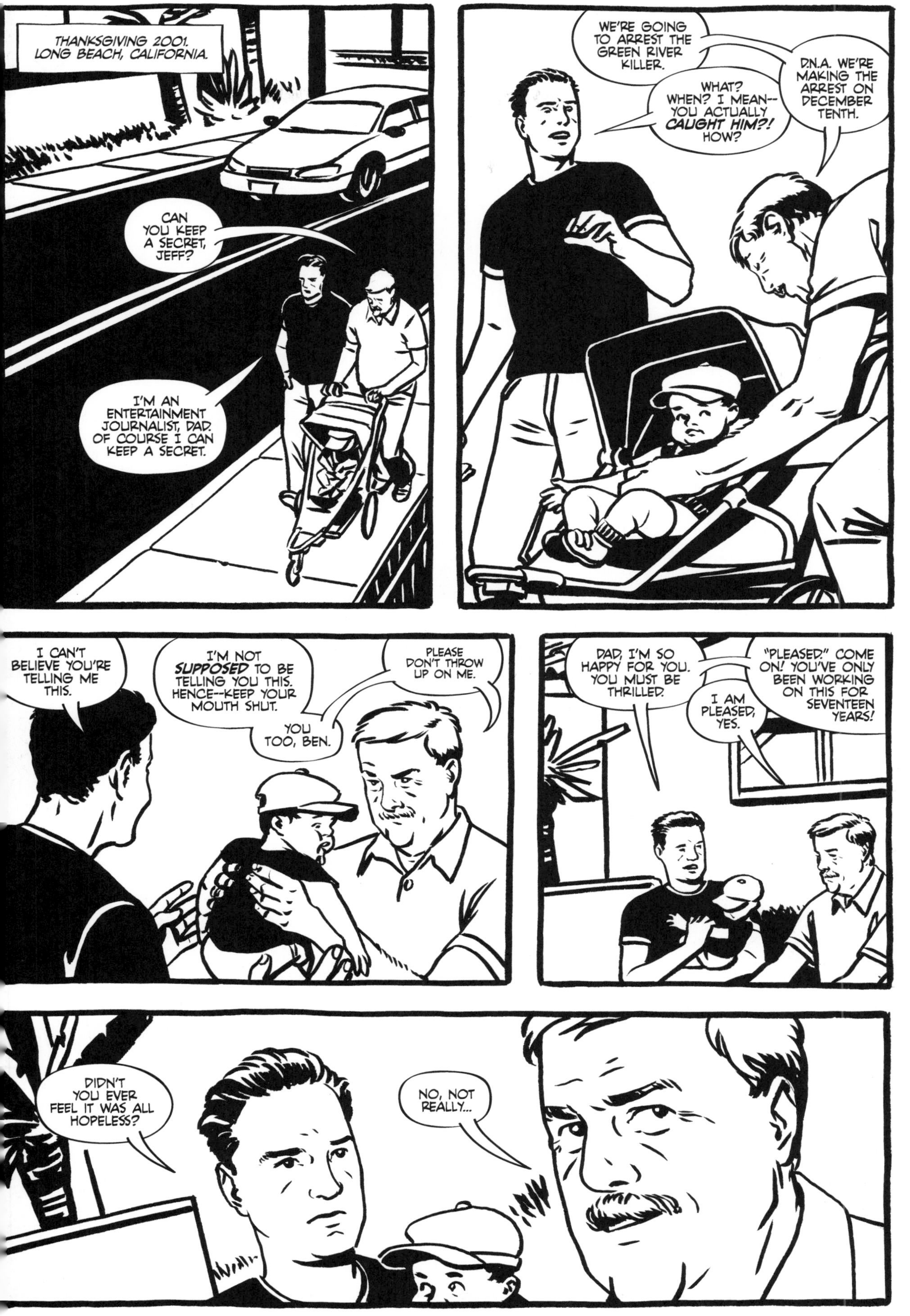
THANKSGIVING 2001. LONG BEACH, CALIFORNIA.
CAN YOU KEEP A SECRET, JEFF?
I'M AN ENTERTAINMENT JOURNALIST, DAD. OF COURSE I CAN KEEP A SECRET.
WE'RE GOING TO ARREST THE GREEN RIVER KILLER.
WHAT? WHEN? I MEAN-- YOU ACTUALLY CAUGHT HIM?! HOW?
D.N.A. WE'RE MAKING THE ARREST ON DECEMBER TENTH.
I CAN'T BELIEVE YOU'RE TELLING ME THIS.
I'M NOT SUPPOSED TO BE TELLING YOU THIS. HENCE--KEEP YOUR MOUTH SHUT.
YOU TOO, BEN.
PLEASE DON'T THROW UP ON ME.
DAD, I'M SO HAPPY FOR YOU. YOU MUST BE THRILLED.
I AM PLEASED, YES.
"PLEASED." COME ON! YOU'VE ONLY BEEN WORKING ON THIS FOR SEVENTEEN YEARS!
DIDN'T YOU EVER FEEL IT WAS ALL HOPELESS?
NO, NOT REALLY...

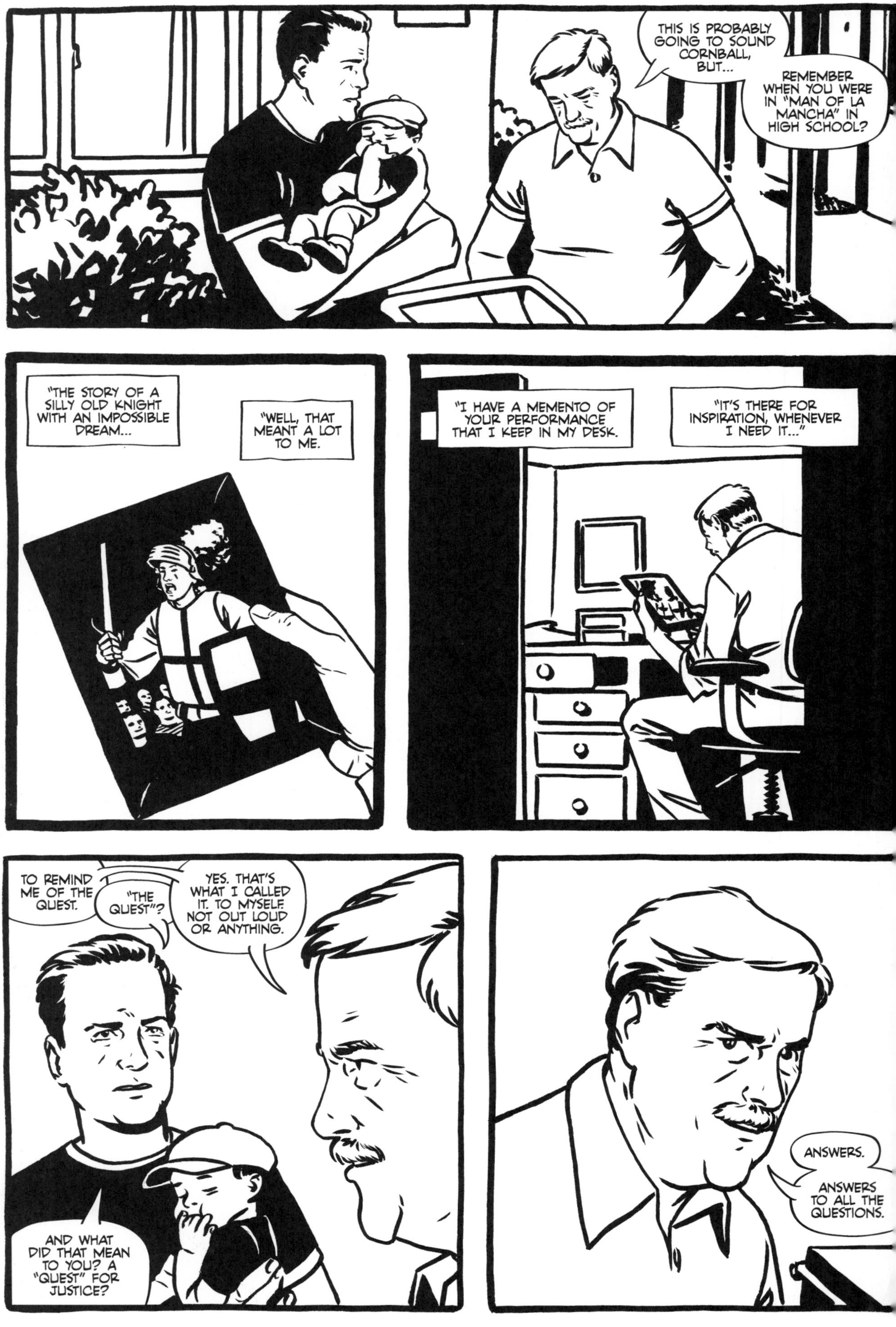

THIS IS PROBABLY GOING TO SOUND CORNBALL, BUT...
REMEMBER WHEN YOU WERE IN "MAN OF LA MANCHA" IN HIGH SCHOOL?
"THE STORY OF A SILLY OLD KNIGHT WITH AN IMPOSSIBLE DREAM...
"WELL, THAT MEANT A LOT TO ME.
"I HAVE A MEMENTO OF YOUR PERFORMANCE THAT I KEEP IN MY DESK.
"IT'S THERE FOR INSPIRATION, WHENEVER I NEED IT..."
TO REMIND ME OF THE QUEST.
"THE QUEST"?
YES. THAT'S WHAT I CALLED IT. TO MYSELF. NOT OUT LOUD OR ANYTHING.
AND WHAT DID THAT MEAN TO YOU? A "QUEST" FOR JUSTICE?
ANSWERS.
ANSWERS TO ALL THE QUESTIONS.

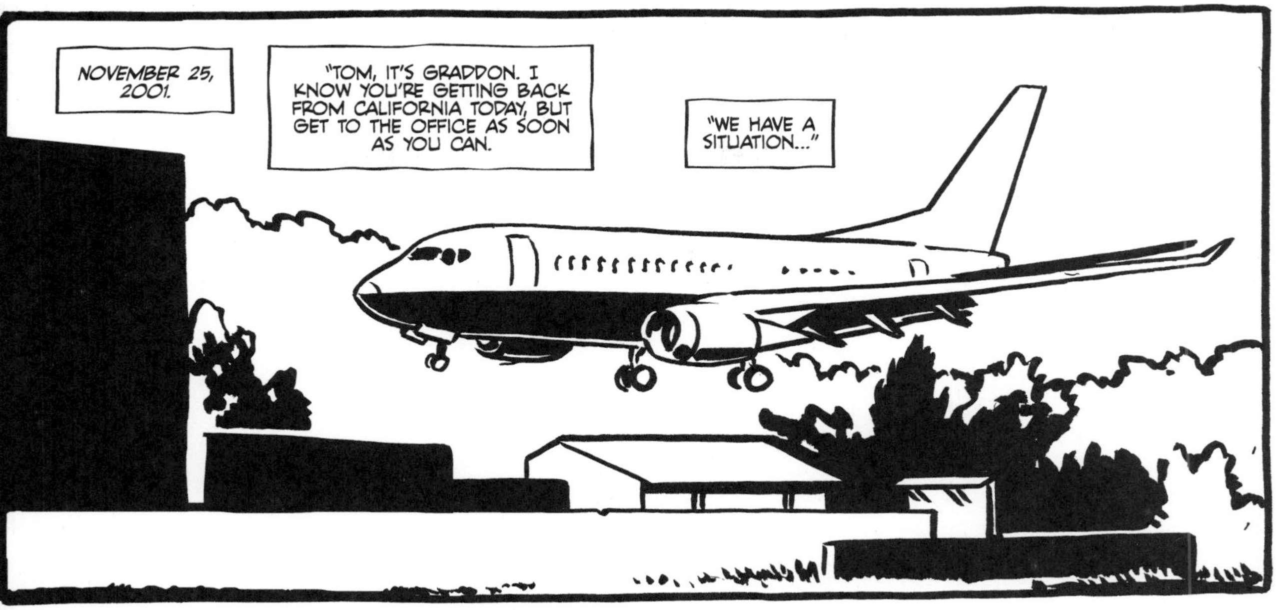
NOVEMBER 25, 2001.
"TOM, IT'S GRADDON. I KNOW YOU'RE GETTING BACK FROM CALIFORNIA TODAY, BUT GET TO THE OFFICE AS SOON AS YOU CAN.
"WE HAVE A SITUATION..."

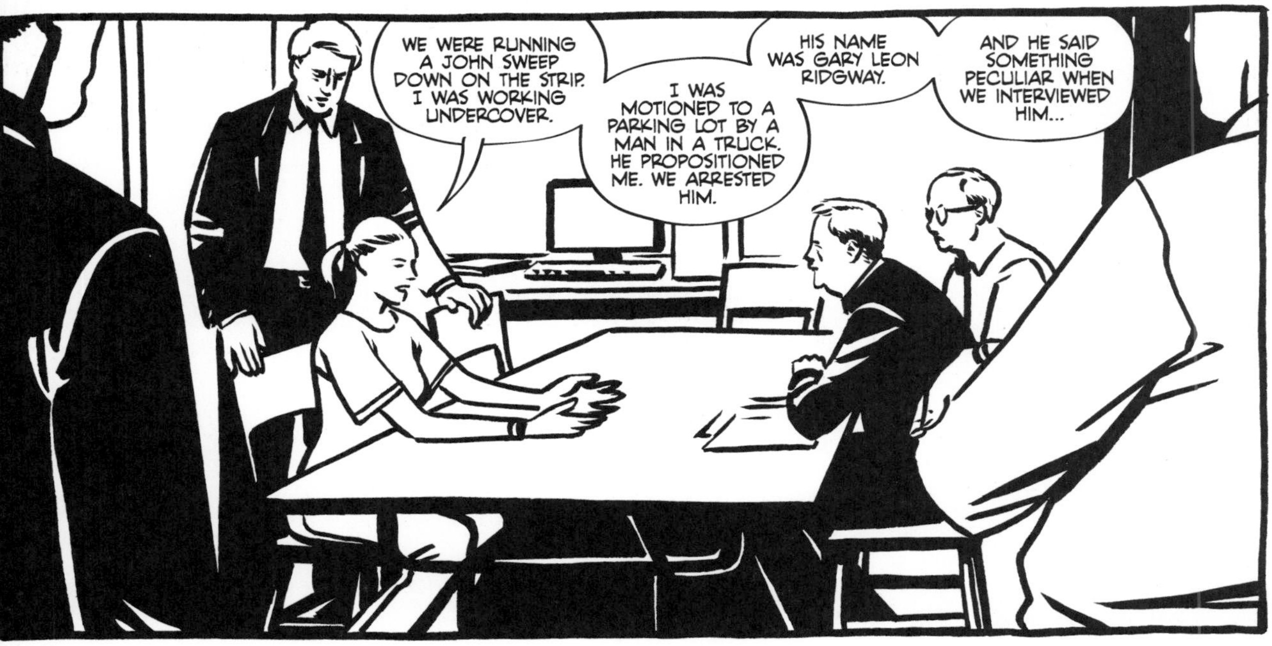
WE WERE RUNNING A JOHN SWEEP DOWN ON THE STRIP. I WAS WORKING UNDERCOVER.
I WAS MOTIONED TO A PARKING LOT BY A MAN IN A TRUCK. HE PROPOSITIONED ME. WE ARRESTED HIM.
HIS NAME WAS GARY LEON RIDGWAY.
AND HE SAID SOMETHING PECULIAR WHEN WE INTERVIEWED HIM...

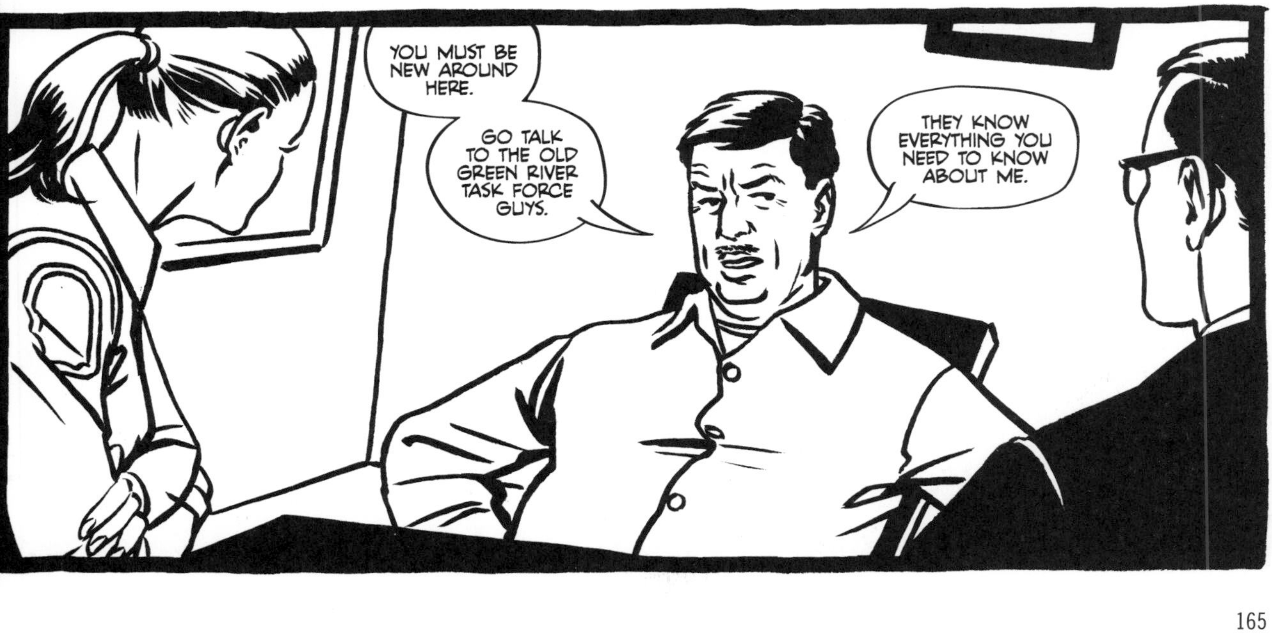
YOU MUST BE NEW AROUND HERE.
GO TALK TO THE OLD GREEN RIVER TASK FORCE GUYS.
THEY KNOW EVERYTHING YOU NEED TO KNOW ABOUT ME.

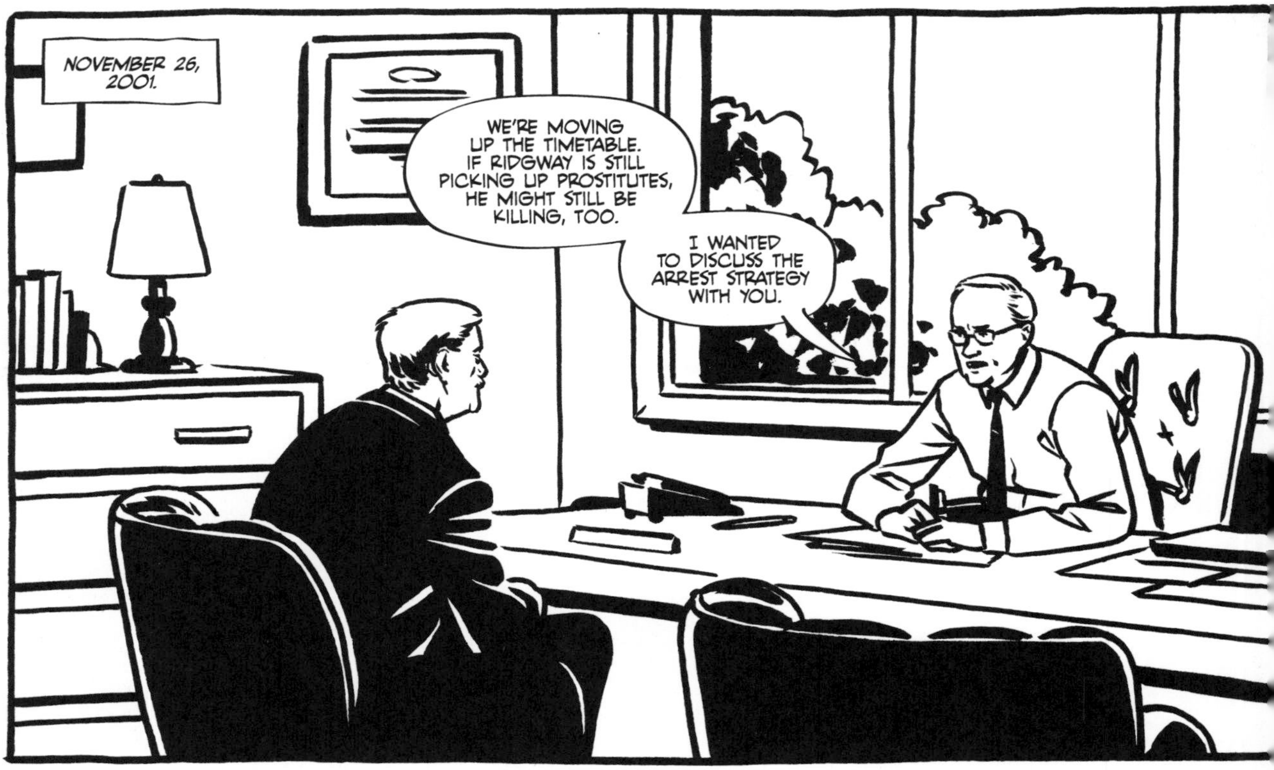
NOVEMBER 26, 2001.
WE'RE MOVING UP THE TIMETABLE. IF RIDGWAY IS STILL PICKING UP PROSTITUTES, HE MIGHT STILL BE KILLING, TOO.
I WANTED TO DISCUSS THE ARREST STRATEGY WITH YOU.

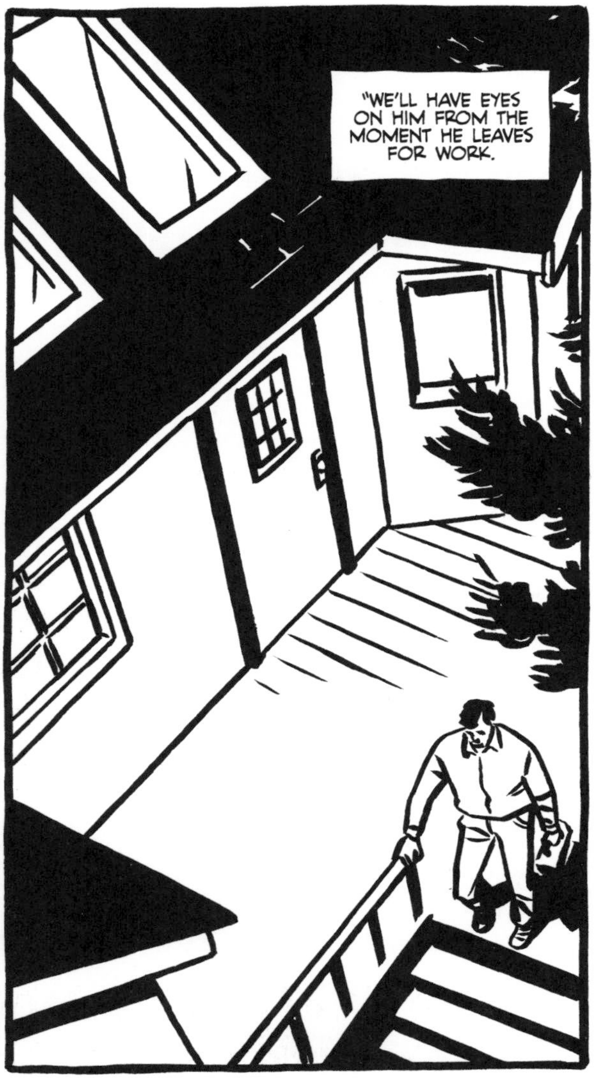
"WE'LL HAVE EYES ON HIM FROM THE MOMENT HE LEAVES FOR WORK.

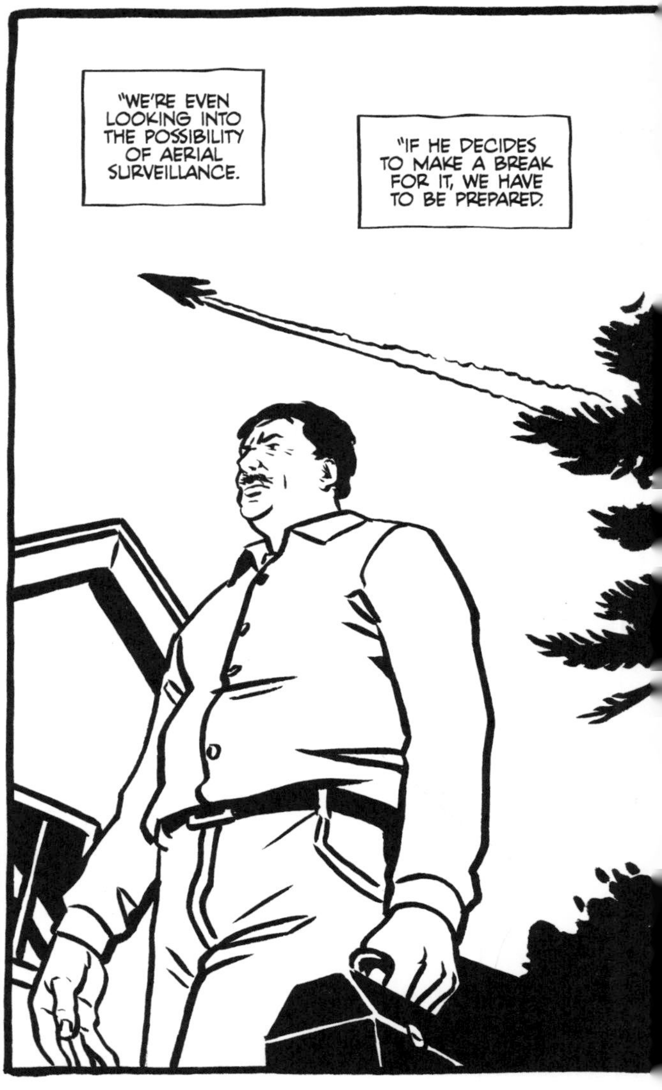
"WE'RE EVEN LOOKING INTO THE POSSIBILITY OF AERIAL SURVEILLANCE.
"IF HE DECIDES TO MAKE A BREAK FOR IT, WE HAVE TO BE PREPARED.

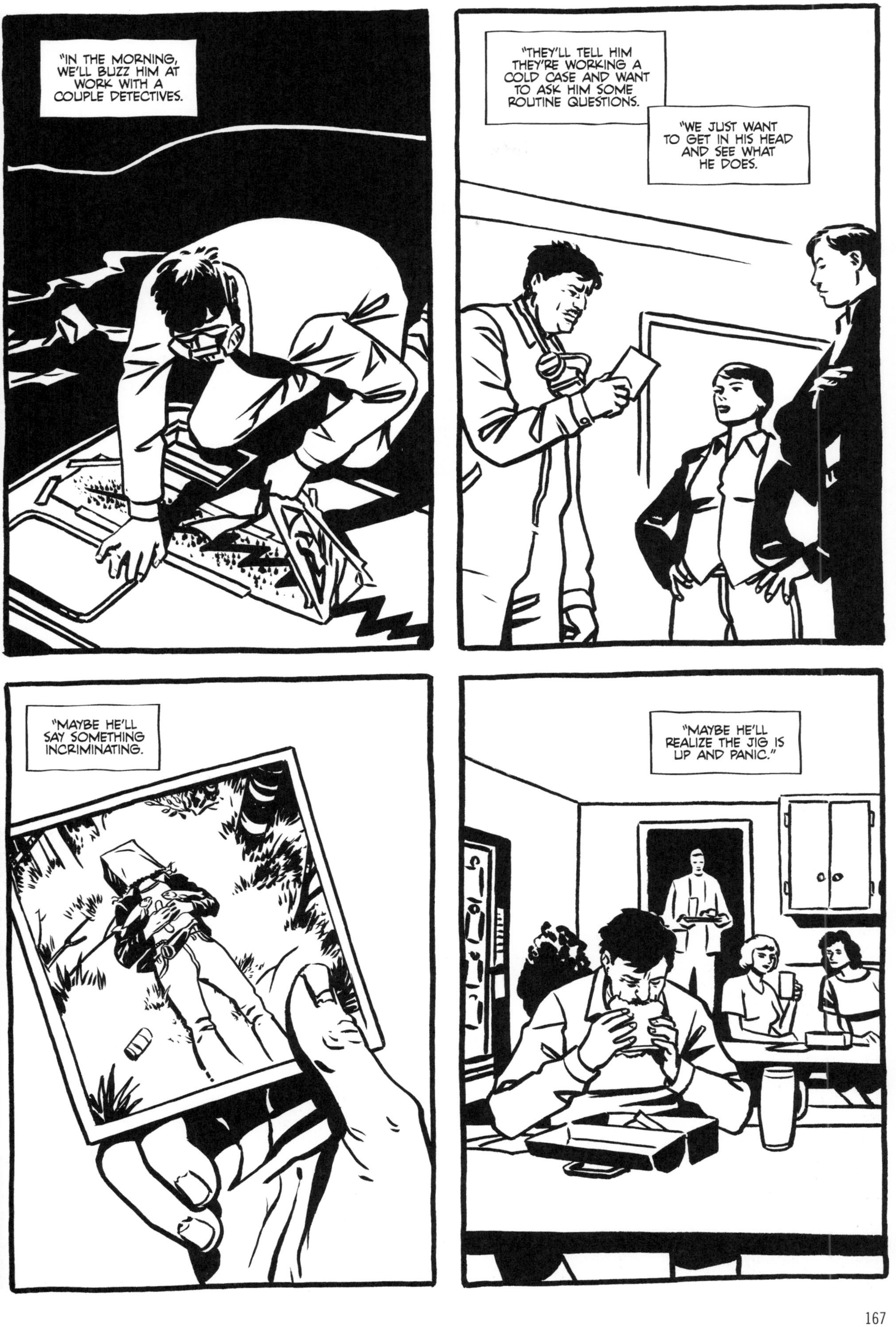
"IN THE MORNING, WE'LL BUZZ HIM AT WORK WITH A COUPLE DETECTIVES.
"THEY'LL TELL HIM THEY'RE WORKING A COLD CASE AND WANT TO ASK HIM SOME ROUTINE QUESTIONS.
"WE JUST WANT TO GET IN HIS HEAD AND SEE WHAT HE DOES.
"MAYBE HE'LL SAY SOMETHING INCRIMINATING.
"MAYBE HE'LL REALIZE THE JIG IS UP AND PANIC."

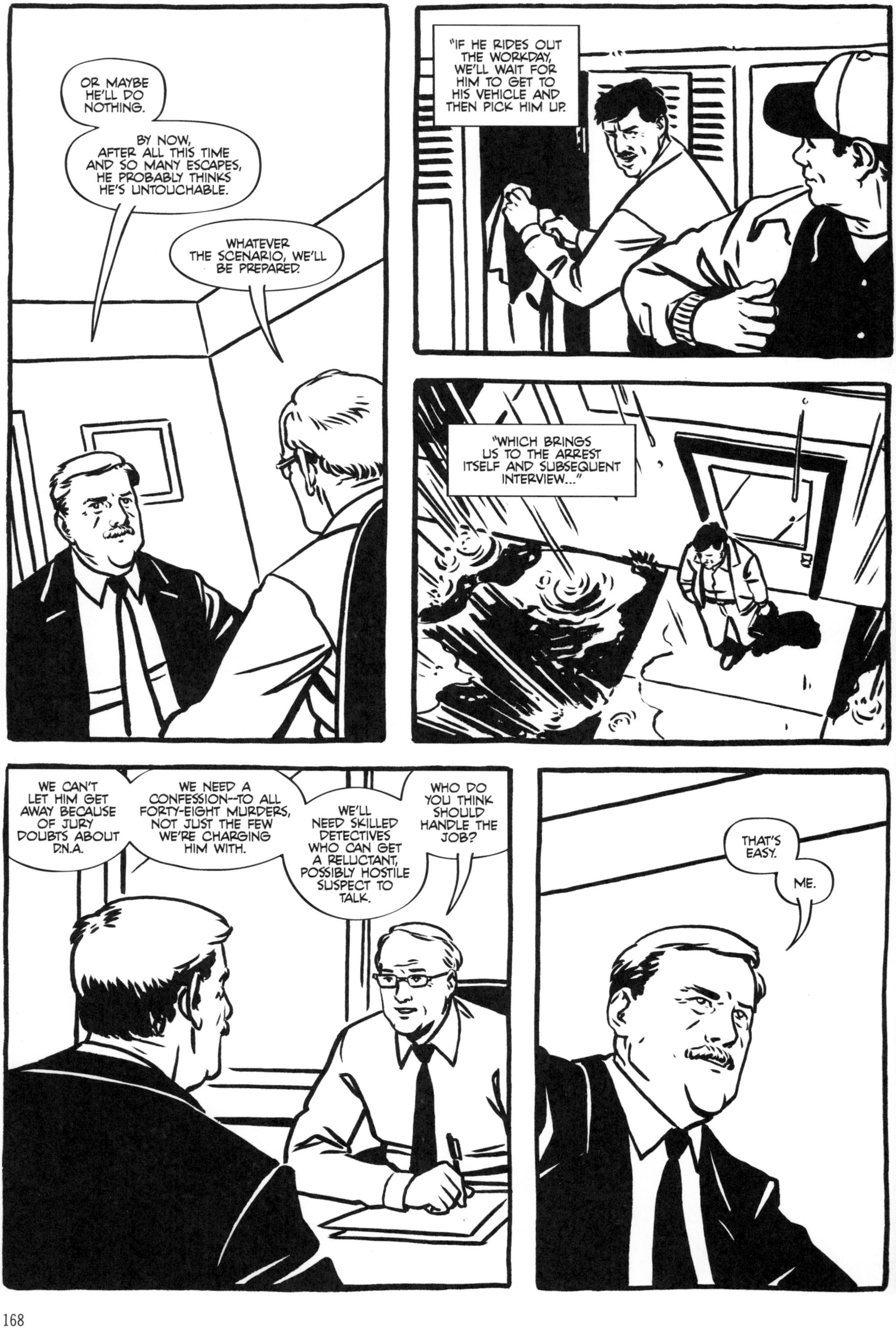
OR MAYBE HE'LL DO NOTHING.
BY NOW, AFTER ALL THIS TIME AND SO MANY ESCAPES, HE PROBABLY THINKS HE'S UNTOUCHABLE.
WHATEVER THE SCENARIO, WE'LL BE PREPARED.
"IF HE RIDES OUT THE WORKDAY, WE'LL WAIT FOR HIM TO GET TO HIS VEHICLE AND THEN PICK HIM UP.
"WHICH BRINGS US TO THE ARREST ITSELF AND SUBSEQUENT INTERVIEW..."
WE CAN'T LET HIM GET AWAY BECAUSE OF JURY DOUBTS ABOUT D.N.A.
WE NEED A CONFESSION--TO ALL FORTY-EIGHT MURDERS, NOT JUST THE FEW WE'RE CHARGING HIM WITH.
WE'LL NEED SKILLED DETECTIVES WHO CAN GET A RELUCTANT, POSSIBLY HOSTILE SUSPECT TO TALK.
WHO DO YOU THINK SHOULD HANDLE THE JOB?
THAT'S EASY.
ME.

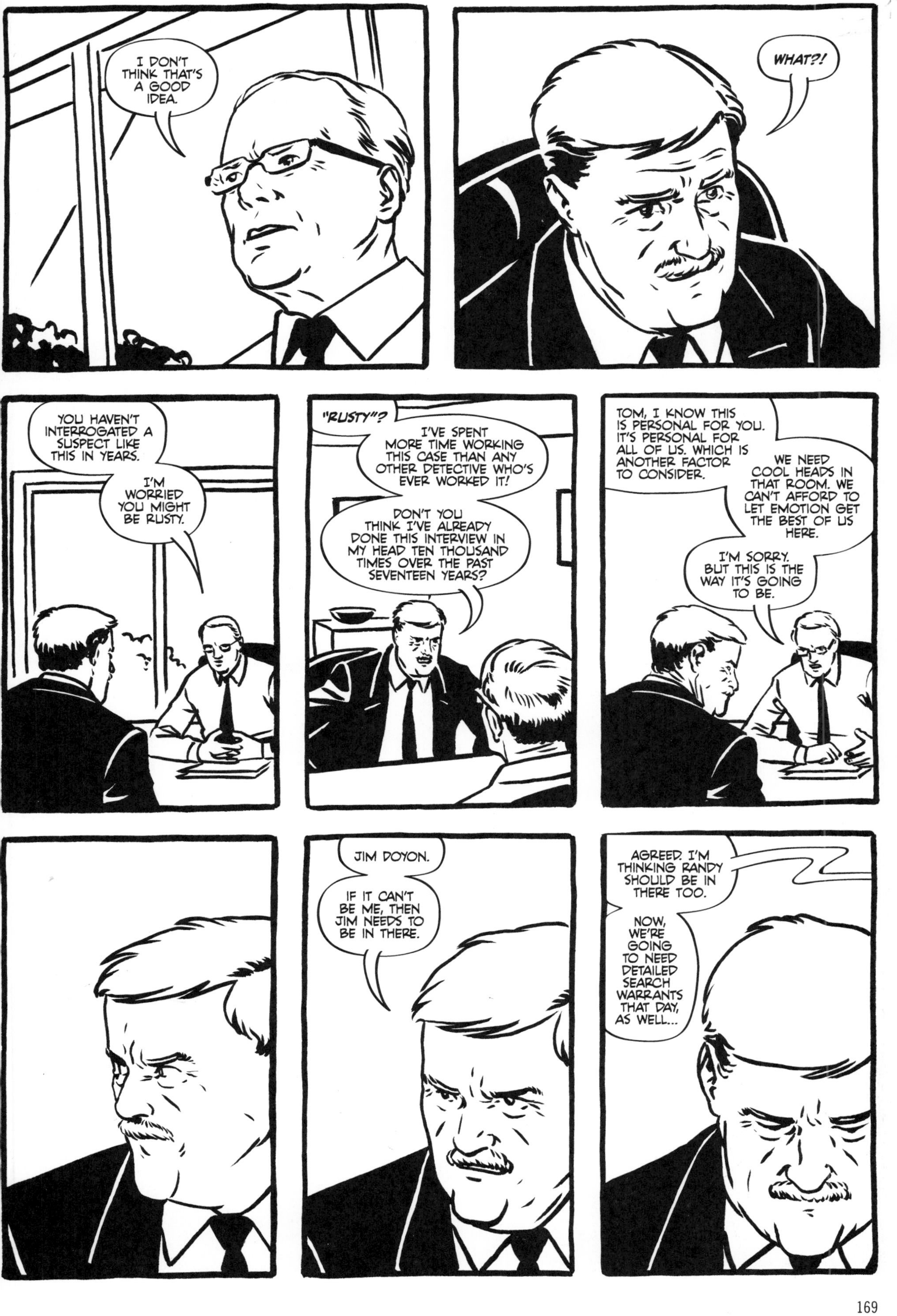
I DON'T THINK THAT'S A GOOD IDEA.
WHAT?!
YOU HAVEN'T INTERROGATED A SUSPECT LIKE THIS IN YEARS.
I'M WORRIED YOU MIGHT BE RUSTY.
"RUSTY"?
I'VE SPENT MORE TIME WORKING THIS CASE THAN ANY OTHER DETECTIVE WHO'S EVER WORKED IT!
DON'T YOU THINK I'VE ALREADY DONE THIS INTERVIEW IN MY HEAD TEN THOUSAND TIMES OVER THE PAST SEVENTEEN YEARS?
TOM, I KNOW THIS IS PERSONAL FOR YOU. IT'S PERSONAL FOR ALL OF US. WHICH IS ANOTHER FACTOR TO CONSIDER.
WE NEED COOL HEADS IN THAT ROOM. WE CAN'T AFFORD TO LET EMOTION GET THE BEST OF US HERE.
I'M SORRY. BUT THIS IS THE WAY IT'S GOING TO BE.
JIM DOYON.
IF IT CAN'T BE ME, THEN JIM NEEDS TO BE IN THERE.
AGREED. I'M THINKING RANDY SHOULD BE IN THERE TOO.
NOW, WE'RE GOING TO NEED DETAILED SEARCH WARRANTS THAT DAY, AS WELL...

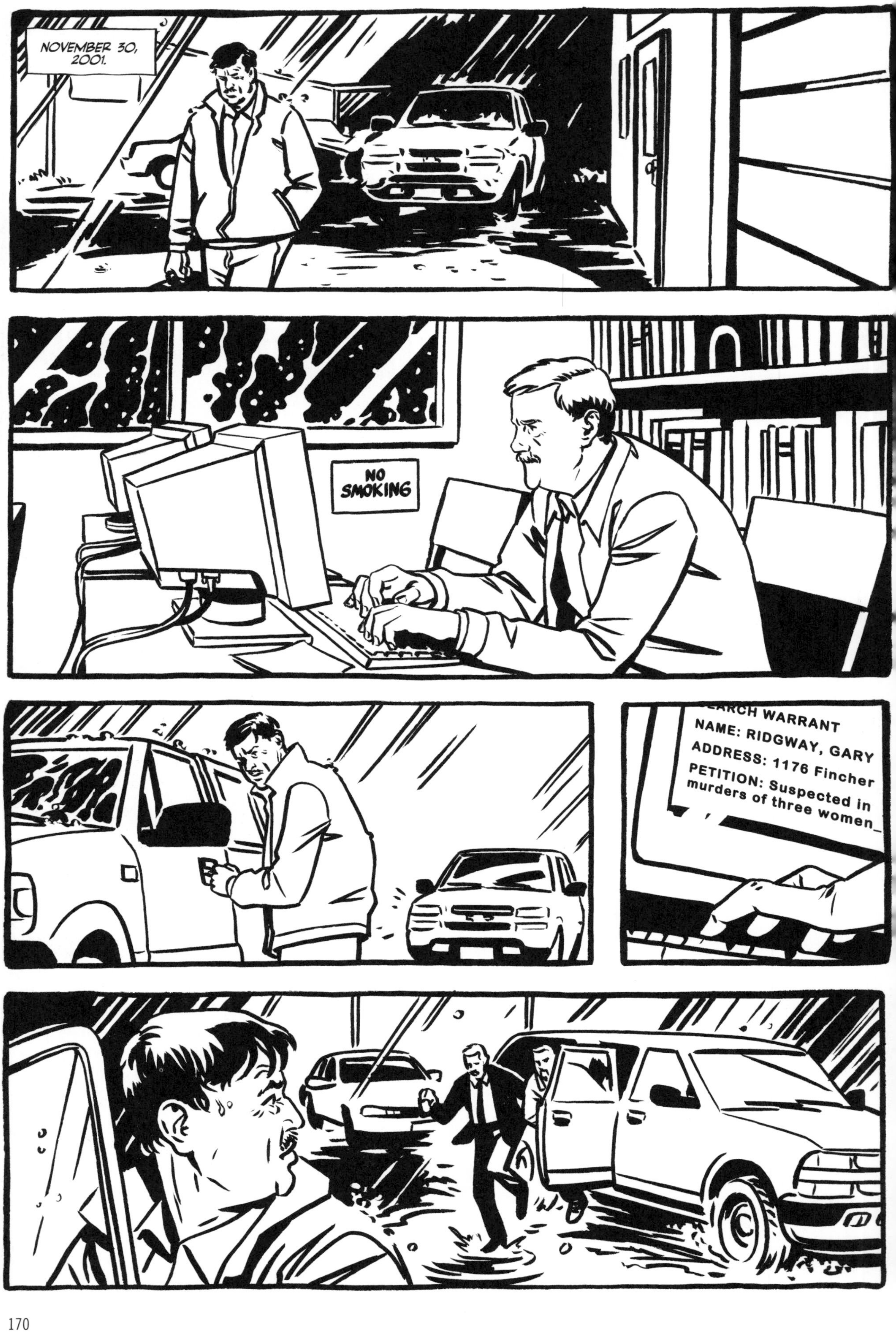
NOVEMBER 30, 2001.
NO SMOKING
ARCH WARRANT
NAME: RIDGWAY, GARY
ADDRESS: 1176 Fincher
PETITION: Suspected in murders of three women_

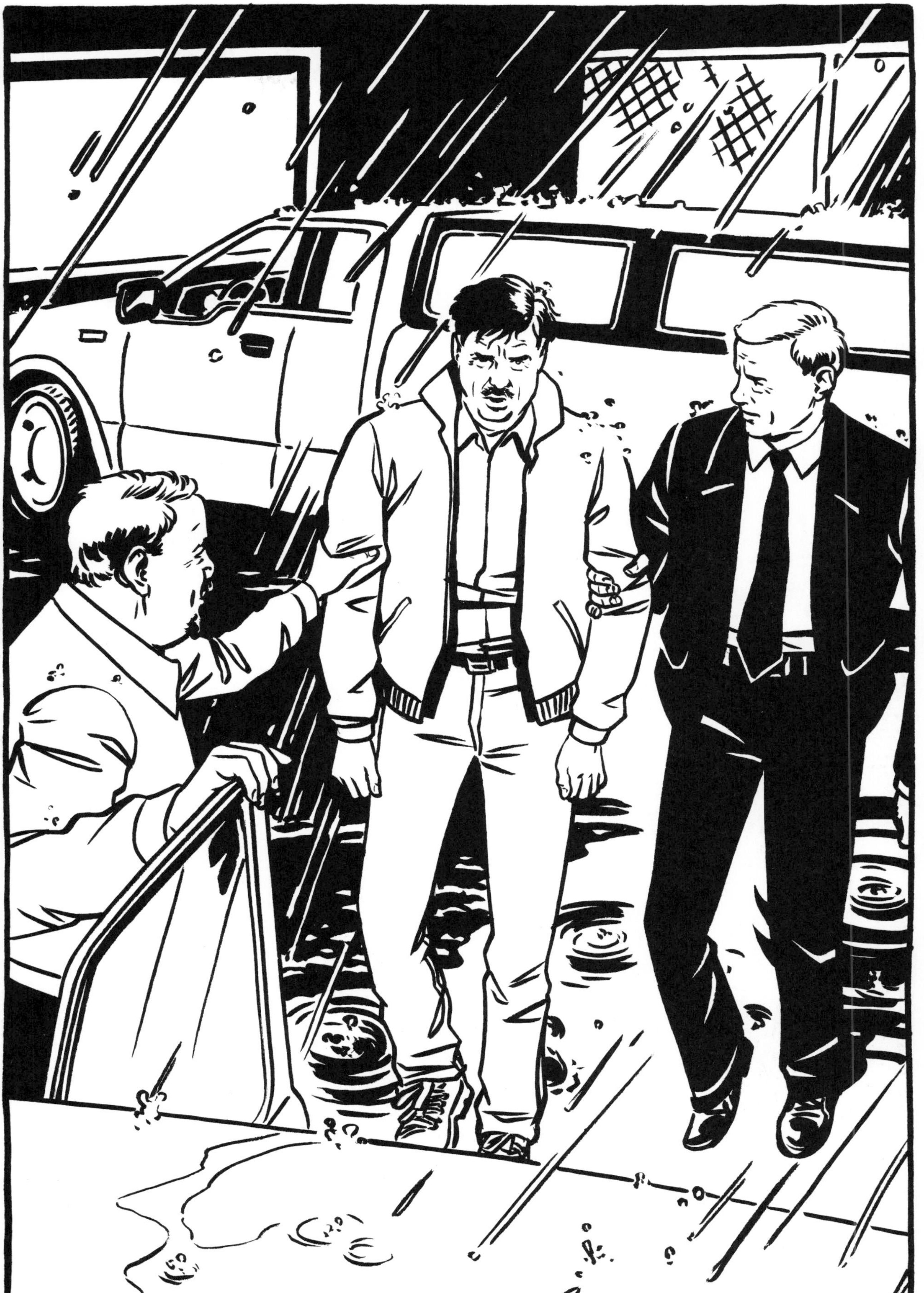

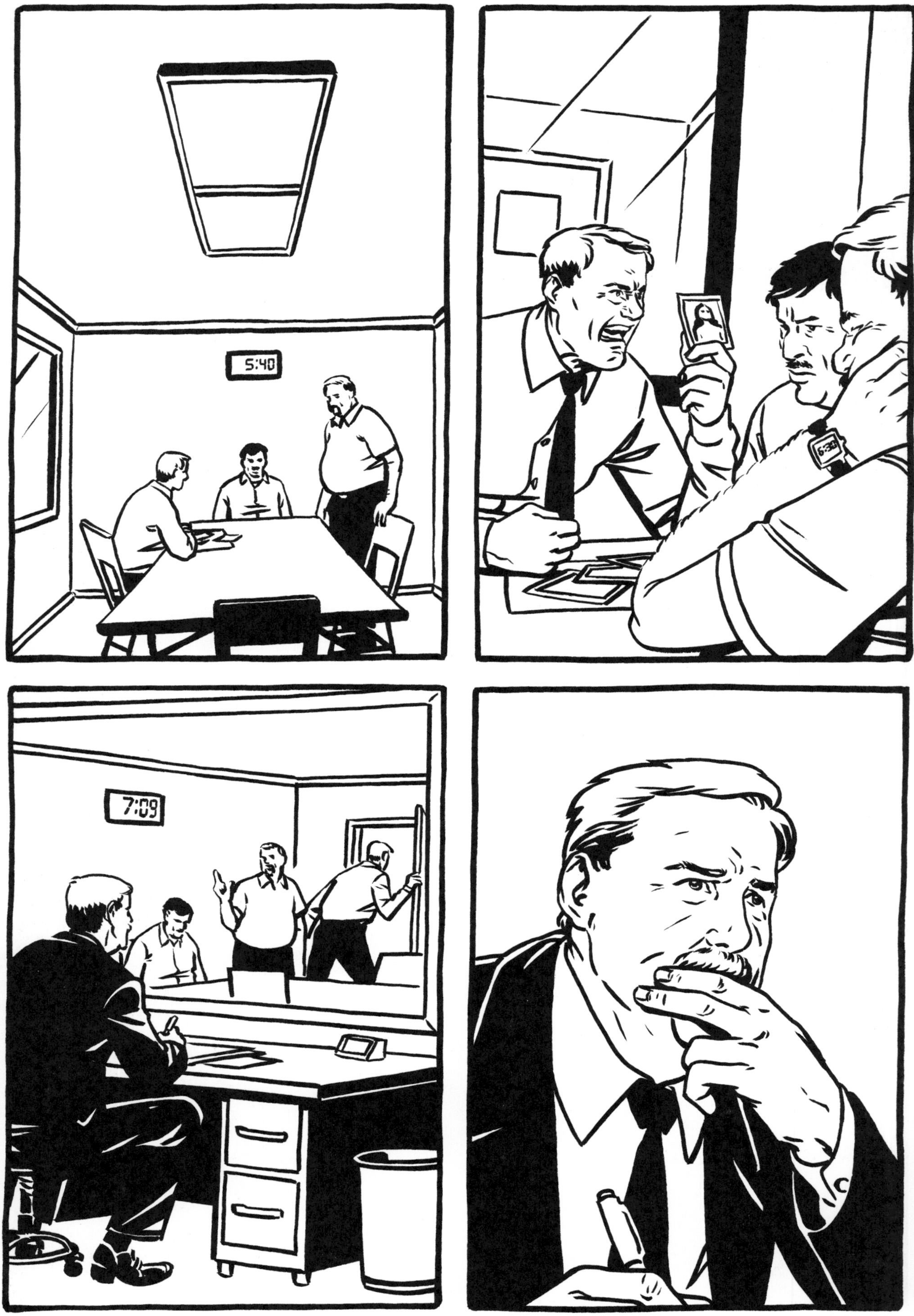

5:40
7:09

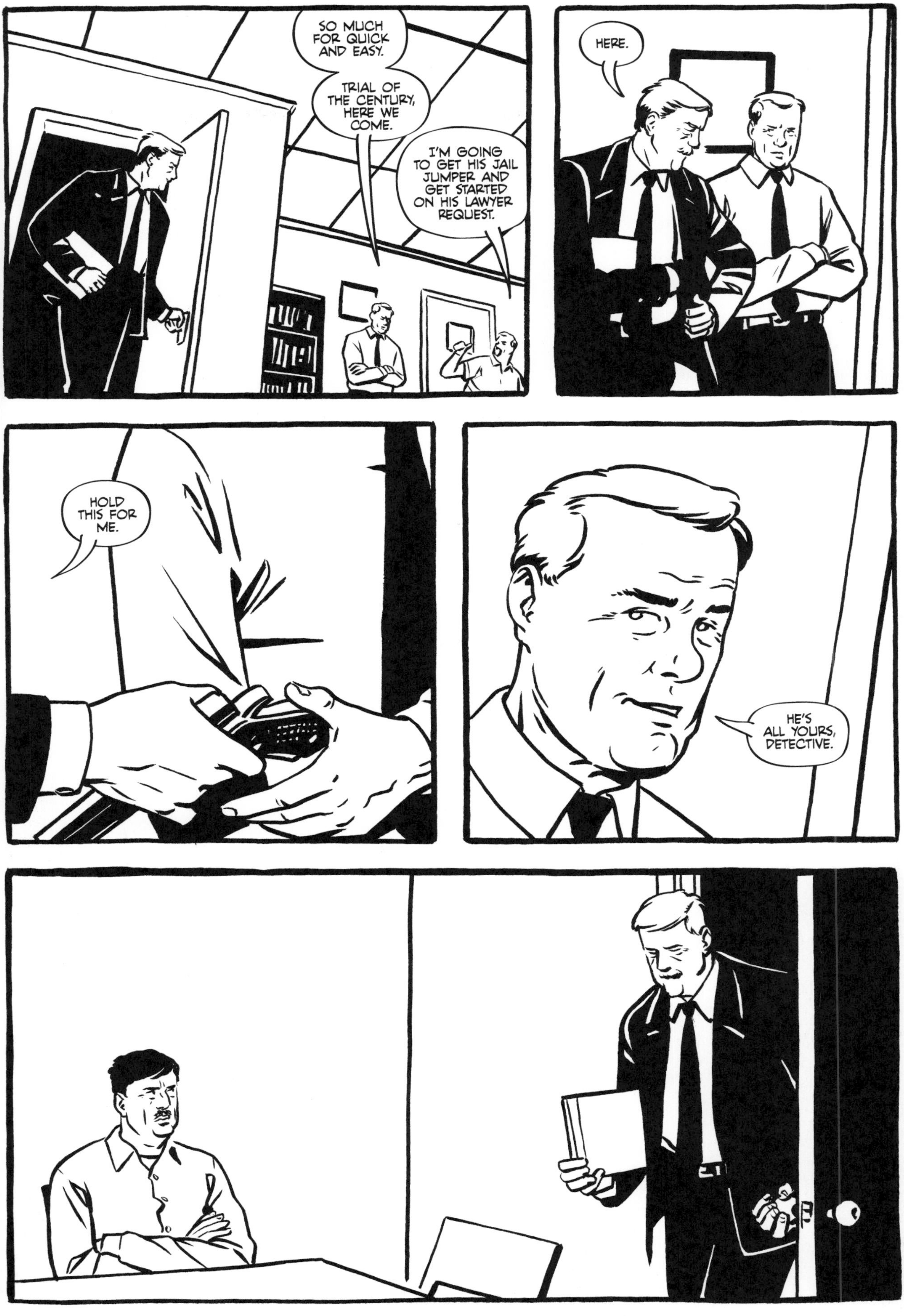
SO MUCH FOR QUICK AND EASY.
TRIAL OF THE CENTURY, HERE WE COME.
I'M GOING TO GET HIS JAIL JUMPER AND GET STARTED ON HIS LAWYER REQUEST.
HERE.
HOLD THIS FOR ME.
HE'S ALL YOURS, DETECTIVE.

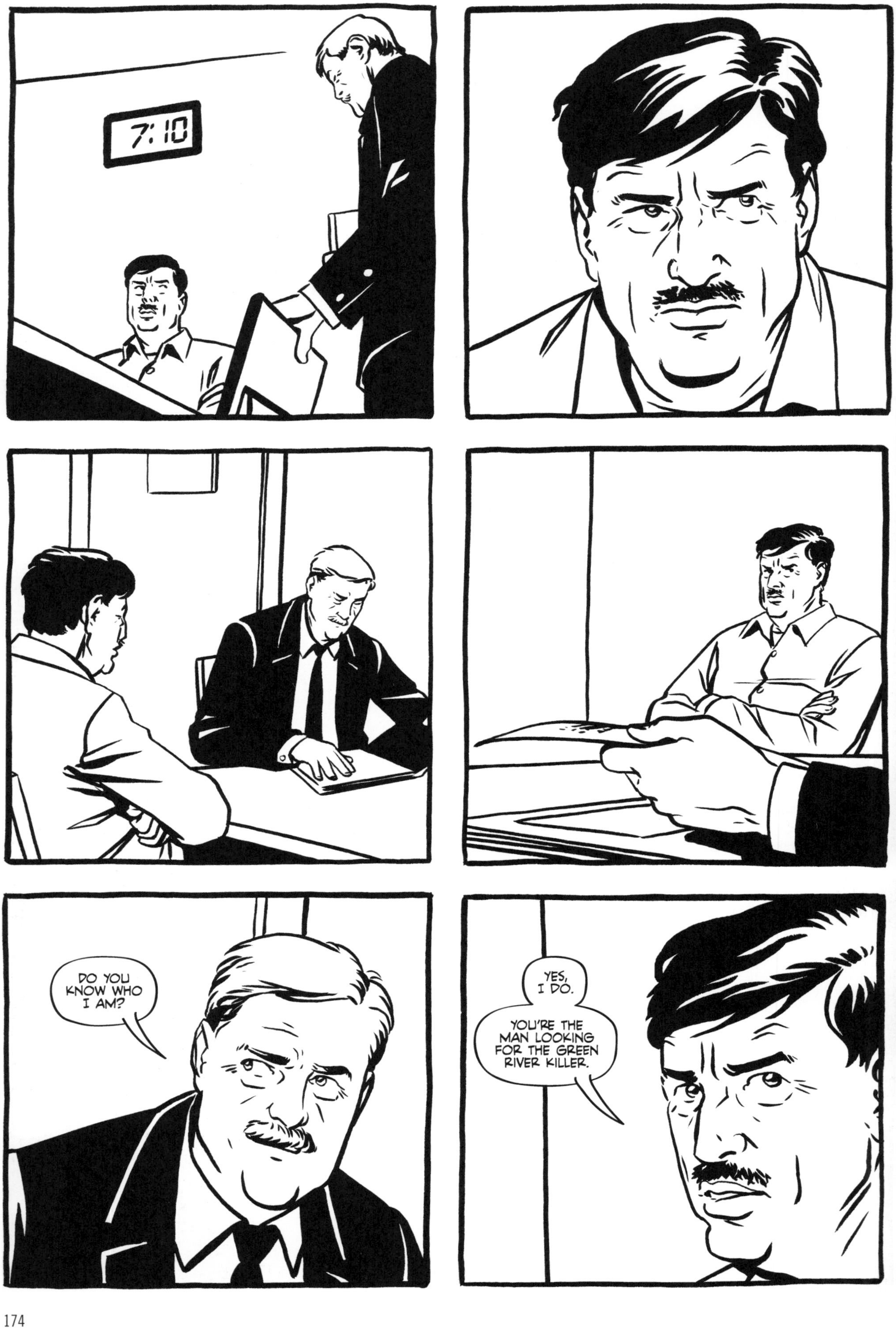
7:10
DO YOU KNOW WHO I AM?
YES, I DO.
YOU'RE THE MAN LOOKING FOR THE GREEN RIVER KILLER.

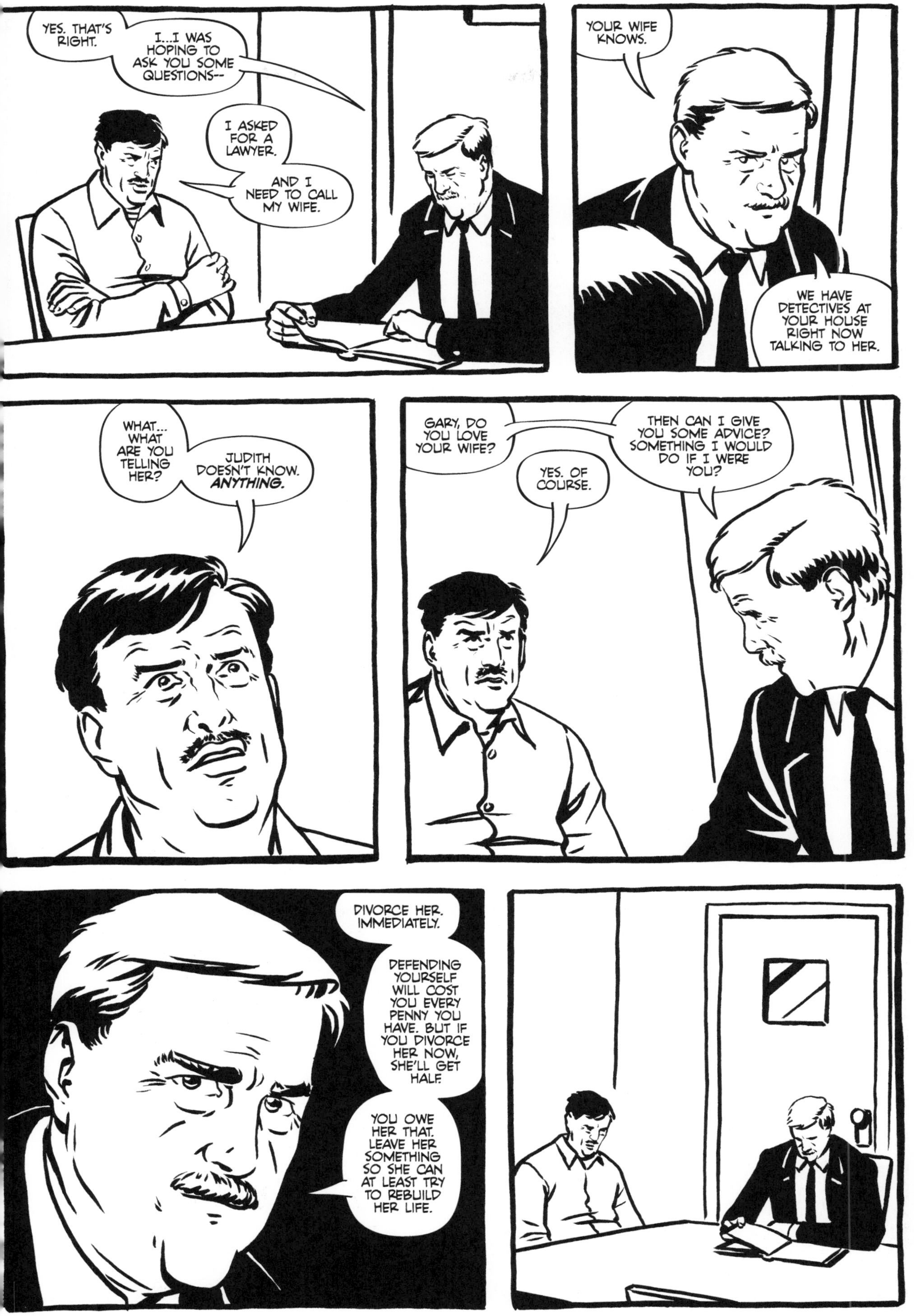
YES. THAT'S RIGHT.
I...I WAS HOPING TO ASK YOU SOME QUESTIONS--
I ASKED FOR A LAWYER.
AND I NEED TO CALL MY WIFE.
YOUR WIFE KNOWS.
WE HAVE DETECTIVES AT YOUR HOUSE RIGHT NOW TALKING TO HER.
WHAT... WHAT ARE YOU TELLING HER?
JUDITH DOESN'T KNOW. *ANYTHING.*
GARY, DO YOU LOVE YOUR WIFE?
YES. OF COURSE.
THEN CAN I GIVE YOU SOME ADVICE? SOMETHING I WOULD DO IF I WERE YOU?
DIVORCE HER. IMMEDIATELY.
DEFENDING YOURSELF WILL COST YOU EVERY PENNY YOU HAVE. BUT IF YOU DIVORCE HER NOW, SHE'LL GET HALF.
YOU OWE HER THAT. LEAVE HER SOMETHING SO SHE CAN AT LEAST TRY TO REBUILD HER LIFE.

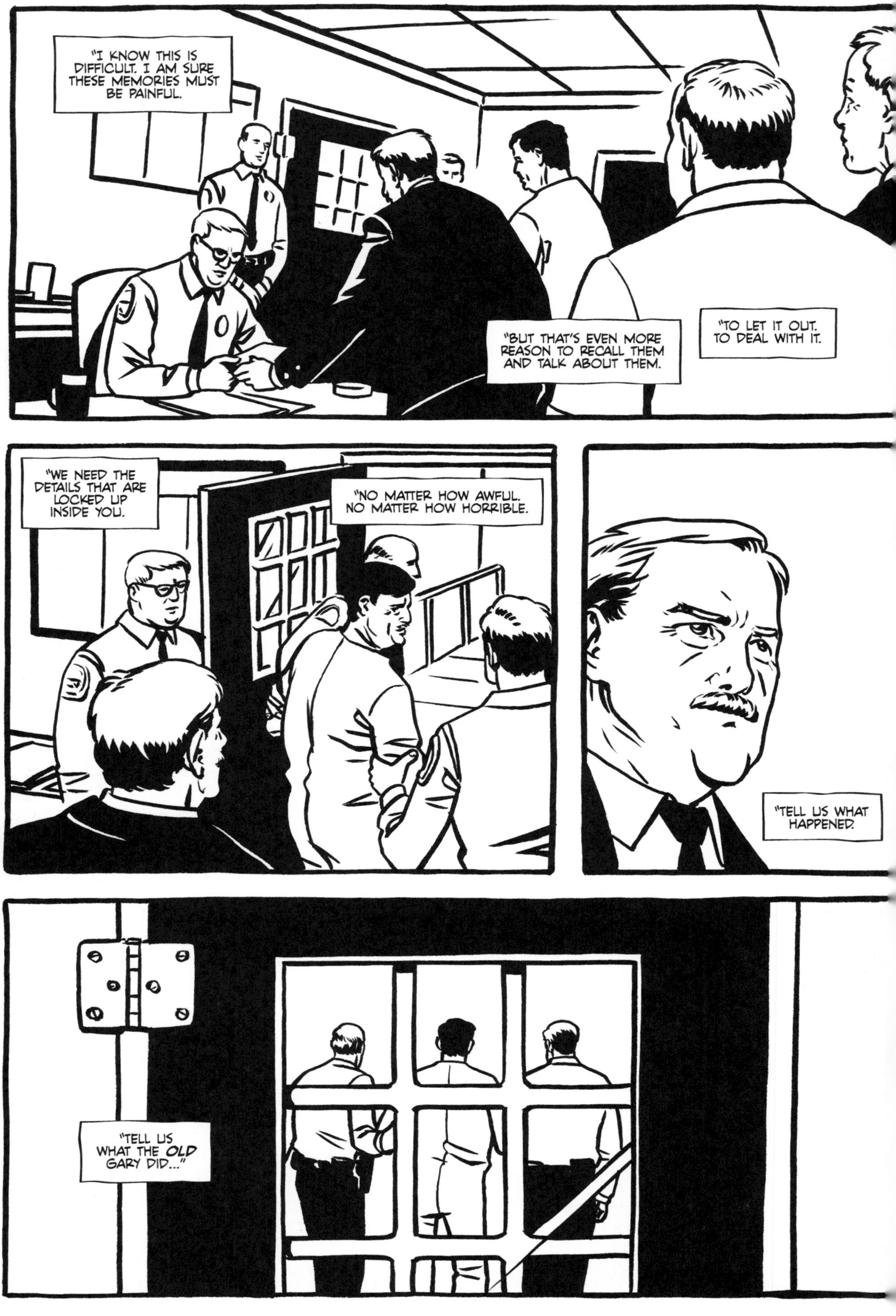
"I KNOW THIS IS DIFFICULT. I AM SURE THESE MEMORIES MUST BE PAINFUL.
"BUT THAT'S EVEN MORE REASON TO RECALL THEM AND TALK ABOUT THEM.
"TO LET IT OUT. TO DEAL WITH IT.
"WE NEED THE DETAILS THAT ARE LOCKED UP INSIDE YOU.
"NO MATTER HOW AWFUL. NO MATTER HOW HORRIBLE.
"TELL US WHAT HAPPENED.
"TELL US WHAT THE *OLD* GARY DID..."

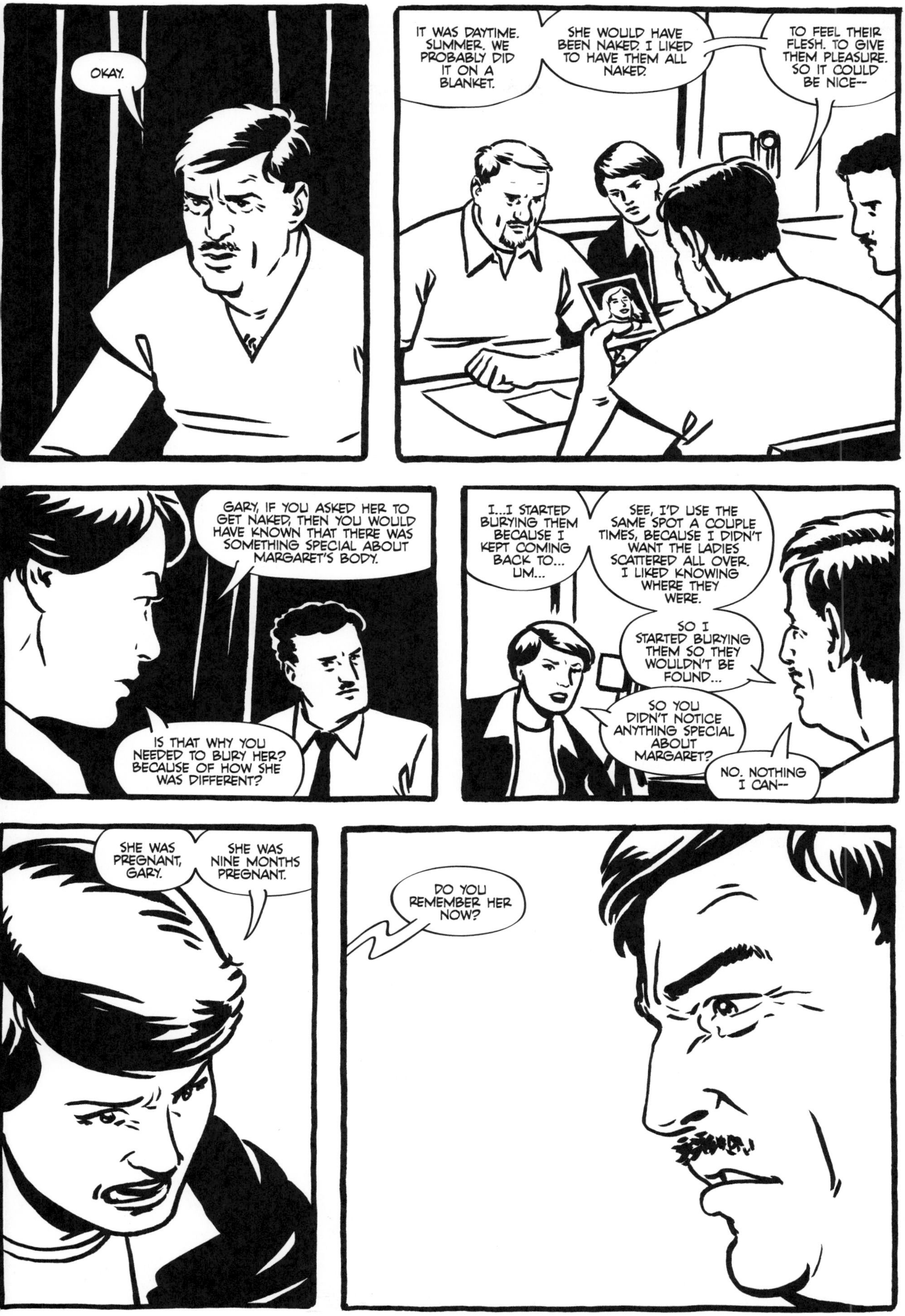
OKAY.
IT WAS DAYTIME. SUMMER. WE PROBABLY DID IT ON A BLANKET.
SHE WOULD HAVE BEEN NAKED. I LIKED TO HAVE THEM ALL NAKED.
TO FEEL THEIR FLESH. TO GIVE THEM PLEASURE. SO IT COULD BE NICE--
GARY, IF YOU ASKED HER TO GET NAKED, THEN YOU WOULD HAVE KNOWN THAT THERE WAS SOMETHING SPECIAL ABOUT MARGARET'S BODY.
IS THAT WHY YOU NEEDED TO BURY HER? BECAUSE OF HOW SHE WAS DIFFERENT?
I...I STARTED BURYING THEM BECAUSE I KEPT COMING BACK TO... UM...
SEE, I'D USE THE SAME SPOT A COUPLE TIMES, BECAUSE I DIDN'T WANT THE LADIES SCATTERED ALL OVER. I LIKED KNOWING WHERE THEY WERE.
SO I STARTED BURYING THEM SO THEY WOULDN'T BE FOUND...
SO YOU DIDN'T NOTICE ANYTHING SPECIAL ABOUT MARGARET?
NO. NOTHING I CAN--
SHE WAS PREGNANT, GARY.
SHE WAS NINE MONTHS PREGNANT.
DO YOU REMEMBER HER NOW?

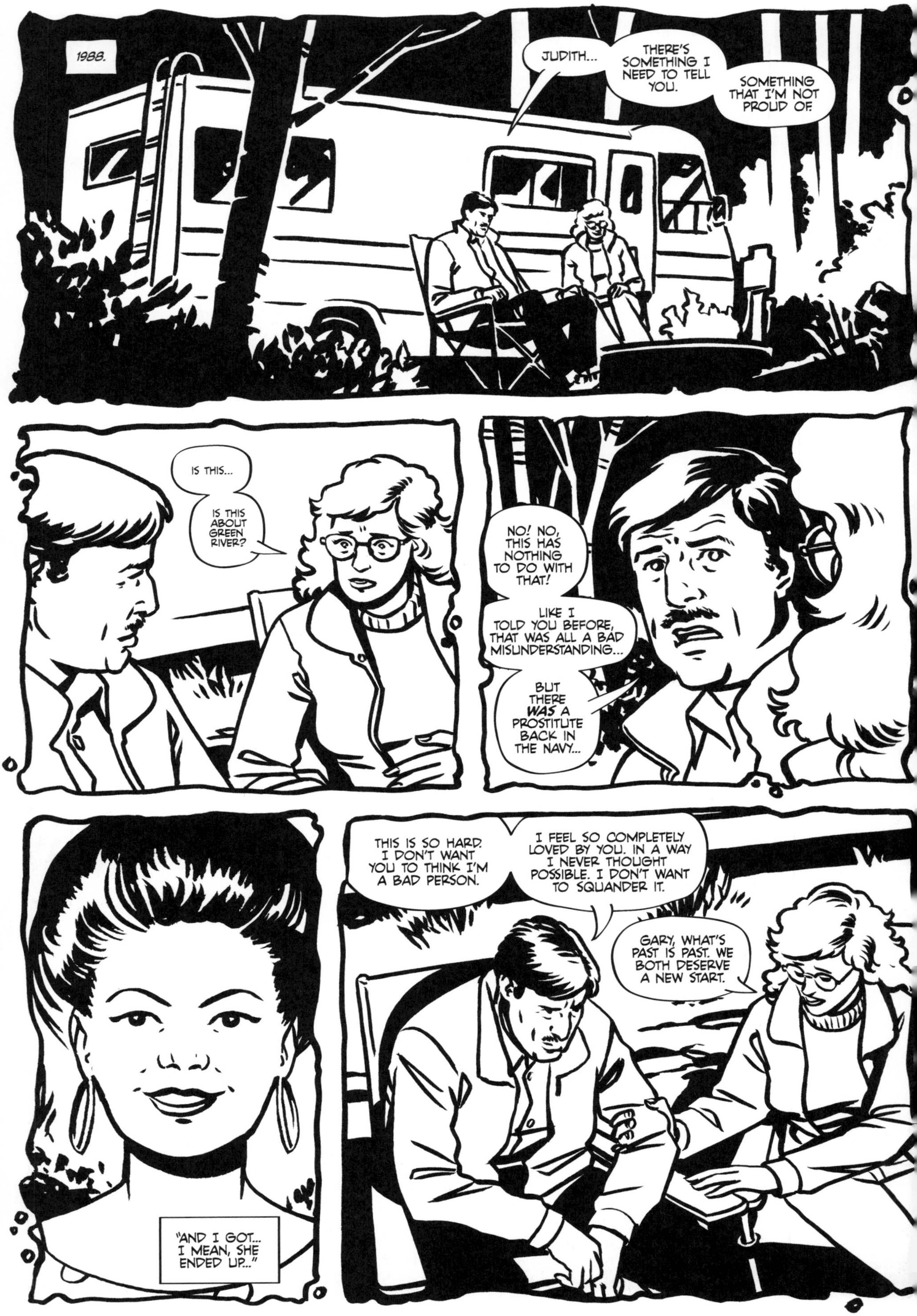
1988.
JUDITH...
THERE'S SOMETHING I NEED TO TELL YOU.
SOMETHING THAT I'M NOT PROUD OF.
IS THIS...
IS THIS ABOUT GREEN RIVER?
NO! NO, THIS HAS NOTHING TO DO WITH THAT!
LIKE I TOLD YOU BEFORE, THAT WAS ALL A BAD MISUNDERSTANDING...
BUT THERE *WAS* A PROSTITUTE BACK IN THE NAVY...
"AND I GOT... I MEAN, SHE ENDED UP..."
THIS IS SO HARD. I DON'T WANT YOU TO THINK I'M A BAD PERSON.
I FEEL SO COMPLETELY LOVED BY YOU. IN A WAY I NEVER THOUGHT POSSIBLE. I DON'T WANT TO SQUANDER IT.
GARY, WHAT'S PAST IS PAST. WE BOTH DESERVE A NEW START.

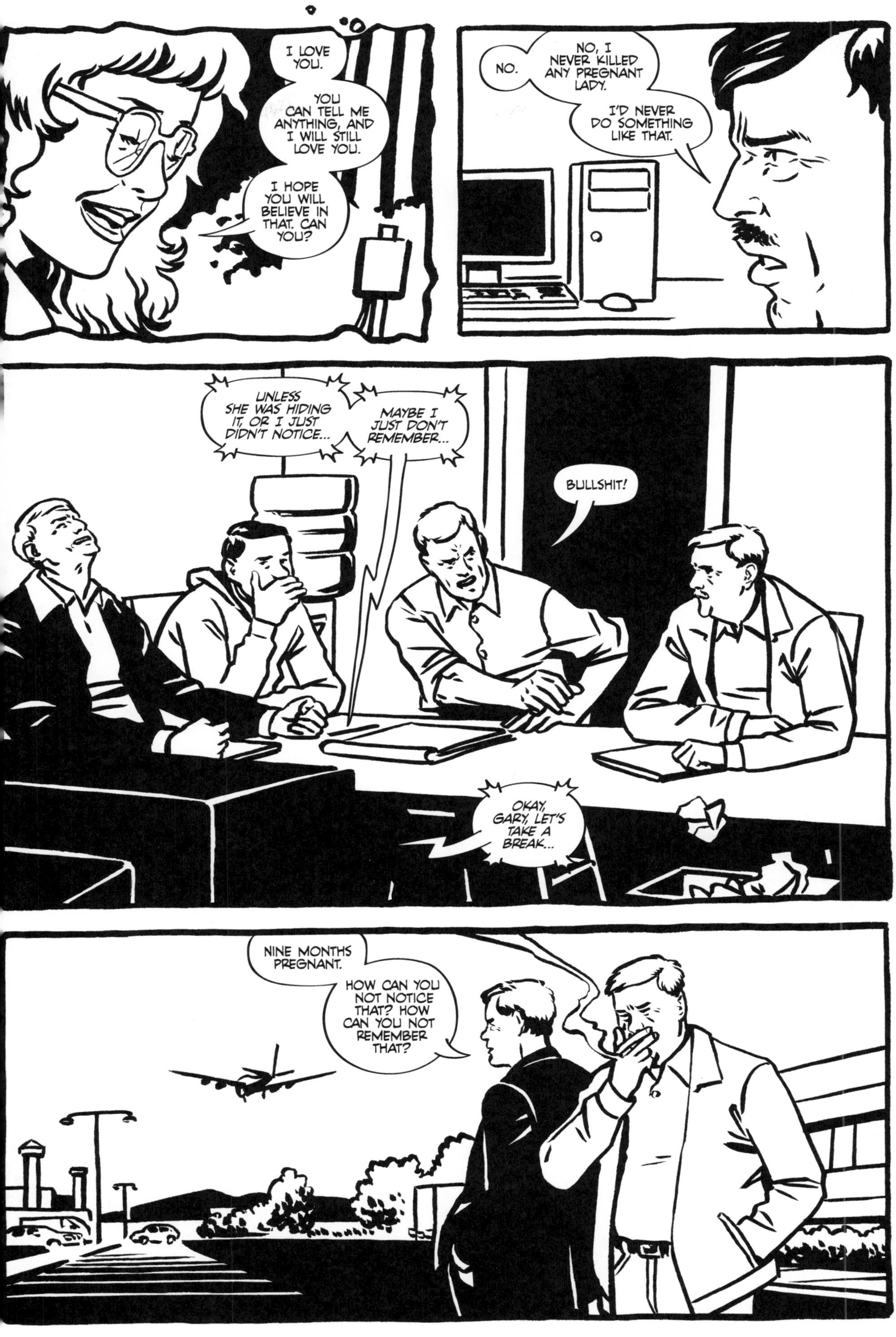
I LOVE YOU.
YOU CAN TELL ME ANYTHING, AND I WILL STILL LOVE YOU.
I HOPE YOU WILL BELIEVE IN THAT. CAN YOU?
NO.
NO, I NEVER KILLED ANY PREGNANT LADY.
I'D NEVER DO SOMETHING LIKE THAT.
UNLESS SHE WAS HIDING IT, OR I JUST DIDN'T NOTICE...
MAYBE I JUST DON'T REMEMBER...
BULLSHIT!
OKAY, GARY, LET'S TAKE A BREAK...
NINE MONTHS PREGNANT.
HOW CAN YOU NOT NOTICE THAT? HOW CAN YOU NOT REMEMBER THAT?

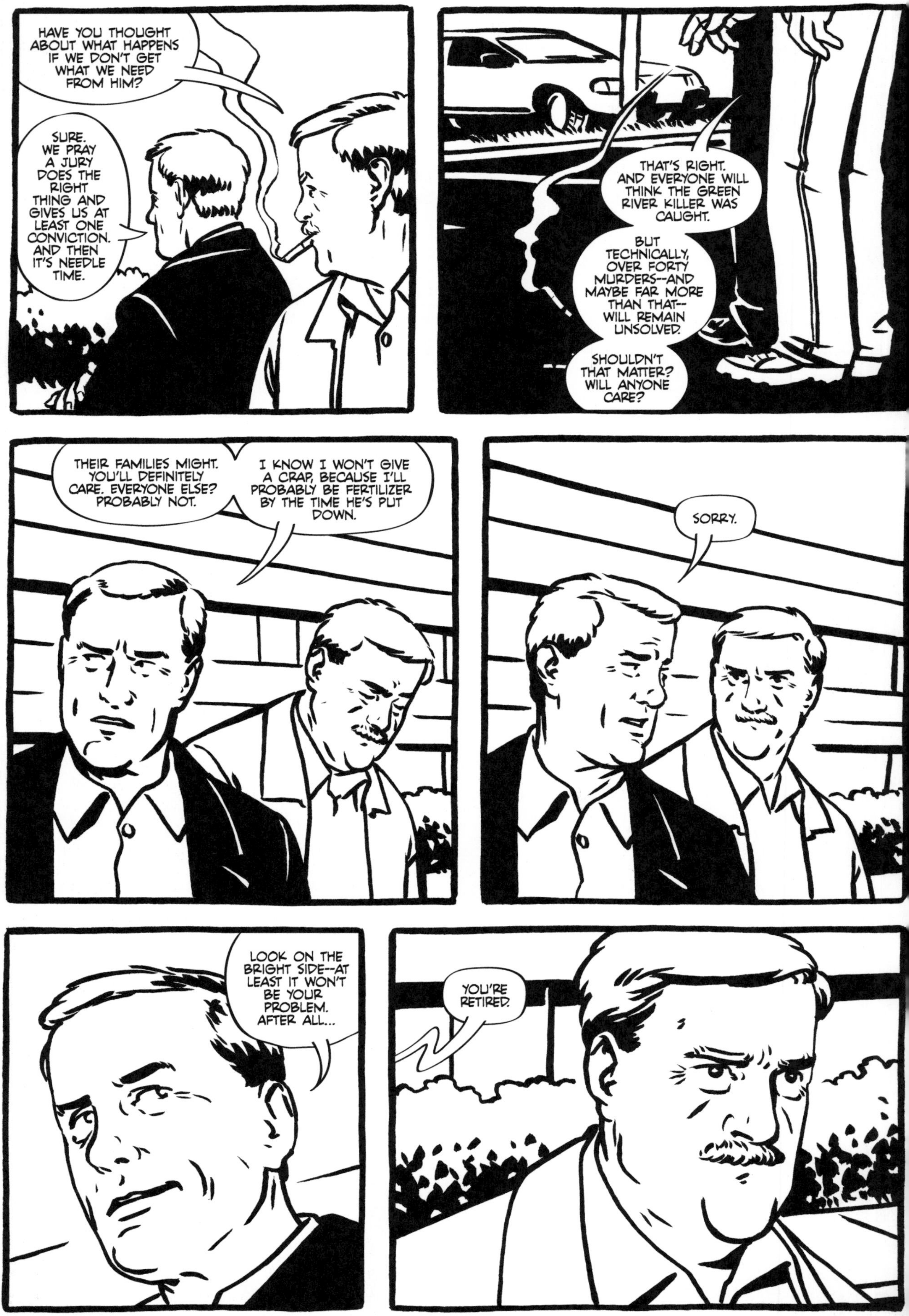
HAVE YOU THOUGHT ABOUT WHAT HAPPENS IF WE DON'T GET WHAT WE NEED FROM HIM?
SURE. WE PRAY A JURY DOES THE RIGHT THING AND GIVES US AT LEAST ONE CONVICTION. AND THEN IT'S NEEDLE TIME.
THAT'S RIGHT. AND EVERYONE WILL THINK THE GREEN RIVER KILLER WAS CAUGHT.
BUT TECHNICALLY, OVER FORTY MURDERS--AND MAYBE FAR MORE THAN THAT--WILL REMAIN UNSOLVED.
SHOULDN'T THAT MATTER? WILL ANYONE CARE?
THEIR FAMILIES MIGHT. YOU'LL DEFINITELY CARE. EVERYONE ELSE? PROBABLY NOT.
I KNOW I WON'T GIVE A CRAP, BECAUSE I'LL PROBABLY BE FERTILIZER BY THE TIME HE'S PUT DOWN.
SORRY.
LOOK ON THE BRIGHT SIDE--AT LEAST IT WON'T BE YOUR PROBLEM. AFTER ALL...
YOU'RE RETIRED.

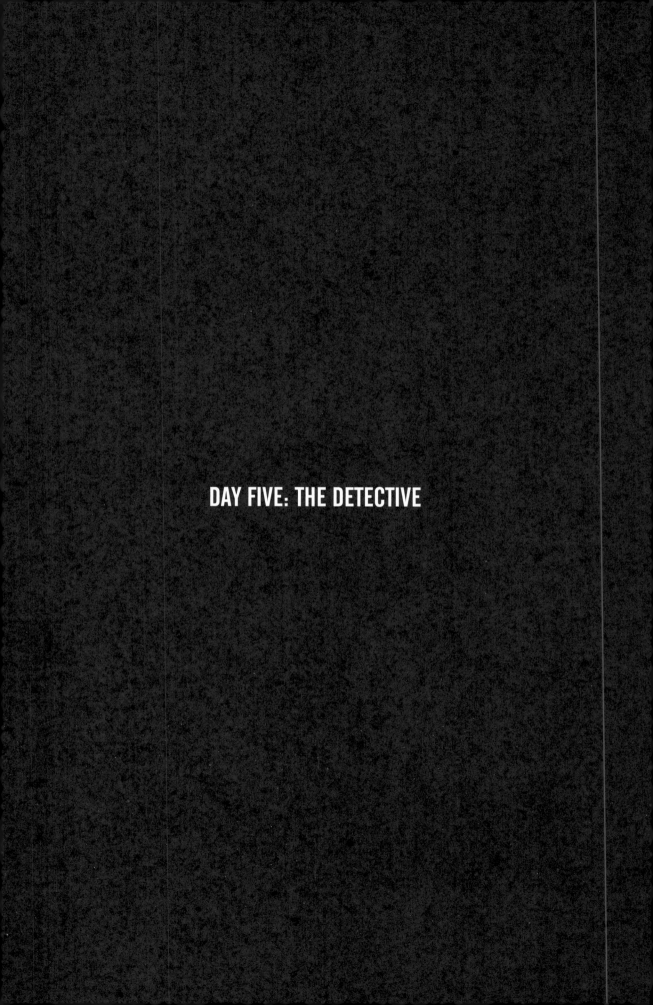

DAY FIVE: THE DETECTIVE

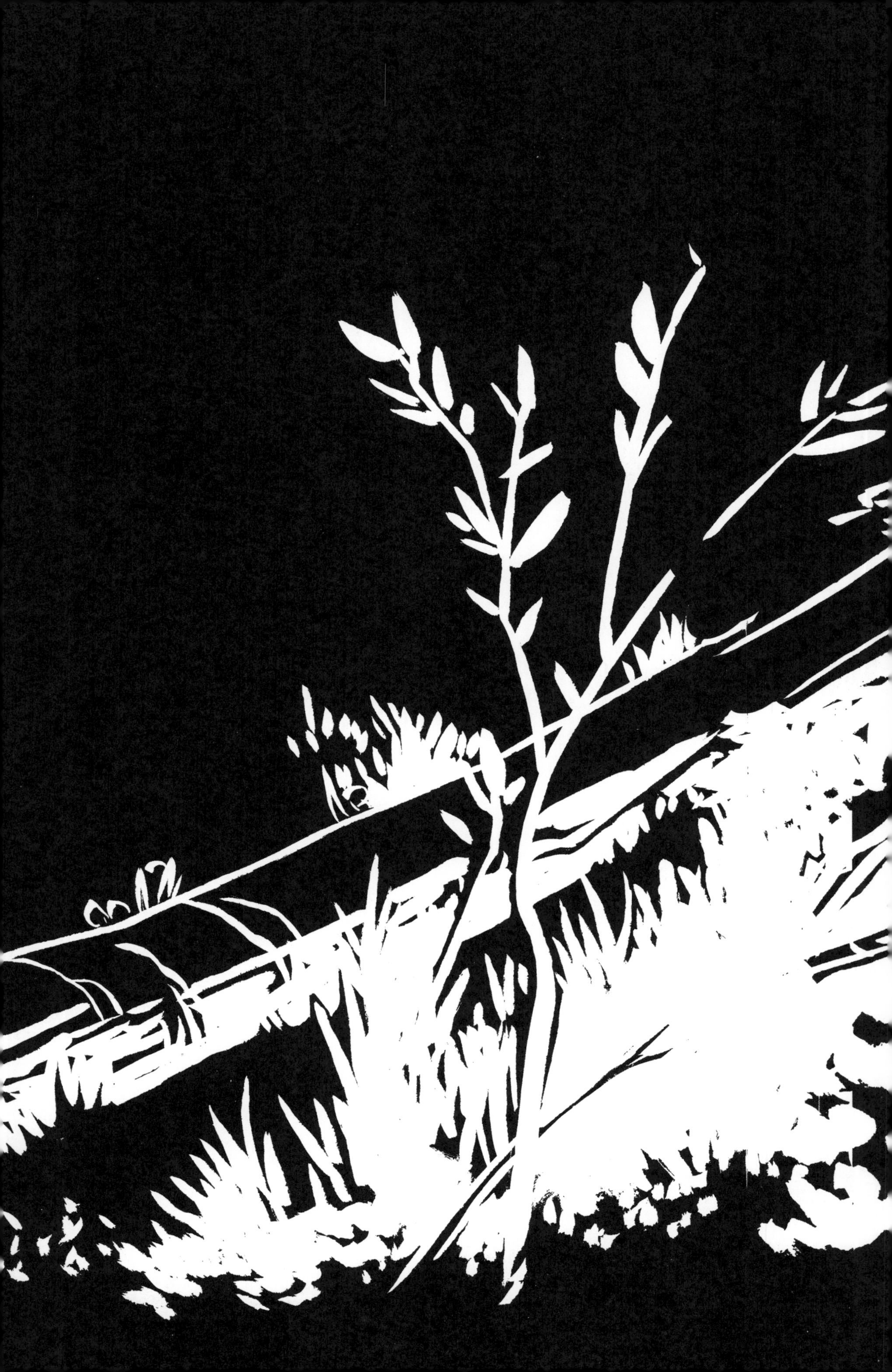

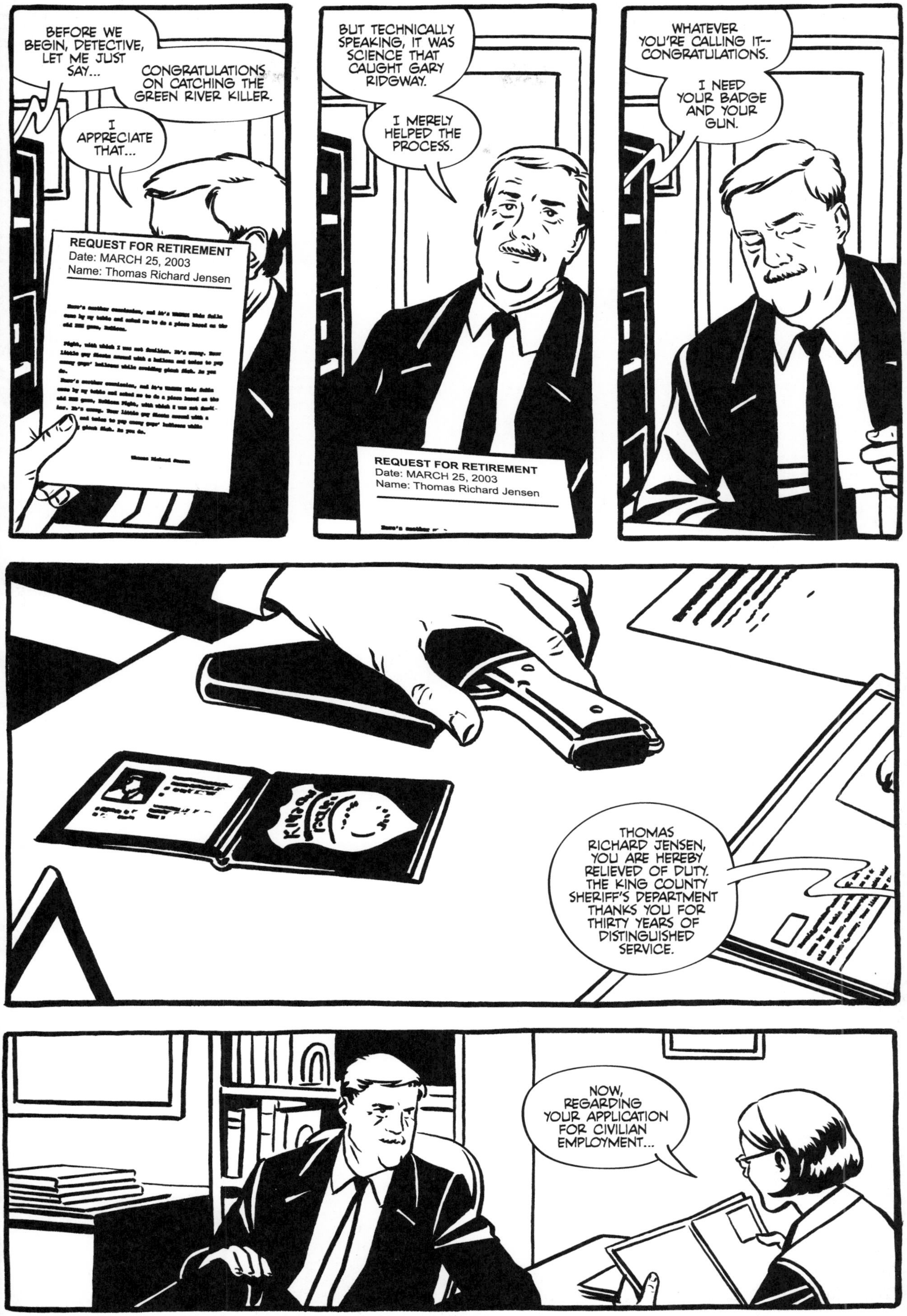
BEFORE WE BEGIN, DETECTIVE, LET ME JUST SAY...
CONGRATULATIONS ON CATCHING THE GREEN RIVER KILLER.
I APPRECIATE THAT...
REQUEST FOR RETIREMENT
Date: MARCH 25, 2003
Name: Thomas Richard Jensen
BUT TECHNICALLY SPEAKING, IT WAS SCIENCE THAT CAUGHT GARY RIDGWAY.
I MERELY HELPED THE PROCESS.
REQUEST FOR RETIREMENT
Date: MARCH 25, 2003
Name: Thomas Richard Jensen
WHATEVER YOU'RE CALLING IT-- CONGRATULATIONS.
I NEED YOUR BADGE AND YOUR GUN.
THOMAS RICHARD JENSEN, YOU ARE HEREBY RELIEVED OF DUTY. THE KING COUNTY SHERIFF'S DEPARTMENT THANKS YOU FOR THIRTY YEARS OF DISTINGUISHED SERVICE.
NOW, REGARDING YOUR APPLICATION FOR CIVILIAN EMPLOYMENT...

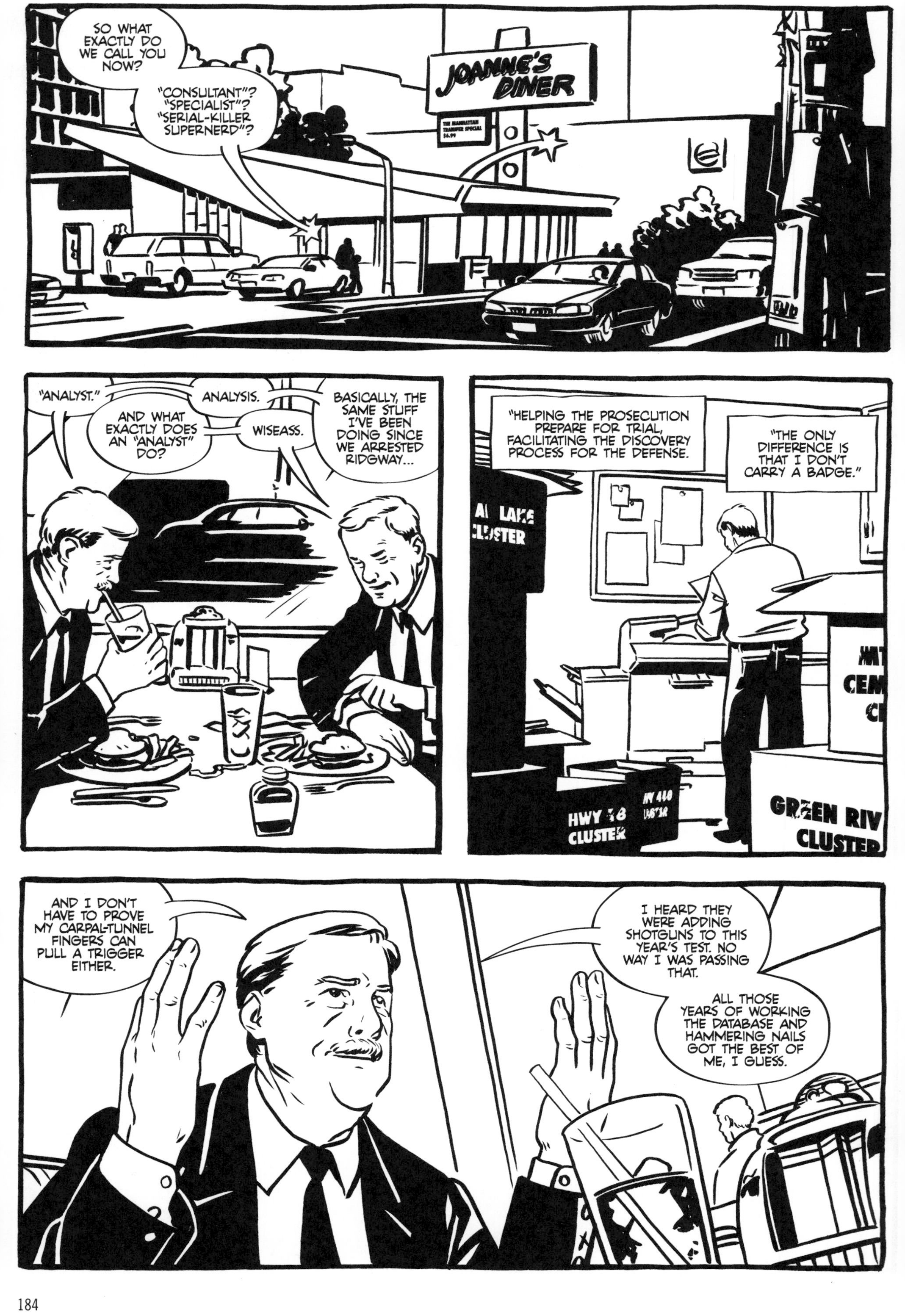

SO WHAT EXACTLY DO WE CALL YOU NOW?
"CONSULTANT"? "SPECIALIST"? "SERIAL-KILLER SUPERNERD"?
JOANNE'S DINER
THE MANHATTAN TRANSFER SPECIAL $6.99
"ANALYST."
ANALYSIS.
AND WHAT EXACTLY DOES AN "ANALYST" DO?
WISEASS.
BASICALLY, THE SAME STUFF I'VE BEEN DOING SINCE WE ARRESTED RIDGWAY...
"HELPING THE PROSECUTION PREPARE FOR TRIAL, FACILITATING THE DISCOVERY PROCESS FOR THE DEFENSE.
"THE ONLY DIFFERENCE IS THAT I DON'T CARRY A BADGE."
CLUSTER
CLUSTER
GREEN RIV
CLUSTER
AND I DON'T HAVE TO PROVE MY CARPAL-TUNNEL FINGERS CAN PULL A TRIGGER EITHER.
I HEARD THEY WERE ADDING SHOTGUNS TO THIS YEAR'S TEST. NO WAY I WAS PASSING THAT.
ALL THOSE YEARS OF WORKING THE DATABASE AND HAMMERING NAILS GOT THE BEST OF ME, I GUESS.

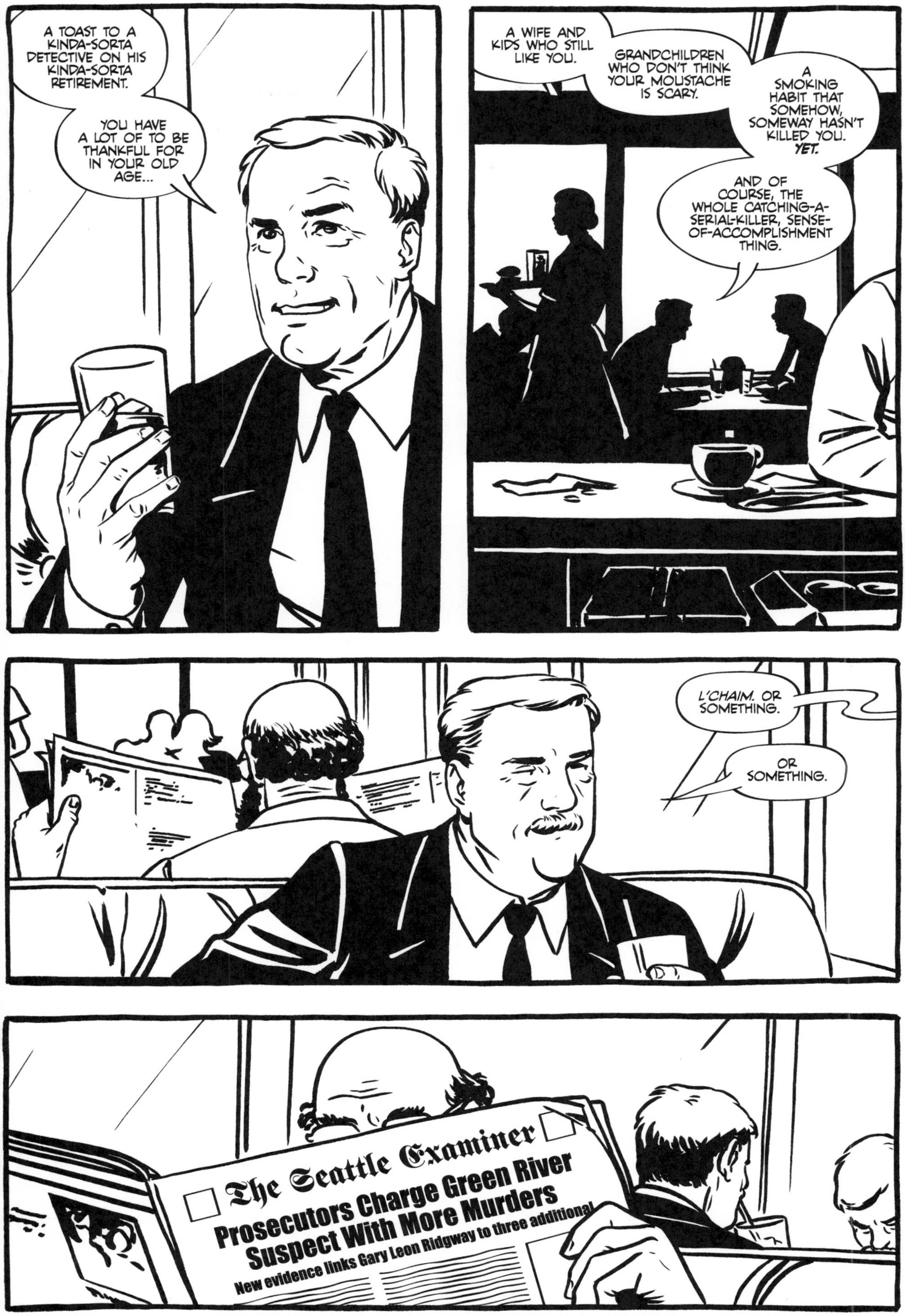
A TOAST TO A KINDA-SORTA DETECTIVE ON HIS KINDA-SORTA RETIREMENT.
YOU HAVE A LOT OF TO BE THANKFUL FOR IN YOUR OLD AGE...
A WIFE AND KIDS WHO STILL LIKE YOU.
GRANDCHILDREN WHO DON'T THINK YOUR MOUSTACHE IS SCARY.
A SMOKING HABIT THAT SOMEHOW, SOMEWAY HASN'T KILLED YOU. *YET.*
AND OF COURSE, THE WHOLE CATCHING-A-SERIAL-KILLER, SENSE-OF-ACCOMPLISHMENT THING.
L'CHAIM. OR SOMETHING.
OR SOMETHING.
The Seattle Examiner
The Seattle Examiner
Prosecutors Charge Green River Suspect With More Murders
New evidence links Gary Leon Ridgway to three additional

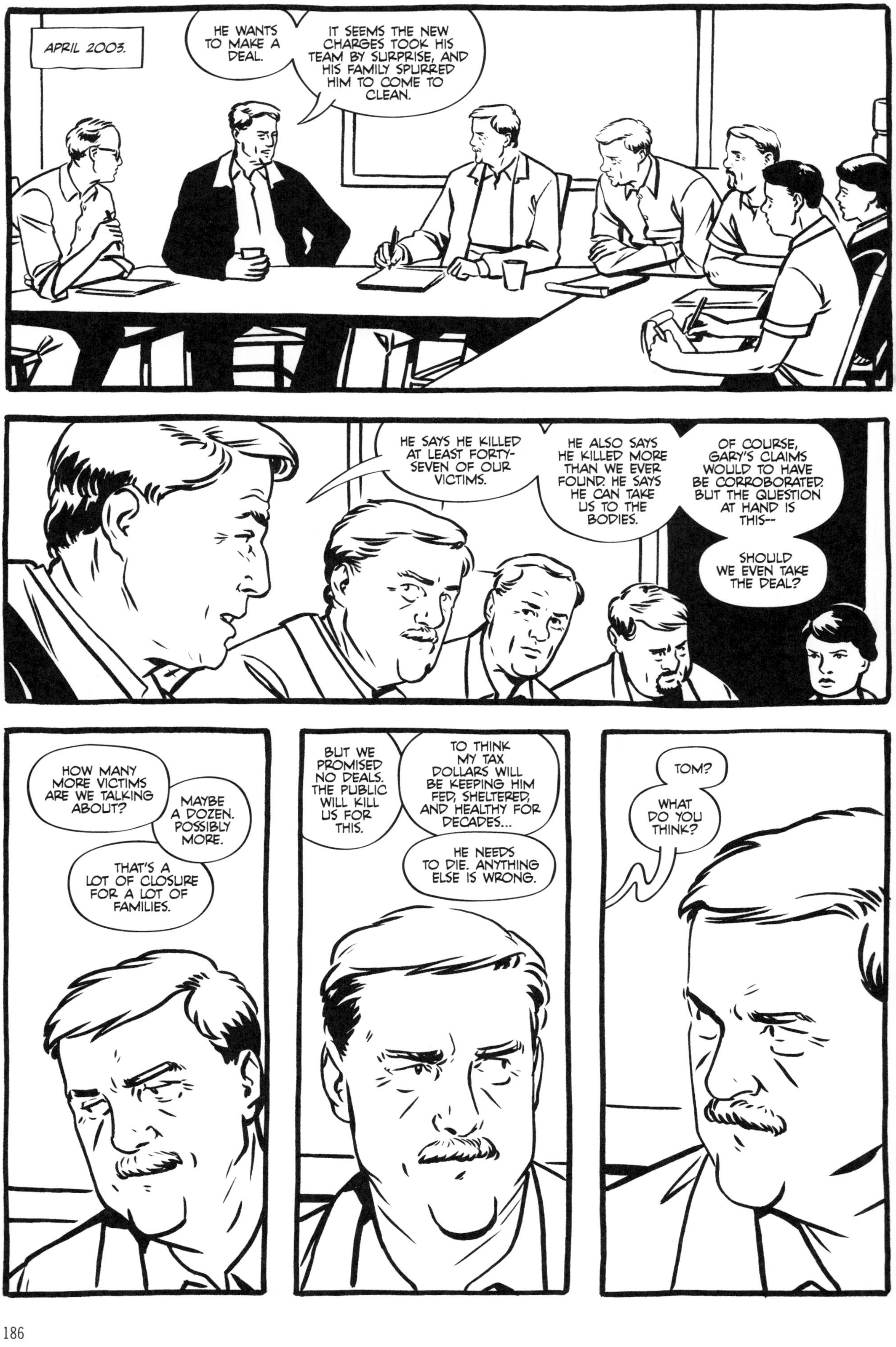

APRIL 2003.
HE WANTS TO MAKE A DEAL.
IT SEEMS THE NEW CHARGES TOOK HIS TEAM BY SURPRISE, AND HIS FAMILY SPURRED HIM TO COME TO CLEAN.
HE SAYS HE KILLED AT LEAST FORTY-SEVEN OF OUR VICTIMS.
HE ALSO SAYS HE KILLED MORE THAN WE EVER FOUND. HE SAYS HE CAN TAKE US TO THE BODIES.
OF COURSE, GARY'S CLAIMS WOULD TO HAVE BE CORROBORATED. BUT THE QUESTION AT HAND IS THIS--
SHOULD WE EVEN TAKE THE DEAL?
HOW MANY MORE VICTIMS ARE WE TALKING ABOUT?
MAYBE A DOZEN. POSSIBLY MORE.
THAT'S A LOT OF CLOSURE FOR A LOT OF FAMILIES.
BUT WE PROMISED NO DEALS. THE PUBLIC WILL KILL US FOR THIS.
TO THINK MY TAX DOLLARS WILL BE KEEPING HIM FED, SHELTERED, AND HEALTHY FOR DECADES...
HE NEEDS TO DIE. ANYTHING ELSE IS WRONG.
TOM?
WHAT DO YOU THINK?

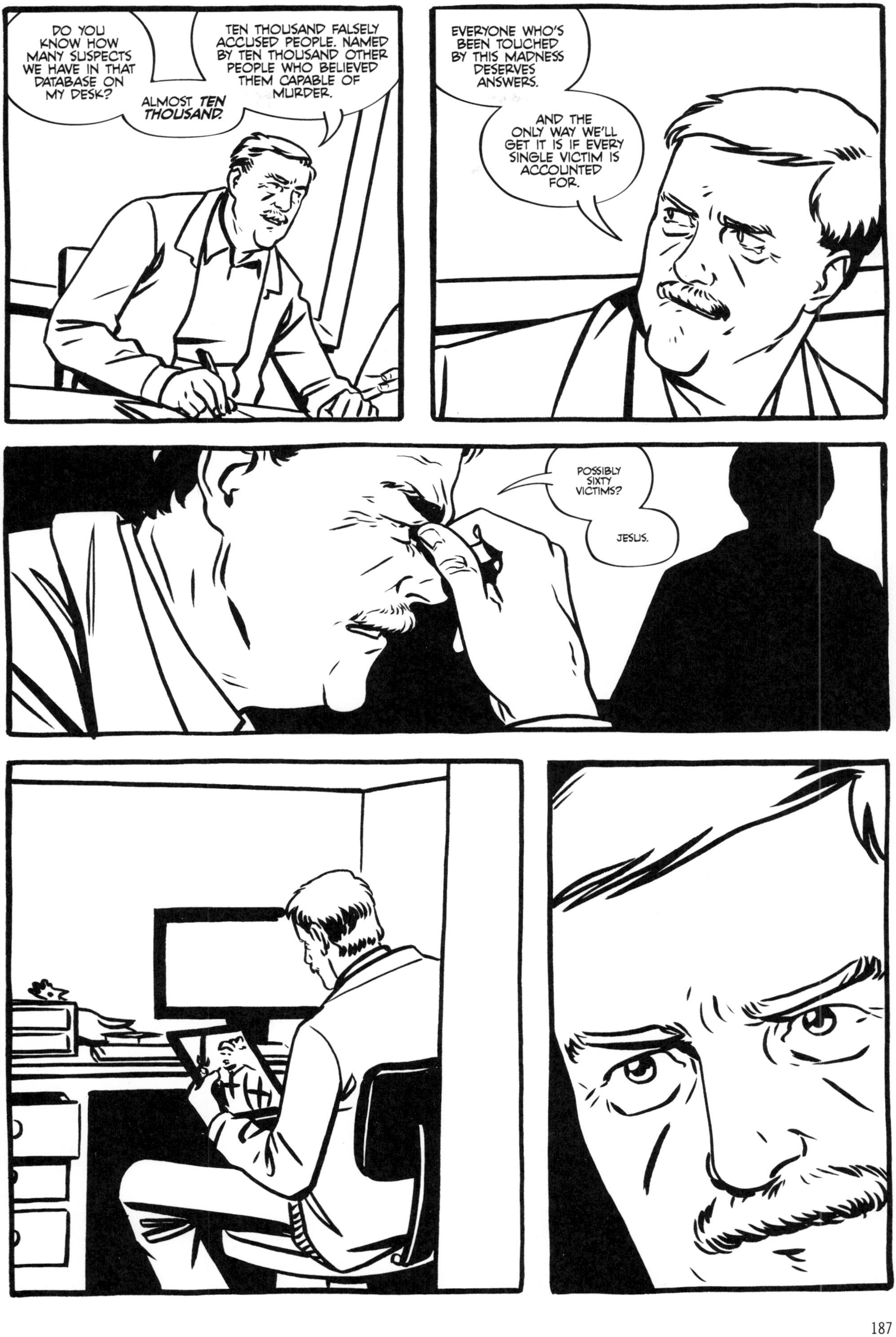
DO YOU KNOW HOW MANY SUSPECTS WE HAVE IN THAT DATABASE ON MY DESK?
ALMOST *TEN THOUSAND.*
TEN THOUSAND FALSELY ACCUSED PEOPLE. NAMED BY TEN THOUSAND OTHER PEOPLE WHO BELIEVED THEM CAPABLE OF MURDER.
EVERYONE WHO'S BEEN TOUCHED BY THIS MADNESS DESERVES ANSWERS.
AND THE ONLY WAY WE'LL GET IT IS IF EVERY SINGLE VICTIM IS ACCOUNTED FOR.
POSSIBLY SIXTY VICTIMS?
JESUS.

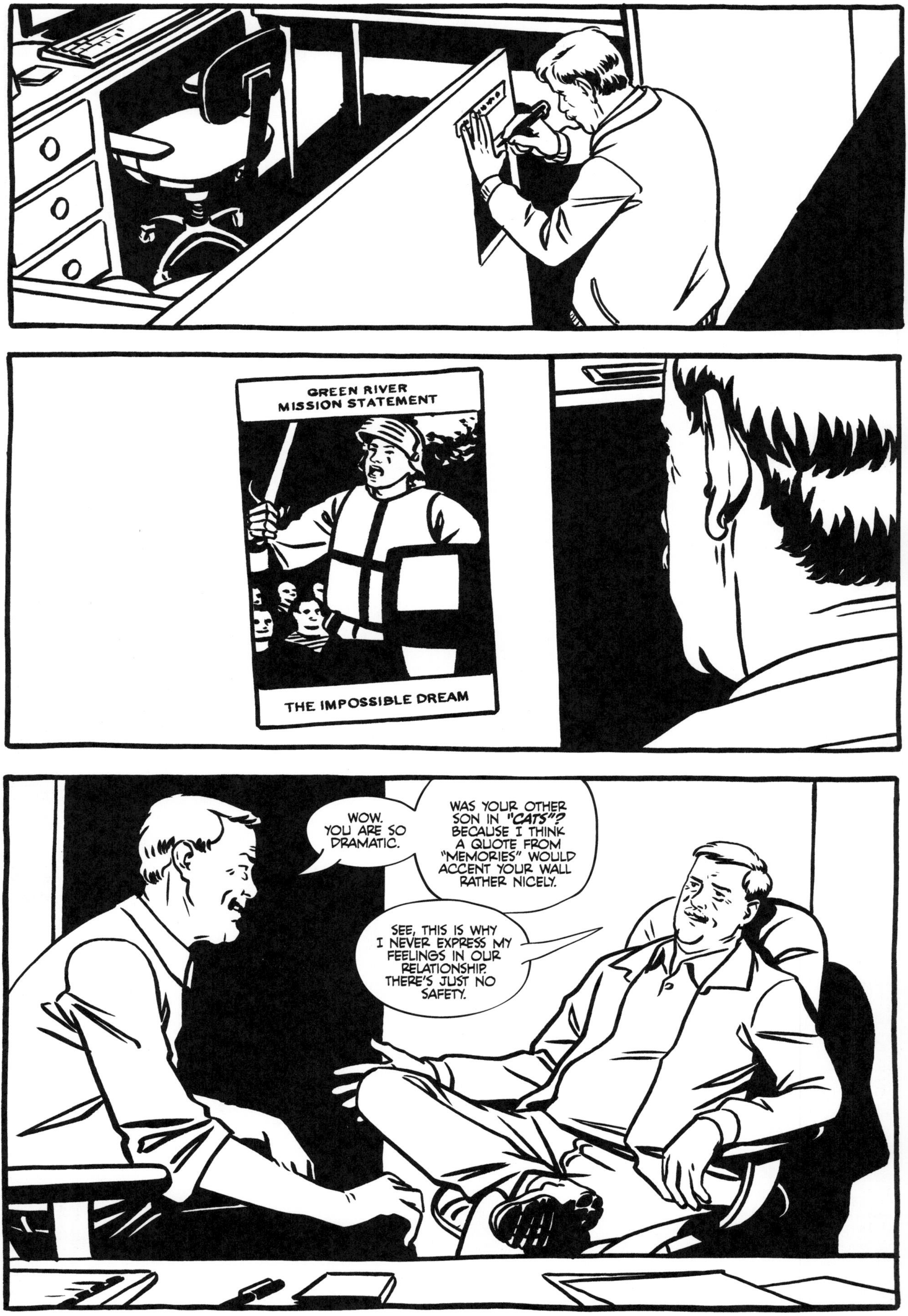
GREEN RIVER
MISSION STATEMENT
THE IMPOSSIBLE DREAM
WOW. YOU ARE SO DRAMATIC.
WAS YOUR OTHER SON IN "CATS"? BECAUSE I THINK A QUOTE FROM "MEMORIES" WOULD ACCENT YOUR WALL RATHER NICELY.
SEE, THIS IS WHY I NEVER EXPRESS MY FEELINGS IN OUR RELATIONSHIP. THERE'S JUST NO SAFETY.

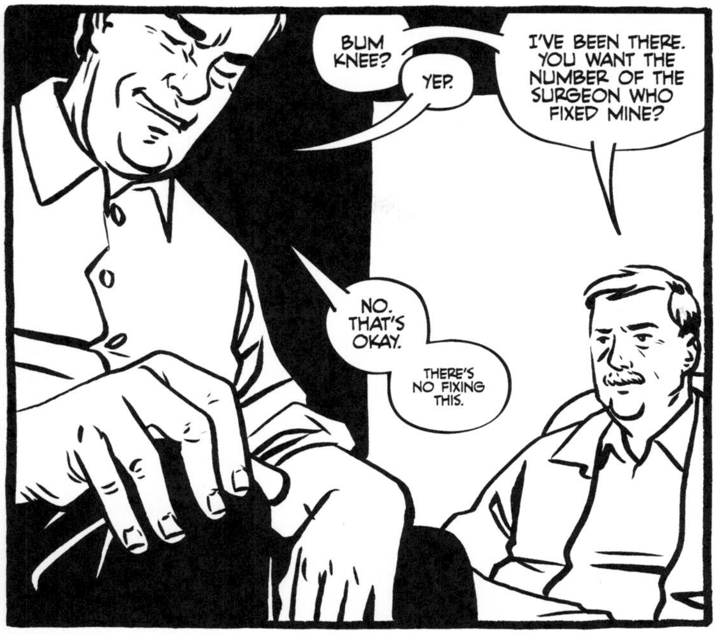
BUM KNEE?
I'VE BEEN THERE. YOU WANT THE NUMBER OF THE SURGEON WHO FIXED MINE?
YEP.
NO. THAT'S OKAY.
THERE'S NO FIXING THIS.

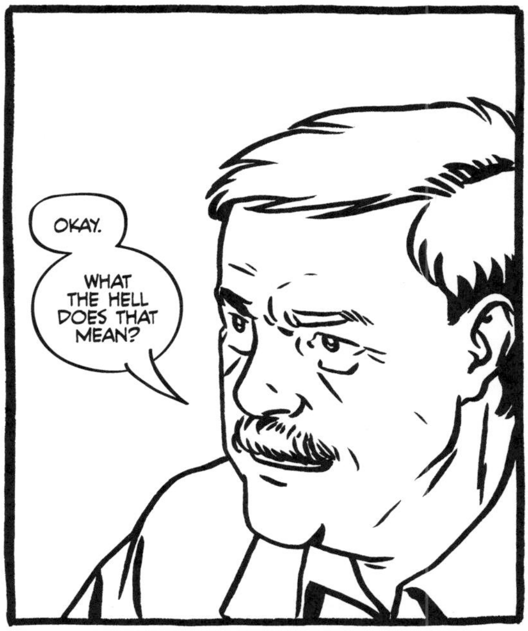
OKAY.
WHAT THE HELL DOES THAT MEAN?

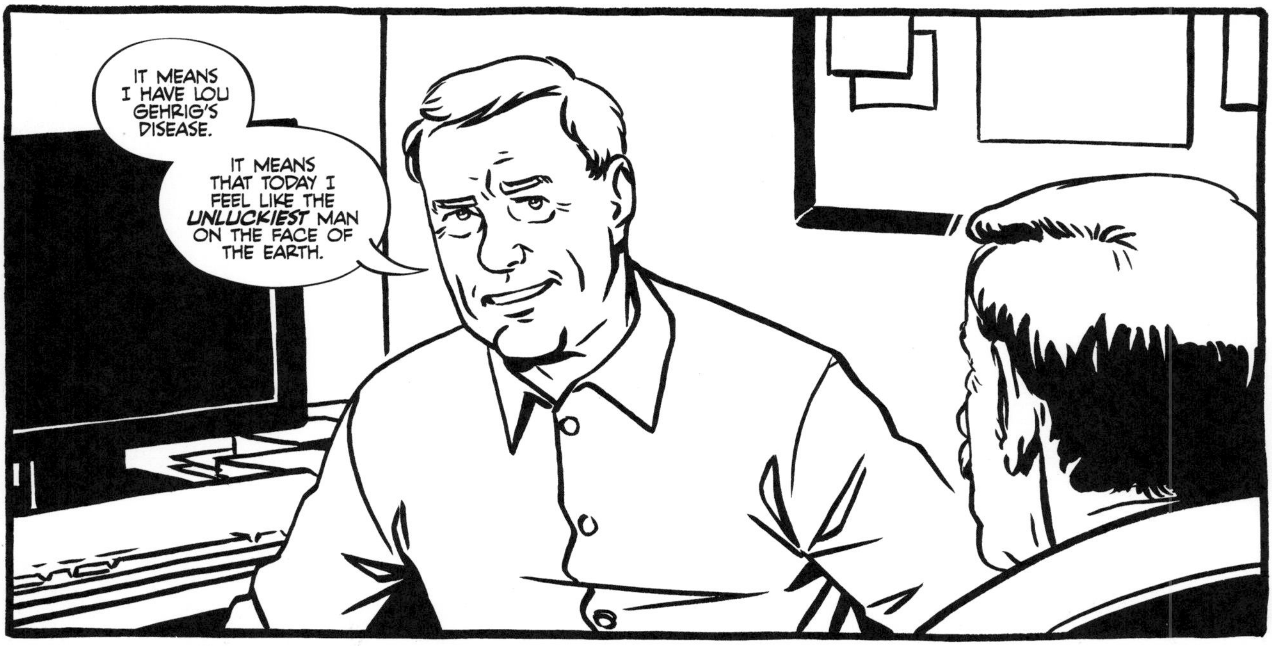
IT MEANS I HAVE LOU GEHRIG'S DISEASE.
IT MEANS THAT TODAY I FEEL LIKE THE UNLUCKIEST MAN ON THE FACE OF THE EARTH.

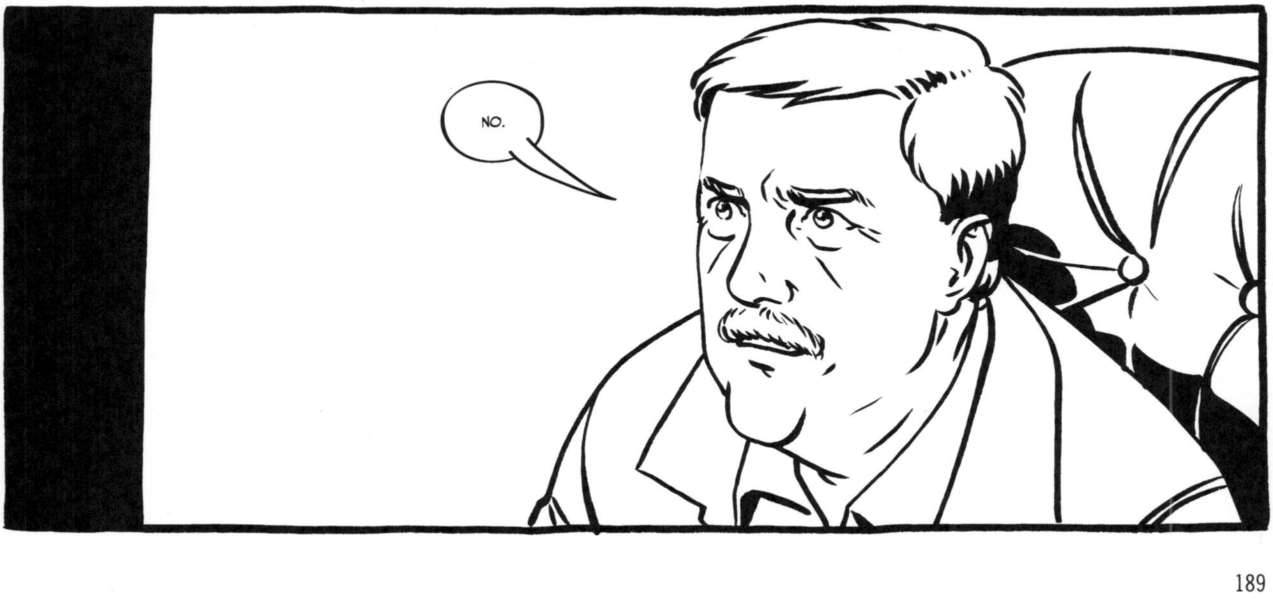
NO.

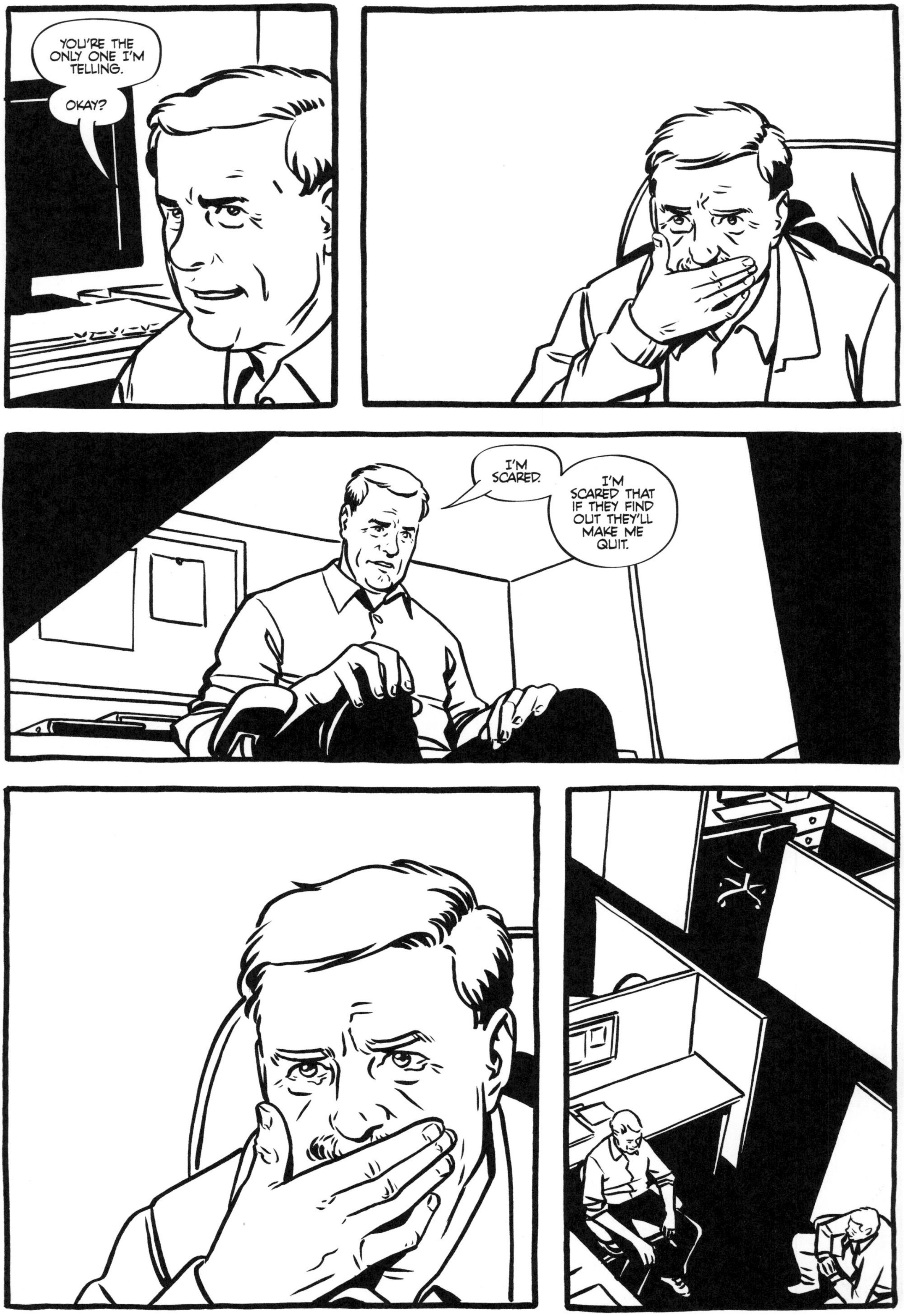
YOU'RE THE ONLY ONE I'M TELLING.
OKAY?
I'M SCARED.
I'M SCARED THAT IF THEY FIND OUT THEY'LL MAKE ME QUIT.

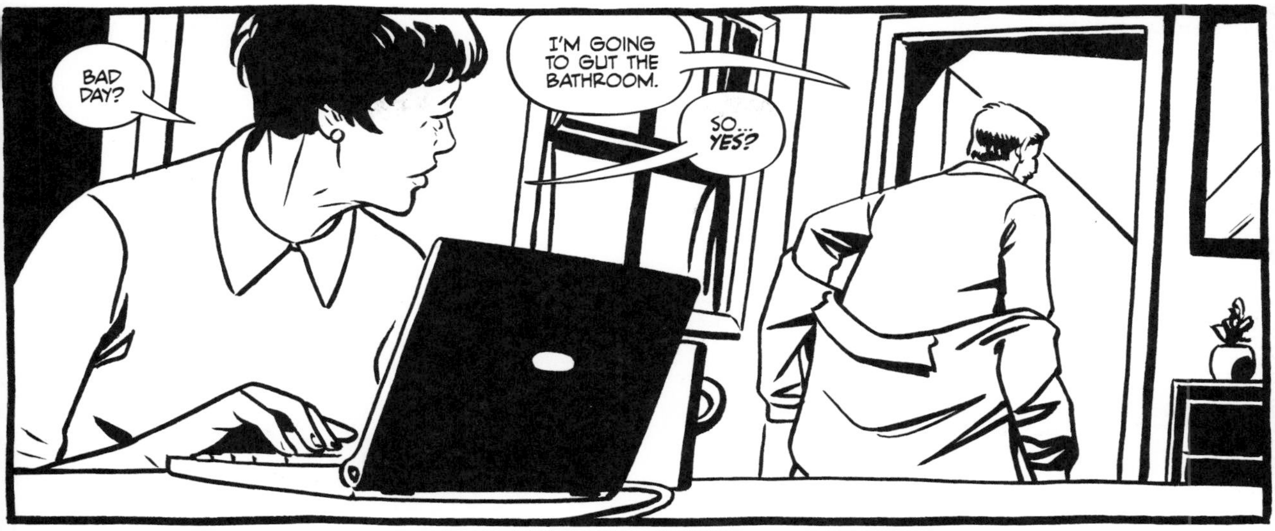
BAD DAY?
I'M GOING TO GUT THE BATHROOM.
SO... YES?

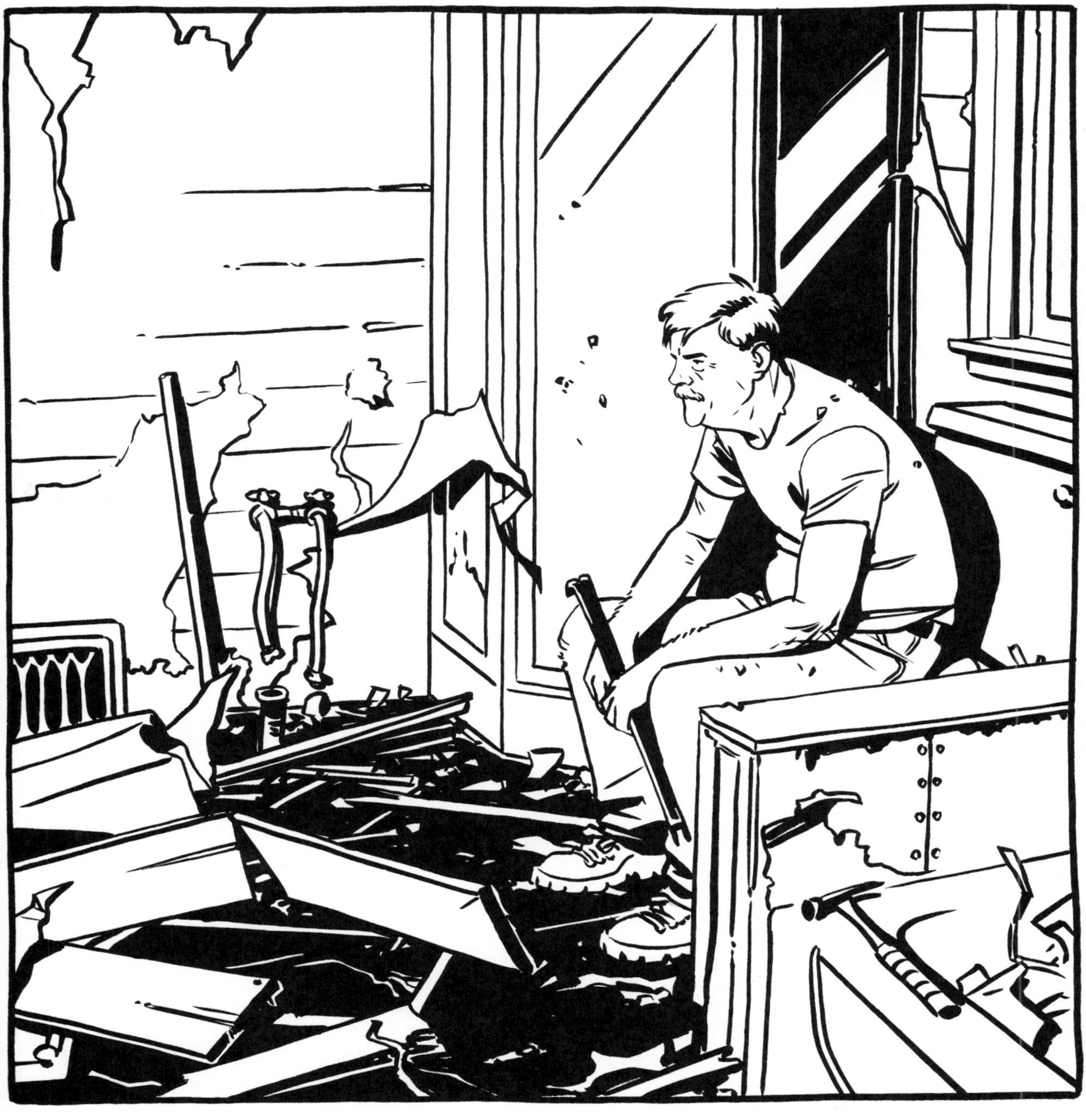

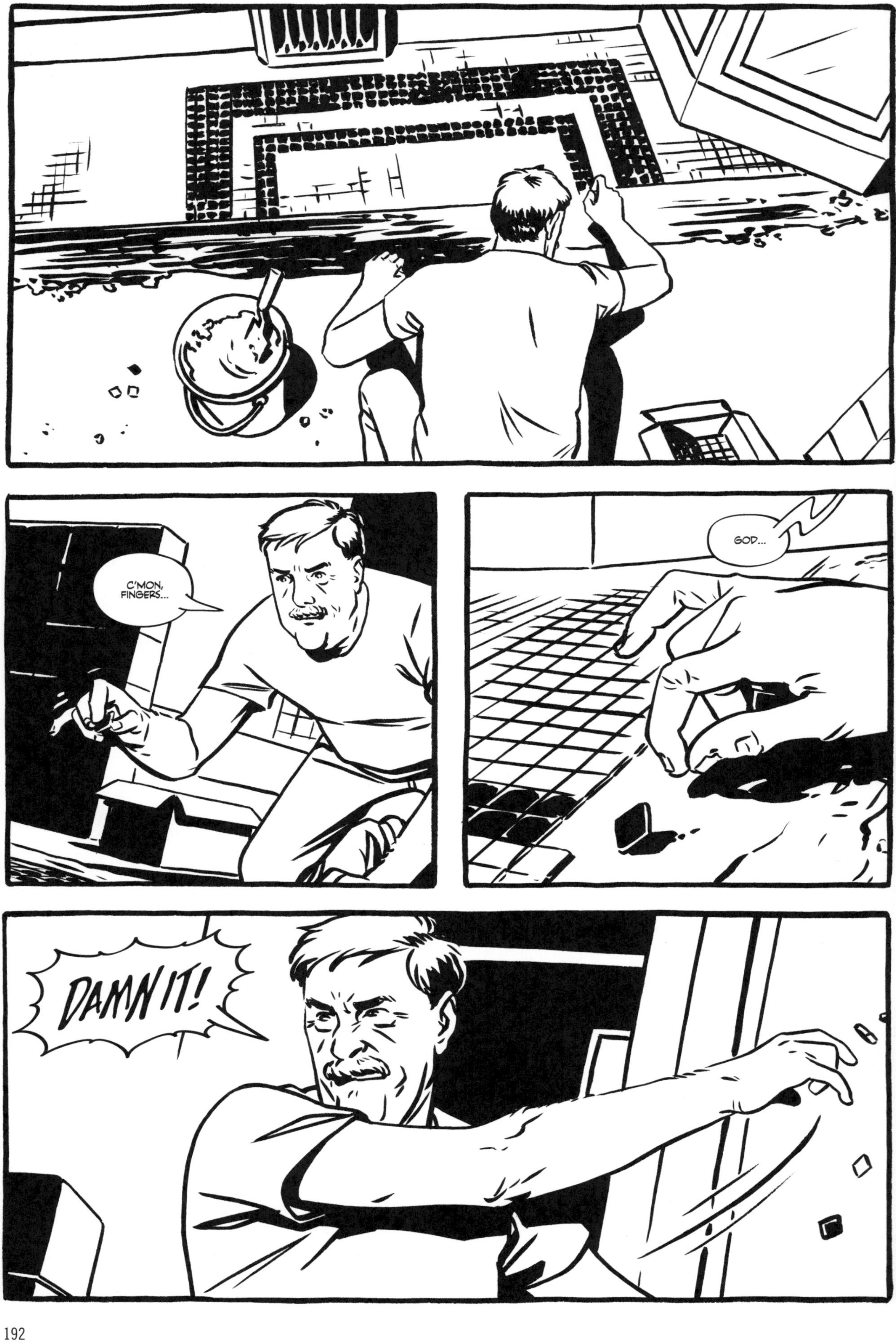
C'MON, FINGERS...
GOD...
DAMN IT!

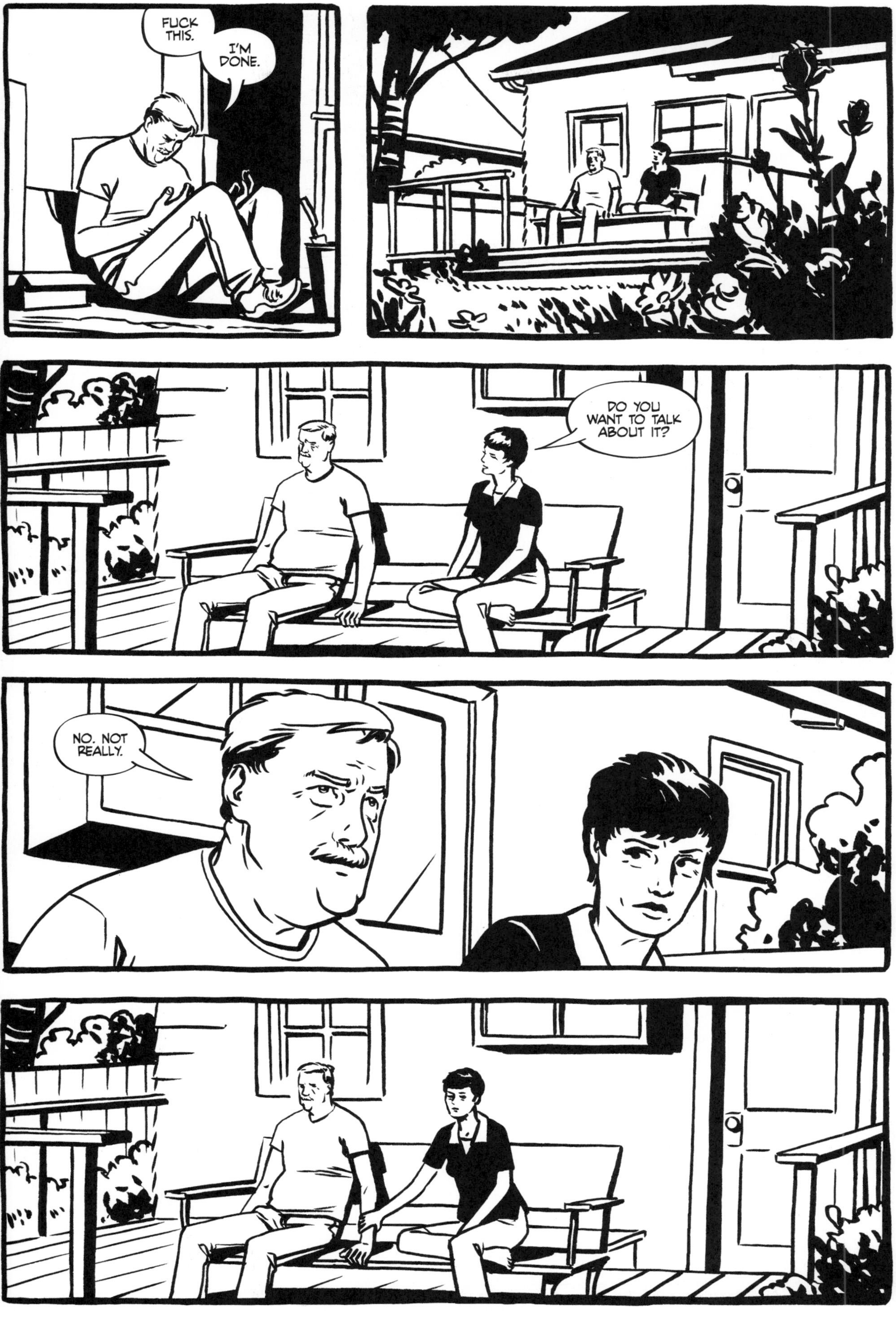
FUCK THIS.
I'M DONE.
DO YOU WANT TO TALK ABOUT IT?
NO. NOT REALLY.

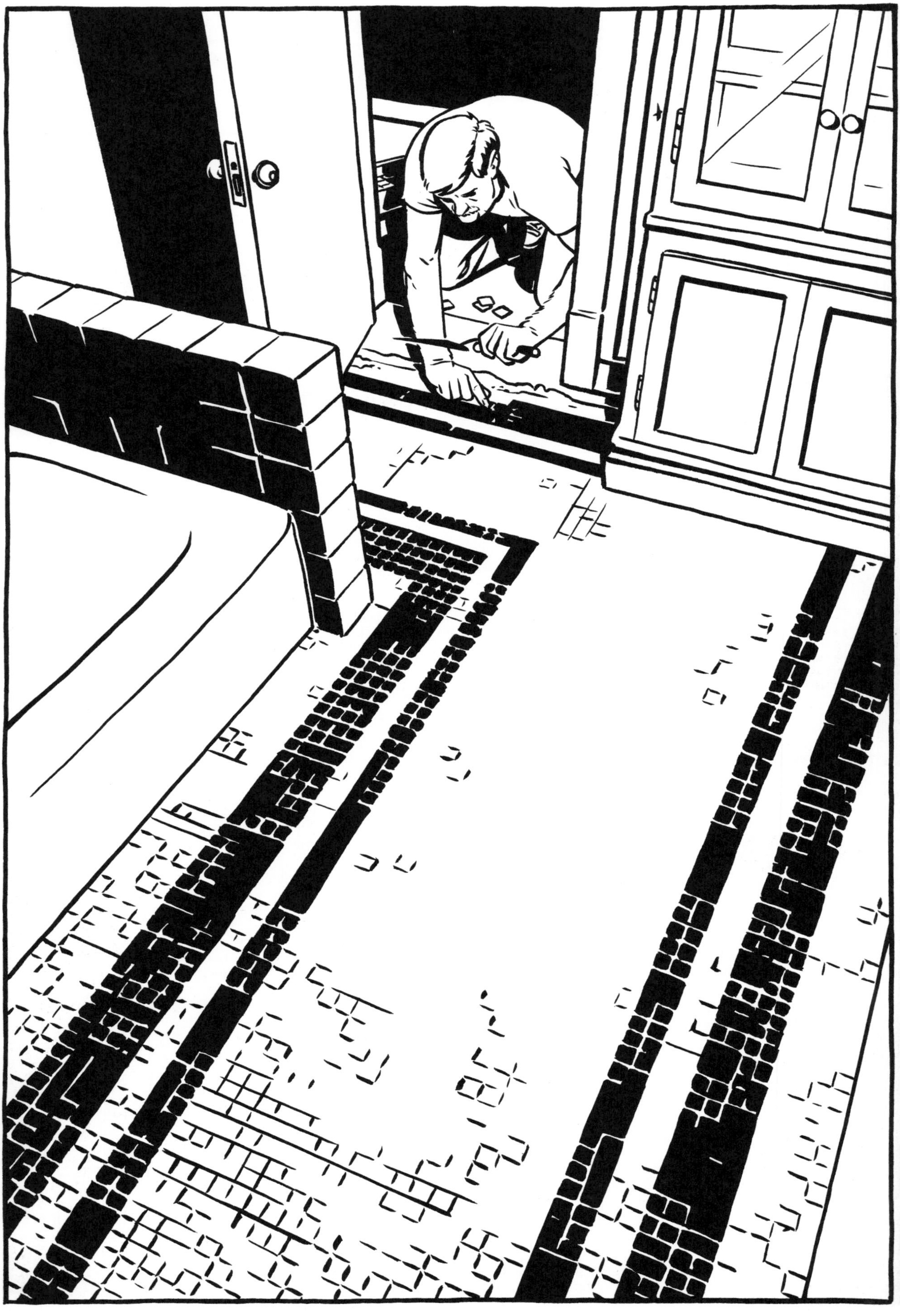

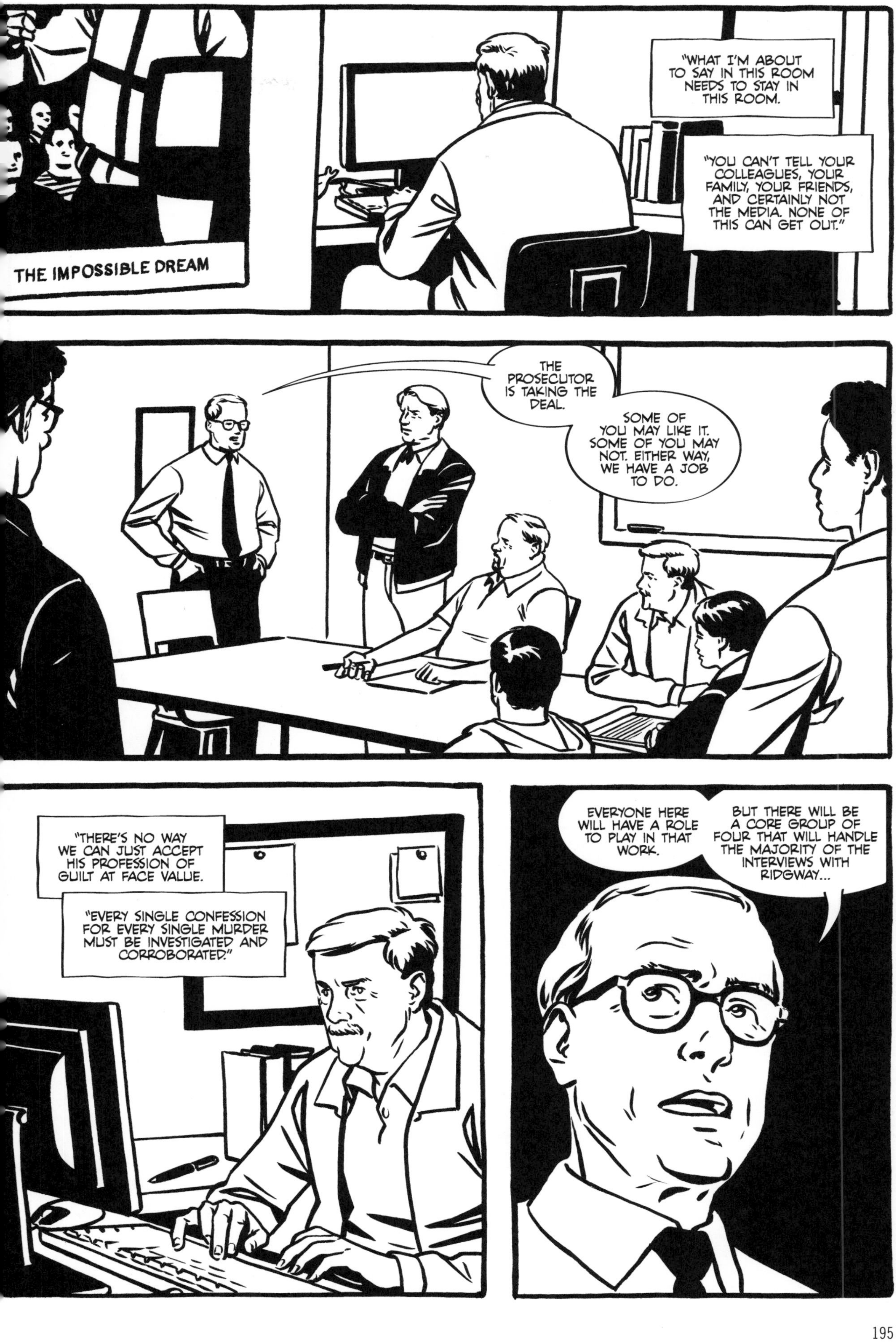
THE IMPOSSIBLE DREAM
"WHAT I'M ABOUT TO SAY IN THIS ROOM NEEDS TO STAY IN THIS ROOM.
"YOU CAN'T TELL YOUR COLLEAGUES, YOUR FAMILY, YOUR FRIENDS, AND CERTAINLY NOT THE MEDIA. NONE OF THIS CAN GET OUT."
THE PROSECUTOR IS TAKING THE DEAL.
SOME OF YOU MAY LIKE IT. SOME OF YOU MAY NOT. EITHER WAY, WE HAVE A JOB TO DO.
"THERE'S NO WAY WE CAN JUST ACCEPT HIS PROFESSION OF GUILT AT FACE VALUE.
"EVERY SINGLE CONFESSION FOR EVERY SINGLE MURDER MUST BE INVESTIGATED AND CORROBORATED."
EVERYONE HERE WILL HAVE A ROLE TO PLAY IN THAT WORK.
BUT THERE WILL BE A CORE GROUP OF FOUR THAT WILL HANDLE THE MAJORITY OF THE INTERVIEWS WITH RIDGWAY...

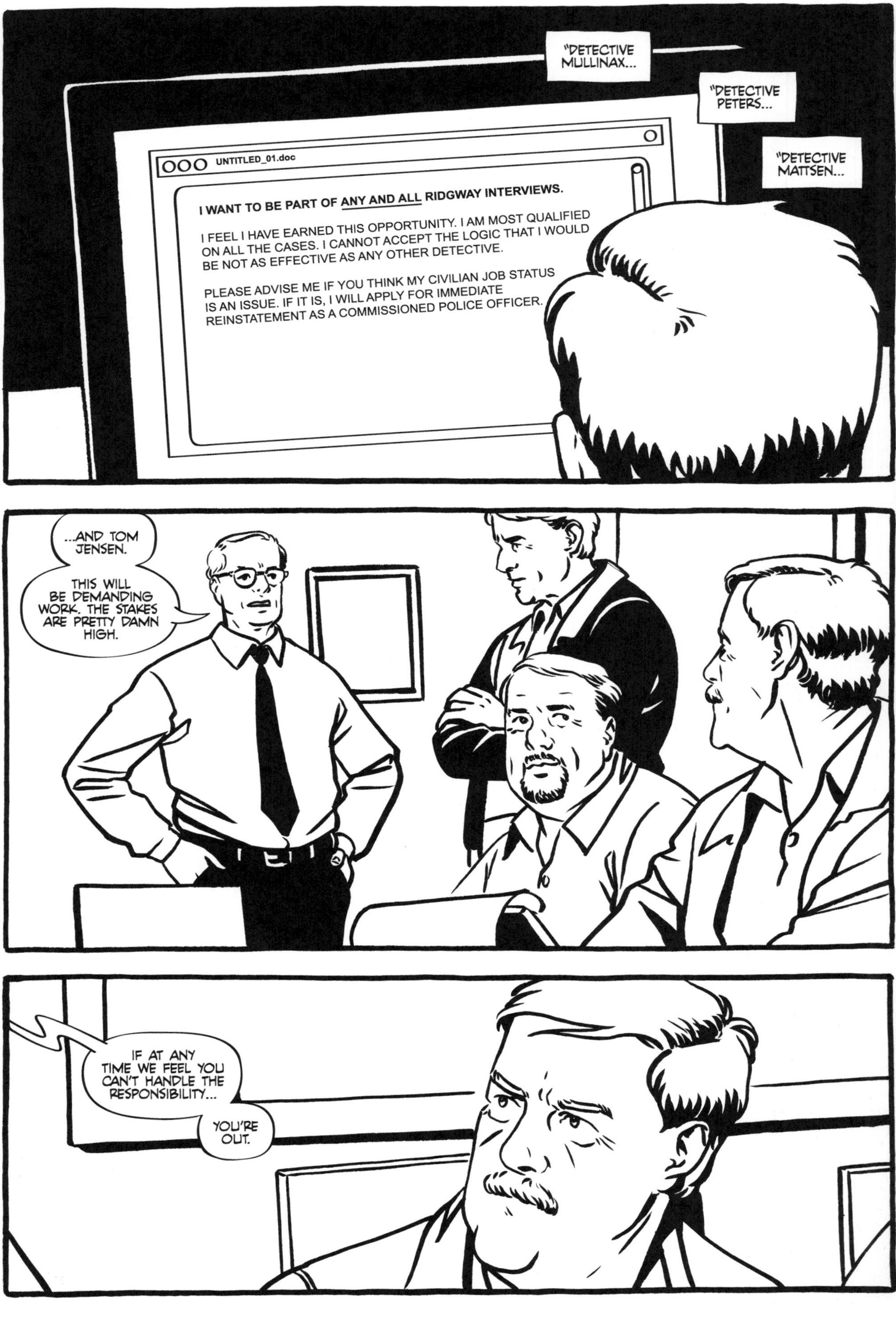
"DETECTIVE MULLINAX...
"DETECTIVE PETERS...
"DETECTIVE MATTSEN...
UNTITLED_01.doc
I WANT TO BE PART OF ANY AND ALL RIDGWAY INTERVIEWS.
I FEEL I HAVE EARNED THIS OPPORTUNITY. I AM MOST QUALIFIED ON ALL THE CASES. I CANNOT ACCEPT THE LOGIC THAT I WOULD BE NOT AS EFFECTIVE AS ANY OTHER DETECTIVE.
PLEASE ADVISE ME IF YOU THINK MY CIVILIAN JOB STATUS IS AN ISSUE. IF IT IS, I WILL APPLY FOR IMMEDIATE REINSTATEMENT AS A COMMISSIONED POLICE OFFICER.
...AND TOM JENSEN.
THIS WILL BE DEMANDING WORK. THE STAKES ARE PRETTY DAMN HIGH.
IF AT ANY TIME WE FEEL YOU CAN'T HANDLE THE RESPONSIBILITY...
YOU'RE OUT.

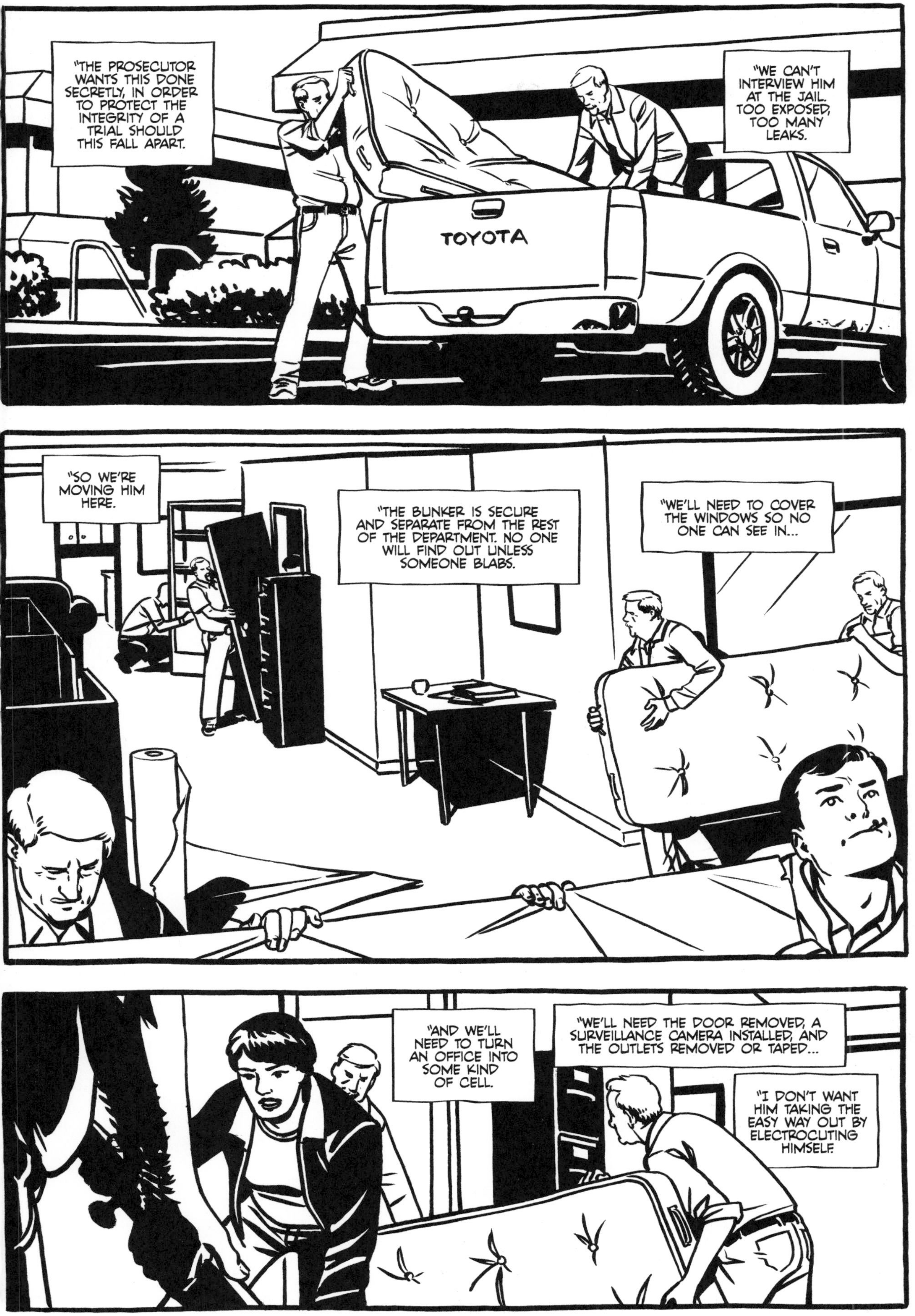
"THE PROSECUTOR WANTS THIS DONE SECRETLY, IN ORDER TO PROTECT THE INTEGRITY OF A TRIAL SHOULD THIS FALL APART.
"WE CAN'T INTERVIEW HIM AT THE JAIL. TOO EXPOSED, TOO MANY LEAKS.
TOYOTA
"SO WE'RE MOVING HIM HERE.
"THE BUNKER IS SECURE AND SEPARATE FROM THE REST OF THE DEPARTMENT. NO ONE WILL FIND OUT UNLESS SOMEONE BLABS.
"WE'LL NEED TO COVER THE WINDOWS SO NO ONE CAN SEE IN...
"AND WE'LL NEED TO TURN AN OFFICE INTO SOME KIND OF CELL.
"WE'LL NEED THE DOOR REMOVED, A SURVEILLANCE CAMERA INSTALLED, AND THE OUTLETS REMOVED OR TAPED...
"I DON'T WANT HIM TAKING THE EASY WAY OUT BY ELECTROCUTING HIMSELF.

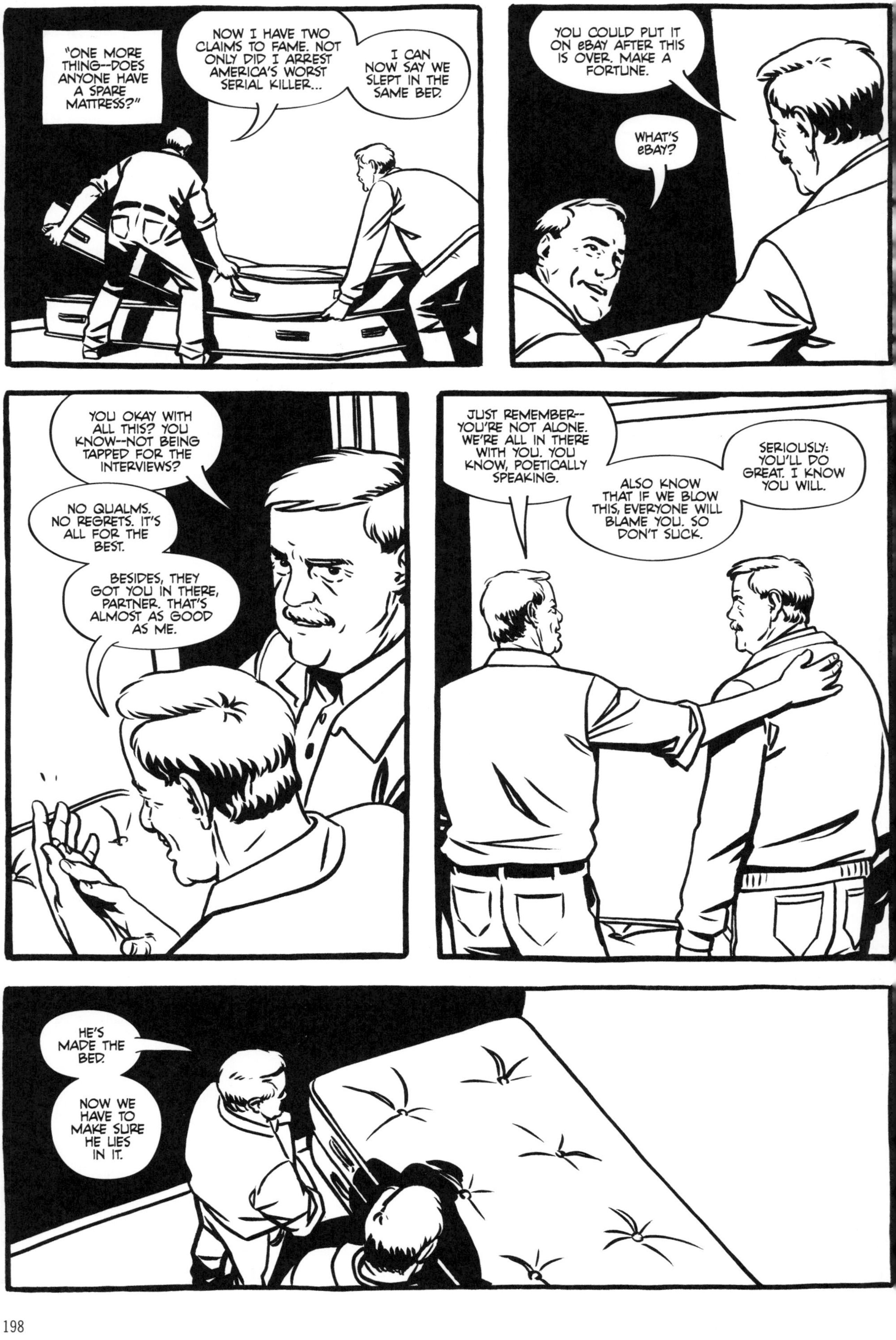
"ONE MORE THING--DOES ANYONE HAVE A SPARE MATTRESS?"
NOW I HAVE TWO CLAIMS TO FAME. NOT ONLY DID I ARREST AMERICA'S WORST SERIAL KILLER...
I CAN NOW SAY WE SLEPT IN THE SAME BED.
YOU COULD PUT IT ON eBAY AFTER THIS IS OVER. MAKE A FORTUNE.
WHAT'S eBAY?
YOU OKAY WITH ALL THIS? YOU KNOW--NOT BEING TAPPED FOR THE INTERVIEWS?
NO QUALMS. NO REGRETS. IT'S ALL FOR THE BEST.
BESIDES, THEY GOT YOU IN THERE, PARTNER. THAT'S ALMOST AS GOOD AS ME.
JUST REMEMBER--YOU'RE NOT ALONE. WE'RE ALL IN THERE WITH YOU. YOU KNOW, POETICALLY SPEAKING.
ALSO KNOW THAT IF WE BLOW THIS, EVERYONE WILL BLAME YOU. SO DON'T SUCK.
SERIOUSLY: YOU'LL DO GREAT. I KNOW YOU WILL.
HE'S MADE THE BED.
NOW WE HAVE TO MAKE SURE HE LIES IN IT.

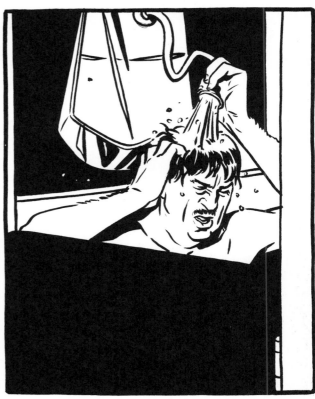

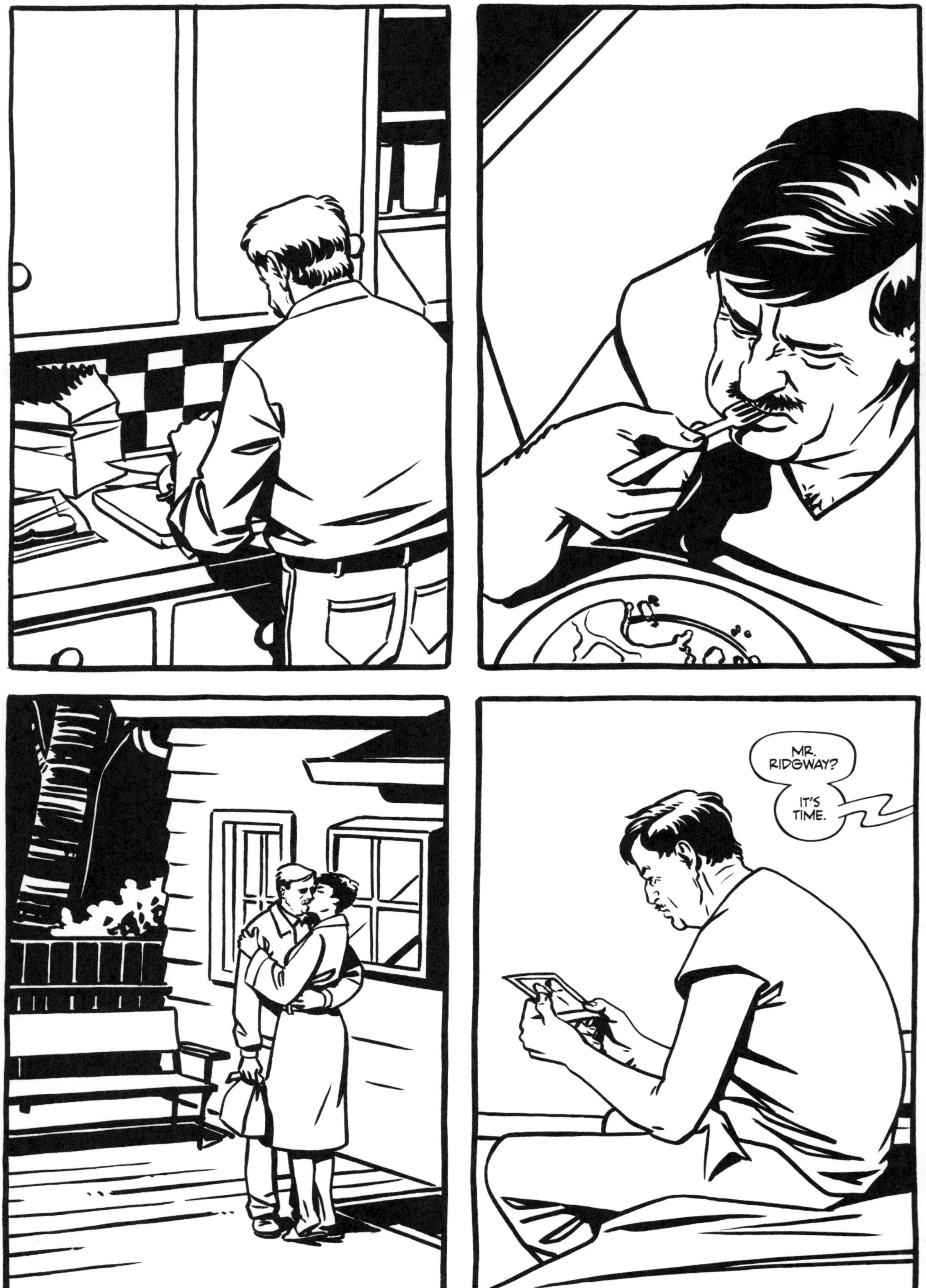
MR. RIDGWAY?
IT'S TIME.

GARY'S ON THE MOVE.

READY TO ROLL?

I AM NOW.

OKAY.

WHAT'S THE DEAL WITH THE SHERLOCK HOLMES QUOTES?

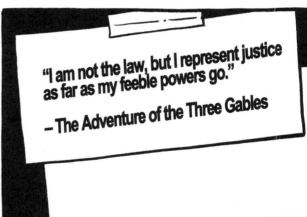

"I am not the law, but I represent justice as far as my feeble powers go."

– The Adventure of the Three Gables

I GOT INTO HOLMES SOON AFTER JOINING THE SHERIFF'S DEPARTMENT--WHILE I WAS STUDYING TO BECOME A DETECTIVE.

I FIGURED IF I WANTED TO BE A GOOD ONE, I BETTER LEARN FROM THE BEST.

IT ALSO HELPED PASS THE TIME DURING SOME SERIOUSLY DULL GRAVEYARD SHIFTS.

GOD, I HATED PATROL...

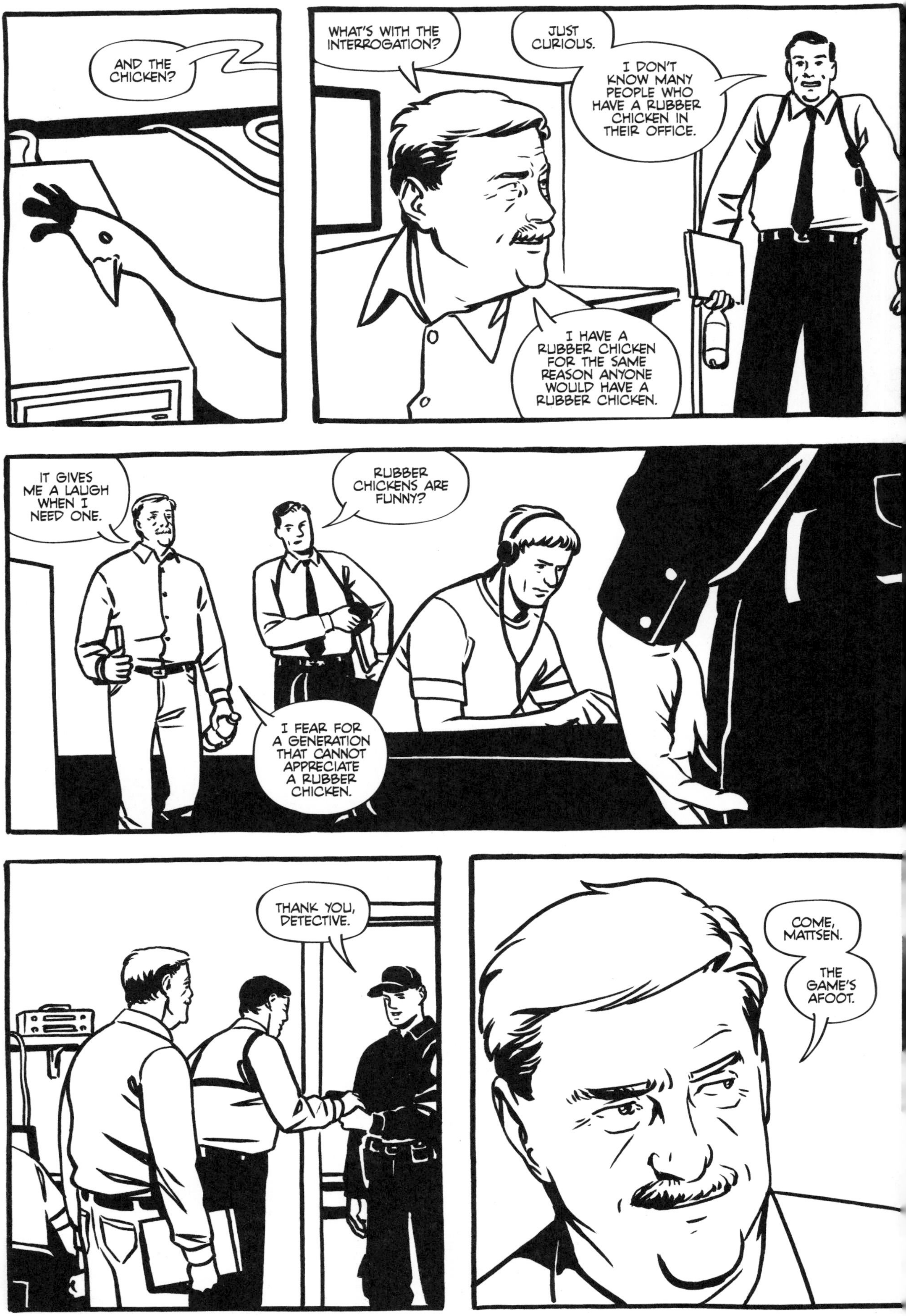
AND THE CHICKEN?
WHAT'S WITH THE INTERROGATION?
JUST CURIOUS.
I DON'T KNOW MANY PEOPLE WHO HAVE A RUBBER CHICKEN IN THEIR OFFICE.
I HAVE A RUBBER CHICKEN FOR THE SAME REASON ANYONE WOULD HAVE A RUBBER CHICKEN.
IT GIVES ME A LAUGH WHEN I NEED ONE.
RUBBER CHICKENS ARE FUNNY?
I FEAR FOR A GENERATION THAT CANNOT APPRECIATE A RUBBER CHICKEN.
THANK YOU, DETECTIVE.
COME, MATTSEN.
THE GAME'S AFOOT.

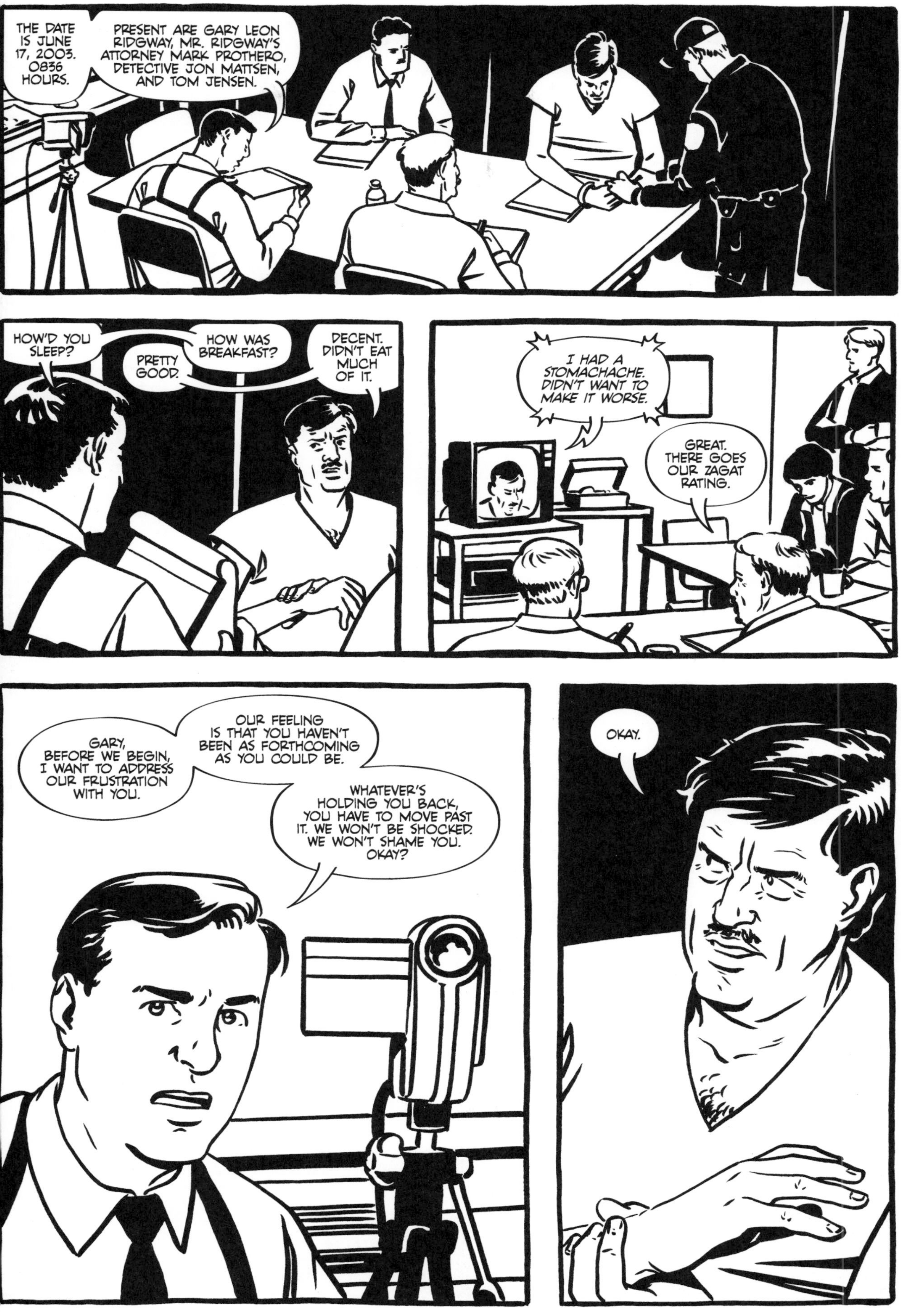
THE DATE IS JUNE 17, 2003. 0836 HOURS.
PRESENT ARE GARY LEON RIDGWAY, MR. RIDGWAY'S ATTORNEY MARK PROTHERO, DETECTIVE JON MATTSEN, AND TOM JENSEN.
HOW'D YOU SLEEP?
PRETTY GOOD.
HOW WAS BREAKFAST?
DECENT. DIDN'T EAT MUCH OF IT.
I HAD A STOMACHACHE. DIDN'T WANT TO MAKE IT WORSE.
GREAT. THERE GOES OUR ZAGAT RATING.
GARY, BEFORE WE BEGIN, I WANT TO ADDRESS OUR FRUSTRATION WITH YOU.
OUR FEELING IS THAT YOU HAVEN'T BEEN AS FORTHCOMING AS YOU COULD BE.
WHATEVER'S HOLDING YOU BACK, YOU HAVE TO MOVE PAST IT. WE WON'T BE SHOCKED. WE WON'T SHAME YOU. OKAY?
OKAY.

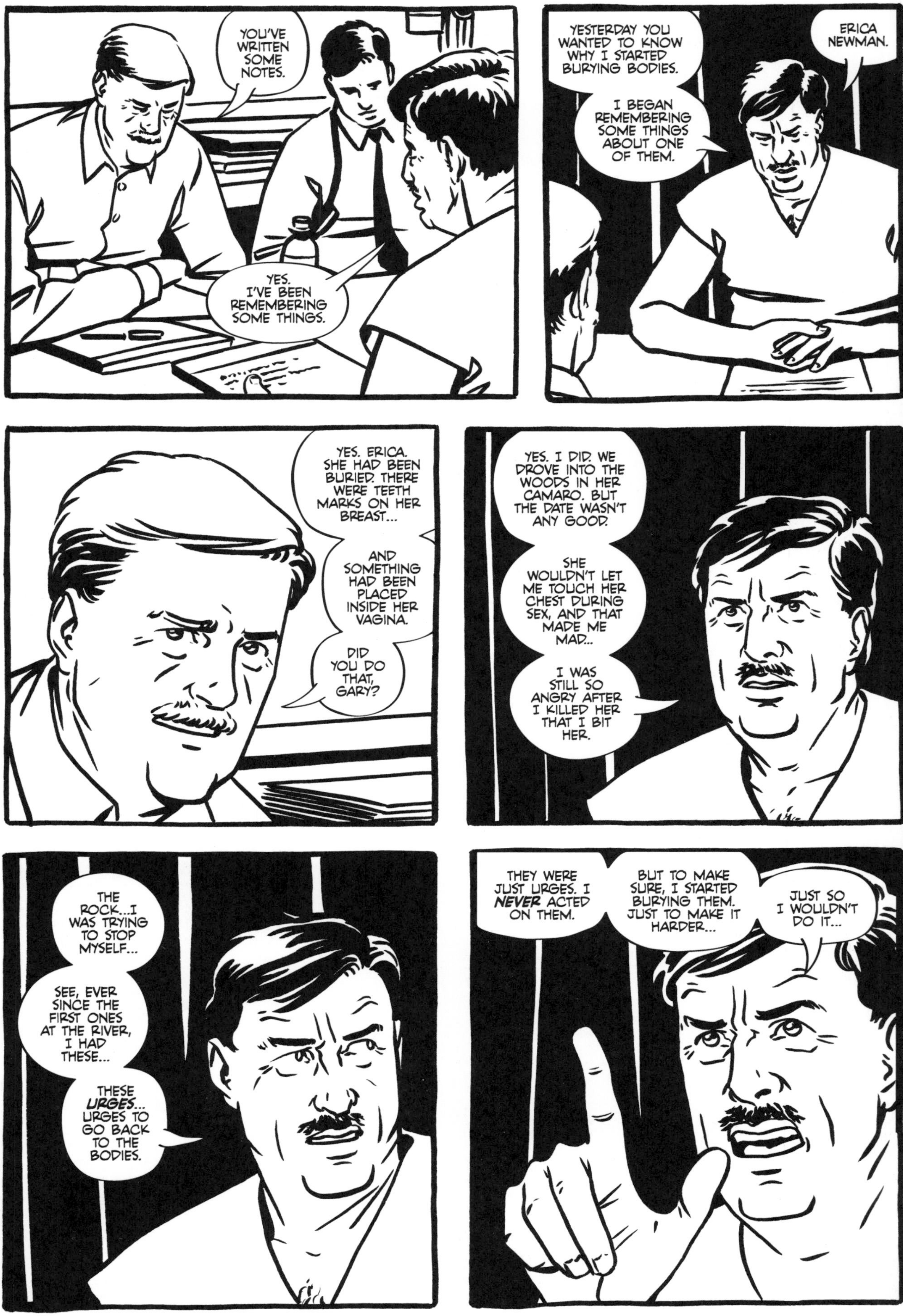
YOU'VE WRITTEN SOME NOTES.
YES. I'VE BEEN REMEMBERING SOME THINGS.
YESTERDAY YOU WANTED TO KNOW WHY I STARTED BURYING BODIES.
I BEGAN REMEMBERING SOME THINGS ABOUT ONE OF THEM.
ERICA NEWMAN.
YES. ERICA. SHE HAD BEEN BURIED. THERE WERE TEETH MARKS ON HER BREAST...
AND SOMETHING HAD BEEN PLACED INSIDE HER VAGINA.
DID YOU DO THAT, GARY?
YES. I DID. WE DROVE INTO THE WOODS IN HER CAMARO. BUT THE DATE WASN'T ANY GOOD.
SHE WOULDN'T LET ME TOUCH HER CHEST DURING SEX, AND THAT MADE ME MAD...
I WAS STILL SO ANGRY AFTER I KILLED HER THAT I BIT HER.
THE ROCK...I WAS TRYING TO STOP MYSELF...
SEE, EVER SINCE THE FIRST ONES AT THE RIVER, I HAD THESE...
THESE ***URGES***... URGES TO GO BACK TO THE BODIES.
THEY WERE JUST URGES. I ***NEVER*** ACTED ON THEM.
BUT TO MAKE SURE, I STARTED BURYING THEM. JUST TO MAKE IT HARDER...
JUST SO I WOULDN'T DO IT...

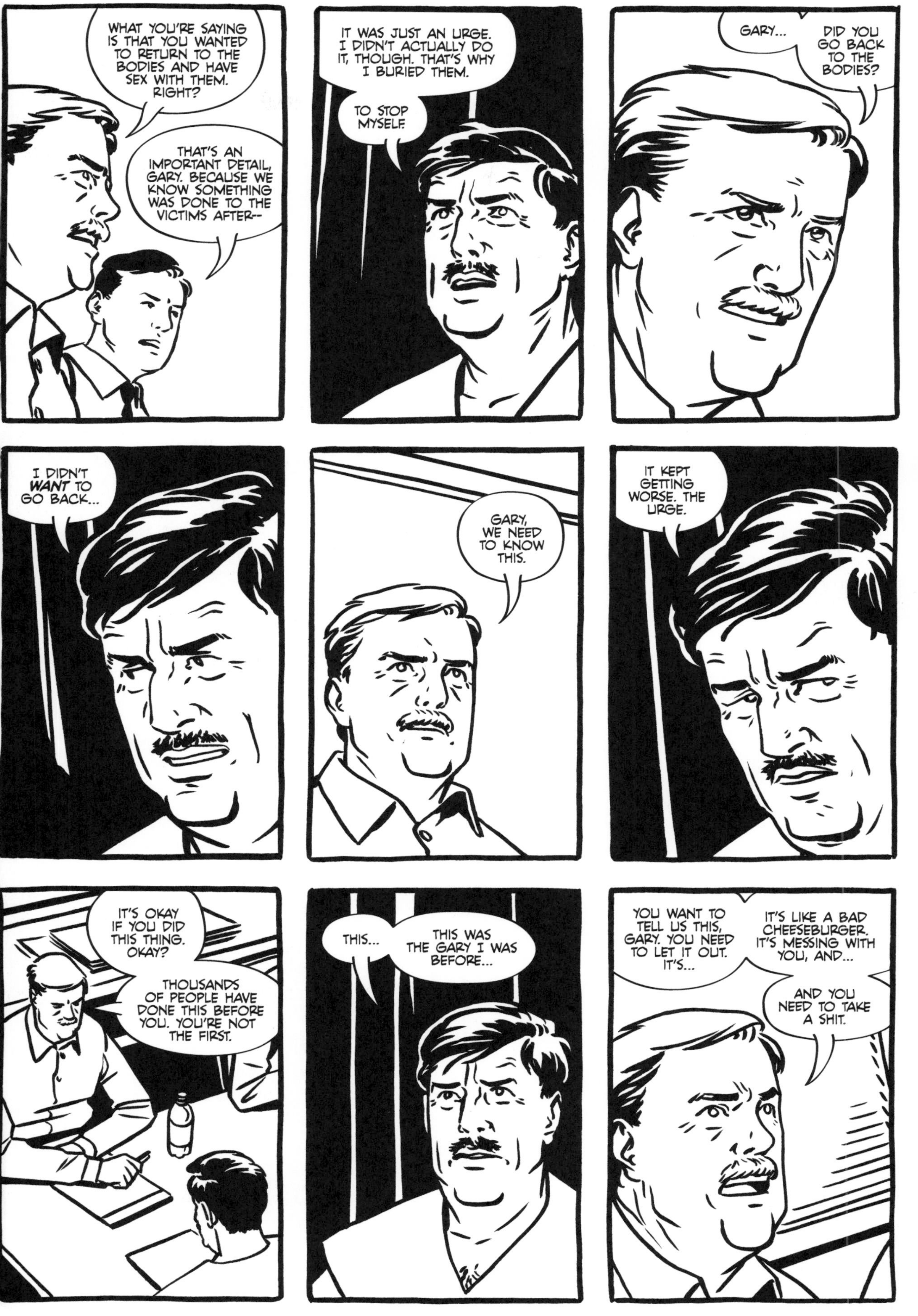
WHAT YOU'RE SAYING IS THAT YOU WANTED TO RETURN TO THE BODIES AND HAVE SEX WITH THEM. RIGHT?
THAT'S AN IMPORTANT DETAIL, GARY. BECAUSE WE KNOW SOMETHING WAS DONE TO THE VICTIMS AFTER--
IT WAS JUST AN URGE. I DIDN'T ACTUALLY DO IT, THOUGH. THAT'S WHY I BURIED THEM.
TO STOP MYSELF.
GARY...
DID YOU GO BACK TO THE BODIES?
I DIDN'T *WANT* TO GO BACK...
GARY, WE NEED TO KNOW THIS.
IT KEPT GETTING WORSE. THE URGE.
IT'S OKAY IF YOU DID THIS THING. OKAY?
THOUSANDS OF PEOPLE HAVE DONE THIS BEFORE YOU. YOU'RE NOT THE FIRST.
THIS...
THIS WAS THE GARY I WAS BEFORE...
YOU WANT TO TELL US THIS, GARY. YOU NEED TO LET IT OUT. IT'S...
IT'S LIKE A BAD CHEESEBURGER. IT'S MESSING WITH YOU, AND...
AND YOU NEED TO TAKE A SHIT.

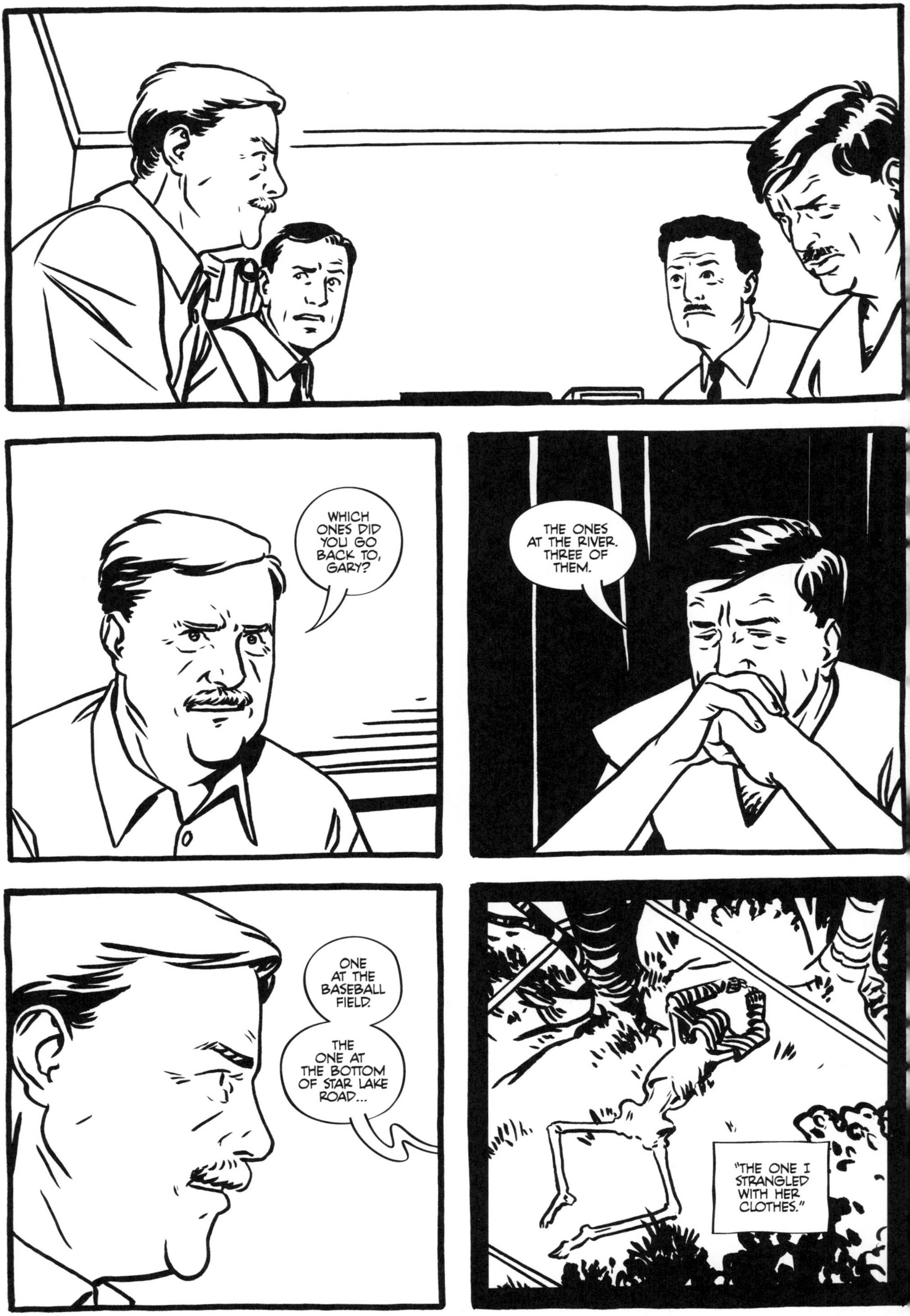

WHICH ONES DID YOU GO BACK TO, GARY?
THE ONES AT THE RIVER. THREE OF THEM.
ONE AT THE BASEBALL FIELD.
THE ONE AT THE BOTTOM OF STAR LAKE ROAD...
"THE ONE I STRANGLED WITH HER CLOTHES."

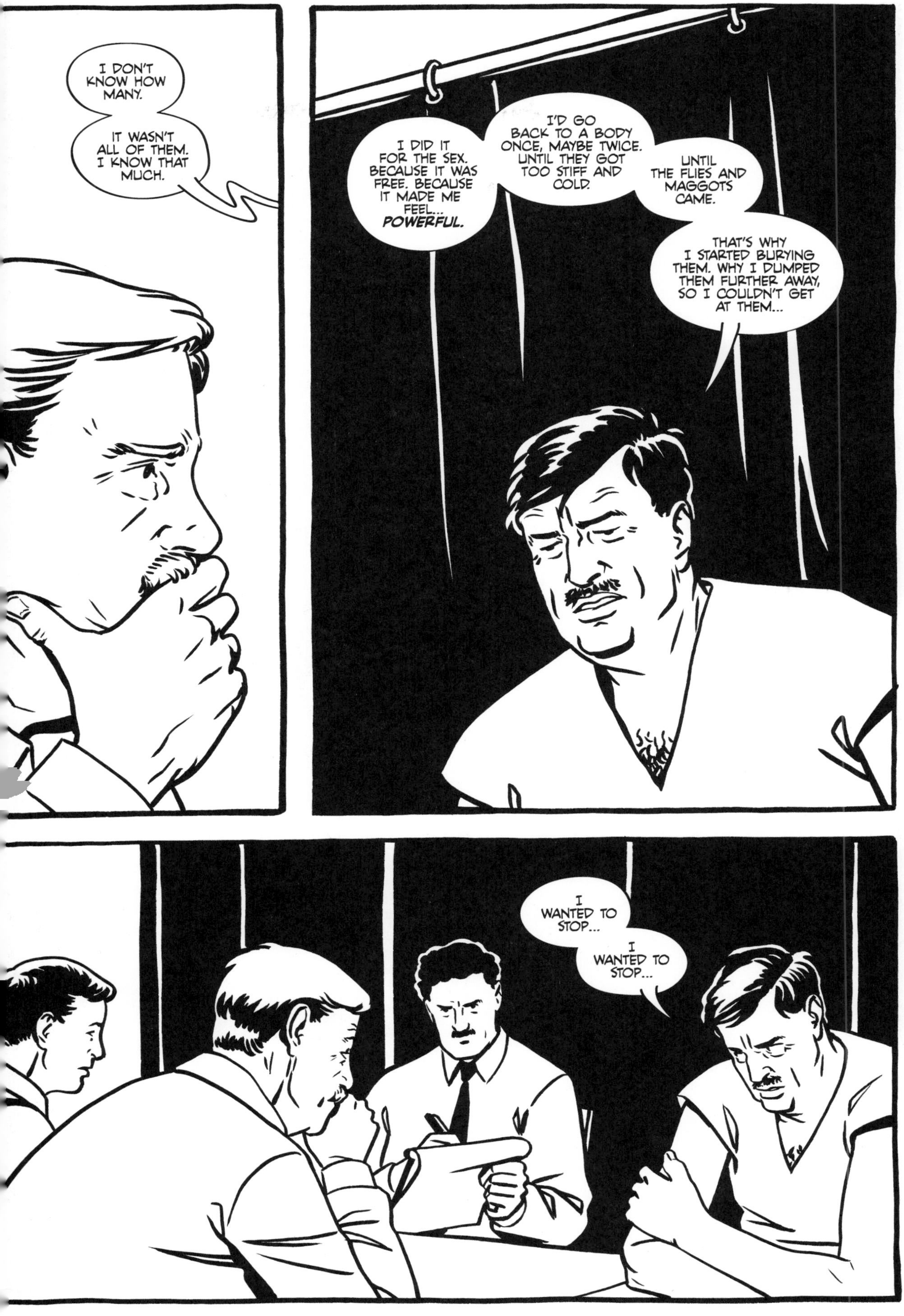
I DON'T KNOW HOW MANY.
IT WASN'T ALL OF THEM. I KNOW THAT MUCH.
I DID IT FOR THE SEX. BECAUSE IT WAS FREE. BECAUSE IT MADE ME FEEL... POWERFUL.
I'D GO BACK TO A BODY ONCE, MAYBE TWICE. UNTIL THEY GOT TOO STIFF AND COLD.
UNTIL THE FLIES AND MAGGOTS CAME.
THAT'S WHY I STARTED BURYING THEM. WHY I DUMPED THEM FURTHER AWAY, SO I COULDN'T GET AT THEM...
I WANTED TO STOP...
I WANTED TO STOP...

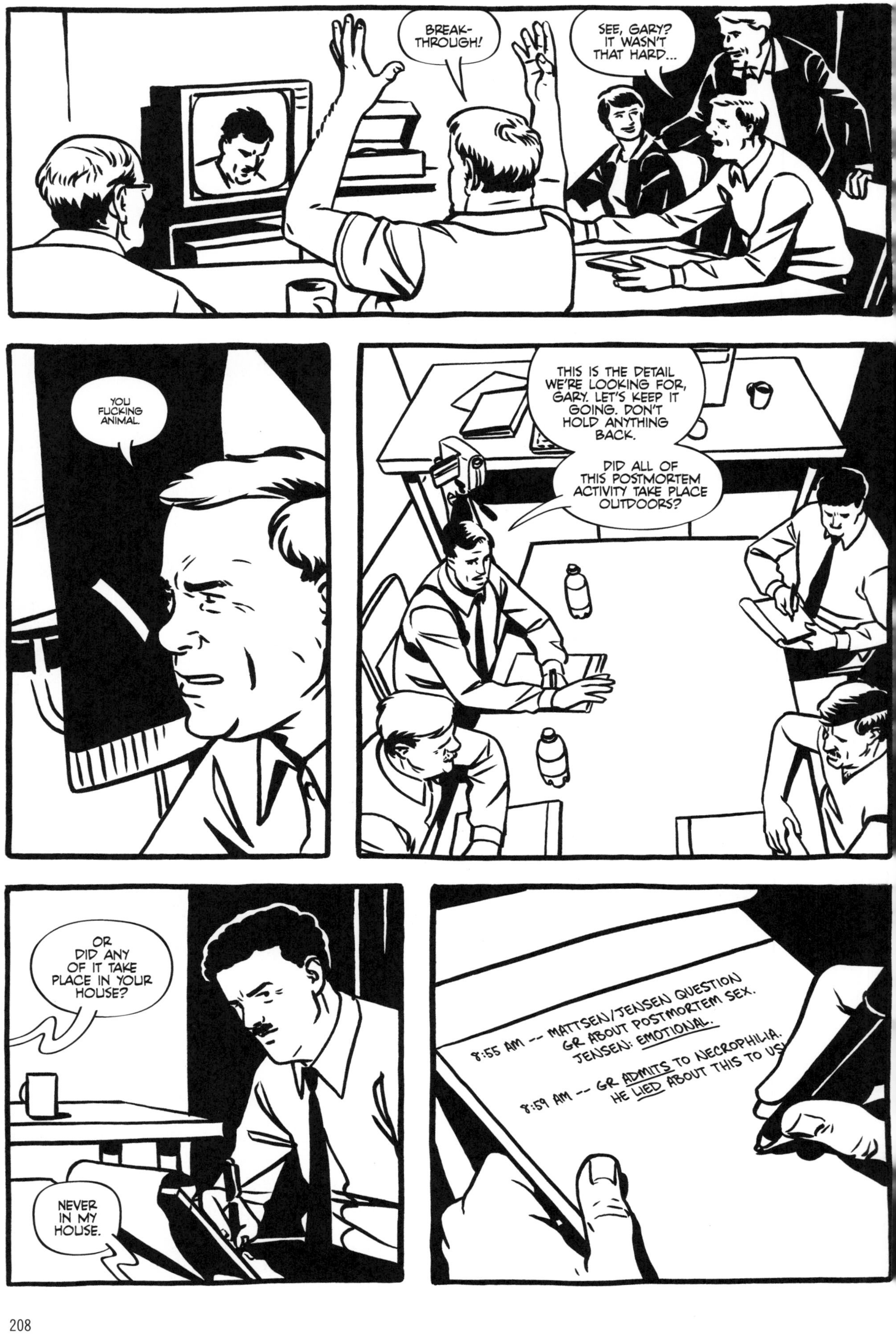
BREAK-THROUGH!
SEE, GARY? IT WASN'T THAT HARD...
YOU FUCKING ANIMAL.
THIS IS THE DETAIL WE'RE LOOKING FOR, GARY. LET'S KEEP IT GOING. DON'T HOLD ANYTHING BACK.
DID ALL OF THIS POSTMORTEM ACTIVITY TAKE PLACE OUTDOORS?
OR DID ANY OF IT TAKE PLACE IN YOUR HOUSE?
NEVER IN MY HOUSE.
8:55 AM -- MATTSEN/JENSEN QUESTION GR ABOUT POSTMORTEM SEX. JENSEN: EMOTIONAL.
8:59 AM -- GR ADMITS TO NECROPHILIA. HE LIED ABOUT THIS TO US

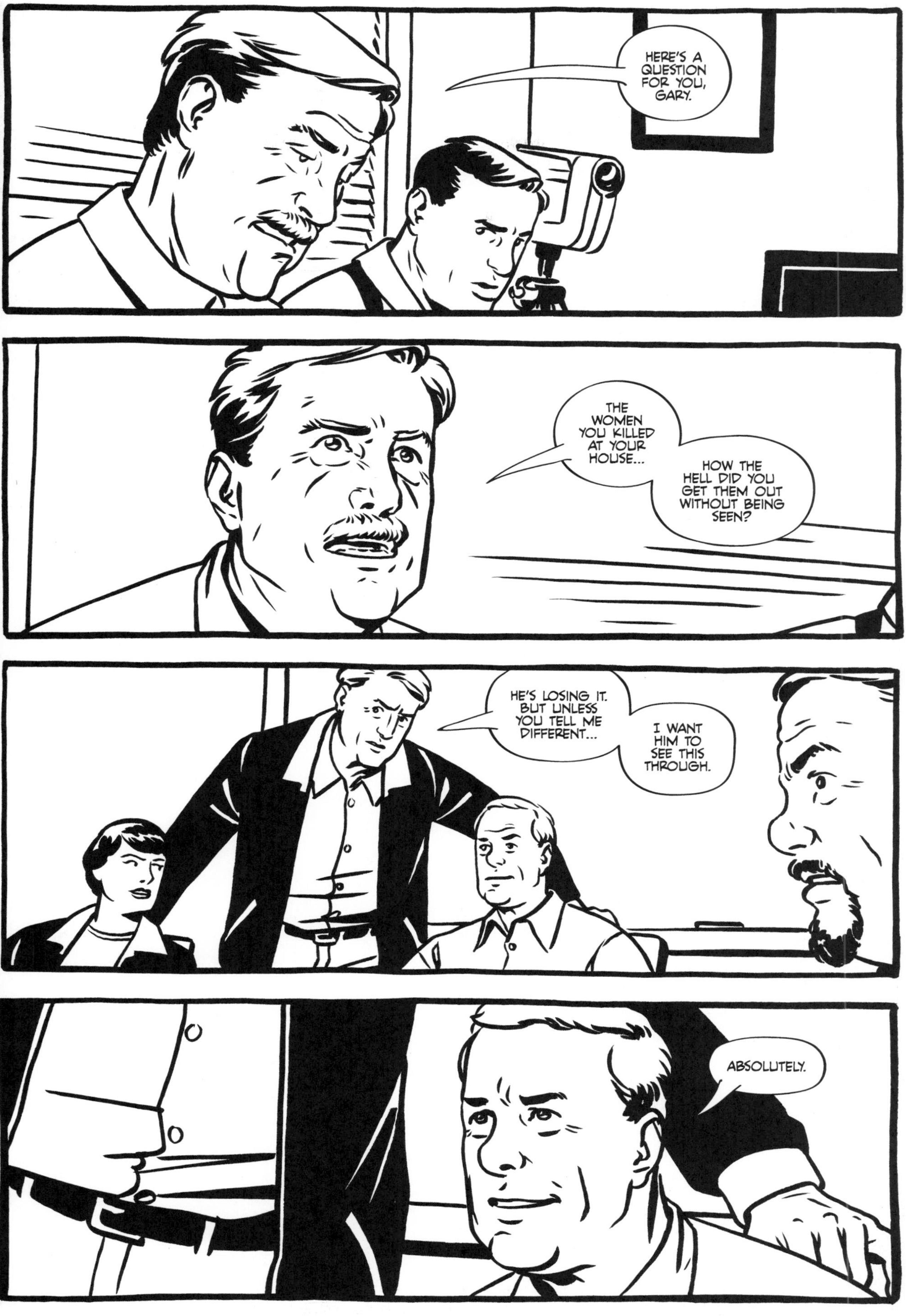
HERE'S A QUESTION FOR YOU, GARY.
THE WOMEN YOU KILLED AT YOUR HOUSE...
HOW THE HELL DID YOU GET THEM OUT WITHOUT BEING SEEN?
HE'S LOSING IT. BUT UNLESS YOU TELL ME DIFFERENT...
I WANT HIM TO SEE THIS THROUGH.
ABSOLUTELY.

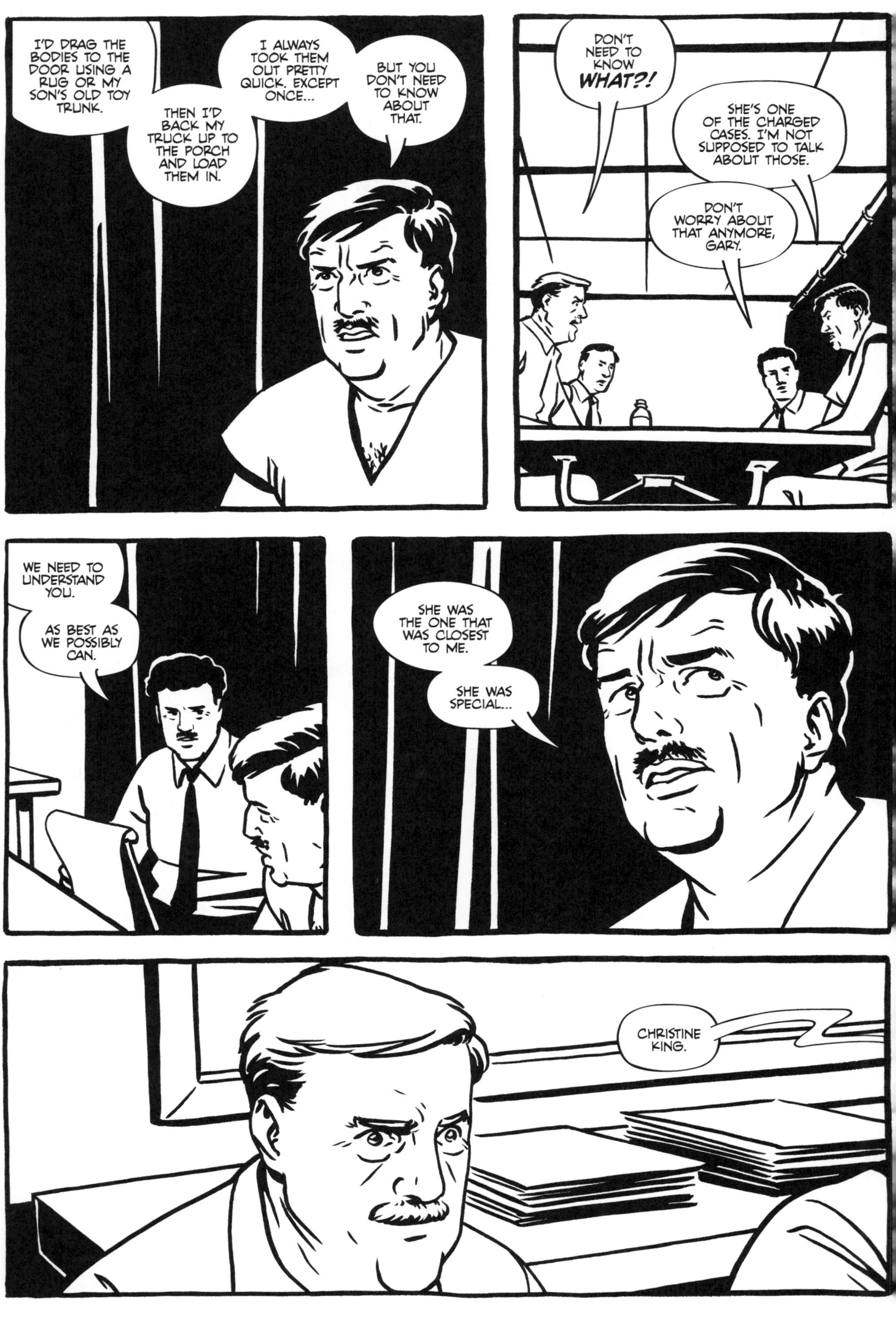
I'D DRAG THE BODIES TO THE DOOR USING A RUG OR MY SON'S OLD TOY TRUNK.
THEN I'D BACK MY TRUCK UP TO THE PORCH AND LOAD THEM IN.
I ALWAYS TOOK THEM OUT PRETTY QUICK. EXCEPT ONCE...
BUT YOU DON'T NEED TO KNOW ABOUT THAT.
DON'T NEED TO KNOW *WHAT?!*
SHE'S ONE OF THE CHARGED CASES. I'M NOT SUPPOSED TO TALK ABOUT THOSE.
DON'T WORRY ABOUT THAT ANYMORE, GARY.
WE NEED TO UNDERSTAND YOU.
AS BEST AS WE POSSIBLY CAN.
SHE WAS THE ONE THAT WAS CLOSEST TO ME.
SHE WAS SPECIAL...
CHRISTINE KING.

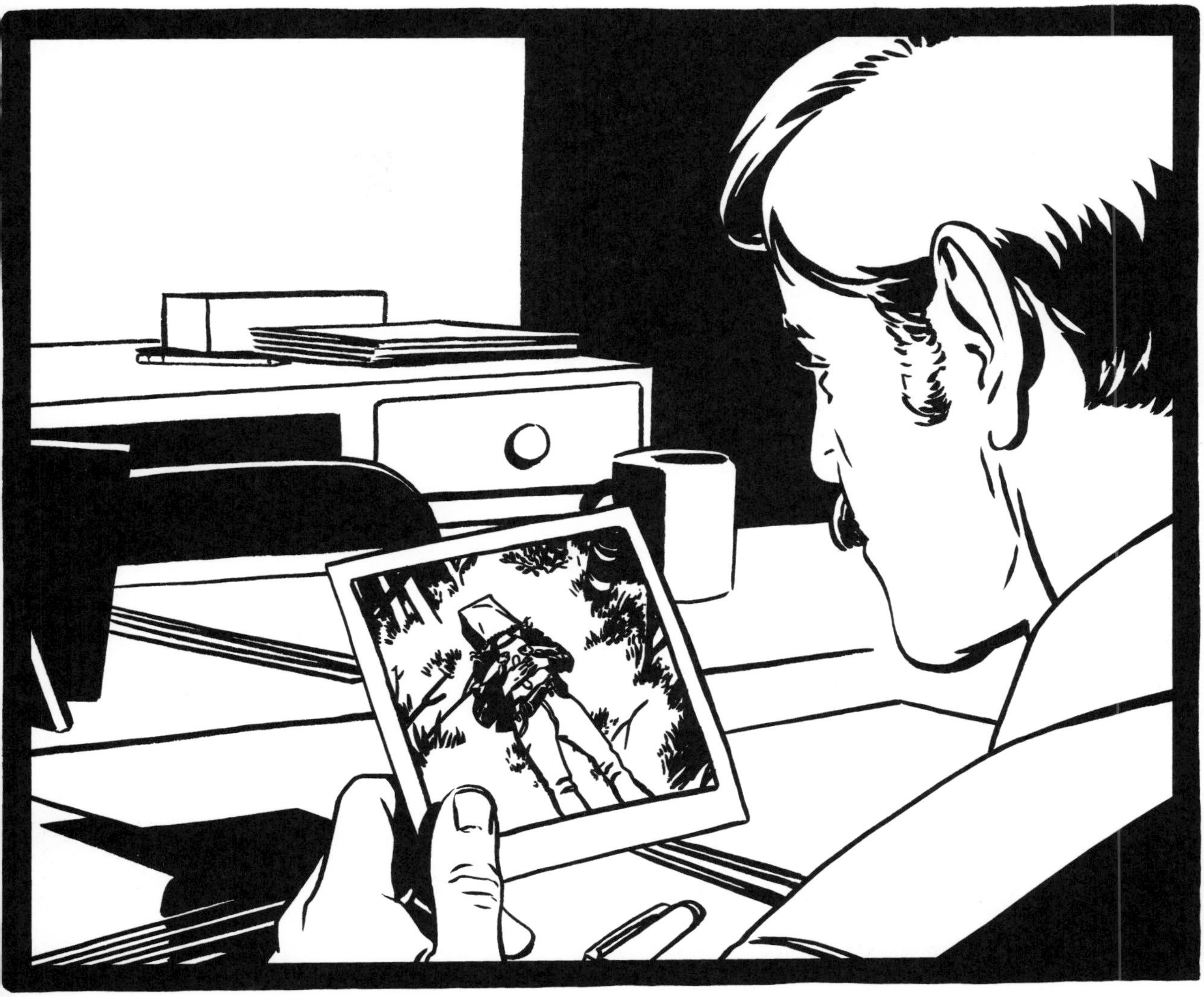

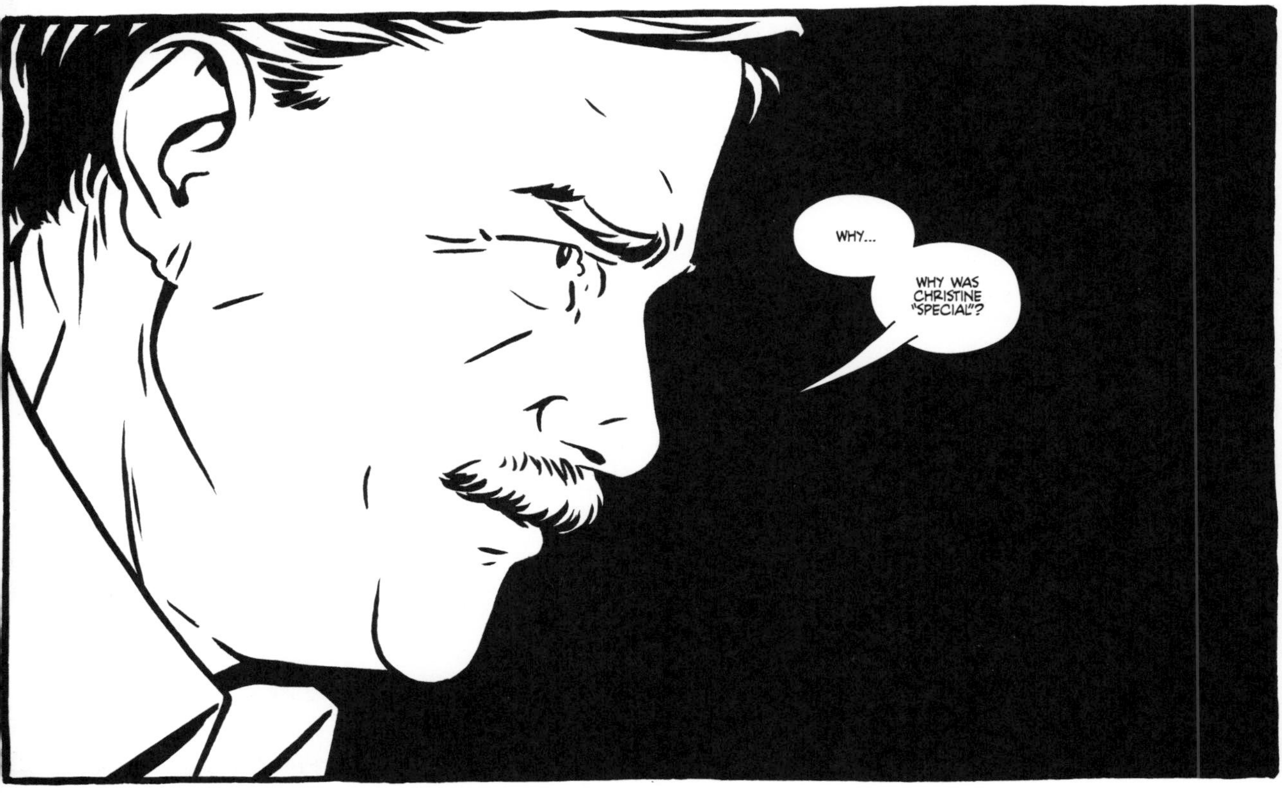
WHY...
WHY WAS CHRISTINE "SPECIAL"?

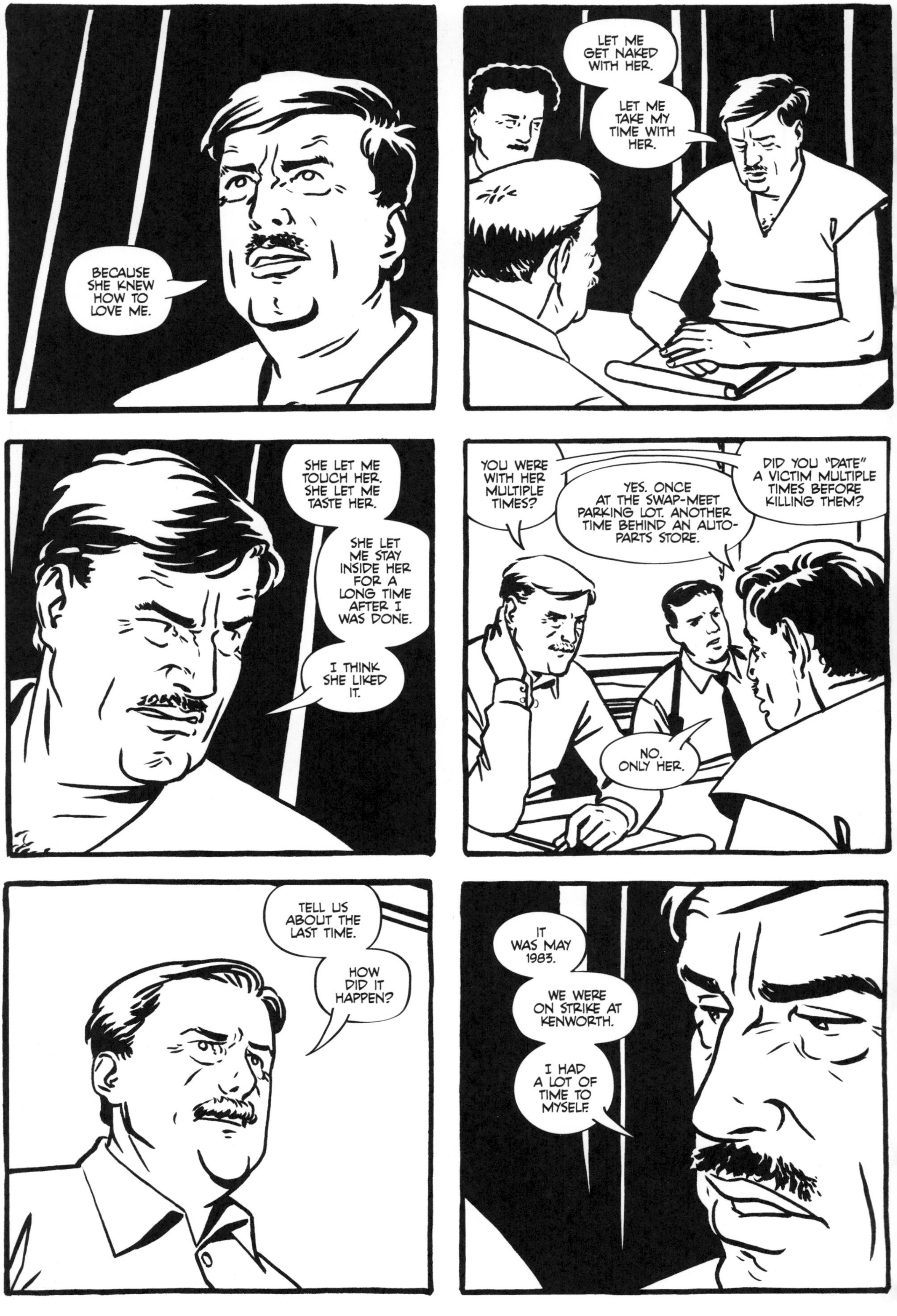
BECAUSE SHE KNEW HOW TO LOVE ME.
LET ME GET NAKED WITH HER.
LET ME TAKE MY TIME WITH HER.
SHE LET ME TOUCH HER. SHE LET ME TASTE HER.
SHE LET ME STAY INSIDE HER FOR A LONG TIME AFTER I WAS DONE.
I THINK SHE LIKED IT.
YOU WERE WITH HER MULTIPLE TIMES?
YES. ONCE AT THE SWAP-MEET PARKING LOT. ANOTHER TIME BEHIND AN AUTO-PARTS STORE.
DID YOU "DATE" A VICTIM MULTIPLE TIMES BEFORE KILLING THEM?
NO. ONLY HER.
TELL US ABOUT THE LAST TIME.
HOW DID IT HAPPEN?
IT WAS MAY 1983.
WE WERE ON STRIKE AT KENWORTH.
I HAD A LOT OF TIME TO MYSELF.

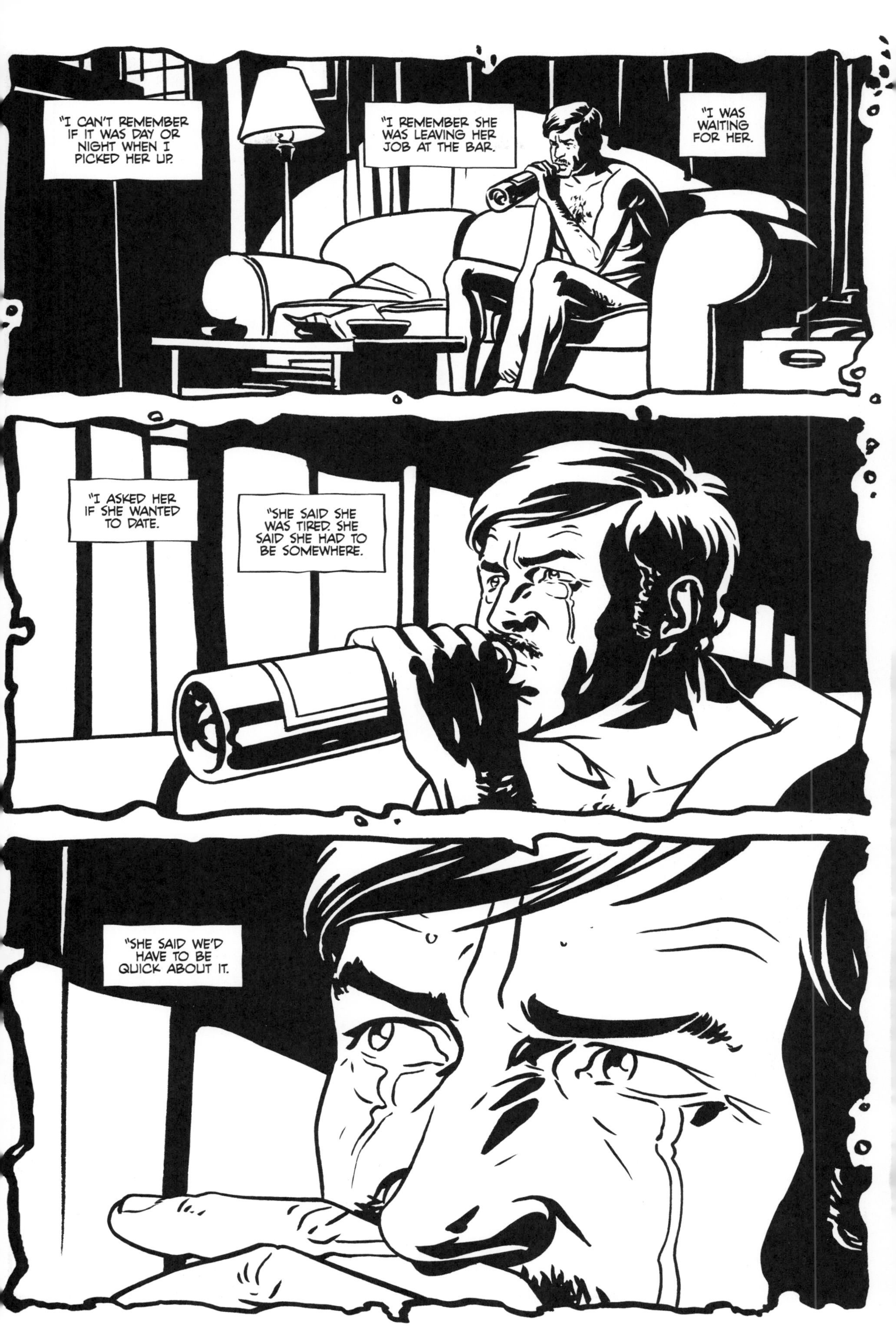
"I CAN'T REMEMBER IF IT WAS DAY OR NIGHT WHEN I PICKED HER UP.
"I REMEMBER SHE WAS LEAVING HER JOB AT THE BAR.
"I WAS WAITING FOR HER.
"I ASKED HER IF SHE WANTED TO DATE.
"SHE SAID SHE WAS TIRED. SHE SAID SHE HAD TO BE SOMEWHERE.
"SHE SAID WE'D HAVE TO BE QUICK ABOUT IT.

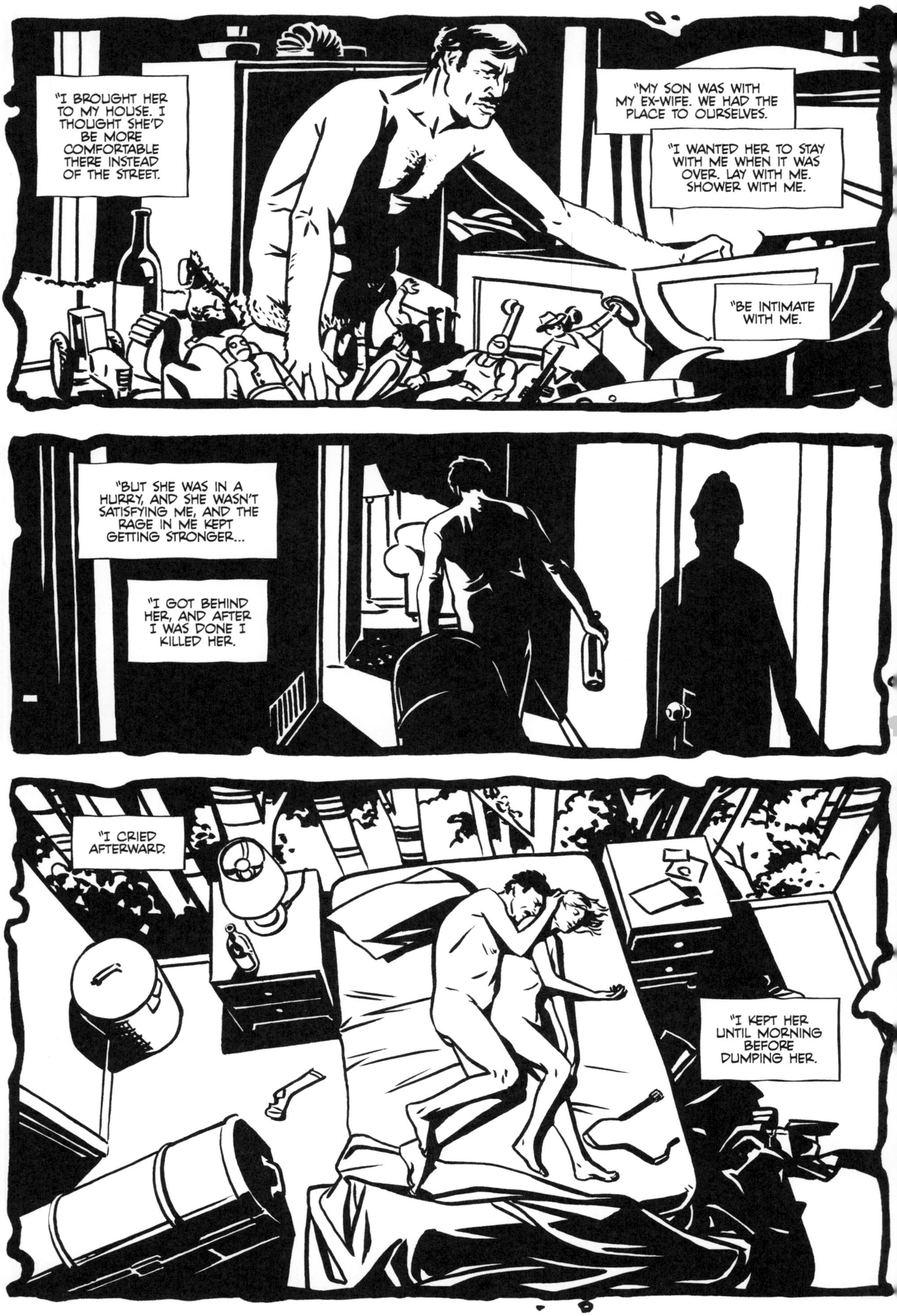
"I BROUGHT HER TO MY HOUSE. I THOUGHT SHE'D BE MORE COMFORTABLE THERE INSTEAD OF THE STREET.
"MY SON WAS WITH MY EX-WIFE. WE HAD THE PLACE TO OURSELVES.
"I WANTED HER TO STAY WITH ME WHEN IT WAS OVER. LAY WITH ME. SHOWER WITH ME.
"BE INTIMATE WITH ME.
"BUT SHE WAS IN A HURRY, AND SHE WASN'T SATISFYING ME, AND THE RAGE IN ME KEPT GETTING STRONGER...
"I GOT BEHIND HER, AND AFTER I WAS DONE I KILLED HER.
"I CRIED AFTERWARD.
"I KEPT HER UNTIL MORNING BEFORE DUMPING HER.

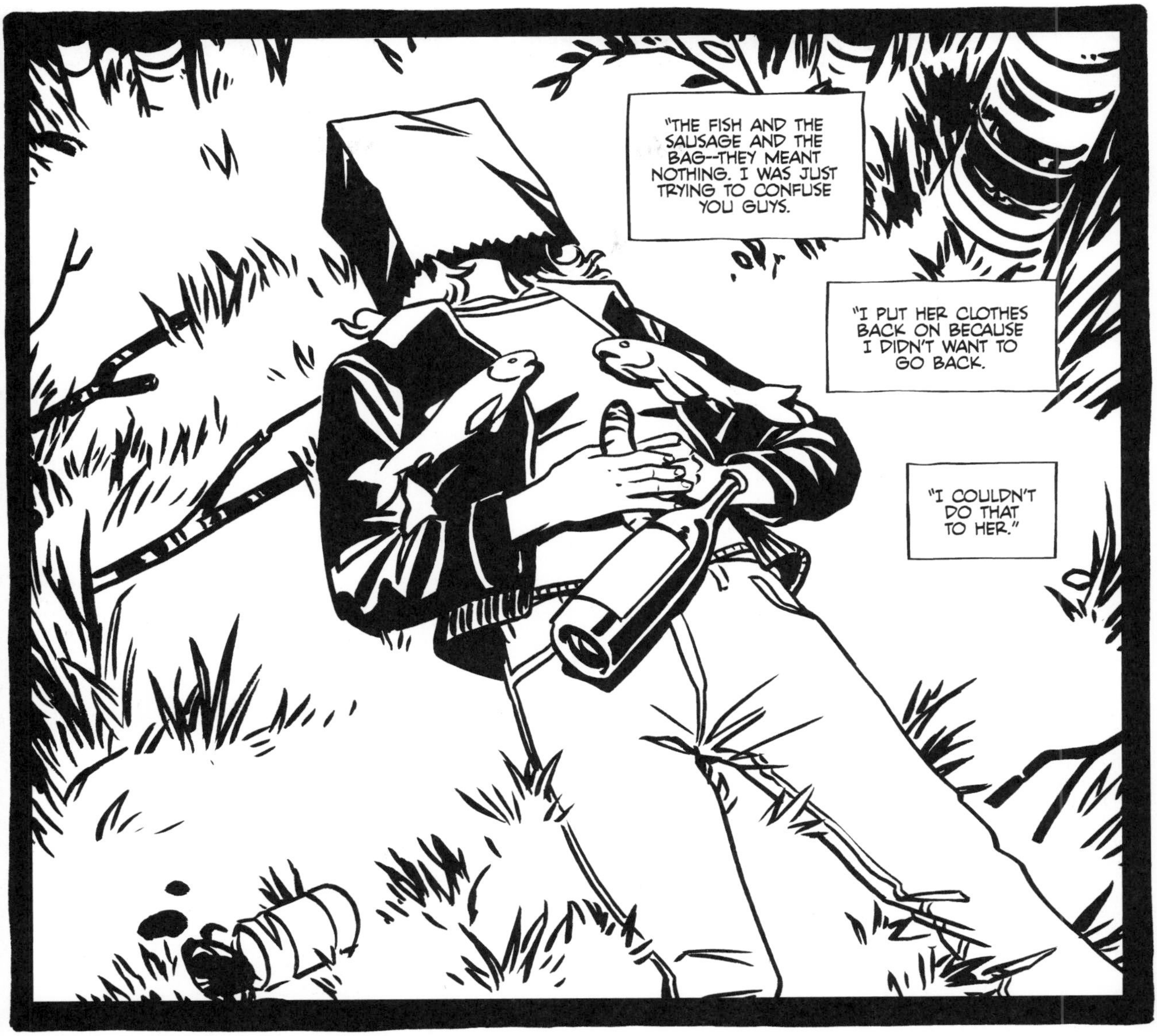
"THE FISH AND THE SAUSAGE AND THE BAG--THEY MEANT NOTHING. I WAS JUST TRYING TO CONFUSE YOU GUYS.
"I PUT HER CLOTHES BACK ON BECAUSE I DIDN'T WANT TO GO BACK.
"I COULDN'T DO THAT TO HER."

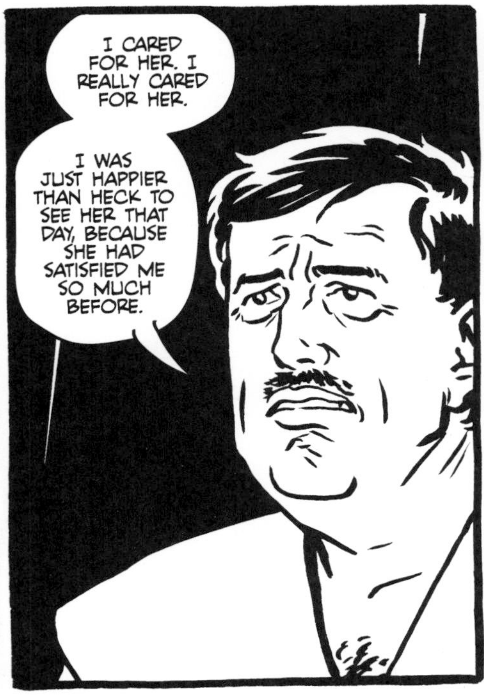
I CARED FOR HER. I REALLY CARED FOR HER.
I WAS JUST HAPPIER THAN HECK TO SEE HER THAT DAY, BECAUSE SHE HAD SATISFIED ME SO MUCH BEFORE.

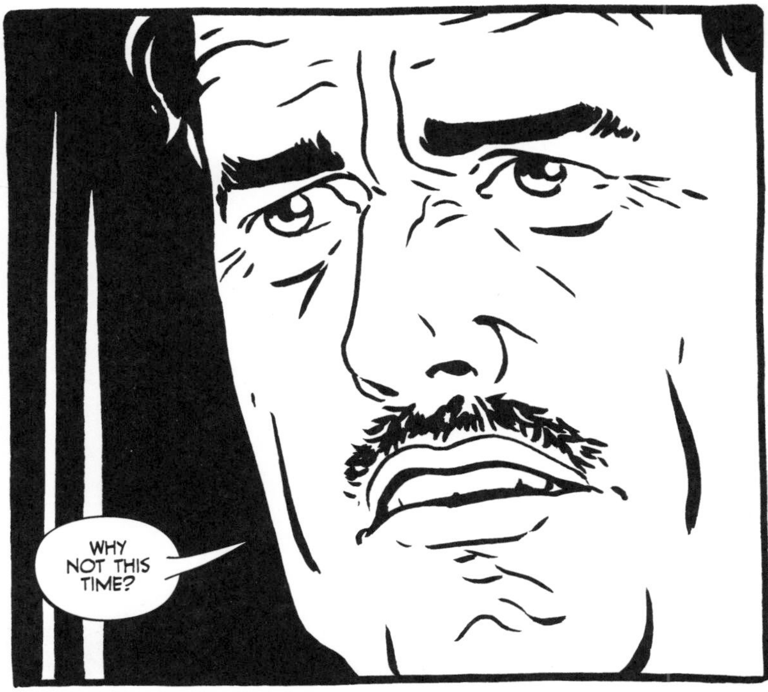
WHY NOT THIS TIME?

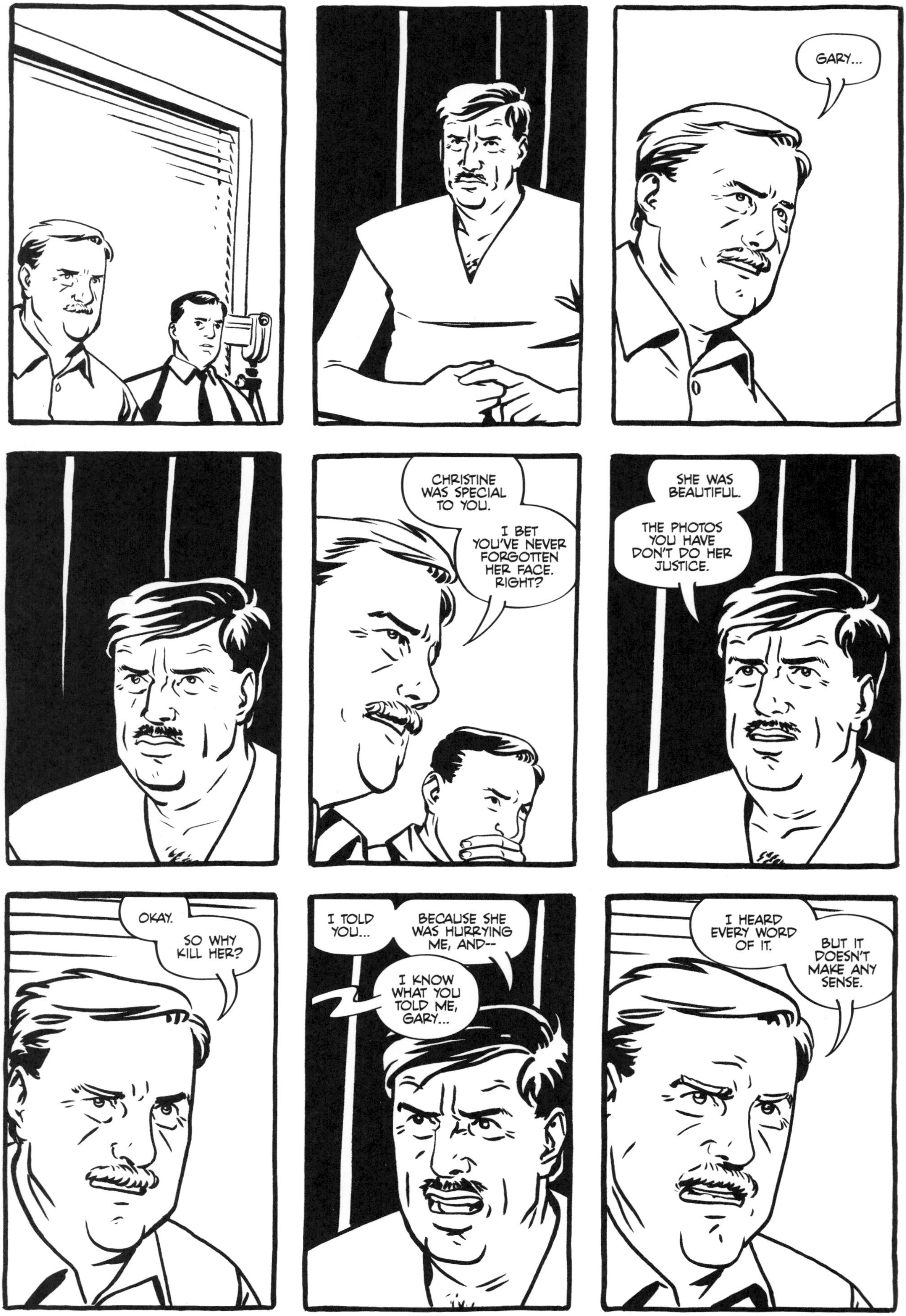
GARY...
CHRISTINE WAS SPECIAL TO YOU.
I BET YOU'VE NEVER FORGOTTEN HER FACE. RIGHT?
SHE WAS BEAUTIFUL.
THE PHOTOS YOU HAVE DON'T DO HER JUSTICE.
OKAY.
SO WHY KILL HER?
I TOLD YOU...
BECAUSE SHE WAS HURRYING ME, AND--
I KNOW WHAT YOU TOLD ME, GARY...
I HEARD EVERY WORD OF IT.
BUT IT DOESN'T MAKE ANY SENSE.

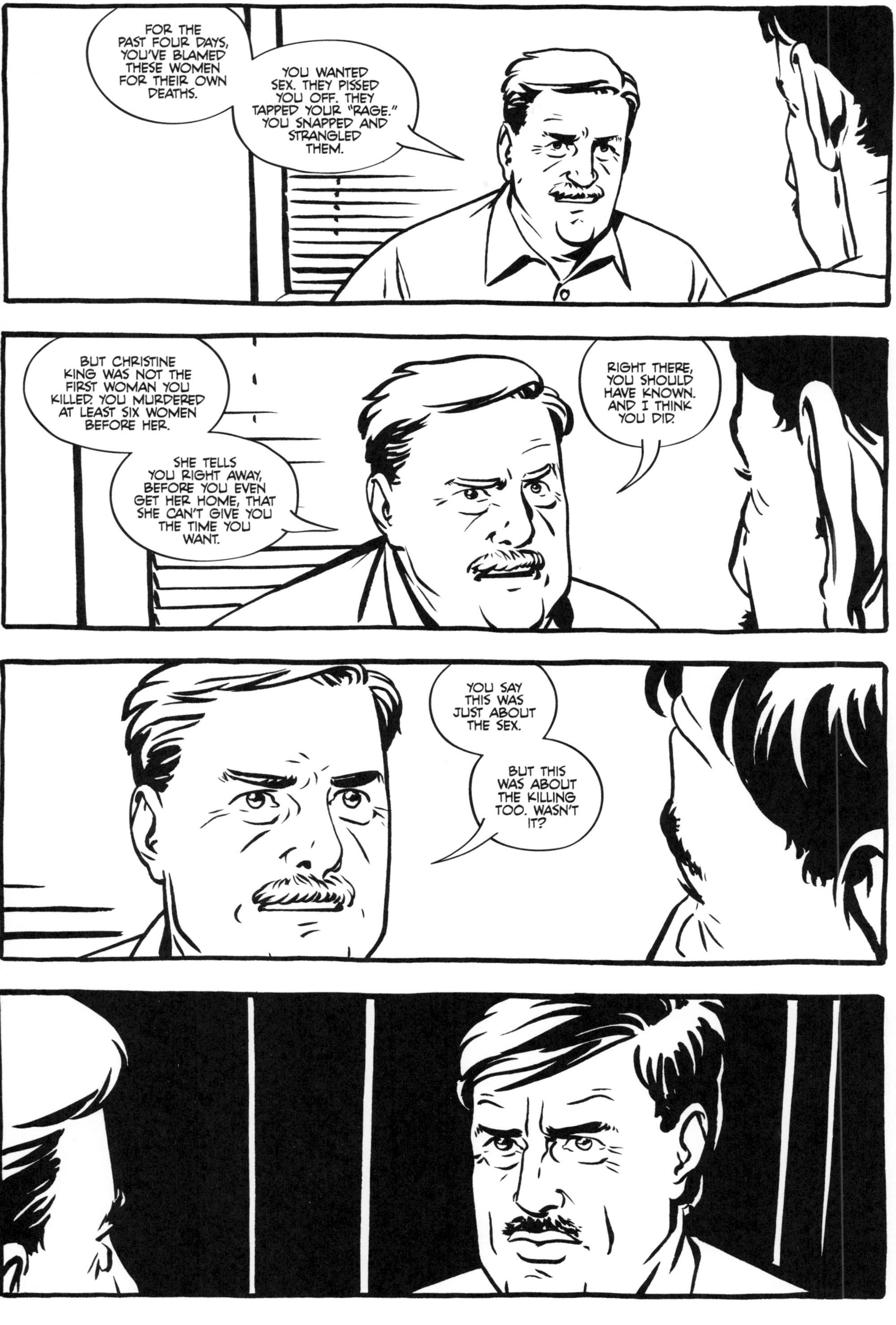
FOR THE PAST FOUR DAYS, YOU'VE BLAMED THESE WOMEN FOR THEIR OWN DEATHS.
YOU WANTED SEX. THEY PISSED YOU OFF. THEY TAPPED YOUR "RAGE." YOU SNAPPED AND STRANGLED THEM.
BUT CHRISTINE KING WAS NOT THE FIRST WOMAN YOU KILLED. YOU MURDERED AT LEAST SIX WOMEN BEFORE HER.
SHE TELLS YOU RIGHT AWAY, BEFORE YOU EVEN GET HER HOME, THAT SHE CAN'T GIVE YOU THE TIME YOU WANT.
RIGHT THERE, YOU SHOULD HAVE KNOWN. AND I THINK YOU DID.
YOU SAY THIS WAS JUST ABOUT THE SEX.
BUT THIS WAS ABOUT THE KILLING TOO. WASN'T IT?

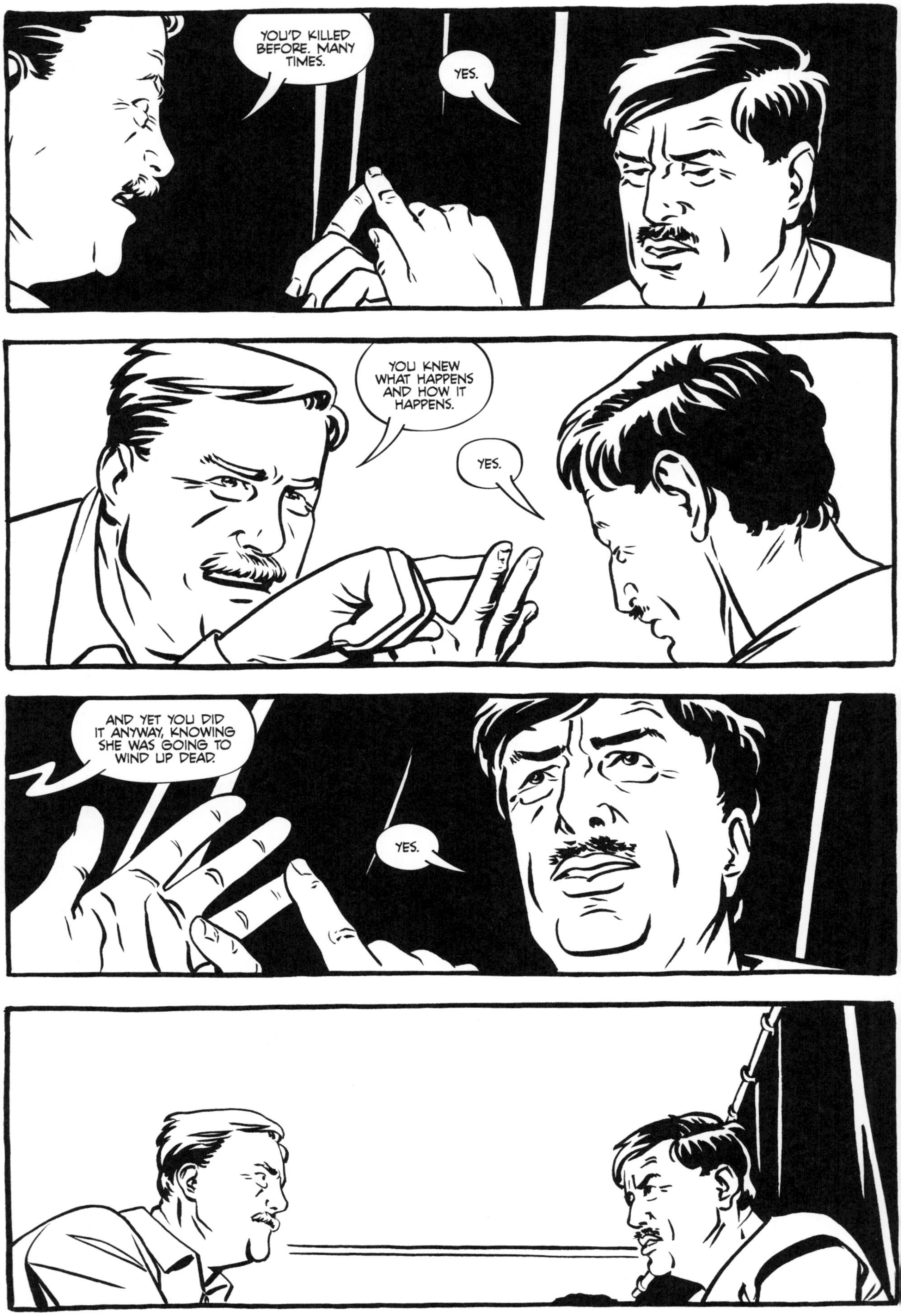
YOU'D KILLED BEFORE. MANY TIMES.
YES.
YOU KNEW WHAT HAPPENS AND HOW IT HAPPENS.
YES.
AND YET YOU DID IT ANYWAY, KNOWING SHE WAS GOING TO WIND UP DEAD.
YES.

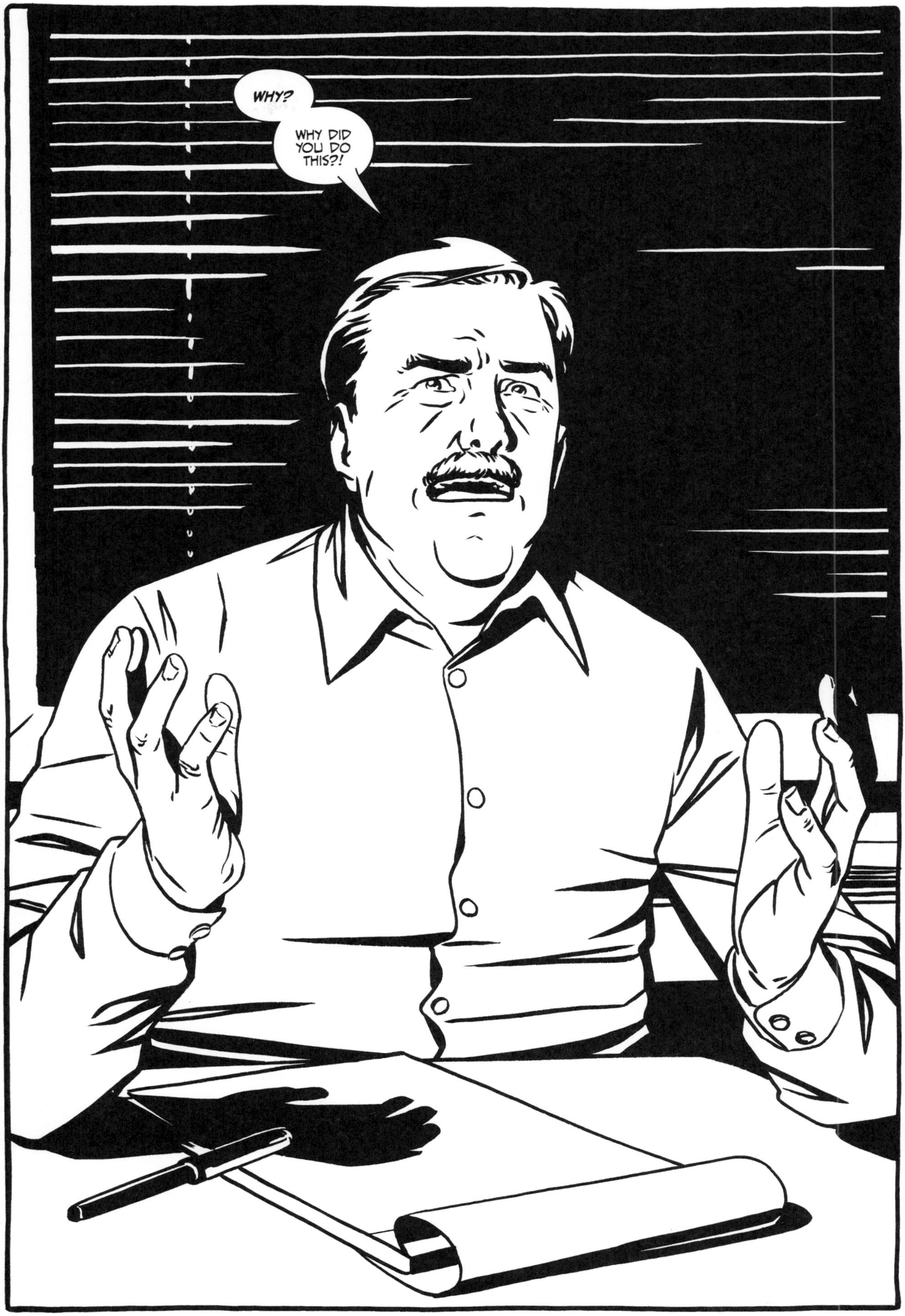
WHY?
WHY DID YOU DO THIS?!

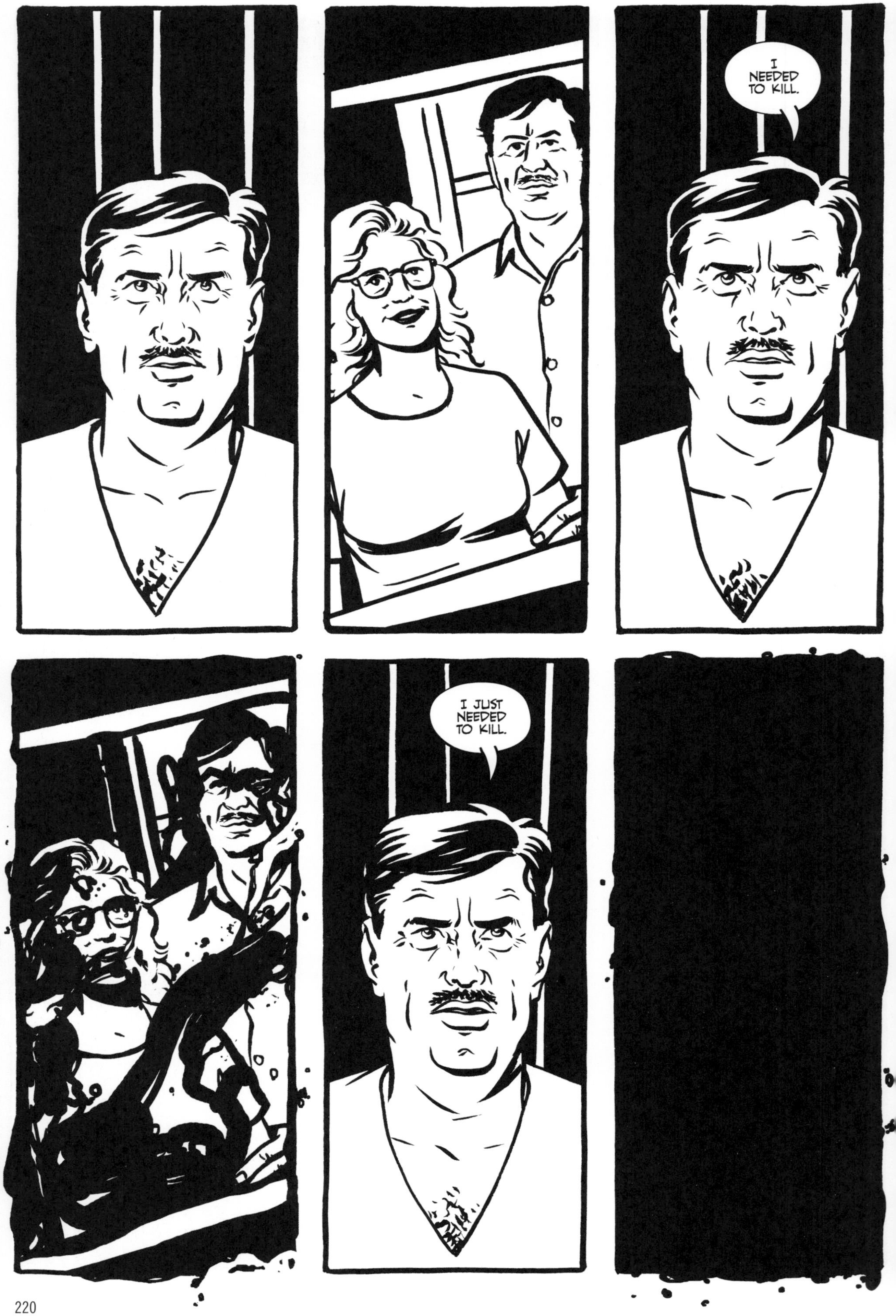
I NEEDED TO KILL.
I JUST NEEDED TO KILL.

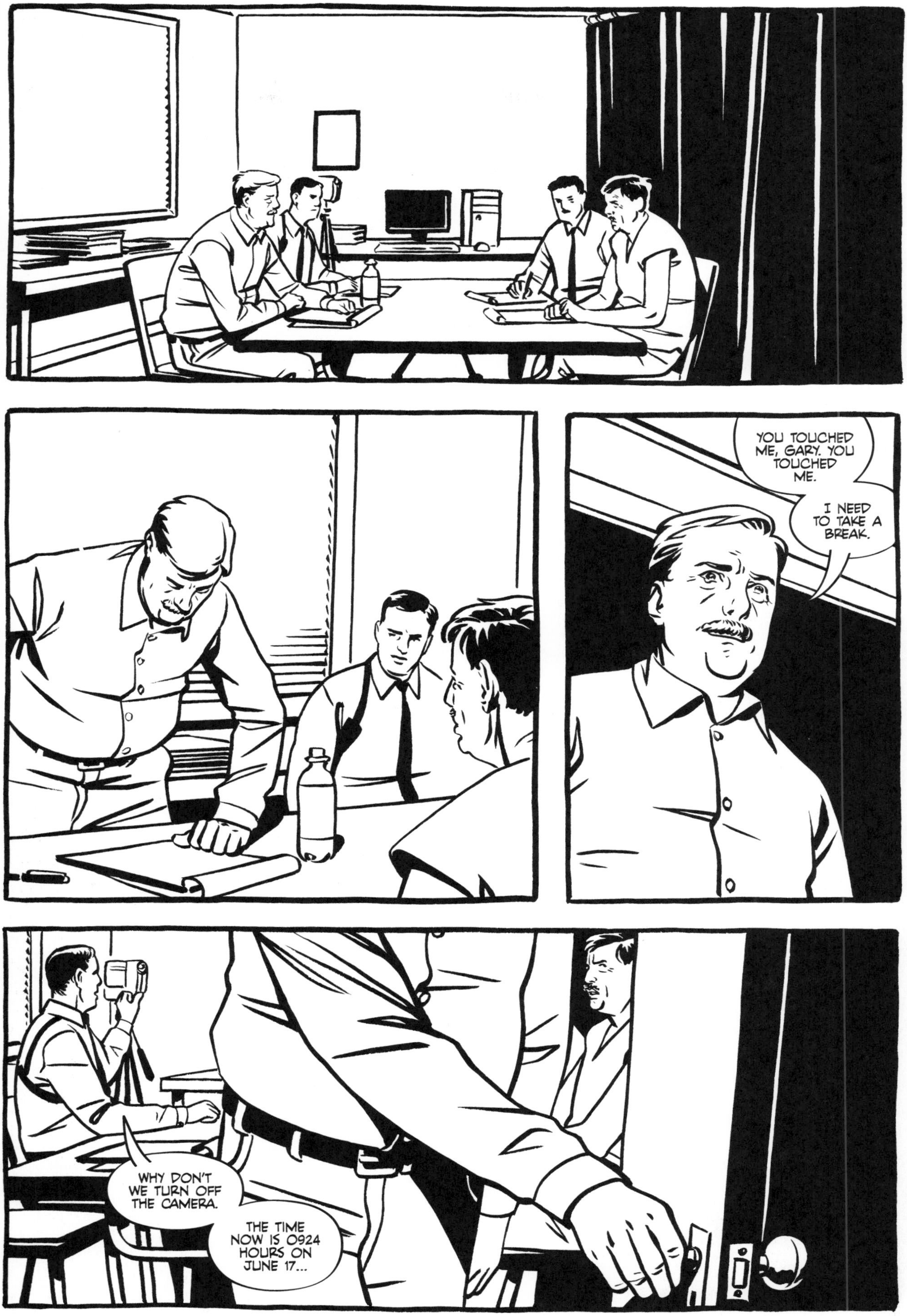
YOU TOUCHED ME, GARY. YOU TOUCHED ME.
I NEED TO TAKE A BREAK.
WHY DON'T WE TURN OFF THE CAMERA.
THE TIME NOW IS 0924 HOURS ON JUNE 17...

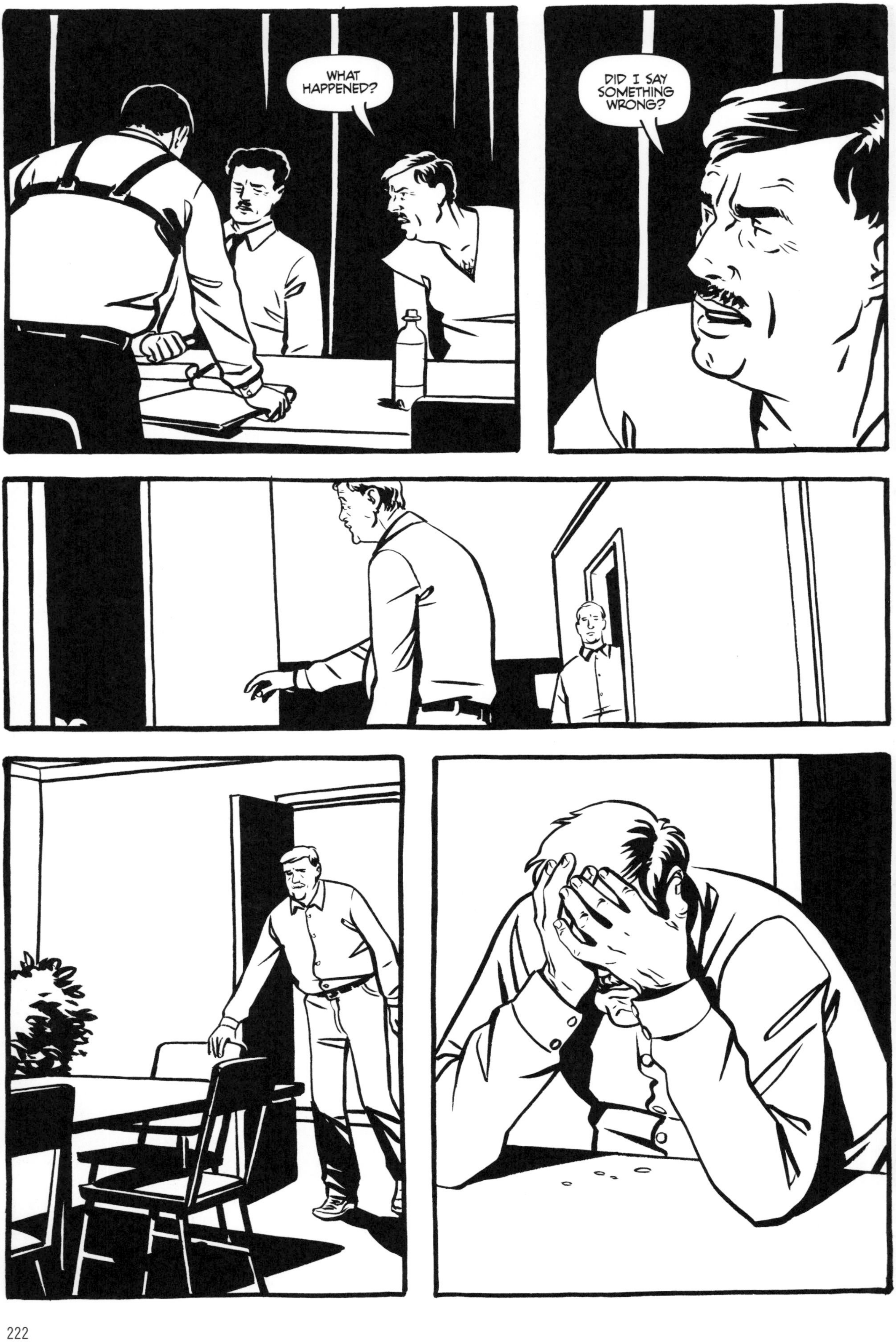
WHAT HAPPENED?
DID I SAY SOMETHING WRONG?

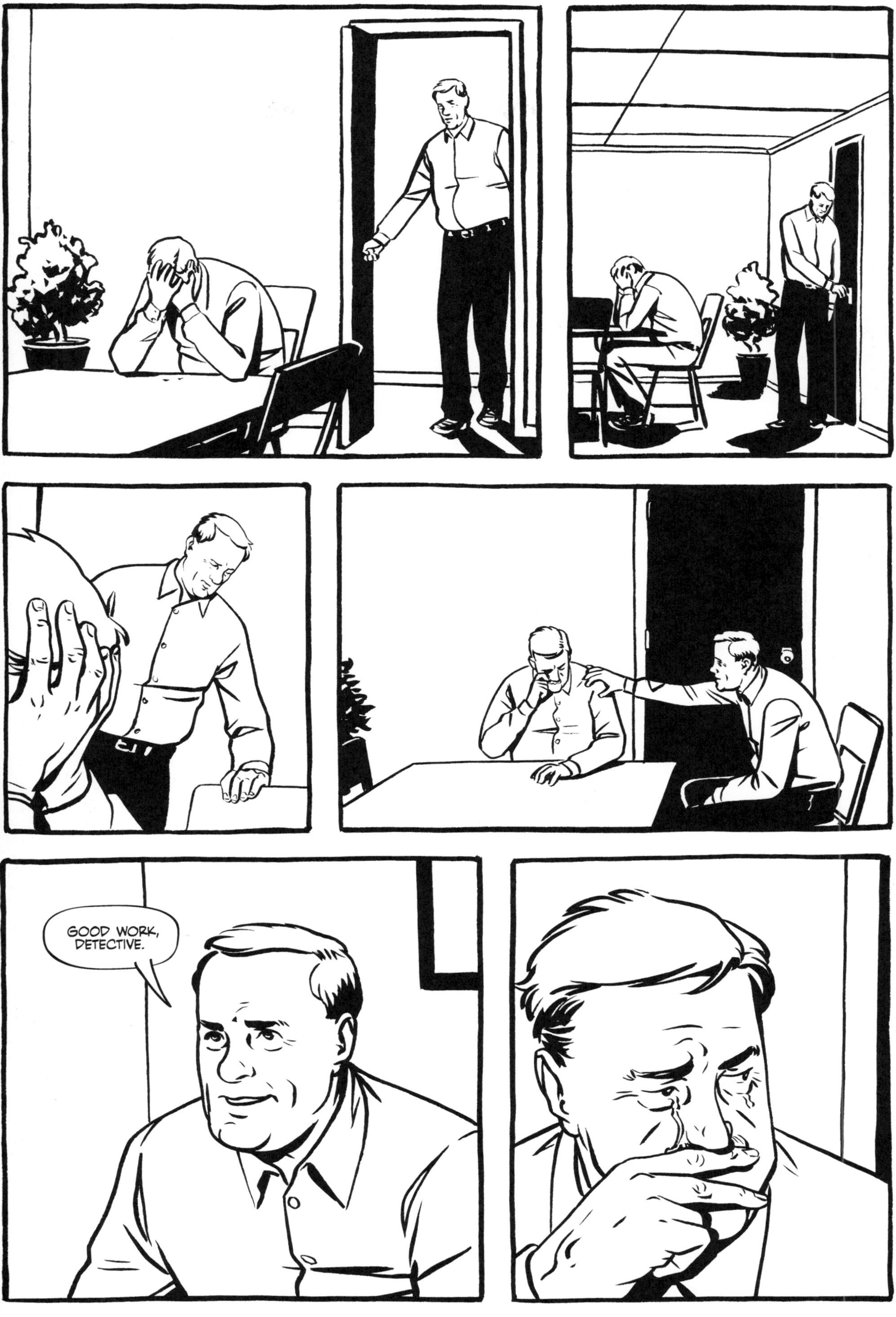
GOOD WORK, DETECTIVE.

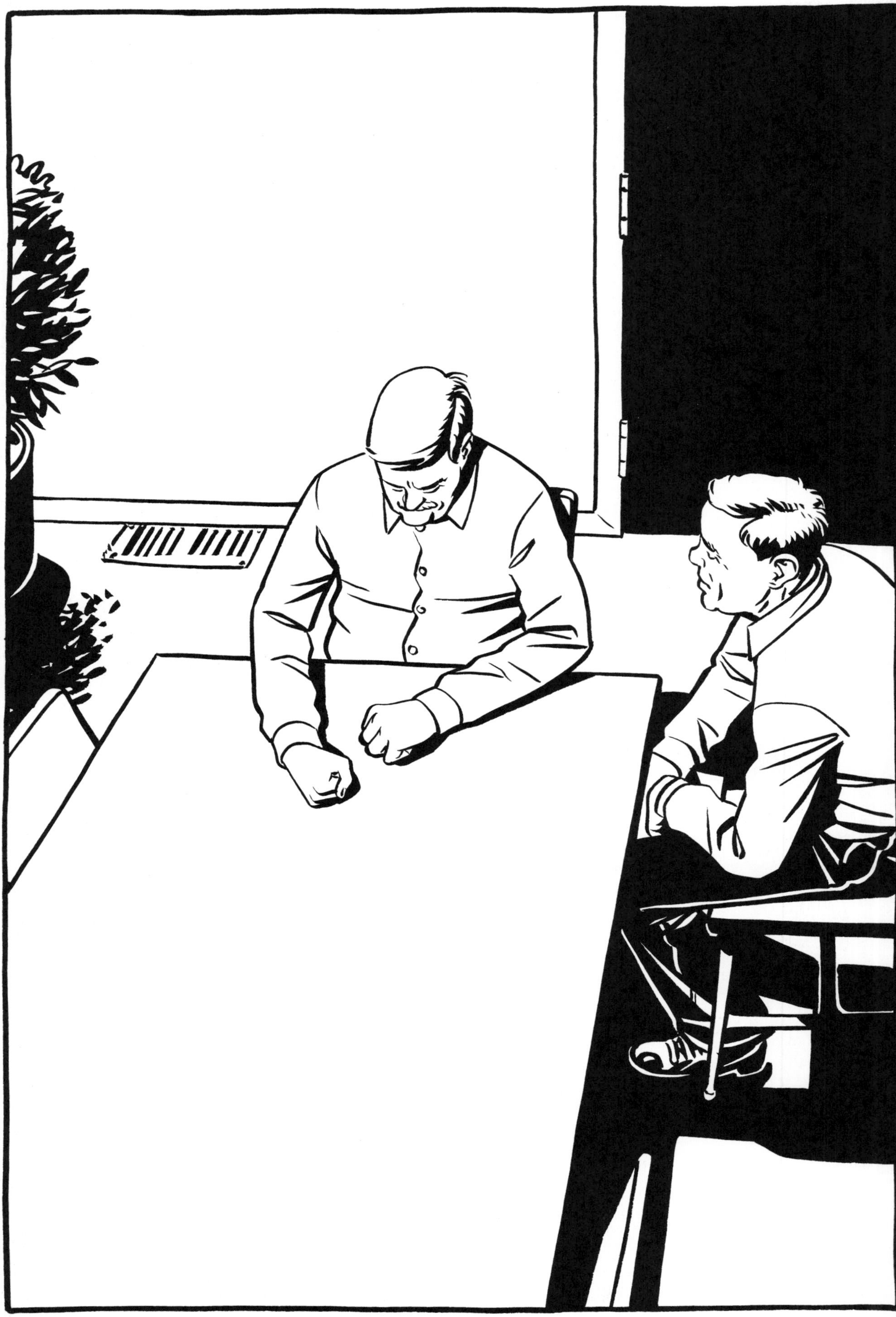

EPILOGUE

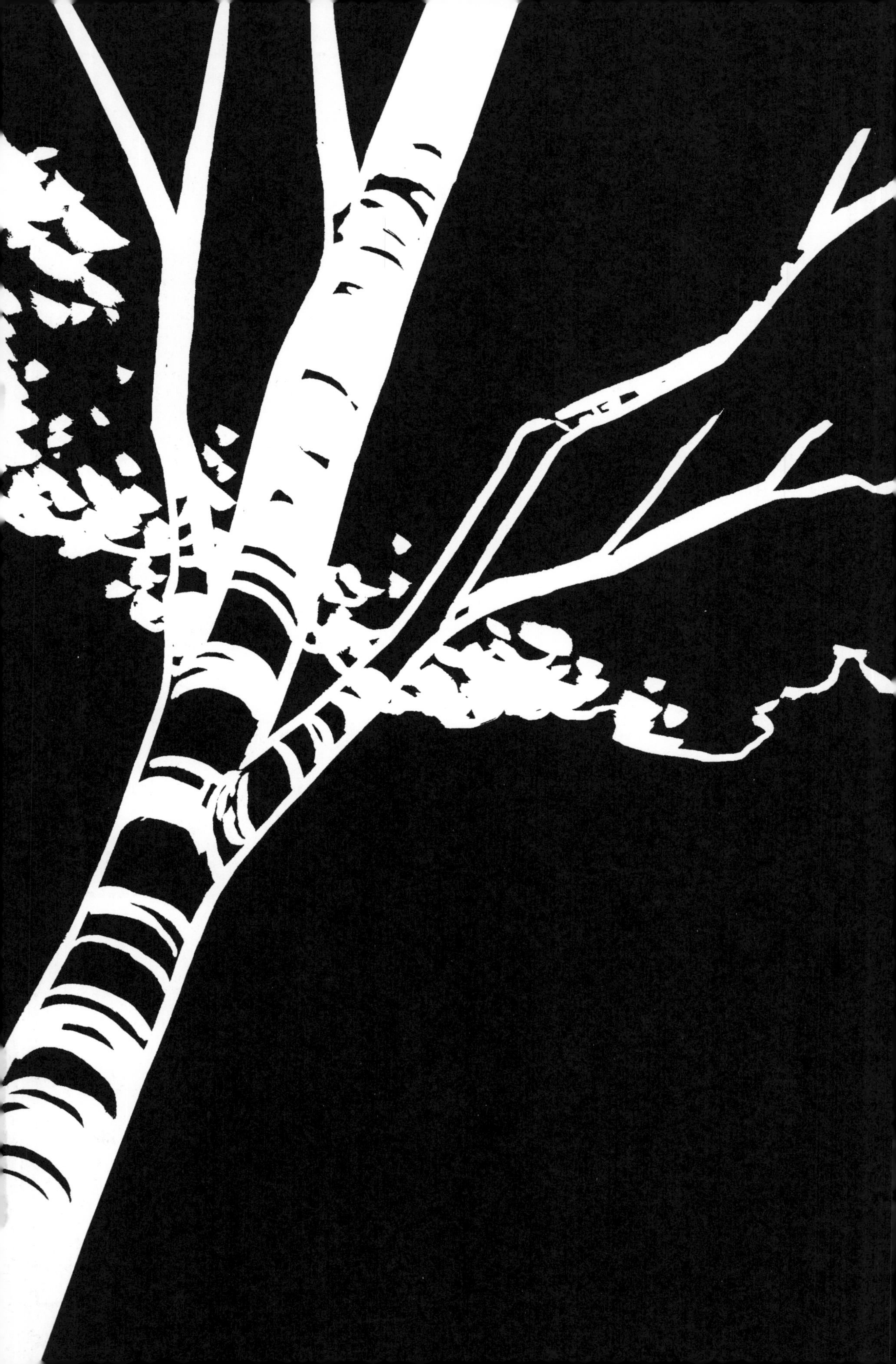

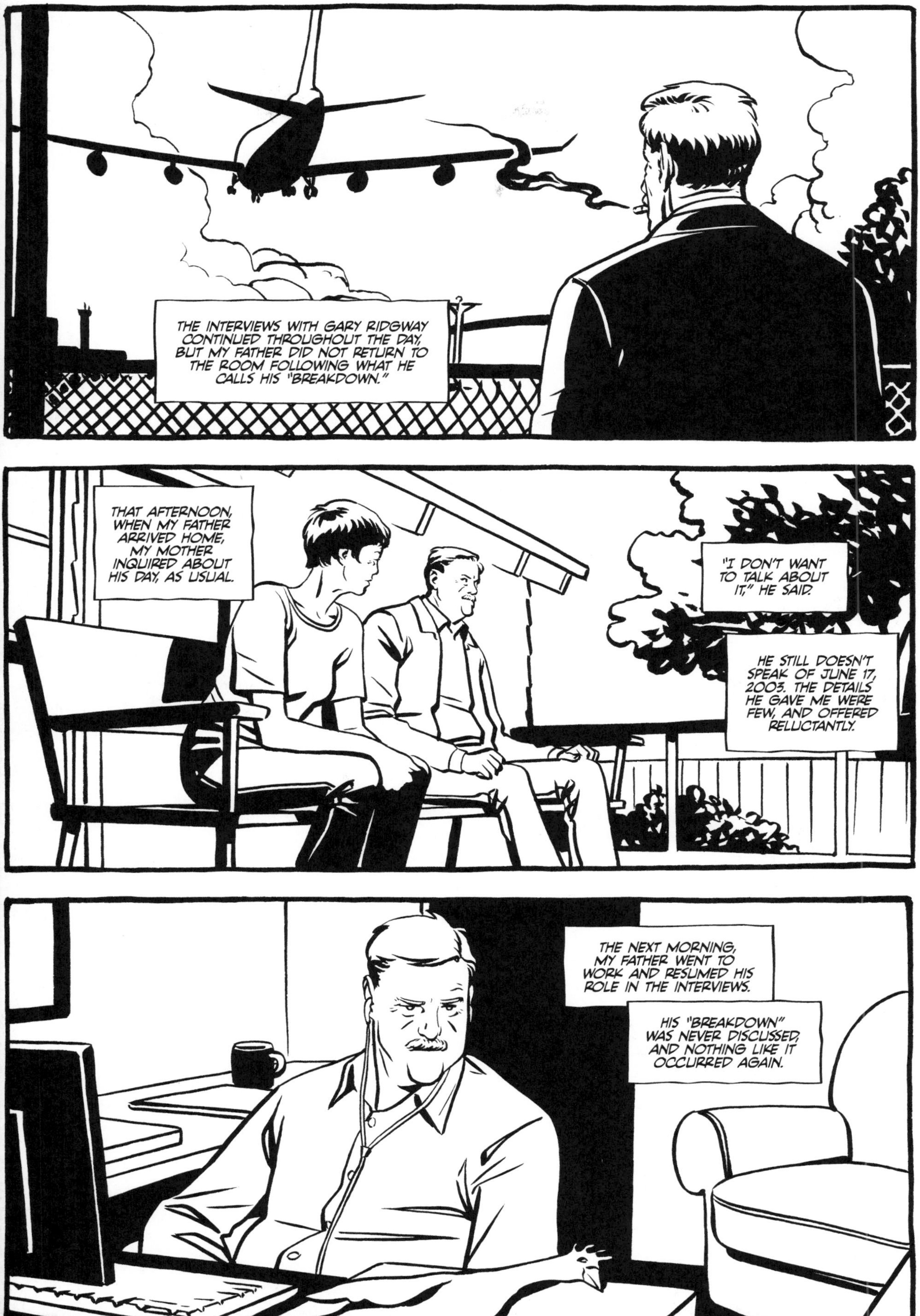
THE INTERVIEWS WITH GARY RIDGWAY CONTINUED THROUGHOUT THE DAY, BUT MY FATHER DID NOT RETURN TO THE ROOM FOLLOWING WHAT HE CALLS HIS "BREAKDOWN."
THAT AFTERNOON, WHEN MY FATHER ARRIVED HOME, MY MOTHER INQUIRED ABOUT HIS DAY, AS USUAL.
"I DON'T WANT TO TALK ABOUT IT," HE SAID.
HE STILL DOESN'T SPEAK OF JUNE 17, 2003. THE DETAILS HE GAVE ME WERE FEW, AND OFFERED RELUCTANTLY.
THE NEXT MORNING, MY FATHER WENT TO WORK AND RESUMED HIS ROLE IN THE INTERVIEWS.
HIS "BREAKDOWN" WAS NEVER DISCUSSED, AND NOTHING LIKE IT OCCURRED AGAIN.

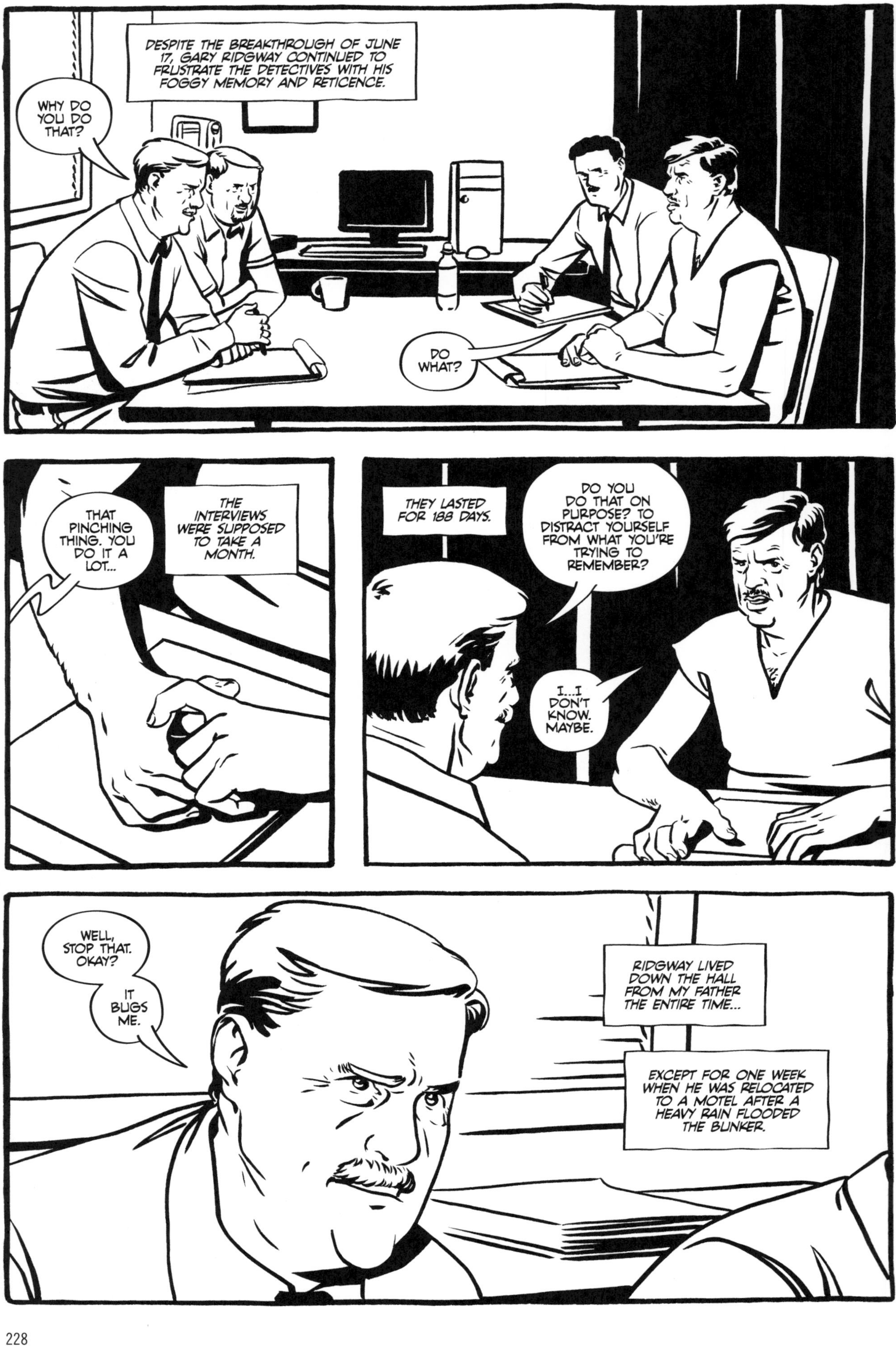
DESPITE THE BREAKTHROUGH OF JUNE 17, GARY RIDGWAY CONTINUED TO FRUSTRATE THE DETECTIVES WITH HIS FOGGY MEMORY AND RETICENCE.
WHY DO YOU DO THAT?
DO WHAT?
THAT PINCHING THING. YOU DO IT A LOT...
THE INTERVIEWS WERE SUPPOSED TO TAKE A MONTH.
THEY LASTED FOR 188 DAYS.
DO YOU DO THAT ON PURPOSE? TO DISTRACT YOURSELF FROM WHAT YOU'RE TRYING TO REMEMBER?
I...I DON'T KNOW. MAYBE.
WELL, STOP THAT. OKAY?
IT BUGS ME.
RIDGWAY LIVED DOWN THE HALL FROM MY FATHER THE ENTIRE TIME...
EXCEPT FOR ONE WEEK WHEN HE WAS RELOCATED TO A MOTEL AFTER A HEAVY RAIN FLOODED THE BUNKER.

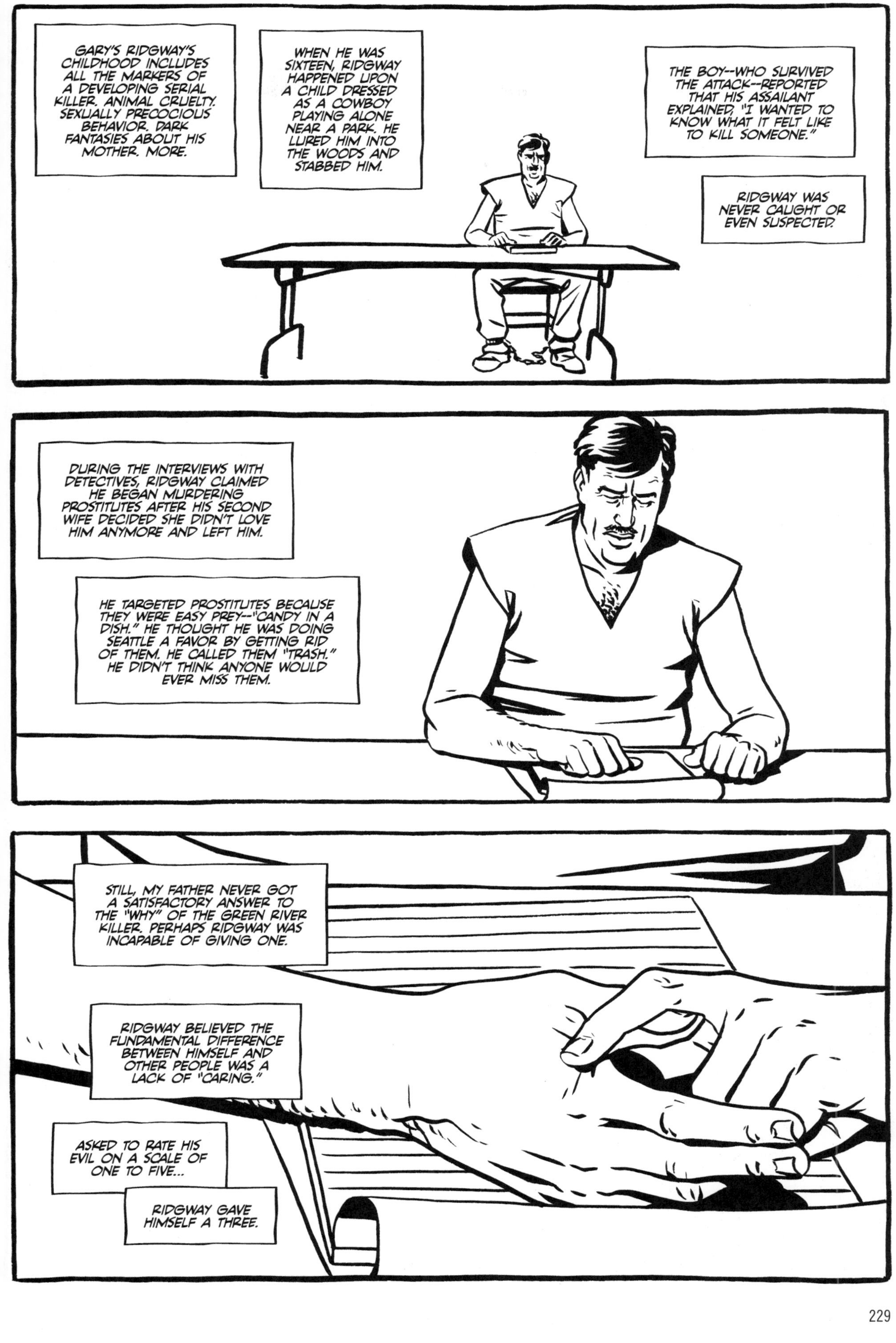
GARY'S RIDGWAY'S CHILDHOOD INCLUDES ALL THE MARKERS OF A DEVELOPING SERIAL KILLER. ANIMAL CRUELTY. SEXUALLY PRECOCIOUS BEHAVIOR. DARK FANTASIES ABOUT HIS MOTHER. MORE.
WHEN HE WAS SIXTEEN, RIDGWAY HAPPENED UPON A CHILD DRESSED AS A COWBOY PLAYING ALONE NEAR A PARK. HE LURED HIM INTO THE WOODS AND STABBED HIM.
THE BOY--WHO SURVIVED THE ATTACK--REPORTED THAT HIS ASSAILANT EXPLAINED, "I WANTED TO KNOW WHAT IT FELT LIKE TO KILL SOMEONE."
RIDGWAY WAS NEVER CAUGHT OR EVEN SUSPECTED.
DURING THE INTERVIEWS WITH DETECTIVES, RIDGWAY CLAIMED HE BEGAN MURDERING PROSTITUTES AFTER HIS SECOND WIFE DECIDED SHE DIDN'T LOVE HIM ANYMORE AND LEFT HIM.
HE TARGETED PROSTITUTES BECAUSE THEY WERE EASY PREY--"CANDY IN A DISH." HE THOUGHT HE WAS DOING SEATTLE A FAVOR BY GETTING RID OF THEM. HE CALLED THEM "TRASH." HE DIDN'T THINK ANYONE WOULD EVER MISS THEM.
STILL, MY FATHER NEVER GOT A SATISFACTORY ANSWER TO THE "WHY" OF THE GREEN RIVER KILLER. PERHAPS RIDGWAY WAS INCAPABLE OF GIVING ONE.
RIDGWAY BELIEVED THE FUNDAMENTAL DIFFERENCE BETWEEN HIMSELF AND OTHER PEOPLE WAS A LACK OF "CARING."
ASKED TO RATE HIS EVIL ON A SCALE OF ONE TO FIVE...
RIDGWAY GAVE HIMSELF A THREE.

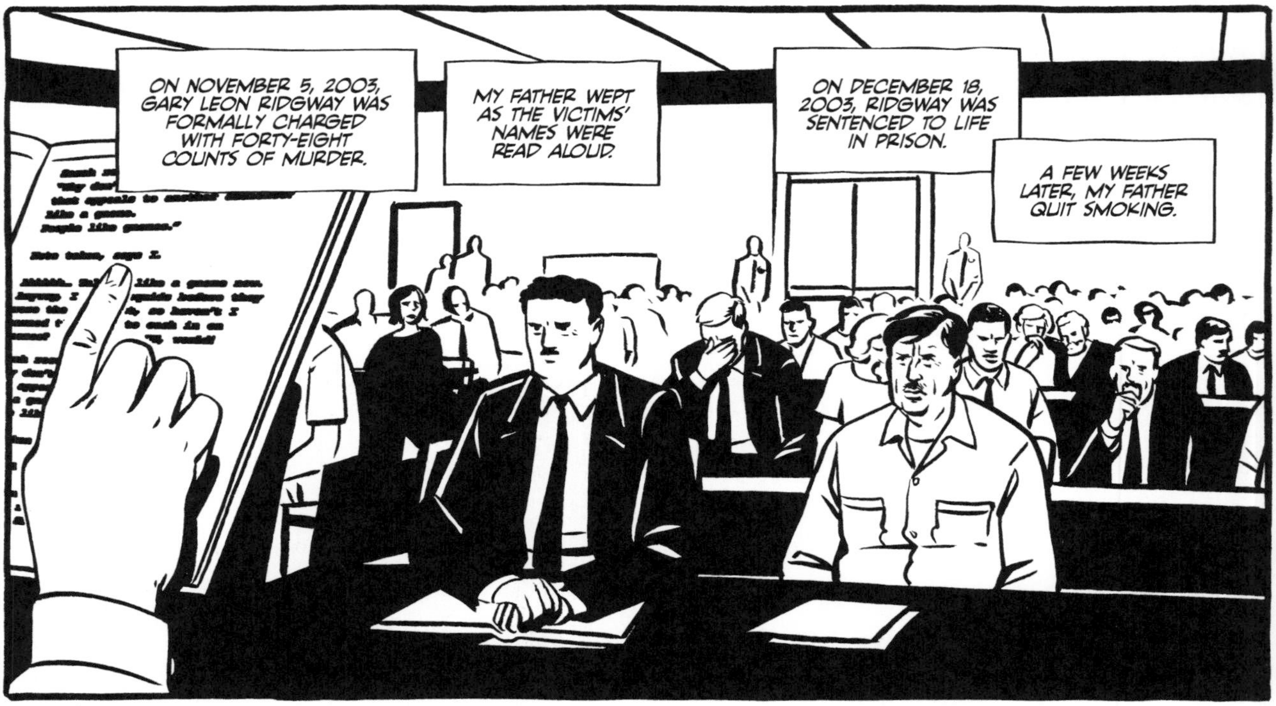
ON NOVEMBER 5, 2003, GARY LEON RIDGWAY WAS FORMALLY CHARGED WITH FORTY-EIGHT COUNTS OF MURDER.
MY FATHER WEPT AS THE VICTIMS' NAMES WERE READ ALOUD.
ON DECEMBER 18, 2003, RIDGWAY WAS SENTENCED TO LIFE IN PRISON.
A FEW WEEKS LATER, MY FATHER QUIT SMOKING.

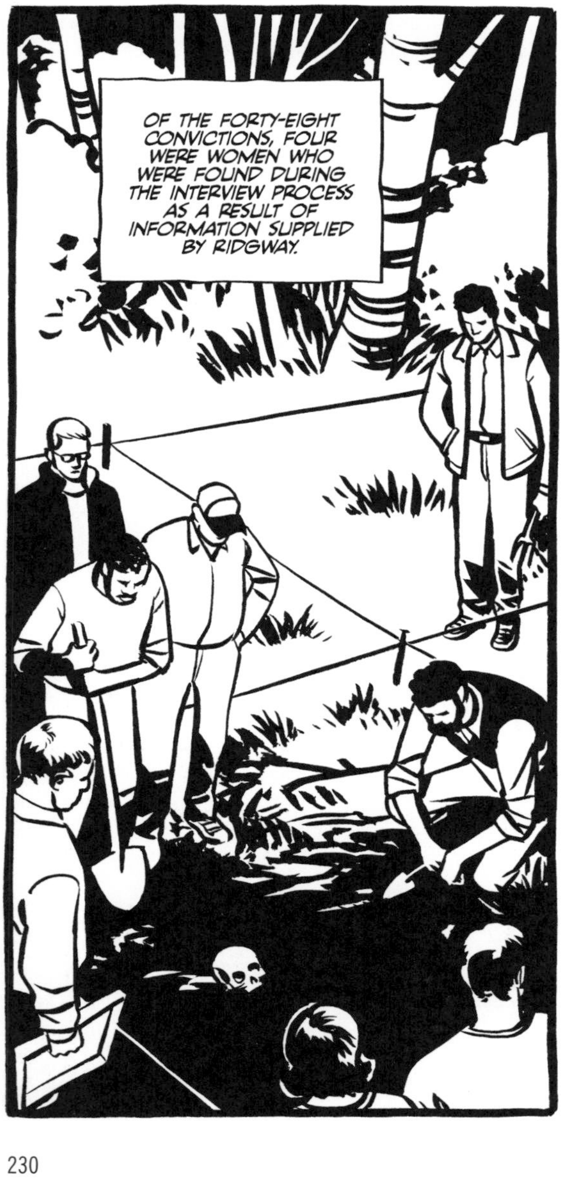
OF THE FORTY-EIGHT CONVICTIONS, FOUR WERE WOMEN WHO WERE FOUND DURING THE INTERVIEW PROCESS AS A RESULT OF INFORMATION SUPPLIED BY RIDGWAY.

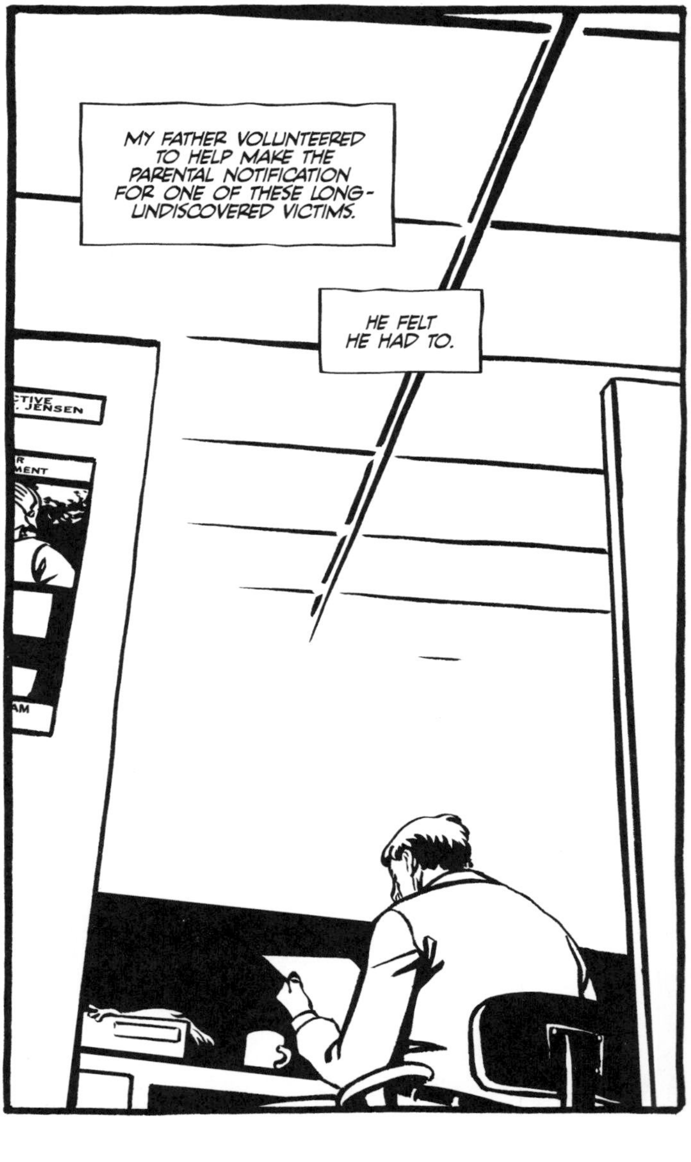
MY FATHER VOLUNTEERED TO HELP MAKE THE PARENTAL NOTIFICATION FOR ONE OF THESE LONG-UNDISCOVERED VICTIMS.
HE FELT HE HAD TO.

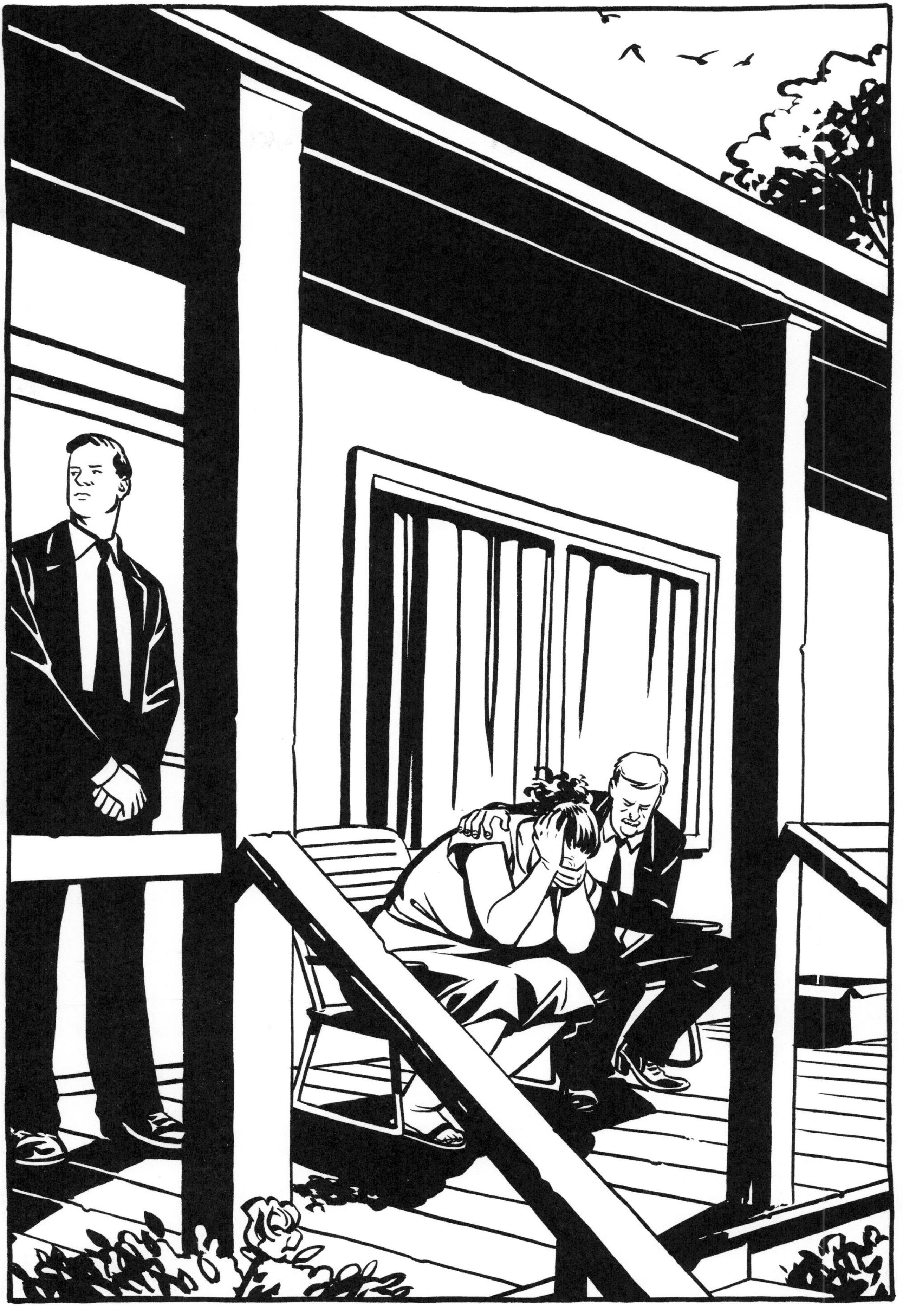

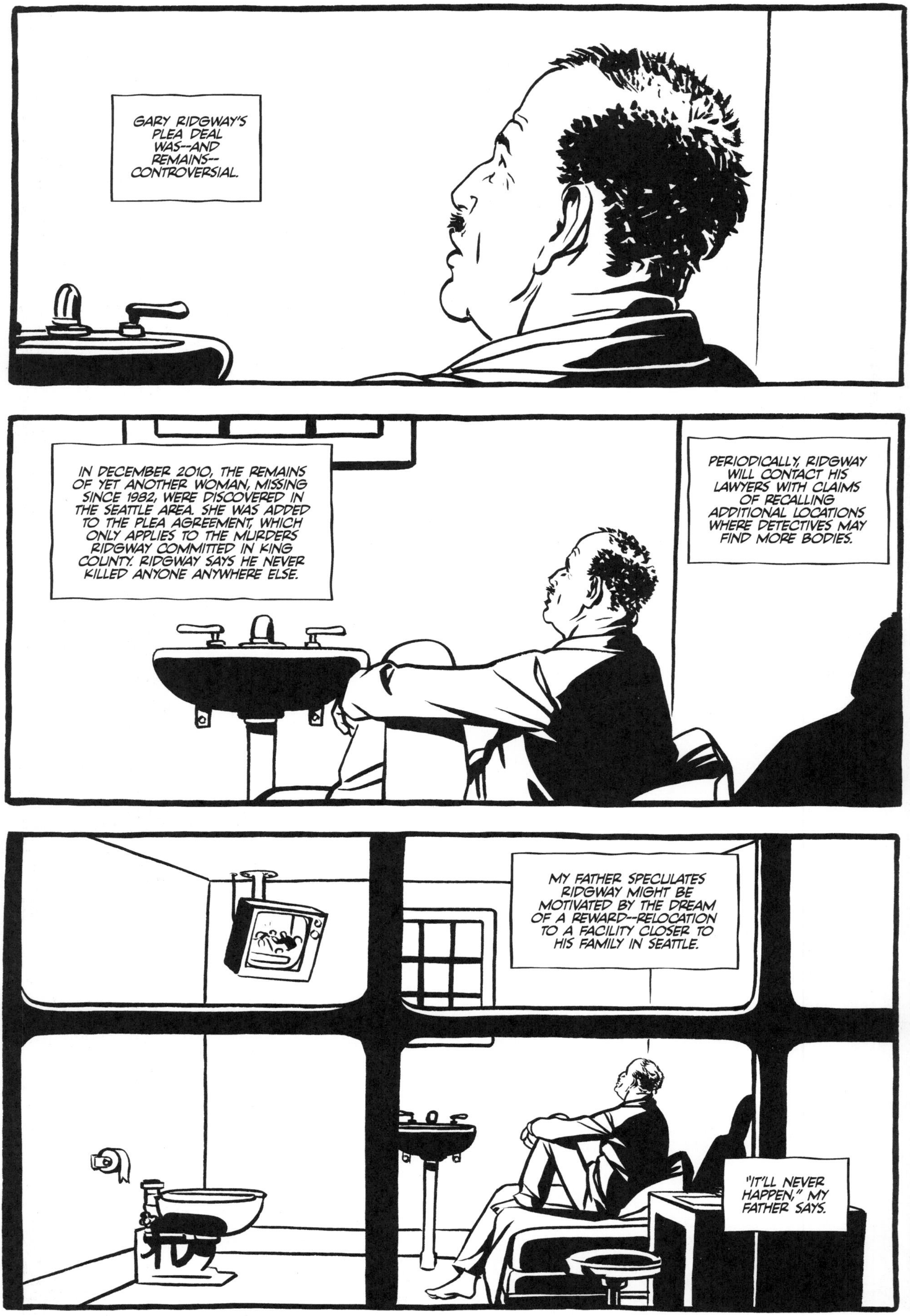
GARY RIDGWAY'S PLEA DEAL WAS--AND REMAINS--CONTROVERSIAL.
IN DECEMBER 2010, THE REMAINS OF YET ANOTHER WOMAN, MISSING SINCE 1982, WERE DISCOVERED IN THE SEATTLE AREA. SHE WAS ADDED TO THE PLEA AGREEMENT, WHICH ONLY APPLIES TO THE MURDERS RIDGWAY COMMITTED IN KING COUNTY. RIDGWAY SAYS HE NEVER KILLED ANYONE ANYWHERE ELSE.
PERIODICALLY, RIDGWAY WILL CONTACT HIS LAWYERS WITH CLAIMS OF RECALLING ADDITIONAL LOCATIONS WHERE DETECTIVES MAY FIND MORE BODIES.
MY FATHER SPECULATES RIDGWAY MIGHT BE MOTIVATED BY THE DREAM OF A REWARD--RELOCATION TO A FACILITY CLOSER TO HIS FAMILY IN SEATTLE.
"IT'LL NEVER HAPPEN," MY FATHER SAYS.

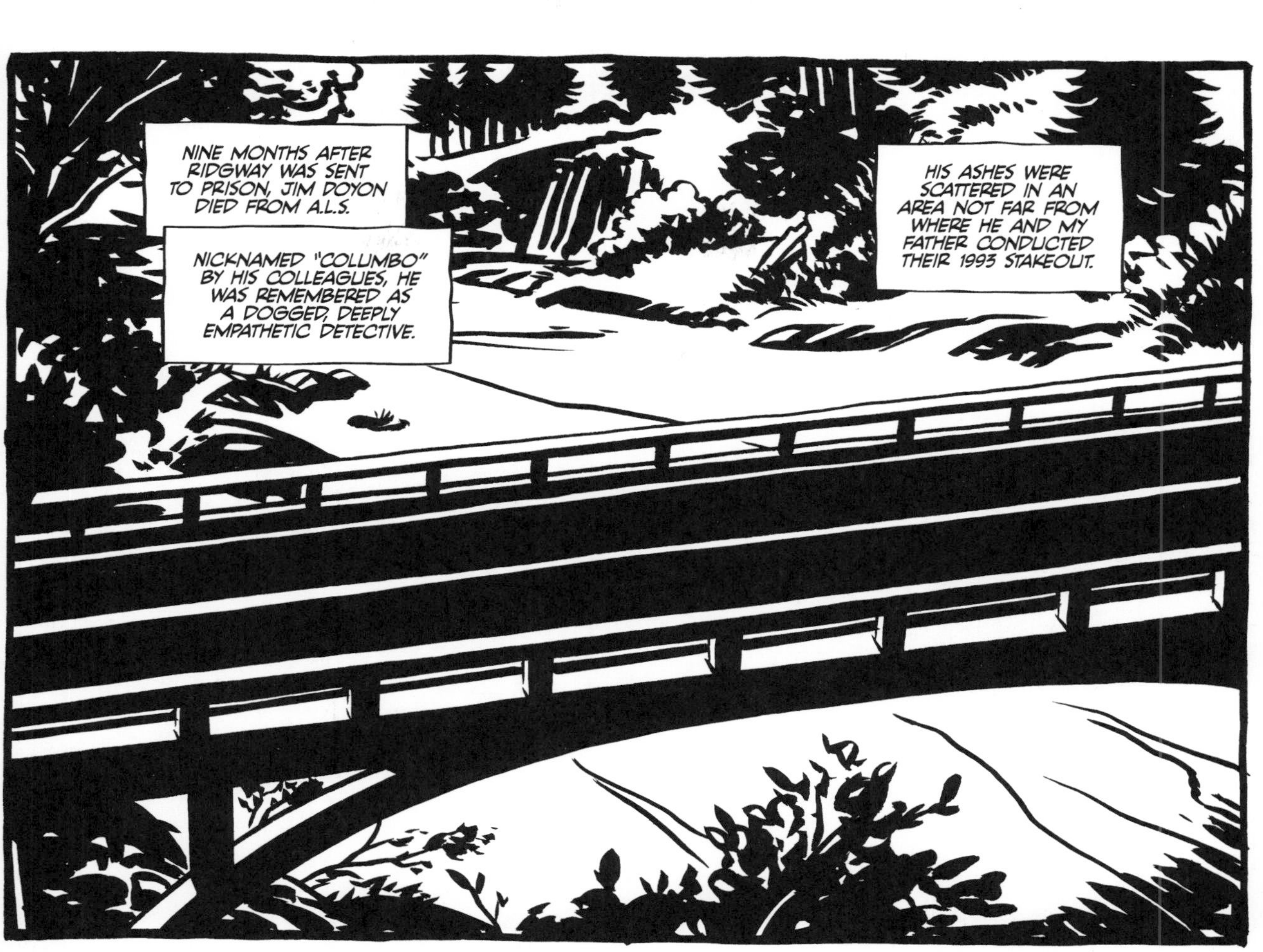
NINE MONTHS AFTER RIDGWAY WAS SENT TO PRISON, JIM DOYON DIED FROM A.L.S.
NICKNAMED "COLUMBO" BY HIS COLLEAGUES, HE WAS REMEMBERED AS A DOGGED, DEEPLY EMPATHETIC DETECTIVE.
HIS ASHES WERE SCATTERED IN AN AREA NOT FAR FROM WHERE HE AND MY FATHER CONDUCTED THEIR 1993 STAKEOUT.

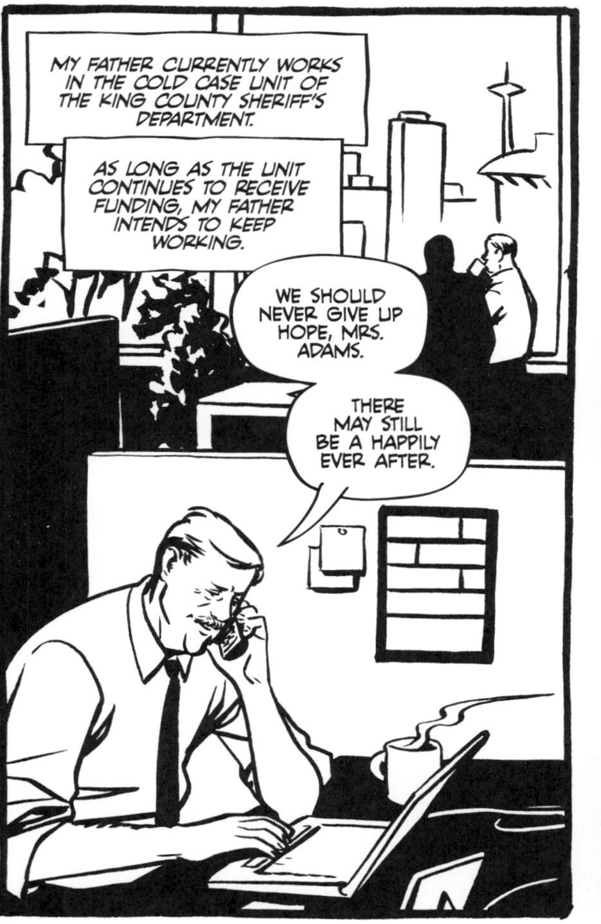
MY FATHER CURRENTLY WORKS IN THE COLD CASE UNIT OF THE KING COUNTY SHERIFF'S DEPARTMENT.
AS LONG AS THE UNIT CONTINUES TO RECEIVE FUNDING, MY FATHER INTENDS TO KEEP WORKING.
WE SHOULD NEVER GIVE UP HOPE, MRS. ADAMS.
THERE MAY STILL BE A HAPPILY EVER AFTER.

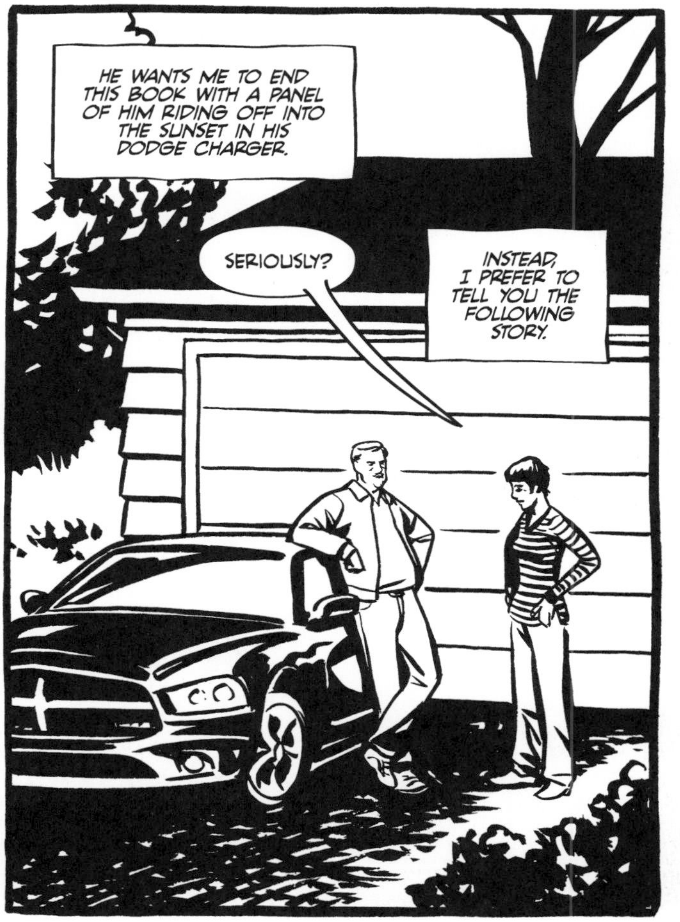
HE WANTS ME TO END THIS BOOK WITH A PANEL OF HIM RIDING OFF INTO THE SUNSET IN HIS DODGE CHARGER.
SERIOUSLY?
INSTEAD, I PREFER TO TELL YOU THE FOLLOWING STORY.

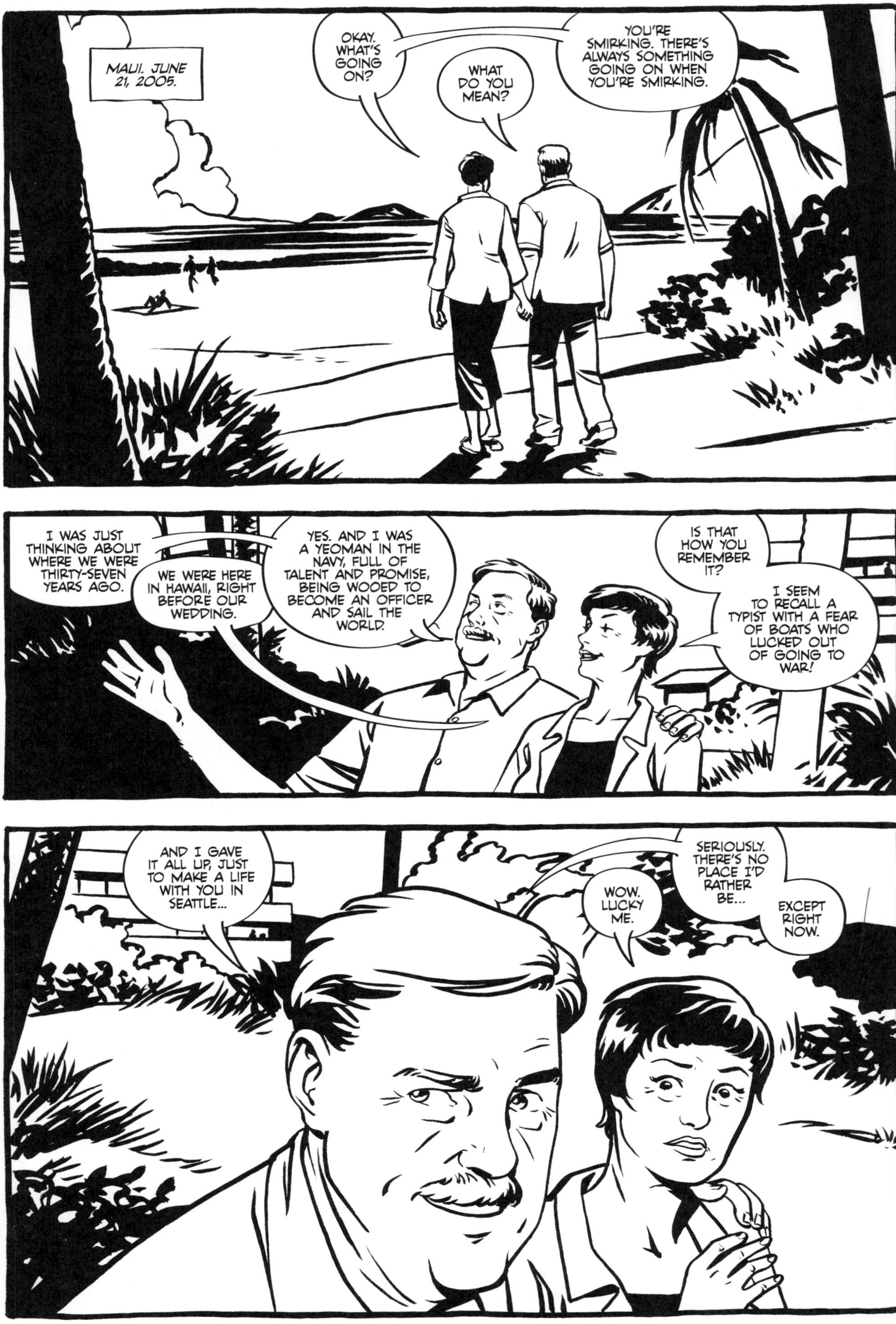
MAUI. JUNE 21, 2005.
OKAY. WHAT'S GOING ON?
WHAT DO YOU MEAN?
YOU'RE SMIRKING. THERE'S ALWAYS SOMETHING GOING ON WHEN YOU'RE SMIRKING.
I WAS JUST THINKING ABOUT WHERE WE WERE THIRTY-SEVEN YEARS AGO.
WE WERE HERE IN HAWAII, RIGHT BEFORE OUR WEDDING.
YES. AND I WAS A YEOMAN IN THE NAVY, FULL OF TALENT AND PROMISE, BEING WOOED TO BECOME AN OFFICER AND SAIL THE WORLD.
IS THAT HOW YOU REMEMBER IT?
I SEEM TO RECALL A TYPIST WITH A FEAR OF BOATS WHO LUCKED OUT OF GOING TO WAR!
AND I GAVE IT ALL UP, JUST TO MAKE A LIFE WITH YOU IN SEATTLE...
WOW. LUCKY ME.
SERIOUSLY. THERE'S NO PLACE I'D RATHER BE...
EXCEPT RIGHT NOW.

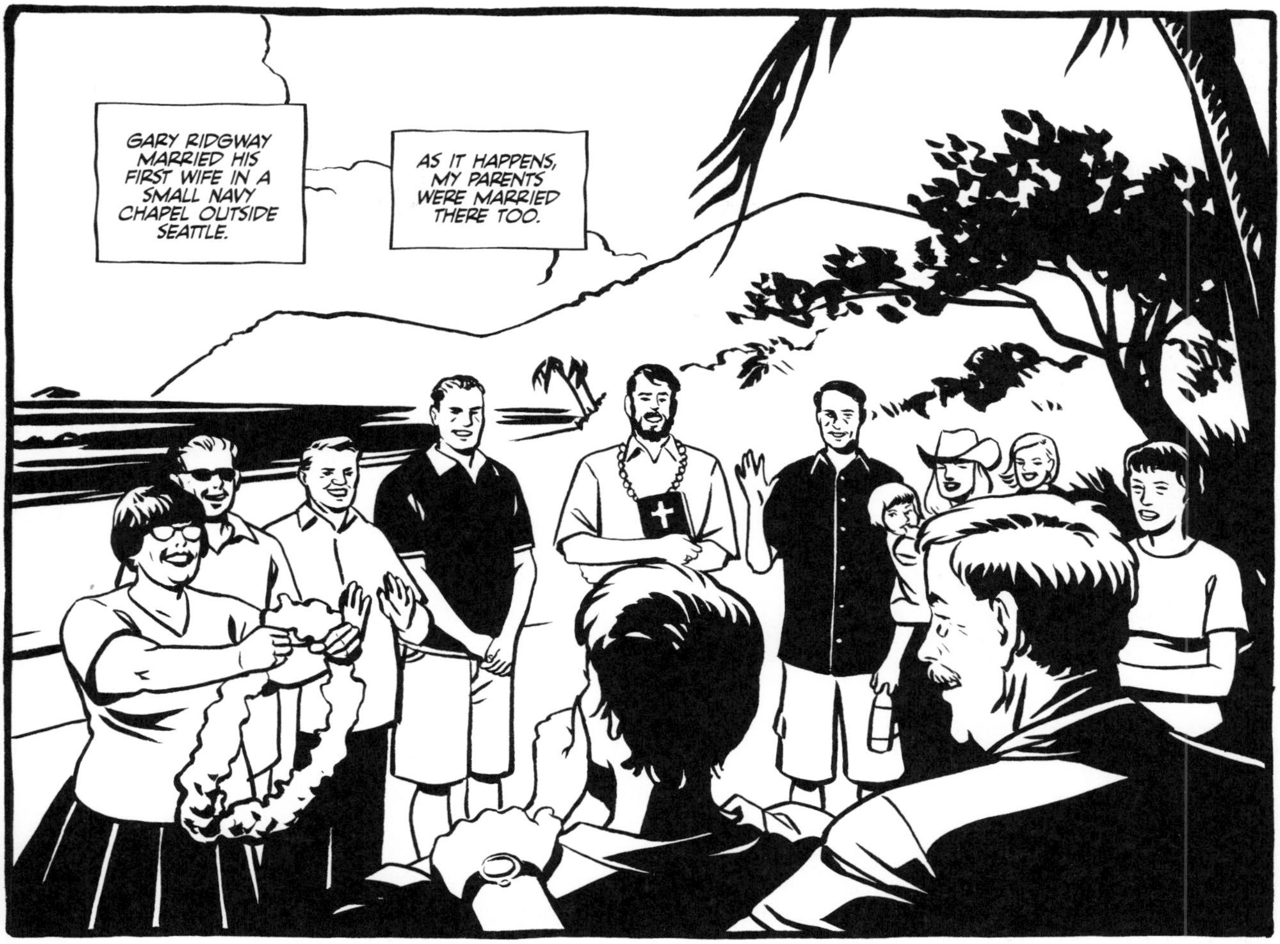
GARY RIDGWAY MARRIED HIS FIRST WIFE IN A SMALL NAVY CHAPEL OUTSIDE SEATTLE.
AS IT HAPPENS, MY PARENTS WERE MARRIED THERE TOO.

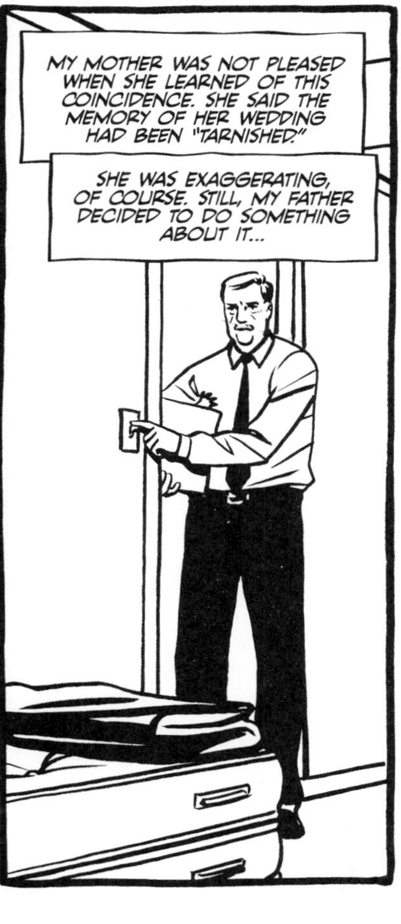
MY MOTHER WAS NOT PLEASED WHEN SHE LEARNED OF THIS COINCIDENCE. SHE SAID THE MEMORY OF HER WEDDING HAD BEEN "TARNISHED."
SHE WAS EXAGGERATING, OF COURSE. STILL, MY FATHER DECIDED TO DO SOMETHING ABOUT IT...

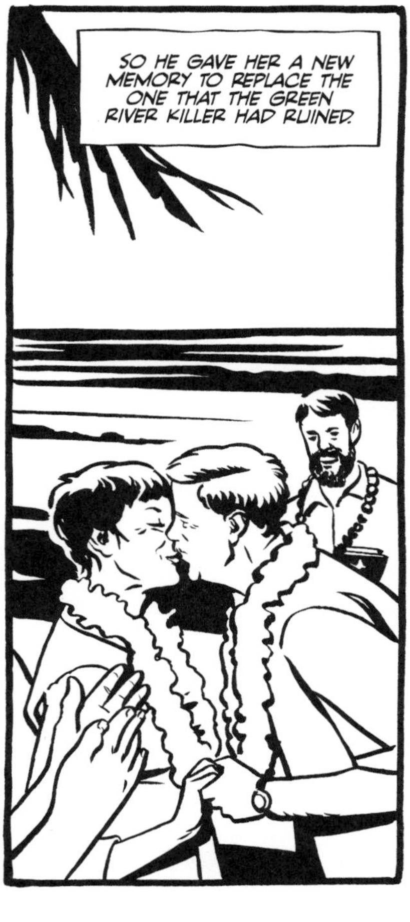
SO HE GAVE HER A NEW MEMORY TO REPLACE THE ONE THAT THE GREEN RIVER KILLER HAD RUINED.

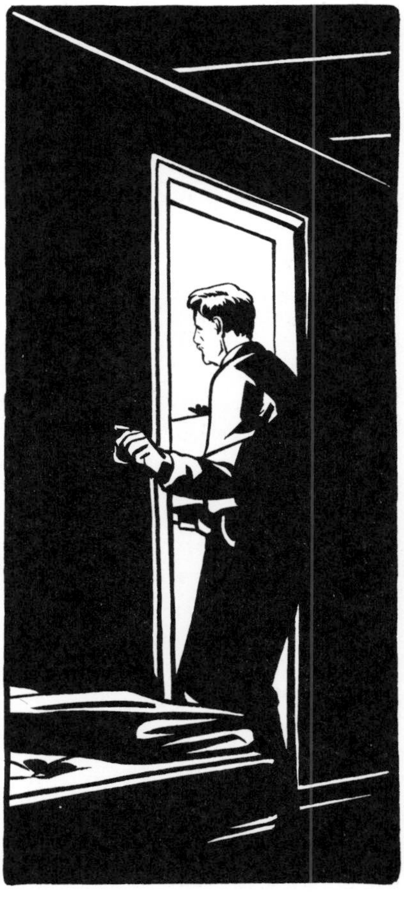

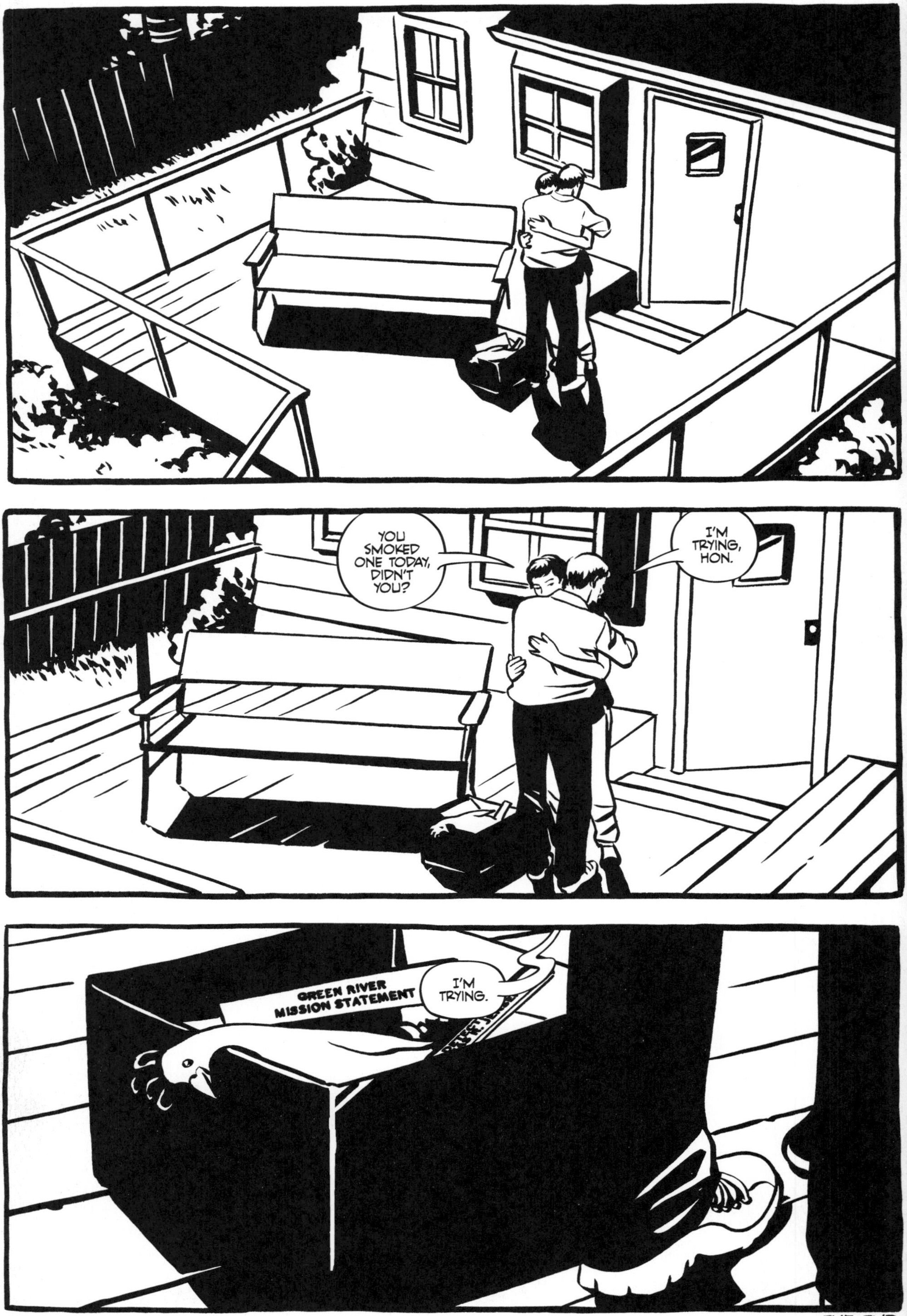
YOU SMOKED ONE TODAY, DIDN'T YOU?
I'M TRYING, HON.
GREEN RIVER MISSION STATEMENT
I'M TRYING.

THE END

ABOUT THE CREATORS

JEFF JENSEN is an author, screenwriter, and journalist living in Lakewood, California. He worked for *Entertainment Weekly* for 18 years, writing cover stories about *Harry Potter*, *Star Wars*, and *Lost* and ultimately serving as the magazine's chief TV critic. With Brad Bird and Damon Lindelof, Jensen cowrote the 2015 film *Tomorrowland*, and with Jonathan Case, he cowrote the prequel novel *Before Tomorrowland*. He's currently working as story editor on the HBO series *Watchmen*.

JONATHAN CASE is a cartoonist, writer, and painter from Portland, Oregon. His creator-owned books include *Dear Creature* and *The New Deal* (nominated for the Harvey, Reuben, and Oregon Book Awards), both published by Dark Horse. He has also worked on classic superhero books like *Batman '66* and *Superman: American Alien* for DC.

Case is currently writing new graphic novels for the Cartoon Network series *Over the Garden Wall* (BOOM!), and writing/illustrating his next original graphic novel, *Little Monarchs* (Holiday House).

LEARN MORE

Green River Killer: A True Detective Story is a graphic novel inspired by true events. It is not intended as history or memoir. The names and some biographical details of the victims and their families have been changed. For the record, Gary Ridgway was represented by a team of lawyers, not just Mark Prothero. Other characters, like Jim Graddon, are composites representing multiple individuals.

The Green River Killer's victims were prostitutes, but to their families they were daughters, sisters, and mothers. They stand for a larger group of women and children victimized through sex and labor exploitation, brought into prostitution by force, fraud, and coercion. To learn more and discover how you can help, please check out the following resources:

- The Polaris Project (PolarisProject.org) runs the National Human Trafficking Resource Center, a nonprofit, nongovernmental organization.

- The Nest Foundation (PlaygroundProject.com) raises public awareness of commercial sexual exploitation of children through their documentary *Playground*, executive produced by George Clooney and Steven Soderbergh, among others.

- The FBI (FBI.gov) provides a wealth of information on human trafficking and the US government's efforts against it.

- Your local nonprofits and law-enforcement offices.

ACKNOWLEDGMENTS

JEFF JENSEN

I wrote this book to gain a better understanding of my father and to express my love for him. I am grateful to the following, who offered insight and encouragement in pursuit of those goals: my wife, Amy Jensen; my mother, Charlaine Jensen; my brother and his wife, Mike and Stephanie Jensen; Phil Jimenez; Dave Reichert, Randy Mullinax, Jon Mattsen, and Mark Prothero; my Seattle family; my community of friends (Pine Tree; Small Group; Grace Brethren Church of Long Beach); my colleagues at *Entertainment Weekly*; Dan Snierson; Ken Tucker; Damon Lindelof, Carlton Cuse, and Jack Bender; Andy Ward and Dan Fierman; Ramon Perez; Marc Bernardin; Craig Thompson; Jonathan Case; Mike Richardson, Scott Allie, Brendan Wright, and everyone at Dark Horse, but especially my editor, Sierra Hahn, whose faith, nurturing, and deep humanity were not only blessings to this book but to my life and my family. Thank you.

JONATHAN CASE

Thanks to Sierra and Jeff for bringing this story to me, and especially to Tom, for seeing it through. A big thanks to my studio mates at Periscope, who helped keep a smile on my face. And to Sarah, for her support and love.

President and Publisher **MIKE RICHARDSON**

Editor **SIERRA HAHN**

Assistant Editor **BRENDAN WRIGHT**

Second Edition Editor **SPENCER CUSHING**

Second Edition Assistant Editor **KONNER KNUDSEN**

Collection Designer **AMY ARENDTS** and **PATRICK SATTERFIELD**

Neil Hankerson *Executive Vice President* · Tom Weddle *Chief Financial Officer* · Randy Stradley *Vice President of Publishing* · Nick McWhorter *Chief Business Development Officer* · Matt Parkinson *Vice President of Marketing* Dale LaFountain *Vice President of Information Technology* · Cara Niece *Vice President of Production and Scheduling* · Mark Bernardi *Vice President of Book Trade and Digital Sales* · Ken Lizzi *General Counsel* · Dave Marshall *Editor in Chief* · Davey Estrada *Editorial Director* · Chris Warner *Senior Books Editor* · Cary Grazzini *Director of Specialty Projects* · Lia Ribacchi *Art Director* · Vanessa Todd-Holmes *Director of Print Purchasing* Matt Dryer *Director of Digital Art and Prepress* · Michael Gombos *Director of International Publishing and Licensing* · Kari Yadro *Director of Custom Programs* · Kari Torson *Director of International Licensing*

Published by Dark Horse Books
A division of Dark Horse Comics LLC
10956 SE Main Street
Milwaukie, OR 97222

DarkHorse.com

Second Edition: January 2019   Digital Edition:
ISBN 978-1-50671-081-5   ISBN 978-1-50671-087-7

10 9 8 7 6 5 4 3 2
Printed in China

Library of Congress Cataloging-in-Publication Data

Names: Jensen, Jeff, author.
Title: Green river killer : a detective story / Jeff Jensen ; illustrated by
  Jonathan Case.
Description: Second Edition. | Milwaukie : Dark Horse Books, 2019. | Revised
  edition of the authors' Green River killer, 2011.
Identifiers: LCCN 2018044707 | ISBN 9781506710815 (hardback)
Subjects: LCSH: Serial murders--Washington (State)--Green River Region (King
  County) | Serial murderers--Washington (State)--Green River Region (King
  County) | Ridgway, Gary Leon, 1949- | Graphic novels--Comic books, strips,
  etc. | BISAC: COMICS & GRAPHIC NOVELS / Crime & Mystery.
Classification: LCC HV6533.W2 J46 2019 | DDC 364.152/32092--dc23
LC record available at https://lccn.loc.gov/2018044707